The World Legal Review

Volume 6

Improving Delivery in Development: The Role of Voice, Social Contract, and Accountability

The World Bank Legal Review
Volume 6
Improving Delivery in Development: The Role of Voice, Social Contract, and Accountability

The World Bank Legal Review is a publication for policy makers and their advisers, judges, attorneys, and other professionals engaged in the field of international development, with a particular focus on law, justice, and development. It offers a combination of legal scholarship, lessons from experience, legal developments, and recent research on the many ways in which the application of the law and the improvement of justice systems promote poverty reduction, economic development, and the rule of law.

The World Bank Legal Review is part of the World Bank Law, Justice and Development Series managed by the Research and Editorial Board of the Bank's Legal Vice Presidency. Publication of *The World Bank Legal Review, Volume 6* was made possible with support from the OPEC Fund for International Development.

The World Bank Legal Review

Volume 6

Improving Delivery in Development: The Role of Voice, Social Contract, and Accountability

Editors

Jan Wouters
Jean Monnet Chair and Professor of International Law and International Organizations, University of Leuven

Alberto Ninio
Deputy General Counsel, Regulatory Affairs and Operations of Vale S.A.

Teresa Doherty
Judge of the Special Court of Sierra Leone

Hassane Cissé
Director of Governance and Inclusive Institutions, Governance Global Practice, The World Bank Group

Production Editor

Elise Wei Tan
Legal Consultant, Legal Vice Presidency, The World Bank

Contents

Foreword

Albie Sachs
Former Judge, Constitutional Court of South Africa

Our South African Bill of Rights goes beyond the political and civil rights that have been provided in most constitutions over the last two and a half centuries. It certainly includes the right to free speech, to equal treatment before the law, to due process, to freedom of religion, to freedom of expression, and, above all, to vote. But it is far more comprehensive.

Coming out of our struggle for human rights and democracy, we South Africans went further and introduced fundamental economic and social rights: the right to have access to adequate housing, health care services, food and water, and social security. Some of the most important cases in which I participated as a Justice of the Constitutional Court concerned this second generation of rights, and the issue of ensuring their progressive realization in the context of limited resources. This is not always easy. Indeed, our very first case on the subject concerned access to expensive dialysis treatment. We had to recognize that we simply did not have the resources to deliver the most expensive forms of health care to everyone. Yet we could not work on the principle that if we could not treat everybody equally, we could not treat anybody at all. The answer to this was a form of rationing based on constitutionally compliant criteria. The applicant died of renal failure two days after the court gave its decision refusing to advance the applicant in the queue for treatment.

Fortunately, there were many other cases where the court was able to prescribe immediate remedies. The work we do as lawyers and judges can be transformative. I have been privileged to be part of the great project of using law to help the poor and vulnerable, and to bring these social and economic rights to life in ways we could never have anticipated. For example, in the seminal *Grootboom* case, we ruled that families who are in crisis through no fault of their own—in this case, mothers and children who have lost their shelter because of floods, fires, or evictions—are constitutionally entitled to emergency shelter. Then, in the *Treatment Action Campaign* case, our court ruled that women living with HIV and about to give birth are entitled, as a matter of right, to have access to antiretroviral (ARV) drugs. One consequence is that South Africa now has one of the largest and most effective ARV programs in the world.

Although these cases have been credited with global impact, the legacy that means the most to me is the message of hope embedded in their outcomes and reasoning. Someone once said that the function of the law is to convert misfortune into justice. These cases do that. They provide that, in appropriate circumstances, manageable responses to extremes of poverty, homelessness, and other desperate circumstances can be achieved by actionable claims in court. Governments are alerted to the fact that they are not doing anyone a favor by providing the basic decencies of a dignified life, but fulfilling their constitutional duties.

Judgments by progressive courts throughout the world have an impact far beyond the particular parties that bring the case to court. They allow us to declare that the poorest and most disadvantaged among us—people living with disease and stigma, people living without shelter—have rights. They affirm human dignity and encourage people to stand up and claim their rights. They promote transparency and accountability in public administration. As lawyers and judges engage with these rights, they affect the lives of millions. And as this message of hope radiates beyond the courtroom, each mother, each child, each immigrant will know that they matter.

In November 2013, as the keynote speaker for the World Bank's annual Law, Justice and Development Week, I had the opportunity to address a global gathering of lawyers, judges, and other people from various disciplines interested in the role of voice, social contract, and accountability, which is also the theme of this volume. The materials collected here offer concrete ideas and motivation to those working to achieve real development impact by using the tools of law and justice, as well as instruments from other disciplines. The chapters that follow make it plain that the world that the World Bank serves is not merely a geographical entity. Nor is it simply a concatenation of economies and markets. It is a planet peopled by human beings with an immense variety of needs and huge differences of life circumstances. One theme that runs through these chapters is that the notion of development cannot be restricted only to attaining measurable material and structural goals, important though this must always be. Development must include promoting the intangibles relating to human dignity and the affirmation of individuals and communities. The multiple voices and perspectives from different parts of the globe represented in this volume all seek an appropriate and commendable blend of the measurable and the intangible.

Preface

Anne-Marie Leroy
Senior Vice President and Group General Counsel
The World Bank

The vast range of development challenges that characterize today's world demand effective solutions. Current development challenges are numerous and include promoting sustainable development and conserving the environment; finding solutions to developing countries' rapid urbanization; generating enhanced social equality along gender, racial, and cultural lines; improving law and justice systems' effectiveness and accessibility; and addressing the wide economic disparity between developed and developing countries. Against this backdrop, if we are to achieve our goals, humanitarian aspirations are essential and desirable, but insufficient. It is crucial that development initiatives are designed and implemented to deliver tangible and positive outcomes. Clearly, finding solutions to today's development challenges will be no small feat—and will require cohesive and committed international cooperation including through multilateral institutions such as the World Bank and the United Nations.

The contributions in *The World Bank Legal Review, Volume 6,* titled *Improving Delivery in Development: The Role of Voice, Social Contract, and Accountability,* examine key values that must underpin development initiatives for effective and efficient development impact. This book showcases a range of development problems, challenges, and solutions. The World Bank's dual goals of eradicating extreme poverty and enabling all countries to share equitably in global economic prosperity are addressed through loans to member countries and the Bank's continued provision of a rich wealth of shared development knowledge, as well as advisory and technical assistance. Yet, if such global development support is to materialize into successful development impact, it must be channeled into projects that from the outset, and through to their completion, are carefully designed and implemented to attain and deliver such targeted and positive outcomes. This fundamental and significant theme of delivering beneficial development impact—to inclusively enhance the lives of all peoples, especially the poor—resonates throughout this book on many levels.

The World Bank Legal Review is a collaborative effort among development practitioners, whose work involves a range of disciplines, including law, economics, sociology, and other social sciences. In this volume, recent, innovative, and cutting-edge perspectives on significant law, justice, and development issues are showcased and shared with all for whom such knowledge is important and relevant. These chapters offer practical solutions to and useful perspectives on current and pressing development issues, which can be adapted by experts all over the world to meet the specific needs of beneficiaries in different local contexts.

This volume has been shaped by the insightful and carefully researched contributions of various law and development experts, and the invaluable guidance provided by our distinguished team of editors: Hassane Cissé, Director of Governance and Inclusive Institutions, Governance Global Practice, the World Bank Group; Alberto Ninio, Deputy General Counsel of Vale; Professor Jan Wouters, Jean Monnet Chair and Professor of International Law and International Organizations, University of Leuven; and Justice Teresa Doherty, who was appointed by the United Nations in 2005 as a judge of the Special Court of Sierra Leone. My appreciation goes out to the editors who have led the direction of this publication.

My sincere appreciation also goes out to Albie Sachs, a former Judge of the Constitutional Court of South Africa, who graciously wrote this volume's foreword. The foreword brings to mind that law and justice systems worldwide are the essential structures on which beneficial development impact may be tangibly and enduringly realized for intended beneficiaries. Relevant development knowledge from other disciplines, pertinent to the design and implementation of development initiatives, also provides essential support to the law in ensuring continued positive development impact. Sachs's wisdom and insights into law, justice, and development, and the core values that must underpin these, enrich the contents of this volume.

The chapters contained in this book explore a variety of themes: human rights and development, sustainable development, urban law and policy, sexual and gender-based violence, enhancing access to justice, regulatory governance, perspectives on anticorruption and stolen assets recovery, and the World Bank Inspection Panel. Contributions under each of these key themes highlight in different ways the importance of delivering positive development impact, and how achieving this goal necessitates consistent engagement with the fundamental concepts of voice, social contract, and accountability. The significance of these three concepts is richly and meaningfully illuminated across the chapters of this book.

Editors and Contributors

Editors

Hassane Cissé is Director, Governance and Inclusive Institutions, Governance Global Practice, at the World Bank. In this capacity, he leads a department composed of teams of experts to support countries in building sustainable, inclusive, and trustworthy governance systems. Key areas of focus include citizen engagement and social accountability mechanisms, institutional reform and strengthening in respect of justice and rule of law institutions, legislatures, independent accountability mechanisms, centers of government, and other areas of public sector management. Previously, Mr. Cissé was Deputy General Counsel, Knowledge and Research, of the World Bank from 2009 to June 2014. In this capacity, he managed the Bank's advisory work on legal and justice reforms, and led the Bank's knowledge activities on law, justice, and development. Prior to this role, he served for several years as Chief Counsel for Operations Policy, and as legal adviser on Governance and Anticorruption. Prior to joining the World Bank in 1997, Mr. Cissé worked at the International Monetary Fund where he started his professional career in 1990. Mr. Cissé has lectured and published widely. He has in particular coedited several volumes of *The World Bank Legal Review*. He serves on several international boards and is a member of the World Economic Forum's Global Agenda Council on Justice and its Meta Council on Global Governance Architecture. Mr. Cissé holds an LL.B. from the Dakar University School of Law, in Senegal, and a Diplôme d'Etudes Approfondies (D.E.A.) in international law from the University of Paris II Panthéon-Assas. He received his D.E.A. in international economic law from the Sorbonne, where he also obtained a D.E.A. in African history. He also holds an LL.M. from Harvard University.

Teresa Doherty is from Northern Ireland. She studied law after working as a civil servant and as a volunteer in Zambia. She worked in legal aid clinics in "no go areas" of Belfast as a student in early 1970s during the "troubles." She was called to the bars of Northern Ireland, New South Wales, and Papua New Guinea. In the latter, she worked from 1976 to 1987 in the Public Solicitor's office and, later, as the provincial legal officer for Morobe Province. She was noted for her civil and constitutional rights work, particularly on prisoners and women's issues. Justice Doherty was the first woman to be elected as a councillor of the Papua New Guinea Law Society. She was appointed as the principal magistrate for the Momase region in 1987 and as a National and, later, Supreme Court judge in 1988, the first woman to hold any high judicial office in the Pacific Islands region. She returned to Northern Ireland and to the bar in late 1997. Justice Doherty was appointed a judge of the High Court of Sierra Leone in 2003 following the civil war in that country and sat in the Court of Appeal. She was appointed by the United Nations in January

2005 as a judge of the Special Court of Sierra Leone and was elected the first presiding judge of Trial Chamber 11. She is currently a parole commissioner for Northern Ireland and a part-time chairman of Appeal Services; she also works on consultancies and speaks internationally. She received a CBE for "outstanding Contribution to the Judiciary and the Community" and an honorary doctor of laws from the University of Ulster. Justice Doherty has written widely on developments in international law and the status of women in the Pacific region. She is also the author of a guide to custody and maintenance law in Papua New Guinea for lay readers, titled *So You Have Been Left Holding the Baby*.

Alberto Ninio is a lawyer with 25 years of experience in regulatory, international, environmental, and corporate responsibility who has also held various technical and managerial positions. He is Deputy General Counsel for Regulatory Affairs and Operations of Vale S.A., the world's leading iron ore–mining company, where his duties focus on all operational issues, including contracts, civil and criminal litigation, environmental and social issues, corporate responsibility and interaction with civil society, governments and regulatory agencies, mining rights, and regulation of energy, ports, and railways in Brazil and abroad. As Chief Counsel of the Legal Vice Presidency of the World Bank for 18 years, he led a series of pioneering environmental initiatives in Latin America, Africa, and Asia, such as structuring investment projects, delivering written and oral defenses, conducting contract negotiations related to funding, and participating in environmental and social studies. Prior to joining the Bank in 1993, he worked as a lawyer at the Environmental Law Institute in Washington, D.C., and in Brazil as a lawyer specializing in foreign investments. He was Professor of Environmental Law at American University and is affiliated with numerous professional organizations. Mr. Ninio holds a degree in environmental law from the National Law School of the Universidade Federal do Rio de Janeiro and a master of international law from American University.

Jan Wouters is Professor of International Law and International Organizations, Jean Monnet Chair Ad Personam EU and Global Governance, and the founding director of the Institute for International Law and of the Leuven Centre for Global Governance Studies, an interdisciplinary center of excellence, at the University of Leuven. As a visiting professor, he teaches EU external relations law at Sciences Po (Paris), Luiss University (Rome), and the College of Europe (Bruges). He is a member of the Royal Flemish Academy of Belgium for Sciences and the Arts; is president of the United Nations Association, Flanders, Belgium; and practices law as Of Counsel at Linklaters, in Brussels. He is the editor of the *International Encyclopedia of Intergovernmental Organizations*, deputy director of the *Revue Belge de Droit International*, and an editorial board member for 10 international journals. He has published widely on international, EU, corporate, and financial law, including more than 50 books, 100 journal articles, and 150 book chapters. His recent books include *Accountability for Human Rights Violations by International Organizations* (Intersentia), *Upgrading the EU's Role as Global Actor* (CEPS), *The European Union and Multilateral Governance* (Palgrave Macmillan), *International Prosecutors* (Oxford), *Informal International Lawmaking* (Oxford), *Private Standards and Global Governance* (Edward Elgar), *China, the European Union, and Global Governance* (Edward Elgar), *The EU's Role in Global Governance* (Oxford), *National Human Rights Institutions in Europe* (Intersentia), and *The Law of EU External Relations* (Oxford). Apart from his participation in many international scientific networks, he advises various international organizations, trains international officials, and often provides commentary on international events in the media. He is the coordinator of a large-scale FP7 Programme FRAME, "Fostering Human Rights among European (External and Internal) Policies," and of the InBev-Baillet Latour EU-China Relations Chair at the University of Leuven.

Contributors

Emmanuelle Amar holds a master's degree in international law from the Université de Montréal and is a member of the Quebec Bar. She is interested in access to justice, international humanitarian law, and international cooperation. Ms. Amar is a research officer at the Cyberjustice Laboratory of the Université de Montréal, where she coordinates a project evaluating the development of cyberjustice worldwide. She previously worked for the International Committee of the Red Cross in Geneva as an intern at the Advisory Service on international humanitarian law. She has also worked in the field of refugee law.

Danielle de Guimarães Germano Arlé graduated in law from the State University of Rio de Janeiro in 1991. She is currently enrolled in a master's degree course in conflict resolution systems at the National University of Lomas Zamora, Argentina. Mrs. Arlé has been a prosecutor at the Ministério Público do Estado de Minas Gerais (MPMG) since June 1992, having previously worked at the Prosecutor's Office for children and young lawbreakers in Belo Horizonte, the capital of the state. Since December 2012, she has been the adviser prosecutor to the Attorney General at Ministério Público for the Institutional School of MPMG. She is also a member of the Study and Mediation Group for Improving Performance of the MPMG, of the Ministério Público's National Council; an MPMG representative in the Global Forum on Law, Justice and Development; and a teacher of courses in adequate dispute treatment within the Brazilian Ministério Público.

Luciano Luz Badini Martins has been a prosecutor in the Ministério Público do Estado de Minas Gerais since June 1993 and was responsible for the prosecutor's public entrance exams. He served as the Attorney General's secretary from 2005 to 2008; as coordinator of the Center for Prosecutors' Operational Support of Environmental Defense, Historical and Cultural Heritage, Housing, and Urban Planning from 2009 to 2012; and as a representative in the State Council for Environmental Policies from 2009 to 2012. He was a coordinator of state prosecutors working on matters related to the São Francisco River from 2002 to 2005, and interstate coordinator from 2009 to 2012. Mr. Badini was presented with a national award in the "Public Prosecutor" category for "Justice without Bureaucracy." Currently, he is the director of the MPMG Institutional School; the president of its Academic, Scientific, and Editorial Council; and president of its memorial. He also is a representative on the Global Forum on Law, Justice and Development.

Letícia Barbabela is a judicial clerk at the Ministério Público do Estado de Minas Gerais (MPMG), where she works at the Anticorruption Special Unit conducting research and writing briefs related to bidding procedures and public procurement. She is a graduate of the Federal University of Minas Gerais's School of Law and holds a postgraduate degree in administrative law from Cândido Mendes University. Before graduation, Miss Barbabela worked in the university's Judicial Assistance Division providing juridical guidance to underserved students and citizens, mainly on matters related to labor law and family law. She participated in the Federal Justice's internship program in Belo Horizonte, analyzing cases involving administrative law and tax law under a judge's supervision. She also received a scholarship to provide tutoring on labor law for fellow students.

Dilek Barlas is Executive Secretary of the World Bank Inspection Panel. Prior to her current position, she served as the Panel's Deputy Executive Secretary, from 2007 to 2014. A Turkish national, Ms. Barlas has more than two decades of experience in the field of development. A lawyer by training, she joined the World Bank in 1992 and served as Senior Counsel in the World Bank Legal Vice Presidency for the Europe and Central Asia Region. As Senior Counsel, she was responsible for the legal aspects of Bank operations in numerous countries; her work included an overseas field assignment to the Bank Office in Ankara, Turkey, from 2004 to 2006. Prior to joining the Bank, Ms. Barlas served with the Undersecretariat of the Treasury and Foreign Trade of Turkey and played a critical role in the preparation of Turkey's antidumping and subsidies legislation. Her private law practice includes work as an associate with White and Case in its Washington, D.C., office. She holds a law degree from the University of Ankara and an LL.M. in international legal studies from the Washington College of Law at American University, Washington, D.C.

Karim Benyekhlef has been a professor at the Université de Montréal's Faculté de droit since 1989, and since 1990 he has worked at the Centre de recherche en droit public, serving as its director from 2006 to 2014. A member of the Quebec Bar since 1985, he practiced at the federal Department of Justice from 1986 to 1989. His areas of teaching and research are information technology law (privacy, domain names, online dispute resolution, freedom of expression), constitutional law (human rights and freedoms), international law, legal theory, and legal history. In 1995, Professor Benyekhlef founded the electronic law journal *Lex Electronica*; he is also the originator of the first online dispute resolution projects: the CyberTribunal project (1996–99), eResolution (1999–2001), and the ECODIR project (2000–). As the director of the Cyberjustice Laboratory, he oversees Towards Cyberjustice, its multidisciplinary international research team, which is composed of 36 researchers from 23 academic institutions and funded by the Social Sciences and Humanities Research Council of Canada. He also holds the Lexum Chair on Legal Information at Université de Montréal.

Stephen Berrisford is an independent consultant working at the intersection between law and urban planning in Southern and Eastern Africa. Previously, he worked for local government in Cape Town and Johannesburg, as well as for the South African Department of Land Affairs, where he was responsible for both the implementation of the first postapartheid planning and land development legislation and the promotion of further legal reforms. In addition to his consulting work for international and South African clients, Mr. Berrisford works with the African Centre for Cities at the University of Cape Town, where he is an Honorary Adjunct Associate Professor, involved in building a platform for improved urban legal reform in Sub-Saharan African countries. He holds an LL.B. and a master of city and regional planning degree from the University of Cape Town, and an M.Phil. from the University of Cambridge. He is coauthor, with the late Patrick McAuslan, of the forthcoming *Urban Legal Guide for Sub-Saharan African Countries*.

Giovanni Bo is Counsel with the South and East Asia and Pacific Practice Group of the World Bank's Legal Vice Presidency. He joined the Bank's Legal Department in 2010 and worked, as an advisory lawyer, in the Environmental and International Law and Operations Policy Practice Groups and, as an operational lawyer, in the Latin America and the Caribbean Practice Group. Prior to joining the Bank, he was a legal researcher at Human Rights Watch and worked for the European Commission in Brussels. He has also practiced European Union law in the Brussels office of Pavia & Ansaldo. A foreign-trained attorney admitted to practice law in the state of New York, he holds an LL.M. in international and comparative law from The George Washington University Law School (2009), an advanced degree in European Union law from the University of Bologna (2007), a certificate in legal studies from University College London (2004), and an LL.B. from the University of Genoa (2004). His recent publications include "The World Bank Group Sanctions System and

Access to Justice for Small and Medium-Size Enterprises" (*The World Bank Legal Review*, vol. 5, 2014).

Francis N. Botchway studied law at universities in Ghana, Canada, and the United States. He was awarded the C. R. Allen Fellowship at the University of Manchester, United Kingdom, where he obtained his Ph.D. Professor Botchway taught at universities in the United Kingdom before moving to Qatar University as the associate dean of law. He was also an adjunct professor at Leuven University, Warwick, Kwame Nkrumah University of Science and Technology, and a visiting professor at the University of Puerto Rico. He is consulted by law firms in the United Kingdom and the United States on transactions and arbitration matters. Governments, institutions, and international organizations also consult him on varied subjects, particularly in international investment, natural resources, and environmental law. He has published books and dozens of journal articles internationally. His latest edited book is titled *Natural Resource Investment and Africa's Development*. He is working on *Defences in International Investment Law* (Routledge).

Valentin Callipel is a project leader at the Cyberjustice Laboratory of the Université de Montréal. In charge of multiple projects focusing on the modernization of the legal system, he combines his expertise in private judicial law with information technology law. Mr. Callipel holds a master's degree in private judicial law from the University of Paris Panthéon-Sorbonne. He also holds an LL.M. in business law from the Université de Montréal and has been admitted as a member of the Paris Bar and the Quebec Bar. Mr. Callipel's interests are centered on the links between law and new technologies, and he is presently focusing one of his several research projects on cyberspace privacy.

Rea Abada Chiongson is a lawyer with almost 20 years of experience on gender, justice, rule of law, and development issues. She was a gender consultant with the World Bank Institute's gender and fragility program. From 2010 to 2013, she also was Gender and Justice Advisor of the Justice for the Poor Program under the Justice Reform Practice Group of the World Bank. Ms. Chiongson worked with the Asian Development Bank, UN Women, the United Nations Development Programme, the United Nations Population Fund, and the Swiss Agency for Development and Cooperation. She developed frameworks for governments and civil societies for assessing compliance of existing national laws with international conventions, leading to several legal, policy, and administrative proposals for gender equality. She also worked with the Ateneo Human Rights Center in the Philippines, providing legal aid and legal empowerment initiatives to marginalized segments of society. Ms. Chiongson earned her B.A. and J.D. degrees from Ateneo de Manila University in the Philippines and her LL.M. from Columbia University, where she was a Fulbright Scholar.

William Coelho is a public prosecutor at the Ministério Público do Estado de Minas Gerais (MPMG), where he works at the Anticorruption Special Unit, investigating and filing actions related to bidding and public procurement fraud. He is a graduate of the National Law University in Rio de Janeiro and holds a postgraduate degree in intelligence and human rights from the Fundação Escola Superior do Ministério Público. Mr. Coelho lectures on the new Brazilian anticorruption law and teaches at the Prosecutor's Institutional School. He is a member of the Scientific Advisory Board at the Brazilian Institute of Criminal Intelligence, a collaborator at the National Council of the Public Ministry, and an Institutional Articulation and Projects adviser at the Brazilian Ministry of Justice. He also represents MPMG at the Global Forum on Law, Justice and Development, as part of the Governance and Anticorruption Thematic Working Group.

Gianluca Crispi is an Italian lawyer with 10 years of experience in supporting policy formulation and the review of urban legal systems. He serves as legal officer in the Urban Legislation Unit of UN-Habitat, providing legislative advice to UN-Habitat's projects and assisting member-states and local authorities in translating urban policies into effectively implementable laws. Mr. Crispi leads the Essential Law Programme, an initiative that analyzes the main constraints of practicability and enforceability of urban legislation in developing countries. Prior to his current position, he worked as research officer for the UN *State of the World's Cities* report, a normative tool geared to informing policy discussion and assisting local governments in designing sustainable urban policies.

Fausto Martin De Sanctis holds a doctorate in criminal law from the University of São Paulo's School of Law and an advanced degree in civil procedure from the Federal University of Brasilia. He is a federal appellate judge in Brazil's Federal Court in São Paulo, deputy director of the Federal Judicial School, a member of the Portuguese-Language Jurists Community, and an Advisory Council member of American University's Washington College of Law on its Brazil-U.S. legal program. Dr. De Sanctis was selected to handle a specialized federal court that exclusively hears complex cases involving financial crimes and money laundering. In 2012, he was a fellow at the Federal Judicial Center in Washington, D.C. He was a public defender in São Paulo, 1989–90, and a State Court judge, also in São Paulo, 1990–91, before being appointed to the Federal Courts. His 18 publications include *Football, Gambling, and Money Laundering: A Global Criminal Justice Perspective* (Springer), *Money Laundering through Art: A Criminal Justice Perspective* (Springer), and *Criminal Law: General Rules* (Forense). He has lectured at numerous universities and international organizations in the United States and Europe.

David D'Hollander is a research fellow at the Leuven Centre for Global Governance Studies at the University of Leuven. His research focuses on the role of human rights and democratic governance within international development policies, with an emphasis on the theory and practice behind rights-based approaches to development cooperation. In addition, he has worked and published on a variety of topics related to sustainable development, particularly regarding market-driven sustainability standards and sustainable procurement. He holds a master's degree in history and a master's degree in conflict and development studies from the University of Ghent, and was a visiting scholar at the Facultad Latinoamericana de Ciencias Sociales (FLACSO—Ecuador). He has contributed to various policy reports for, inter alia, the European Commission, the European Parliament, and the Belgian federal and regional governments.

Adrian Di Giovanni, LL.M., New York University; LL.B., University of Toronto; B.A., McGill University, is Senior Program Officer, Law and Development at the International Development Research Centre (IDRC) in Ottawa, where he has been initiating a portfolio of research projects focusing on public law and accountability in the global South. Before joining the IDRC, Di Giovanni worked for the Canadian Department of Justice's Human Rights Law Section, where he provided legal advice on Canada's Charter of Rights and Freedoms and represented Canada in litigation before UN human rights tribunals and the Inter-American Commission on Human Rights. Di Giovanni is also an alumnus of the World Bank's Legal Department and a part-time professor at the University of Ottawa's Faculty of Common Law. He is a member of the Law Society of Upper Canada and an honorary member of the Uganda Law Society.

Frank A. Fariello Jr. is a Lead Counsel with the Operations Policy Practice Group of the World Bank's Legal Vice Presidency. He is the Bank's primary legal focal point for its Governance and Anticorruption Strategy and is legal adviser to the Bank's Governance Global Practice. Mr. Fariello recently concluded a comprehensive review of the Bank's sanctions system, and is coordinating an ongoing multi-institutional study on the Drivers of Corruption in IFI operations. Since joining the Bank in 2005, he has also worked on a range of other legal policy issues, including the Legal Harmonization Initiative, Bank engagement in the criminal justice sector, and the legal aspects of the Bank's Middle-Income Countries strategy. He is Vice Chair of the American Bar Association's International Anticorruption Committee. His recent publications include several chapters in previous volumes of *The World Bank Legal Review* and in the *George Washington Law Review*. He has lectured at the Joint Vienna Institute, George Mason University, and the New York University School of Law. Prior to joining the Bank, he was Special Adviser to the Vice President of the International Fund for Agricultural Development (IFAD) and Senior Counsel in IFAD's Office of the General Counsel. Prior to IFAD, he practiced corporate law in a number of New York–based law firms, including Skadden, Arps, Slate, Meagher & Flom. He holds a B.A. in history from Brown University and a J.D. from New York University Law School. He is admitted to practice law in the state of New York.

Camilla Gandini is a gender specialist at the World Bank with a focus on gender-based violence (GBV), male gender issues, and masculinity. She is currently a researcher on sexual trafficking of children at the School of Advanced International Studies, Johns Hopkins University. Previously, Ms. Gandini worked with the European Commission to support the government of Pernambuco, Brazil, in the design and implementation of public policy for violence prevention and social cohesion. She also was a researcher at the African Gender Institute, University of Cape Town, where she investigated structural violence, GBV, and masculinity and femininity identity issues. Ms. Gandini has substantial experience working directly with local NGOs and community-based projects in Brazil, Costa Rica, and South Africa. She worked at the operational level on preventing violence against women, promoting men-women cooperation, coordinating crisis interventions, and supervising women and children protection efforts. She earned her M.A. in anthropology and ethnology from the University of Bologna, and an M.A. in human rights and conflict management from the Sant' Anna School of Advanced Studies in Italy.

Matthew Glasser's legal career began in 1977 as a municipal bond counsel and then as Broomfield's City Attorney in Colorado, and he has also worked as a registered professional lobbyist in Washington, D.C., on behalf of Colorado cities. Before joining the World Bank's urban sector team in 2003, Mr. Glasser worked as an adviser in the South African National Treasury, where he helped develop regulatory frameworks for municipal borrowing and financial emergencies. For more than 20 years, he has worked with national and local governments in Africa, Asia, and Europe on policy and legislation regarding urban finance and development. Mr. Glasser is working on a book exploring the legal, regulatory, and institutional framework within which the developing world's cities operate. He obtained his J.D. from Cornell University Law School and his B.A. and M.B.A. from the University of Colorado.

Felipe Gómez Isa is Professor of Public International Law and a researcher at the Institute of Human Rights of the University of Deusto, in Bilbao, Spain. He is the national director of the European Master's in Human Rights and Democratization, (E.MA.) Program, organized by 42 European universities in the framework of the European Inter-University Centre for Human Rights and Democratization, in Venice, Italy. He was also the Spanish representative to the UN Working Group for the Elaboration of an Optional Protocol to the CEDAW (1997–1999). Mr. Gómez Isa has been a visiting professor in several European, Latin American, Asian, and U.S. universities. His publications include *The Right to Development in Public International Law* (University of Deusto), *Privatisation and Human Rights in the Age of Globalisation* (coedited with Koen de Feyter; Intersentia), *International Human Rights Law in a Global Context* (coedited with Koen de Feyter; University of Deusto), *Rethinking Transitions: Equality and Social Justice in Societies Emerging from Conflict* (coedited with Gaby Oré, Intersentia), and "Freedom from Want from a Local Perspective: Evolution and Challenges Ahead," in *The Local Relevance of Human Rights* (Cambridge).

Emmanuel D. Kam Yogo holds a Ph.D. in law from the University of Leiden. He is a senior lecturer, and the coordinator of the Research Group on Natural Resources Law at the University of Douala's Faculty of Legal and Political Sciences. He also lectures at the International Relations Institute of Cameroon and at the National School of Administration and Magistracy of Cameroon. He is an associate fellow of the Centre for International Sustainable Development Law, an associate professor of the Faculty of Law of Laval University in Quebec, and a member of the International Law Association. Dr. Kam Yogo has published various articles and chapters in peer-reviewed journals and books on environmental law, human rights, economic law, and constitutional law. He has served as a consultant for the Central Africa Forests Commission and for the German Cooperation Agency in Cameroon.

Robert Kibugi is a lecturer in law at the Centre for Advanced Studies in Environmental Law and the University of Nairobi's School of Law, and has previously taught at the Faculty of Law, University of Ottawa. His legal and policy research agenda focuses on public participation in natural resource governance; land use law for sustainable development; climate change, including the role of law and policy in the adaptation and mitigation to climate change; and energy law, water resources management and rights, water, and sanitation. He holds an LL.B. and a LL.M. from the University of Nairobi School of Law, and an LL.D. from the University of Ottawa School of Law, and is an advocate of the High Court of Kenya. He has published various chapters and articles in peer-reviewed books and journals.

Stephen Kingah, LL.M. and Ph.D. (in law) is a research fellow at the United Nations University Institute on Comparative Regional Integration Studies in Bruges, Belgium. Previously, he worked as a research fellow at the Institute for European Studies at the Free University of Brussels. He also served as an ad hoc administrator at the European Union Commission, where he was in charge of relations between the European Union and international financial institutions, including the World Bank and the African Development Bank. He has taught in various universities in Africa, Latin America, and Europe. Dr. Kingah teaches at the University of Maastricht's Master's Program in Governance and Public Policy. He has published in many international peer-reviewed journals, including *International and Comparative Law Quarterly*, *European Foreign Affairs Review*, and *International Organizations Law Review*. He is working on topics such as asset recovery, international law in emerging markets, access to medicine, and the interaction between human rights and free trade agreements.

Karin Lukas is Senior Researcher and Head of Team at the Ludwig Boltzmann Institute of Human Rights. In January 2011, she joined the European Committee of Social Rights of the Council of Europe. She has been a consultant for various national and international organizations, such as the UN Development Programme and the Austrian Ministry for Foreign Affairs. She has done research as well as project-related activities in the field of human rights, in particular women's rights, development cooperation, and business since 2001. Dr. Lukas holds an LL.M. in gender and the law (American University), an E.MA. in human rights and democratization (University of Padova), and a Ph.D. in legal studies (University of Vienna). She works on the issues of labor rights in global production networks, and international as well as company-based complaint mechanisms.

Rajeev Malhotra bridges the world of academics and policy making. He is a professor and the executive director at the Centre for Development and Finance, School of Government and Public Policy, O. P. Jindal Global University, in the Delhi National Capital Region. A development economist with over 25 years of experience, he worked with the government of India until August 2012, as the economic adviser to the then Union finance minister. From 2002 to 2008, he worked at the UN Office of the High Commissioner for Human Rights in Geneva, and prior to that at the Planning Commission, New Delhi. He has published on methodological issues in estimation of poverty, human development, human rights indicators, right to development, fiscal policy, and specific issues on the Indian economy. His most recent publications include *India Public Policy Report 2014* (Oxford) and *A Critical Decade: Policies for India's Development* (Oxford). He is interested in researching and writing on macroeconomic issues in development policy and on human rights in development. He has a master's degree in economics from the Delhi School of Economics, University of Delhi, and also from the London School of Economics.

Siobhán McInerney-Lankford is Senior Counsel in the World Bank Legal Vice Presidency and a recognized expert in international human rights law, advising the Bank in this area since 2002. She regularly represents the Bank in international human rights fora, including the United Nations, the European Union, and the Organisation for Economic Co-operation and Development (OECD). She has published widely on human rights law and its links to development and is Adjunct Professor at American University's Washington

College of Law, having also taught at the Venice Master's program and the UN Summer Academy. She is cochair of the Human Rights Interest Group of the American Society of International Law, cochair of the GFLJD Community of Practice on Human Rights and Development and adviser to the Health, Nutrition, and Population and Governance Global Practices. Dr. McInerney-Lankford holds an LL.B. from Trinity College, Dublin, an LL.M. from Harvard Law School, and a B.C.L. and D.Phil. in EU human rights law from Oxford University. In 2010 and 2011, she was named among the Irish Legal 100 by the *Irish Voice* newspaper. Before joining the Bank, she worked in private practice in Washington, D.C. She is admitted to practice law in the state of Rhode Island.

Axel Marx is Deputy-Director of the Leuven Centre for Global Governance Studies, University of Leuven. He studied sociology and political science in Leuven, Hull (M.A.), and Cambridge (M.Phil.), and holds a Ph.D. from the University of Leuven. His research mainly focuses on global governance, sustainability standards, non-state market regulation, human rights, international development, and research methodology. His international academic publications have appeared, inter alia, in *European Political Science Review*, *Regulation and Governance*, *Political Research Quarterly*, *Research in Sociology of Organizations*, *Journal of Socio-Economics*, *Globalizations*, and *Sociological Methodology*. As an academic expert, he has contributed to over 15 policy reports for, inter alia, the United Nations Industrial Development Organization, the European Commission, the European Parliament, the Committee of the Regions, and Belgian federal and regional governments.

Benoit Mayer is a Ph.D. candidate at the Faculty of Law in the National University of Singapore. He holds an M.A. in political sciences from Sciences Po Lyon and an LL.M. from McGill University. His research focuses on international governance in the fields of climate change, migration, and development, with a particular interest in analyzing law as a tool for social progress. He has coauthored a book on environmental migration (Presses de Sciences Po), coedited a volume on critical international law (Oxford), and published more than a dozen peer-reviewed articles in, among other journals, the *European Journal of International Law*, the *Chinese Journal of International Law*, the *Asian Journal of International Law*, and *Climatic Change*. He received the 2010 CISDL-IDLO Award of Excellence in Legal Scholarship on Sustainable Development.

Morigiwa Yasutomo is Professor of Philosophy of Law at the Graduate School of Law, Nagoya University. He teaches legal theory, legal ethics, and anticorruption in English and Japanese. His interests range from the theory of justice to legal assistance programs, engaging not only with philosophers of law but also with legal professionals in many countries. After beginning his career at the University of Tokyo, he worked on theories of law and language at Oxford University. He is now active in work on interpretation and in promoting the practical import of legal philosophy, explaining to the practicing jurist the nature of professional responsibility. The legal ethics textbook he edited has been translated into Chinese and Mongolian. He was the acting president of the International Association of Philosophy of Law and Social Philosophy from 2009 to 2011, and has been a director since 2003. He is also a director of the International Association of Legal Ethics and the Japan Association of Legal Philosophy, as well as a member of the editorial boards of leading journals in the philosophy of law and legal ethics.

Maria Mousmouti (LL.M., Ph.D.) is Executive Director of the Centre for European Constitutional Law, an associate research fellow of the Institute of Advanced Legal Studies (IALS) of the University of London, and a codirector of the Sir William Dale Legislative Drafting Clinic (IALS). She specializes in different aspects of legislating and quality of legislation and is coordinating the research cooperation between the IALS and UN-Habitat on improving the quality of urban legislation. Her work throughout the years consists in supporting reform initiatives through research and capacity building in areas related to public administration, human rights, and the quality of regulatory systems and legislation in more than 20 countries. Recent projects include assistance to the Serbian Parliament in the process of EU integration, assessing the impacts of legislation on gender, measuring administrative burdens and reducing bureaucracy, improving the regulatory environment in Syria, and enhancing judicial independence in Azerbaijan.

Waafas Ofosu-Amaah, a lawyer, served as the Regional Coordinator for the World Bank Group's Leadership, Learning and Innovation (LLI; formerly World Bank Institute) Vice Presidency until her retirement in October 2014. Prior to this assignment, she was a Senior Operations Officer with WBI's Fragile and Conflict-Affected States unit. She was a Senior Gender Specialist with the Gender and Development Anchor in the Poverty Reduction and Economic Management Vice Presidency for over 10 years. Ms. Ofosu-Amaah's thematic areas of expertise include integrating gender issues into emerging development themes, especially conflict and fragility, governance, law, and HIV/AIDS. She also coordinated the World Bank Group's Gender Action Plan, "Gender Equality as Smart Economics." Prior to joining the Bank, she consulted for various international organizations and NGOs on environmental, gender equality, and development issues. She designed a three-year global program on gender equality and the advancement of women for the United Nations Development Programme (UNDP) and assisted UNDP staff and management in developing "Guidance Note on Gender Mainstreaming." Ms. Ofosu-Amaah was called to the bar of England and Wales in 1976. She has a master's degree in law from London University (Queen Mary College) and an M.B.A. from the University of Maryland.

Damilola S. Olawuyi is Director of the Institute for Oil and Gas, Energy, Environment, and Sustainable Development, Afe Babalola University, Nigeria and an energy associate with the global law firm Norton Rose Fulbright LLP in Calgary, Canada. Dr. Olawuyi's legal and policy research agenda cuts across broad areas of public international law, specifically natural resources, energy, and the environment. He has published over two dozen journal articles, as well as three books in these areas of law. Dr. Olawuyi holds a D.Phil. in energy and environmental law from the University of Oxford, an LL.M. from Harvard Law School, another LL.M. from the University of Calgary, and a diploma in international environmental law from the United Nations Institute for Training and Research, in Switzerland. He earned his LL.B. from Igbinedion University in Nigeria, and his B.L. degree from the Nigerian Law School. Dr. Olawuyi is the vice president of the International Law Association (Nigerian Branch), the editor-in-chief of Nigeria's *Journal of Sustainable Development Law and Policy*, and an associate fellow of the Center for Sustainable Development Law in Montreal.

Nightingale Rukuba-Ngaiza is Senior Counsel, Latin America and the Caribbean, Eastern Europe and Central Asia Practice Group in the World Bank's Legal Vice Presidency. She has implemented several legal and judicial reform projects, including being Task Manager for the Kenya Judicial Performance Improvement Project, the first stand-alone, Bank-financed judicial reform project in Africa and the second-largest judiciary project in the Bank's portfolio. She joined the Bank in 1996 and worked with the Social Development Department on a range of social development issues. She also worked as an advisory lawyer in the Environmental and International Law Practice Group and as an operational lawyer in the Africa Practice Group. Prior to joining the Bank, she served as a consultant to the Bank and the United Nations on a range of issues. Dr. Rukuba-Ngaiza's recent publications include *Judicial Reform: A Journey of Turmoil and Opportunities in Achieving Prosperity in Kenya* (World Bank). She holds an LL.B. from Makerere University, Uganda, an LL.M. from Columbia Law School, and a Ph.D. in law, policy, and society from Northeastern University. She is licensed to practice law in New York and Uganda.

Tatiana Tassoni has worked in the field of accountability and compliance review for close to 13 years since joining the World Bank Inspection Panel where she is Senior Operations Officer. At the Panel she works closely with Panel members on complaints received concerning a wide variety of development projects, including large infrastructure projects and other investments and policy reform projects and programs. She has been the lead Secretariat staff for 15 Panel investigations and has been involved in the review of over 50 requests for inspection in many countries. She has been a guest lecturer on independent accountability and the Inspection Panel at American University, and has represented the Panel in a number of meetings and conferences on accountability and the right to recourse. Prior to joining the Panel, she practiced law in an Italian law firm and worked with a nonprofit organization in Washington, D.C., focusing her research on workers and women's rights, domestically and internationally. She holds a law degree from Italy and an LL.M. in international law from the Washington College of Law, American University.

Rene Urueña is an associate professor and the director of the Master's Program in International Law at Universidad de Los Andes (Colombia), where he also belongs to the Global Justice and Human Rights Clinic. He earned his doctorate in law at the University of Helsinki and holds a postgraduate degree in economics. He has been a visiting professor of international law at the University of Utah and a fellow at the Institute for International Law and Justice, New York University. He has published on international law and global governance, and leads a project on interinstitutional relations and economic development.

Emilio C. Viano has earned an LL.B. and three master's degrees in law, an M.A. in sociology and anthropology, and a Ph.D. (summa cum laude) in the sociology of law (New York University). Recently, he has taught and undertaken research chiefly at American University's School of Public Affairs and Washington College of Law, and he has also been a professor at a number of universities around the world. His work in law, criminal justice issues, and governance has been recognized by his election as president of the International Society for Criminology and as a member of the Board of Directors of the International Association of Penal Law (Paris). He is a member of the Task Force for the Creation of the World Security University. Most recently, he was the program chair organizing the World Congress of Criminology, 2014, in Mexico. He was also the general rapporteur on cybercrime for the International Association of Penal Law. Dr. Viano has consulted worldwide, especially in the developing world and particularly on security issues. He has published extensively, often speaks at international conferences and universities, and frequently appears as a political analyst on television and radio stations worldwide.

Waikwa Wanyoike is Executive Director of Katiba Institute, an organization based in Nairobi, Kenya, which works to promote constitutionalism and the rule of law in Kenya. He practices constitutional law as a public interest litigator and appears regularly at the High Court, Court of Appeal, and the Supreme Court of Kenya on groundbreaking constitutional matters. Mr. Wanyoike also advises government and nongovernmental agencies on constitutional implementation and policy reforms. Previously, he practiced law in Toronto, with an emphasis on criminal, immigration, constitutional, human rights, and refugee law. He regularly represented clients before various Canadian courts and administrative tribunals. He also taught advocacy at

York University's Osgoode Hall Law School. Mr. Wanyoike was educated at Kenyatta University in Nairobi and York University in Toronto; he received his J.D. from Queen's University in Kingston, Canada. He is called to the bar in Ontario, a member of the Law Society of Upper Canada, an advocate of the High Court of Kenya, and a member of the Law Society of Kenya. He was the winner of the 2010 Precedent Setter Award for excellence in practice of law and his contribution to the community in Ontario, Canada.

Jane Weru is trained as a lawyer and holds a master's degree in NGO management from the London School of Economics. From 1993 to 2001, she worked with Kituo Cha Sheria, a legal and human rights organization in Nairobi. Her work focused on public interest litigation on behalf of communities threatened with forceful eviction. In 2001, she helped found Pamoja Trust, a nonprofit organization that mobilized and supported movements of the urban poor by providing technical, legal, and financial support to urban poor movements. Ms. Weru is the executive director and founder member of Akiba Mashinani Trust (AMT), a nonprofit organization working on developing innovative community-led solutions to housing and land-tenure problems for the urban poor in Kenya. AMT is the financing facility of the Kenya Federation of Slum Dwellers (MuunganowaWanavijiji). She was also a member of the Millennium Project's task force on "improving the lives of slum dwellers." She is a member of the Provincial Commissioners Informal Settlements Committee, a board member of Slum/Shack Dwellers International, and the team leader for the Kenya Railway Relocation Action Plan.

Yvonne Wong is an entrepreneur, legal consultant, and academic, based in Yangon, Myanmar. Dr. Wong is an expert in sovereign debt and international finance and banking law. Her current research looks at Myanmar's evolving banking and finance system. Her recent publications include "Restructuring Responsibility for Greece's Sovereign Debt: The Need for a Truth and Reconciliation Audit" (*Law in Context*) and her book *Sovereign Finance and the Poverty of Nations: Odious Debt in International Law* (Elgar). Dr. Wong has worked as a lawyer, consultant, and academic in various jurisdictions. She was recently in private practice in Cambodia and, prior to that, on the faculty of the Law School at the University of New South Wales, in Sydney. Dr. Wong is a member of the New York State Bar and admitted to practice in New South Wales. She obtained her BCommerce/LL.B. from University of Sydney, and her LL.M. and J.S.D. from the University of California, Berkeley, Law School.

The World Bank Legal Review

Volume 6

Improving Delivery in Development: The Role of Voice, Social Contract, and Accountability

Improving Delivery in Development

The Role of Voice, Social Contract, and Accountability

HASSANE CISSÉ

In recent years, a much-needed spotlight has been cast on the meaning and significance of delivery in development.[1] Particularly, the key importance of effective and successful delivery systems in development was emphasized, clearly and publicly, by Jim Yong Kim, President of the World Bank Group.[2] Kim cast a brighter spotlight on, first, the significance of effective and successful delivery of development outcomes as a fundamental goal and priority undertaken and focused on at the level of individual states. Second, and more significantly, he emphasized the fact that these state-level efforts would be supported as key priorities on a multilateral level by the World Bank.[3] He also articulated strategic and practical first steps toward achieving this goal in 2012.[4]

The author sincerely extends his gratitude to Elise Wei Tan, for her invaluable research, insights, and assistance during the preparation and successful completion of this chapter. The author also extends his sincere appreciation to the other editors, Alberto Ninio, Jan Wouters, and Teresa Doherty, for their invaluable input in shaping this introduction.

1 At a multilateral level, the delivery of outcomes and results in development has come under greater scrutiny and has acquired greater visible significance. *See* Jim Yong Kim, *Delivering on Development: Harnessing Knowledge to Build Prosperity and End Poverty* (keynote speech to the World Knowledge Forum, Seoul, Republic of Korea, Oct. 8, 2012), http://www.worldbank.org/en/news/speech/2012/10/08/delivering-development-harnessing-knowledge-build-prosperity-end-poverty. This speech places delivery at the center of development, and became the thematic basis of the World Bank Group's annual conference, Law, Justice and Development Week 2013, *Towards a Science of Delivery in Development: How Can Law and Justice Help Translate Voice, Social Contract, and Accountability into Development Impact?* (World Bank H.Q., D.C., Nov. 18–22, 2013).

2 *Id. See* also Jim Yong Kim, *Opening Remarks at Law, Justice and Development Week 2013* (World Bank H.Q., D.C., Nov. 18, 2013), http://web.worldbank.org/WBSITE/EXTERNAL/TOPICS/EXTLAWJUSTICE/0,,content MDK:23507046~pagePK:210058~piPK:210062~theSitePK:445634,00.html.

3 *See* Kim, *Delivering on Development*, *supra* note 1.

4 Kim stated that the World Bank Group would support "three self-selected countries" to create "national delivery knowledge hubs for development." These hubs would organize people and resources to address delivery issues in alignment with national policies and encourage and distribute relevant learning and knowledge to others. Kim also stated that the World Bank Group would realign more of its efforts onto measuring the delivery of results and outcomes of the development projects that come under its purview, and that the World Bank Group would, through specific learning strategies, teach its staff delivery skills essential to bringing about the successful delivery of development results and outcomes. *Id.*

There is an important reason why delivery in development has acquired a more central priority and gained clear support at both the multilateral and the national levels, and why it has received greater attention in policy, legal, and other academic circles. Developing countries often have the means and the capacity to produce overarching development directions and to formulate implementable development programs that, on paper, are fully consistent and projected to be effective. However, the observable and practical reality is that such policies and directions, even when consistent throughout, often either do not or only inadequately obtain their desired or targeted results when implemented on the ground. This phenomenon replicates itself in various development initiatives throughout the world and in varying contexts and demands urgent solutions and answers to the following questions:

> How should development goals and accompanying efforts to achieve them be carefully crafted, managed, and targeted to achieve the most effective results in an efficient manner? What are the right ways and correct methods through which development goals can be selected, and policies, programs, and other supporting initiatives designed and implemented on the ground, such that successful outcomes can result?

These questions, in accord with recent literature in development studies, clearly illuminate the central role of *delivery* in actualizing positive, effective, and efficient development impact. Such impact should ideally be in the form of tangible, appropriate, and measurable outcomes for targeted beneficiaries.[5]

5 Measuring results is important in order to accurately monitor a development program's attainment of desired goals and objectives. This, coupled with transparent dissemination of information on a program's progress, are part of a wider accountability system under which policy makers, legislators, project implementers, beneficiaries, and other stakeholders are held accountable with respect to duties and obligations owed one another under the development program. Measuring results also enables all stakeholders to internalize a program's workability and, consequently, actively participate in proposing and making necessary changes so that the program may continue to be effective.

In broad terms, *delivery* may be understood as getting goods and services to people in a way that meets their expectations.[6] More specifically—in the context of delivering development outcomes and as shaped by the range of development topics discussed in this volume—*delivery* means getting goods and services such as material infrastructure,[7] education, health care, economic development, social protections,[8] and other beneficial social or economic support systems to targeted beneficiaries.[9] Such targeted beneficiaries of development initiatives, whether instituted at the multilateral, national, or subnational level, through formal or informal institutions, or a combination of these entities, are ultimately recipients who require effective and efficient delivery of outcomes if they are to transcend the interlocking social, political, and economic factors that hold them in relative poverty or disadvantage. Such entrenched and interlocking factors operate to prevent beneficiaries from justly and equitably sharing in their nation's wider social and economic assets. By extension, if such beneficiaries continually remain unsupported by successful delivery of outcomes, they also remain continually impeded from a fair and equitable enjoyment of the various social and economic benefits wrought by globalization and economic integration in the wider international community.[10]

In order to make some headway and find answers to the questions posed above, it is important to evaluate and assess the usefulness and practical

---

6 Kim, *Delivering on Development, supra* note 1.

7 Examples of material infrastructure include roads and other transport infrastructure, energy, water, and other power systems.

8 Social protections include, for example, gender equality, indigenous peoples' rights, and an evident and practiced social ethos and culture of anticorruption.

9 Some of these examples in notes 7 and 8 are briefly mentioned in Kim, *Delivering on Development, supra* note 1.

10 In this volume, the existence of deeply interconnected social, political, economic, and other factors that prevent disadvantaged groups in society from sharing in and reaping benefits from national and global economic progress is specifically discussed in the context of indigenous peoples' rights. *See* especially chapter 4, *The Curse of Riches: Sharing Nature's Wealth Equitably?* by Emilio Viano. See generally, chapter 3, *The Right to Development: Translating Indigenous Voice(s) into Development Theory and Practice,* by Felipe Gómez Isa.

impact that the concepts of voice,[11] social contract,[12] and accountability[13] have

---

11 In general terms, honoring the value and concept "voice" in development includes acknowledging and recognizing the importance of, as well as practically ensuring that the views, perspectives, values, and concerns—be they social, economic, cultural, or political—of all stakeholders, including beneficiaries, are heard and understood. It intersects with human rights operational principles of participation and inclusion. This volume contains some insightful discussions on human rights principles, such as participation and inclusion, as they are incorporated or evident in development. *See* chapter 1, *Human Rights and Service Delivery: A Review of Current Policies, Practices, and Challenges* by Axel Marx, Siobhán McInerney-Lankford, Jan Wouters, and David D'Hollander. *See* also chapter 2, *Delivering Development and Good Governance: Making Human Rights Count,* by Rajeev Malhotra.

12 The meaning of "social contract" has its original roots in modern moral and political theory, such as the writings of Thomas Hobbes, John Locke, and Jean-Jacques Rousseau. For a succinct yet comprehensive overview of the history and development of the term, see the website *Internet Encyclopedia of Philosophy: A Peer-Reviewed Academic Resource,* s.v. "Social Contract Theory," http://www.iep.utm.edu/soc-cont/. A brief and succinct legal definition of a social contract is "[t]he express or implied agreement between citizens and their government by which individuals agree to surrender certain freedoms in exchange for mutual protection" (emphasis added). *See Black's Law Dictionary* 1517 (Bryan A. Garner ed., 9th ed., 2009). A social contract is an *agreement—a consensual and formalized apportionment of rights and obligations agreed inter se amongst peoples in society, and agreed especially with their government*—that "form[s] the foundation of political society." *See Black's Law Dictionary* 1517. In the foregoing sense, the meaning of a social contract, therefore, conventionally includes reference to the constitution of a country and its provisions. For a brief further explanation on how a nation-state's constitution may be appropriately conceived as a social contract, see *infra* note 26. In this conceptual vein, a social contract may also conceivably include other major and overarching national laws that define key rights and obligations of the state with respect to its citizens, and also the attendant rights and obligations among citizens, inter se, under such overarching national laws. This idea of a social contract in the foregoing sense of meaning constitutional and national law is actively engaged with by many chapters in this book. It is significant, however, that some chapters in this book reflect the concept of a social contract in a much broader and more fluid sense. Generally, such chapters describe or reflect the concept of a social contract in the sense of being *a set of preexisting and informal or unwritten rights and obligations among parties, who collectively coexist in a particular society, community, or socioeconomic group, which is not national in character.* Generally speaking, in this volume, illustrations of such networks of informal or unwritten rights and obligations *among such parties* in their society, community, or group include authors' descriptions of *unwritten understandings or norms—mainly social or economic in nature*—that are *commonly shared or accepted among such parties* and that thereby crucially determine what such parties consider to be *valid and acceptable codes of interaction or behavior.* One specific illustration of a social contract conceived in this broader sense and that surfaces in some of this volume's chapters is the complex network of shared relationships among individuals or groups with respect to their rights and use of property or shared resources (e.g., entrenched and complex relationships among different socioeconomic groups in urban settings that allocate rights over limited urban resources, or among individuals with respect to a commonly shared natural resource). Other variations of the concept of a social contract as conceived in its much broader and more fluid sense, besides this, have surfaced in this volume.

13 Accountability draws its current meaning from the vast range of preexisting writings and discussions on the subject. In general terms, accountability includes two key aspects. First, it involves recognizing the practical value of governance and accountability mechanisms and devising appropriate such mechanisms to ensure that stakeholders of a development initiative are held to account in fulfilling their responsibilities to ensure successful outcomes. Second, it involves establishing effective avenues of recourse or redress available to affected persons when stakeholders' responsibilities and obligations are not fulfilled or affected parties' or stakeholders' rights are not honored or met.

on shaping such outcomes for beneficiaries. At this point, two broad observations can be made.

First, the fundamental significance of voice, social contract, and accountability in delivering successful development outcomes is, arguably, most accurately and usefully illuminated when these concepts are examined in the light of the highly specific development contexts and practical challenges that necessitate their careful application. In this way, one may apprehend how these concepts may be adhered to and applied, in reality and in practice, in such unique or specific contexts, so as to deliver effective and carefully targeted development outcomes.[14] Conceivably, assessing the importance of these concepts through a lens that is too broad, abstract, or general would dilute a precise and accurate apprehension of such concepts' fundamentality in providing solutions to specific and practical development challenges. It bears noting that many of the chapters in this volume demonstrate that such concepts are an indispensable part of an effective and practical solution to a specific development problem.[15] Each chapter, in its discussion of a particular development challenge or issue situated in a unique or specific context, combines with the others to collectively showcase varied examples and case studies on how positive development impact ultimately originates, both directly and indirectly, from a contextually sensitive engagement with and application of these three concepts. Conversely, many chapters also demonstrate or evaluate the less-than-desirable results and outcomes that occur when such key concepts are ignored or not adhered to in development initiatives.[16]

Our second observation builds on the first one above. As just highlighted above, the rich and complex significance of voice, social contract, and accountability is most accurately fleshed out, and is also comprehended in its most purposeful way, when derived from and examined in precise alignment with

---

14 Of particular note is chapter 10, *Confronting Complexity: Using Action-Research to Build Voice, Accountability, and Justice in Nairobi's Mukuru Informal Settlements*, by Jane Weru, Waikwa Wanyoike, and Adrian Di Giovanni. In this chapter, the authors demonstrate how these concepts are effectively harnessed and, in highly practical terms, materialized into positive outcomes and solutions for slum dwellers.

15 Some chapters of note that reflect how these concepts are essential in delivering effective, practical solutions include, chapter 15, *ICT-Driven Strategies for Modernizing and Reforming Access to Justice Mechanisms in Developing Countries*, by Karim Benyekhlef, Emmanuelle Amar, and Valentin Callipel; chapters 7 and 8 on community forestry laws, *Conceptualizing Regulatory Frameworks to Forge Citizen Roles to Deliver Sustainable Natural Resource Management in Kenya*, by Robert Kibugi; and *The Impact of the Legal Framework of Community Forestry on the Development of Rural Areas in Cameroon*, by Emmanuel D. Kam Yogo; and chapter 12, *Justice Sector Delivery of Services in the Context of Fragility and Conflict: What Is Being Done to Address Sexual and Gender-Based Violence?* by Waafas Ofosu-Amaah, Rea Abada Chiongson, and Camilla Gandini.

16 One chapter, the primary focus of which is on how and where such concepts are not adequately adhered to, found that less-than-desirable practical development consequences are the likely result. See chapter 5, *Fostering Accountability in Large-Scale Environmental Projects: Lessons from CDM and REDD+ Projects*, by Damilola S. Olawuyi. *See* also chapter 9, *Urban Law: A Key to Accountable Urban Government and Effective Urban Service Delivery*, by Matt Glasser and Stephen Berrisford.

the highly specific development challenges and contexts within which these concepts are usefully applied or adhered to. It is on this basis of understanding that this volume's broad coverage of different development challenges, specific case studies, and varying contexts brings to light for the reader an important recurrent theme—namely, that improving the delivery of targeted development outcomes crucially and foundationally *pivots* on the ability to successfully harness and integrate these concepts into the *practical actualization* of development efforts. It is through specific observation of how such practical actualization of successful development impact is ultimately derived from a concerted adherence to these concepts—as they manifest in real and specific development contexts—that the rich and complex meaning, and significance, of such concepts can be usefully understood. In this way, the wide-ranging chapters in this book, covering a wide array of development challenges and their unique contexts, constitute a fertile and practical basis on which the evolving meaning, usefulness, and significance of these three concepts are both elucidated and enriched.

The Structure, Key Themes, and Specific Issues Covered in This Volume

An accurate discussion of this volume's overarching themes of voice, social contract, and accountability requires a detailed engagement with the specific discussions contained in the chapters, which cover a wide variety of development issues. Yet there must be a genuine attempt to do the seemingly impossible: draw together these assorted chapters into an organized and broadly unified structure, without sacrificing the chapters' rich and detailed content. Inevitably, a difficult compromise between the general and the specific must be attempted. Accordingly, the sections below engage with the various chapters individually under several key and broad thematic areas. The reader, of course, must also navigate and meaningfully engage with the wide assortment of development issues, challenges, and solutions discussed herein. It is intended, therefore, that this introductory chapter be practically useful in assisting the reader in this respect. In this light, the chapters and thematic areas discussed below are aligned with the thematic sequence in which they appear in the volume. Insomuch as it is impossible and unhelpful to reiterate every detail in the chapters, only the more salient, valuable, or unique insights relevant to the book's overarching themes are underscored as each chapter is discussed.

Most importantly, the sections below are written in a way that addresses and appeals to the interests of a broad range of readers. Readers with specific interests in only one or some thematic areas may proceed directly to those sections that discuss chapters that engage his or her specific areas of interest. For such readers, this approach is recommended. For other readers, reading the sections below in sequence and in their entirety will provide a more complete overview of the many diverse, useful, and complex development themes and issues covered, which, in various ways and with different emphases, are relevant to the book's themes of voice, social contract, and accountability.

Structurally, in addition to this introduction and the concluding remarks, this volume consists of 24 chapters, arranged under the following 7 broad themes: part I, "Human Rights and Development," chapters 1–4; part II, "Sustainable Development," chapters 5–8; part III, "Urban Law and Policy," chapters 9–11; part IV, "Sexual and Gender-Based Violence," chapters 12–13; part V, "Improving Access to Justice," chapters 14–16; part VI, "Anticorruption and Stolen Assets Recovery," chapters 17–21; and part VII, "Perspectives on the World Bank Inspection Panel," chapters 22–24. On the whole, these themes and chapters provide a rich assortment of examples and incisive analyses on a wide variety of key, current, and, in some cases, pioneering and controversial development issues.[17] They offer the reader numerous opportunities to examine the importance of voice, social contract, and accountability as essential concepts that underpin the attainment of successful outcomes across a variety of development challenges.

While this introduction examines the above thematic areas and the individual chapters subsumed under them in sequence, illuminating their specific significance, the concluding remarks offer a succinct overview and observations by an experienced practitioner,[18] briefly rounding up from his perspective the substance and value of these chapters.

Part I: Human Rights and Development

This first thematic part, aptly introduced in chapters 1 and 2, begins by offering the reader two broad and differing perspectives on human rights approaches to development.

Chapter 1, "Human Rights and Service Delivery: A Review of Current Policies, Practices, and Challenges," by Axel Marx, Siobhán McInerney-Lankford, Jan Wouters, and David D'Hollander, focuses on human rights–based approaches (HRBAs) to development. The authors first examine the foundational origins of HRBAs, discussing the ways in which human rights operational principles—namely, participation, nondiscrimination, inclusion, rule of law, and accountability—have influenced, both conceptually and practically, the goal-setting, design, and implementation of development projects

17 For example, in chapter 16, *Courts and Regulatory Governance in Latin America: Improving Delivery in Development by Managing Institutional Interplay,* by Rene Urueña, recent and innovative theories on regulation inform the author's views and observations. In addition, chapter 21, *Measures for Asset Recovery: A Multiactor Global Fund for Recovered Stolen Assets,* by Stephen Kingah, engages with well-known controversies surrounding the topic. Chapters 22–24, on the Bank's Inspection Panel, contain differing views, reflecting a degree of controversy that surrounds the work of this multilateral accountability mechanism.

18 The final chapter, "Concluding Remarks," is written by Alberto Ninio, one of the editors of this volume.

and other initiatives across a range of development areas.[19] These human rights principles are inherently expressive of and contain significant overlaps with the cornerstone concepts of voice, social contract, and accountability.

Against this wider backdrop of development initiatives, the authors proceed to highlight and delineate the much narrower and more specific subset of HRBAs. Although by their nature HRBAs are difficult to define with exactness, HRBAs are generally *more centrally* focused on the practical utilization and application of human rights principles, unlike other forms of development initiatives. The application of human rights principles in HRBAs is present throughout the evolving process and lifetime of the development initiative.[20] Specifically, the chapter elucidates the conceptual and ethical desirability of HRBAs, fueled by values of fairness and equitability generally contained in human rights principles. The authors, however, also candidly discuss the various practical, contextual, organizational, and cross-border challenges in delivering development outcomes under HRBAs,[21] and demonstrate the difficulties in navigating and balancing complex quantitative and qualitative methods of measuring the delivery of development outcomes under HRBAs. On this latter topic, the chapter realistically assesses the practical challenges faced by HRBAs in measuring and monitoring the delivery of targeted development outcomes, such that the measurements of results obtained align precisely with specific human rights goals or principles that are a more central priority in HRBAs. In the round, this chapter highlights the desirable intrinsic ideals and values embedded in HRBAs while underscoring several complex practical and contextual difficulties that challenge their widespread implementation.

An interesting counterpoint to the perspectives presented in chapter 1 is provided by Rajeev Malhotra in chapter 2, "Delivering Development and Good Governance: Making Human Rights Count." Malhotra's consideration of the integration of human rights into development initiatives extends beyond the conventional scope of HRBAs, as delineated by the authors in chapter 1.[22] Against a broad backdrop of challenges wrought by globalization and the integration of states, Malhotra offers his view that human rights principles play an essential and necessary governance role in development initiatives, both within individual states and on a multilateral platform. He

19 The authors demonstrate that human rights and development, although largely occupying independent legal and academic domains and deriving from different originating sources, have developed in parallel, and in today's context, the issues and concerns they each address significantly converge and overlap.

20 Note that the chapter's focus is on human rights operational principles as they are incorporated into HRBAs.

21 The authors highlight difficulties such as the necessity for organizational and institutional reform—particularly the widespread organizational internalization of the knowledge and principles underpinning HRBAs—which is needed in order that HRBAs are properly implemented and deliver positive impact. Cross-border challenges include situations where HRBAs conceived at an institution's headquarters are often not easily adaptable to foreign contexts and realities when they are implemented.

22 See especially, Malhotra's explanation at note 10 of chapter 2.

makes explicitly clear that human rights operational principles, discussed briefly above, align with the concepts of voice, social contract, and accountability. Significantly, the reader is offered a relatively optimistic view on the practical feasibility of incorporating human rights into development initiatives. Although Malhotra acknowledges that incorporating human rights into development initiatives brings with it practical and operational challenges, he does not consider these challenges insurmountable. He focuses on and proposes a detailed framework—a solution—that demonstrates how human rights approaches to development in the broadest sense[23] might be designed, practically advanced, and its well-crafted outcomes successfully delivered to beneficiaries. Specifically, this framework addresses how development goals, conceived and shaped by human rights substantive and operational principles, may be created, measured, and monitored by relevant and carefully selected human rights–based indicators. These indicators are chosen specifically to match with the attributes of a particular human right, or set of rights, targeted for achievement in a specific development initiative or project. Throughout this process, human rights operational principles, called "cross-cutting norms" by the author, are continually in play during these efforts of measuring delivered outcomes. Through his proposed framework—and with a wider consideration of concrete examples of successes and shortcomings, mostly drawn from India's experience with incorporating human rights into development initiatives—Malhotra invites the reader to reevaluate not merely the inherent value of human rights approaches to development but, more significantly, the practical feasibility of delivering, measuring, and monitoring targeted outcomes under such approaches.

The next two chapters of part I, chapters 3 and 4, examine the specific issue of indigenous peoples' rights in a development context. These chapters complement each other and are discussed together. Chapter 3, "The Right to Development: Translating Indigenous Voice(s) into Development Theory and Practice," by Felipe Gómez Isa, and chapter 4, "The Curse of Riches: Sharing Nature's Wealth Equitably?" by Emilio Viano, consider how economic development in states, driven forward by national and transnational economic pressures, has encroached on and violated indigenous peoples' rights. These chapters also recognize a need for states to acknowledge indigenous peoples' voices—their perspectives, concerns, and way of life—and to incorporate them into state development policies and initiatives. More specifically, Viano and Gómez Isa consider this broad issue through very different lenses, and each clearly emphasizes a very different aspect of the same issue.

In "The Right to Development," Gómez Isa analyzes and evaluates the gradual evolution of international law, largely influenced by the United Nations (UN) and other multilateral organizations, in enshrining and honoring indigenous peoples' rights. The UN Declaration of the Right to Development, the International Labour Organization's Convention 169, and the UN

---

23 *Id.*

Declaration on the Rights of Indigenous Peoples, which Gómez Isa keeps as his central focus, are multilateral commitments established by individual states working with one another and that declare support in honoring, maintaining, and securing indigenous peoples' rights within their state borders. Similarly, in chapter 4, "The Curse of Riches," Viano acknowledges such multilateral efforts to preserve indigenous peoples' rights as a clearly positive step, but the central focus of Viano's broad and revealing account is on how historical and current realities—particularly the interlocking *globalized* web of multilateral financial institutions,[24] the evolving financial mechanisms easing large global transfers of money into and out of developing countries, and the rapid growth of multinational corporations (what he terms an international "revolving door" phenomenon),[25] coupled with pressure to advance economic development in terms of natural resources exploitation—collectively impede the way that indigenous peoples' rights are addressed and incorporated in development initiatives. Viano examines the implementation of solutions, including the impact of the Inter-American Human Rights system, and multilaterally instituted model contracts and best practices. He concludes that although progress has gradually been made, it remains inadequate against the force of interlocking globalized pressures that drive forward economic development against indigenous peoples' voice, rights, and interests. Gómez Isa's solution is *buen vivir,* the concept of "living well" enshrined in Ecuador's Constitution.[26] He suggests that this example represents a clear legal step toward honoring in law indigenous peoples' voice, rights, and way of life. Yet he also acknowledges that such a concept is not yet sufficiently clarified in law to be of practical advantage. Although Gómez Isa does not state as much, his chapter leaves the reader with a sense that even if *buen vivir* is further developed legally, it will inevitably be subject to much controversy with respect to navigating fairly and equitably among the competing interests of economic development, which is particularly acute in developing countries, while trying to preserve indigenous peoples' voice, rights, and way of life.

---

24 For example, the International Monetary Fund and the World Bank.

25 For an explanation of what Viano specifically means by this, see the section titled "The Revolving Door Effect" in the main text of chapter 4, *The Curse of Riches.*

26 The constitution of a nation-state is a social contract in that, first, it contains a set of rights and obligations that the state is legally bound by and expected to honor, with respect to its people, and second, it contains a set of legal rights and obligations that all peoples in that state have consensually agreed to with respect to one another, inter se, and also with the state. In this sense, enshrining rights and concepts in constitutions, if justiciable, accord a degree of power to those who can assert them, including indigenous peoples. For an explanation of the term "social contract" as used in in this volume, *see supra* note 12.

Part II: Sustainable Development

Chapter 5, "Fostering Accountability in Large-Scale Environmental Projects: Lessons from CDM and REDD+ Projects," by Damilola Olawuyi, casts a spotlight on the inadequate incorporation of both substantive and operational human rights in the design, implementation, and delivery of development outcomes under the Kyoto Protocol's Clean Development Mechanism (CDM) and the UN REDD+ projects. Olawuyi examines the nature and practical realities of multilateral cooperation in such projects, as well as the international legal regime, policies, and regulations that govern CDM and REDD+ projects. In so doing, he undertakes a careful analysis of how these programs create ways in which human rights infringements can, and do, occur. He points out gaps in existing multilateral governance and accountability mechanisms that oversee and impact such projects and that result in inadequate safeguards of the social, cultural, and economic rights of peoples affected by those projects. His views are supported by a range of concrete and well-known instances where the implementation of such projects has raised human rights concerns within the international community. A convincing case is made that the lack of human rights considerations—particularly the absence of incorporating human rights operational principles into the multilateral legal and accountability mechanisms governing such projects—has obstructed the fair and equitable delivery of development outcomes. The failure to centralize these human rights concerns, both multilaterally and by states, has caused glaring lapses in the delivery of beneficial outcomes in such projects. Ultimately, beneficial outcomes must be derived through a sincere engagement with and comprehension of the voice and contextual realities experienced by such projects' stakeholders and beneficiaries.[27]

Where chapter 5 examines the role and effects of multilateral and globally oriented legal and accountability regimes in influencing the delivery of outcomes in environmental projects, chapter 6, "The Constitutional Regime for Resource Governance in Africa: The Difficult March toward Accountability," by Francis N. Botchway and Nightingale Rukuba-Ngaiza, undertakes a comparative study of how states' constitutions—namely, those of Botswana, Ghana, Kenya, and South Sudan—influence and safeguard states' prudent natural resource governance in varying ways and degrees of effectiveness. In a broad sense, constitutional provisions may be regarded and evaluated in the sense of being a formal and legally binding social contract made between the state and its people, and also among citizens, inter se, to honor and respect one another's mutual rights, duties, and obligations.[28] These four constitutions reflect varying and progressive efforts at making governments accountable

27 Although the author does not explicitly discuss this, for CDM and REDD+ projects to deliver genuinely successful and positive outcomes for all beneficiaries and stakeholders over the long term, governments must sincerely engage with preexisting informal or unwritten social contracts that characterize or affect the relationships among such projects' beneficiaries and stakeholders. For an explanation of the meaning of a social contract as conceived in this broader sense, *see supra* note 12.

28 *See* especially *supra* note 26.

for their natural resource governance. Each constitution attempts to harness citizens' voice—in terms of citizens' capacity to assert their constitutionally enshrined rights that reflect nationally held values and entitlements—in holding governments and other actors, including foreign private investors, accountable in delivering equitable, prudent, and sustainable exploitation of natural resources. Different provisions in each of these countries' constitutions varyingly advance some way toward—yet crucially also fall short of—instituting clearly justiciable constitutional oversight and sufficient accountability safeguards, which ensure governments' accountability to citizens for their effective management and governance over natural resources.[29] Of particular interest is the authors' analysis of the ways that constitutional provisions delineate, shape, and influence governmental decision-making processes (e.g., through parliaments or state regulatory bodies), which ultimately confer on governments the mandate to execute natural resource contracts with foreign investors. The authors conclude that such provisions, in varying ways across the four constitutions, lack adequate accountability safeguards that ensure governments' transparent decision making and prudent natural resource governance. The chapter concludes by examining the difficulties and relative disempowerment of states to extract themselves from unfairly instituted or negotiated contracts made with large foreign investors, a practice that often dates back to the unfair exploitation of colonial times.

Chapters 7 and 8 are discussed together because they feature complementary country-specific case studies, of Kenya and Cameroon, that show how specific legal regimes govern and deliver sustainable natural resource management through citizen participation. Chapter 7, "Conceptualizing Regulatory Frameworks to Forge Citizen Roles to Deliver Sustainable Natural Resource Management in Kenya," by Robert Kibugi, examines Kenyan laws on community forestry and water resource management; chapter 8, "The Impact of the Legal Framework of Community Forestry on the Development of Rural Areas in Cameroon," by Emmanuel D. Kam Yogo, focuses solely on Cameroonian laws on community forestry. Both authors examine how the respective legal regimes on community forestry operate in practice, mandating the state's cooperative engagement with participating citizens' voice. Such legal regimes necessitate that the state and citizens interact, allowing citizens to communicate among themselves and with the state their views, including their economic, social, and other reasons for using forests; their methods to generate sustainable use; and other relevant contextual circumstances that affect their use of forests.

Under both legal regimes, where informal and preexisting social relationships exist among persons, either because they share a common interest in the use of or interaction with a forest, or because they have a social, cultural, or

29 Constitutional provisions examined by the authors include those governing property rights, environmental protection, as well as provisions that confer power on parliaments, as representatives of all citizens, to enter into contracts with foreign investors for natural resource exploitation.

traditional relationship with one another in connection with the use of a forest, these social relationships may form the foundational basis of formalized legal contracts later signed and agreed on between such persons and the state, allowing the former to use forests sustainably.[30] Under both Kenyan and Cameroonian laws, such legal contracts are overarchingly governed by accountability measures stipulated in law that support both citizens' and the state's rights and duties with respect to one another concerning the sustainable use of forests.[31]

Both chapters express a largely favorable view of the community forestry legal regimes they discuss. In both countries, community forestry laws and regulations clearly incorporate participating citizens' voice. In so doing, such laws and regulations simultaneously mandate and empower state authorities to understand and engage with the preexisting, and informal or unwritten, social rights, obligations, and understandings among participating citizens, in their interactions with one another, and in their use of a forest.[32] Such engagement with preexisting and informal social contracts[33] among participating citizens ultimately constitutes the firm underlying basis on which the abovementioned formal legal agreements are made between participating citizens and the state. In this way, citizens' accountability to the state, and among themselves, concerning their sustainable use of forests is legitimately fostered.

Kibugi, however, raises some criticisms of Kenya's community forestry legal regime, suggesting that legal inconsistencies obfuscate the correct way that laws should be applied. Consequently, in practice, citizens' voice may not be as adequately or satisfactorily honored and incorporated into the legal processes governing community forestry as may be ideal or intended. Further, if, because of legal inconsistencies, accountability and dispute resolution measures are incorrectly applied in practice, increased costs and complications for participating citizens may constrain the effective functioning of such measures as equitable governance and accountability mechanisms through which the state's and citizens' rights and obligations are upheld. Finally, Kibugi also examines water resource management in Kenya and shows that the relevant governing laws similarly attempt to incorporate citizens' and stakeholders' voices into decision-making processes. However, imprecise legal stipulations regarding stakeholders' and citizens' participation in key governance and decision-making bodies, combined with the lack of accurate citizen education and transparency by decision-making bodies, may entail that citizens'

---

30 Such preexisting and informal social relationships, or networks of entrenched understandings, rights, and obligations that exist among such persons, with respect to their use of a forest, may be said to reflect the broader and more fluid meaning of a social contract as has surfaced in some chapters in this volume. For an explanation of the much broader sense in which the concept of a social contract is reflected in this volume, *see supra* note 12.

31 Note, however, that the state adopts a supervisory and monitoring role over community forestry activities.

32 *Supra* note 30.

33 *Id.*

and stakeholders' voices—their concerns and contextual realities—are not adequately addressed in decisions ultimately taken. In these ways, Kibugi highlights clearly that in Kenya, the delivery of fair and equitable outcomes for stakeholders and citizens is challenged with respect to both water resource management and community forestry.

Part III: Urban Law and Policy

Part III opens with chapter 9, "Urban Law: A Key to Accountable Urban Government and Effective Urban Service Delivery," by Matt Glasser and Stephen Berrisford. The authors suggest that urban legislation may conceivably be viewed in the sense of being a social contract governing and apportioning urban rights, duties, and obligations among urban dwellers.[34] Ideally, urban legislation should be contextually appropriate, and when applied on the ground, it should effectively deliver and support the fair and equitable apportionment of economic, social, cultural, and other benefits that urban dwellers derive from urban settings. The authors synthesize important lessons derived from four key areas of urban legislation and policy covered during the World Bank's Law, Justice and Development Week in 2013: titling and tenure rights in urban settings of developing countries; what constitutes effective urban legislation and how this may be delivered; the contextual realities of urban law and its implementation in African countries; and tax and insolvency legislation that shapes behaviors and circumstances leading up to and in the aftermath of the insolvency of subnational or municipal governments. Drawing from a variety of illustrative and insightful examples, the authors examine how urban legislation and policies, when implemented, often fall short of their ideal function in delivering and maintaining a fair and equitable apportionment of the various social, economic, and other benefits that urban settings offer residents. This chapter illuminates some causes of the disparity between urban legislation's ideal function and the contextual realities that demonstrate that the ideal function of urban legislation has not been delivered or realized on the ground. From the authors' coverage of the four key areas, it becomes broadly discernible that when such disparity exists, two things have occurred. First, the goals, design, and implementation of urban legislation have not been adequately influenced by, nor has legislation properly addressed, various stakeholders' voice—namely, their varied perspectives, contextual realities and needs—or the complex social relationships that characterize such stakeholders' lives and existence.[35] When policies' or legislation's

34 For an explanation of the meaning of a social contract as used conventionally, as well as in the much broader and fluid sense with which it is engaged within this volume, *see supra* note 15. Berrisford and Glasser's brief discussion of urban legislation as a social contract apportioning rights, duties, and obligations among dwellers in urban settings departs from the narrow and conventional meaning of a social contract and includes elements of the much broader sense with which this term is alluded to or reflected in some of this volume's chapters.

35 Who exactly these stakeholders are would logically be determined by the particular legislative, policy, or urban initiative at issue and its impact. Broadly speaking, they may include

content and architecture do not accede to and honor the value of voice, as just detailed, the goals, design, and implementation of urban laws and policies are unlikely to be consistent with stakeholders' needs and contextual realities. Consequently, the resultant urban legislation and policies implemented are unable, in practice, to truly represent, shape beneficially, or deliver fair and equitable solutions to urban residents and other stakeholders. Second, following this premise, any accountability or governance mechanism instituted and purported to benefit stakeholders is unlikely to function as intended due to inadequate understanding and addressing of contextual realities that determine the workability and effectiveness of the mechanisms. Glasser and Berrisford do not explicitly state the above two points, but their chapter is a revealing overview that showcases in the foregoing light that the interlocking concepts of voice, social contract,[36] and accountability are essential to the goals, design, and implementation of urban law and policy. In the absence of these concepts, the successful delivery of properly targeted economic, social, and other outcomes to beneficiaries and stakeholders through urban legislation will not be achieved.

Chapters 10 and 11 both illustrate in further detail the key aspects that Berrisford and Glasser's chapter raise. First, in chapter 10, "Confronting Complexity: Using Action-Research to Build Voice, Accountability, and Justice in Nairobi's Mukuru Informal Settlements," by Jane Weru, Waikwa Wanyoike, and Adrian Di Giovanni, we are confronted with an action-research initiative set in Mukuru, a pair of slum settlements in Nairobi, Kenya. The authors describe and evaluate researchers' efforts, with an eye firmly fixed on contextual realities and practicalities, to conduct extensive legal and other research to understand the shape and nature of urban problems experienced by Mukuru's slum dwellers. Such research opens avenues through which slum dwellers' and other stakeholders' voices may be understood and addressed. Specifically, it involves first-hand and practical interaction with slum residents to comprehend the complex network of urban problems that are rooted in complex and interlocking relationships established between slum residents and other stakeholders (e.g., landowners and utilities service providers).[37] Ultimately, it is on this basis of contextual research that researchers have found creative and contextually sensitive ways—such as through litigation based on residents' constitutional property rights and public advocacy—to progressively deliver improvements to slum residents' living conditions.

The key value of this urban initiative is that, instituted at the grassroots level, assessments of problems and creations of solutions are carried out in

---

urban dwellers from the widest range of social and economic groups, relevant state institutions, and private sector investors in cities.

36 *Supra* note 34.

37 The authors' description of the complex and interlocking relationships between slum residents and other stakeholders reflects the concept of a social contract in the broader, more fluid sense, as has descriptively surfaced in some of this volume's chapters. For an explanation of this kind of social contract, *see supra* note 12.

a direct, hands-on, and contextually sensitive manner. Valuably impressed on the reader are the many practical solutions to problems creatively derived from researchers' context-specific engagement with and practical application of the concepts of voice, social contract,[38] and accountability to deliver beneficial outcomes. One such outcome is the use of the Kenyan Constitution as the legal basis of ongoing litigation that asserts Mukuru residents' rights when threatened by the state or other stakeholders.[39] Furthermore, through harnessing such concepts in researchers' cooperation with Mukuru residents, new legal and planning tools and practical strategies of engagement (e.g., public advocacy) that improve residents' living conditions have been delivered. As the authors showcase clearly, these evolving and progressive outcomes have been derived from research and other activities that are necessarily multidisciplinary in nature and draw on the values and concepts of voice, social contract, and accountability.

Ending part III is chapter 11, "'Good' Legislation as a Means of Ensuring Voice, Accountability, and the Delivery of Results in Urban Development," by Maria Mousmouti and Gianluca Crispi. Demonstrating first that urban legislation functions as a social contract that navigates a complex web of competing interests,[40] the authors illuminate the meaning of "good" legislation. For example, "good" legislation is simple, easily understood and implemented, and delivers effective and efficient outcomes for urban residents and other stakeholders. One problem illuminated in Glasser and Berrisford's chapter is that urban legislation, when implemented, often falls far short of its ideal and intended objectives.[41] Among a range of solutions, Mousmouti and Crispi suggest that such incongruity is appropriately addressed by "evidence-based law making." This refers to law making that derives its goals, design, and implementation from harnessing the value of voice to discover, comprehend, and gather evidence on the contextual realities and urban problems faced by residents and stakeholders so that they may be addressed. In so doing, such legislation is designed so that, first, it may be implemented harmoniously with contextual realities and, second, where beneficial and appropriate, it may also more equitably reshape any preexisting social relationships, formal and informal, that may not currently, fairly, or optimally apportion economic, social, and other benefits among urban residents and other stake-

38 *Id.*

39 As understood in its conventional sense, a nation-state's constitution is a social contract on which rights are justiciable. For an explanation of a nation-state's constitution as a social contract, *see supra* note 26. *See* also *supra* note 12.

40 Although not explicitly stated by the authors, their description of urban legislation accords with Glasser and Berrisford's concept of urban legislation as a social contract apportioning rights and obligations among private and public sector stakeholders, including residents, with respect to numerous shared resources and other aspects of urban living. *See supra* note 34 and its accompanying discussion in the main text. For an explanation of the broader and more fluid sense of a social contract as reflected in this volume, *see supra* note 12.

41 This problem is particularly acute in the rapidly growing cities in developing countries.

holders.[42] Highlighted also is the importance of accurately assessing the financial and institutional capacity of state and urban institutions as part of contextual realities to be addressed so that legislative efforts can be properly enforced in practice and accountability and monitoring efforts effectively and efficiently carried out by state and urban authorities. Throughout the chapter, the authors repeatedly illuminate that understanding contextual realities, in alignment with the concepts of voice and social contract[43] and on which urban legislation may be designed and implemented, is fundamental and indispensable if beneficial, workable, and enforceable urban legislative outcomes are to be delivered to urban residents and stakeholders. In this vein, legislation that is clear, contextually sensitive, and easily complied with in practice is legislation that can also easily hold residents and stakeholders accountable.

Part IV: Sexual and Gender-Based Violence

Part IV commences with chapter 12, "Justice Sector Delivery of Services in the Context of Fragility and Conflict: What Is Being Done to Address Sexual and Gender-Based Violence?" by Waafas Ofosu-Amaah, Rea Abada Chiongson, and Camilla Gandini. This chapter offers a thorough and comprehensive overview of a range of problems and issues, and proposes a variety of useful context-appropriate and gender-sensitive solutions that address sexual and gender-based violence (SGBV) in fragility and conflict situations (FCS). The authors' key focus is on justice sector and related reforms that may effectively deliver justice and redress to victims as well as successfully hold perpetrators accountable. Solutions proposed, however, affect more than the justice sector and the delivery of justice outcomes; they also draw on and have wider implications with respect to invoking beneficial change in societal mind-sets, behaviors, and other social norms on which SGBV is deemed acceptable in certain communities and thereby recurrently perpetuated.[44]

This chapter demonstrates that justice sector reforms and the delivery of justice, especially in FCS, clearly cannot function in isolation from wider institutional and other societal reforms. Specifically, justice sector reforms that address SGBV in FCS face unique challenges, including fragmented state and justice institutions, limited access to justice, lack of rule of law, and minimal resources. In FCS, delivering effective prosecution and other context- and gender-sensitive forms of redress for SGBV victims through justice institutions is especially difficult. This is often because of a network of deeply entrenched social values and norms in certain communities, which impede female (and sometimes male) victims' voice—their grievances, experiences, and perspectives—from being aired and addressed, both within and beyond available channels of redress in justice institutions. This network of entrenched societal

42 *Supra* note 40.

43 *Id.*

44 Although the authors mainly cover SGBV issues as perpetuated against women, they acknowledge that men can similarly be victims.

norms obstructing the voice of SGBV victims is internalized and experienced by men and women in their communities, and it strictly governs what those communities regard as appropriate gender behavior, mind-sets, and values. On a separate but related note, the authors observe that where formal and informal justice systems exist to address SGBV, they often operate in alignment with preexisting social, economic, or other biases toward educated or more socially empowered perpetuators. Although the authors primarily focus on a range of justice sector reforms, it is made clear that at bottom, an underlying solution to SGBV—because it is both preventative and an essential catalyst to attain victims' redress—is to progressively change the nature and shape of such social mind-sets, behaviors, and norms internalized by communities, such that victims and potential victims of SGBV are more empowered and their voices better heard and understood. Doing so is clearly necessary to catalyze and enable the effective workability of many of the targeted reforms proposed by the authors. The range of solutions offered for enabling or supporting delivery of justice to SGBV victims are crucially centered around strategies for strengthening, empowering, or finding avenues for victims' voice to be aired, understood, accurately interpreted, and made evidentially helpful during investigation and adjudicatory processes relating to courts of law or other forums where justice is sought. Such solutions ideally should not operate alone but should work in an integrated manner.[45]

Chapter 13, "Sexual Violence in Conflict: Can There Be Justice?" by Teresa Doherty, offers insightful observations on the historical development and evolution of women's sexual rights in law and as adjudicated by courts, specifically, as these rights pertain to sexual crimes perpetuated against women during conflict and war. Doherty charts evolving international laws and cases that came before courts of justice and that had an impact (or lack thereof) on protecting women's sexual rights during war and conflict. She observes that it is only after World War II that a gradual but tangible shift toward more satisfactory international laws protecting women from rape and sexual assault during war and conflict occurred. The author notes, however, that postwar criminal tribunals in Nuremberg and Tokyo did not prosecute sexual crimes; it was only later, at the international criminal tribunals, namely, the International Criminal Tribunal for the Former Yugoslavia, the International Criminal Tribunal for Rwanda, and the Special Court of Sierra Leone, that sexual crimes during war and conflict were progressively prosecuted more often and in increasing number. Doherty points out that today there is international consensus and recognition that rape during war is torture, an act of terror, and an act of genocide; it is a war crime and a crime against humanity.[46] Further reforms and changes in mind-sets remain necessary.

---

45 In addition, such solutions' workability clearly requires the integration of knowledge from many relevant disciplines beyond the legal, for example, from medicine, education, or psychology. A multidisciplinary approach is required.

46 See note 38 and its accompanying main text in chapter 13, *Sexual Violence in Conflict: Can There Be Justice?* by Teresa Doherty.

One key question that Doherty examines—in the light of past prosecutions and with an eye toward the future—is: What needs to change, and how may such change be brought about, in order that perpetrators of sexual war crimes may be held criminally accountable for their acts?[47] Doherty, with her experienced view as a former judge at the Special Court of Sierra Leone, shows that contrary to popular perception, female victims often and actively seek that their voice—namely, their suffering, grievances, and perspectives—be understood openly in a court of law where judicial redress may be sought. Inaccurate and prevalent perceptions that women must be shielded from further harm caused by putting them through a rigorous and detailed adjudicatory process involving examination and cross-examination are contrary to reality and need to be eschewed. Such attitudes prevent the strengthening and empowerment of women's voices in courts of law, where prosecutions can occur and perpetrators held accountable. Doherty also observes that the inability of courts to successfully prosecute perpetuators and deliver justice to victims of sexual war crimes is often due to evidentiary challenges. Cultural and linguistic barriers to a court's accurate interpretation of witnesses' evidence may operate in practice to prevent this. Further, obtaining medically relevant and other useful corroborative evidence of sexual violence is valuable at trial. This is not easily done if the knowledge base and efficiency of other systems (e.g., those that are medical or psychological in nature) that support the prosecution of sexual war crimes are not adequately equipped to perform this role. It is impossible to capture Doherty's many rich and revealing insights. She concludes by acknowledging that, although much progress has encouragingly been made over time, there remains room for "all participants in the justice system"[48] to integrate their efforts to ensure that perpetrators can be effectively and consistently prosecuted and justice delivered to victims.

The authors of chapters 12 and 13 adopt different perspectives and emphasize different aspects of the problem of SGBV. Taken together, these two chapters offer the reader a rich and thorough consideration of some specific practical challenges—in law and as relevant to justice systems and institutions—which characterize the search for solutions and the delivery of justice outcomes in this area.

Part V: Improving Access to Justice

The subject matter of the first two chapters in part V—chapter 14, "The Ministério Público of the State of Minas Gerais and the ADR Experience," by Danielle de Guimarães Germano Arlé and Luciano Luz Badini Martins, and chapter 15, "ICT-Driven Strategies for Reforming Access to Justice Mechanisms in Developing Countries," by Karim Benyekhlef, Emmanuelle Amar,

47 Under international law, perpetuators' accountability may be viewed as extending to their victims, wider society, and even the international community.

48 As discussed in this chapter, such participants include, for example, judges, investigators, medical witnesses, and court interpreters.

and Valentin Callipel—is vastly different, but both examine in detail unique and innovative initiatives that improve beneficiaries' access to justice.

In chapter 14, the authors discuss the creation of, and the unique alternative dispute resolution (ADR) activities undertaken by the Ministério Público of the State of Minas Gerais (MPMG) in Brazil. For the authors, ADR is not ADR as understood conventionally; in this chapter, ADR refers to the highly unique objectives, methods, and approaches taken in a range of areas in dispute resolution as carried out by the MPMG. The MPMG is independent from the three branches of the Brazilian government and may be considered a fourth governance institution. Focusing on civil disputes connected with environmental issues, the authors describe ADR-derived solutions that, because of their flexibility and practicality, are relevant to affected parties and stakeholders as well as contextually appropriate. ADR includes negotiations and pretrial mediations between the MPMG and individual or corporate persons who have perpetrated a wrong against society at large (e.g., they have caused damage to the environment through industrial or economic activities) or against affected select groups or other affected persons. The ADR process is evidently aligned with the value of voice in the sense of giving affected or disputing parties a chance to express grievances or perspectives outside a court of law, with the intent of reaching some kind of resolution. Reaching a resolution, in its ultimate form, includes a process of understanding the contextual realities in which are situated complex governing laws, for example, the country's constitutional protections[49] and other national laws. Simultaneously, reaching a resolution also involves comprehending and engaging with informal networks of preexisting social relationships, patterns of behavior, and other social norms that are practised among affected stakeholders, communities, or other parties.[50] These norms may have been violated by individual persons or corporations. ADR navigates and finds solutions to interparty disputes or violations of the public interest, and incorporates into such solutions, first, the voice of disputing parties and other affected stakeholders and, second, contextual realities that include the existence of, and in some cases also the violation of, constitutional or national laws, or a contravention of informal yet entrenched social norms that exist among affected parties.[51] It is clear that because ADR is instituted on the foundational values of voice and honoring preexisting social relationships and other social norms[52] through negotiations that are sensitive to contexts and parties' concerns, solutions consensually reached acquire a degree of legitimacy. In this light, the ADR process itself becomes an effective governance mechanism that supports parties' account-

---

49 *See supra* note 39.

50 Such networks of preexisting social relationships, patterns of behavior, and other social norms reflect the broader meaning of a social contract as alluded to in this volume. For an explanation of the broader sense of the concept of a social contract as reflected in this volume, *see supra* note 12.

51 *Id.*

52 *Id.*

ability in meeting obligations under a consensually derived resolution.[53] In the foregoing light, ADR contains many valuable lessons on how the concepts of voice, social contract, and accountability may be harnessed and utilized to deliver an ADR system that gives beneficiaries an improved and legitimate access to justice outside the traditional court system, yet functioning in a way that remains complementary to it.[54]

In chapter 15, "ICT-Driven Strategies," increasing the efficiency and effectiveness of stakeholders' access to and attainment of justice outcomes is an overarching goal. However, unlike in chapter 14, where the MPMG's ADR system creates justice outcomes and exists outside traditional courts, Benyekhlef, Amar, and Callipel discuss enhancing access to justice by improving preexisting justice systems, structures, and processes through the use of information and communication technology (ICT) innovations. The authors explain in detail that first, understanding the voice—in other words, the specific needs, concerns, and problems—of justice actors and other stakeholders who interact with the justice system, using a multidisciplinary approach, and second, understanding the contextual practicalities in which current justice systems, structures, and processes operate is fundamental. Acquiring an understanding of both enables designing and implementing contextually specific and highly targeted ICT innovations to existing justice systems, processes, and structures, such that effective and efficient access to justice can be delivered. The use of ICT in justice systems is not new but has produced varying degrees of success. The authors examine the causes for failure or inadequate delivery of outcomes and propose various contextually sensitive methodologies and solutions to circumvent such a result. In this vein, they emphasize that ICT initiatives must adequately examine and understand contextual realities that characterize both the nature of problems faced and the existing advantages experienced by justice system users, stakeholders, and actors. If this is not the case, overly general or imprecise solutions are developed, which, when applied, do not sufficiently address contextual specificities, and, consequently, such initiatives are considerably less likely to deliver intended results. Voice—in the specific sense of understanding the contextual and practical realities that characterize justice systems' use by justice actors and stakeholders, including such users' mind-sets, and other cultural or socioeconomic factors affect-

53 This is further supported by the fact that, practically speaking, not honoring such ADR agreements may ultimately cause an action to be instituted in a court of law, with potentially undesirable legal and practical consequences.

54 The authors do not discuss this at length, but it is clear that ADR can also be a repository of case-related knowledge and, in theory, a potential agent for change. Over time, the MPMG clearly gains experience and expertise in being able to address disputes or violations similar to ones that have occurred previously. If a repeated recurrence or pattern of prior similar cases emerges, the similar ways in which affected stakeholder and party perspectives and disputes have been understood and negotiated, and the way that their rights and obligations have been clarified, become new understandings that may progressively become more regularized and well accepted not just by the directly affected parties but also by the MPMG, and perhaps even by wider society. In this sense, ADR may potentially become an agent for positive change with respect to certain recurrent issues that affect the public interest.

ing such users' nature and ability to interact with justice systems—needs to be honored and addressed when developing ICT initiatives to deliver better access to justice. In addition, instituting contextually appropriate monitoring and accountability mechanisms to ensure that designed ICT solutions achieve intended results is essential. Crucially, the authors refute the notion that ICT use invariably delivers improved access to justice; more accurately, they credibly suggest that if ICT innovations are to deliver positive outcomes, appropriately harnessing the value of voice to understand contextual realities and addressing these realities in highly targeted and contextually specific solutions is key.

Chapter 16, "Courts and Regulatory Governance in Latin America: Improving Delivery in Development by Managing Institutional Interplay," by Rene Urueña, engages with cutting-edge concepts of regulatory governance and examines the ways in which independent regulatory agencies (IRAs), and specifically courts, interact with one another and synergistically create just and workable regulatory solutions to a shared problem. Urueña's empirical observations and approach deviate from top-down conceptions of regulatory governance. Instead, he demonstrates that courts' and IRAs' active interactions with one another and with other stakeholders, actors, experts, and other players in local, national, and international contexts are organic and evolutionary. Any given context—whether local, national, or transnational—within which IRAs and courts interact is called a "regulatory space." Thus, regulatory solutions to problems are not derived and implemented in a static top-down way by courts and IRAs acting in individual isolation. Rather, solutions are achieved through courts and IRAs using one another and other stakeholders, actors, experts, and other players within a given regulatory space as continual catalysts and stimuli for new workable ideas. In this way, solutions to problems are organically shaped and ultimately derived.

The above process is discussed predominantly in the light of concrete examples involving courts' regulatory and supervisory influence and role in Colombia and Argentina. The author demonstrates that in these specific Latin American contexts, such interactions and activities in regulatory spaces that involve courts and IRAs—which are organic, contextually informative, and evolutionary—generate contextually relevant understandings and knowledge on which creative and contextually appropriate solutions are devised. In this process, courts play a key role as catalyst and facilitator. Interaction between courts and IRAs, and among IRAs under court supervision, draw from and open up avenues for hearing and understanding the voice of IRAs, affected stakeholders, actors, experts, and other relevant players; when this happens, courts working with IRAs are able to generate just initiatives and solutions that incorporate these perspectives. In addition, this interactive process clarifies the preexisting scope of IRAs' operations and interactions with one another and also, where appropriate, creates new and more effective formal and informal understandings and interactions, both among IRAs, and between IRAs and affected stakeholders.[55] This enables the creation and delivery of beneficial, legitimate, and contextually workable regulatory outcomes. Finally, based on contextual knowledge and awareness derived from such organic interactions, courts and IRAs are able to establish workable, effective, and efficient accountability mechanisms through which just outcomes to regulatory problems can be delivered and continually ensured. As Urueña demonstrates, courts' interactions with IRAs are often the essential catalyst for generating beneficial regulatory outcomes through a process that aligns with the concepts and values of voice, social contract,[56] and accountability.[57] Such contextually driven, organic, and evolutionary interactions among courts and IRAs, as well as with stakeholders, experts, and other players, are observed to be what in actuality delivers just and viable regulatory solutions, not top-down approaches.

Part VI: Anticorruption and Stolen Assets Recovery

Broadly speaking, anticorruption laws and policies safeguard against assets being misused by public officials or persons from the private sector[58] for private or personal gains, and such misuse being carried out in ways or with objectives that violate the public interest. In this broad sense, anticorruption laws and policies have the ultimate objective of safeguarding the public interest against such acts that contravene it. In addition, such law and policies seek to make those who carry out corrupt acts accountable under the law and to act as a deterrent, where appropriate. In most jurisdictions, criminal or civil legal actions, and often both, are available against persons alleged or found to be guilty of corruption.

Part VI opens with chapter 17, "The New Brazilian Anticorruption Law: Federation Challenges and Institutional Roles," by William Coelho and Letícia Barbabela, which is appropriately followed by "Voice and Accountability: Improving the Delivery of Anticorruption and Anti–Money Laundering Strategies in Brazil," by Fausto Martin De Sanctis. Chapters 17 and 18 are discussed together, as they are similarly concerned with developments in anticorruption law and policy in Brazil.

---

55 Conceivably, this interactive process reflects clarification of, and redefining beneficially, preexisting social contracts in the broad sense of meaning IRAs' established operational scope, usual practices, and interactions with one another and also with affected stakeholders. For an explanation of the broader and less-conventional meaning of a social contract, *see supra* note 15.

56 *Id.*

57 Urueña also reveals the important multidisciplinary nature of solving regulatory problems, where experts from a range of disciplines assist in the supervisory role of courts; in addition, expertise, knowledge, and solutions to local problems are derived from organic interactions that involve not just local and national sources or IRAs but also multilateral institutions and sources.

58 The meaning of "persons" as used here includes individuals, companies, and employees of companies.

In chapter 17, Coelho and Barbabela offer the reader a broad overview of past developments in the anticorruption and anti–money laundering legal regime in Brazil, with a special focus on the history and legislative process of one of the most recent legal reforms, namely, the new Anticorruption Law (new ACL), Act No. 12,846/2013. The authors examine the provisions in the new ACL closely, examining its advantages and shortcomings, and evaluate the challenges that Brazilian public institutions face in applying the new law. These challenges include the lack of uniformity and consistency in decisions made throughout Brazil's expansive and diverse federal system, an inefficient judicial system, administrative and resource-related difficulties that impede poorer municipalities in correctly applying the new ACL, and the vast problem of coordinating the many accountability and oversight institutions that play a key role in ensuring that Brazilian anticorruption laws deliver their intended results. The authors also examine specifically the key role played by the Office of the Comptroller General and the Ministério Público, and the importance of incorporating an anticorruption ethos into the business culture of private sector corporations. Overall, the chapter offers many revealing insights into the challenges faced, as well as key solutions and advantages that can deliver progressive and positive outcomes in Brazil's continued efforts in combating corruption.

Chapter 18, written by De Sanctis, a federal appellate judge in Brazil's Federal Court in São Paulo, considers national strategies undertaken by the Brazilian government to combat corruption and money laundering. The first of these he examines is the National Strategy for Combating Corruption and Money Laundering, which endeavors to deliver more efficient and effective investigation and prosecution processes pertaining to money laundering crimes through cooperation with various government and civil society sectors and organizations. Briefly highlighted are Brazil's international anticorruption efforts, because Brazil is a signatory to various key multilateral anticorruption conventions[59] and consequently has promulgated a range of anticorruption and anti–money laundering national legislation, such as the new ACL. De Sanctis's perspective as a federal appellate judge is most valuable and insightful in his critique of the Brazilian judicial system and the systemic challenges to courts and judges in effectively and efficiently adjudicating money laundering and corruption crimes. He notes that in the current and evolving context of new anticorruption and anti–money laundering initiatives, many beneficial innovations have been delivered, such as specialized courts for financial crimes and money laundering. However, there is currently considerable pressure placed on judges and courts to adjudicate cases fairly and efficiently but without sufficient administrative support. In addition, other procedural and

59 As discussed by De Sanctis, these would be the UN Convention against Corruption (the Mérida Convention), enacted in 2006, the Inter-American Convention against Corruption of 2002, and the Convention on Combating Bribery of Foreign Public Officials in International Business Transactions (the OECD Convention) of 2000. Brazil has also received an invitation to join the Open Government Partnership launched by the Obama administration in the United States in 2010.

systemic reforms need to occur if justice, in the form of fair, successful, and efficient prosecutions of corrupt actors, is to be effectively delivered. Coordination of various actors and stakeholders (e.g., the police, federal prosecutors, and the Council for Financial Intelligence Unit) must also take place in an integrated way to support prosecutions and judicial processes if fair, effective, and efficient justice outcomes against corruption and corrupt actors are to result. This chapter highlights that new anticorruption legislative initiatives in Brazil encouragingly reflect strong political will to combat corruption. However, long entrenched and complex judicial, administrative, and other institutional systemic shortcomings need to be overcome to deliver fair and successful justice outcomes that consistently hold corrupt actors accountable.

Chapter 19, "Development-Oriented Alternatives to Debarment as an Anticorruption Accountability Tool," by Frank A. Fariello Jr. and Giovanni Bo, critiques the predominant and frequent use of debarment by the World Bank in its system of international sanctions against corrupt actors and persons.[60] The authors examine the proper use and value of debarment in the light of other alternatives, and ultimately propose that community service, undertaken by corrupt parties, be included in the range of Bank sanctions against corruption.

Among other insights, Fariello and Bo carefully examine the premises and rationale behind the accepted view that debarment is a workable and effective deterrent against corruption. They conclude that this proposition is at best a credible assumption but that there is no concrete basis on which to accept that it is indisputably true. The authors firmly acknowledge the potential and actual benefits of debarment as an anticorruption tool, making clear that it should by no means be removed from the World Bank's sanctions system; however, they candidly highlight the less-discussed controversies surrounding debarment. This includes, for example, resultant anticompetitive effects in markets where the debarred party is one of a very few willing bidders for Bank-financed projects, which could drive up costs to the Bank.[61] Another effect is that debarment may apply pressure on governments requiring Bank financing to find other sources that apply fewer safeguards and legal constraints on financed projects. These and other effects discussed may indirectly constrain the fulfillment of the Bank's development objectives. Reparative and preventative anticorruption alternatives to debarment are examined in a candid light.[62] The authors highlight that in spite of their benefits, each of these alternatives contains inherent difficulties that mitigate its potential posi-

---

60 The meaning of *persons* as used here, in the context of Fariello and Bo's chapter, includes individuals and corporations.

61 Thee authors also acknowledge that debarment may have a sanitizing effect on unclean markets where corrupt persons, including corporations, exert a collusive effect on other persons in the same market who compete for involvement or investments in Bank-financed projects.

62 Alternatives to debarment examined in this chapter include making corrupt parties institute integrity compliance programs, mandating financial restitution to compensate for harms caused by corrupt acts, and participating in the Voluntary Disclosure Program.

tive effects. The authors therefore make a valuable and innovative proposition: instituting community service as a remedy of restitution for corrupt acts and behavior by persons who transact business with the Bank or who are involved in Bank-financed projects is an attractive and viable alternative to debarment. The advantages and challenges of community service are covered in detail, and the authors conclude that as a Bank sanctions tool, community service needs to be carefully managed on multiple fronts. For example, Bank policies need to define the circumstances and persons for which such sanction is appropriate, how the project's scope or scale should be decided, and the procedural and operational rules governing this sanction's application. On the whole, the authors are optimistic that community service is an attractive and viable anticorruption sanctions tool and should be included among other Bank sanctions that hold corrupt actors accountable.

The last chapter in this part that focuses solely on anticorruption is chapter 20, "Making Delivery a Priority: A Philosophical Perspective on Corruption and a Strategy for Remedy," by Morigiwa Yasutomo, who presents the reader with a novel and refreshing perspective on anticorruption laws and policies. Through the lens of legal philosophy, Morigiwa first examines what corruption is, its origins, and its causes; he then discusses the roots and evolution of legitimate decision making undertaken in the public interest, as distinct from private interests. Next, he conducts a revealing examination of the reasons for the existence of corruption, with "corruption" defined as public officials acting in their private interest in a way that contravenes the public interest. Morigiwa explores the paradox that, although from a collective vantage point, the benefits of honoring the public interest are clearly understood and rationally should be upheld, corrupt acts are still undertaken by individual public officials who, from their individual vantage points, consider such corrupt acts rational undertakings. The author terms this the "situational rationality" of corruption, and the causes of this are in turn termed the "drivers of corruption."

Morigiwa posits three principles that should be borne in mind in the design of anticorruption policy that diminishes the drivers of corruption and, consequently, the situational rationality of corruption. The first principle is to increase the relative personal cost over the personal gains of corruptive behavior through sanctions or other means, such that corruptive behavior becomes situationally irrational to the public official. The second principle is that of aligning public officials' private interests and concerns with the public interest, such that attainment of the former is also an achievement of the latter.[63] The more complex third principle highlights how society's collective rationalization and appreciation of the public interest, as distinct from private benefits and interests, may usefully evolve. Thus, the maintenance of society's collec-

---

63 An illustration of the second principle is as follows. Increasing the relative private benefit that accrues to public officials for performing acts consistent with the public interest, or for not performing corrupt acts, can have the effect of rendering corruptive behavior no longer situationally rational. The second principle is in a sense the flip side of the first principle.

tive rationalization and appreciation of the desirability of honoring or acting in the public interest to equitably distribute collective benefits to all is an ethos that ultimately prevents or works against corruptive behavior.[64] The author's argument ultimately leads to his apt observation that public officials need not, and in actuality do not, always rationalize and appreciate the costs and benefits of their acts before undertaking them. Instead, where rule of law exists, public officials' automatic compliance with law through their acts demonstrates that the "authority of law" is what preempts rational meanderings or weighing up of personal costs and benefits before lawful acts are undertaken. Clearly, where rule of law exists, all laws, including those that directly or indirectly discourage or prevent corruption, mandate compliance by their sheer existence. In this light, effective anticorruption policy necessitates creating, and strengthening, the rule of law to effectively prevent corrupt behavior. In addition, all three of the above-mentioned principles may usefully feature in the design of effective anticorruption policy, working together to bolster its impact.

Morigiwa's underlying reasoning and perspective is one whereby policy makers and legislators are offered a systematic framework to conceptualize key principles and the fundamental objectives that the design of anticorruption initiatives should seek to deliver.

Closely related to anticorruption policy and the accountability issues that it raises is the recovery of public assets stolen by corrupt public officials and other individuals. On this topic, chapter 21, "Measures for Asset Recovery: A Multiactor Global Fund for Recovered Stolen Assets," by Stephen Kingah, offers some detailed insights. Kingah first examines a range of reasons that justify resources spent on and transnational cooperative efforts undertaken toward the recovery of stolen assets. Such reasons relate to the establishment of greater justice and fairness to people of states whose public assets are stolen, the need to hold culpable public officials firmly accountable, and the deterrence of current and future perpetrators of corruption and money laundering crimes. Kingah undertakes a close examination of the global and regional multilateral rules and institutions that support the recovery of stolen assets. Chief among these is the UN Convention Against Corruption (UNCAC).[65] In addition to examining the international laws and cooperative efforts undertaken to facilitate recovery of stolen assets, Kingah rigorously presents his perspective, supported by a range of examples, on some key challenges faced by countries involved in recovering stolen assets. These challenges include the inherent legal difficulties in establishing the right to seize traced assets located in foreign jurisdictions as well as the high cost of the recovery and tracing process. Kingah acknowledges that international cooperation is key and proposes a unique solution, namely, a global fund he calls the Global Stolen Asset Recovery Fund (GSARF). The GSARF does not currently exist in any form, but as envisaged by the author it would be a multilaterally supported fund

---

64 *See* pages 488–492 of chapter 20, "Making Delivery a Priority."

65 *See supra* note 59.

that draws cooperative and targeted operative support from countries and multilateral institutions at the global, regional, and national levels. Kingah discusses in detail what he conceives would be the potential ideal objectives and operations of the GSARF. In his view, this potential solution for the future holds promise in addressing the challenges encountered in recovering stolen assets. Although Kingah clearly underscores the ideal objectives and benefits of the GSARF as he envisions it, he clearly highlights that key multilateral challenges in the current context prevent its creation.[66] Overall, Kingah presents a candid and detailed perspective on the highly complex challenges of stolen asset recovery, which, as he makes clear, cannot be adequately addressed without highly integrated, systematic, and cooperative efforts undertaken by the international community. GSARF may be one possible solution instituted at a future time, but it can materialize only when current key challenges to its creation cease to exist and when multilateral conditions have evolved sufficiently to accommodate it.[67]

Part VII: Perspectives on the World Bank Inspection Panel

This last part of the volume consists of three chapters, each offering different perspectives on the World Bank Inspection Panel ("the Panel"). All three detail the Panel's operational framework and scope of authority. In varying degrees, each chapter provides a comparative and revealing counterpoint to the others. It is impossible to cover all points raised, but some of the more interesting and essential insights are discussed below.

The first contribution is chapter 22, "Improving Service Delivery through Voice and Accountability: The Experience of the World Bank Inspection Panel," by Dilek Barlas and Tatiana Tassoni. Barlas, the Panel's Executive Secretary, and Tassoni, one of the Panel's Senior Operations Officers, present an invaluable insider's perspective of the Panel's work. They underscore that the Panel is the first multilateral accountability mechanism that has an independent and overarching authority to investigate its own organization's compliance with internal operational and safeguard policies in the design, appraisal, and implementation of Bank-financed projects. With their insider's perspective, the authors explain the ways that the Panel operates in alignment with the concepts of voice, social contract,[68] and accountability. They justify the Panel's existence as an accountability mechanism as follows. Put succinctly, the Bank's operational and safeguard policies are incorporated into the terms

---

66 As discussed by Kingah, the first challenge is that such a fund would operate under specified governing terms and conditions and therefore would be likely to contravene UNCAC's approach, which holds that asset recovery should be unconditional. The second challenge is that, according to the author's understanding, to date, the World Bank has not indicated support for such a fund.

67 *Id.*

68 For an explanation of how the concept of social contract is used and engaged within this volume, *see supra* note 12.

and frameworks of the formal financing agreements that the Bank makes with the governments of its member countries; this is done to ultimately ensure that Bank financing confers intended social protections and economic benefits on development projects' ultimate beneficiaries and stakeholders, in accordance with such policies. In this light, the mandatory and governing effect of such policies extends beyond the terms contained in the four corners of the financing agreement and its parties; in actuality, these policies may be viewed as an expression of a unique kind of social contract that the Bank has established between itself and the beneficiaries and stakeholders of the development projects that it finances.[69] The justification for this proposition is that such policies, which inform the financing agreement signed between the Bank and governments, reflect the Bank's intention and mandate to confer economic benefits and social protections enshrined in such policies to ultimate beneficiaries and stakeholders of Bank-financed projects. It is on this basis that beneficiaries or other stakeholders who experience harm or potential harm that is caused by Bank Management's contraventions of the Bank's policies have the right to make their voice—their resultant grievances, perspectives, and unique contextual circumstances—heard, understood, and addressed through the Panel. The Panel, then, functions as a legitimate accountability mechanism through which beneficiaries' voice can be aired and understood, Bank Management consequently held to account, and, where appropriate, action plans instituted to address the problem.

In the above light, the authors demonstrate that the Panel draws its objectives and operation from the concepts of voice, social contract, and accountability. In evaluating the Panel's operational and procedural framework, the authors also clarify and critique the roles and duties of the Board of Executive Directors and Bank Management at various key stages, offering the reader an opportunity to assess the advantages and limitations of the Panel's decision-making processes. Highlighted also is the indispensable role and invaluable impact of the Panel on the Bank as a whole. Cases before the Panel have led to major clarifications of the scope of policies' application where gaps or inconsistencies had formerly existed, and, in some cases, useful, additional guidelines were developed for staff on key issues. Although the authors acknowledge limitations of the Panel,[70] they also point out its advantages, and in the end present a positive view of the Panel as an accountability mechanism.

---

69 On this note, consider in particular the broader meaning of a social contract as it is reflected in this volume. For an explanation of this broader meaning of a social contract, see note 15. Note that this unique social contract between the Bank and the beneficiaries and stakeholders of Bank-financed projects is not a preexisting relationship or set of rights and obligations between parties in the sense that it can only spring into existence on the execution of financing documents between the Bank and the governments of its member countries. However, it is a social contract insofar as on such execution, an *informal set of rights and obligations in the form of these operational and safeguard policies* comes to exist between the Bank and its projects' beneficiaries and stakeholders.

70 They acknowledge, for example, that the Panel has no mandate to ensure that Bank Management complies with its action plans to remedy the concerns brought up by requesters, and that it can investigate only those issues that have close links to a violation of Bank policies.

Chapter 23, "The World Bank's Inspection Panel: A Tool for Accountability?" by Yvonne Wong and Benoit Mayer, examines the Panel through a markedly different lens than that used by Barlas and Tassoni. Wong and Mayer adopt an outsider's perspective—at times even a local beneficiary's or stakeholder's viewpoint—in their critique of the Panel. An interesting aspect, not discussed by other chapters in detail, is their analysis of the extremely limited legal avenues traditionally available to individuals who seek compensation or some form of redress for harms done by projects financed by international or multilateral organizations. Long-standing legal tradition has never given individuals direct recourse against international organizations as a party to a legal dispute. In light of this, the Panel's key value as an accountability mechanism in the multilateral landscape is that it allows individuals harmed by Bank-financed projects to *directly* institute a complaint through the Panel against Bank Management; in effect, the Panel process confers on individuals *direct power* to institute an inquiry and investigation process against a multilateral organization, which is a significant shift away from prior legal tradition. The authors also consider, through the eyes of local beneficiaries of Bank-financed projects, why the Panel's global reach as an accountability mechanism—in theory, over all Bank-financed projects—may not be as extensive as often envisaged. Insufficient awareness of the Panel's existence and processes on the part of local beneficiaries, sometimes located in remote or inaccessible areas; linguistic and cultural barriers; and high financial and even political costs to beneficiaries resorting to the Panel are cited as credible reasons why complaints may fail to be instituted with the Panel. The authors also examine in detail the way that an outsider may perceive the Panel's procedural mechanisms and the interlocking roles played by the Panel members, the Board of Executive Directors, and Bank Management in terms of the Panel's transparency, independence from political influences, and inherent ability to be an effective accountability mechanism. The authors signal the desirability for targeted and appropriate reforms in several respects. Also duly noted are limitations on the Panel's ability to enforce and monitor the actual implementation of remedies or solutions to address complaints. Although the authors clearly adopt a relatively critical view of the Panel through an outsider's lens, emphasizing different aspects of the Panel's work compared with Barlas and Tassoni's more positive viewpoint, the authors also discuss its various advantages, some of which are also discussed by Barlas and Tassoni. Wong and Mayer ultimately conclude that despite the Panel's limitations and shortcomings, its existence is a clear step in the right direction toward making multilateral organizations accountable for the ways that their policies shape the design and implementation of their projects, and these policies' ultimate impact on local beneficiaries and stakeholders.

The final contribution, chapter 24, "The Inspection Panel of the World Bank: An Effective Extrajudicial Complaint Mechanism?" by Karin Lukas, is a relatively short chapter that complements the other two on the Panel. Lukas examines the Panel's work in the evolving context of the Bank's current and ongoing initiatives to review its environmental and social safeguard policies, the overarching object of which is to refine and make beneficial changes to its operational policies, such that they continue to remain relevant in the current global and multilateral context. Any changes made to existing policies may affect the Panel's future decisions as well as the types of cases that come before it. One of Lukas's main concerns is the way that human rights issues—for example, involuntary resettlement, sufficient participation of and consultations with affected beneficiaries and stakeholders, and honoring indigenous peoples' rights—have surfaced in the past with respect to some Bank-financed projects. It is in this light that she critiques the Panel's role and impact, as well as the manner in which Bank-financed projects have been undertaken. She acknowledges that the Panel's complaints process has enhanced public awareness and also provided solutions to human rights concerns that would otherwise have had no practically viable avenues of legal recourse within national borders. Some of Lukas's key criticisms pertain to the procedural aspects of the Panel's processes. Among other concerns, she notes the limited powers of the Panel to independently institute an investigation into a project (the Board's approval is required to do so), as well as the Panel's inability to exert an oversight or enforcement mandate over the implementation of approved action plans by Bank Management. Some of Lukas's criticisms are also discussed and addressed by Barlas and Tassoni, providing the reader of both chapters with revealing and insightful avenues to exercise judgment with respect to some of the concerns and controversies revolving around the Panel's work and procedures. Lukas concludes that in spite of her criticisms, the Panel as an accountability mechanism generally functions to positive effect. She also highlights that it remains to be seen how ongoing Bank policy reforms will ultimately shape the Panel's processes, work, and impact.

The above three chapters offer the reader both complementary and differing perspectives on the Panel's work. Specific issues on which they disagree or offer differing viewpoints or considerations present readers with a platform on which to evaluate and formulate their own views about the Panel's role and function as a multilateral accountability mechanism with a global reach.

Concluding Remarks

This volume's chapters contain many useful, highly insightful, and innovative ideas. Collectively, they evaluate a wide spectrum of current and ongoing delivery challenges and issues, situated in very diverse social, economic, and cultural contexts. Development areas, challenges, and solutions examined throughout these chapters are operative and relevant on multilateral, national, or subnational levels, and often on varying combinations of these levels. As this introductory chapter has shown, each chapter is highly specific and uniquely different from the others in its elucidation of subject matter. This is especially clear when chapters that engage with broadly similar development issues are arranged alongside one another under one of the broad themes outlined above; despite being thematically grouped together, each discrete chapter reflects a unique viewpoint on a problem. Inevitably, and more often than not, even within the broad thematic areas, each chapter emphasizes very different aspects of the same development issue or problem relative to the others. At other times, the discrete chapters placed side by side simply bring to light their respective author or authors' special expertise and specialized engagement with a particular narrower subject under a broader theme. Notably, when these chapters are considered individually and collectively in the light of their highly specific and diverse character, two key and related points come to light.

The first point concerns the fundamentality and significance of the concepts of voice, social contract, and accountability in delivering successful development results. These concepts are most accurately and usefully illuminated when they are examined as an integral part of the highly specific development contexts and practical challenges that necessitate their application or adherence. The manner in which these concepts are—or should be—realistically adhered to, and the practical form and specific solutions that they manifest to create successful development impact, are inescapably determined and shaped by the unique development context and specific challenges toward which such concepts are applied or made integral. Conceivably, assessing such concepts' importance through a lens that is too broad, abstract, or general would likely dilute or perhaps obfuscate a more precise, accurate, and useful apprehension of those concepts' fundamentality in addressing specific development challenges in practical ways.

The second point builds on the first. Throughout the chapters' diverse and discretely unique coverage of different development challenges and their specific contexts, an important common theme emerges: namely, improving delivery of development outcomes crucially and foundationally pivots on the ability to successfully harness and integrate these concepts into the practical actualization of carefully targeted development efforts. It is through specific observation of how such practical actualization of successful development impact is ultimately derived from a concerted adherence to these concepts, as they manifest in specific and unique development contexts, that the rich, complex meaning and significance of those concepts can be comprehended. The diverse chapters, highly specific in nature and covering an array of different development challenges, concerns, and their unique contexts, function as a fertile platform on which the meaning and also the fundamentality of these three concepts in development can be appreciated.

Significantly, and in addition to the above observations, every chapter in this book directly or indirectly demonstrates that a multidisciplinary approach in crafting, designing, and implementing development initiatives is indispensable if the successful delivery of outcomes is to be realized Throughout these chapters, the message that no development problem or issue can be examined solely through a discrete economic, social, political, scientific, or other lens is reiterated in varying ways. These chapters make crystal clear that development challenges or problems require conjoined solutions that derive from a wide variety of disciplines. Relevant efforts, concepts, and tools, and the knowledge of experts from various disciplines need to be coordinated and applied to solve development problems and deliver successful results. In this light, these chapters discretely and collectively support Jim Yong Kim's words, that the successful delivery of well-crafted development outcomes "will have to be multidisciplinary from the outset . . . draw[ing] on the natural sciences; the social sciences; engineering and applied mathematics; and the business disciplines; [and] also humanities fields like history and ethics," and that "collaboration and communication, as people and institutions problem-solve together," is essential in identifying, designing, and delivering appropriate solutions to development problems.[71]

In the foregoing light, then, these chapters, spanning a diverse variety of development areas, challenges, and their specific contexts, demonstrate the many ways in which voice, social contract, and accountability are fundamental and ineradicable concepts that create a stronger likelihood of successful development impact. Where possible, these concepts should ideally constitute the foundations of every stage of putting forth and making real any development initiative. Although contextual and practical realities may threaten to constrain the expression of the concepts of voice, social contract, and accountability in development efforts, the fundamental nature of these concepts in ultimately delivering successful development impact is such that, where possible, difficulties or challenges should be sensitively worked through and resolved. These concepts should ideally be infused into and influence the selection and setting of development goals and the planning, design, and implementation of development initiatives to generate positive development impact. Doing this, and adopting a sensible multidisciplinary approach, will greatly strengthen the likelihood of successfully delivering targeted development outcomes and realizing beneficial development impact.

71 Kim, *Delivering on Development*, *supra* note 1.

PART I

Human Rights and Development

1
Human Rights and Service Delivery
A Review of Current Policies, Practices, and Challenges

Axel Marx, Siobhán McInerney-Lankford, Jan Wouters, and David D'Hollander

The World Bank, in its 2004 World Development Report, *Making Services Work for Poor People,* recognized that accountability among citizens, service providers, and policy makers was key to understanding the failure or success in the delivery of basic services to poor people. Since then, the concepts of social contract, voice, and accountability have gained prominence in development policy and discourse. These concepts are closely connected with a number of human rights principles that have become embedded in the policies of development actors and consolidated into more explicit policy frameworks known as "human rights–based approaches" (HRBAs) to development.[1] These human rights principles constitute a set of policy principles that imply neither a clear legal foundation nor legal obligations. As such, they remain loosely defined and conceptualized.

This chapter analyzes these principles and offers a critical analysis of HRBAs by situating them in the context of broader donor efforts to integrate human rights considerations into development. It assesses the strengths and weaknesses of a HRBA as a policy concept in light of the human rights principles on which it is founded, and considers whether and how these principles are in fact realized to secure more effective service delivery processes (and outcomes). Implicit in the adoption of HRBAs is an emphasis on the "how" (processes to deliver services) of development rather than exclusively on the "what" (service being delivered). The chapter first charts the emergence of HRBAs. Next, it offers conceptual clarification around the common characteristics of a HRBA. In a third section, two contentious issues are identified: the difficulty of measuring the impact of a HRBA, and the organizational and institutional challenges linked to adopting a HRBA. The chapter concludes

---

The views expressed in this chapter are those of the authors and do not necessarily reflect the views of the Board of Executive Directors of the World Bank or the governments they represent. Responsibility for errors or omissions remains with the authors. Axel Marx, Jan Wouters, and David D'Hollander acknowledge support by the Flemish government (Policy Research Centre) and the European Commission–FRAME project (grant agreement no. 320,000) for research on human rights and development cooperation.

1 It should be noted that, in principle, a HRBA can apply to any development service, including a service initiated by a government for its own citizens. However, this chapter discusses the notion of HRBA in the context of bilateral or multilateral development cooperation.

with a discussion of how the underlying principles of a HRBA have been integrated into other development policies and processes that are not explicitly based on human rights.

The Emergence of Human Rights-Based Approaches

Human rights and development work have long been viewed as operating in "parallel streams," addressing similar problems and sharing compatible goals but existing relatively independent of one another.[2] Both the human rights and development communities avail themselves of progressive and transformative self-understandings, and share the aim to "bring into being new worlds that are more prosperous, more humanly fulfilling, and more just."[3] More often than not, the operational focus of development and human rights activities is focused on the same target groups and subject areas.[4] Despite this convergence, more explicit synergies between human rights and development policy began to take root only in the early 1990s. Since then, the more deliberate integration of human rights in development policy has been pursued by donors in various ways.[5] Although there is an increasing awareness of development challenges in the human rights community, perhaps more fundamental is the shift in perceptions about the role of human rights within the international development community. Beyond being "moral considerations," human rights are recognized as having a potential instrumental role in making development interventions more efficient through improving the governance processes that underpin service delivery.[6] As a result, a growing convergence is evident between development and human rights on a number of levels,[7] and several strategies have been developed to integrate human rights in development cooperation policies. Human rights, democracy, and good governance have traditionally been the subjects of various forms of

---

2 M. Darrow & A. Tomas, *Power, Capture, and Conflict: A Call for Human Rights Accountability in Development Cooperation*, 27(2) Human Rights Q. 471–538 (2005); S. McInerney-Lankford, *Human Rights and Development: A Comment on Challenges and Opportunities from a Legal Perspective*, 1(1) J. Human Rights Practice 51–82 (2009).

3 R. Archer, *Linking Rights and Development: Some Critical Challenges* in *Rights-Based Approaches to Development: Exploring the Potential and Pitfalls* 26 (S. Hickey & D. Mitlin eds., Kumarian 2009).

4 H.-O. Sano, *Development and Human Rights: The Necessary, but Partial Integration of Human Rights and Development*, 22(3) Human Rights Q. 734, 735 (2000).

5 Org. Econ. Co-Operation & Dev. & World Bank, *Integrating Human Rights into Development: Donor Approaches, Experiences, and Challenges*, 2nd ed. (Org. Econ. Co-Operation & Dev.; World Bank 2013).

6 *Id.*, at 74.

7 McInerney-Lankford, *supra* note 2, identifies (a) an overlap in obligations, as the right to development is increasingly, but not unanimously, recognized as a human right; (b) a factual or substantive overlap, as human rights organizations and development agencies address similar problems regarding poverty, inequality, and exclusion; and (c) an overlap or convergence of principles, such as participation, transparency, and equality, which are currently shared by both the development and the human rights communities.

"targeted support," separate from "traditional" development sectors such as agricultural development, infrastructure, or education.[8] Donors established separate organizational units and funding instruments, but human rights and democratic governance were not necessarily considered a core aspect of development work in other intervention areas.[9]

To make human rights an integral aspect of their development work, several donors have moved toward more comprehensive approaches to integrating human rights into development, shifting away from addressing human rights as merely a subcomponent of democracy promotion or "political aid." Policies for human rights mainstreaming have since been developed to ensure that human rights are accounted for in all types of development interventions, in some cases to promote greater policy coherence or to draw more systematically on human rights tools and methodology.

This move toward more comprehensive approaches is often characterized as "mainstreaming," which the European Commission defines as "the process of integrating human rights and democratization issues into all aspects of EU policy decision making and implementation."[10] HRBAs take mainstreaming a step further by aiming to provide a more coherent framework toward integrating human rights across all sectors of development policy, and by reconceptualizing development processes in terms of rights and duties. Within the UN system in particular, the concept of a HRBA was born out of the need to have a more comprehensive, coherent, and systematic understanding of "mainstreaming" human rights across agencies.[11] To harmonize the various experiences within the United Nations, a UN Common Understanding (UNCU) on a HRBA was agreed on at the working level in 2003 and subsequently adopted by the UN Development Group (UNDG).[12]

According to the UNCU, a HRBA requires that

1. All programmes of development cooperation, policies, and technical assistance should further the realization of human rights as laid down in the Universal Declaration of Human Rights and other international human rights instruments;

---

8 P. Uvin, *Human Rights and Development* (Kumarian 2004); Sano, *supra* note 4.

9 European Commn., *Thematic Evaluation of the European Commission Support to Respect of Human Rights and Fundamental Freedoms (Including Solidarity with Victims of Repression)*, vol. 1: *Final Report* 70 (Evaluation commissioned by the European Commn. 2011), http://ec.europa.eu /europeaid/how/evaluation/evaluation_reports/2011/1298_docs_en.htm.

10 European Commn., *The European Union: Furthering Human Rights and Democracy across the Globe* 13 (European Commn., Directorate-Gen. External Rel., Luxembourg 2006).

11 G. Oberleitner, *A Decade of Mainstreaming Human Rights in the UN: Achievements, Failures, Challenges*, 26(3) Netherlands Q. Human Rights 359, 361 (2008).

12 The United Nations *Statement of Common Understanding on Human Rights-Based Approaches to Development Cooperation and Programming* can be consulted at http://hrbaportal.org/the-human -rights-based-approach-to-development-cooperation-towards-a-common-understanding -among-un-agencies#sthash.Vk4JorX7.dpuf.

2. Human rights standards contained in, and principles derived from, the Universal Declaration of Human Rights and other international human rights instruments guide all development cooperation and programming in all sectors and in all phases of the programming process;
3. Development cooperation contributes to the development of the capacities of "duty-bearers" to meet their obligations and/or of "rights-holders" to claim their rights.

The Office of the High Commissioner for Human Rights (OHCHR) further defines a HRBA as "a conceptual framework for the process of human development that is normatively based on international human rights standards and operationally directed to promoting and protecting human rights."[13] An increasing number of development actors, including UN development agencies and several bilateral European donors, have adopted HRBAs. Recently, the European Union, the world's largest donor, adopted a HRBA.[14] Other donors have also adopted similar policies and strategies.

By definition, HRBAs are founded on normative and legal justifications (states have a legal duty to respect, protect, and fulfill human rights, including beyond their domestic territory), but they may also be underpinned with instrumental objectives.[15] Such instrumental perspectives see a HRBA as a way to increase the impact and effectiveness of service delivery by amplifying the "voice" of citizens and enhancing the responsiveness and accountability of service providers. HRBAs are therefore essentially about supporting "active citizens" who are aware of, and able to claim, their rights.[16] As phrased by the Swedish International Development Cooperation Agency (SIDA), raising the standard of living for the poor can be achieved more easily through working with HRBAs, because they can "make cooperation more efficient through contributing to the identification of the people who are discriminated against and the power structures in society that affect poor people's lives."[17]

---

13 Off. U.N. High Commr. Human Rights, *Frequently Asked Questions on a Human Rights-Based Approach to Development Cooperation' Strategies* 15 (U.N. High Commr. Human Rights 2006).

14 Council of the European Union, *EU Strategic Framework and Action Plan on Human Rights and Democracy* 10 (Council of the European Union 2012), http://www.consilium.europa.eu/uedocs/cms_data/docs/pressdata/EN/foraff/131173.pdf.

15 Org. Econ. Co-Operation & Dev. & World Bank, *supra* note 5; Darrow & Tomas, *supra* note 2; L.-H. Piron, *Rights-Based Approaches and Bilateral Aid Agencies: More Than a Metaphor?*, 36(1) IDS Bull. 19–30 (2005).

16 A. Cornwall, & C. Nyamu-Musembi, *Putting the "Rights-Based Approach" to Development into Perspective*, 25(8) Third World Q. 1415–37 (2004).

17 Swedish Intl. Dev. Cooperation Agency & Swedish Ministry For. Affairs, *A Democracy and Human Rights Approach to Development Co-operation* 1 (policy document adopted by the Swedish Intl. Dev. Cooperation Agency & Swedish Ministry For. Affairs 2001).

HRBAs within the Broader Context of Donor Approaches to Integrating Human Rights in Development

A HRBA is one of several approaches to integrating human rights into development. It is, moreover, not a unitary concept; rather, it covers a range of definitions and interpretations.[18] Donors define their human rights priorities in different ways and, equally, approach human rights in their policies and activities in distinct manners. A range of policy strategies exists among donors that explicitly espouses human rights. Although these strategies are evolving, sometimes overlapping, and often undertaken simultaneously, at least four basic categories can be identified.

First, at the policy level, human rights have been integrated into policies on aid allocation, which have in turn been made conditional on compliance with human rights obligations and adherence to democratic governance. Second, donors undertake human rights dialogues with partners to complement development interventions. Third, several donors support human rights projects that may target the realization of specific rights, the protection of particular groups, or the support of human rights organizations or processes. Fourth, donors have developed human rights mainstreaming policies under which donors integrate human rights and thematic terms across a range of sectors, or with respect to particular groups such as children, women, persons with disabilities, or indigenous peoples. Given these different policy reforms and initiatives, it is therefore possible for development actors to integrate human rights without having adopted a rights-based approach as a full-fledged, explicit policy position. Although HRBAs are understood to cover all of the aforementioned policy options, they also refer to a more specific approach to planning development interventions. This chapter relies on that more-confined interpretation of a HRBA as the reference point for analysis.

In addition, it should be noted that some donors do not rely explicitly on the human rights framework but nevertheless can be said to integrate human rights more implicitly through a range of human rights–related interventions. The interplay and overlap between such implicit approaches and HRBAs are discussed next.

Implementing Human Rights-Based Approaches: Policies and Practices

The policy documents of donors and development agencies in which a HRBA is adopted are often aspirational and prescriptive, remaining vague about operational and organizational changes they imply. Inasmuch as a HRBA is an "umbrella concept," it covers a broad variety of practices, from which

18 It is for this reason that this chapter refers throughout to "HRBAs" or "a HRBA" rather than to "the HRBA."

donors tend to pick and choose combinations of elements to put into use.[19] Despite the comprehensive transformation proposed in theory, the adoption of a HRBA does not in practice imply an "all or nothing choice," as there are "many degrees and levels of engagement."[20]

Notwithstanding the conceptual complexity, authors and agencies have tried to capture the essential features of a HRBA and apply them in a range of distinct mechanisms, instruments, and tools.[21] A feature common to different interpretations of HRBAs is the application of human rights principles throughout the process of development. These principles, as defined by the UNCU, are universality and inalienability, indivisibility, interdependence and interrelatedness, equality and nondiscrimination, participation and inclusion, and accountability and rule of law.[22] The principles are *derived* from human rights treaties, and their application is determined on the basis of their functionality (i.e., the extent to which they gear the development process more directly toward the realization of human rights) and their practicality (i.e., the extent to which they provide development practitioners with clear and effective guidance).[23]

While each of these human rights principles has relevance for development, a distinction can be drawn between structural and operational principles. Structural principles describe features of human rights law and affirm the universality and inalienability, indivisibility, interdependence, and interrelatedness of human rights. These principles apply more generally to all human rights requiring that all donor (and partner) actions comply with the international legal human rights framework, and mandate certain key elements in the framework's interpretation, such as the equal importance of all human rights (indivisibility) or the applicability of human rights in all contexts (universality).[24]

The operational principles derived from human rights pertain more to their application in context; they include participation, accountability, nondiscrimination, inclusion, and rule of law. Although this categorization is not strict and there may be significant overlap between them, the latter group of principles relates more to the "how" than the "what." This group of prin-

---

19 H. Miller, *From Rights-Based" to "Rights-Framed" Approaches: A Social Constructionist View of Human Rights Practice,* 14(6) Intl. J. Human Rights 915, 919 (2010).

20 Swiss Dev. Cooperation, *Integrating Human Rights and Poverty Reduction: Towards a Human Rights Based Approach for SDC* 20 (working paper, Swiss Dev. Cooperation 2004).

21 Off. U.N. High Commr. Human Rights, *supra* note 13; Cornwall & Nyamu-Musembi, *supra* note 16; V. Gauri & S. Gloppen, *Human Rights Based Approaches to Development: Concepts, Evidence, and Policy* (Policy Research Working Paper No. 5938, World Bank 2012).

22 These are sometimes summarized in the acronym PANEL (participation, accountability, nondiscrimination, empowerment, and linkages to human rights standards).

23 For an elaborate discussion of how these principles are derived from the human rights framework, *see* Darrow & Tomas, *supra* note 2, at 501.

24 B. I. Hamm, *A Human Rights Approach to Development,* 23(4) Human Rights Q., 1005, 1012 (2001).

ciples evidences a greater degree of convergence with development work and is especially relevant in the context of a HRBA. In addition, through the work of UN treaty bodies or special procedures, other human rights principles have emerged providing more specific operational guidance on the interpretation and implementation of particular rights (particularly economic, social, and cultural rights). These principles include accessibility, adaptability, acceptability, and affordability. The following discussion explores the operational principles in greater detail, because these are the principles most commonly included in HRBAs adopted by donor agencies.

Nondiscrimination and Equality

Among the principles that have direct operational implications for development policy and programming, revealing the strongest elements of convergence between development and human rights, are nondiscrimination and equality. These principles relate to the concepts of social exclusion and deprivation, whereby certain groups or individuals are denied basic entitlements due the entire population but enjoyed only by the rest of the population. These particular principles require a focus on development processes and scrutiny of how a development initiative is implemented; who it includes and excludes; how it takes account of representation, voice, and dissent; and, ultimately, who benefits from it. HRBAs introduce a clear normative and legal basis for development practitioners to systematically address discrimination and its underlying causes, including making allowances for affirmative action and "special measures."[25] In the first instance, this can imply using disaggregated data on development indicators to enhance the identification of patterns of exclusion faced by poor people, vulnerable groups, and minorities. Donors adopting a HRBA have emphasized the establishment of "equitable" and "inclusive" service delivery systems at the country level.

In addition to women's rights and gender equality, a HRBA urges donors to consider all forms of discrimination, thereby broadening the scope of inquiry and scrutiny for other suspect classifications and other vulnerable groups. Moreover, unequal access to basic services is often caused by lack of finances to pay for services and transport, creating patterns of exclusion that may become entrenched but are potentially less obvious.[26] A principal critique of the Millennium Development Goals (MDGs) from a human rights perspective was precisely this framework's inability to account for different forms of inequality within a given national context or to address development goals beyond aggregate targets, thereby potentially failing to reach the poorest and most vulnerable groups.[27] The OHCHR has encouraged the application of a

---

25 Darrow & Tomas, *supra* note 2, at 505.

26 Org. Econ. Co-Operation & Dev. Network on Governance, *Linking Human Rights and Aid Effectiveness for Better Development Results: Practical Experience from the Health Sector* 17 (Org. Econ. Co-Operation & Dev. Network on Governance 2008).

27 M. Darrow, *The Millennium Development Goals: Milestones or Millstones? Human Rights Priorities for the Post-2015 Development Agenda,* 15 Yale Human Rights & Dev. L. J. 65–66 (Mar. 2012).

HRBA to the MDG framework, which could imply creating additional targets for particular groups and disaggregating indicators.[28]

In addressing discrimination and exclusion in development planning, some donors use a "targeted approach," designing new programs that target specific vulnerable or excluded groups. In doing this, donors adopt different priority groups and demographics. In its human rights strategy for foreign policy, the Dutch Ministry of Foreign Affairs identified discrimination against religious minorities as well as discrimination based on sexual orientation as key action points.[29] The Danish development cooperation agency, however, has invested considerably in the area of indigenous peoples' rights and has adopted this as a transversal theme in its strategy.[30] In some instances, initiatives address structural or systemic discrimination against certain groups by encouraging legal reform. UNICEF, for example, takes as an objective the elimination of discriminatory laws that allow girls to marry before the compulsory school-leaving age or prescribe different school-leaving ages for girls and boys.[31] In addition to "targeting," donors have endeavored to embed the principle of nondiscrimination by developing safeguard mechanisms and "inclusion policies" within sector-wide programs to ensure equal access to public services.

Participation and Empowerment

Instead of mere consultation, a HRBA requires donors to enable "active, free and meaningful participation" in any development intervention undertaken, not just those directly related to political governance. Accordingly, participation becomes both a means and an aim of development.[32] In SIDA's human rights strategy, participation is conceived as a way to ensure sustainable results as well as a goal in itself; it helps people be more aware that "they have the right to demand change and social justice."[33] Participation in this sense implies "empowerment."[34] The objective of a HRBA is to embed and institu-

---

28 Off. U.N. High Commr. Human Rights, *Claiming the Millennium Development Goals: A Human Rights Approach* 9–10 (2008).

29 Dutch Ministry For. Affairs, *Naar een Menswaardig bestaan: Een mensenrechtenstrategie voor het buitenlands beleid* [Toward a dignified existence: Human rights strategy for foreign affairs] (Dutch Ministry For. Affairs 2007).

30 Danish Intl. Dev. Agency, *Strategy for Danish Support to Indigenous Peoples* (Ministry For. Affairs 2004).

31 UNICEF, *A Human Rights-Based Approach to Education for All: A Framework for the Realization of Children's Right to Education and Rights within Education* 53 (UNICEF 2007).

32 Off. U.N. High Commr. Human Rights, *supra* note 13.

33 Swedish Ministry For. Affairs, *Change for Freedom: Policy for Democratic Development and Human Rights in Swedish Development Cooperation, 2010–2014* (Swedish Ministry For. Affairs 2010).

34 According to the World Bank's *Sourcebook on Empowerment and Poverty Reduction*, "empowerment" refers to the "expansion of assets and capabilities of poor people to participate in, negotiate with, influence, control, and hold accountable institutions that affect their lives." *See* World Bank, *Empowerment and Poverty Reduction: A Sourcebook* 11 (World Bank 2002).

tionalize participation in a way that it becomes self-sustaining.[35] The inclusiveness and transparency of the participatory process become a central concern, as poor and excluded groups are often not equally represented in participatory processes, because of practical impediments, lack of awareness, or more structural legal and institutional obstacles. Investing in the capacities of poor and disadvantaged groups to participate becomes crucial.[36] Transparency and access to information—for example, by making information available in accessible formats and minority languages—comes to the fore as key elements in fostering meaningful participation.[37]

Participation can be enhanced by creating new channels and mechanisms and/or building the capacity of existing community-based or civil society organizations to work with human rights.[38] Illustrative of the first approach is the Department for International Development's (DFID's) Participatory Rights Assessment Methodologies (PRAMs) project, which presents a working method to facilitate people's own identification and assessment of their rights and open up new channels of institutional engagement between citizens and duty bearers.[39] Organizing participatory spaces and supporting local organizations or NGOs to engage in rights-based participation are common strategies. Investing in participation and inclusion through local organizations implies that these organizations are themselves representative and functioning in a participatory manner.[40] Hence, in the selection of local partner organizations, more attention should be paid to inclusiveness and local embeddedness. The latter has gained increased attention, as several authors argue that donors should not try to impose an "artificial" associational model, but should focus on working with existing practices of self-organization within local communities.[41]

One of the consequences, and challenges, of the "rights-version" of participation and empowerment is that it can potentially "sharpen the political edges" of development.[42] Accordingly, programs have been canceled for political reasons, for example, when a partner government perceives funding as support for the opposition.[43] Moreover, the efficiency of the "confrontational"

---

35 Darrow & Tomas, *supra* note 2, at 506.

36 *Id.*, at 510.

37 U.N. Dev. Programme, *Mainstreaming Human Rights in Development Policies and Programming: UNDP Experiences* (U.N. Dev. Programme, Bureau Dev. Policy 2012). *See* also consultation requirements in World Bank safeguards as well as the access to information policy, which illustrate how this can be secured without HRBA.

38 Off. U.N. High Commr. Human Rights, *supra* note 13, at 26–27.

39 J. Blackburn et al., *Operationalising the Rights Agenda: Participatory Rights Assessment in Peru and Malawi*, 36(1) IDS Bull. 91, 93 (2005).

40 U.N. Dev. Programme, *supra* note 37.

41 D. Booth & D. Cammack, *Solving Collective Action Problems* 115 (Zed 2013).

42 Cornwall & Nyamu-Musembi, *supra* note 16, at 1418.

43 Overseas Dev. Inst. *DFID Human Rights Practice Review Synthesis Report* 7 (Overseas Dev. Inst. 2008).

use of human rights has also been questioned; in several contexts it may not be constructive or result in greater vulnerability for already vulnerable groups.[44] Uvin notes that in some contexts the adoption of human rights language with a clear political tone might endanger the local personnel and the complex network of local relationships on which development agencies rely.[45] Longer-term research indicates that framing demands for accountability in terms of human rights standards can lead to increased legitimacy of citizen demands, but in some cases it can also "backfire."[46]

Accountability, Transparency, and Rule of Law

The principle of "accountability" is central to all iterations of a HRBA.[47] Within the development community, the notion of "accountability" is often understood as the capacity of donors to hold NGOs and governmental partners answerable for their performance, although it may also define the ability of partners to hold donors to account, or citizens of both donor and partner countries to hold their governments to account.

In the context of a HRBA, accountability is defined as the capacity of beneficiaries (i.e., rights-holders) to actively claim their rights and hold their own government, as well as donors and other actors, accountable. Instead of supporting an indefinite number of isolated technical interventions, a HRBA underlines the need for development actors to address structural change and the potential of "transforming state-society relations," with the final aim of "strengthening the social contract."[48] As stated by the OHCHR, "the most important source of added value in the human rights approach is the emphasis it places on the accountability of policy-makers and other actors."[49] More generally, it has been argued that the very essence of the contribution made by integrating human rights into development is the introduction of accountability through the notion of rights and duties, and the introduction of legal accountability through the underpinning of international human rights law.[50]

---

44 S. Patel & D. Mitlin, *Reinterpreting the Rights-Based Approach: A Grassroots Perspective on Rights and Development* in *Rights-Based Approaches to Development: Exploring the Potential and Pitfalls* (S. Hickey & D. Mitlin eds., Kumarian 2009).

45 Uvin, *supra* note 8, at 149.

46 Decade of Collaborative Research on Citizen Engagement, *Blurring the Boundaries: Citizen Action across States and Societies: A Summary of Findings from a Decade of Collaborative Research on Citizen Engagement* 44 (Dev. Research Ctr. Citizenship, Participation & Accountability, Brighton 2011).

47 P. Uvin, *From the Right to Development to the Rights-Based Approach: How "Human Rights" Entered Development*, 17(4–5) Dev. Practice 597, 601–2 (2007).

48 Piron, *supra* note 15, at 22.

49 Off. U.N. High Commr. Human Rights, *Draft Guidelines: A Human Rights Approach to Poverty Reduction Strategies* para. 31 (2002).

50 S. McInerney-Lankford, *Human Rights and Development: A Comment on Challenges and Opportunities from a Legal Perspective,* 1(1) J. Human Rights Practice 51–82 (2009).

While direct support for human rights and democracy focuses mostly on political accountability (e.g., support for fair and transparent electoral processes and strengthening multiparty systems), a HRBA aspires to make enhanced accountability the main outcome in any area of development programming. This requires insight into various political, legal, and institutional dimensions of development work. Practitioners within agencies such as UNDP are therefore expected to develop a thorough understanding of the legal dimensions of their operating context, which includes national legislation, adherence to regional charters or agreements, and ratification of human rights treaties or other international agreements.[51] A strategy adopted by some donors is to advocate for the alignment of national legislation with the relevant provisions of the international human rights framework. For example, the Austrian Development Agency supports states in codifying the right to water and sanitation in laws and regulations.[52]

Closely linked to the issue of accountability is the principle of redress and the focus on effective rule of law and a functional justice system. Several development agencies use the human rights framework as a standard for justice reform and the performance of judiciaries.[53] Working with a HRBA broadens the scope of rule of law programs by addressing structural barriers and emphasizing access to justice or legal empowerment for excluded people.[54] This generally implies some awareness-raising activities about human rights and making legal services accessible in terms of language, procedures, affordable legal aid and lawyers, or the integration of informal and traditional legal systems.

A HRBA implies a focus not only on formal legal accountability but also on informal processes of accountability.[55] Donors can enhance accountability through nonlegal means, sometimes under the label of "social accountability," which is applied by many donors, including ones not explicitly accepting of a HRBA approach. The latter includes initiatives as different as participatory budgeting, administrative procedures acts, social audits, citizen report cards, organizing public debates, or other approaches to greater citizen participation in public service delivery.[56] In the health sector, experiences with these types

---

51 U.N. Dev. Programme, *supra* note 37.

52 Austrian Dev. Agency, *Focus: Right to Water and Sanitation* (Austrian Dev. Agency 2012).

53 A. Tomas, *Reforms That Benefit Poor People: Practical Solutions and Dilemmas of Rights-Based Approaches to Legal and Justice Reform* in *Reinventing Development? Translating Rights-Based Approaches from Theory into Practice* (P. Gready & J. Ensor eds., Zed 2005); Swedish Intl. Dev. Cooperation Agency, *A Guide to Equal Access to Justice Programmes* (Swedish Intl. Dev. Cooperation Agency 2010).

54 Donors who work on legal empowerment or access to justice programs, such as the U.S. Agency for Intl. Dev. and the World Bank, do not refer explicitly to the human rights framework. *See* Org. Econ. Co-Operation & Dev. & World Bank, *supra* note 5, at 231.

55 Darrow & Tomas, *supra* note 2, at 487–88; Off. U.N. High Commr. Human Rights, *supra* note 13, at 24.

56 Darrow & Tomas, *supra* note 2, at 488; J. Ackerman, *Human Rights and Social Accountability* 6 (Soc. Dev. Papers: Participation and Civic Engagement, Paper No. 86, World Bank 2005).

of social accountability[57] processes in East Africa have included supporting the capacity of local organizations to monitor the rights of patients and the management of the health budget.[58] While the concept of social accountability is closely related to applying a HRBA, it may not always provide legal recourse, may suffer from a lack of bottom-up engagement, and may remain concentrated on localized dynamics.[59] In this sense, social accountability initiatives, such as the use of citizen scorecards, are ideally integrated into a more comprehensive HRBA.[60]

Finally, in adopting a HRBA, donors acknowledge the need to be held accountable themselves by the recipients of aid,[61] which is reflected in the principle of mutual accountability in the Paris Declaration on Aid Effectiveness. Hence, human rights norms and standards can be part of the mutual accountability frameworks between partners, whereby both sides are held accountable for their contributions to the realization of human rights.[62] On the project level, accountability to beneficiaries can lead to the establishment of redress and complaint mechanisms. This is evident in UNDP's Water Governance Facility program in Kenya, where communities and consumers were enabled to voice their dissatisfaction and address corruption in water services through complaints mechanisms.[63]

The extent to which donors are legally accountable for their human rights impacts is a contested issue,[64] and, accordingly, the integration of human rights into accountability mechanisms for development projects is still largely uncharted terrain. For example, the Danish International Development Agency enables people experiencing adverse consequences from its development policy to complain directly to Danish embassies.[65]

---

57 Social accountability can be understood as "a form of accountability which emerges from actions by citizens and civil society organizations (CSOs) aimed at holding the state to account, as well as efforts by government and other actors (media, private sector, donors) to support these actions." *See* U.N. Dev. Programme, *Fostering Social Accountability: From Principle to Practice—Guidance Note* 9 (U.N. Dev. Programme 2010).

58 Org. Econ. Co-Operation & Dev., Network on Governance, *supra* note 26, at 6.

59 Ackerman, *supra* note 56, at 6.

60 *Id.*, at 26–27.

61 L.-H. Piron, *Human Rights and Poverty Reduction: The Role of Human Rights in Promoting Donor Accountability* 2 (Overseas Dev. Inst. 2005).

62 Org. Econ. Co-Operation & Dev. & World Bank, *supra* note 5, at 84.

63 Kenya Water for Health Org., *Human Rights Based Approach to Reforms in the Kenya Water Sector* (Kenya Water for Health Org. 2009).

64 Org. Econ. Co-Operation & Dev. & World Bank, *supra* note 5, at 84.

65 Danish Intl. Dev. Agency, *The Right to a Better Life: Strategy for Denmark's Development Cooperation* 11 (Ministry For. Affairs of Denmark 2012).

A Human Rights-Based Approach to Service Delivery: Issues and Challenges

The value added of human rights policies is still debated within the development community. The tension between the more technical outlook of "traditional" development programming and the normative underpinnings of HRBAs is most evident at the evaluation stage.[66] This has gained prominence in recent times as concepts such as evidence-based or results-based management and "value for money" in aid collections have become influential. Several stakeholders have raised concerns that this might lead donors to be increasingly driven toward "what's measureable" instead of "what matters."[67] There is arguably growing pressure on human rights policies and HRBA programming to prove their effectiveness and impact. This section explores a number of challenges confronting a HRBA to development, including measurability and organizational challenges.

Measuring the Impact of HRBAs

Although the concept of a HRBA to development is now more than a decade old, the evidence of its operational impact is scarce and its "added value" remains contested.[68] Even for donors that have explicitly committed themselves to adopting a HRBA, the evidence of whether it has achieved the policy goals it aimed to advance is limited. Applying quantitative measurement methods to HRBAs and other human rights policies presents several theoretical and operational difficulties. Chief among these is the challenge of measuring concepts such as human rights, which are the subject of competing and context-dependent definitions, or the challenge of establishing a causal nexus between the adoption of legal or policy norms on human rights, on the one hand, and a particular outcome in a development intervention, on the other. Empirical evidence and evidentiary tools related to human rights themselves are scarce, which further compounds the challenges of measurement.

However, the UNCU emphasizes the importance of including "measurable goals and targets."[69] Similarly, OHCHR underlines that there is no inherent

---

66 L. T. Munro, *The Human Rights-Based Approach to Programming: A Contradiction in Terms?*, in *Rights-based Approaches to Development: Exploring the Potential and Pitfalls* (S. Hickey & D. Mitlin eds., Kumarian 2009).

67 Intl. Council Human Rights Policy, *No Perfect Measure: Rethinking Evaluation and Assessment of Human Rights Work* 4 (Intl. Council Human Rights Policy 2012).

68 S. Kindornay, J. Ron, & C. Carpenter, *Rights-Based Approaches to Development: Implications for NGOs*, 34(2) Human Rights Q. 472, 497 (2012). Few empirical studies exist which provide an in-depth assessment of the implementation of a HRBA in a recipient country. An interesting exception is a study by Hisayo Katsui et al. on a human rights–based approach in Finland's development cooperation with special focus on gender and disability in Ethiopia and Kenya. *See* Hisayo Katsui et al., *Reducing Inequalities: A Human Rights-Based Approach in Finland's Development Cooperation with Special Focus on Gender and Disability—A Case Study on Ethiopia and Kenya* (Åbo Akademi University, Inst. Human Rights 2014).

69 U.N. Common Understanding, *The Human Rights Based Approach to Development Cooperation: Towards a Common Understanding among UN Agencies* (Stamford Interagency Workshop on a

contradiction between a HRBA and results-based management.[70] As a HRBA aims to strengthen the relationship between citizen (rights-holder) and state (duty-bearer) in all thematic areas of development, the central question becomes whether integrating a HRBA in areas such as education or health contributes to the achievement of outcomes related to health and education. In addition to such outcome goals, a HRBA also provides a new layer of evaluation as it puts emphasis on the integration of human rights principles throughout the process of an intervention. Both HRBA outcomes and process goals face a measurement challenge.

The challenge of how to measure the "HRBA quality" of development processes at the program/project level has emerged as a key issue. Development actors committed to HRBAs recommend the development and use of "process indicators" to meet the challenge. However, there are significant conceptual, methodological, and practical challenges in using indicators to measure the quality of development processes. Innovative evaluation practices that assess governance processes through quantitative methods are emerging,[71] but such long-term, rigorous evaluation efforts seem to remain the exception rather than the rule.

Donors have also explored adjusting evaluation frameworks in order to advance the integration of human rights–based outcome goals. This implies incorporating human rights indicators, but also the collection and analysis of disaggregated data, and the use of more participatory methods of monitoring and evaluation interventions.[72] Various indicators are currently used by donors to assess human rights performance, mostly as part of a larger set of traditional development (and human development) indicators.[73] Depending on which strategy is applied to integrate human rights into development policy, donors will rely on different sets of indicators.[74] Progress in reconciling human rights programs and programming with results-based management has led to the progressive development of evaluation methods[75] and results-based human rights indicators.[76]

Human Rights-Based Approach in the Context of UN Reform 2003).

70 Off. U.N. High Commr. Human Rights, *supra* note 13, at 31.

71 M. Humphreys, R. Sanchez de la Sierra, & P. Van der Windt, *Social and Economic Impacts of Tuungane: Final Report on the Effects of a Community Driven Reconstruction Program in Eastern Democratic Republic of Congo* (Columbia University Press 2012).

72 Off. U.N. High Commr. Human Rights, *supra* note 13, at 31.

73 S. McInerney-Lankford & H. Sano, *Human Rights Indicators in Development: An Introduction* 31 (World Bank report, 2010).

74 *Id.*, at 40.

75 U.N. Dev. Group, *Results-Based Management Handbook: Strengthening RBM Harmonization for Improved Development Results* (U.N. Dev. Group 2010), http://www.un.cv/files/UNDG%20RBM%20Handbook.pdf.

76 McInerney-Lankford & Sano, *supra* note 73, at 40.

However, a strong focus on measurement risks obscuring the fact that one is measuring very different contexts with different temporal dimensions. The prevalent "evaluation culture" preoccupied with "technical, quantitative checklists" has been criticized as incapable of capturing the long-term impacts of human rights–based development cooperation.[77] Instead, evaluation formats based on quantitative and qualitative data, covering diverse outcomes and impacts on legislation, policy, and the behavior of society as a whole would be required.[78]

A more qualitative approach may be more appropriate to unravel the complexities and added value of a HRBA, but it would make comparability between projects more difficult. One should also note that change induced by HRBA processes is by definition incremental and additive, which makes it potentially difficult to capture by an evaluation at the project level. As a recent study by Andrews clearly demonstrates, structural institutional change, which a HRBA aims to advance, is in no way linear. A sustained series of projects, interventions, and initiatives, which build on one another and generate learning effects, is necessary to bring about structural institutional reform.[79] Donors with a short-term, "programmatic" vision of development cooperation might be ill-advised to engage with such nonlinear processes. This is not to argue against the use of more quantitative assessment, but rather to caution against relying on it exclusively. In addition, evaluations should not be interpreted in isolation, and aggregated data are needed over longer periods of time in order to allow conclusions to be drawn.

HRBAs and the Challenge of Organizational Reform

A HRBA redefines development challenges as legal and political issues that might otherwise be seen through a purely technical lens. This structural or institutional approach implies a shift toward a view of service delivery as a complex process of interaction between citizens and service providers, underpinned by an intricate web of formal and informal institutions and governance dynamics. Instead of temporarily satisfying needs through "simple" service delivery, a HRBA methodology identifies rights and duties, explores why these cannot be realized, determines what action is needed to realize the rights or to discharge the duties, and assesses the "capacity gap," and seeks to close that gap by developing local capacities that outlast the donor's intervention."[80] Traditional human rights work is often associated with support to civil society and grass-roots organizations. As a more comprehensive concept, a HRBA brings together "state-centered and society-centered inter-

---

77 P. Gready, *Reasons to Be Cautious about Evidence and Evaluation: Rights-Based Approaches to Development and the Emerging Culture of Evaluation*, 1(3) J. Human Rights Practice, 383 (2009).

78 *Id.*, at 399.

79 M. Andrews, *The Limits of Institutional Reform in Development: Changing Rules for Realistic Solutions* (Cambridge U. Press 2013).

80 Org. Econ. Co-Operation & Dev. & World Bank, *supra* note 5, at 85–86.

ventions" and underlines how "state institutions need to be strengthened and citizens need to be empowered."[81]

The transformation toward a HRBA implies an organizational shift and reform on multiple levels. If donors commit to human rights in their policies, they "must be willing to apply the rights agenda to all of their own actions."[82] A HRBA therefore requires "inward looking change" with significant organizational commitments and consequences ranging from the strategic to the operational.[83] Some organizations endorse a HRBA on paper but have not invested in the necessary institutional transformation to implement it.[84] Indeed, various authors have argued that the adoption of HRBAs has been more rhetorical than anything else.[85] To adequately analyze the strategic, organizational, and operational implications, institution-wide assessment is required.

To date, only a handful of donors have commissioned self-assessments that shed light on this issue. Some donor agencies have also established new focal point positions or recruited external experts to capacitate staff on the operational implication of working with human rights. However, the internal capacity of most donors remains limited in this regard, whereby a small number of staff, backed by weak organizational structures, are tasked with mainstreaming human rights or a HRBA across an entire organization.[86] An evaluation of the European Commission's human rights mainstreaming policy found that systems to monitor and evaluate progress on mainstreaming were absent, and the responsible unit faced structural limitations and a lack of high-level support.[87] A review of UNICEF's policy found considerable variation in staff understanding of a HRBA.[88] The report concluded that, despite more than 10 years of experience of working with human rights in development, the implementation of a HRBA is still a "work in progress" within UNICEF.

Finally, decentralization presents another organizational obstacle, as considerable efforts are needed to bridge the gap between the human rights policy designed at headquarters and its practical application at the country and local levels. A review of DFID's human rights policy revealed that the use of human

81 Piron, *supra* note 15, at 25.

82 Uvin, *supra* note 47, at 604.

83 W. Vandenhole et al., *In Lieu of a Conclusion: Some Cross-Cutting Issues and Their Policy Implications*, in *Human Rights and Development in the New Millennium: Towards a Theory of Change* 295 (P. Gready & W. Vandenhole eds., Routledge 2014).

84 Org. Econ. Co-Operation & Dev. & World Bank, *supra* note 5, at 24–25.

85 Uvin, *supra* note 47; Kindornay, et al., *supra* note 68, at 497.

86 Org. Econ. Co-Operation & Dev. & World Bank, *supra* note 5, at 100–101.

87 European Commn., *Thematic Evaluation of the European Commission Support to Respect of Human Rights and Fundamental Freedoms (Including Solidarity with Victims of Repression)*, vol. 1: *Final Report* 19 (evaluation commissioned by the European Commn. 2011), http://ec.europa.eu/europeaid/how/evaluation/evaluation_reports/2011/1298_docs_en.htm.

88 UNICEF, *Global Evaluation of the Application of the Human Rights-Based Approach to UNICEF Programming* 39 (UNICEF 2012).

rights principles is highly dependent on country context and country team.[89] A study on the adoption of a HRBA by three large NGOs found that the planned transition to a HRBA at headquarters resulted in widespread incoherence and was only partially implemented at the level of country offices.[90] Evaluations of donor policies identify similar issues regarding the "dilution" of the human rights component at lower organizational levels.[91] For certain country/field offices, a human rights policy might be more difficult to apply because of the political or cultural context. Here, a flexible and adaptable understanding of a HRBA may be more efficient. Nevertheless, this further complicates the questions of how to effectively operationalize and institutionalize a comprehensive HRBA for a significant number of countries.

The question of the adaptability to local contexts has gained increased attention.[92] A HRBA faces the challenge of generating sufficient ownership by local stakeholders. In certain country contexts or specific sectors within a country, donors have found strong resonance with local stakeholders in introducing a HRBA. In other contexts, the adoption of a HRBA has remained largely a donor-driven effort. Both the nature of the local "policy space" as well as the capacity of local actors can constrain or enable the integration of human rights into development initiatives. Indeed, when "domestic constellations of power and interests" do not favor human rights–based reforms, the process is likely to remain superficial.[93]

Conclusion: Human Rights in Development Projects and Service Delivery

This chapter explored the concept of a HRBA to development cooperation, including its challenges and potential benefits. While in doctrinaire terms, a HRBA implies a foundation in legal obligations and legal accountability, the principles (particularly nonstructural) of the UNCU have themselves found expression in a far wider set of contexts. As Sano recently argued, "there are strong overlaps between human rights- and governance-based development policies, often to a degree that it remains impossible to distinguish one from the other."[94]

---

89 L.-H. Piron, & F. Watkins, *DFID Human Rights Review: A Review of How DFID Has Integrated Human Rights into Its Work* 78 (Overseas Dev. Inst. 2004).

90 S. Plipat, *Developmentizing Human Rights: How Development NGOs Interpret and Implement a Human Rights-Based Approach to Development Policy* 295 (Ph.D. dissertation, U. Pittsburgh 2005).

91 European Commn., *supra* note 87, at 17.

92 Booth & Cammack, *supra* note 41.

93 L. Pritchett, M. Woolcock, & M. Andrews, *Looking Like a State: Techniques of Persistent Failure in State Capability for Implementation* (CID Working Paper No. 239, Ctr. Global Dev., Harvard 2012).

94 H.-O. Sano, *The Drivers of Human Rights Change in Development*, in *Human Rights and Development in the New Millennium: Towards a Theory of Change,* 35 (P. Gready & W. Vandenhole eds.,

In addition to this, the UNCU augurs the possibility of distinguishing between "unique" and "essential" elements of a HRBA. Unique elements are those related directly to the nature of human rights and their correlative duties.[95] These include using the recommendations of international human rights bodies and mechanisms, assessing the capacity of rights-holders to claim their rights or duty-bearers to fulfill their obligations, and developing strategies specifically aimed at building those capacities. Essential elements include recognizing people as autonomous actors, central to their own development (not passive recipients of services or charity); valuing participation; promoting empowerment; and linking such bottom-up demands for better governance with enhanced responsiveness from service providers. Many of these elements, both unique and essential, are features of development policy and are considered part of good development practice.[96]

The widespread reflection of these elements signal the possibility of identifying a broader convergence between human rights and development at the level of principles, and also indicate the potential for a far wider set of development actors to contribute to human rights realization through their policies and activities. For organizations that have not adopted a HRBA and do not work explicitly on human rights, these principles provide reference points for integrating human rights into their work, even if only in implicit terms. However, this also presents the risk of what Uvin has called "rhetorical repackaging": the superficial use of human rights language to reframe development activities. In a similar vein, characterizing any intervention undertaken in the spheres covered by a human rights treaty as supporting the realization of rights may be criticized for presuming or overstating the positive influence of development on human rights. At the same time, too rigid or formalistic an approach toward what constitutes human rights–based development work risks undervaluing the substantial, albeit indirect, positive impacts of projects undertaken with an implicit human rights approach. An independent review of the Australian aid program found it rich with activities that advanced human rights, but it also concluded that the program needed to communicate more clearly its connection to human rights.[97] Some development actors frame entire programs or approaches in terms of human rights principles, underscoring both the latter's intrinsic and instrumental importance. For instance, a recent World Bank report on inclusion observes: "inclusion has both intrinsic and instrumental value for development and shared prosperity."[98] This is consistent with the emphasis on nondiscrimination inherent to HRBAs.

Routledge 2014).

95 B. Mayo, *What Are Human Rights?*, in *Political Theory and the Rights of Man* 72 (D. D. Raphael ed., Indiana U. Press 1967).

96 Org. Econ. Co-Operation & Dev. & World Bank, *supra* note 5, at 73. *See* also U.N. Common Understanding, *supra* note 69.

97 Australian Ministry For. Affairs, *Independent Review of Aid Effectiveness* 9 (Australian Ministry For. Affairs 2011).

98 World Bank, *Inclusion Matters: The Foundation for Shared Prosperity* 249 (World Bank 2013).

Participation is another principle that evidences significant overlaps, and to which a wide range of donor activities can be said to offer support, even without embracing it explicitly as a human rights principle. In addition, participation is linked to improved accountability through enabling redress mechanisms to function. The international human rights framework offers an accountability framework at the international level, emphasizing the need to document and monitor practices regularly, providing recommendations and opportunities for redress or compensation, and demanding justification for noncompliance. Development actors, for their part, have increasingly emphasized accountability, whether through the programs they fund or the mechanisms they have established to ensure compliance with their own policies and accountability for their own operations (e.g., the World Bank Inspection Panel). The question of donor accountability can also relate to a variety of internal and "programmatic" solutions for providing various forms of (nonlegal) accountability mechanisms (e.g., complaint mechanisms at the project/program level). Similarly, the issue of citizen-state accountability and its impact on the effective delivery of services to poor people is addressed by a number of donors that have not formally adopted a HRBA. Social accountability initiatives undertaken by the World Bank are one practical example of this.

More generally, innovative methods for understanding and tackling governance problems within development work are contributing to an expanding field of perspectives and tools for tackling institutional change in developing countries.[99] These approaches and practices imply human rights principles, particularly through their focus on enhancing accountability in service delivery, but without framing the approach in terms of rights-holders and duty-bearers or linking processes of change to obligations within the human rights framework. However, while donors working with such implicit approaches often rely on human rights principles in their development activities, donors who have adopted a HRBA commit themselves, at least in theory, to do so systematically as a legal and normative imperative.

99 Andrews, *supra* note 79.

2

Delivering Development and Good Governance

Making Human Rights Count

RAJEEV MALHOTRA

Most nations face the perennial challenge of improving development outcomes and good governance, particularly at the grassroots level. Although policy makers, academics, and development practitioners have found fertile ground for research on this subject, durable and effective solutions remain elusive. Part of the problem is that analysts seek grand narratives rooted in ideological preferences that tend to oversimplify the issues and the linkages as well as causality underpinning the desired outcomes. The problem also relates to the inadequate use of evidence in policy making and institutional weaknesses in public delivery. As a result, solutions to complex issues have often been suboptimal. Over time, the lack of effective development outcomes leads to a loss of credibility in regard to state agency, to fatigue and frustration among development stakeholders, to inadequate participation in the design and implementation of policies, and eventually to public helplessness and indifference to state action. Lack of beneficial development thus perpetuates the vicious cycle of poor performance in the delivery of public goods, especially in developing countries.

This situation, however, does not imply a lack of research space for policy frameworks with universal applicability. Generic solutions to the common problems of accountability, transparency, and equity in the access to public goods and services, if suitably adapted to the local context, could improve development and governance outcomes. Indeed, the distilled development wisdom and governance practices of Western nations have guided the recent successful economic, social, and political transformation of East Asian countries as well as countries in other parts of the world. At the same time, nations that have succeeded in overcoming the shackles of poverty and underdevelopment and have sustained high growth for long periods have invariably done so by adapting and charting their own unique course to development.[1]

The views expressed in this chapter are solely those of the author and do not reflect the position of the Government of India, from which he is on long-term leave, or the organization for which he currently works.

1 This is evidenced by the rise of China and, to a lesser extent, the emergence of Brazil, India, Indonesia, Turkey, Botswana, and Chile in recent times and the industrialized East Asian economies and Japan in previous decades. None of the successfully industrialized economies conformed to the dominant development thinking of the time. They evolved their own policy mixes and paths, taking advantage of a favorable global economy. They adopted a

Since World War II, at least two trends have been discernible at the global level that are relevant to this chapter. The first relates to rapid economic integration and the globalization of nations;[2] the second is the growing democratization of the polity across nations, which embodies the social and political facets of globalization.[3] These trends feed on each other and appear to be irreversible in most parts of the world.

The current era of globalization has been characterized by an extended period of economic expansion, the gradual dilution of borders between nation-states, and the rapid growth of market liberalism, all riding on an explosive deployment of information, communication, and transportation technology. These trends have raised people's expectations of the markets to deliver sustained global prosperity. Although significant progress has been seen for a great part of humanity for most of this period, some countries have grown faster than others, and some have seen a rise in income inequalities in the course of their development. Some regions have not benefited from the average improvement in global prosperity.[4]

In recent decades, systemic market failures have brought disappointment and economic disruption in both the developed and the developing world. Globalized economies have rapidly transmitted local weaknesses across borders, resulting in increased economic volatility and serious dislocation of economic activity in many countries. This was the experience with the East Asian currency crisis in late 1990s and in the wake of the 2008 global financial crisis. The resulting situation has encouraged development practitioners to seek a

---

heterodox strategy involving a combination of proactive state shepherding of economic agents and allocation of domestic capital, a step up in the rate of savings and capital accumulation, gradual economic liberalization with a guarded opening up of the economy (using capital controls and active exchange rate management), and a limited prioritization of the social development agenda. They engineered a structural transformation that shaped and honed their economic comparative advantage and propelled them to a higher growth trajectory and rapid development.

2 Economic globalization can be seen as the international integration of commodity, capital, and labor markets. For the period 1950–2007, world trade expanded by 6.2 percent, which was more than the growth of 3.8 percent in world gross domestic product (GDP). This was also more than the trade expansion in the earlier wave of globalization from 1850 to 1913. Similarly, from 1950 to 1973, global foreign direct investment stock as a proportion of world GDP was 5.2 percent, which increased fivefold to 25.2 percent from 1974 to 2007. *See* World Trade Organization, http://www.wto.org/english/res_e/booksp_e/anrep_e/wtr08-2b_e.pdf.

3 In its 1999 *Freedom in the World Survey*, Freedom House reported that in 1900, no country could claim full universal suffrage or regular elections, and only 5 percent of the world's people were able to vote for their leaders. By 1990, this count had grown to 69 countries and 64 percent of the world's people. Since then, 49 members have been added to the world democratic community, reaching 118 in 2013. Freedom House, *Freedom in the World 2013*, http://www.freedomhouse.org/report/freedom-world/freedom-world-2013#.U32y6MKKDmQ.

4 The vast majority of the world's low- and middle-income countries saw a sharp slowdown in economic growth in the period 1980–2000 as compared with the period 1960–1980. The period 2000–2010 saw a rebound in growth to the levels seen in the period 1960–1980 for most of these countries, along with an improvement in their social indicators. *See*, for example, Mark Weisbrot & Rebecca Ray, *The Scorecard on Development, 1960–2010: Closing the Gap?* DESA Working Paper No. 106, ST/ESA/2011/DWP/106 (June 2011).

more proactive role for states in the development process. A well-founded case has been made for a larger regulatory role for states in macroeconomic coordination and financial system stability at the global level.[5] Thus, a state is expected to provide an effective social protection floor as insurance against the economic uncertainties of a deeply globalized world; at the same time, it must coordinate and cooperate with other states, parastatal actors, and supranational agencies to foster a stable economic environment for sustained global growth and prosperity.

The democratization of societies has long been a human aspiration. An electoral democracy is considered among the best governance options for building state capacity to steer, deliver, and sustain human development.[6] However, evidence from the second half of the 20th century suggests that most nations that took that route did not realize the goals to the degree they desired.[7] The states that held back the process of democratizing their societies in favor of building an effective (authoritarian/centralized) developmental state—for example, some nations in Southeast Asia—witnessed unprecedented improvement in social and economic conditions. Yet a model of authoritarian governance, even when it is benevolent, is not likely to be an option in today's world. The empowerment of local stakeholders, including the media, and the unifying and aspirational influence of globalization make a centralized authoritarian model of governance difficult to sustain. Indeed, the trend in growth of electoral democracies in the past couple of decades has only accelerated.[8]

It is necessary, therefore, to analyze how an evolving electoral democracy could deliver development and governance more effectively, just as it is necessary to address the demands of globalization to secure and sustain development and good governance. Even as developing countries evolve their institutional framework and deepen democracy to overcome (where required) the weaknesses of an electoral democratic system, it is desirable to explore

---

5 United Nations, *Report of Commission of Experts on Reforms of the International Monetary and Financial System* (Stiglitz Commission) (Sept. 2009), http://www.un.org/ga/econcrisissummit/docs/FinalReport_CoE.pdf; and World Bank staff, *Rebalancing Growth and Development: An Interconnected Agenda* (World Bank Oct. 2011).

6 Freedom House defines an "electoral democracy" as a country or nonindependent territory such as Hong Kong with a two- or multiparty political system, regular elections, universal suffrage, and access to media for parties reflecting a representative spectrum of national opinion (see Freedom House, *supra* note 3).

7 In India, the first few decades of the postindependence period yielded less-than-desired growth in income. The inadequate trickle-down of benefits to the poor and the political-economy compulsions of vote-bank electoral politics led India to adopt a slew of redistributive development programs with an emphasis on meeting the basic minimum needs of the people. These policy preferences, in the face of slow growth in per capita income, poor targeting, implementation weaknesses, and leakages, resulted in suboptimal outcomes, a gradual buildup of policy contradictions, and economic instability, which, one could argue, have been addressed only partially in the context of the economic reforms initiated since the early 1990s.

8 Freedom House, *supra* note 3.

other factors and models that could support the governance of a social transformation process that moves in the desired direction and at the required pace.

This chapter explores the role of human rights and how their implementation can be tailored to the specific needs of countries in delivering development and good governance. The next section discusses why human rights matter for improving development delivery in the present global context. It elaborates on the human rights–based approach as commonly understood in the literature. The following section presents the human rights indicators framework and shows how this schema can be used to operationalize a human rights approach to development and good governance and, in the process, bridge the development and the human rights discourses. The concluding section discusses how such an approach to improve development delivery and governance is unfolding in India and its consequences for India's economy and society at large.

Why Do Human Rights Matter for Development and Good Governance?

A nation's policy to improve development and governance effectiveness can be meaningfully anchored in human rights standards and the process of their implementation. As universally recognized values, human rights standards provide a normative basis for development and governance agenda setting in a society. At the same time, human rights principles and crosscutting norms offer the means and the methodology to harness the potential development and governance outcomes for human well-being. The notion of "good governance" can be related and benchmarked to a process that supports and sustains enjoyment of human rights. In an era when nations are challenged by the process of globalization and its attendant consequences, including the expectations of people regarding development and governance processes, equally pressing concerns arise out of the growing momentum for democratization and decentralization of governance within nations. These apparently competing trends necessitate the use of a framework that not only focuses on realizing socially desired outcomes but also ensures that conduct of that process is in compliance with certain valued principles, including those of equity, inclusion, and nondiscrimination.

To begin with, although globalization is a vital element in the transformation of societies and a means to enjoy growing prosperity, it has the potential to contribute to despair, social dissonance, and economic hardship, as seen, for example, in the post–2008 financial crisis world.[9] Rising prosperity, inexpensive communications, cross-border networks, and global footloose capital are contributing to a shift of power from the state to the people and nonstate

---

9 *See*, for example, Joseph E. Stiglitz, *Globalization and Its Discontents* (W. W. Norton 2002); *Governing Globalisation: Issues and Institutions* (Deepak Nayyar ed., Oxford U. Press 2002); Jagdish Bhagwati, *In Defense of Globalization* (Oxford U. Press 2004).

actors. More important, the impact of globalization on people is being felt directly through social media. People are drawing inspiration and sustenance from each other in implementing major changes in their societies. The Arab Spring is evidence of this trend, as are social mobilization efforts in India, Bangladesh, Thailand, and several other countries.[10] Globally, there is an overwhelming buildup of support for common values and norms to anchor and guide policies for the social, political, and economic transformation of nations and to meet the concerns and rising aspirations of people. Such values and the objectives of social change that they serve are embodied in international human rights instruments and the standard-setting process spearheaded, for example, by the United Nations. Thus, in the face of a rapid convergence of purpose across what were in the past insurmountable cultural, social, and political barriers, especially in the developing world, there is a case for creating policy space and means to improve governance and development delivery anchored in the universal human rights normative framework.

Second, given the political and social consequences of globalization and the absence of recourse to authoritarian developmentalism (a model that has successfully delivered rapid economic and social transformation in several countries), there is a role for a human rights approach to support development and secure good governance.[11] This role seeks to make democracies, particularly electoral democracies in the developing world, more inclusive, accountable, and effective in delivering rapid development. It calls for a deepening of democracy and electoral system reform based on a human rights framework.

In the exercise of taking democracy from the national and subnational electoral politics to broad-based participation at the local level and in the process of improving development and governance outcomes, the notions of *voice, social contract,* and *accountability* come to the forefront. Each notion, in its operational context, stands to gain by being anchored in human rights standards

---

10 "Arab Spring" refers to the civil unrest followed by a wave of demonstrations in the Arab world that surfaced in 2010 and resulted in regime change in countries including Tunisia, the Arab Republic of Egypt, and the Republic of Yemen and widespread protests in several other countries. In India, there was civil society mobilization to strengthen laws and enforcement to address issues such as violence against women (in Dec. 2012) and corruption (in 2010 and 2011). In Bangladesh, the focus was on crimes committed by collaborators of the regime during the war of their independence. In Thailand, the focus was on regime change.

11 In this chapter, the term "human rights approach" is preferred over "human rights–based approach." In the development literature, particularly in the programming context, "human rights–based approach" is more commonly used. It gives primacy to the crosscutting norms or standards on procedural human rights (such as the right to nondiscrimination and equality in the Universal Declaration of Human Rights arts. 1, 2, and 7, or the right to participate in public affairs in art. 21) in its articulation. However, for a more general articulation of the approach that encompasses human rights standards and obligations related to both procedural and substantive human rights (such as the right to liberty and security of person, art. 3, or the right to education, art. 26), the use of "human rights approach" is more appropriate. Substantive human rights have a relatively clear content and may also have a progressive component in their realization. Procedural human rights are critical to the process of realizing substantive rights and may be easier to define and operationalize in the specific context of substantive rights, for example, the right to nondiscrimination in the context of the right to education.

and the state parties' obligations that flow from implementing those standards. Human rights are universal legal guarantees protecting individuals and groups against actions and omissions that interfere with fundamental freedoms, entitlements, and human dignity.[12] An underlying feature of human rights is the identification of rights holders who, by virtue of being human, have a claim over certain entitlements, and duty bearers, who are legally bound to meet the entitlements associated with those claims. Thus, there are rights of individuals and there are correlate obligations, primarily for the state. The latter encompasses the human rights obligation to respect, protect, and fulfill and the obligation of conduct and results that empower the voice of development stakeholders, that strengthen the foundations of social contract in society, and that improve the accountability of public agencies in delivering development and good governance.[13]

The notion of voice highlights the importance of effective participation and meaningful stakeholder consultations in the decision making, implementation, and assessment of development and governance modalities that affect human well-being. The idea of social contract relates to a paradigm that recognizes the rights and obligations of parties and is guided by a sense of justice and equity in the use of available common resources in furthering the well-being of people. Such a paradigm must evolve in keeping with the needs of the times and the changing context of societies and could benefit from being explicitly anchored in a value system that has a universal acceptance and perpetual relevance. The concept of accountability implies effective development delivery and good governance, with recourse to redress mechanisms for individuals whose legitimate claims are not met. The very construct of a human right involving a normative standard with universal appeal (such as the right to take part in public affairs or the right to nondiscrimination and equality) and benchmarks of conduct in the form of specific obligations that need to be fulfilled in implementing those standards lends power to the notion of voice, social contract, and accountability in delivering improved development and governance outcomes.

Third, human rights by virtue of being embedded in a legal framework (and if effectively enforced) have the potential to rapidly alter the power relations and structural constraints of a decadent social order (e.g., the caste system in India or entrenched discrimination on grounds of color, sex, race, or religion elsewhere) that are at the root of persistent inequalities and deprivation within and across social groups in a society. Electoral democracies due to their context and weaknesses (such as in India, with its inherent dependence

---

12 *Frequently Asked Questions on Human Rights Based Approach to Development Cooperation* 1 (United Nations publication, sales No. E.06.XIV.10).

13 In the human rights literature, these are referred to as the Maastricht principles, which define the scope of state obligations, generally in the national context, but could apply to the nature of state obligations at the international level. *See "Maastricht Guidelines" on Violations of Economic, Social, and Cultural Rights* (Maastricht, Netherlands, Jan. 22–26, 1997). *See* also United Nations, *Human Rights Indicators: A Guide to Measurement and Implementation* 10–13 (U.N. Off. High Commr. Human Rights 2012).

on vote-bank politics, limitations of the first-past-the-post criterion in multi-cornered electoral contests, and a protracted decision-making process) may not always be able to overcome these constraints quickly enough and, therefore, need support to deliver development and good governance to facilitate the desired social transformation. Moreover, by providing a normative basis for the development and governance process, as well as a strategy involving well-defined redress and accountability mechanisms, a human rights framework can be used to implement and sustain social transformation.

Fourth, it is necessary to recognize and invoke the value-added of a human rights approach over a good development approach. The latter also recognizes many of the human rights crosscutting norms such as transparency, accountability, participation, and ownership of the policies and practices in seeking desirable social outcomes. A human rights approach to development agenda setting and its implementation can be distinguished in terms of an explicit focus on empowerment (of individuals, communities, and nations through specific legal entitlements anchored in international human rights instruments and by altering the governance structure of the development process) and accountability of development stakeholders (the various duty bearers, individually and collectively) to protect and promote human dignity and well-being. A human rights approach leverages legal systems to improve accountability, providing redress and addressing the vital concerns of equity (fairness in the distribution of development benefits and access to opportunities), equality (in publicly guided social outcomes and under the rule of law), and nondiscrimination (under prohibited grounds by law) in the development and governance process.[14] Most important, unlike a developmental approach, a human rights approach leverages the power of its normative framework to influence policy interventions in ensuring the well-being of all.

A human rights approach is not just about respecting and protecting legal entitlements. It is also about promoting public policies and programs that facilitate the enjoyment of human rights. Thus, implementing human rights requires an ad infinitum assessment of the efforts made by duty bearers in meeting their obligations, irrespective of whether those obligations are directed at promoting a right or protecting it. This requires engaging a diverse set of stakeholders at the national and subnational levels, including human rights practitioners, civil society organizations, policy makers, development practitioners, and administrative agencies encompassing social, economic, judicial, and law enforcement services. The human rights approach operates on a platform involving a larger set of stakeholders than does a development approach and is therefore a source of potential strength in providing holistic and durable solutions to improving development effectiveness and good governance.

---

14 United Nations, *The Future We Want* (U.N. Conf. Sustainable Dev. [Rio+20] 2012), http://www.un.org/en/sustainablefuture; United Nations, *Realizing the Future We Want for All: Report to the Secretary-General*, especially *Towards Freedom from Fear and Want: Human Rights in the Post-2015 Agenda* (Thematic Think Piece, May 2012).

Some practitioners argue that a human rights approach is resource intensive. It requires public interventions to create legal entitlements for people, which could undermine the fiscal sustainability of the development process and the overall macroeconomic environment for growth. This is the argument extended, for example, in the case of India, where during 2004–2014, the federal (central) government, led by the United Progressive Alliance, created legal entitlements for individuals to access public information, education, and limited basic work opportunities (confined to unskilled labor) in rural areas. The government at that time also took steps to create legal entitlements to health services and food security. In the process, the government may have expanded its financial liabilities ahead of its ability to raise the required resources, thereby compromising the fiscal balance of the economy. This happened at a time when the post–global-financial crisis slowdown in economic growth impacted the government's revenue buoyancy. However, this need not be the case if the creation of legal entitlements is selectively and cautiously undertaken and accompanies a comprehensive rationalization of extant subsidies and social transfers in the society. The creation of new entitlements, particularly in resource-constrained developing countries, must also take into account a revamping of publicly provided services, notably education and public health, making them accountable to institutions of local governance for improved efficiency in delivery.

Sustaining high growth can be a meaningful attribute in the objective function of a human rights approach to development because of the opportunities that it could generate for the society at large, and in relaxing the resource constraints for public interventions. Arjun Sengupta, the first UN Independent Expert on the Right to Development, makes a credible case for including economic growth as a right-to-development attribute to avoid the perception of a trade-off between a human rights approach and a policy focus on sustaining economic growth.[15]

Also a human rights approach has important resource-neutral components that have a direct bearing on the lives of the poor and deprived, as well as on overall governance standards in the society, that impacts the well-being of all. There is ample evidence to suggest that the poor are disproportionately affected by corruption and are often denied the benefits of rule of law in practice. Rule of law and administration of justice are cornerstones of the social and economic transformation of a society. Overcoming corruption requires transparency in administration, the elimination of discretionary powers vested in or deliberately acquired by public officials and agencies, improved oversight systems, incisive investigations, time-bound adjudication, and effective enforcement of law. All these measures, if effectively implemented through a human rights approach, can improve development delivery and governance.

Fifth, human rights can bring a certain purpose and vigor to the approach used to address the development and governance challenges of globalization

---

15 *See* U.N. doc. /CN.4/2002 /WG.18/6.

and the sustainability of efforts at the international level. Indeed, international cooperation holds the key to delivering desired outcomes, and incorporating the human rights principles of accountability and solidarity could strengthen the framework of cooperation. This is relevant in the post-2008 global financial crisis world, where policy options exercised in the national interest in one country have had detrimental consequences for recovery in other countries, and particularly so in some emerging economies. The commitment to international cooperation must be raised to the level of a collective obligation for global development, equality, and sustainability. Political commitment to international cooperation must recognize mutual and reciprocal responsibilities among nations, taking into account their respective capacities and resources and subject to effective accountability mechanisms. An operational framework for addressing this issue may not necessarily require new international modalities; rather, it requires better implementation and monitoring of existing international human rights instruments and mechanisms. In that process, a strategic use of human rights indicators, goals, and targets could play a significant role. Thus, sustained global economic recovery from a financial crisis could benefit from a human rights approach to global agenda setting and development cooperation.

Notwithstanding the ethical appeal and the conceptual feasibility of a human rights approach to development and good governance, the challenge to operationalize it is a serious one. For the human rights discourse to provide a normative and an instrumental guide to public policy, a language of rights must exist that can be accessed and used by policy makers and other stakeholders. This language has to be less prescriptive and legalistic than a legal narrative, and more concrete, accessible, and practicable to a broader set of stakeholders, including policy makers and public service providers. Such language requires the creative use of qualitative and quantitative human rights indicators. The next section outlines how the identification of such indicators can help operationalize a human rights approach to development delivery and good governance.

Operationalizing the Human Rights Approach

The identification and application of human rights indicators in goal setting, policy articulation, implementation, and assessment is a potent way to incorporate human rights in the development and governance agenda at the national and international levels.[16] More important, these indicators can pro-

---

16 This section draws on Rajeev Malhotra, *Towards Implementing the Right to Development: A Framework for Indicators and Monitoring Methods*, in *Development as a Human Rights* (Bard A. Andreasson & Stephen P. Marks eds., Harvard U. Press 2006); the work done by the author of this chapter in preparing U.N. Off. High Commr. Human Rights 2012 (*see* United Nations, *supra* note 13); Rajeev Malhotra, *Implementing the Right to Development: Towards Operational Criteria and Monitoring Framework*, in *Realizing the Right to Development: Essays in Commemoration of 25 Years of the United Nations Declaration on the Right to Development* (U.N. Off. High Commr. Human Rights 2013); and Rajeev Malhotra, *India Public Policy Report 2014: Tackling*

vide a framework in which to operationalize and monitor the implementation of a rights approach in its role of protecting as well as promoting human rights for human well-being. Human rights indicators also provide a meaningful platform for the convergence of human rights and development discourses, in the process supporting improvement in public delivery and governance outcomes for human well-being. A human rights indicator

> is specific information on the state or condition of an object, event, activity or an outcome that can be related to human rights norms and standards; that addresses and reflects the human rights principles and concerns; and that can be used to assess and monitor the promotion and implementation of human rights.[17]

It is, therefore, a useful tool for articulating and advancing claims on duty bearers and in providing benchmarks to guide and monitor the implementation of a duty bearer's obligations and related policy response. The use of human rights indicators also promotes accountability and redress, thereby contributing to the value of a human rights approach.

The catalog of human rights is articulated in various human rights instruments. Their content is constantly elaborated on and clarified by different mechanisms under the international human rights system and human rights jurisprudence as it evolves.[18] The complex and evolving nature of human rights standards makes it necessary to have a well-structured framework that can assist in interpreting the normative standards, promote their implementation, and assess stakeholder compliance for improving development delivery and governance.

The framework as detailed by the UN Office of the High Commissioner for Human Rights builds a common approach to identifying indicators for promoting and monitoring civil and political rights, as well as economic, social, and cultural rights.[19] It contributes to strengthening the notion of the interrelatedness, interdependence, and indivisibility of all human rights. In ensuring

---

Poverty, Hunger, and Malnutrition (Oxford U. Press 2014).

17 *See* United Nations, *supra* note 13, ch. 1. Defined in this manner, some indicators might be unique human rights indicators because they owe their existence to specific human rights norms or standards and are generally not used in other contexts. This could be the case, for example, with indicators such as the number of extrajudicial, summary, or arbitrary executions; the reported number of victims of torture by the police and the paramilitary forces; or the number of children who do not have access to primary education because of discrimination. At the same time, there could be a large number of other indicators, such as commonly used socioeconomic statistics (e.g., human development indicators used in the UN Development Programme's Human Development reports) that could meet (at least implicitly) all the definitional requirements of a human rights indicator as laid out here. In these cases, to the extent that such indicators relate to human rights standards and principles and could be used for human rights assessments, it is helpful to consider them human rights indicators.

18 It includes the general comments and recommendations of the various treaty monitoring committees and the work of the special procedures of the Human Rights Council. *See id.*

19 *Id.*

that the framework is workable, the focus is on using information and data sets that are commonly available and based on standardized data-generating mechanisms (such as official administrative statistics), which most states parties (to human rights treaties and other international agreements) find acceptable and administratively feasible to compile and follow. Furthermore, the framework focuses on identifying indicators for specific substantive and procedural human rights, as well as for crosscutting human rights norms.[20] These are then used as building blocks for elaborating on indicators at the level of human rights treaties or for specific human rights thematic issues such as violence against women.

Anchoring Indicators in Human Rights Standards: The Importance of Attributes

The conceptual framework used to identify human rights indicators requires that selected indicators be anchored in the normative content of a right, as enumerated in the relevant articles of the treaties and general comments of treaty monitoring committees. This is ensured by taking a two-part approach that includes identifying the attributes of a human right, followed by identifying a cluster of indicators that unpack specific aspects of implementing the associated standard.[21] An attribute of a right reduces the relevant narrative on the legal standard into a concrete categorization. This facilitates indicator selection and makes explicit the link between the indicator, on the one hand, and the relevant normative standards, on the other. Considerations in the identification of attributes include the need for the attributes to be nonoverlapping or mutually exclusive in their scope and based on an exhaustive reading of the standard so that no part of the standard is overlooked in the choice of the attributes of a human right or in identifying the indicators for that right; collectively, the attributes of a right should reflect the essence of the normative content of that right.

Thus, in the case of the right to nondiscrimination and equality, the attributes identified are "equality before the law and protection of person," "access to an adequate standard of living, health and education," "equality of livelihood opportunities," and "special measures including for participation in decision-making." In the case of the right to education, the attributes identified are "universal primary education," "accessibility to secondary and higher education," "curricula and educational resources," and "educational opportunities and freedom" (see tables 1, 2, 3, 4, and 5 at the end of this chapter).[22]

---

20 *Supra* note 11.

21 United Nations, *supra* note 13, ch. 2.

22 In the case of the human rights where illustrative indicators have been identified (*see* United Nations, *supra* note 13), on average, four attributes are able to capture reasonably the essence of the normative content of those rights.

Measuring Human Rights Commitments, Efforts, and Results

Having identified the attributes of a human right, the next step is to implement a consistent approach to selecting and designing indicators for the normative standards and the obligations corresponding to those attributes. In that context, the framework focuses on measuring three aspects:

- The commitments of duty bearers to their human rights obligations
- The efforts they undertake in implementing those obligations in the form of policies and public programs, irrespective of whether such efforts are directed at respecting, protecting, or promoting the standards
- The results of a duty bearer's efforts to support the realization and enjoyment of human rights by the people

Consequently, the framework uses a cluster of indicators—namely, structural, process, and outcome indicators, or, in other words, commitments, efforts, and results indicators—to measure the different facets of a duty bearer's obligations.

Structural indicators capture the ratification and adoption of legal instruments and the existence as well as the creation of basic institutional mechanisms deemed necessary for the promotion and protection of human rights. They reflect the commitment and the intent of a state to implement the accepted standards once it has ratified a human rights treaty. Foremost, structural indicators focus on the enactment and the enforcement of domestic law as relevant to a right. They also focus on the policy framework and strategies required by a state to implement the standards and the corresponding obligations on a right, particularly in the form of government's stated policy position, for example, on free elementary education or on affirmative action for minorities and marginalized sections of the population. Structural indicators set the basis for the justiciability of the standard and its related obligations in the domestic legal system.

Process indicators measure the duty bearer's efforts to transform human rights commitments into desired results. Unlike structural indicators, these indicators seek to continuously assess the policies and specific measures being undertaken by a duty bearer in implementing its commitments on the ground. A process indicator links state policy measures with milestones that, over time, could result in the desired human rights outcomes. By defining process indicators in terms of an implicit cause-and-effect relationship and as a monitorable intermediate between commitments and results, the conduct of the process and the accountability of a state for its human rights obligations can be better assessed.

There are two important considerations in the selection and formulation of process indicators. It is necessary to ensure that a process indicator links a structural indicator to its corresponding outcome indicator, preferably through a conceptual and/or an empirical relationship, and that a process indicator explicitly brings out some measure of an effort being undertaken by a duty bearer in implementing its obligation. Also, it is desirable that a process indicator be measured in terms of the physical milestone that it generates, rather than in terms of the public expenditure that goes into the process.[23]

Outcome indicators capture individual and collective attainments that reflect the enjoyment of human rights in a given context. An outcome indicator consolidates over time the impact of various underlying processes that can be captured by one or more process indicators. For example, life expectancy or mortality indicators could be a function of immunization programs for children, public health awareness of the population, accessibility to adequate nutrition, or a reduction in physical violence and crime in a society. It is sometimes helpful to view process and outcome indicators as flow and stock variables, respectively. An outcome indicator, or a stock variable, is often slow moving and less sensitive to capturing momentary changes than a process indicator.[24] However, it reflects more appropriately, and perhaps more comprehensively, the sense of well-being that an individual enjoys as a result of the desired (public) action. Process and outcome indicators may not always be mutually exclusive. A process indicator for one human right can be an outcome indicator for another right.[25]

Indicators of Crosscutting Human Rights Norms

The indicators that capture crosscutting human rights norms or principles need not be exclusively identified with a specific human right; they are meant to capture the extent to which the process of implementing and realizing human rights respects, protects, and promotes, for example, nondiscrimination and equality, participation, transparency, access to remedy, and accountability.[26] There is no easy or unique way to reflect these transversal norms and principles explicitly in the selection of indicators. When capturing the norm of nondiscrimination and equality in the selection of structural, process, and outcome indicators, for example, a starting point is to seek disaggregated data

---

23 Experience across countries and across regions within a country reveals that there is no monotonic relationship between public expenditure and the physical outcome that such expenditure generates. The physical outcome is a function of resources and other institutional and noninstitutional factors that vary from place to place, making it difficult to interpret indicators on public expenditure (*see* also note 24).

24 Some similarity in process and outcome indicators derives from the fact that any process can be measured in terms of the inputs going into a process or in terms of the immediate outputs that the process generates. Thus, a process indicator of the immunization of children can be measured in terms of the public expenditure going into immunization programs (which is the input variant) or in terms of the proportion of children covered under the program (which is an output variant). Both these indicators are process indicators. They contribute to lowering child mortality, which is an outcome indicator because it captures the consolidated impact of the immunization program over a period of time and can be directly related to the enjoyment of the right to health attribute on child mortality and health care.

25 For example, the proportion of people covered by health insurance can be categorized as a process indicator for the right to health and as an outcome indicator for the right to social security.

26 The list of crosscutting norms is neither sacrosanct nor complete.

about discrimination on such grounds as sex, disability, ethnicity, religion, language, and social or regional affiliation. Or it can also be addressed as a procedural right that has a bearing on the realization of a specific substantive right and hence is defined in reference to that right. Thus, the procedural standard on nondiscrimination and equality could be assessed in the context of the realization of the right to education or to work opportunities across different population segments.

In the case of the human rights principle of participation, the objective is to reflect whether local stakeholders have a say in the adoption and implementation of measures that a duty bearer takes in order to fulfill its obligations. At a more aggregative level, changes in the magnitude of indicators such as the Gini coefficient or the share of income accruing to the bottom population decile could be used. Such indicators reflect the distribution of household consumption expenditure and income in the population and help researchers assess whether a society encourages participation, inclusion, and equality in the distribution of returns from the development process. Indicators on work participation rates and educational attainment of the population in general and of specific groups in particular (e.g., women and minorities) could be useful in this context.

The first steps in the implementation of the principle of accountability are being taken as one translates the normative content of a right into relevant and reliable quantitative and qualitative indicators. Indeed, the availability of information sensitive to human rights, and collection and dissemination of that information through independent mechanisms using transparent procedures, reinforces accountability. Moreover, the process indicators, by definition, seek to promote accountability of the duty bearer in discharging its human rights obligations.

Each of the categories of indicators, through their respective information sets, highlights the steps being undertaken by states to meet their human rights obligations, be it respecting, protecting, or fulfilling a right or determining the obligations of conduct and result that underpin the implementation of human rights standards. Human rights obligations are captured through indicators that reflect human entitlements, acts of commission or omission of public policy, outcomes that influence human well-being, and legal and administrative mechanisms of accountability and redress. The collective use of structural, process, and outcome indicators helps in establishing the value of a rights approach to monitoring and assessment.[27] Moreover, the use of said configura-

---

27 *See* Malhotra, *Towards Implementing the Right to Development, supra* note 16, for details. The need to monitor the outcomes, as well as the underlying processes in undertaking human rights assessments, is not equally recognized in the two sets of human rights: the civil and political rights, and the economic, social, and cultural rights. In the case of the latter, it is more obvious to accept it. In many situations, particularly in the context of developing countries, these rights can be realized only progressively because of resource constraints. In such cases, it is logical to monitor the process of the progressive realization of the human right. However, even the civil and political rights that are ratified and guaranteed by a state and can in principle be enjoyed must be protected ad infinitum. It is recognized in the literature that the implementation and realization of civil and political rights require resources as well as time—for example, to set up the requisite judicial and executive institutions and to design policy and regulatory and enforcement frameworks to protect those rights. In other words,

tion of indicators also encourages the use of contextually relevant, available, and potentially quantifiable information for populating the chosen indicators.

Figure 1 shows the framework for identifying human rights indicators. Steps used in elaborating indicators on the standards and obligations related to a specific human right are depicted on the left. Methods to tweak the framework to identify indicators on human rights thematic issues, such as violence against women, that may involve implementing standards on more than one human right, are shown on the right. The middle section depicts crosscutting norms applicable to the elaboration of the indicators. Using this framework, tables 1, 2, 3, 4, and 5 identify indicators for some procedural and substantive rights and on the issue of violence against women.

Figure 1. Framework for human rights indicators

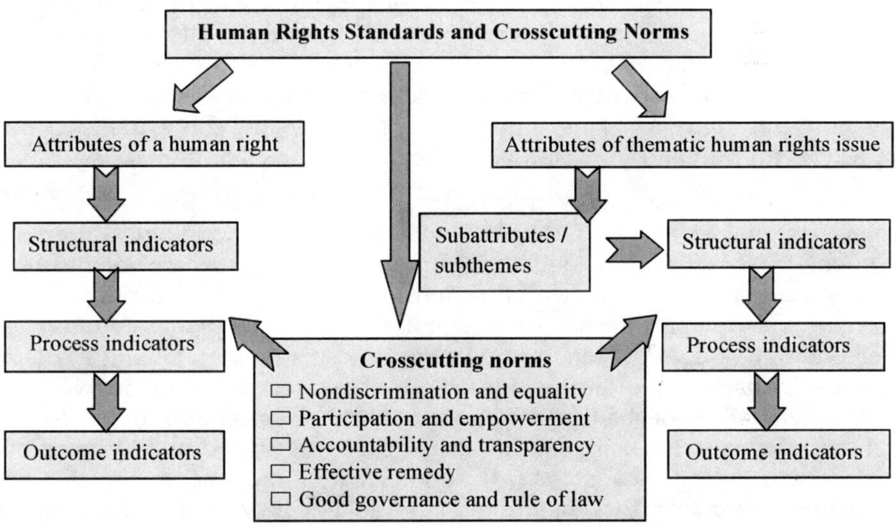

Violence against women (table 4) is a human rights thematic issue that cuts across civil, cultural, economic, political, and social rights, and thus its indicators need to reflect multiple standards. A life-cycle perspective is best used to identify the attributes of violence against women. Phases, events, and situations where a woman is likely to experience violation of her physical and mental integrity are considered to identify the attributes, namely, sexual and reproductive health and harmful traditional practices; domestic violence; violence at work, forced labor, and trafficking; community violence and abuse by law enforcement officials; and violence in conflict, postconflict, and emergency situations. These are then further decomposed to isolate subthemes related to the applicable human rights standards around which the indicators are identified.

---

in monitoring the realization of the civil and political rights, it is also important to assess the conduct of the process that supports the protection of such rights.

The elaboration of indicators on different rights and on the issue of violence against women is presented in a matrix format in tables 1 through 5. The normative standard as captured in the attributes of a right is placed on the horizontal axis and the different categories of indicators—the structural, process, and outcome indicators—appear on the vertical axis (under each attribute) to permit a systematic coverage of the normative standard and the corresponding obligations of the right.

Given the framework presented here for identifying human rights indicators, the use of a standardized template is desirable. Because each table exhibits the range of indicators that are relevant to adequately capture the normative content and the corresponding obligations of a human rights standard, it permits stakeholders to make an informed choice in selecting a few indicators from among the set to meet the specific needs of the context. Some structural and process indicators presented in the tables cut across more than one attribute. Similarly, some outcome indicators are relevant for more than one attribute or common to a set of process indicators. In all these instances, a meaningful choice of indicators can help in limiting the overall basket of indicators required to articulate policy and monitor the implementation of the human rights approach. This template also facilitates the contextualization of indicators for human rights standards that are universal in their scope.[28]

A conceptual framework that helps in identifying indicators for use in human rights assessments must be backed by a robust methodological approach to populate those indicators with the required data. Indicators are not meaningful in promoting the implementation and monitoring of human rights unless they are explicitly and precisely defined; based on an acceptable standardized methodology of data collection, processing, and dissemination; and available on a regular basis. The indicators identified in the tables are based on two types of data-generating mechanisms: indicators that are or can be compiled by official statistical systems using census, statistical surveys, and/or administrative records; and indicators or standardized information more generally compiled by national human rights institutions and civil society sources focusing on alleged violations reported by victims, witnesses, or others. The intention here is to explore and exhaust the use of commonly available information, particularly from objective data sets that can be easily quantified for tracking human rights implementation, and in the process contribute to operationalizing the approach and assisting in its acceptance by the stakeholders.[29]

Although appropriate indicators may help in identifying development outcomes/goals that embody normative human rights concerns and facilitate the articulation of the required policy interventions, it is the implementation of those policies that ultimately helps in attaining the desired outcomes and goals. Besides its conceptual appeal, the human rights approach to develop-

---

28 *See* United Nations, *supra* note 13, ch. 4.

29 *Id.*, ch. 3.

ment and good governance needs an adequate empirical basis to be considered a serious option for application across different contexts.

Does the Rights Approach Work? Some Evidence and Concluding Remarks

There are only a few examples of a well-articulated human rights approach being used to improve development delivery and governance practice. Between 2004 and 2014, India's federal government adopted a strategy for inclusive development that included creating new entitlements and strengthening others by providing limited legal guarantees on some aspects of life seen as vital for an individual's well-being and inclusion in the economic and social mainstream of society. The motivation behind the approach was to remove political, social, economic, and bureaucratic barriers to empowerment of marginalized segments of the society. The initiative gave shape to a human rights approach to the social protection floor, or the social safety net.

India's efforts in this regard include the following:

- The Mahatma Gandhi National Rural Employment Guarantee Act (2005) provides for 100 days of unskilled manual labor to every rural household on demand within 15 days ordinarily within a distance of five kilometers of the place of residence and at an inflation-indexed wage rate.
- The Right to Education Act (2009) provides for free education for children up to 14 years of age in keeping with norms and benchmark, including those related to school infrastructure, curriculum, and nutrition, through the provision of midday meals at schools.
- The National Food Security Act (2013) provides for subsidized cereals for up to 67 percent of the population, with greater entitlements for destitute families.
- The Draft National Health Bill (2009) seeks to provide universal health entitlement to all citizens (a major part of this initiative in the rural areas is being implemented under the National Rural Health Mission); and social pensions, under the National Social Assistance Programme, that are being gradually expanded for persons in old age and single woman pensioners.[30]

In addition, initiatives on housing for rural and urban areas with limited entitlements to affordable housing for the urban poor are being implemented. These measures seek to improve the current entitlements of the poor and enhance the scope of their future exchange entitlements.[31] Moreover, the

---

30 The draft bill is still under consideration.

31 *See* A. K. Sen, *Starvation and Exchange Entitlements: A General Approach and Its Application to the Great Bengal Famine,* 1 Cambridge J. Economics (1977); A. K. Sen, *Poverty and Famines* (Oxford U. Press 1981) for an elaboration of the notion of entitlements and the importance of improving the exchange entitlements of the poor and the marginalized to lift them out of their chronic deprivation.

human rights approach is bringing about greater accountability and transparency in the implementation and delivery of India's public programs in the social welfare sector.

Although it is too simplistic to make a definitive conclusion about the impact of these interventions in the short span of their implementation, the evidence suggests that trends in selected outcome/process indicators for these interventions show a significant improvement. This evidence includes indicators such as private real rural wage rates (influenced by the implementation of the employment guarantee program in rural areas), rural inequality in household consumption, school enrollment rates, nutrition status of children, health indicators on child and maternal mortality, and head count incidence of poverty.[32]

Two other measures that are contributing to the empowerment of people, particularly the marginalized, are the creation of a right to information (for information in the public domain) and the formalization of an identity instrument to improve people's access to public service delivery and their entitlements. The Right to Information Act (2005) has been instrumental in bringing greater transparency and accountability in the functioning of public agencies at the federal and the state levels. It has contributed to unearthing corruption and political scams in the allocation of scarce public resources. The Unique Identification Authority of India was set up in 2009 to create a universally acceptable identity instrument called *Aadhaar* and address the critical gap in the effective delivery of public services to the intended beneficiaries. It provides a digital identity to every individual, making each individual a part of the economy. This initiative has the potential to radically improve the delivery efficiency of social welfare programs when it is fully rolled out, including by supporting location portability for accessing public benefits and social transfers.[33] If the targeted population groups are correctly identified and the significant inefficiencies associated with India's public programs are monitored, government subsidies will decrease, improving the fiscal space for other reforms. This potential is attested to by the success of pilot programs implemented using the *Aadhaar* platform.

The results from India's gradually evolving human rights approach to social protection floor appear promising. However, potential pitfalls need to be avoided. The rights approach, which focused on selected issues and is being implemented in a few sectors, must be seen as part of a larger policy reform process—a process that, while seeking to expand the overall opportunities for people (through sustained high and inclusive growth), supports a social safety net to check unintended and unanticipated consequences for a growing market economy in an globalized world. Legal entitlements for meet-

---

32 *See* Malhotra, *India Public Policy Report*, *supra* note 16, for details on some of these indicators and related assessment.

33 Location portability of benefits will help poor migrant labor, which is forced to give up welfare entitlements as it migrates in search of work to avail those benefits in the new place of work.

ing basic needs must be created selectively, without undermining the fiscal sustainability of the growth process in the medium term and long term.

Over the past few years, several provincial governments (state governments) in India have taken the initiative to legislate a right to public services with the explicit objective of improving accountability in public delivery and addressing corruption. These efforts include statuary laws that guarantee time-bound delivery of various public services provided by the government along with mechanisms for redress, with provisions for punishing the public servant who fails to fulfill his or her mandated responsibilities. The Madhya Pradesh government was the first to take a lead in this regard in 2010; many other provincial governments have followed since then. India's federal government introduced the right of citizens for time-bound delivery of goods and services and redress of their grievances bill in the parliament in December 2011. The proposed bill would have made it mandatory for every public authority to publish a Citizen's Charter listing the goods and services provided by a public authority, the person or agency responsible for providing the goods or services, the time frame within which the goods or services must be provided, and the category of people entitled to the service. Unfortunately, the bill lapsed.

As of April 1, 2014, India's federal government made it mandatory for business entities (with net worth, turnover, and net profits above specified thresholds) to spend at least 2 percent of their net profits on certain activities under the corporate social responsibility (CSR) initiative. This provision in the Companies Act (2013) makes India perhaps the only country that has a legislative basis for CSR spending. Although the practice of CSR activities is not new to India, the new legislation has significantly increased likely CSR spending and provides a structured business responsibility to India's development agenda.

To sum up, a human rights approach is an option for countries seeking to speed up their social transformation in the face of hurdles imposed by an unjust historical social order and political economy weaknesses in decision-making processes. It also promises results for countries that are grappling with corruption and accountability issues in public agencies and need to decentralize their governance systems to improve development delivery. It is not just an approach that seeks to protect legal entitlements; this approach is about promoting an equitable and just process of development and change using normative considerations and creating a cohesive society with empowered individuals engaged with social causes in the collective interest. It is about coordinating state and nonstate actors to contribute to the process of social transformation through a framework of rights and responsibilities.

Although universal in its scope and relevance, a human rights approach can be contextualized to meet the needs of countries at different levels of development, quality of institutions, and aspirations. In that context, the framework to identify and design human rights indicators outlined in this chapter could play a significant role. The challenge is to weave the identified indicators creatively but purposefully into the fabric of policy articulation, implementation, and assessment so they can guide the transformation of the society.

Table 1. Indicators of the right to liberty and security of persons (Universal Declaration of Human Rights [UDHR], Art. 3)

	Arrest and Detention Based on Criminal Charges	Administrative Deprivation of Liberty
Structural	• International human rights treaties relevant to the right to liberty and security of person • Date of entry into force and coverage of the right to liberty and security of persons in the • Date of entry into force and coverage of domestic laws for implementing the right to • Time frame and coverage of policy and administrative framework against arbitrary grounds (e.g., immigration, mental impairment, educational purposes, vagrancy) • Type of accreditation of national human rights institutions by the rules of procedure of	
	• Legal time limits for an arrested or detained person before being informed of the reason or having the case reviewed by an authority exercising judicial power; and for the trial	
Process	• Proportion of received complaints on the right to liberty and security of persons mechanisms and the proportion of these responded to effectively by the government • Proportion of communications sent by the UN Working Group on Arbitrary Detention • Proportion of law enforcement officials (including police, military, and state security punishment	
	• Number/proportion of arrests or entries into detention (pre- and pending trial) on the basis of a court order or due to action taken directly by executive authorities in the reporting period • Number/proportion of defendants released from pre- and trial detentions in exchange for bail or due to nonfiling of charges in the reporting period	• Number/proportion of arrests or entries into detention under national administrative provisions (e.g., security, immigration control, mental impairment and other medical grounds, educational purposes, drug addiction, financial obligations) in the reporting period • Number/proportion of releases from administrative detentions in the reporting period
Outcome	• Number of detentions per 100,000 population, on the basis of a court order or due to action by executive authorities at the end of the reporting period • Reported cases of arbitrary detentions, including posttrial detentions (e.g., as reported to the UN Working Group on Arbitrary Detention) in the reporting period	
All indicators should be disaggregated by prohibited grounds of discrimination, as applicable		

Effective Review by Court	Security from Crime and Abuse by Law Enforcement Officials
ratified by the state constitution or other forms of superior law liberty and security of persons deprivations of liberty, whether based on criminal charges, sentences, or decisions by a court or administrative the international coordinating committee of national institutions	
for the arrest or detention; before being brought to duration of a person in detention	• Time frame and coverage of policy and administrative framework on security, handling of criminality, and abuses by law enforcement officials
investigated and adjudicated by the national human rights institution, human rights ombudsperson, or other responded to effectively by the government force) trained in rules of conduct concerning proportional use of force, arrest, detention, interrogation, or	
• Proportion of cases where the time for arrested or detained persons before being informed of the reasons of arrest; before receiving notice of the charge (in a legal sense); or before being informed of the reasons for administrative detention exceeded the respective legally stipulated time limit • Number of habeas corpus and similar petitions filed in courts in the reporting period • Proportion of bail applications accepted by the court in the reporting period • Proportion of arrested or detained persons provided with access to a counselor or legal aid • Proportion of cases subject to review by a higher court or appellate body • Reported cases where pre- and trial detentions exceeded the legally stipulated time limit in the reporting period	• Proportion of law enforcement officials formally investigated for physical and nonphysical abuse or crime, including arbitrary arrest and detention (based on criminal or administrative grounds) • Proportion of formal investigations of law enforcement officials resulting in disciplinary actions or prosecution in the reporting period • Proportion of uniformed police and other law enforcement officials with visible government-provided identification (e.g., name or number) • Number of persons arrested, adjudicated, convicted or serving sentence for violent crime (including homicide, rape, assault) per 100,000 population in the reporting period • Proportion of law enforcement officials killed in line of duty in the reporting period • Firearms owners per 100,000 population/number of firearms licenses withdrawn in the reporting period • Proportion of violent crimes with the use of firearms • Proportion of violent crimes reported to the police (victimization survey) in the reporting period
• Proportion of arrests and detentions declared unlawful by national courts • Proportion of victims released and compensated after arrests or detentions declared unlawful by judicial authority	• Proportion of population feeling "unsafe" (e.g., walking alone in area after dark or alone at home at night) • Incidence and prevalence of physical and nonphysical abuse or crime, including by law enforcement officials in line of duty, per 100,000 population, in the reporting period

Table 2. Indicators of the right to participate in public affairs (UDHR, Art. 21)

	Exercise of Legislative, Executive, and Administrative Powers
Structural	• International human rights treaties, relevant to the right to participate in public • Date of entry into force and coverage of the right to participate in public affairs • Date of entry into force and coverage of domestic laws for implementing the association, and assembly • Date of entry into force of universal suffrage, right to vote, right to stand for with respect to the right to participate in public affairs at the national and • Quota, time frame, and coverage of temporary and special measures for • Type of accreditation of national human rights institutions by the rules of • Number of registered and/or active nongovernmental organizations (NGOs)
	• Periodicity of executive and legislative elections at the national and local levels • Date of entry into force and coverage of laws establishing an independent national electoral body
Process	• Proportion of received complaints on the right to participate in public affairs other mechanisms and the proportion of these responded to effectively by
	• Number of suffrages (election, referendum, and plebiscite) at national and local levels held during the reporting period • Number of legislations adopted by national and subnational legislatures during the reporting period • Proportion of elections and sessions of nationally and locally elected bodies held as per the schedule laid out by constitutional or statutory bodies • Proportion of election campaign expenditures at the national and subnational levels met through public funding • Proportion of elected personnel whose term of service was interrupted, by cause of interruption • Proportion of women and target groups included in the membership of national political parties or presented as candidate for election
Outcome	• Proportion of seats in parliament,* elected, and appointed bodies at subnational and local levels held by women and target groups
All indicators should be disaggregated by prohibited grounds of discrimination, as applicable ** Millennium Development Goal (MDG)–related indicator*	

Universal and Equal Suffrage	Access to Public Service Positions
affairs, ratified by the state in the constitution or other forms of superior law right to participate in public affairs, including freedom of opinion, expression, information, media, election, legal provisions defining citizenship, and limitations (including age limits) on permanent residents local levels targeted populations in legislative, executive, judicial, and appointed bodies procedure of the international coordinating committee of national institutions per 100,000 persons involved in the promotion and protection of the right to participate in public affairs	
	• Date of entry into force and coverage of legal provisions guaranteeing access to public service positions without discrimination • Date of entry into force and coverage of administrative tribunals or dedicated judicial redress mechanism for public service matters
investigated and adjudicated by the national human rights institution, human rights ombudsperson, or the government	
• Proportion of the voting-age population registered to vote • Reported irregularities (intimidation, corruption, or arbitrary interference) with registration, maintenance, and review of electoral rolls • Number of complaints per elected position recorded and addressed in the election process by national and subnational electoral authorities • Share of public expenditure on national and subnational elections spent on voter education and registration campaigns • Number of political parties registered or recognized at the national level • Proportion of voting age population not affiliated with political parties	• Proportion of vacancies in (selected) public authorities at the national and subnational levels filled through the selection of women and candidates from target population groups • Proportion of cases filed in administrative tribunals and dedicated judicial redress mechanisms for public service matters adjudicated and finally disposed during the reporting period • Proportion of positions in the public service reserved for nationals or citizens
• Average voter turnout in national and local elections, by sex and target groups • Proportion of invalid and blank votes in elections to national and subnational legislatures	• Reported cases of denial of access to public service or position on account of discrimination • Proportion of public service positions held by women and members of target groups

Table 3. Indicators of the right to education (UDHR, Art. 26)

	Universal Primary Education	Accessibility to Secondary an Higher Education
Structural	• International human rights treaties, relevant to the right to education, ratified by the • Date of entry into force and coverage of the right to education in the constitution or • Date of entry into force and coverage of domestic laws for implementing the right to educational institutions barrier free, and inclusive education (e.g., children with • Date of entry into force and coverage of domestic law on the freedom of individuals • Number of registered and/or active NGOs per 100,000 persons involved in the	
	• Time frame and coverage of the plan of action adopted by the state to implement the principle of compulsory primary education free of charge for all • Stipulated duration of compulsory education and minimum age for admission into school	• Time frame and coverage of national working and street children) • Time frame and coverage of national • Date of entry into force and coverage of • Proportion of education institutions at • Proportion of education institutions with
Process	• Proportion of received complaints on the right to education investigated and and the proportion of these responded to effectively by the government • Public expenditure on primary, secondary, and higher education as proportion of proportion of public expenditure on education*	
	• Net primary enrollment ratio* by target groups, including children with disabilities • Drop-out rate for primary education by grades for target groups • Proportion of enrolled children in public primary education institutions • Proportion of students (by target groups) covered under publicly supported additional financial programs or incentives for primary education • Proportion of public schools with user charges for services other than tuition fees • Proportion of primary education teachers fully qualified and trained • Proportion of children getting education in their mother tongue • Proportion of students in grade 1 who attended preschool	• Transition rate to secondary education by target groups • Gross enrollment ratio for secondary and higher education by target groups • Drop-out rate for secondary education by grades for target groups • Proportion of enrolled students in public secondary and higher education institutions • Share of annual household expenditures on education per child enrolled in public secondary or high school • Proportion of students (by target groups) receiving public support or grant for secondary education • Proportion of secondary or higher education teachers fully qualified and trained • Proportion of students enrolled in vocational education programs at secondary and postsecondary level
Outcome	• Ratios of girls to boys in primary education* by grades for target groups • Proportion of students starting grade 1 who reach grade 5 (primary completion rate)* • Proportion of out-of-school children in primary education age group	• Ratio of girls to boys in secondary or higher education* by grades • Proportion of children completing secondary education (secondary completion rate) • Number of graduates (first-level university degree) per 1,000 population
	• Youth (15–24 years)* and adult (15+) literacy rates (i.e., reading, writing, calculating,	

All indicators should be disaggregated by prohibited grounds of discrimination, as applicable.

** MDG-related indicator*

Curricula and Educational Resources	Educational Opportunity and Freedom
state other form of superior law education, including prohibition of corporal punishment, discrimination in access to education, making disabilities, children in detention, migrant children, indigenous children) and groups (including minorities) to establish and direct educational institutions promotion and protection of the right to education	
policy on education for all, including provision for temporary and special measures for target groups (e.g., policy on vocational and technical education regulatory framework, including standardized curricula for education at all levels all levels teaching human rights/number of hours in curricula on human rights education mechanisms (student council) for students to participate in matters affecting them	
adjudicated by the national human rights institution, human rights ombudsperson, or other mechanisms gross national income; net official development assistance (ODA) for education received or provided as	
• Proportion of schools or institutions conforming to stipulated national requirements on academic and physical facilities • Periodicity of curricula revision at all levels • Number of educational institutions by level recognized or derecognized during the reporting period by relevant regulatory body • Average salary of schoolteachers as a percentage of regulated minimum wages • Proportion of teachers at all levels completing mandatory in-service training during reporting period • Ratio of students to teaching staff, in primary, secondary, public, and private education	• Proportion of education institutions engaged in "active learning" activities • Proportion of adult population covered under basic education programs • Proportion of students, by level, enrolled in distance and continuing education programs • Number of institutions of ethnic, linguistic minority, and religious population groups recognized or extended public support • Proportion of labor force availing retraining or skill enhancement at public or supported institutions • Proportion of higher learning institutions enjoying managerial and academic autonomy • Personal computers in use per 100 population*
• (Improvement in) density of primary, secondary, and higher education facilities in the reporting period	• Proportion of women and targeted population with professional or university qualification
problem-solving, and other life skills)	

Table 4. Indicators of violence against women (UDHR, arts. 1-5 and 16)

	Sexual and Reproductive Health and Harmful Traditional Practices	Domestic Violence
Structural	• International human rights treaties, relevant to the elimination of discrimination against women, • Date of entry into force and coverage of the principle of nondiscrimination between men and • Date of entry into force and coverage of domestic law(s) criminalizing VAW, including rape, • Date of entry into force and coverage of legal act instituting an independent oversight body with • Time frame and coverage of policy or action plan for the elimination of discrimination and all for • Number of registered or active nongovernmental organizations and full-time equivalent	
	• Time frame and coverage of policy to eliminate harmful traditional practices (HTP), including female genital mutilation, early or forced marriage, honor killing or maiming, and fetal sex determination • Legally stipulated minimum age for marriage	• Date of entry into force and coverage of legislation criminalizing marital rape and incest • Date of entry into force and coverage of legislations protecting gender equality and women's ability to leave abusive relationships (e.g., equal inheritance, asset ownership, divorce)
Process	• Proportion of received complaints on all forms of VAW investigated and adjudicated by the responded effectively by the government • Proportion of public social sector expenditure on national awareness-raising campaign on all • Number of perpetrators of VAW (including HTP, domestic violence, trafficking, sexual	
	• Proportion of women of reproductive age, or whose partner is using contraception and effective preventive measures against sexually transmittable diseases (e.g., HIV/AIDS)* • Unmet need for family planning* • Number of safe and unsafe abortions per 1,000 women of reproductive age • Proportion of women whose age at marriage is below 18 years# • Proportion of managerial and other leader positions (e.g., religious leader) occupied by women	• Proportion of women reporting forms of domestic violence to law enforcement officials or initiating legal action • Number of available places in shelters and refuges per 1,000 population (urban and rural) • Number of adopted civil protection orders prohibiting perpetrators of domestic violence from further contact with the victim(s) • Proportion of men and women who think that abuse or violence against women is acceptable or tolerable
Outcome	• Proportion of women subjected to female genital mutilation# • Sex ratio at birth and ages 5–9 years • Maternal mortality ratio* and proportion of deaths due to unsafe abortions	• Proportion of women who have experienced physical and/or sexual violence by current or former partner in the last 12 months/during lifetime# • Proportion of women subjected to psychological and/or economic violence by the intimate partner#
	• Femicide rates (e.g., murder by intimate partner, sexual murder, killing of prostitutes, honor • Proportion of women who have experienced physical, sexual, and psychological violence during • Proportion of victim-survivors of physical, sexual, or mental violence, including trafficking and • Suicide rates by sex	
	All indicators should be disaggregated by prohibited grounds of discrimination, as applicable **** MDG-related indicator*** ***# United Nations Economic Commission for Europe indicator***	

Violence at Work, Forced Labor, and Trafficking	Community Violence and Abuse by Law Enforcement Officials	Violence and (Post-) Conflict and Emergency Situations
including all forms of violence against women (VAW), ratified by the state without reservations women and prohibition of all forms of VAW in the constitution or other forms of superior law domestic violence, trafficking, traditional harmful practices, stalking, and childhood sexual abuse specific VAW mandate (e.g., accredited national human rights institution) of violence against women and including data collection and dissemination program employment (per 100,000 persons) involved in the protection against VAW		
• Time frame and coverage of policy or program against workplace sexual harassment • Time frame and coverage of policy to combat trafficking, sexual exploitation, and forced labor and provide protection and access to remedy for victims	• Date of entry into force and coverage of legislation defining rape in relation to a lack of consent rather than use of force • Time frame and coverage of policy to combat community violence and abuse by police forces	• Time frame and coverage of policy or program to prevent or address sexual violence in conflict, postconflict, or emergency situations • Time frame and coverage of special measures for participation of women in peace processes
national human rights institution, human rights ombudsperson, or other mechanism and the proportion of these forms of VAW (including HTP) and on national prevention program integrated into school curriculum exploitation, and forced labor) arrested, adjudicated, convicted, and serving sentences (by type of sentence)		
• Proportion of and frequency of business organizations inspected for conformity with labor standards • Proportion of migrants working in the sex industry • Proportion of informal sector workers (e.g. domestic workers) shifted to formal sector employment	• Proportion of new recruits to police, social work, psychology, health (doctors, nurses and others), education (teachers) completing a core curriculum on all forms of VAW • Proportion of victims of rape who had access to emergency contraception or safe abortion, prophylaxis for sexually transmitted infections/HIV • Proportion of sexual crimes (e.g. rape) reported to the police (population survey) • Proportion of formal investigations of law enforcement officials for VAW cases resulting in disciplinary actions or prosecution	• Proportion of health staff trained in medical management and support for victims of sexual and other violence • Proportion of victims of sexual and other violence accessing appropriate medical, psycho-social and legal services • Proportion of reported cases of sexual or other violence where victims (or related third parties) initiated legal action • Proportion of expenditure on relief and emergency assistance devoted to women and child welfare
• Reported cases of women/men victims of trafficking (within and across countries), sexual exploitation, or forced labor • Proportion of working women who have been victims of workplace sexual abuse/ harassment	• Proportion of women/men who report feeling unsafe in public places or limiting their activities because of safety or harassment • Proportion of women who have experienced physical violence or rape/sexual assault during the last year (lifetime) #	• Reported cases of death, rape (attempted or completed) and other violence against women ncidents that occurred in conflict, postconflict, or emergency situations
killing, female infanticide, dowry deaths) the last year (lifetime), by severity of violence, relationship to the perpetrator, and frequency# forced labor, who received assistance, compensation, and rehabilitation services		

Table 5. Indicators of the right to nondiscrimination and equality (UDHR, Arts. 1, 2, and 7)

<table>
<tr><th rowspan="2"></th><th rowspan="2">Equality before Law and Protection of Persons</th><th>Direct or Indirect Discrimination by Public Nullifying or Impairing</th></tr>
<tr><th>Access to an Adequate Standard of Living, Health, and Education</th></tr>
<tr><td rowspan="2">Structural</td><td colspan="2">• International human rights treaties relevant to the right to nondiscrimination and
• Date of entry into force and coverage of NDE, including the list of prohibited
• Date of entry into force and coverage of domestic laws for implementing NDE,
• Date of entry into force and coverage of legal act constituting a body responsible
• Periodicity and coverage of the collection and dissemination of data relevant to
• Number of registered or active NGOs and full-time equivalent employment (per</td></tr>
<tr><td>• Time frame and coverage of policy and programs to ensure equal protection, security, and handling of crimes (including hate crimes and abuses by law enforcement officials)
• Date of entry into force and coverage of domestic laws ensuring equal access to justice and treatment, including for married, unmarried couples, single parents, and other target groups</td><td>• Time frame and coverage of policy or program for equal access to education at all levels
• Time frame and coverage of policy and programs to provide protection from discriminatory practices interfering with access to food, health, social security, and housing</td></tr>
<tr><td rowspan="2">Process</td><td colspan="2">• Proportion of received complaints on cases of direct and indirect discrimination other mechanisms (e.g., an equal opportunity commission) and the proportion
• Proportion of targeted population (e.g., law enforcement officials) trained on</td></tr>
<tr><td>• Proportion of victims of discrimination and bias-driven violence provided with legal aid
• Number of persons (including law enforcement officials) arrested, adjudicated, convicted, or serving sentence for discrimination and bias-driven violence per 100,000 population
• Proportion of women reporting forms of violence against self or children initiating legal action or seeking help from police or counseling centers
• Proportion of requests for legal assistance and free interpreters being met (criminal and civil proceedings)
• Proportion of lawsuits related to property where women appear in person or through council as plaintiff or respondent</td><td>• Ratio of targeted population (e.g., girls) in the relevant population group in primary and higher education levels* and by kind of schools (e.g., public, private, special school)*
• Proportion of health care professionals (landlords) handling requests from potential patients (candidates) in a nondiscriminatory manner (source: discrimination testing survey)
• Proportion of public buildings with facilities for persons with physical disabilities
• Proportion of targeted populations that was extended sustainable access to an improved water source, sanitation,* electricity, and garbage disposal</td></tr>
</table>

and Private Actors Equality of Opportunity for Livelihood	Special Measures, Including for Participation in Decision Making
equality (NDE) ratified by the state grounds of discrimination (see list below), in the constitution, or other forms of superior law including on the prohibition of advocacy constituting incitement to discrimination and hatred for promoting and protecting NDE assess the implementation of NDE 100,000 persons) involved in the promotion and protection of NDE	
• Time frame and coverage of policies for equal access to decent work • Time frame and coverage of policy for the elimination of forced labor and other abuses at work, including domestic work	• Time frame and coverage of policy to implement special and temporary measures to ensure or accelerate equality in the enjoyment of human rights • Date of entry into force and coverage of quotas or other special measures for targeted populations in legislative, executive, judicial, and other appointed bodies
investigated and adjudicated by the national human rights institution, human rights ombudspersons, or responded to effectively by the government implementing a code of conduct for the elimination of discriminatory practices	
• Proportion of enterprises (e.g., government contractors) that conform with certified discrimination-free business and workplace practices (e.g., no HIV test requirements) • Proportion of job vacancy announcements stipulating that among equally qualified (or comparable) candidates a person from targeted population groups will be selected (e.g., women, minority) • Proportion of employers handling applications of candidates in a non-discriminatory manner (e.g., ILO discrimination testing survey) • Proportion of employees (e.g., migrant workers) reporting discrimination and abuse at work who initiated legal or administrative action • Proportion of time dedicated to unpaid domestic work and caregiving charged to women	• Proportion of targeted population groups accessing positive action or preferential treatment measures aiming at promoting de facto equality (e.g., financial assistance, training) • Proportion of education institutions at all levels teaching human rights and promoting understanding among population groups (e.g., ethnic groups) • Proportion of members of trade unions and political parties who are women or from other targeted population groups and the proportion thereof presented as candidates for election

Outcome	• Prevalence/incidence of crimes, including hate crime and domestic violence, by target population groups • Reported cases of arbitrary killing, detention, disappearance. and torture from population groups ordinarily subject to risk of discriminatory treatment • Conviction rates for indigent defendants provided with legal representation as a proportion of conviction rates for defendants with lawyer of their own choice	• Educational attainments (e.g., youth and adult literacy rates) by targeted population groups* • Birth, mortality, and life expectancy rates disaggregated by targeted population groups • Proportion of targeted populations below after social transfers*
	• Reported number of victims of direct and indirect discrimination and hate crimes period	
All indicators should be disaggregated by prohibited grounds of discrimination, as applicable. **** MDG-related indicator***		

• Employment-to-population ratios* by targeted population groups • Wage gap ratios for targeted population groups	• Proportion of relevant positions (e.g., managerial) in the public and private sectors held by targeted population groups • Proportion of seats in elected and appointed bodies at subnational and local levels held by targeted population groups*
national poverty line (and Gini indices) before and	
and proportion of victims (or relatives) who received compensation and rehabilitation in the reporting	

3

The Right to Development

Translating Indigenous Voice(s) into Development Theory and Practice

FELIPE GÓMEZ ISA

Indigenous peoples have been largely excluded from the evolution of international human rights law since 1945. When the General Assembly of the United Nations adopted the Declaration on the Right to Development in 1986,[1] indigenous peoples were not recognized as subjects of this new right, although proposals pertaining to indigenous peoples were under discussion during the drafting process. This unacceptable lacuna was overcome by the adoption of the UN Declaration on the Rights of Indigenous Peoples (UNDRIP) in 2007.[2] Indigenous voices were the driving force behind the long and difficult process that led to the adoption of this instrument. The UNDRIP recognizes indigenous peoples as holders of the right to development and their right to free, prior, and informed consent in the design and implementation of development projects affecting their lives, territories, and natural resources.

A major challenge in integrating indigenous peoples' rights into international law is the frenzied race to explore ancestral territories in order to exploit the natural resources these lands contain. This race must be reconciled with respect for the right to development, as well as indigenous peoples' right to make meaningful decisions about the definition of development and specific priorities related to the concept. In this regard, it is interesting that the Declaration on the Right to Development makes no reference to indigenous peoples being entitled to this right. This is, indeed, one of the declaration's major omissions. The adoption by the International Labour Organization of Convention 169 in 1989 and UNDRIP in 2007 bridged this gap by explicitly acknowledging the entitlement of indigenous peoples to the right to development.

This chapter discusses how the recognition of indigenous peoples as subjects of the right to development can be viewed as a way to consider indigenous peoples as actors in their own development. Participation is a core principle of the right to development as enshrined in the UN Declaration on the Right to Development. Participation can increase the ownership and empowerment of the ultimate beneficiaries of development. The participation of indigenous

---

1 *Declaration on the Right to Development*, A/Res 41/128 (Dec. 4, 1986). For a reflection on the right to development on the occasion of the 25th anniversary of the declaration, *see* United Nations, *Realizing the Right to Development: Essays in Commemoration of 25 Years of the United Nations Declaration on the Right to Development*, HR/PUB/12/4 (2013).

2 *Declaration on the Rights of Indigenous Peoples*, A/Res 61/295 (Sept. 13, 2007).

peoples in all relevant phases of the development cycle may pave the way to improving the delivery system[3] and creating effective accountability mechanisms. No development project should be implemented without the meaningful consent and participation of those primarily affected. The last section of this chapter explores the potential of *sumak lawsay* (a Quechuan word that refers to an indigenous paradigm on development also known as *buen vivir,* or "living well") to incorporate indigenous voices in how development is theorized, framed, and practiced.

Subjects of the Right to Development in the UN Declaration

The Declaration on the Right to Development is consistent with the principle of the indivisibility and interdependence of individual rights and collective rights. Article 1.1 sets forth who is entitled to the right to development: "The right to development is an inalienable human right by virtue of which *every human person and all peoples* are entitled to participate in, contribute to, and enjoy economic, social, cultural and political development, in which all human rights and fundamental freedoms can be fully realized" (emphasis added). Article 2.1 underscores that "the human person is the central subject of development and should be the active participant and beneficiary of the right to development."

The Declaration on the Right to Development opts for a balanced and nuanced position, seeking to synthesize the issues that affect persons entitled to development and to achieve an equilibrium between the individual and the collective facets of this basic human right. Thus, as Bedjaoui posits, "the Declaration on the Right to Development defines, in a balanced and equitable manner, the right to development as a right that is both collective as well as individual."[4] The same position is upheld by Claude-Albert Colliard, in whose view "the Declaration sanctions the balance struck between the individual and the collective dimensions of the right to development."[5]

In Article 1.1, the right is conferred on "every human person" and "all peoples," while Article 2.1 underscores that it is the human person who is "the central subject of development." The declaration aspires to integrate different notions about who is entitled to the right to development, notions that often are at odds with each other. This aspiration helps explain the relative hetero-

---

3 According to Jim Yong Kim, president of the World Bank, "*Delivery* is an elegant word for getting goods and services to people in a way that meets their expectations." Jim Yong Kim, keynote speech, *Delivering on Development: Harnessing Knowledge to Build Prosperity and End Poverty*, (World Knowledge Forum, Oct. 8, 2012), http://www.worldbank.org/en/news/speech/2012/10/08/delivering-development-harnessing-knowledge-build-prosperity-end-poverty.

4 Mohamed Bedjaoui, *The Right to Development*, in *International Law: Achievements and Prospects* 1182 (Mohamed Bedjauoui ed., UNESCO; Martinus Nijhoff 1991).

5 Claude-Albert Colliard, *L'Adoption par l'Assemblée Générale de la Declaration sur le Droit au Développement (4 Décembre 1986)*, 33 Annuaire Français de Droit International 614, 623 (1987).

geneity of the declaration when it comes to defining who is entitled to the right to development. In the preamble, the declaration makes a reference to the fact that development is a prerogative of states, without clarifying what it defines as a state;[6] Article 1 confers this right on human persons and peoples, without making a specific reference to states as entitled entities[7] and without defining, at any point, people. Article 2.1 seems to define a kind of a hierarchy, one that benefits the individual aspects of the right to development. As Maria Magdalena Kenig-Witkowska points out, "This multi-faceted and heterogeneous definition of the persons entitled to the right to development is insufficiently clear and may even threaten its implementation."[8] In truth, the Declaration on the Right to Development was a compromise reached after lengthy and difficult negotiations and an excruciatingly complex and delicate process.[9]

The Declaration on the Right to Development does underscore the importance of the human person as "the central subject of development," as defined in Article 2.1. This approach to the right to development, stemming from the needs of the human person and taking his or her participation into account, is, according to Gillian Triggs and other authors, "a very positive approach."[10] It implies that any and all processes of development necessarily call on the individual, whose participation and expectations really do matter.[11] In line with this understanding of the importance of the individual in the perception of the right to development, the Declaration on the Right to Development reinforces the basic tenet of respect for human rights and fundamental freedoms. The

---

6 According to Koen De Feyter, the preamble's use of the term "nations" or "states" in the English-language version is an "indirect reference" to states, although he declares that this perspective does not surface again in the operative part of the declaration, even though the term "nations" does appear in the declaration. Koen De Feyter, *The Human Rights Approach to Development* 387 (Ph.D. dissertation, U. Instelling Antwerpen 1992).

7 Art. 2.3, although not specifically referring to the state during the process of development, does refer to it as one of the subjects entitled to the right to development. This article stipulates that "states have the right and the duty to formulate appropriate national development policies that aim at the constant improvement of the well-being of the entire population and of all individuals, on the basis of their active, free and meaningful participation in development and in the fair distribution of the benefits resulting therefrom."

8 Maria Magdalena Kenig-Witkowska, *The UN Declaration on the Right to Development in the Light of Its Travaux Préparatoires*, in *International Law and Development* 382 (Paul De Waart, Paul Peters, & Erik Denters eds., Martinus Nijhoff 1988).

9 Notwithstanding the efforts made to achieve consensus regarding this and other problematic aspects of the declaration, the United States voted against the declaration, and other relevant Western countries abstained from voting.

10 Gillian Triggs, *The Rights of Peoples and Individual Rights: Conflict or Harmony?* in *The Rights of Peoples* 156 (James Crawford ed., Clarendon 1988).

11 This step will have tremendous consequences on the thinking about development because it implicitly acknowledges that any process of development has, as its ultimate aim, the men and women involved and their participation in the process. Ultimately, the goal is to advance toward human development along the lines of the United Nations Development Programme (UNDP), in other words, the type of development that has as its main priorities such basic needs as education, health care, a dwelling, and the protection of basic human rights. *See* also *Human Rights and Development: Towards Mutual Reinforcement* (Philip Alston & Mary Robinson eds., Oxford U. Press 2006).

declaration assumes that true development is not possible in the absence of scrupulous respect of human rights and fundamental freedoms.

Numerous and varied references are made to the protection of human rights in the declaration. In the preamble, the General Assembly states that it is "concerned at the existence of serious obstacles to development, as well as to the complete fulfillment of human beings and of peoples, constituted, inter alia, by the denial of civil, political, economic, social and cultural rights, and considering that all human rights and fundamental freedoms are indivisible and interdependent."[12] In Article 3, the declaration specifies that human rights are an important element for development to be achieved: "States should take steps to eliminate obstacles to development resulting from failure to observe civil and political rights, as well as economic, social and cultural rights."

Yet indigenous peoples are not mentioned in the Declaration on the Right to Development. They are one of the declaration's "great forgotten."[13]

Indigenous Peoples Have the Right to Development

Many people today believe that the right to development is an individual and a collective right and that, in order to guarantee this entitlement, it is essential to encourage the participation of subnational entities in all actions geared toward development. The right to development thus is, as Koen De Feyter puts it, a "multidimensional" right.[14] In other words, the right to development pertains not only to "peoples" but also to "minorities and indigenous peoples."[15] Increasing the size of the group of subjects entitled to development is an attempt to secure the participation of those entities targeted by development, or what Konrad Ginther denominates as "the intermediate structures."[16] Ginther believes that if the right to development is guaranteed to structures that lie between the individual, the people, and the state, the domestic function of the right to development can be consolidated. In other words, the broadest possible participation is ensured of all those subjects whose absence would make it impossible to achieve an authentic and real development process.[17]

---

12 *Declaration on the Right to Development*, annex, at para. 10.

13 Indigenous peoples have been an "absent humanity" since the adoption of the Universal Declaration on Human Rights in 1948. *See* B. Clavero, *De los Ecos a las Voces, de las Leyes Indigenistas a los Derechos Indígenas* in *Derechos de los Pueblos Indígenas* 37 (Servicio Central de Publicaciones del Gobierno Vasco 1998).

14 *See* De Feyter, *supra* note 6, at 550.

15 *Id.*, at 272.

16 Konrad Ginther, *The Domestic Policy Function of a Right of Peoples to Development: Popular Participation a New Hope for Development and a Challenge for the Discipline*, in *The Right to Development in International Law* 69 (Subrata Roy Chowdhury, Erik Denters, & Paul De Waart eds., Martinus Nijhoff 1992).

17 Rodolfo Stavenhagen's introduction to the concept of ethno development is an alternative mode of development that underscores the role of subnational entities in the process of development. From the vantage point of ethno development, the state and society alike benefit from a diversity of development strategies determined by the different ethnic groups

It is along these lines that many authors have recognized that ethnic groups, minorities, and indigenous peoples are entitled to the right to development.[18] Indigenous peoples are among the groups of persons who have most suffered the brunt of inadequate development policies and their interests have not been taken into account, nor have their needs and specific worldviews been addressed.[19] Despite the fact that indigenous peoples are not mentioned in the Declaration on the Right to Development, many authors have upheld their inclusion among the groups that are or that should be entitled to the right to development. De Feyter highlights the need to include indigenous peoples among those who are entitled to the right to development to preserve their identity, and, indeed, to survive.[20] Many other authors have studied the right to development and its relationship with indigenous peoples.[21]

The Global Consultation on the Realization of the Right to Development as a Human Right, which took place in Geneva in January 1990, underscored the adverse situation that indigenous peoples were in, focusing on the fact that "the most frequent and destructive violations of the rights of indigenous peoples are a direct result of development strategies that do not respect the right to self-determination,"[22] a right that is closely linked to the right to development.[23] In line with this vision, the World Conference on Human Rights in

---

involved. Ethno development implies the establishment of broad swathes of autonomy for ethnic groups with regard to decisions having to do with the use of resources with development in mind. *See* Rodolfo Stavenhagen, *Ethno Development: A Neglected Dimension in Development Thinking,* in *Ethnic Violence, Development, and Human Rights* 1551 (SIM 1985).

18 Romualdo Bermejo Garcia and Jose Dougan Beaca, for example, believe that ethnic groups and minorities may also avail themselves of the right to development, although the Declaration on the Right to Development does not explicitly mention them. Romualdo Bermejo Garcia & Jose Dougan Beaca, *El Derecho al Desarrollo: Un Derecho Complejo con Contenido Variable,* 8 Anuario de Derecho Internacional 239 (1985); this position is also upheld (with nuanced differences) by Ian Brownlie, *The Human Right to Development* 19 (Commonwealth Secretariat Human Rights Unit Occasional Paper 1989).

19 *See Report of the United Nations Technical Conference on Practical Experience in the Realization of Sustainable and Environmentally Sound Self-Development of Indigenous Peoples* (Ctr. World Indigenous Stud. 1992); Gabe Mugarik, *Pueblos Indígenas: Nuestra Visión del Desarrollo* (Icaria 1995); M. Simon, *Indigenous Peoples and the Right to Development: An Inuit Perspective* 26 (paper presented at the conference *Global Consultation on the Realization of the Right to Development as a Human Right,* U.N. Off. at Geneva, Jan. 8–12, 1990) [hereinafter Global Consultation Conference]; J. W. Spellman, *Development through Indigenous Resources* 31 (paper presented at the Global Consultation Conference); Ted Moses, *Indigenous Peoples and International Development Policies,* in *Global Consultation* 18 (paper presented at the Global Consultation Conference); *La Voz de los Pueblos Indígenas* (Alexander Ewen ed., Palma de Mallorca 1995).

20 *See* De Feyter, *supra* note 6, at 476.

21 Paul Coe, *The Right to Development Must Also Address Indigenous Peoples and Economies,* in *Global Consultation* 38 (paper presented at the Global Consultation Conference); H. Bull, *Indigenous Peoples and the Right to Development* 25 (paper presented at the Global Consultation Conference).

22 *Global Consultation on the Realization of the Right to Development as a Human Right: Report by the Secretary General Pursuant to Commission on Human Rights Resolution,* 1989/45, E/CN.4/1990/9 /REV.1, at 29 (Sept. 26, 1990).

23 Art. 1.2 of the *Declaration on the Right to Development* proclaims that "the human right to development also implies the full realization of the right of peoples to self-determination."

Vienna in 1993 devoted part of its final declaration to recognizing the importance of guaranteeing the development and welfare of indigenous peoples. In Paragraph 20, the Vienna Declaration and Programme of Action "recognizes the inherent dignity and the unique contribution of indigenous people to the development and plurality of society and strongly reaffirms the commitment of the international community to their economic, social and cultural well-being and their enjoyment of the fruits of sustainable development."[24]

The Right to Development of Indigenous Peoples in ILO Convention 169

In an attempt to correct the omission in the Declaration on the Right to Development, the International Labour Organization adopted Convention 169, known as the Indigenous and Tribal Peoples Convention, on June 27, 1989. The convention contains acknowledgment of specific collective rights from the vantage point of the development of indigenous peoples. Specifically, Article 7 states that "the peoples concerned shall have the right to decide their own priorities for the process of development as it affects their lives, beliefs, institutions and spiritual well-being . . . and to exercise control, to the extent possible, over their own economic, social and cultural development." Article 13 states that governments shall respect the special importance for the cultures and spiritual values of the peoples concerned of their relationship with the lands or territories . . . and *in particular the collective aspects of this relationship*" (emphasis added). The collective dimension of the relationship between indigenous peoples and their lands and territories is one of the most relevant elements of indigenous peoples' worldview. That is why indigenous ownership goes well beyond individual ownership. These aspects are essential if indigenous peoples are to develop adequately; any development of this nature calls for an understanding and inclusion of the special relationship that links them to their territories.[25] Article 14 of the convention recognizes the right to collective ownership of indigenous peoples. By virtue of this provision, "the rights of ownership and possession of the peoples concerned over the lands which they traditionally occupy shall be recognized."

---

24 *Report on the World Conference on Human Rights*, A/CONF.157/DC/1/Add.1 (June 24, 1993).

25 The relationship of indigenous peoples to their ancestral territories and the collective nature of the property thereof was acknowledged in the judgment of the Inter-American Court of Human Rights in *Awas Tingni v. Nicaragua* by reason of specific concessions to log in traditional Awas Tingni lands; *see* Inter-American Court of Human Rights, *Case of the Mayagna (Sumo) Awas Tingni Community v. Nicaragua*, judgment of Aug. 31, 2001. *See* James Anaya and Claudio Grossman, *The Case of Awas Tingni v. Nicaragua: A New Step in the International Law of Indigenous Peoples* 12(1) Ariz. J. Intl. Comp. L. 1–16 (2002). *See* also Inter-American Court of Human Rights, *Case of the Yakye Axa Indigenous Community v. Paraguay*, judgment of June 17, 2005; Inter-American Court of Human Rights, *Case of the Xákmok Kásek Indigenous Community v. Paraguay*, judgment of Aug. 24, 2010.

The Inclusion of the Right to Development in the UNDRIP

Even though the right to development of indigenous peoples is explicitly set forth in a number of provisions in the UNDRIP,[26] thus correcting the omission in the Declaration on the Right to Development, the recognition of the right to development together with the right to self-determination of all peoples was fraught throughout the long and complex preparation of the declaration.[27]

Indigenous Peoples and Historical Wrongs

History is often used as a cloak under which to hide, justify, and validate wrongdoings, supremacist abuse, and exploitation under the guise of "discovery,"[28] "evangelization," "the sacred trust of civilization,"[29] "progress," and "development." European nations that benefited from colonialism and the despoilment of indigenous peoples for centuries used international law as a tool to uphold their expansionist interests. The concept of *terra nullius* was useful in justifying the occupation and expropriation of indigenous territories in America as well as in Africa.[30]

The efforts to make amends for past injustices "form an important part of the search for justice in the present."[31] Effects of past abuse—colonialism, slavery, the expropriation of indigenous territories—continue to be felt and to contribute to current inequalities and discriminatory attitudes, which are for the most part structural in nature. Indigenous peoples the world over are increasingly standing up for their right to reparation for past and present abusive behavior and injustices inflicted on them.

One rationale used to defend the right to reparation for historical wrongdoing is that the adverse effects of past mistakes persist, for example, in the current inequalities and social exclusion that afflict groups such as indigenous

---

26 Daniel Oliva Martínez, *El Derecho al Desarrollo de los Pueblos Indígenas: La Evolución Conceptual y su Inclusión en la Declaración de las Naciones Unidas*, in *La Declaración Sobre los Derechos de los Pueblos Indígenas* 233–65 (Natalia Alvarez Molinero, Daniel Oliva Martínez, & Nieves Garcia-Falces eds., Los Libros de la Catarata 2009).

27 A rigorous assessment of the difficulties that this project had to overcome and discussions about the right to development are included in Catherine Brolmann & Marjolein Zieck, *Some Remarks on the Draft Declaration on the Rights of Indigenous Peoples* 8(1) Leiden J. Intl. L. 103–13 (1995). *See* also Claire Chartres & Rodolfo Stavenhagen, *Making the Declaration Work: The United Nations Declaration on the Rights of Indigenous Peoples* (Intl. Work Group for Indigenous Affairs 2009).

28 *See* the discussion on the framework of the Spanish conquest of the Americas in Tzvetan Todorov, *La Conquista de América: El Problema del Otro* (Siglo XXI 1987).

29 This term was used well into the 20th century within the framework of the first "international organization," the League of Nations. *See* art. 22 of the Covenant of the League of Nations (1919).

30 Effective occupation and de facto control of the territory sufficed in and of themselves for the acquisition of sovereign rights over these territories; *see* Antonio Cassese, *International Law* 28 (Oxford U. Press 2005).

31 John Torpey, *Introduction: Politics and the Past*, in *Politics and the Past: On Repairing Historical Injustices* 26 (John Torpey ed., Rowman & Littlefield 2003).

peoples.[32] The UN Committee on the Elimination of Racial Discrimination makes reference to the fact that "in many regions of the world indigenous peoples have been, and are still being, discriminated against and deprived of their human rights. . . . [T]hey have lost their land and resources to colonists, commercial companies and State enterprises." Thus, "the preservation of their culture and their historical identity has been and still is jeopardized."[33] Indigenous peoples are among the peoples with the highest poverty levels and lowest possibilities of development in the world.[34] A report published by the United Nations High Commissioner for Human Rights in 2006 noted,

> Indigenous peoples are discriminated against within society, have generally weak political participation and lack equal access to economic, social and cultural rights. They may be harmed by or excluded from development projects and do not benefit fully from strategies to meet the Millennium Development Goals (MDGs). . . . They have less access to justice and security and are often implicated in conflict. They are also victims of serious human rights violations.[35]

In the face of ongoing discrimination, "it will be very difficult to overcome (its) after-effects in the absence of a clear admission of wrongdoing and of just reparation either to the victims or their descendants."[36]

Although restitution is a modality of reparation that appeases many indigenous peoples in cases that center on claims regarding the dispossession of ancestral territories,[37] it is also a complex and controversial measure. Conflict may arise about the rights of persons who, in good faith, occupy territories in the present. Consequently, the UN Committee for the Elimination of Racial Discrimination

> calls upon States parties to recognize and protect the rights of indigenous peoples to own, develop, control and use their communal

---

32 The other side of this argument is that some states, private businesses, and individuals became very rich at the expense of the victims of past abusive behavior. The economic gap between the haves and the have-nots has continued to grow. This seems to call for "the returning of accumulated wealth by those who became unjustly rich to those who were deprived and to their descendants." Dinah Shelton, *The World of Atonement: Reparations for Historical Injustices,* 50(3) Netherlands Intl. L. Rev. 305 (2003).

33 Committee on the Elimination of Racial Discrimination, *General Recommendation 23, Rights of Indigenous Peoples,* UN Doc. A/52/18, annex V, at 122, para. 3 (1997).

34 A study by the World Bank showed that the income levels of the indigenous peoples of Latin America, as well as indicators of human development such as education and conditions of health, "systematically lag far behind those equivalent standards of the remainder of the population." Gillete Hall & Anthony Patrinos, *Pueblos Indígenas: Pobreza y Desarrollo Humano en América Latina: 1994–2004* (World Bank 2005).

35 *Report of the High Commissioner for Human Rights on Indigenous Issues,* E/CN.4/2006/77, at para. 2 (Feb. 27, 2006).

36 Bartolomé Clavero, *El Orden de los Poderes: Historias Constituyentes de la Trinidad Constitucional* 293 (Trotta 2007).

37 Víctor Toledo Llancaqueo, *Políticas Indígenas y Derechos Territoriales en América Latina: 1990–2004: Las Fronteras Indígenas de la Globalización?,* in *Pueblos Indígenas: Estado y Democracia* 67–102 (Pablo Dávalos ed., CLACSO 2005).

> lands, territories and resources and, where they have been deprived of their lands and territories traditionally owned or otherwise inhabited or used without their free and informed consent, to take steps to return those lands and territories. Only when this is for factual reasons not possible, the right to just, fair and prompt compensation should substitute the right to restitution. Such compensation should, as far as possible, take the form of lands and territories.[38]

The UNDRIP is a landmark in the progressive recognition of the obligation to offer reparation to indigenous peoples for historical injustices. Its very adoption was interpreted by some as a token of a commitment to the past and compensation for a process of exploitation and dispossession that has not concluded.[39] But what is most important is that it explicitly tackles the issue of historical injustices. In the preamble, the General Assembly of the United Nations states that it is "concerned that indigenous peoples have suffered from historic injustices as a result of, inter alia, their colonization and dispossession of their lands, territories and resources, thus preventing them from exercising, in particular, *their right to development* in accordance with their own needs and interests" (emphasis added).[40]

This discerning statement establishes a causal link between colonization and the dispossession of the lands, territories, and resources that were wrested from indigenous peoples in the past and their inability to effectively exercise their right to development, which continues to be a problem. Thus, access to and control of indigenous peoples' territories, lands, and resources are fundamental tools to guarantee the right to development by indigenous peoples. The General Assembly of the United Nations is "convinced that control by indigenous peoples over developments affecting them and their lands, territories and resources will enable them to maintain and strengthen their institutions, cultures and traditions, and to promote their development in accordance with their aspirations and needs."[41]

The Right to Development in the UNDRIP

The recognition of the right to development of indigenous peoples is closely linked to their right to self-determination.[42] Ultimately, the UNDRIP aspires to establish necessary preconditions in the economic and social domains that are essential for indigenous peoples to exercise their right to self-determination.

---

38 *General Recommendation 23, supra* note 33, at para. 5.

39 Miguel Concha Malo, *Lucha por la Dignidad y los Derechos Humanos Individuales y Colectivos de los Pueblos de América Latina*, in *Responsabilidad Histórica: Preguntas del Nuevo al Viejo Mundo*, 321 (Reyes Mate ed., Anthropos 2007).

40 Para. 6 of the pmbl.

41 Para. 10 of the pmbl.

42 Dalee Sambo Dorough, *The Indigenous Human Right to Development*, 1–2 Indigenous Affairs 77 (2010).

As Article 3 notes, "Indigenous peoples have the right to self-determination. By virtue of that right they freely determine their political status and *freely pursue their economic, social and cultural development*" (emphasis added).

The clearest assertion regarding the acknowledgment of the right to development of indigenous peoples is contained in Article 23, which reads:

> Indigenous peoples have the right to determine and develop priorities and strategies for exercising their right to development. In particular, indigenous peoples have the right to be actively involved in developing and determining health, housing and other economic and social programmes affecting them and, as far as possible, to administer such programmes through their own institutions.

The logical consequence of the right to development for indigenous peoples is that they can determine priorities with regard both to issues related to development and to projects carried out on their territories. Indeed, a main challenge is presented by the knowledge that under the heading of *development* lurks projects and activities that directly attack the identity, lifestyles, and environmental balance that are characteristic of indigenous peoples. Projects may represent a serious threat to the worldview of indigenous peoples and to their right to development, for instance, projects related to the extractive industry, as detailed with concern by James Anaya, UN special rapporteur on the rights of indigenous peoples.[43] Article 32.2 of the UNDRIP defends the principle of free, prior, and informed consent regarding those projects that affect indigenous peoples:[44]

> States shall consult and cooperate in good faith with the indigenous peoples concerned through their own representative institutions in order to obtain their free and informed consent prior to the approval of any project affecting their lands or territories and other resources, particularly in connection with the development, utilization or exploitation of mineral, water or other resources.

---

43 For the rapporteur, "there is a fundamental problem with the current model of natural resource extraction in which the plans are developed by the corporation, with perhaps some involvement by the State, but with little or no involvement of the affected indigenous community or people, and in which the corporation is in control of the extractive operation and is the primary beneficiary of it." He is convinced that "new and different models and business practices for natural resource extraction need to be examined, models that are more conducive to indigenous peoples' self-determination and their right to pursue their own priorities for development. In his future work on extractive industries, the Special Rapporteur plans to examine various models of natural resource extraction in which indigenous peoples have greater control and benefits than is typically the case under the standard corporate model, drawing on a review of the experiences of indigenous peoples in various locations." *Report of the Special Rapporteur on the Rights of Indigenous Peoples*, A/HRC/21/47, at paras. 86 & 87 (Jul. 6, 2012).

44 *See* the progressive precedents in the field of free, prior, and informed consent by the Inter-American Court of Human Rights in the Inter-American Court of Human Rights case of the *Saramaka People v. Suriname* judgment of Nov. 28, 2007. A similar line of thought was expressed by the Constitutional Court of Colombia in a landmark case regarding the descendants of African peoples in the Valle del Cauca; *see* Judgment T-1045A/10 (2010).

The difficulties in the implementation of the declaration are a sign of the obstacles that indigenous peoples must overcome to ensure their right to development.[45]

Indigenous Peoples and the Paradigm of *Buen Vivir*

The indigenous peoples of Latin America coined the term *buen vivir*[46] to refer to the paradigm that includes their claims within the scope of development.[47] Mirna Cunningham, an indigenous Miskito and current chair of the UN Permanent Forum of Indigenous Issues, notes that *buen vivir* refers to the

> deep spiritual bond that we indigenous peoples maintain with Mother Earth; it also has to do with the economic relations that, based on our own systems and institutions, govern our productive lives and exchange relations; "Buen Vivir" has to do with our indigenous identity that is the foundation allowing us to proclaim who we are, where we come from and where we are going.[48]

Ultimately, *buen vivir* and the close relationship binding indigenous peoples with *la pacha mama* (nature) are based on the duality and complementarity that are an essential element of the indigenous worldview.

The constitution of Ecuador and that of Bolivia, examples of plurinational constitutionalism, both include the concept of *buen vivir*.[49] The constitution of Ecuador, adopted in 2008, introduced a series of concepts that are the result of the worldview of the indigenous people who inhabit the country. The preamble acknowledges the "millennia-old roots" of different peoples residing in the country and of the tremendous relevance of *pacha mama,* "of which we

---

45 Another interesting case is that of the acknowledgment by the African Commission on Human and Peoples' Rights of the right to development of the Endorois people. In May 2009, the African Commission stated that the forcible eviction of the Endorois people from their traditional lands near Lake Bogoria by the government of Kenya without prior consultation and with no provision for compensation was a violation of a number of rights under the African Convention on Human and Peoples' Rights. Specifically, the state was found to have violated the right to development of the Endorois people. *Centre for Minority Rights Development (Kenya) and Minority Rights Group International on Behalf of Endorois Welfare Council v. Kenya*, Communication 276/2003, at para. 298.

46 The term in Quechuan is *Sumak Kawsay*; in the Aymara language, it is *suma qamaña*.

47 *See* Maité Niel, *El Concepto del Buen Vivir* (Universidad Carlos III, 2011).

48 Mirna Cunningham, *Living Well: The Indigenous Latin American Perspective,* 1–2 Indigenous Affairs 53 (2010).

49 Art. 8 of the constitution of Bolivia of 2009 states that "I. The State assumes and promotes the following ethical-moral principles of a pluralistic society: ama qhilla, ama llulla, ama suwa (do not be lazy, do not lie, do not steal), suma qamaña ("Vivir Bien"), ñandereko (live in harmony), teko kavi (live well), ivi maraei (land without evil) and qhapaj ñan (noble life or path). II. The State's foundations are the values of unity, equality, inclusion, dignity, freedom, solidarity, reciprocity, respect, complementarity, harmony, transparency, balance, equal opportunities, social and gender equity in participation in life, common welfare, responsibility, social justice, distribution and redistribution of social product and goods, in order to live a good life."

are a part and which is vital to our existence." The authors of the constitution state their desire to construct "a new way of living together . . . appreciating the diversity of nature and living in harmony with it," with the goal of achieving *buen vivir*. The constitution enshrines the "rights relevant" to *buen vivir*, including the right to access water, the right to food security, and the right to live in a healthy and balanced environment. What is perhaps most novel in this constitution is the recognition of the rights of nature. The rights of nature could well be construed as the contribution by indigenous peoples to modern constitutionalism in particular and to humankind in general.[50] As Article 71 states, "Nature or *Pacha Mama*, where life takes place and reproduces itself, is entitled to the right to be totally respected and to ensure that its life cycles, structure, functions and evolutionary processes be maintained and regenerated." The rights of nature, because they are recognized as pertaining to nature itself and not to the human people who inhabit nature, lie "outside of the systematically homocentric Western sphere."[51]

Despite its appealing qualities, the *buen vivir* concept needs further conceptual clarification and definition of specifics for it to truly serve indigenous peoples as a road map for proposals for development. As Efraín Jaramillo, a Colombian anthropologist, points out, *buen vivir* is a concept that is too weak, too superficial, and suffering from too many loopholes to be truly useful as a tool for social and economic transformation,[52] or more specifically in the effective exercise by indigenous peoples of their right to development.

Conclusions and the Way Forward

The progressive recognition of indigenous peoples' rights represents a major conceptual shift in the field of human rights. The acceptance of indigenous peoples as subjects of their own right to development may pave the way for their empowerment and increased self-esteem, thus creating avenues for better and more appropriate development. Participation in the development process is an integral component of the right to development as enshrined both in the UN Declaration on the Right to Development and in the UNDRIP. The emerging paradigm of *buen vivir* has the potential to incorporate indigenous cosmo-visions and views on development, but it needs greater conceptual clarification and practical elucidation to become a tool for emancipation and change.

---

50 José Aylwin, *The Contribution of Indigenous Peoples' Legal Systems to International Human Rights Law: The Experience of Latin America* 5 (paper presented at the international conference *The Contribution of Non-Western Legal Systems to International Human Rights Law*, Sept. 13–14, 2010).

51 Raquel Irigoyen, *El Pluralismo Jurídico en la Historia Constitucional Latinoamericana: De la Sujeción a la Descolonización* 10 (Instituto Internacional de Derecho y Sociedad 2009).

52 Efraín Jaramillo, *Mother Earth and Living Well: New Paradigms for Indigenous Struggles?*, 1–2 Indigenous Affairs 61 (2010).

4
The Curse of Riches
Sharing Nature's Wealth Equitably?

Emilio C. Viano

The exploration for and exploitation of resources through extractive industries is not a new phenomenon but rather a chronic situation that has endured for centuries. This chapter examines the role that the state, multinationals, and international financial institutions (IFIs) play in the clash over natural resources, where indigenous peoples' voice and rights are often ignored and disregarded. It examines current efforts and policies intended to recognize and respect indigenous peoples' rights and to honor a social contract. It demonstrates that current practices do not address key issues, including that of accountability, and that a concerted effort must be undertaken to change the equation and dynamics of power and dominion and use of the earth's riches. This chapter suggests that development must be redefined, crafted, and targeted in a way that takes into account and balances all legitimate claims to the earth's wealth, thus fulfilling the tenet of "translating voice, social contract, and accountability into development."[1]

Contrasting Rights and Claims

Driven by an increasing realization that the earth's riches are limited, spurred by the fierce competition that globalization has unleashed, and using increasingly sophisticated technology for discovery and exploitation, states and corporations have been motivated to go, literally, where no outsider has gone before. The natural resources in some of the earth's most remote and inhospitable locations became available for exploitation when new states sprang up in the post–World War II postcolonial period. Elites and dominant groups, empowered to maintain security and promote trade, "developed" natural resources, often igniting conflicts with indigenous peoples. In an enduring cycle, these clashes frequently led to the growth of the military and to arms races, which in turn led to debt, thereby generating the need to appropriate resources to pay off the debt.

The conflict over the issue of who owns natural resources has been central to the rise of nationalism and the assertion of ethnic identity throughout the world. Today, first nation (indigenous) peoples realize that without their resource base, they have no future. They—and many other interested

---

1 Peter Hjertholm & Howard White, *Foreign Aid in Historic Perspective: Background and Trends*, in *Foreign Aid and Development: Lessons Learnt and Directions for the Future* 80–102 (Finn Tarp ed., Routledge 2000).

parties—believe that modern states, some of them relatively young, cannot legitimately and fully, without reservation, lay claim to resources that indigenous peoples have utilized and maintained for centuries. The consequences of such exploitation are thus the subject of fierce disputes (e.g., damage and destruction of ancestral lands, food and water sources, and way of life).

Ironically, improving economic conditions worldwide and the growing wealth of many people in emerging economies have made the hunt for and exploitation of natural resources ever more urgent. This trend legitimizes the process, given the increasing demand for consumer goods and technological items. Development industries help states seize resources and put them for sale on the world market through projects such as mining, oil exploration, and hydroelectric development and less tangible actions such as colonization (which takes land), transportation (which eventually takes land, timber, minerals, and other resources), and credit (which finances the appropriation and/or processing of salable resources).[2] States have traditionally received considerable help from other states and international organizations in appropriating these resources.

One issue that is rarely addressed when development projects are launched is who owns the resources to begin with? Whose agreement is needed before proceeding? How can interested parties voice their concerns and objections? What is an equitable formula for sharing earnings and mitigating displacement and environmental pollution and destruction? What requirements does a social contract place on multinationals and on governments authorizing massive projects, allocating resources, and sharing proceeds? Which accountability systems should be in place to make sure those agreements and contracts are honored and fulfilled?

Laws introduced in the past few decades by ruling groups often deny indigenous peoples' claims to resources. Such laws, many indigenous groups argue, should not and do not take precedence over their own historical claims to resources. The issue of who has rights to resources is being fought out on a case-by-case basis in the streets, in the forests, on the high seas, and in the courts. At stake is not only the complex issue of ownership but also the value of the resources and who has the right to manage, extract, and consume them.[3]

International institutions, including the United Nations and the World Bank, and some multinational companies (MNCs) have voiced concern over the adverse impact of resource extraction on the lives of indigenous communities; at the same time, they continue to fund such activities.[4] The scale and scope of problems confronting indigenous peoples caused by mineral extraction projects endorsed by governments, international agencies, and MNCs

---

2 Samir Amin, *Capitalism in the Age of Globalization: The Management of Contemporary Society* (Zed 2006).

3 Jean-Marie Baland & Jean-Philippe Platteau, *Halting Degradation of Natural Resources: Is There a Role for Rural Communities?* (U.N. Food & Agric. Org. 1996).

4 *See* the sections on foreign direct investment and MNCs and on the role and function of IFIs.

are monumental and growing, creating a paradox.[5] In spite of the burgeoning number of international charters and national laws asserting the rights of indigenous peoples, indigenous peoples still find themselves systematically subject to discrimination, dispossession, and impoverishment.[6]

The fact is that indigenous peoples, even when shunted away to places thought to be barren and unproductive, often inhabit areas with vast natural resources that are coveted by the extractive industry. However, as in years past, these groups are rarely consulted in decisions about whether and how to go about mining or building dams or harvesting lumber from the forests. They are normally not offered or trained to take up employment in projects that take advantage of and profit from their lands. Activism and advocacy efforts are drawing attention to the strain and disconnect between the development discourse in the developed world and the aspirations of indigenous groups who often have centuries-old links with their land.[7]

A Landscape of Development, Dispossession, and Hegemony

The land is not seen by indigenous people merely as a source of riches to be exploited (or to be destroyed, for example, through open-pit mining). The land is often seen as an ancestral cradle, a sacred place, a spiritual base, and a source of inspiration, values, and identity.[8] The link between indigenous peoples and their land is integral to, and inseparable from, indigenous peoples' identity. Thus, issues of identity are essential to grasp if one is to comprehend how and why indigenous peoples relate to and respond to neoliberal capitalism in the way that they do.[9]

Because of its intrinsic dynamics and needs, globalization is often perceived by indigenous people as undermining the sustainability of the ecosystems on which they have depended for millennia as well as their unique identity.[10] Some indigenous peoples view economic development, often presented as a panacea for all ills and problems facing a particular society or

---

5 Edmund Terence Gomez & Suzana Sawyer, *State, Capital, Multinational Institutions, and Indigenous Peoples*, in *The Politics of Resource Extraction: Indigenous People, Multinational Corporations, and the State* 33–45 (Edmund Terence Gomez & Suzana Sawyer eds., Palgrave Macmillan 2012).

6 For an example, *see* Walden Bello & Shea Cunningham, *A Siamese Tragedy: Development and Degradation in Modern Thailand* (Zed 1999).

7 Noam Chomsky, *Profit over People: Neoliberalism and Global Order* (Seven Stories 1998).

8 United Nations, *Prevention of Discrimination and Protection of Indigenous Peoples*, Report of the Working Group on Indigenous Populations on its 19th Sess., subcomm. on the Promotion & Protection of Human Rights, 53rd Sess., Agenda item 5(b), UN Doc. E/CN.4/Sub.2/2001/17 (Aug. 9, 2001), http://daccessddsny.un.org/doc/UNDOC/GEN/G01/149/79/PDF/G0114979.pdf.

9 Makere Stewart-Harawira, *The New Imperial Order: Indigenous Responses to Globalization* 152–55 (Zed 2005).

10 Michael Löwy & Charlotte C. Stanley, *Toward an International Resistance against Capitalist Globalization*, 29(6) Latin American Perspectives 127–31 (2002).

group, as an instrument to justify and impose assimilation. This view is reinforced by countless examples in the history of relations between the "developed" world and indigenous populations where economic development has taken place without any input from indigenous people.[11] Development is often defined as the equivalent of becoming, acting, and living like Westerners—as attaining the level and status of Western civilization.[12] This perception has eroded, obscures, and ignores any sense of indigenous identity.

Regardless of much talk about human rights and democracy, in some ways, our globalized society and economy has not progressed much since European explorers and entrepreneurs encountered indigenous populations in different parts of the world and colonized them. Medieval and Renaissance Europeans assumed that they were the model of what humans should be and that indigenous peoples were thus, by definition, inferior, backward, and uncivilized; in the name of "civilizing" indigenous peoples and protecting them, indigenous peoples could be subjugated and exploited. For survival and the attainment of opportunities in a colonial world, the best hope for indigenous populations was to become "civilized," that is, to become how Europeans saw and defined themselves.[13] Until this elusive point was reached, indigenous peoples could be exploited, and their natural resources and land could be plundered with state support.[14]

Europeans, in addition to Australians, North Americans, and others, exploited resources that they encountered in other peoples' territories. Often, such colonial discourse characterized indigenous peoples as lazy, ignorant, or incapable of properly managing and using their own natural resources, and this attitude was considered an impediment to "progress." (Sometimes, it seems that attitudes have changed little over the centuries.)

---

11 The literature supporting and praising development in the Omo River valley in Ethiopia clearly reflects these patronizing attitudes, values, and approaches. *See* Verónica Potes, *The Duty to Accommodate Aboriginal Peoples Rights: Substantive Consultation?*, 19(1) J. Envtl. L. & Practice 27–45 (2006).

12 This mentality still appears in current statements and literature written to defend Western-style projects dispossessing indigenous people of their land and way of life with patronizing language that repeats and reinforces stereotypes about the lack of "utility" and "productivity" of indigenous people's use of the land and water resources. For a current example, *see* http://aigaforum.com/articles/The-Omo-Kraz-Sugar-development-Project-English.pdf and http://www.slideshare.net/meresaf/the-omokuraz-sugar-development-project.

13 Guido Abbattista, *European Encounters in the Age of Expansion* (2011), http://ieg-ego.eu/en/threads/backgrounds/european-encounters/guido-abbattista-european-encounters-in-the-age-of-expansion.

14 From the start of European exploration and expansion in various parts of the world, it was common practice to capture individuals or families or groups of indigenous, considered "exotic," and take them to Europe to illustrate their "otherness" and, by visibly demonstrating their "backwardness," reaffirm European superiority and supremacy and legitimize its exploitative colonial conquests. *See* Suzana Sawyer & Edmund Terence Gomez, *On Indigenous Identity and a Language of Rights*, in *The Politics of Resource Extraction: Indigenous People, Multinational Corporations, and the State* 9 (Edmund Terence Gomez & Suzana Sawyer eds., Palgrave Macmillan 2012).

The effort to resist the homogenizing dynamics of globalization forced the introduction of an alternative vision that accommodates both economic development and group identity.[15] This can be seen in the paradox of today's commercial transactions, where producers of goods want to conquer global markets while they fiercely defend, to the point of appearing parochial, the denomination of origin of their products. The concepts of appellation or denomination of origin and of geographical indicators are growing in importance in international trade,[16] and the European Union is especially active in promoting and defending these concepts on behalf of its member-states.[17]

Foreign Direct Investment and MNCs: A New Wave of Conquests and Exploitation

By the 20th century, powerful European countries or their successor states founded by European settlers, including the United States, had claimed practically all the "global South." This opened the door for foreign companies (often based in the colonial powers) to engage in foreign direct investment (FDI), which typically allowed them to exert a significant degree of influence and control over the companies, and the countries, in which the investment was made.

FDI has grown substantially in the last 25 years in both volume and geographical reach. FDI is measured by the foreign ownership of productive assets, such as factories, mines, agricultural land, and forested land; its increase is often considered an indication of growing economic globalization. Most FDI takes place in emerging countries in the industries of raw materials and minerals exploitation, agricultural products, meat, and lumber. Most FDI has been concentrated in and has had an impact on lands occupied or claimed by indigenous groups. FDI has also provided a major platform through which MNCs operate in more than one country through subsidiaries that engage in the exploitation of raw materials. Subsidiaries offer easy access to and allow MNCs to dominate markets, benefit from cheaper labor, and enjoy attendant reduction in costs, as well as take advantage of benefits provided by permissive legislation in favor of their interests in various areas across countries.

---

15 Kevin Hindle, Robert B. Anderson, Robert J. Giberson, & Bob Kayseas, *Relating Practice to Theory in Indigenous Entrepreneurship: A Pilot Investigation of the Kitsaki Partnership Portfolio,* 29(1–2) Am. Indian Q. 1–23 (Winter–Spring 2005).

16 Ekaterine Egutia, *Marketing and Protecting Geographical Indication of Georgia Abroad* (Natl. Intell. Prop. Ctr. 2013), www.sakpatenti.org.ge.

17 Http://ec.europa.eu/agriculture/quality/index_en.htm. *See* also *EU and US: Opposing Views of Geographic Indications of Origin* (Mar. 5, 2010) http://www.fr.com/TrademarkThoughts-Fall2008/; and *Geographical Indications: Systems, Registration, Use, and Protection in China and Europe,* http://www.ipr2.org/gi. For the complications and possible contradictions of promoting free trade while enforcing all these origin and geographical limitations, *see* Danielle B. Shalov, *Will the European Union Prove to Be Lactose Intolerant?: The European Union's Attempt to Strike a Delicate Balance between Protecting Appellation of Origin for Cheese and the Promotion of Free Movement of Goods between Member States,* 11 Cardozo J. Intl. & Comp. L. 1099 (Spring 2004).

MNCs carry weight and influence because of the globalization process that gives them access to national economies—many MNCs have more capital and thus, negotiating power, than most countries, particularly smaller developing countries.

MNC Involvement in Elections and the Exertion of Undue Influence on National Laws

A major point of entry for an MNC into the policy-making and legislative process of a country is the elections cycle. Modern elections are extremely expensive. Although not all elections cost as much as the 2012 U.S. presidential campaign,[18] elections everywhere have become sophisticated and complicated affairs, requiring highly skilled advisers, planners, and executing staffers and the use of expensive media. Political parties and politicians welcome large individual and corporate donations and rely on money provided by corporate leaders. And corporations are happy to oblige.[19] A politician who wins an election may be indebted to those who "invested" in the campaign.[20] Thus, political contributions are often made on the basis of expected returns from the winning campaign. Some individual and corporate donors donate to multiple candidates in an election to ensure that, regardless of the result, their access and influence to high-level politicians and decision makers will be guaranteed. In many countries, the upper levels of government are controlled or strongly influenced by those who contributed to electoral campaigns. Thus, corporations may gain significant influence in local or national policy-making in any country.

This is especially true of foreign corporations and interests in developing countries where financial tycoons are still a rare phenomenon. A foreign corporation's access to hard currency gives it a sizeable opening to buy influence. This situation has been made even easier with the restructuring of the financial sector and the modernization and liberalization of financial operations and markets demanded by international financial institutions (IFIs) as a condition for financing development. The elimination of restrictions on currency speculation or conversion; the guarantee of repatriation of profits; and the right of foreign investors to attain, purchase, or keep a majority equity stake

18 According to an estimate by the nonpartisan Center for Responsive Politics, the reelection of President Barack Obama in the United States in 2012 reportedly cost around $6 billion, $700 million more than the previous "most expensive election" in history—2008. Not all elections will cost that much; *see* http://www.thewire.com/politics/2012/11/most-expensive-election-history-numbers/58745/.

19 In the United States, there has been controversy over recent Supreme Court decisions that struck down limits on independent campaign spending by corporations and unions. *See Citizens United v. Federal Election Commission*, 558 U.S. ___ (2010). Consequent to this decision, the court eliminated a decades-old cap on the total amount any individual can contribute to federal candidates. *See McCutchteon et al. v. Federal Election Commission*, 572 U.S. ____ (2014).

20 It has been said, for example, that the Obama administration's strong support for gays in the military and for gay marriage has been in acknowledgment of the substantial fundraising for his election and reelection campaigns conducted by the LGBT community, especially in California.

in domestic companies have enhanced the role that MNCs can play in national politics. MNCs have become major and important players in economic policy-making decisions in certain countries as those countries seek greater access to power. MNCs can thus get at and exploit natural resources; invest and move large amounts of money in and out of a country; and set up local companies that have access to a large amount of capital and therefore can drive other local companies out of business so as to monopolize access to resources and dictate policies, salaries, prices, and quantities on the basis of the MNC's interests. Jurisdictions often compete to attract investments and foreign companies that might bring jobs, revenues, and development.

Laws evolve to foster a favorable climate for businesses involved in trade, mining, commercial farming, manufacturing, and assembling so that MNCs are enticed to establish themselves in "business-friendly countries." In such an environment, labor laws, environmental laws, and laws aimed at protecting indigenous populations and their lands are not a priority, and assurances are given to indigenous people and environmentalists with a wink and a nod to the investors that such assurances will not be enforced.[21]

The Revolving Door Effect

Another dynamic that facilitates the corrupting and damaging influence of the MNCs on the government is the so-called revolving door that allows key and influential people to circulate and be recycled among government, business, IFIs, and MNCs.[22] These people are like a Trojan horse that infiltrates the halls of government and influences policy making in favor of MNCs' interests and plans. They have a strong voice and are able to silence dissenting opinions, allowing MNCs to facilitate and expedite policies, financial decisions, and projects that benefit themselves and to defeat attempts for transparency, consumer protection, regulation, and accountability. The goal, especially in smaller and weaker countries, is to gain control of the government and thereby of valuable and rare resources to establish the MNCs' control of the developing economy.

One effect of the revolving door is that a certain vision of reality is propagated by those who go through it—a vision that includes a certain conception of the economy, what is good for a country, what will revive the economy, and what will generate prosperity, power, and influence. A social construction that ensures that a certain definition of what is good and right economically for a country, according to the interests of a particular business sector, is accepted and becomes part of the general population's understanding, lexicon, and assessment of reality. There is no desire or consciousness of giving a voice to those most impacted by these decisions or to honor the tenet of a

---

21 David Sogge, *"TWO: Who Is Aiding Whom?,"* in *Give and Take: What's the Matter with Foreign Aid?* 24–39 (David Sogge ed., Zed 2002).

22 *See, e.g., Corruption Confusion: Congressional Staff and the Revolving Door Problem* https://politicalscience.stanford.edu/sites/default/files/workshop-materials/Corruption_Confusion10.pdf.

social contract. "Creating jobs" often seems to be a secular dogma that secures a green light for a project regardless of the havoc and damage it may visit on a country, society, or particular group, including indigenous peoples.

The power of big corporations and the overt or covert support they receive from various levels of governments and from IFIs are visible in many parts of the world where the territories of indigenous groups are used for mining, hydroelectric plants, highways, vast plantations, fracking, tourism, and sports without their consent, input, and compensation; without opportunities for training and employment, viable relocation, housing, and education; and in the absence of accountability measures when things go wrong.

The Role and Function of IFIs

In the last 30 years, an increasing number of developing countries have been supervised by IFIs and MNCs that work in close cooperation and coordination with each other and with developed countries.[23] The International Monetary Fund (IMF) and the World Bank are the best known, and their names often elicit strong reactions in favor of or against such multilateral institutions. This situation of transnational financial organizations controlling developing countries reflects the increasingly strong and complex ties between states, IFIs, and MNCs.[24] These linkages of power have an impact on decisions pertaining to extractive industry investments that affect local and indigenous communities. Such linkages have existed in different forms and in varying degrees of cooperation for a long time. In the modern sense, however, they have become deeper, firmer, and more systematic and are an integral part of institutional operations.[25]

The United Nations and influential leaders first started two decades ago to propose and promote the advantages of public-private partnerships that would make development plans and projects feasible. In 2006, the UN General Assembly adopted the resolution "Toward Global Partnerships," which calls for stronger partnerships with the private sector.[26] The idea was to advance the public good, especially in poor countries, by organizing shared business ventures that would profit everyone.[27] That same year, the report of the Secretary-General's High-Level Panel on UN System-Wide Coherence stressed

---

23 *See*, for example, John Pilger, *The New Rulers of the World* (Verso 2002).

24 Eric Neumayer, *The Determinants of Aid Allocation by Regional Multilateral Development Banks and United Nations Agencies*, 47(1) Intl. Stud. Q. 101–22 (2003).

25 *See*, for example, David Craig with Richard Brooks, *Plundering the Private Sector: How New Labour Are Letting Consultants Run off with £70 Billion of Our Money* (Constable 2006); ALTER EU, *Bursting the Brussels Bubble: The Battle to Expose Corporate Lobbying at the Heart of the EU* (Corp. Europe Observatory 2010).

26 U.N.G.A. Res. A/RES/60/215.

27 Simon Zadek, *The Logic of Collaborative Governance: Corporate Responsibility, Accountability, and the Social Contract* (Corp. Soc. Resp. Initiative Working Paper No. 17, John F. Kennedy Sch. Govt., Harv. U. 2006).

public-private partnerships as a dynamic way to realize sustainable development.[28] High on the list of objectives pursued by these public and private partnerships are the obliteration of poverty, the introduction and support of economic development in sustainable forms, and environmental protection. However, there has been considerable concern about how ties between governments, IFIs, and MNCs grow into patterns of action that undercut the very objectives that all purportedly want to reach,[29] depriving the populations that they ostensibly want to serve of their input (voice) and of just benefits in violation of the social contract with little or no consequences for those in power (accountability).[30]

The impact that this web of connections and powerful interests has on indigenous peoples and their interests is a particularly sensitive area. As some experts have pointed out,[31] regardless of their claims of being neutral, IFIs depend on, and are under the influence, of their most prominent member and donor countries, which usually are developed countries.[32] As a consequence, the financial aid distributed by international financial organizations and the conditions that accompany it strongly reflect the political and economic agenda of the member-states that provide the bulk of the funding.[33] Different than the United Nations and some other international organizations where each member, regardless of size or population, has one vote to cast, IFIs make decisions using a weighted system of voting. How many votes a member country has depends on a formula that takes into account a number of variables, the most important one being how much money the country contributes to the resources of the IFI. For this reason, the largest share of voting power at the World Bank is held by the United States (15.85 percent),[34] Japan (6.84 percent), China (4.42 percent),[35] Germany (4.00 percent), and the United Kingdom

---

28 *Delivering as One,* Report of the U.N. Secretary-General's High-Level Panel 2006, para. 74, http://www.un.org/en/ga/deliveringasone/.

29 *See,* for example, Christopher J. Fariss, *The Strategic Substitution of United States Foreign Aid,* 6 For. Policy Analysis 107–31 (2010). The results of this study demonstrate over a robust set of models that as human rights on the ground worsen, the probability for a state to be selected into the food aid recipient pool increases and, once selected, so too does the allotment of food aid.

30 Raymond F. Hopkins, *Political Economy of Foreign Aid,* in *Foreign Aid and Development: Lessons Learnt and Directions for the Future,* 423–49 (Finn Tarp, ed., Routledge 2000).

31 Korinna Horta, *The State, International Institutions, and Indigenous Peoples in Chad and Cameroon,* in *The Politics of Resource Extraction: Indigenous People, Multinational Corporations, and the State* 204 (Edmund Terence Gomez & Suzana Sawyer eds., Palgrave Macmillan 2012).

32 Christopher Kilby & Axel Dreher, *The Impact of Aid on Growth Revisited: Do Donor Motives Matter?,* 107(3) Econ. Letters 338–40 (2009).

33 Wil Hout, *The Politics of Aid Selectivity: Good Governance Criteria in World Bank, U.S. and Dutch Development Assistance* (Routledge 2007); Axel Dreher & Nathan Jensen, *Independent Actor or Agent? An Empirical Analysis of the Impact of U.S. Interests on IMF Conditions* (Leitner Working Paper, 2004).

34 Robert H. Wade, *U.S. Hegemony and the World Bank: The Fight over People and Ideas,* 9(2) Rev. Intl. Political Economy 215–43 (2002).

35 Ngaire Woods, *Whose Aid? Whose Influence? China, Emerging Donors, and the Silent Revolution*

(3.75 percent).[36] In 2010, the voting power allocation formula was modified to increase the voice of developing countries such as China. However, the United States' percentage of voting power was not reduced. The member-states providing the largest amount of funds sit on the executive boards of the World Bank and the IMF. Other member-states are grouped into constituencies and are collectively represented by region. Thus, these latter member-states have reduced decision-making power, that is, relatively little voice.[37] According to Dreher and Sturm,[38] the power of the United States in IFIs is revealed by the fact that developing countries that are close allies of the United States and vote with it most of the time in the United Nations and other international forums receive IMF loans more easily and with more favorable terms than those who are not close U.S. allies.[39]

This web of mutual interests between IFIs and developed and developing countries results in a potent and well-entrenched, complex, and institutionalized network of control and submission founded on financial considerations.[40] This is why IFIs are often perceived as oblique conduits for the more powerful

---

in Development Assistance, 84(6) Intl. Affairs 1205–21 (2008); and Arjan de Haan, *Will China Change International Development as We Know It?* (ISS Working Paper No. 475, (Den Haag Inst. Soc. Stud. 2009).

36 Robert H. Wade & Jakob Vestergaard, *The Future of the World Bank: Why More "Voice" Reform Is Needed* (paper presented at the *Conference on the Future of the World Bank and IMF*, Williams College, Sept. 27–28, 2012), http://cde.williams.edu/wp-content/uploads/2012/10/The-Future-of-the-World-Bank_RWade.pdf.

37 Ngaire Woods, *Order, Justice, the IMF, and the World Bank*, in *Order and Justice in International Relations* 83 (Rosemary Foot, John Lewis Gaddis, & Andrew Hurrell eds., Oxford U. Press 2003).

38 Axel Dreher & Jan-Egbert Sturm, *Do IMF and World Bank Influence Voting in the UN General Assembly?* (Swiss Fed. Inst. Tech. & KOF Swiss Econ. Inst. 2005).

39 T. Y. Wang, *U.S. Foreign Aid and UN Voting: An Analysis of Important Issues*, 43(1) Intl. Stud. Q. 199–210 (1999); Christopher Kilby, *The Political Economy of Conditionality: An Empirical Analysis of World Bank Loan Disbursements*, 89 J. Dev. Econ. 51–61 (2009); Ilyana Kuziemko & Eric Werker, *How Much Is a Seat on the Security Council Worth? Foreign Aid and Bribery at the United Nations*, 114(5) J. Political Economy 905–30 (2006); Charles W. Kegley & Steven W. Hook, *U.S. Foreign Aid and UN Voting: Did Reagan's Linkage Strategy Buy Deference or Defiance?*, 35(3) Intl. Stud. Q. 295–312 (1991); Axel Dreher, Peter Nunnenkamp, & Rainer Thiele, *Does U.S. Aid Buy UN General Assembly Votes? A Disaggregated Analysis*, 136 Pub. Choice 139–64 (2008); Paul Nelson, *Whose Civil Society? Whose Governance? Decision-Making and Practice in the New Agenda at the Inter-American Development Bank and the World Bank*, 6(4) Global Governance 405–31, at 421 (October–December 2000). *See* also Robert K. Fleck & Christopher Kilby, *How Do Political Changes Influence U.S. Bilateral Aid Allocations? Evidence from Panel Data*, 10(2) Rev. Dev. Economics 210–23 (2006). This is not limited to the World Bank and IMF. For the influence of the United States and Japan on the Asian Development Bank's decisions, *see* Christopher Kilby, *Donor Influence in Multilateral Development Banks: The Case of the Asian Development Bank*, 1(2) Rev. Intl. Organizations 173–95 (2006).

40 Lewis G. Irwin, *Dancing the Foreign Aid Appropriations Dance: Recurring Themes in the Modern Congresses*, 20(2) Pub. Budgeting & Fin. 30–48 (2000); Robert Cassen, Richard Jolly, John Mathieson, & John Sewell, *Overview*, in *Rich Country Interests and Third World Development*, 1–40 (Robert Cassen, Richard Jolly, John Sewell, & Robert Wood eds., Croom Helm 1982). *See* also Steven W. Hook, *Foreign Aid in Comparative Perspective: Regime Dynamics and Donor Interest*, in *Foreign Aid and Foreign Policy: Lessons for the Next Half Century*, 86–105 (Louis A. Picard, Robert Groelsema, & Terry F. Buss eds., M. E. Sharpe 2008).

developed member-states to protect and advance their economic clout, objectives, and interests in the developing world.[41] By means of technical assistance loans, the IMF and the World Bank and related banks and organizations have played key roles in setting up energy sections in the national economic systems of several countries and in substantially amplifying extraction activities of minerals and hydrocarbons.[42] The absence of accountability and transparency in regard to IFIs has allowed malfeasance and corruption to take root.[43] Development projects and the institutions themselves are not directly answerable to any supervisory outside organ,[44] which emboldens certain states to impose their will and apply pressure on IFIs to make decisions contrary to their own policies and benchmarks.[45]

---

41 Robert K. Fleck & Christopher Kilby, *World Bank Independence: A Model and Statistical Analysis of U.S. Influence,* 10(2) Rev. Dev. Economics 224–40 (2006). According to this study, the empirical analysis, motivated by a model of agency-donor interaction, yields results largely consistent with significant U.S. influence over World Bank lending. *See* also D. P. Clarke, *Trade versus Aid: Distributions of Third World Developmental Assistance,* 39(4) Economic Development and Cultural Change 829–37 (1991).

42 *The World Bank in Extractive Industries: 2012 Annual Review,* http://www-wds.worldbank.org/external/default/WDSContentServer/WDSP/IB/2013/05/22/000445729_20130522190042/Rendered/PDF/778660AR0WBG0E00Box377313B00PUBLIC0.pdf. *See* also http://www.worldbank.org/en/topic/extractiveindustries/research and the six volumes http://web.worldbank.org/WBSITE/EXTERNAL/TOPICS/EXTOGMC/0,,contentMDK:20306686~menuPK:336936~pagePK:148956~piPK:216618~theSitePK:336930,00.html. *See* also World Bank, Oil, Gas, and Mining Policy Division, *Companion Matrix on EITI Mainstreaming Linkages, World Bank Oil and Gas Mining Unit (SEGOM) and EITI Multi-Donor Trust Fund* (World Bank; MDTF), http://siteresources.worldbank.org/EXTOGMC/Resources/COCPObrochureFINAL.pdf?resourceurlname=COCPObrochureFINAL.pdf. Moreover, *see* World Bank Information Center and Global Witness, *Assessment of International Monetary Fund and World Bank Group Extractive Industries Transparency Implementation* (2008), http://www.bicusa.org/en/Document.11479.pdf; *Mining Community Development Agreements: Source Book* (vol. 2 of 4): http://documents.worldbank.org/curated/en/2012/03/16523320/mining-community-development-agreements-source-book.

43 William Easterly, *Can Foreign Aid Buy Growth?* 17(3) J. Econ. Perspectives 23–48 (2003); William Easterly, Ross Levine, & David Roodman, *New Data, New Doubt: Revisiting Aid, Policies and Growth* (Ctr. Global Dev. Working Paper No. 26, Ctr. Global Dev. 2003).

44 Nafeez Ahmed, *World Bank and UN Carbon Offset Scheme "Complicit" in Genocidal Land Grabs—NGOs,* Guardian (July 3, 2014), http://www.theguardian.com/environment/earth-insight/2014/jul/03/world-bank-un-redd-genocide-land-carbon-grab-sengwer-kenya.

45 *Rich Country Interests and Third World Development,* 215–47 (Robert Cassen, Richard Jolly, John Sewell, & Robert Wood eds., Croom Helm 1982); Derek Headey, *Foreign Aid and Foreign Policy: How Donors Undermine the Effectiveness of Overseas Development Assistance* (CEPA Working Paper Series No. 05/2005 Sch. Economics, U. Queensland 2005).

A current example is a report by the NGO The Forest People: *How the World Bank Is Implicated in Today's Embobut Evictions* (Cherangany Hills Projects, Kenya), http://www.forestpeoples.org/sites/fpp/files/news/2013/12/How%20the%20World%20Bank%20is%20implicated%20in%20today's%20Embobut%20Evictions.pdf.

A letter to the World Bank on March 12, 2014, by No REDD in Africa network (Nran)—a group of African civil society organizations—signed by more than 60 international NGOs—accused the Bank of "both admitting its complicity in the forced relocation of the Sengwer People as well as offering to collude with the Kenyan government to cover-up cultural genocide." As "carbon credit financier and broker," the World Bank is "aiding and abetting the forced relocation of an entire Indigenous People through its Natural Resource Management Plan (NRMP) which includes REDD (Reducing Emissions from Deforestation and Forest

IFIs are not monolithic. There may be strongly divergent opinions within them about promoting, approving, or carrying out extractive industry projects. For example, the World Bank and the Asian Development Bank influenced the Philippine government to adopt the Indigenous People's Rights Act of 1997.[46] However, both organizations had earlier advocated the introduction and the approval by the Philippines of the Mining Act of 1995, legislation that counters the objectives of the Indigenous People's Rights Act.[47] Another example is the Inter-American Development Bank, which supported the Camisea River project in Peru while it wavered over funding the project and supported the establishment of public agencies to supervise the project.[48] When a major Cameroon-Chad oil pipeline project was proposed and approved, there were serious disagreements over the project within the World Bank about its implementation,[49] though disagreeing voices were eventually silenced.[50]

Such incongruities can be explained by the fact that these IFIs do not consider their policies affecting indigenous groups as being incompatible with their position on the extraction of oil or mineral riches. Such development may eventually assist in reducing poverty by bringing in foreign capital and channeling it into the national and local economy. If one accepts the trickle-down theory of wealth sharing,[51] then this is a sensible approach. However,

---

Degradation), in the Cherangany Hills," said the letter. According to Ahmed, *supra* note 44, "the World Bank Carbon Fund's approach to defining carbon rights has been widely criticised by civil society groups for creating conflict between new property rights to carbon, and existing statutory and customarily held rights of local communities. The lack of clear safeguards and measures opens up an unprecedented opportunity for corporate and government land grabbing." Edmund Terence Gomez & Suzana Sawyer, *State, Capital, Multinational Institutions, and Indigenous Peoples*, in *The Politics of Resource Extraction: Indigenous People, Multinational Corporations, and the State* 1–9 (Edmund Terence Gomez & Suzana Sawyer, eds., Palgrave Macmillan 2012).

46 A recent evaluation of the implementation of the Indigenous People's Rights Act (IPRA) states, "The indigenous people of The Philippines continue to figure in social discrimination, economic marginalization, and political disempowerment, albeit the presence of IPRA and the existence of the National Commission for the Indigenous People. Subject to socio-economic and political exclusion, they have remained the most disadvantaged people, representing the poorest of the poor and the most vulnerable sector." *The Struggle Continues: Uphold the Rights of Indigenous People* 2 (IAG policy brief, Apr. 2011).

47 Raymundo D. Rovillos & Victoria Tauli-Corpuz, *Development, Power, and Identity Politics in the Philippines*, in *The Politics of Resource Extraction: Indigenous People, Multinational Corporations, and the State* 129 (Edmund Terence Gomez & Suzana Sawyer eds., Palgrave Macmillan 2012).

48 Patricia Urteaga-Crovetto, *The Broker State and the "Inevitability" of Progress: The Camisea Project and Indigenous Peoples in Peru*, in *The Politics of Resource Extraction: Indigenous People, Multinational Corporations, and the State* 103 (Edmund Terence Gomez & Suzana Sawyer eds., Palgrave Macmillan 2012).

49 Genoveva Hernandez Uriz, *To Lend or Not to Lend: Oil, Human Rights, and the World Bank's Internal Contradictions*, 14 Harv. Hum. Rights J. 197 (Spring 2001); Dustin D. Sharp, *Requiem for a Pipedream: Oil, the World Bank, and the Need for Human Rights Assessment*, 25 Emory Intl. L. Rev. 379 (2011).

50 Kathleen Grimes, *Environmental Justice Case Study: The Chad-Cameroon Oil and Pipeline Project* (2000), http://www.umich.edu/~snre492/Jones/pipe.htm.

51 The trickle-down theory has been used derisively to describe a popular version of conser-

this theory has been criticized by many economists and officials. Among others, Pope Francis has condemned growing inequality and unfettered economic markets.[52]

Accountability Issues

A number of studies and evaluations have shown that IFIs play a major role in assessing and establishing the conditions and the granting of resource extraction contracts. However, when it comes to accountability, they have neglected or even declined to restrain or correct and penalize governments or multinationals for contravening the conditions of agreements.[53] There are instances when IFIs have failed to discipline recipients of funds for sabotaging the public agencies that were funded by these IFIs to supervise the extraction of underground riches.[54] Regulatory agencies, through the revolving door phenomenon, maintain cozy relationships with the industries that they supposedly regulate and often are regulated by those they are meant to oversee.[55] Thus, the absence of supervision by international institutions causes—particularly, from the viewpoint of outsiders—perceptions of IFI support for the undisturbed progress and earnings by MNCs.[56] Foreign direct investments are by their nature harmful and pernicious even as they are crucial to supporting the global economy and current lifestyle.[57] Foreign direct investments also

---

vative economic philosophy that argues that allowing the wealthy to run their businesses unencumbered by regulation or taxation bears economic benefits that lead to more jobs and income for the rest of society. Various economists and officials have rejected the theory, believing that it is contradicted by economic evidence. Philippe Aghion & Patrick Bolton, *A Theory of Trickle-Down Growth and Development*, 64(2) Rev. Econ. Stud. 151–72 (1997).

52 Zachary A. Goldfarb & Michelle Boorstein, *Pope Francis Denounces "Trickle-Down" Economic Theories in Critique of Inequality*, Washington Post (Nov. 26, 2013). In a meeting with UN secretary-general Ban Ki-moon and the heads of major UN agencies on May 9, 2014, Pope Francis called for governments to redistribute wealth to the poor in a new spirit of generosity to help curb the "economy of exclusion" taking hold today—this is a clear call for giving "voice" and respecting an equitable "social contract" extended to the poor. He voiced a similar message to the World Economic Forum in January 2014. *See* http://www.nydailynews.com/news/world/pope-francis-urges-legitimate-redistribution-wealth-article-1.1785861#ixzz31VelYi4F.

53 For an in-depth analysis of the interaction of the various actors on this project, *see* Ben Naanenm, *The Nigerian State, Multinational Oil Corporations, and the Indigenous Communities of the Niger Delta*, in *The Politics of Resource Extraction: Indigenous People, Multinational Corporations, and the State* 153–79 (Edmund Terence Gomez & Suzana Sawyer eds., Palgrave Macmillan 2012).

54 Urteaga-Crovetto, *supra* note 48.

55 Seojou Kang, *Agree to Reform? The Political Economy of Conditionality Variation in International Monetary Fund Lending, 1983–1997*, 46 European J. Political Research 685–720 (2007).

56 Edmund Terence Gomez & Suzana Sawyer, *State, Capital, Multinational Institutions, and Indigenous Peoples*, in *The Politics of Resource Extraction: Indigenous People, Multinational Corporations, and the State* 35 (Edmund Terence Gomez & Suzana Sawyer eds., Palgrave Macmillan 2012).

57 *See* Saleem H. Ali, *Mining, the Environment, and Indigenous Development Conflicts* (U. Arizona Press 2003).

advance economic development in states and communities that accept and adopt development goals.[58]

Indigenous groups at times endorse and are behind certain development programs. Some MNCs engage in business practices and use methodologies that favor environmental sustainability. In such situations, having an MNC deliver a project is considerably less injurious to indigenous populations and the environment than the alternative.[59] In these cases, foreign direct investment may offer both drawbacks and opportunities to indigenous peoples. Developing countries can be too weak to effectively protect human and indigenous rights, even if sympathetic to them, or, when it comes to prioritizing development outcomes, they may inevitably favor economic gains over indigenous populations' rights and title to land.[60]

Rebalancing the Scale

Some progress is being made internationally to protect the rights of indigenous peoples by giving them voice and calling for the establishment of social contracts and greater accountability. Some examples are presented here.

The Inter-American Human Rights System

Some human rights conventions and jurisprudence have attempted to redress violations of the rights of the indigenous peoples. The American Declaration of the Rights and Duties of Man (1948) and the American Convention on Human Rights (1978) do not particularly refer to indigenous groups, although the bodies created to interpret and enforce these instruments, the Inter-American Commission on Human Rights and the Inter-American Court of Human Rights, have allocated and bestowed some rights on these groups. Many states that are members of the Organization of American States are party to international conventions such as the International Labour Organization that address indigenous rights in detail.[61]

---

58 *See* OECD, *Foreign Direct Investment for Development: Maximising Benefits, Minimising Costs* 5 (2002) http://www.oecd.org.proxyau.wrlc.org/dataoecd/47/51/1959815.pdf.

59 *See* Nicola Borregaard et al., *Foreigners in the Forests: Saviors or Invaders?*, in *Rethinking Foreign Investment for Sustainable Development: Lessons from Latin America* 147 (Kevin P. Gallagher & Daniel Chudnovsky eds., Anthem 2010).

60 *See* Vassilis P. Tzevelekos, *In Search of Alternative Solutions: Can the State of Origin Be Held Internationally Responsible for Investors' Human Rights Abuses That Are Not Attributable to It?* 35 Brookings J. Intl. L. 155, 207 (2010).

61 The International Labour Organization (ILO) is the first international institution that paid attention to indigenous issues, beginning in 1957 with the adoption of ILO Convention 107 for the protection of indigenous, tribal, and semitribal populations. Following the thinking at the time, ILO Convention 107 adopted an "integrationist" approach, with the goal of assimilating indigenous peoples into the dominant culture, most often Western, and into the national society, an agenda that was criticized and discarded, at least officially, afterward. In 1989, this convention was revised and amended, becoming ILO Convention 169 concerning indigenous and tribal peoples in independent countries. Presently, ILO Convention 169 is the only binding instrument that specifically covers the need to protect the rights of in-

Both the Inter-American Commission on Human Rights and the Inter-American Court of Human Rights have asserted and reinforced the rights of indigenous people confronted with encroachment on their territory by outsiders that intend to carry out extractive activities. However, the American Declaration of the Rights and Duties of Man and the American Convention on Human Rights do not offer effective and viable remedies to indigenous groups affected by outsiders because they mandate that claims can be lodged only against member-states, not against a private party such as an MNC. Moreover, as in the case of most international tribunals, there is no machinery that ensures the enforcement of the commission or the court's decision.

Additionally, not all countries in the Americas, notably the United States and Canada, have accepted the jurisdiction of the Inter-American Court of Human Rights. Canadian mining companies are the largest and most active in the world:[62] five of the ten largest gold mining companies in the world are Canadian. Seventy-five percent of mining companies in the world are headquartered in Canada and for a good reason: Canada offers the best protection from accountability and redress.[63] For example, while American mining companies can be prosecuted for environmental and social policies abroad under the U.S. Alien Tort Statute, Canada does not have any such legal mechanisms to hold companies accountable.[64]

This situation is similar with other international organisms, such as the United Nations, that have been instituted to protect human rights. Thus, multinationals do not have much to fear from the inter-American system or from the UN human rights system for similar reasons.[65]

UN Declaration on the Rights of Indigenous Peoples

On September 13, 2007, the UN General Assembly adopted the UN Declaration on the Rights of Indigenous Peoples (UNDRIP), which affirms that several individual and collective rights of indigenous people exist and that states have the duty to recognize them. These include the right to self-determination; of nonremoval from lands or territories without "free, prior, and informed consent"; restitution and compensation for land and resources that indigenous

---

digenous peoples. It is noteworthy that only 22 out of the 192 UN member states have ratified this document. With the exception of Fiji and Nepal, they are all in Central and South America and Europe.

62 http://www.mining.ca/resources/mining-facts.

63 http://en.wikipedia.org/wiki/Largest_gold_companies. For criticism of the record of Canadian mining companies worldwide and for current struggles by indigenous peoples with this sector, *see* www.polarisinstitute.org or miningwatch.ca. *See* also http://globaljournalist.org /2013/10/when-canadian-mining-companies-take-over-the-world/.

64 Kelly Patterson, *Open Veins: Bloody Conflicts Are Erupting around the World over Canadian Mining Projects,* Ottawa Citizen, B1 (Oct. 1, 2005), http://www.lexisnexis.com.proxyau.wrlc.org /hottopics/lnacademic/?verb=sr&csi=143838.

65 Cristina Baez et al., *Multinational Enterprises and Human Rights,* 8 U. Miami Intl. & Comp. L. Rev. 183, 186 (2000).

peoples traditionally owned, or occupied, or used that were confiscated; security in the enjoyment of their own means of subsistence and development and free engagement in traditional economic activities; conservation of medicinal plants, animals, and minerals and of their environment and of the productivity of their lands or territories and resources; maintenance and protection of archaeological sites; and the ability to determine their own priorities for the development or use of their lands and resources. States have the duty to establish effective legal mechanisms to enforce indigenous rights and to consult and cooperate in good faith with indigenous peoples in order to obtain their free and informed consent prior to approving "any project affecting their lands and other resources, especially if connected with the development, utilization or exploitation of mineral, water or other resources."

It must be stressed that UNDRIP is a declaration, not a treaty, and therefore it is not legally binding. The 2007 declaration represents the culmination of a negotiation process that began in 1971.[66] Four countries voted against UNDRIP: Australia, Canada, New Zealand, and the United States.[67] They especially objected to the right to self-determination and the right to redress from displacement from ancestral lands.[68] These four countries did not accept the provision that states must consult and cooperate in good faith with indigenous peoples in order to obtain their free and informed consent before approving extractive projects that will affect them.[69] Articles 2, 19, and 31 remind states to act with restraint and good faith when dealing with indigenous peoples, especially taking into account the major losses that these people incurred at the hands of the state in past years and the considerable risks that the extractive industry presents to them.[70]

Will UNDRIP make an important difference in the lives of indigenous peoples? Not likely. As it applies to any law or treaty, it is one thing to adopt or endorse a declaration; it is another to implement it.[71] As with most human

---

66 Robert T. Coulter, *The UN Declaration on the Rights of Indigenous Peoples: A Historic Change in International Law*, 45 Idaho L. Rev. 539, 544–45 (2009).

67 All four countries later switched their positions to "supporting" the declaration as a nonlegally binding document.

68 Aliza Gail Organick, *Listening to Indigenous Voices: What the UN Declaration on the Rights of Indigenous Peoples Means for U.S. Tribes*, 16 UC Davis J. Intl. L. & Policy 171, 178 (2009).

69 George K Foster, *Foreign Investment and Indigenous Peoples: Options for Promoting Equilibrium between Economic Development and Indigenous Rights*, 33(4) Mich. J. Intl. L. 27 (July 2012).

70 A month after President Obama announced in December 2010 that the United States would support UNDRIP, the U.S. State Department clarified that position by stating that "the United States understands [the importance of a] call for a process of meaningful consultation with tribal leaders, but not necessarily the agreement of those leaders, before the actions addressed in those consultations are taken." *See* more at http://www.culturalsurvival.org/news/united-states/victory-us-endorses-un-declaration-rights-indigenous-peoples#sthash.06NvUV9w.dpuf.

71 Shortly after President Obama declared that the United States would lend its support to UNDRIP, the commitment of the United States to UNDRIP and to genuine consultation and taking indigenous people's interests into account was tested by the proposed TransCanada Keystone XL Pipeline. If constructed, the Keystone XL pipeline would transport hundreds of thousands of barrels of crude oil from Alberta to Nebraska, crossing six states over thousands

rights instruments, there is a chasm between the words on paper and their real-life application.[72] History will tell if countries that adopted UNDRIP give priority to adopting laws and allocate funds needed to make UNDRIP's ideals a reality.[73] Some countries will take UNDRIP more seriously than others.[74] Even if a country adopts corresponding laws, those laws must be enforced.

Issues Involving Rules, Standards, and Model Contracts

Recently, a number of standards, model contracts, and other documents have been produced to facilitate agreements between multinationals and their counterparts, including indigenous ones. These documents represent important advances in giving indigenous peoples a voice, offer protection in the nature of a social contract, and contain accountability measures.

The Guidelines for Multinational Enterprises of the Organisation for Economic Co-operation and Development (OECD) are the most comprehensive set of government-backed recommendations on responsible business conduct.[75] The governments adhering to these guidelines aim to encourage and maximize the positive impact that multinational enterprises can make on sustainable development and ongoing social progress. They are nonbinding, and therefore their efficacy is limited. The OECD has set up a network of national contact points to investigate accusations of noncompliance by MNCs. However,

---

of square miles of indigenous lands. Because the proposed pipeline must cross an international border, the project must obtain a presidential permit from the State Department before it can be built. In September 2011, indigenous leaders delivered to the president "The Mother Earth Accord," a rejection of the pipeline grounded on "the principles of traditional indigenous knowledge, spiritual values, and respectful use of the land." It is a clear invocation of the right to free, prior, and informed consent (FPIC) as provided by UNDRIP and the president's first major chance to demonstrate his administration's acceptance of the declaration by honoring the tribes' decision. The position of indigenous leaders is that, without the right to decide what happens on their lands, indigenous people are left with no control of their assets, and therefore no say in their future. TransCanada, responsible for the construction and operation of the pipeline, reportedly stated that it has "no legal obligation to work with the tribes," adding, "We do it because we have a policy. We believe it's a good, neighborly thing to do." Tribal leaders complain that the U.S. State Department is not living up to UNDRIP's consultation requirement, raising questions about the Obama administration's commitment to indigenous rights. One of the obstacles is the indigenous leaders' insistence that negotiations be conducted on nation-to-nation basis. Pressure to allow the pipeline is enormous. The pushback is also strong. No decision had been announced as of August 2014. For the source of quotations included in this note, *see Decision Time for Keystone XL: Was Obama's UNDRIP Endorsement an Empty Promise?* First Peoples Worldwide Newsletter (June 4, 2013), http://firstpeoples.org/wp/decision-time-for-keystone-xl-was-obamas-undrip-endorsement-an-empty-promise/.

72 Julian Burger, *The UN Declaration on the Rights of Indigenous Peoples: From Advocacy to Implementation*, in *Reflections on the UN Declaration on the Rights of Indigenous Peoples* (Stephen Allen & Alexandra Xanthaki eds., Hart Publg. 2011).

73 Rodolfo Stavenhagen, *Making the Declaration on the Rights of Indigenous Peoples Work: The Challenge Ahead*, in *Reflections on the UN Declaration on the Rights of Indigenous Peoples* 147, 158–59 (Stephen Allen & Alexandra Xanthaki eds., Hart Publg. 2011).

74 For example, Bolivia incorporated UNDRIP verbatim into domestic law on Nov. 7, 2007.

75 http://mneguidelines.oecd.org.

the national contact points can only make recommendations to MNCs;[76] they cannot promulgate binding orders.

The UN Guiding Principles on Business and Human Rights (UNGPs) is a global standard for preventing and addressing the risk of adverse impacts on human rights caused by business activity.[77] On June 16, 2011, the UN Human Rights Council unanimously endorsed the UNGPs—the first attempt to address corporate human rights responsibility endorsed by the United Nations. The three pillars that form the guiding principles offer a profile for how states and businesses should act:

- The state has a duty to protect human rights.
- There is a corporate responsibility to respect human rights.
- Victims of business-related abuses have access to remedies.

The UNGPs have been well received by states, civil society organizations, and the private sector.[78] A major objective is that MNCs "should avoid infringing on the human rights of others and should address adverse human rights impacts with which they are involved."[79] However, although this is a positive attempt to regulate MNCs, it is a nonbinding solution and therefore limited in its impact.[80]

The World Bank Group has developed and ratified a number of standards to manage and shepherd its lending decisions.[81] The World Bank Group offers financial and technical assistance to the governments of developing countries; the International Finance Corporation finances projects by the private sector in the developing world; the Multilateral Investment Guarantee Agency furnishes political risk insurance to foreign investors. Sometimes projects that are funded or insured entail the extraction of natural resources on lands owned or occupied by indigenous peoples. The World Bank Group is aware that such projects present a major risk to indigenous people,[82] and it created an Inspection Panel and a Compliance Advisor Ombudsman to oversee compliance.

---

76 *See* Anna Triponel, *Business & Human Rights Law: Diverging Trends in the United States and France*, 23 Am. U. Intl. L. Rev. 855, 911 (2008). *See* also Jernej Letnar Cernic, *Human Rights Law and Business: Corporate Responsibility for Fundamental Human Rights* (Europa L. Publg. 2010).

77 *Guiding Principles on Business and Human Rights: Implementing the United Nations "Protect, Respect, and Remedy" Framework*, Hum. Rights Council, U.N. Doc. A/HRC/17/31 (Mar. 21, 2011).

78 George K. Foster, *Foreign Investment and Indigenous Peoples: Options for Promoting Equilibrium between Economic Development and Indigenous Rights* 33(4) Mich. J. Intl. L. 627 (July 2012).

79 Cernic, *supra* note 76, at 13.

80 http://www.un.org/esa/socdev/unpfii/documents/DRIPS_en.pdf. For a critical examination of the declaration, *see* Robin Perry, *Balancing Rights or Building Rights? Reconciling the Right to Use Customary Systems of Law with Competing Human Rights in Pursuit of Indigenous Sovereignty*, 24 Harv. Hum. Rights J. 71 (Summer 2011).

81 Hout, *supra* note 33.

82 Evaristus Oshionebo, *World Bank and Sustainable Development of Natural Resources in Developing Countries*, 27 J. Energy & Nat. Res. L. 193, 219–20 (2009).

To prevent, minimize, or ameliorate such risk, the World Bank Group also created a set of social and environmental standards to provide guidance to staff dealing with such projects. These standards were not developed to provide worldwide rules for businesses on social and environmental issues, but evolved as policy documents created to provide guidance to World Bank staff. Initially not publicly available, they have emerged as an influential source of de facto global rules and are now being adopted by corporations, private and public financial institutions, governments, and export credit agencies.[83] Some of these standards were formulated to protect indigenous peoples.

Internationally, there is a legislative void in the area of developing standards of acceptable environmental and social behavior. For those who feel pressure to adopt some form of international standards, the World Bank Group standards may suffice. Corporate and governmental officers can protect themselves by accepting and professing the social and environmental standards of the World Bank, lending them international armor and cachet of social and environmental respectability.[84]

Even if the standards contain shortcomings or they are insufficiently implemented, they are the minimum floor on which any project that is socially and environmentally sound and acceptable should stand. This adoption of the World Bank standards by outside corporate and governmental entities is aptly explained in the work of Neil Gunningham, Robert Kagan, and Dorothy Thornton, who expounded on the concept of a "social license to operate" in the extractive industries world.[85] Attempting to explain the variation of compliance with environmental standards by 14 pulp manufacturing plants in the United States, Canada, Australia, and New Zealand, these researchers found that discrepancies are not necessarily due to differences in regulation in each country. Rather, what accounts for variations is the complex interaction between tightening regulations and a social license to operate (especially arising from pressure from the community and environmental activists), economic constraints, and differences in corporate environmental management style.

The social license to operate is much wider than a legal license. There is a palpable need as well as a strong expectation to observe a social license, which is connected to social media. Bearing in mind that reputation is one of the most valuable assets of an individual or corporation, activists in these times of "regulation by information" have a variety of tools available. Although the technology behind these tools is new, the dynamic is old. To protect themselves from potential reputational damage and crises, MNCs and government entities embrace the World Bank's standards because, as Anne-Marie Slaughter

---

83 Natasha Affolder, *Cachet Not Cash: Another Sort of World Bank Group Borrowing,* 14 Mich. St. J. Intl. L. 141 (2006).

84 *See id.,* at 147.

85 Neil Gunningham, Robert Kagan, & Dorothy Thornton, *Shades of Green: Business, Regulation, and Environment* (Stanford U. Press 2003).

explains, the World Bank "provides guidance, saves transaction costs, and offers the luxury of security. The value of such guidance rises concomitantly with both uncertainty and complexity, circumstances likely to arise more and more frequently in a world of complex rules and technical regulations."[86]

To add complexity to the argument, when it comes to the impact of the World Bank Group standards, some observers believe that their impact has been unsatisfactory and only partial.[87] Parties within the World Bank do not implement or enforce these standards consistently.[88] As one critic has said, "the [World Bank Group] has yet to achieve appreciable results in its drive towards sustainable development of natural resources. The [World Bank Group's] safeguard policies are frequently violated by project owners. Thus, today, many extractive projects supported by the [World Bank Group] continue to pose serious environmental and social risks to host communities."[89]

The International Bar Association's Model Mining Development Agreement offers a menu of model contracts that include environmental and social restrictions for agreements between governments and mining companies.[90] The model agreement is intended to be utilized not just by governments and extractive companies but also by other stakeholders such as nongovernmental organizations (NGOs), indigenous peoples groups, members of parliaments, and others involved in extractive businesses. The Model Mining Development Agreement has the same inherent shortcoming of other similar attempts: multinationals and governments are under no obligation to insert its terms into their contracts.

The above-mentioned guidelines, standards, rules, and model agreements represent important efforts, creativity, and advances to provide voice, social contract norms, and some accountability for indigenous peoples. However, they cannot be relied on to offer needed protection to indigenous peoples and to the environment against the challenges and perils posed by FDI projects, especially those that occur in the extractive industries.[91]

---

86 Anne-Marie Slaughter, *Sovereignty and Power in a Networked World Order*, 40 Stan. J. Intl. L. 283, 300 (2004).

87 George K. Foster, *Foreign Investment and Indigenous Peoples: Options for Promoting Equilibrium between Economic Development and Indigenous Rights*, 33(4) Mich. J. Intl. L. 627, 643 (Summer 2012); James H. Lebovic & Erik Voeten, *The Cost of Shame: International Organizations and Foreign Aid in the Punishing of Human Rights Violators*, 46(1) J. Peace Research. 79–97 (2009).

88 Dana Clark, *Boundaries in the Field of Human Rights: The World Bank and Human Rights: The Need for Greater Accountability*, 15 Harv. Hum. Rights J. 205 (Spring 2002).

89 *See id.*, at 203.

90 Maître François Serres, *The Model Mining Development Agreement*, http://www.aflsf.org/downloads/capicity_building/05.F.SERRESThe%20IBA's%20Model%20Mining%20Agreement.pdf.

91 Rhona K. M. Smith, *The International Impact of Creative Problem Solving: Resolving the Plight of Indigenous Peoples*, 34 Cal. W. L. Rev. 411, 413 (1998).

Conclusion

Increasingly, since the 1980s, IFIs and other development banks have supported, facilitated, and funded the liberalization of mining, oil, and lumber business areas. They have embraced public-private collaboration as a way to anchor such projects on solid financial, legal, and ethical bases and to raise the awareness of the challenges that accompany most extraction ventures.[92] Today, it is generally regarded that public-private partnerships among governments, MNCs, and IFIs are a positive tool for increasing society's welfare through the elimination of poverty, the advancement of sustainable models of economic development, and the protection of the environment.[93] However, not everyone agrees with this view, and the historical record is not as positive as many may wish to believe—particularly in the area of how indigenous peoples' rights have been eroded and disregarded.[94] Several international organizations, among them the United Nations and IFIs, have expressed their alarm over the negative consequences that minerals, oil, and timber extraction operations have had and continue to have on the subsistence and way of life for indigenous populations in various parts of the world.[95] These concerns are in alignment with that of a few MNCs involved in extraction industry activities that have begun espousing principles of corporate social responsibility.[96] These parties and organizations agree on the urgent need to empower indigenous people with a voice so that governments and the private sector can make choices that will have a fair and positive impact on their lifestyle and their future.[97]

---

92 Tomohisa Hattori, *The Moral Politics of Foreign Aid*, 29 Rev. Intl. Stud. 229–47 (2003). This article identifies the donations of states to multilateral grant-giving organizations as the ethical core of a larger institutionalization of foreign aid in the postwar era as a collective endeavor of the former colonizing states. What in a bilateral face-to-face relation signals and euphemizes the material hierarchies of the postwar world is transformed in this process into a virtuous practice, ethically justified as contributing to the peace and prosperity of the community of states.

93 Raymond F. Hopkins, *Political Economy of Foreign Aid*, in *Foreign Aid and Development: Lessons Learnt and Directions for the Future*, 423–49 (Finn Tarp ed., Routledge 2000); Henrik Hansen & Finn Tarp, *Aid Effectiveness Disputed*, 12(3) J. Intl. Dev. 375–98 (2000).

94 Curtis M. Jolly & M. A. Gadbois, *Foreign Aid as a Promotional Strategy*, 18(1) Rev. Black Political Econ. 59–74 (1989).

95 Alex Mourmouras & Peter Rangazas, *Foreign Aid with Voracious Politics*, IMF Staff Papers, vol. 56, 786–810 (2009).

96 A definition of corporate social responsibility is "Corporate initiative to assess and take responsibility for the company's effects on the environment and impact on social welfare. The term generally applies to company efforts that go beyond what may be required by regulators or environmental protection groups. Corporate social responsibility may also be referred to as "corporate citizenship" and can involve incurring short-term costs that do not provide an immediate financial benefit to the company, but instead promote positive social and environmental change." http://www.investopedia.com/terms/c/corp-social-responsibility.asp. For an analysis of this concept and its applications to management, *see* Adam Lindgreen & Valérie Swaen, *Special Issue: Corporate Social Responsibility*, 10(1) Intl. J. Mgt. Reviews (Mar. 2010).

97 One example of this is through inclusive consultative approaches.

Some international organizations and governments have developed and approved charters, guidelines, rules, and laws—social contracts of sorts—that protect the rights and the welfare of indigenous peoples. Ideally, these tools provide indigenous peoples the power to request changes, reformulate, endorse, or even reject projects put forward by governments, MNCs, or international organizations, or all three, depending on certain variables, including how indigenous peoples' ways of life may or will experience an impact. In reality, however, the challenges confronting indigenous peoples because of extractive industry projects that are approved and financed by governments, MNCs, and IFIs are complex and bewildering.[98]

The unequal balance of power evident in negotiations between MNCs, the state, and international financial organizations on one side and indigenous groups on the other can be extreme.[99] Despite the international declarations, amendments of state constitutions, and favorable national legislation that purport to support and protect the rights of indigenous peoples, most of these people, especially those affected by projects in the extractive industries, face more, not less, discrimination, exploitation, loss of territory and livelihood, poverty, and racism as a result of these projects. Herein lies a paradox.[100]

While the quantity of national and international legal mechanisms that admit and accept the rights of indigenous peoples is increasing, so is the marginalization of most indigenous peoples.[101] This is due not merely to a disconnect between the law on the books and its application in the real world or to the discrepancy between a de jure and de facto acceptance of indigenous rights. The cause runs deeper and farther. A powerful and interlocking network of worldwide economics, trade, consumer demand, international financing, multinationals' interests, free market greed, pressure exerted by international markets, and global competition for power, influence, and dominance create and nourish this phenomenon and paradox.[102]

There is a need to understand and analyze the structures and dynamics of power unleashed by neoliberal financial reforms and by an increase in extraction activities that require large amounts of capital. The effort to find space

---

98 Jim Kolbe, *Lessons and New Directions for Foreign Assistance*, 26(2) Wash. Q. 189–98 (2003).

99 For an analysis of the interaction of these variables to the detriment of indigenous communities, *see* Jon Altman, *Indigenous Rights, Mining Corporations, and the Australian State*, in *The Politics of Resource Extraction: Indigenous People, Multinational Corporations, and the State* 47–74 (Edmund Terence Gomez & Suzana Sawyer eds., Palgrave Macmillan 2012).

100 Suzana Sawyer & Edmund Terence Gomez, *Conclusion: Attending to the Paradox: Public Governance and Inclusive International Platforms*, in *The Politics of Resource Extraction: Indigenous People, Multinational Corporations, and the State* 253–59 (Edmund Terence Gomez and Suzana Sawyer eds., Palgrave Macmillan 2012).

101 Roger C. Riddell, *Does Foreign Aid Really Work?* (Oxford U. Press 2008).

102 Steven W. Hook, *Foreign Aid in Comparative Perspective: Regime Dynamics and Donor Interest*, in *Foreign Aid and Foreign Policy: Lessons for the Next Half Century* 86–105 (Louis A. Picard, Robert Groelsema, & Terry F. Buss eds., M. E. Sharpe 2008); Derek Headey, *Foreign Aid and Foreign Policy: How Donors Undermine the Effectiveness of Overseas Development Assistance* (CEPA Working Paper Series No. 05/2005, Sch. Economics, U. Queensland 2005).

in this complex equation for human rights—namely, for indigenous rights to land and indigenous peoples' right to their ways of life and identity; for a reasonable voice to express indigenous concerns with respect to proposed projects; and for an equitable compensation system—is complex and fraught with difficulties.[103] Various actors, including IFIs, international organizations, NGOs, state actors, and indigenous groups themselves, which are weak compared with the rest, should interact and compete to define the rules, guidelines, and apparatus of governance with respect to the projects and activities of extractive industries.[104] A global debate on defining and applying indigenous rights needs to take place.

Committing to finding a solution is imperative and for the common good. A balance must be struck between improving lives; extracting from the earth what humans need; protecting the environment; and honoring the rights, traditions, way of life, and identity of indigenous peoples who are intricately connected with the land. This chapter underscores the concept that indigenous peoples deserve and must be allowed to have a voice in protecting their rights, needs, and ways of life with respect to extractive industries' activities and projects. Accountability mechanisms must be put in place to protect these voices, rights, and needs and to craft equitable compensation agreements.

The key word here is *balance*. What is currently a grossly imbalanced approach to extractive industries' projects, an approach that favors the private sector and MNCs, must be realigned so that indigenous peoples' rights, needs, and interests are fairly acknowledged, factored in, and addressed.

---

103 For an analysis of the interplay of these factors, *see* Megan Davis, *Identity, Power, and Rights: The State, International Institutions, and Indigenous Peoples in Canada*, in *The Politics of Resource Extraction: Indigenous People, Multinational Corporations, and the State* 230–52 (Edmund Terence Gomez & Suzana Sawyer eds., Palgrave Macmillan 2012).

104 Carol Lancaster, *Foreign Aid in the Twenty-First Century: What Purposes?*, in *Foreign Aid and Foreign Policy: Lessons for the Next Half Century* 39–50 (Louis A. Picard, Robert Groelsema, & Terry F. Buss eds., M. E. Sharpe 2008).

PART II

Sustainable Development

5
Fostering Accountability in Large-Scale Environmental Projects
Lessons from CDM and REDD+ Projects

Damilola S. Olawuyi

Over the last decade, concern has grown and evidence has mounted that projects aimed at combating environmental problems ("environmental projects") increasingly produce serious human rights consequences, especially in developing countries. Often-cited examples include the human rights impacts of the Three Gorges Dam project in China,[1] the Changuinola (Chan 75) hydroelectric dam project in Panama,[2] and the West African Gas Pipeline project in Nigeria and Ghana.[3] Efforts to design projects that reduce the emission of greenhouse gases under the Clean Development Mechanism (CDM) of the Kyoto Protocol—including projects aimed at reducing emissions from deforestation and forest degradation and increasing the sustainable management of forests, conservation of forest carbon stocks, and enhancement of forest carbon stocks (REDD+)—have only intensified these concerns.[4]

---

1 B. Mayer, *Judicial Review of Human Rights Impacts of Hydroelectric Projects* (Ctr. for Intl. Sustainable Dev. L. 2012); P. Fearnside, *Greenhouse Gas Emissions from Hydroelectric Dams: Controversies Provide a Springboard for Rethinking a Supposedly "Clean" Energy Source,* 66(1–2) Climatic Change 1–8 (2004); S. Aird, *China's Three Gorges: The Impact of Dam Construction on Emerging Human Rights,* 8(2) Human Rights Brief 24 (2001); B. Wehrli, *Climate Science: Renewable but Not Carbon-Free,* 4(9) Nature Geoscience 585 (2011); K. Hoshour & J. Kalafut, *A Growing Global Crisis: Development-Induced Displacement and Resettlement* (issue paper, Intl. Accountability Project 2010).

2 C. Patrick Morris, *Hydroelectric Development and the Human Rights of Indigenous People,* in *The Struggle for the Land: Indigenous Insight and Industrial Empire in the Semiarid World* 193 (Paul A. Olson ed., U. of Nebraska–Lincoln, Ctr. Great Plains Stud. 1990); D. Cullenward & D. Victor, *An Editorial Comment: The Dam Debate and Its Discontents,* 75 Climatic Change 81 (2006); Ivan B. T. Lima et al., *Methane Emissions from Large Dams as Renewable Energy Resources: A Developing Nation Perspective,* 13(2) Mitigation & Adaptation Strategies for Global Change 193 (2006); L. Liu et al., *Unexpected CH4 Emission from the Three Gorges Reservoir and Its Implications,* 31(5) Acta Ecologica Sinica 233 (2011).

3 The West African Gas Pipeline project has been described as a human rights, environmental, and economic disaster. *See* Friends of the Earth International, *The New West African Gas Pipeline: Project Enshrines Energy Monopoly of Chevron and Shell in the Region* (2005), http://www.globalresearch.ca/the-new-west-african-gas-pipeline/912.

4 The Kyoto Protocol establishes three flexible mechanisms that allow industrialized countries to achieve their emission reduction objectives by earning emission reduction credits anywhere in the world, at the lowest cost possible. Joint implementation and emission trading take place between two industrialized countries with emission reduction targets. Because developing countries do not have emission reduction targets under the Kyoto Protocol, they are only eligible to take part in the CDM, which is a cooperative mechanism that allows developed countries to invest in developing countries in exchange for emission reduction

The CDM was designed to provide a cooperative mechanism that allows developed countries to invest in developing countries in exchange for emission reduction credits.[5] While it provides industrialized countries additional opportunities to earn emission reduction credits in the host country at the lowest cost possible, it provides reciprocal opportunities for the host country to derive social, environmental, and economic gains from the project. Through the CDM, a host country could attract capital for projects that assist in the shift to a more-prosperous but less-carbon-intensive economy; attract technology transfer through projects that replace old, dirty, and inefficient fossil fuel technology with cleaner ones; create new industries using environmentally sustainable technologies; and help define investment priorities in projects that meet sustainable development goals.[6] CDM projects could also result in social benefits such as rural development, employment, and poverty alleviation.[7] Estimates indicate that with over 5,200 registered CDM projects in over 80 countries, the CDM has mobilized more than US$215.4 billion in investments in developing countries, thereby providing opportunities for socioeconomic growth and poverty alleviation in many developing countries.[8]

Despite the significant promise of the CDM, its implementation and delivery has been fraught with a plenitude of challenges.[9] For example, the CDM

---

credits. There are also human rights issues in emission trading in joint implementation; however, the focus here is on the CDM because it has attracted the most protests and court cases. It is also the only mechanism with a global coverage, as it can happen between any developed country and a developing country party to the Kyoto Protocol. This global reach has generated more concerns, especially in developing countries with perennially bad human rights records. Despite the focus on the CDM, though, proposals in this chapter could be applicable to the human rights issues in all three mechanisms.

5 *See* U.N. Conf. Trade & Dev. Earth Council, *An Implementation Guide to the Clean Development Mechanism* (2003), http://unctad.org/en/Docs/ditcted20031_en.pdf.

6 United Nations Environmental Programme (UNEP), *CDM Information Book* 2–3 (UNEP 2004); K. Olsen & J. Fenhann, *Sustainable Development Benefits of Clean Development Mechanism Projects: A New Methodology for Sustainability Assessment Based on Text Analysis of the Project Design Documents Submitted for Validation,* 36(8) Energy Policy 2819–30 (2008).

7 Olsen & Fenhann, *supra* note 6.

8 *See* the 2012 report of the U.N. Framework Convention on Climate Change (UNFCCC), *Benefits of the Clean Development Mechanism 2012,* http://cdm.unfccc.int/about/dev_ben/ABC_2012.pdf. According to the report, the total investment in registered or soon-to-be-registered CDM projects as of June 2012 was estimated at US$215.4 billion.

9 *See,* generally, H. Haugen, *What Role for Human Rights in Clean Development Mechanism, REDD+, and Green Climate Fund Projects?,* 5(1) Nordic Envtl. L.J. 51–70 (2013); N. Roht-Arriaza, *Human Rights in the Climate Change Regime* 1(2) J. Human Rights & Env. (2010), in which the author identifies areas where current climate change regimes may cause human rights violations in local communities. These include some projects under the Clean Development Mechanism, large hydropower and biomass projects, use of biofuels, choices on energy and adaptation, and REDD+ projects. *See* also D. Driesen, *Sustainable Development and Market Liberalism's Shotgun Wedding: Emissions Trading under the Kyoto Protocol* 83(1) Ind. L.J. 21 (2008); K. Umamaheswaran & A. Michaelowa, *Additionality and Sustainable Development Issues Regarding CDM Projects in Energy Efficiency Sector* (HWWA Discussion Paper No. 346, Hamburg Inst. of Intl. Economics 2006); UNDP, *Fighting Climate Change: Human Solidarity in a Divided World* 1 (UNDP 2007); *Climate Change and Human Health: Risks and Responses* (A. McMichael et al. eds., World Health Organization [WHO] 2003); I. Rowlands, *The Kyoto Protocol's Clean*

has been criticized for not delivering on its sustainable development promises.[10] A number of CDM projects approved by the CDM Executive Board (CDMEB) have been criticized for resulting in the violation of fundamental human rights in developing countries.[11] There have been concerns related to the displacement of locals from ancestral homes and farmlands to allow projects to be located therein.[12] There have also been concerns about pollution caused by the transfer of outdated and inefficient technologies for emission credits.[13] Other human rights concerns include the lack of opportunities for participation by citizens in project planning and implementation,[14] siting of

---

Development Mechanism: A Sustainability Assessment, 22 Third World Q. 795 (2001); M. Doelle, *From Hot Air to Action? Climate Change, Compliance, and the Future of International Environmental Law* 29 (Carswell 2005); International Council on Human Rights Policy (ICHRP), *Climate Change and Human Rights: A Rough Guide* 12–14 (ICHRP 2008).

10 *See* P. Bond, *Politics of Climate Justice: Paralysis Above, Movements Below* (U. of KwaZulu-Natal Press 2012); A. Michaelowa, *The Future of the Clean Development Mechanism,* in *Climate Change Policies* (Emilio Cerdá & Xavier Labandeira eds., Edward Elgar 2011); Haugen, *supra* note 9; E. Boyd et al., *Reforming the CDM for Sustainable Development: Lessons Learned and Policy Futures,* 12 Envtl. Sci. & Policy 820–31 (2009): C. Voigt, *Is the Clean Development Mechanism Sustainable? Some Critical Aspects,* 8(2) Sustainable Dev. L. & Policy 15 (2008); D. Behn, *Linking Climate Change Mitigation and Poverty Reduction: Using Kyoto's Clean Development Mechanism to Promote Energy Development on the African Continent,* ch. 13 in *Poverty Alleviation and Environmental Law* (Yves Le Bouthillier et al. eds., Edward Elgar 2012); S. Headon, *Whose Sustainable Development? Sustainable Development under the Kyoto Protocol: The "Coldplay Effect" and the CDM Gold Standard,* 20 Colo. J. Intl. Envtl. L. & Policy 127 (2009); B. Pillai, *Moving Forward to 2012: An Evaluation of the Clean Development Mechanism,* 18 N.Y.U. Envtl. L.J. 357–411 (2010).

11 *See* T. Griffiths & F. Martone, *Seeing "REDD"? Forests, Climate Change Mitigation, and the Rights of Indigenous Peoples and Local Communities* (report prepared for the Forest Peoples Program, May 2009), http://www.rightsandresources.org/documents/files/doc_923.pdf. *See,* generally, E. Meijer, *The International Institutions of the Clean Development Mechanism Brought before National Courts: Limiting Jurisdictional Immunity to Achieve Access to Justice,* 39 N.Y.U. J. Intl. L. & Pol. 873 (2007). *See* also J. Santa Barbara, *The False Promise of Biofuels* (Spec. Rpt., Intl. Forum Globalization & Inst. Policy Stud. 2007); E. Holt-Giménez & I. Kenfield, *When Renewable Isn't Sustainable: Agrofuels and the Inconvenient Truths behind the 2007 U.S. Energy Independence and Security Act* (Food First Policy Brief No. 13: Agrofuels, Inst. for Food and Dev. Policy 2008).

12 *See* A. de Sherbinin et al., *Preparing for Resettlement Associated with Climate Change,* 334(6055) Sci. 456–57 (2011); R. Bronen, *Climate-Induced Community Relocations: Creating an Adaptive Governance Framework Based in Human Rights Doctrine,* 35 N.Y.U. Rev. L. & Soc. Change 357–407 (2011); K. Hoshour & J. Kalafut, *A Growing Global Crisis: Development-Induced Displacement and Resettlement* (Intl. Accountability Project Issue Paper 2010); J. McAdam, *Climate Change, Forced Migration, and International Law* (Oxford U. Press 2012); B. Mayer, *International Legal Challenges of Climate-Induced Migration: Proposal for an International Legal Framework,* 22 Colo. J. Intl. Envtl. L. & Policy 357–416 (2011); *Climate Change and Displacement: Multidisciplinary Perspectives* (J. McAdam ed., Hart Publg. 2010); *Forced Migration Review: Climate Change and Displacements* (M. Couldrey & M. Herson eds., Oxford Refugees Stud. Ctr. 2008); B. Petterson, *Development-Induced Displacement: Internal Affair or International Human Rights Issue?,* 12 Forced Migration Rev. 19 (2002).

13 *See,* generally, P. Lucas & T. Patzek, *The Disastrous Local and Global Impacts of Tropical Biofuel Production,* Energy Tribune 19 (Mar. 2007). *See* also Carbon Trade Watch, *Groups Slam Nigeria's Submission of Gas Flare Reductions for Carbon Credits,* Mar. 6, 2006, http://www.carbontradewatch.org/index.php?option=com_content&task=view&id=171&Itemid=36.

14 *See* F. Seymour, *Forests, Climate Change, and Human Rights: Managing Risks and Trade-offs* in *Human Rights and Climate Change* 207 (S. Humphreys ed., Cambridge U. Press 2010); S.

projects in poor and vulnerable communities, lack of governmental accountability on projects, and absence of judicial and quasi-judicial remedies for victims of the above-mentioned problems.[15]

Due to these problems, the credibility and integrity of the CDM, as well as large-scale, project-based mechanisms, have been questioned.[16] Due to ineffective delivery and implementation, projects that carry undoubted potential for sustainable development have met with resistance, criticism, and protest from local communities.[17] The CDM has in fact been labeled as a "Cheap and Corrupt Development Mechanism."[18] These gaps in the implementation of the CDM, as well as the high incidence of human rights violations resulting from large-scale environmental projects, have further increased the calls for a more transparent, accountable, and human rights–based approach to development in general. For example, in 2012, a coalition of developing countries petitioned the United Nations to seek powers to withdraw approvals of emission reduction projects if evidence emerged that the projects had breached human rights or harmed the environment.[19] The petition emphasizes how policy measures

---

Jodoin, *From Copenhagen to Cancun: A Changing Climate for Human Rights in the UNFCCC?* (Ctr. Intl. Sustainable Dev. L. [CISDL] & Intl. Dev. L. Org. [IDLO] Working Paper Ser., Jan. 2011), http://www.idlo.int/Download.aspx?Id=282&LinkUrl=Publications/3_JodoinSébastien%20_ChangingClimateforHumanRights.pdf&FileName=3_JodoinSébastien%20_ChangingClimateforHumanRights.pdf.

15 *See Petition to the Inter-American Commission on Human Rights Seeking Relief from Violations Resulting from Global Warming Caused by Acts and Omissions of the United States, by the Inuit People of the Arctic Regions of the United States and Canada* (Dec. 7, 2005). The IACHR informed the petitioners that it would not consider the petition because the information it provided was not sufficient for making a determination and that no legally enforceable right had been violated, available at http://inuitcircumpolar.com/files/uploads/iccfiles/ FINALPetitionICC.pdf.

16 *See* L. Pottinger, *The CDM's Hydro Hall of Shame*, in *Bad Deal for the Planet: Why Carbon Offsets Aren't Working . . . and How to Create a Fair Global Climate Accord* (Dams, Rivers and People Report 2008, International Rivers 2008); S. McInerney-Lankford, *Climate Change and Human Rights: An Introduction to Legal Issues*, 33(2) Harv. Envtl. L. Rev. 431–37 (2009); Oxfam, *Climate Wrongs and Human Rights: Putting People at the Heart of Climate-Change Policy* (Oxfam Briefing Paper on Climate Change and Human Rights 2008), http://www.oxfam.org.uk/resources/policy/climate_change/downloads/bp117_climatewrongs.pdf. *See* also C. Aminzadeh, *A Moral Imperative: The Human Rights Implications of Climate Change*, 30 Hastings Intl. & Comp. L. Rev. 259 (2007); and M. Limon, *Human Rights and Climate Change: Constructing a Case for Political Action* 33(2) Harv. Envtl. L. Rev. 451 (2009).

17 *See* German Energy Transition, *Carbon Credits Tarnished by Human Rights Disgrace*, http://www.euractiv.com/climate-environment/carbon-credits-tarnished-human-r-news-508068; R. Doornbusch & R. Steenblik, *Biofuels: Is the Cure Worse Than the Disease?* (background paper prepared for Organisation for Economic Co-operation and Development [OECD] meeting in Paris, Sept. 11–12, 2007), http://www.oecd.org/sd-roundtable/39411732.pdf.

18 *See* Down to Earth Group, *Issues: Flexibility Mechanisms*, Down to Earth magazine (Nov. 15, 2005). *See* also Ctr. Sci. & Env., *Current CDM Design Corrupt and "Unclean"* http://www.cseindia.org/node/3031. This rather sentimental condemnation of the CDM is arguably debatable; while it is easy to acknowledge the flaws in the current implementation of the CDM, this chapter argues that the CDM could stimulate real economic, social, and environmental growth in developing countries if properly restructured to be more transparent, accountable, and rights-based.

19 Point Carbon, *CDM Host Nations Ask U.N. for Power to Ban Projects*, http://www.pointcarbon.com/news/1.1802068.

and projects intended to advance environmental goals can have serious negative impacts if not properly designed and shaped by robust accountability safeguards.

This chapter explores and discusses the legal and normative frameworks for promoting accountability in large-scale environmental projects. It examines how lessons learned from CDM and REDD+ projects could inform thoughts on the value and requirements of mainstreaming international law principles on accountability into the design and implementation of large-scale environmental projects. It argues that the need for international organizations, national authorities, and relevant actors to ensure accountability in the design, delivery, and implementation of environmental projects must be understood as a fundamental human right of local communities and not as a mere add-on.

This chapter is divided into four sections. After this introductory section, section 2 examines key accountability questions and concerns regarding the design and implementation of CDM and REDD+ projects. Section 3 analyzes the essential requirements and scope of an accountability framework that holds governments and relevant actors involved in the design of environmental projects to their responsibilities and ensures that recourse is available to affected persons when obligations are not fulfilled. In section 4, the chapter concludes that, to promote accountability in the delivery of large-scale environmental projects, international bodies, governments, and national authorities must transcend needs-based approaches, which treat accountability as an add-on and bring accountability and human rights principles to the table only when a project has come under protest, experienced a problem, or been petitioned. Policy makers must begin to understand and mainstream accountability frameworks as part of the "rules of the game" when approving, planning, designing, and implementing projects. To be effective, such accountability frameworks require project planners and authorities to demonstrate that the substantive and procedural human rights of the public—such as access to information, participation, and access to justice—have been considered and that structural conditions ensuring that these rights are protected, respected, and fulfilled have been put in place before the project is approved. Such a framework also provides opportunities that enable the public to demand a review or cessation of projects that produce unanticipated consequences after approval.

Key Accountability Concerns in CDM and REDD+ Projects

A review of the key concerns associated with CDM projects focuses mainly on the lack of accountability and transparency by national authorities and project proponents in the design and implementation of the projects. Generally, the CDM rules and procedures require host countries to confirm that a CDM project will contribute to its national sustainable development goals.[20] Con-

---

20 Modalities and Procedures of the Clean Development Mechanism, UNFCCC, 3/CMP.1, Annex.to Decision 3/CMP.1, para. 40(a).

sequently, matters related to the sustainable development of a CDM project are determined by the government of the project's host country.[21] As such, projects have been approved at the national level, despite concerns about their impact on the rights of local communities. There have also been allegations of collusion between national authorities and project proponents in approving projects, even in the face of gross human rights violations.

Examples of projects that have dominated international discussions include the Aguan biogas CDM project in Honduras,[22] the Barro Blanco hydroelectric power plant CDM project in Panama,[23] and the Kwale CDM project in Nigeria.[24] Taking the Kwale project as an example, the aim of the project was to tackle the perennial concern of gas flaring in Nigeria,[25] through the capture and recovery of associated gas that would otherwise be flared at the Kwale

---

21 According to the spokesperson for the CDM Executive Board: "The allegations are deplorable. If human life has been taken, or human rights violated in any other way, it is a flagrant violation of the most fundamental principles of the United Nations. . . . However the CDM board has no mandate to investigate human rights abuses. Any matters related to the sustainable development of the project are determined by the government that hosts the project, in this case the de-facto government of Honduras." *See* Climate Connections, *Carbon Trade Group Backs Call to Check Credits on Human Rights* (2011), http://climate-connections.org/2011/04/18/carbon-trade-group-backs-call-to-check -credits-on-human-rights/.

22 *See* BIOMASS Hub, *Human Rights Violations Linked to CDM Biogas Project in Honduras* (2011), http://biomasshub.com/human-rights-violations-linked-cdm-biogas-honduras/. *See* also CDM Watch, *United Nations under Pressure to Denounce Human Rights Abuses in Carbon Offsetting Scheme* (press release, Apr. 18, 2011), http://www.cdm-watch.org/?p=1872.

23 The Ngöbe, numbering about 170,000 people, are the largest indigenous group in Panama, with the majority still living in their traditional lands in western Panama. *See* International Rivers, *Letter to the CDM Executive Board Regarding the Barro Blanco Hydroelectric Project* (Feb. 9, 2011), http://www.internationalrivers.org/resources/letter-to-the-cdm-executive-board-regarding-the-barro-blanco-hydroelectric-project-3078. *See* also the petition by the organizations Cultural Survival and Alianza para la Conservación y el Desarrollo (Alliance for Conservation and Development), *Human Rights Violations by the Government of Panama against the Ngöbe Indigenous Communities and Individuals in the Changuinola River Valley, Bocas del Toro, Panama* 32–33 (Mar. 28, 2008), http://www.cidh.oas.org/annualrep/2009eng/Panama286.08eng.htm.

24 *See* F. Allen et al., *Niger Delta Oil Flares, Broken Laws, Pollution and Oppression*, ch. 4 in *Why the Carbon Trading Gamble and the Clean Development Mechanism Won't Save the Planet from Climate Change and How African Civil Society Is Resisting* (report by the U. of KwaZulu-Natal, Ctr. for Civil Soc. & Dartmouth College, Climate Jus. Research Project, Apr. 2012). *See* also N. Bassey, *Foreword*, in *Mired in a Fossil Trap: The Nigerian CDM Report* (Envtl. Rights Action/Friends of the Earth, May 2011); Carbon Trade Watch, *supra* note 13.

25 One of the main environmental issues in Nigeria is the problem of gas flaring. Nigeria is reputed to flare more natural gas associated with oil extraction than any other country on the planet. Estimates suggest that of the 3.5 billion cubic feet of associated gas produced annually, 2.5 billion cubic feet, or about 70 percent, is wasted via flaring. This equals about 25 percent of the United Kingdom's total natural gas consumption and is the equivalent to 40 percent of the entire African continent's gas consumption. *See Flames of Hell: Gas Flaring in the Niger Delta* http://www.saction.org/home/saction_image/flames_of_hell.pdf. *See* also Environmental Rights Action (ERA), *Harmful Gas Flaring in Nigeria* (fact sheet); Vanguard, *Nigeria Loses $150 Billion to Gas Flare in 36 Years* (Lagos, July 12, 2008), 3; ERA & Friends of the Earth Nigeria, *Gas Flaring in Nigeria: A Human Rights, Environmental, and Economic Monstrosity* (June 2005), http://www.climatelaw.org/cases/case-documents/nigeria/gas-flaring-in-nigeria.pdf.

Oil-Gas Processing Plant.[26] Despite its potential and promise, it was the lack of transparency in the approval process, the inadequate opportunities for stakeholder consultation and participation, and the lack of a transparent environmental impact assessment (EIA) on the short- and long-term impacts of the project that gained the most attention and publicity.[27] Environmental groups in Nigeria raised concerns that the project proponents failed to address key environmental concerns on the long-term impacts of the project on local communities by not conducting a transparent EIA that could provide comprehensive details on the short- and long-term impact of the project.[28] Allegedly, the EIA for this project was conducted as a smokescreen, after the project had already been approved by the Nigerian-designated national authority for the CDM and registered by the CDMEB. The project proponents failed to demonstrate through an EIA that the long-term effects of the project had been considered and mitigated where necessary. There were also questions about whether appropriate infrastructure had been put in place to deal with the possibilities of pipeline rupture and leakage of the captured gas. Furthermore, community leaders sought to know whether project proponents would utilize associated gas, as was laid out in the Project Design Document, or the cheaper nonassociated gas in the gas recovery and utilization phase of the project. Additionally, there were claims that in its previous independent power plant projects the company mostly used easier-to-process and less-expensive nonassociated gas instead of the agreed-on associated gas. These questions were not adequately answered, which consequently fueled public mistrust about CDM implementation in Nigeria in general.[29] Furthermore, the consultation process was allegedly deceptive, as community leaders were told by the Nigerian government that the project was an electrical power project aimed at bringing electricity to the community.[30]

Most importantly, the "additionality" of this project was not sufficiently demonstrated to the local communities; therefore, it was perceived as an opportunity for oil companies operating in the Niger Delta to receive carbon credits for reducing gas flaring—an act expressly prohibited by Nigerian law in the first place. Project proponents failed to demonstrate how the Kwale

---

26 *See* UNFCCC, *Kwale CDM Project Monitoring Report: Recovery of Associated Gas That Would Otherwise Be Flared at Kwale Oil-Gas Processing Plant, Nigeria* (2007), UNFCCC/ Document ID: CDM0553-MR01. The recovery and utilization of flared gases through this project started in 2006. As of 2010, the total emissions reduction generated by the project was estimated to be above 791,325 tons of CO_2 (equivalent).

27 *See* F. Onojiribholo, *Kwale Chief Laments Plight of Communities,* Daily Independent (Aug. 16, 2011); Allen et al., *supra* note 24. *See* also Bassey, *supra* note 24; Carbon Trade Watch, *supra* note 13.

28 *See* K. Adeyemo, *Nigerians Oppose Climate Development Projects,* Tribune (Ibadan) 3 (Sept. 12, 2010).

29 Onojiribholo, *supra* note 27.

30 *See* F. Allen, P. Bond, & K. Sharife, *The CDM in Africa Can't Deliver the Money: Report to the United Nations CDM Executive Board "Call for Inputs on the Policy Dialogue"* (report by the U. of KwaZulu-Natal Ctr. for Civ. Soc., Durban, Jan. 21, 2012) regarding CDM flaws in South Africa and Nigeria; Carbon Trade Watch, *supra* note 13.

CDM project—which had existed since 1987 as a gas recovery and utilization project, and which was simply repackaged and labeled as a CDM project in 2005—would bring additional emission reduction and sustainability benefits to the country when compared with its pre-CDM scenario. This lack of detailed information fueled the public perception that the project was an indirect effort by project proponents to gain cheap carbon reduction credits for a problem it was meant to address without the CDM.[31] These are questions that arguably could have been addressed with more transparent stakeholder participation and a more transparent information disclosure system.

Projects aimed at reducing emissions from deforestation and forest degradation, and increasing the sustainable management of forests, conservation of forest carbon stocks, and enhancement of forest carbon stocks (REDD+) offer another example. Scientific studies show that deforestation and forest degradation, through agricultural expansion, conversion to pastureland, infrastructure development, and destructive logging and fires account for nearly 20 percent of global greenhouse gas emissions, more than the entire global transportation sector and second only to the energy sector.[32] The United Nations therefore recommends REDD+ as a mechanism to compensate countries that prevent deforestation and forest degradation that would otherwise occur. REDD+ allows industrialized countries to gain credits by engaging in forest conservation and efforts that protect trees from being cut down.[33] Estimates suggest that REDD+ projects have a potential of producing emission reductions of up to 7.8 billion tons per year.[34]

A number of developing countries have demonstrated a willingness to execute REDD+ projects by granting multinationals permission to execute them; Nigeria is a good example.[35] However, REDD+ has had a very rough start in many countries, as instanced by the Noel Kempff project in Bolivia, the Rimba Raya REDD project in Indonesia, the Shell/Gazprom REDD+ project in Nigeria, and the New Forests project in Uganda.[36] The Noel Kempff project, for example, has been criticized as a carbon scam for engendering land grabs and as lacking the potential to deliver on its carbon mitigation claims.[37] In

---

31 Envtl. Rights Action, *Nigeria: Learning Clean Development Mechanism (CDM) Lessons* (Sept. 2012), http://www.eraction.org/publications/learningcdmlessons.pdf.

32 *See* A. Angelsen et al., *Reducing Emissions from Deforestation and Forest Degradation: An Options Assessment Report* 3–4 (Meridien Inst. 2009).

33 R. O'Sullivan et al., *Should REDD+ Be Included in the CDM? Analysis of Issues and Options* (policy paper prepared for the CDM Policy Dialogue, June 2012), http://www.cdmpolicydialogue.org/research/1030_Redd.pdf.

34 Angelsen et al., *supra* note 32, at 3–4.

35 S. Ogidan, *Nigeria to Earn N 34.44 Billion Yearly in Tree Planting,* Nigerian Compass (Lagos) (Feb. 14, 2011).

36 D. Forgarty, *Shell Bankrolls REDD Project in Nigeria,* http://climatevoices.wordpress.com/2010/09/07/shell-bankrolls-redd/.

37 Green Peace International, *Carbon Scam: Noel Kempff Climate Action Project and the Push for Sub-national Forest Offsets,* http://www.greenpeace.org/usa/en/media-center/reports/carbon-scam-noel-kempff-clima/.

Uganda, more than 22,000 peasants with land titles were allegedly evicted from the Mubende and Kiboga districts to make way for the REDD+ project sponsored by the UK-based New Forests Company.[38] There have also been claims that the process that led to the approval of Shell Canada for REDD+ projects in Nigeria was the decision of the Nigerian authorities alone, without the consent and approval of the indigenous communities who owned the lands and trees in question.[39] What followed were pockets of protests and demonstrations.[40]

Is Accountability Taken Seriously in Project Delivery?

The United Nations Framework Convention on Climate Change (UNFCCC), the Kyoto Protocol, and the CDM "Modalities and Procedures" (CDM rules) fail to establish robust accountability mechanisms and procedures that mandate national authorities to demonstrate that the substantive and procedural human rights of the public—such as access to information, access to justice, and participation—have been considered, and that structural conditions to ensure these rights are protected, respected, and fulfilled both before and after approval. They also fail to provide reciprocal opportunities for stakeholders or private individuals whose consultative rights or human rights in general have been infringed on; such opportunities take the form of projects to seek redress, to challenge the approval of such projects, or to seek the review of already approved projects.

For example, the Kyoto Compliance Committee only examines questions of implementation with obligations under the Kyoto Protocol; these are mainly issues relating to estimation, reporting, and verification of emissions and credits of Annex I parties, and to overall compliance by parties with their emission reduction obligations.[41] Given that the Kyoto Protocol itself does not expressly

---

38 No REDD Africa, *The Worst REDD-Type Projects in Africa: Continent Grab for Carbon Colonialism*, http://www.no-redd-africa.org/index.php/16-redd-players/84-the-worst-redd-type-projects-in-africa-continent-grab-for-carbon-colonialism.

39 As the official spokesperson of the indigenous community noted: "Forests in Cross Rivers State—some of the few remaining tracks of mangrove and rainforest reserve in the world targeted for REDD are in grave danger due to the scheme, hence the need for participants to uncover any cover-ups by government which is detrimental to community forests and the environment. To us, carbon trading/market mechanism promoted by the REDD are false solutions to climate change; REDD promotes deforestation, more plantation and corporate land grabs." *See* REDD Monitor, *Shell REDD Project Slammed by Indigenous Environmental Network and Friends of the Earth Nigeria* (2010), http://www.redd-monitor.org/2010/09/08/indigenous-en vironmental-network-and-friends-of-the-earth-nigeria-denounce-shell-redd-project/.

40 *See* C. Lang, *Shell Project Slammed in Nigeria* (Sept. 2010), http://www.redd-monitor.org/2010/09/08/indigenous-environmental-network-and-friends-of-the-earth-nigeria-denounce-shell-redd-project/.

41 Some of the overall weaknesses of the Kyoto Compliance Mechanism and Procedures with respect to monitoring and verifying emission reductions have been exhaustively identified elsewhere. *See* M. Doelle, *Early Experience with the Kyoto Compliance System: Possible Lessons for MEA Compliance System Design*, http://law.dal.ca/Files/MEL_Institute/Doelle_Kyoto_Compliance_Final_Draft.pdf; S. Oberthür & R. Lefeber, *Holding Countries to Account: The Kyoto*

include human rights obligations or respect for human rights in the design and execution of climate change responses, the Kyoto Compliance Committee does not have the mandate to consider compliance with human rights.[42] As such, issues relating to how projects or measures aimed at achieving emission reductions affect human rights fall outside the mandate and expertise of the enforcement or facilitative branches of the compliance committee.[43] This gap must be addressed if parties to the UNFCCC and the Kyoto Protocol are truly serious about giving effect to the Cancun Decision that "'Parties should in all climate change actions respect human rights."[44] It is not enough to simply

---

Protocol's Compliance System Revisited after Four Years of Experience, 1 Climate L. 133–58 (2010); J. Brunnée, *A Fine Balance: Facilitation and Enforcement in the Design of a Compliance for the Kyoto Protocol,* 13 Tul. Envtl. L.J. 223 (2000). *See* also M. Doelle, *From Hot Air to Action? Climate Change, Compliance and the Future of International Environmental Law* (Carswell 2005); C. Breidenich & D. Bodansky, *Measurement, Reporting, and Verification in a Post-2012 Climate Agreement* (Pew Ctr. on Global Climate Change 2009), http://www.pewclimate.org/doc Uploads/mrv-report.pdf; P. Rodgers Kalas & A. Herwig, *Dispute Resolution under the Kyoto Protocol,* 27 Ecology L.Q. 53 (2000); D. Victor, *Enforcing International Law: Implications for an Effective Global Warming Regime,* 10 Duke Envtl. L. & Policy Forum 147 (1999).

42 The Compliance Committee is made up of two branches: the facilitative branch and an enforcement branch. The facilitative branch provides advice and assistance to parties to promote compliance; the enforcement branch has the responsibility to determine consequences for parties not meeting their emission reduction commitments. Reviewing the human rights impacts of emission reduction projects is not listed as one of the functions or mandates of either branch of the Compliance Committee. *See Procedures and Mechanisms Relating to Compliance under the Kyoto Protocol,* Annex, sec. VII, para. 1, Dec. 24/CP.7.

43 The enforcement branch of the Kyoto Compliance Committee has to date been confronted with eight questions of implementation related to a party's compliance with its Kyoto commitments. The cases involved Greece, Canada, Croatia, Bulgaria, Romania, Ukraine, Lithuania, and the Slovak Republic. Procedurally, a question of implementation can be brought before the Compliance Committee either by a party to the Kyoto Protocol or by an expert review team (ERT). The Bureau of the Committee then determines whether it comes under the jurisdiction of the enforcement branch (EB) or the facilitative branch (FB) or both. Once the EB receives a question of implementation from the bureau, it conducts a preliminary review of the issue raised and makes a determination whether to proceed. A human rights question will most likely stop at this stage, as it falls outside the jurisdiction of the committee. For issues coming under its jurisdiction, the party under investigation is informed of the decision of the EB to proceed. Such party has the right to request a hearing and make written submissions. The EB will usually hear from the party, the ERT, any other party, and any independent experts that it feels are needed to resolve the issue raised. The EB can also request specific information from the party under investigation and can consider submissions from nonparties. Timelines are set for the major steps in the process. After the hearing, the EB makes a preliminary finding as to whether the party is in compliance. The party has an opportunity to comment on the preliminary finding. If it does not, the preliminary finding stands as the final decision of the EB. If the party submits comments on the preliminary finding, the EB issues a final decision in light of the comments filed. The EB has to give reasons for its decisions. A finding of noncompliance will result in a range of consequences depending on the nature of the violation. A key part of the process is the preparation of a compliance plan within three months of the determination of noncompliance, with regular updates thereafter on the implementation of the compliance plan. Key substantive requirements for the compliance plan are set out in sec. XV(6) of the Compliance Procedures. For a comprehensive overview of the process, *see* Oberthür & Lefeber, *supra* note 41; Doelle, *Early Experience supra* note 41.

44 *See* para. 8 of the Cancun Agreements: "Outcome of the work of the Ad Hoc Working Group on Long-term Cooperative Action under the Convention which noted Resolution 10/4 of the

include human rights paragraphs or safeguards in the climate change regime; these must be accompanied by a reform in governance structures to establish robust systems to monitor and enforce compliance with human rights.

The current Compliance Committee does not have powers to receive compliance complaints from the public. Compliance issues can be referred only by a party to the Kyoto Protocol or by an expert review team (ERT).[45] Private individuals or members of the public do not have access to request a review or a question of implementation under the current compliance rules. This further narrows the scope of the committee and reduces the impacts it could make with respect to investigating questions of implementation or complaints by members of the public.

Apart from the Compliance Committee, the CDMEB and its accredited project verifiers (called designated operational entities, or DOEs), which verify all projects before registration, do not have the mandate to consider projects from a human rights standpoint.[46] Rather, both the CDMEB and the DOEs examine the technical requirements of projects and whether the projects have met the national requirements of the host country. For example, the CDMEB, in response to allegations of fraud and procedural impunities brought against DOEs, established a complaint procedure in 2010. This procedure allows the public to bring forward complaints about fraud or unethical behavior by a DOE or to challenge a DOE that has not complied with its own accredited system and/or the CDM requirements.[47] However, despite the potential of this new complaint procedure, its efficacy has been hindered by the fact that respect for human rights is not one of the CDM requirements; thus, DOEs, just like the CDMEB, do not have powers to consider the human rights impact of a project. This gap makes it impossible for individuals to approach the executive board to review projects that affect their human rights, leaving states as the only option for redress.

United Nations Human Rights Council on human rights and climate change on the adverse direct and indirect effects of climate change on the effective enjoyment of human rights." *See* also CDM Policy Dialogue, *Climate Change, Carbon Markets and the CDM: A Call to Action: Recommendations of the High Level Panel on the CDM Policy Dialogue* (2012), http://www.cdmpolicydialogue.org/report/ues_en.pdf.

45 *See* annexes to Decisions 4/CMP.2 and 4/CMP.4 on the Compliance Committee, FCCC/KP/CMP/2006/Add.1 (Mar. 2, 2007), 17; FCCC/KP/CMP/2008/11/Add.1, at 14 (Mar. 19, 2009).

46 DOEs are independent auditors who have been accredited by the CDMEB to assess and validate whether a project meets all the eligibility requirements of the CDM and to certify whether the project has achieved greenhouse gas emission reductions. They are responsible for verifying the accuracy of the project description documents, ensuring that proposed CDM project activities meet all requirements established by the CDMEB, and submitting the project proposals to the CDMEB for registration. *See* UNFCCC, *Designated Operational Entities (DOE)*, http://cdm.unfccc.int/DOE/index.html. *See* also para. 27(e) of the *CDM Modalities & Procedures*, which provides that the executive board maintain a publicly available list of designated operational entities.

47 CDMEB, *Appendix 3: Handling of Complaints against an AE/DOE*, in *Procedure for Accrediting Operational Entities by the Executive Board of the Clean Development Mechanism (CDM)*, http://cdm.unfccc.int/Reference/Procedures/accr_proc01.pdf.

Another gap is the fact that individuals are not recognized under the CDM Rules and cannot request a project review. Currently, only governments or three CDMEB members can request a review of projects under the CDM rules.[48] As expected, it would be most unlikely for states that have approved projects to instigate such review processes. Stakeholders whose rights are violated do not currently have any way to request a review of a CDM project prior to registration. Nor does the Kyoto Protocol confer on the CDMEB the authority to refuse a project based on human rights complaints or the discretion to hear appeals from members of the public whose rights may be affected by a project, even in cases such as the Aguan gas project, which received several petitions indicating significant infringements of human rights. Similarly, the Kyoto Protocol does not contain any requirement or provision that provides access to justice or administrative recourse to individuals or the public when any human right is violated or when proper processes and procedures have not been followed in the design and execution of a project.[49] Dispute resolution mechanisms established in the Kyoto Protocol relate to disputes between any two or more parties concerning the interpretation or application of the UNFCCC convention and which also applies *mutatis mutandis* to the protocol.[50] The focus is on disputes between parties; this provision does not establish a complaint mechanism or project appeal panel through which the public can file disputes, complaints, or grievances. Similarly, the CDM rules fail to establish complaint mechanisms and appeal procedures for stakeholders or private individuals whose consultative rights or human rights in general have been infringed to seek redress, to block the approval of CDM projects, or to seek the review of already approved projects. This freezes out those members of the public, whose fundamental human rights might be repressed by host countries.

These gaps create a one-way mechanism in which the decision of the state is final and most often rubber-stamped by the international supervisory body. This has entrenched a culture of "approvals" that excludes the common citizen, whose fundamental human rights may be repressed by the home state and that repression endorsed by the UNFCCC. Grievance mechanisms support the identification of any adverse human rights impact as part of the human rights due diligence on a project; they also make it possible for grievances, once identified, to be addressed and for any adverse impact to be remediated early and directly by project proponents, thereby preventing harm

---

48 *CDM Modalities & Procedures,* 3/CMP.1 (2005), http://cdm.unfccc.int/Reference/COPMOP/08a01.pdf.

49 Art. 19 of the Kyoto Protocol and art. 14 of the UNFCCC provide only for dispute settlement among parties. Art. 14 of the UNFCCC, which applies *mutatis mutandis* to art. 19 of the Kyoto Protocol, reads: "In the event of a dispute between any two or more Parties concerning the interpretation or application of the Convention, the Parties concerned shall seek a settlement of the dispute through negotiation or any other peaceful means of their own choice." *See* Kalas & Herwig, *supra* note 41.

50 Art. 19, Kyoto Protocol; art. 14, UNFCCC.

from being compounded and grievances from escalating.[51] As new project information emerges, new human rights issues could also emerge. As such, it is not enough to provide only updated information on projects; there must also be a project-review, dispute resolution platform for stakeholders to seek a review of projects and to address any human rights concerns that might arise. A review mechanism complements wider stakeholder engagement as it provides opportunities for stakeholders to raise emerging issues that were not discussed or during the preapproval consultations. While REDD+ projects would contribute to climate change mitigation, taking a large proportion of land from the indigenous communities by brute force without providing compensation or settlement options is a major human rights concern.

Furthermore, placing the decision to host a project in the hands of national governments that would be interested in such projects has led to the approval of questionable projects, even projects that lead to loss of life and the violation of human rights. Arguably, states have been more concerned with hosting climate change projects at all costs, irrespective of the human rights consequences of such projects. Due to the scramble among developing countries to host CDM projects, there have been increased tendencies to lower sustainability standards and to encourage foreign CDM projects despite their potential short- and long-term effects on human rights.[52] These concerns are most serious in developing countries with abysmal human rights records.[53]

More accountability and transparency should be demanded from national governments regarding the process of approving projects that could alter the lifestyles and existence of inhabitants who depend on these forests for peasant farming and food. Lack of information and participation has led to a misunderstanding of the genuine intentions behind projects, and there is the charge that states cloak project-description documents in such secrecy that citizens

---

51 *Id.*

52 M. Jung, *Host Country Attractiveness for CDM Non-sink Projects* Energy Policy 2174 (2006); A. Silayan, *Equitable Distribution of CDM Projects among Developing Countries* 1 (HWWA Report No. 255, Hamburg Inst. Intl. Economics 2005); K. Olsen, *The Clean Development Mechanism's Contribution to Sustainable Development: A Review of the Literature,* 84(1) Climatic Change 59–73 (2007).

53 In Nigeria, for example, six emission reduction projects have been subjects of intense petition and court actions over human rights violations. These projects include the Kwale Project, the Ovade Ogharefe Project, the Lafarge Cement Project, the West African Gas Project, the Asuokpu/Umutu Gas Recovery and Marketing Facility Project, and the Cross River Reducing Emissions from Deforestation and Degradation (REDD) Project, currently being executed in Nigeria by Shell. The violations range from land grabs without compensation, assault on indigenes, killings, lack of participation in the decision-making process, and the displacement of residents of affected areas. For each of these projects, it is reported that the environmental impact assessments were put together only as a smokescreen and forwarded to the CDMEB after Nigerian authorities had already approved the projects. These projects were still approved and registered by the CDMEB despite the protests. *See* Adeyemo, *supra* note 28, at 3; *REDD under Fire in Nigeria,* http://uk.oneworld.net/article/view/165950/1/246; Akanimo Sampson, *Don't Sell Forests: Groups Urge Nigerian Govts* (press release, *Scoop,* Aug. 27, 2010). *See* also Carbon Trade Watch, *supra* note 13; Bank Info. Ctr., *Local Groups Say Project Will Not End Gas Flaring, Could Exacerbate Conflicts in the Niger Delta,* http://www.bicusa.org/en/Project.39.aspx.

find it hard to know how these projects might affect them in both the short and the long term.[54] Peasants and community members, most of whom are uneducated, understandably construe projects as an attempt to forcefully grab their lands, subject them to servitude, and destroy their means of existence. A transparent, informative, and participatory approach arguably could have addressed these concerns. As Aristotle once wrote, "All men by nature desire to know."[55] There is a need for national authorities to establish a transparent and accessible public disclosure system that provides citizens with up-to-date information on projects that could affect their lives.

The absence of EIAs, the lack of participation and inclusion, and the lack of remedies for victims raise genuine concerns regarding the need for more accountability by national authorities in the design and implementation of environmental projects, and in the process of approving such projects, especially the need to demonstrate that all the short- and long-term human rights impacts of a project have been considered before granting host-country approval to that project.

The CDM process demonstrates how a viable environmental project could result in large-scale human rights problems if not properly equipped with robust accountability principles and frameworks. The examples discussed underline the need to promote more accountability in the design of environmental projects.[56]

Legal Framework for Ensuring Accountability in Projects

Accountability has increasingly gained recognition under international law as a prerequisite for the protection, fulfillment, and realization of human rights. It has been described as the obligation to demonstrate that a project has been conducted in accordance with agreed-on rules and standards and to report fairly and accurately on performance results vis-à-vis mandated roles and/or plans.[57] Accountability is the obligation of relevant authorities to review, monitor, and enforce compliance with human rights standards and obligations in the design and execution of environmental projects.[58] It encompasses the

---

54 *See* Onojiribholo, *supra* note 27.

55 Aristotle, *Metaphysics*, bk. 7 Clarendon (1924), http://classics.mit.edu/Aristotle/metaphysics.1.i.html.

56 S. Humphreys, ed., *Human Rights and Climate Change* 23 (Cambridge U. Press 2010). *See* also S. Lankford, M. Darrow, & L. Rajamani, *Human Rights and Climate Change: A Review of the International Legal Dimensions* (World Bank 2011), in which the authors argue that policy measures designed to address climate change may affect the realization of human rights. Human rights principles, both substantive and procedural, would be relevant to the design and implementation of effective responses to climate change, particularly in relation to adaptation and to some extent also to mitigation (56–57).

57 OECD, *Public Sector Transparency and Accountability: Making It Happen* 7 (OECD 2002).

58 *See* One World Trust, *2011 Pathways to Accountability II, the Revised Global Accountability Framework*, http://oneworldtrust.org/publications/doc_download/470-pathways-to-accountability-ii.

structural conditions, the processes, the indicators, and the outcomes through which governance systems review and monitor the practical impacts of a project on the human rights of the public. As such, an accountable regime measures, reviews, and monitors the level at which human rights are respected and fulfilled in the implementation of projects, programs, and mandates.

Accountability may be measured by a set of indicators that include identifying the unintended impacts of projects on human rights; identifying which actors are having an impact on the realization of rights; revealing whether the obligations of these actors are being met; giving early warning of potential violations, prompting preventive action; enhancing social consensus on difficult trade-offs to be made in the face of resource constraints; and exposing issues that have been neglected or silenced.[59]

Virtually every human rights instrument creates mechanisms for monitoring compliance and for reporting violations.[60] The Commission on Human Rights also establishes special rapporteurs, expert committees, and working groups to gather human rights compliance information and to recommend actions for noncompliance. Such recommended actions and reports are often not legally binding, but they provide guidance and reference points on the mechanisms for ensuring greater accountability in the performance of human rights obligations at the international level. The Aarhus Convention is an example of an environmental agreement that establishes compliance mechanisms that monitor the protection and fulfillment of procedural human rights.[61]

Similarly, the United Nations has in different nonbinding resolutions identified accountability as part of the founding principles of transparency and effective public administration.[62] The UN General Assembly, for example, has adopted Resolution 60/260 on Accountability.[63] This resolution emphasizes the importance of strengthened accountability within the United Nations and the need for all UN agencies to ensure greater accountability within their spheres of operation for the effective and efficient implementation of legislative mandates and for the best use of human and financial resources.

---

59 S. Lankford & H. Sano, *Human Rights Indicators in Development: An Introduction* (World Bank 2010). *See* also UNDP, *Using Indicators for Human Rights Accountability*, http://hdr.undp.org/en/media/hdr_2000_ch5.pdf.

60 *See* United Nations, *Delegation of Authority and Accountability*, Rpt. of the UN Joint Inspection Unit, JIU/REP/2004/7 13 (2004).

61 For example, art. 15 of the Aarhus Convention provides that "the meeting of the parties shall establish, on a consensus basis, optional arrangements of a nonconfrontational, nonjudicial, and consultative nature for reviewing compliance with the provisions of this convention. These arrangements shall allow for appropriate public involvement and may include the option of considering communications from members of the public on matters related to this convention."

62 *See* A/RES/49/136 of 1994, A/RES/50/225 of 1996, A/RES/53/201 of 1999, A/RES/56/213 of 2002, A/RES/57/277 of 2002, and A/RES/58/231 of 2004.

63 United Nations, *Investing in the United Nations: For a Stronger Organization Worldwide*, G.A. Res., A/RES/60/260 (May 16, 2006).

Despite these resolutions and declarations, however, the lack of accountability within the UN systems and other international development agencies has received scholarly attention over the last decade.[64] Accountability concerns include the prevalent development paradigm that fails to hold corporations liable for human rights violations in project constructions.[65] Another concern is the failure of development agencies to establish clear and compulsory human rights benchmarks that must be met before projects are approved or funded.[66] For example, the CDMEB has been variously condemned for its lack of accountability and transparency, in registering CDM projects and failing to hold countries to account for projects that produce human rights impacts.[67] This has led to increased calls for an approach that hinges development on respect for human rights requirements on accountability.[68] Respect for the human rights of local communities in the delivery of development projects cannot continue to be thought of as a mere add-on. It is necessary to transcend the prevailing needs-based approach to a human rights–based approach, which recognizes the need for accountability and transparency by such key actors as project proponents, national authorities, development agencies, and funding partners as a fundamental human right of local communities where projects are located.

There is also a need for public bodies such as national authorities to mainstream human rights–based benchmarks or indicators into local rules and procedures governing the approval and execution of environmental projects, such that compliance with human rights obligations would be measured side-by-side with environmental goals such as emission reductions. This would also include establishing rewards and sanctions for successes and failures in

---

64 *See* E. Brown Weiss, *Accountability and International Law: Reflections from Water Projects* (lecture delivered at the U. of Oxford, Feb. 23, 2012). *See* also O. Hathaway, *Do Human Rights Treaties Make a Difference?* 11(8) Yale L.J. (2002); *Envisioning Reform: Enhancing UN Accountability in the Twenty-First Century*, 5–8 (S. Kuyama & M. Fowler eds., U.N. U. Press 2009).

65 *See* E. Brown Weiss, *On Being Accountable in a Kaleidoscopic World*, 1 Asian J. Intl. L. 21–32 (2011). *See* also E. Brown Weiss, P. Lallas & A. Herken, *The World Bank Inspection Panel: Participation and Accountability*, in Kuyama & Fowler, *supra* note 64; J. Conant, *Massive UN-Supported African Palm Plantations Leading to Oppression, Kidnapping, and Murder* (2012), http://www.alternet.org/environment/149778/why_u.n.-backed_carbon_credit_schemes_may_be_fueling_land_grabs%2C_kidnappings_and_murder?page=entire. *See* also G. Monbiot, *North Biofuel Appetite Causing South Starvation*, Hindu (Nov. 7, 2007); S. Jodoin, *Lost in Translation: Human Rights in the Climate Change Negotiations* (Legal Working Paper, Ctr. Intl. Sustainable Dev. L. Jan. 2010), http://www.cisdl.org/pdf/working_papers_climate/Jodoin.pdf.

66 *See* S. Nanwani, *Improving Accountability at the Asian Development Bank* in Kuyama & Fowler, *supra* note 64; R. Keohane, *Global Governance and Democratic Accountability*, in *Global Governance and Public Accountability* (D. Held & M. Koenig-Archibugi eds., Blackwell 2005).

67 *See* A. Filmozer, *CDM Projects Affect Human Rights* (Feb. 2011), http://www.cdm-watch.org/wordpress/wp-content/. *See* also Climate Connections, *Carbon Trade Group Backs Call to Check Credits on Human Rights* (Climate Connections 2011), http://climate-connections.org/2011/04/18/carbon-trade-group-backs-call-to-check-credits-on-human-rights/.

68 *See* Brown Weiss, *supra* note 64; Hathaway, *supra* note 64; A. Johl & S. Duyck, *Promoting Human Rights in the Future Climate Regime*, 15(3) Ethics, Policy & Env. 300 (2012); D. Olawuyi, *Towards a Transparent and Accountable Clean Development Mechanism: Legal and Institutional Imperatives*, 2(2) Nordic Envtl. L.J. 33–52 (2012).

complying with established benchmarks.[69] Accountability benchmarks would provide stakeholders an opportunity to understand how national authorities, project proponents, and funding agencies have discharged, or failed to discharge, their human rights obligations, and an opportunity for these public bodies to demonstrate their human rights compliance through mandatory compliance and implementation reports.[70]

Ensuring accountability will require the establishment of a legal framework that compels project actors to transparently demonstrate that the rights of stakeholders have been considered, respected, and protected in the design of projects. Such a framework will also provide opportunities for stakeholders to freely obtain project information and provide the essential structural conditions that make it possible to monitor compliance with human rights standards.[71] There is also a need to establish and empower compliance committees and review teams that would be responsible for monitoring compliance. Such institutions must be independent and should not be easily influenced by governmental interests or pressure; for example, through a monitoring committee or expert review team that would inspect project locations to ensure that projects are being executed based on approved guidelines and methodologies.

To give effect to an accountability regime, such review structures must be equipped with the resources to perform spot assessments, fact-findings, and investigations, such that they could gather firsthand information on the true impacts of a project on the human rights of host communities. A good example is the problem-solving approach adopted by the World Bank Inspection Panel (WBIP).[72] Despite the conflicting opinion on the efficiency and legacy of the WBIP with respect to transparency and accountability,[73] the panel is an

---

69 B. Andreassen & H. Otto Sano, *Human Rights Based Approaches Indicators* 1 (Norwegian Ctr. Human Rights 2004).

70 *See Global Responsibilities: Who Must Deliver on Human Rights?* (A. Kuper ed., Routledge 2005).

71 This builds on the framework by the UN Special Rapporteur on how the attainment of the human rights to health can be measured. *See* P. Hunt, *Interim Report of the Special Rapporteur of the Commission on Human Rights on the Right of Everyone to Enjoy the Highest Attainable Standard of Physical and Mental Health,* U.N.G.A., 58th sess. agenda item 117 (c), U.N.G.A., paras. 14–29 (Oct. 10, 2003).

72 In the 1980s, similar concerns began to emerge on how development projects sponsored by the International Bank for Reconstruction and Development (World Bank) were producing negative environmental and social impacts in developing countries. The World Bank responded in September 1993 by establishing the World Bank Inspection Panel to serve as an independent investigative forum through which individuals or communities who believe that they are or are likely to be harmed by a World Bank–funded project to bring their concerns directly before the Board of Executive Directors of the World Bank. The panel has been established to provide people directly and adversely affected by a Bank-financed project with an independent forum through which they can request the Bank to act in accordance with its own policies and procedures. *See* Intl. Bank Reconstruction & Dev., Inspection Panel, *Panel Operating Procedures* (Aug. 19, 1994), http://www.worldbank .org/inspectionpanel.

73 D. Clark, *The Rise and Fall of Accountability,* 6(3) Watershed 52–55 (2001); R. Bisell, *Recent Practice of the Inspection Panel of the World Bank,* 91 Am. J. Intl. L. (1997); D. Bradlow, *The World Bank, the IMF, and Human Rights,* Transnational L. & Contemporary Problems 47–90 (1996);

example of how accountability mechanisms can detect and check the excesses that arise when large-scale infrastructural projects sponsored by developed countries or international development agencies are implemented in developing countries. The WBIP example, if improved upon, could provide a good example of how international organizations, treaty bodies, and development institutions can monitor large-scale projects to ensure transparency, stakeholder participation, accountability, and compliance with international best practices and law.[74]

At the national level, such inspection and review panels may be established within relevant ministries and departments to ensure that projects are being implemented according to approved plans. Such panels would be empowered to receive complaints directly from members of the public and to issue stop orders for projects that threaten the fulfillment of human rights of the public.

Conclusion

Despite growing evidence that large-scale environmental projects, when not appropriately designed, may result in human rights problems, the needs-based approach arguably prevails in the implementation and delivery of many environmental projects. This is an approach that treats human rights as an add-on, or that brings human rights to the table only when a project has come under protest, experienced a problem, or been petitioned. The recent protests challenging the execution of many CDM and REDD+ projects are excellent examples of why this approach is not the way forward. The absence of robust accountability principles that allow the public to play a more active role in the approval of projects, demand reviews of approved CDM projects, and approach the CDMEB to review or block a project has engendered a culture of approval in which projects that negatively affect human rights are still approved by the host-country government and registered by the CDMEB. This chapter has discussed the need for a human rights–based approach that mainstreams robust accountability principles in the design, implementation, and delivery of environmental projects.

D. Clark, *The World Bank and Human Rights: The Need for Greater Accountability* 15 Harv. Human Rights J. 205–26 (2002).

74 E. Carrasco & A. Guernsey, *The World Bank's Inspection Panel: Promoting True Accountability through Arbitration*, 41(3) Cornell Intl. L.J. (2008); A. Ninio, *Environmental Audit in the International Context: The Experience of the World Bank Inspection Panel*, in *Ten Years after Rio 92: Sustainable Development and Law*, Proceedings of the 6th Intl. Conf. on Envtl. L., São Paulo, Brazil (June 2002); L. Boisson de Chazournes, *Compliance with International Standards—The Contribution of the World Bank Inspection Panel*, in *The Inspection Panel of the World Bank: A Different Complaints Procedure* (G. Alfredsson & Rolf Ring eds., Martinus Nijhoff 2001); A. Rigo Sureda, *Process Integrity and Institutional Independence in International Organizations: The Inspection Panel and the Sanctions Committee of the World Bank*, in *International Organizations and International Dispute Settlement* (L. Boisson de Chazournes, Cesare P. R. Romano, & Ruth Mackenzie eds., Transnational 2002); D. Hunter, *Using the World Bank Inspection Panel to Defend the Interests of Project-Affected People*, 4(1) Chi. J. Intl. L. 201–11 (2003).

Accountability frameworks provide the platform for national authorities to demonstrate that the substantive and procedural human rights of the public such as access to information, participation, and access to justice have been considered and that structural conditions ensure that these rights are protected, respected, and fulfilled prior to approval and put in place after approval. Accountability principles also provide reciprocal opportunities that enable the public to demand a review or cessation of projects that produce unanticipated consequences after approval.

Accountability frameworks will focus on providing the structural conditions and processes that allow the public to have a say on what project should be approved or continued, and to call for inspections and reviews of projects to ensure that they are implemented in accord with approved guidelines. Thus, human rights responses and language will not be introduced only when a demand or protest already exists; rather, they will be mainstreamed as part of the project approval process. By carrying stakeholders along in project design, and by providing opportunities for them to demand project reviews and inspections, the room for tensions, protests, and marginalization is reduced, and possibly eliminated. In this way, projects that bring significant environmental benefits and gains will not be hindered by local protests.

6

The Constitutional Regime for Resource Governance in Africa

The Difficult March toward Accountability

FRANCIS N. BOTCHWAY AND NIGHTINGALE RUKUBA-NGAIZA

Given the vital role that natural resources have played in Africa's economic and political history, it is inevitable that natural resources are addressed in the constitutions of many African countries. South Africa, Angola, the Democratic Republic of Congo, Republic of Congo, Ghana, and Nigeria are blessed with resources such as gold, diamonds, oil, gas, fertile soils, and an excellent climate.[1] Libya, Algeria, Chad, and Equatorial Guinea have one particular resource: fossil fuel. Every country on the continent has wildlife, forests, fertile land, fisheries, hard rock minerals, silica, or abundant sunshine that could be tapped for solar energy.

To what extent are these resources regulated by the constitutions and legislation of African countries? How do the constitutional provisions on natural resources provide for accountability and effective public participation in resource transactions and the ensuing benefits? In the face of growing complaints about the inequities of resource contracts, what options do constitutional regimes suggest? This chapter examines these questions and argues that various constitutions embody good faith progressive efforts to provide for meaningful public participation and to hold governments accountable for their stewardship of resources. However, close analysis of these constitutional provisions reveals that the provisions on accountability and resource use are not comprehensive enough, and sometimes their application has not yielded desired results. In this regard, constitutional provisions are not a sufficiently effective basis for meaningful public participation in the oversight of resources or in redressing the consequences of negative resource exploitation and unfair contracting processes.[2]

At the theoretical level, the framework for analyzing the nature and effectiveness of accountability in this regard is based on the explanation provided

---

1 Hlako Choma, *The Impact of Mining Rights on the Local Communities of the Limpopo Province, South Africa: A Comparative Study*, U.S.-China L. Rev. 14–15 (2009); TWN, *Mining, Development, and Social Conflicts in Africa* (TWN 2001).

2 *See* Shelton Davis & Nightingale Rukuba-Ngaiza, *Meaningful Consultations in Environmental Assessment*, http://www-wds.worldbank.org/external/default/WDSContentServer/WDSP/IB/2000/11/17/000094946_00110805370994/Rendered/PDF/multi_page.pdf, which explains the main principles underlying effective public participation.

by Frederick Stapenhurst and Mitchell O'Brien, who identify accountability as "when there is a relationship where an individual or body, and the performance of tasks or functions by that individual or body, are subject to another's oversight, direction or request that they provide information or justification for their actions."[3] Constitutions establish relationships among various bodies and individuals and provide for checks and balances in the administration of the countries. Stapenhurst and O'Brien propose that horizontal accountability deals with the reporting relations between or among state institutions with the possibility of censure or sanctions for poor performance.[4] Accountability "is the capacity of state institutions to check abuses by other public agencies and branches of government, or the requirement for agencies to report sideways."[5] In this chapter, accountability is a process that manifests in rights over land, parliamentary oversight, environmental rights, and stewardship.

Parliaments and other institutions have oversight over natural resource management in African countries. There are also opportunities for judicial redress of grievances against the state or any person in the exercise of the state's powers of eminent domain or compulsory acquisition of property and for the enforcement of environmental rights. These are integral to horizontal accountability.

In this chapter, accountability is applied at two levels: first, at the level of parliamentary or institutional oversight over resource transactions; and second, at the level of governmental stewardship of land and resources in relation to owners and communities. Governmental stewardship extends to environmental protection. At its heart is the social contract between the state and its people vis-à-vis the commercial contract between the state and investors in the natural resource business. The state is entrusted with the oversight of natural resources by law and has responsibility for the general economy and protection of the environment in the interest and for the benefit of the people. To execute this trust, the government invites investors to exploit resources. To what extent do these arrangements reflect the social contract that the state has with its people? If the arrangements do not meet the expectations of the people, what options can be pursued that balance the interests of the investors with those of the people?

---

3 Frederick Stapenhurst & Mitchell O'Brien, *Accountability in Governance* 1 (2005), http://siteresources.worldbank.org/PUBLICSECTORANDGOVERNANCE/Resources/AccountabilityGovernance.pdf; Stefano Migliorisi & Clay Wescott, in *A Review of World Bank Support for Accountability Institutions in the Context of Governance and Anti-corruption* (IEG Working Paper 2011/5, 3, 2011), state that "accountability refers to the process of holding to account, overseeing and keeping in check those persons who are entrusted with public responsibilities in the fulfillment of their tasks or functions."

4 *Id. See* also Nicole Maldonado, *The World Bank's Evolving Concept of Good Governance and Its Impact on Human Rights* 6–7 (paper presented at a workshop on development and international organizations, Stockholm, May 2010).

5 Stapenhurst & O'Brien, *supra* note 3. Although vertical accountability, which involves citizens' direct action through media and other outlets, is relevant, it entails more diffused options, with law playing a less prominent role. This chapter is focused on the constitutional regime for natural resource governance.

In addressing these questions, this chapter analyzes the natural resources constitutional provisions of four African countries: Botswana, Ghana, Kenya, and South Sudan. These countries are very resource dependent and represent the east, west, south, and central/northern parts of Africa. In addition, their respective constitutional evolutions have significant implications for natural resource governance. Botswana has the oldest surviving constitution and South Sudan the youngest constitution in Africa. Ghana's Constitution of 1992 has generated considerable judicial and scholarly jurisprudence, and its natural resource provisions served as a model for the Kenya Constitution.[6] This chapter evaluates these provisions comprehensively; identifies differences, strengths, and weaknesses in their reflection of the spirit and letter of accountability and transparency; and points to their investment or transactional ramifications.

Constitutional Provisions That Relate to Natural Resources

Constitutional provisions on natural resources can be categorized into four main groups:

- Provisions that are found in human rights chapters or sections of constitutions, particularly the right to property and public taking, or eminent domain
- Provisions that directly and specifically relate to institutional control and transparency in the allocation of resources
- Provisions that relate to environmental protection
- Miscellaneous constitutional sources that form the basis of resource legislation, enforcement, and expression

The key elements under miscellaneous provisions are those that place the government in the position of trustee for the management of natural resources and those that evince a range of international obligations including resource management.

These four themes express the *problematiques* involved in development delivery, accountability, voice, and social contract. For example, provisions on the right to property place the government as the guarantor of those rights yet at the same time give the government limited powers to take land or property for public purposes. In return, the public through the government compensates the original owner. This is a key element of the social contract between the state and its people. The accountability, transparency, and participation ethos are reflected in the parliamentary or institutional oversight over resource transactions.

---

6 Charles Odidi Okidi, *How Constitutional Entrenchment Could Mitigate Conflicts and Poverty in Resource-Rich African Countries*, 37(2–3) Envtl. Policy and L. 167–69 (2007).

Right to Property and the Public Domain

At independence, many African countries did not include natural resource provisions in their constitutions. The exceptions to this are Zimbabwe, Namibia, South Africa, and South Sudan. In these countries, the struggle for independence involved a significant fight over natural resources (e.g., Namibia over Walvis Bay and South Sudan over Abeyie and the oil pipelines through Sudan). These constitutions assembled analogous provisions such as human rights, in particular the right to property, and applied the concepts to natural resources.[7] All African constitutions have provisions regarding land and property rights. The Constitution of Botswana, one of the few constitutions in Africa enacted at independence (in 1966) and still in force, provides that "no property of any description shall be compulsorily taken possession of, and no interest in or right over property of any description shall be compulsorily acquired."[8] This is a classic element of many African constitutions and is intended to protect property taken or acquired from indigenous peoples. It also reflects some of the values of the departing colonial authorities.[9]

Chapter 2 of the Botswana Constitution, particularly Articles 3(c), 8, and 9, can be interpreted as the constitutional foundation for the regulation of that country's natural resources. Article 3(c) describes the protection of fundamental rights and freedoms of the individual to include the "protection of the privacy of . . . home and other property and from deprivation of property without compensation." This right is subject to the rights of others or the public interest. This principle is fleshed out in Articles 8 and 9, which constitute the direct source of regulation of natural resources in Botswana. Article 8(1) provides:

> No property of any description shall be compulsorily taken possession of, and no interest in or right over property of any description shall be compulsorily acquired, except where the following conditions are satisfied, that is to say (a) the taking of possession or acquisition is necessary or expedient (i) in the interests of defence, public safety, public order, public morality, public health, town and coun-

---

7 The human rights provisions in many former British colonies were more at the insistence of the new African governments than the departing British colonial authorities. *See* Geoffrey Bing, *Reap the Whirlwind* (MacGibbon & Kee 1968). British legal academics and colonialists did not believe that it was important to have human rights provisions in a constitution. Jeremy Bentham considered it the old desire of ruling over posterity and dismissed it as "nonsense upon stilts." *See The Works of Jeremy Bentham* vol. 2, 489–529 (John Bowring ed., Tait 1843). *See* also Joseph Jaconelli, *Enacting a Bill of Rights* 12–13 (Clarendon 1980). The exceptions such as in Kenya; South Africa; and Hong Kong SAR, China were to protect the European minority in the former colonies. *See* Wai Lun Max Wong, *Re-ordering Hong Kong: De-colonization and the Hong Kong Bill of Rights Ordinance* (unpublished Ph.D. thesis, School of Oriental & African Stud. 2005).

8 Constitution of Botswana, art. 8(1).

9 The United Kingdom held the view that rights need not be codified. This is a reflection of the common law position that what is not prohibited by law is permitted. The only time there is a deviation from this position is when rights are needed to protect the European minority in the independent African or Asian country or to shore up social stability. *See* A. V. Dicey, *Introduction to the Study of the Law of the Constitution* 199 (10th ed., St. Martin's 1959).

> try planning or land settlement; (ii) in order to secure the development or utilization of that, or other, property for a purpose beneficial to the community; or (iii) *in order to secure the development or utilization of the mineral resources of Botswana and* (b) provision is made by a law applicable to that taking of possession or acquisition (i) for the prompt payment of adequate compensation; and (ii) securing to any person having an interest in or right over the property a right of access to the High Court, either direct or on appeal from any other authority, for the determination of his interest or right, the legality of the taking of possession or acquisition of the property, interest or right, and the amount of any compensation to which he is entitled, and for the purpose of obtaining prompt payment of that compensation. (emphasis added)

Botswana's economy is largely dependent on diamonds and other natural resources.[10] The country is one of the few in the world, and the only one in Sub-Saharan Africa, that has managed its resources for its peoples' benefit.[11] Surprisingly, Article 8(1) is the first and most articulate provision in its constitution relating to natural resources. Interestingly, at independence, the country had no known natural resource of contemporary significance. Diamonds were discovered in commercial quantities a year after independence, in 1967, and this resource has formed the fulcrum of the country's development.[12] Given the association of Africa with natural resources, the constitution envisaged the exploration and development of natural resources in circumstances where private property rights might be infringed on or would have an impact. The constitution thus permits the compulsory acquisition of property "*in order to secure the development or utilization of mineral resources*" (emphasis added).

A closely related provision is Article 9, on the protection of privacy of home and other property. However, Article 9(1) covers laws that provide for the violation of the privacy of home and other property where such property is "reasonably required in the interests of defence, public safety, public order, public morality, public health, town and country planning, *the development and utilization of mineral resources, . . . in order to secure the development or utilization of any property for a purpose beneficial to the community*" (emphasis added). In compliance with the Hull doctrine of expropriation,[13] the Botswana Constitution

---

10 *See* African Development Bank, *Botswana: 2009–13* (Country Strategy Paper 2009), http://www.afdb.org/fileadmin/uploads/afdb/Documents/Project-and-Operations/BOTSWANA_2009%20%E2%80%93%202013%20COUNTRY%20STRATEGY%20PAPER.pdf.

11 *Id.*

12 *See* Rhuks Ako & Nilopar Uddin, *Good Governance and Resource Management in Africa*, in *Natural Resource Investment and Africa's Development* 35 (F. Botchway ed., Edward Elgar 2011).

13 The Hull doctrine calls for the prompt payment of adequate compensation for the expropriation of property. Although compensation is accepted practice, the Hull standard of prompt, effective, and adequate compensation is not a generally accepted standard. *See* Frank Dawson & Burns H. Weston, *Prompt, Adequate, and Effective: A Universal Standard of Compensation?*, 30 Fordham L. Rev. 736–37 (1961–62). *See* also Adeoye Akinsanya, *International Protection of Direct Foreign Investments in the Third World*, 36 Intl. & Comp. L. Q. 60 (1987); Ian Brownlie, *Principles of Public International Law* 543–44 (7th ed., Oxford U. Press 2008).

provides for the prompt payment of adequate compensation for any compulsory acquisition. To ensure that the legal process is followed and the government is held accountable for the cost of the acquisition or expropriation, the judicial process is available for aggrieved interest holders and claimants to ventilate their concerns.[14] In many ways, this provision is targeted more at nonnative owners of land or resources than at native owners.[15] The provision emanates from Western notions of property rights and compensation for nationalization of property claimed by Western interests.[16] And the subsequent subsection provides:

> [N]o person who is entitled to compensation under this section shall be prevented from remitting, within a reasonable time after he has received any amount of that compensation, the whole of that amount (free from any deduction, charge or tax . . .) to any country of his choice outside Botswana.[17]

Such provisions were aimed at protecting the interests of the European minority in the decolonizing country.[18]

Although the judicial process offers a way to ensure some level of accountability and gives voice to aggrieved stakeholders to contest an acquisition, it does not remove opacity in the allocation of exploration and production rights for natural resources. Admittedly, the right to question the legality of the taking of the property for mineral development opens a window into the acquisition of the property.[19] However, the right to question that legality is conferred only on a person with interest or right to the property in question.[20] It is possible that the "community benefit" clause in Articles 9 and 18 can be interpreted to provide *locus standi,* or standing to the community affected by the taking or acquisition to voice its grievance and to challenge the legality of

---

14 Constitution of Botswana, art. 8(1)b, ii.

15 *See* Wong, *supra* note 7.

16 *See Amodu Tijani v. Secretary to the Govt. of Southern Nigeria* (1921) 2 AC 403, and *Oyekana v. Adele* (1957) 2 All ER 789–90.

17 Botswana Constitution, art. 9(2).

18 *See* Wong, Jaconelli, Bentham, Dicey, *supra* notes 7 and 9, on the British colonial view of human rights.

19 Constitution of Botswana, art. 9.

20 *Id.*, at art. 18, which is a general protective provision, formulated in a way that limits the right of redress in court to a person with interest in the subject matter. Article 18(1) states that "if any person alleges that any of the provisions of sections 3–16 of this constitution has been or is being or is likely to be contravened *in relation to him*" (emphasis added). This is very different from art. 2(1) in the Ghana Constitution of 1992, which provides, "A person who alleges that (a) an enactment or anything contained in or done, under the authority of that or any other enactment; or (b) any act or omission of any person; is inconsistent with, or is in contravention of a provision of this Constitution, may bring an action in the Supreme Court for a declaration to that effect." The Kenya Constitution also removes any conditions or qualifications for a person seeking to enforce the constitutional provisions on property and environmental rights. *See* Constitution of Kenya, arts. 22 and 70.

the acquisition.[21] However, not only would such a party have to prove that he or she is a member of the community affected, but he or she also could be required to prove that his or her property interest is affected.[22]

Many of the more recent African constitutions make provisions for property rights. They also provide for transparency in the administration of the country's natural resources. Chapter 5 of the 1992 Constitution of Ghana makes comprehensive provisions for the protection of human rights and for the purposes of this work property. Article 20 is an expanded version of a similar provision in the Botswana Constitution; it provides that "no property of any description, or interest in or right over any property, shall be compulsorily taken possession of or acquired by the State unless the following conditions are satisfied." It then lists the circumstances under which an acquisition is permissible.[23] The conditions are not very different from those in the Botswana Constitution, except that there is no explicit reference to "mineral resources." However, the fact that the provision covers property of any description means it includes natural resources. An additional difference is that the Ghana Constitution mandates that property so acquired must be used in the public interest, and, if the original public purpose or interest for which it was acquired changes, the previous owner should be given first refusal priority to retake the property.[24] This novel provision enhances the accountability ethic of the constitution by ensuring that the state will not take property in the name of the public and then transfer it to private interests, including mining.

The Kenya Constitution of 2010 is one of the newest constitutions on the continent. It is much more comprehensive and covers wide-ranging subjects, unlike many others. As do other constitutions, it includes significant provisions on land and property rights. Every citizen of Kenya has the right, individually or in groups, including citizen-owned corporate entities, to acquire or own property of any description anywhere in the country.[25] Noncitizens are limited to maximum leasehold interest of 99 years.[26] Parliament is prohibited

---

21 In *Attorney General v. Unity Dow*, [1992] LRC (Cons) 623, the Court of Appeal, per its president, A. N. E Amissah, held that Article 18 is broad enough to allow standing to a woman who challenged the constitutionality of the citizenship law. Amissah stated that the constitutional provision granting standing could not be whittled away by common law, Roman-Dutch law, or any other law.

22 *Id.* In the *Unity Dow* case, Justice Amissah ruled that the woman applicant had suffered injury personally because the citizenship of her children was adversely affected by the Citizenship Act. *See* Bonine, *infra* note 60, at 253–54.

23 The conditions all revolve around the public interest. They are "(a) the taking of possession or acquisition is necessary in the interest of defence, public safety, public order, public morality, public health, town and country planning or the development or utilization of property in such a manner as to promote the public benefit. (b) the necessity for the acquisition is clearly stated and is such as to provide reasonable justification for causing any hardship that may result to any person who has an interest in or right over the property."

24 Constitution of Ghana, art. 20(5), (6).

25 Constitution of Kenya, art. 40.

26 *Id.*, at art. 65.

from enacting laws that allow the state or any person "to arbitrarily deprive a person of property of any description or of any interest in, or right over, any property of any description."[27] The state cannot take property from any person except for public purposes in accordance with the constitution and following due process of law. The process must include prompt payment of just compensation, and the judicial process is open to aggrieved persons to seek redress.[28]

The power and capacity of the state to take land for natural resource development and the giving of voice to stakeholders to question the process is interesting. Apart from the broad public purpose exception to compulsory acquisition, two exceptions relating to natural resources exist in the Kenya Constitution. The first is Article 42, regarding the right of every person to a clean and healthy environment, with the right to protect the environment for present and future generations. Whereas Article 42, like Article 36(9) in the Ghana Constitution, is vague and hardly justiciable, Chapter 5, Part 2, of the Kenya Constitution is comprehensive and effective. The capacity for compulsory acquisition is vested only in the state and in no other entity or person.[29] This is important in view of the dealings of property and natural resources.[30] In Ghana, the Minerals and Mining Act vests all mineral resources in their natural state in the president in trust for the people.[31] However, land is owned by stools or communities, families, private persons, and, to a limited extent, the state.[32] A private person who wants to exploit mineral resources needs a mineral license from the state and land tenure from the landowner. Yet, the law states that "where the Minister grants a mineral right, the Minister shall determine the land subject to the grant."[33] This can be interpreted as effectively expropriating private land for the purposes of a private company's exploitation of the mineral resource. The Kenya provisions follow a similar vein. The state may acquire land in the public interest and then allow a private company to exploit it for profit.

---

27 *Id.*, at art. 40(2).

28 *Id.*, at art. 40(3).

29 *Id.*, at art. 40(3), "the state shall not deprive a person of property of any description, or of any interest in, or right over, property of any description," and compare it with Article 40(1): "subject to article 65, every person has the right, either individually or in association with others, to acquire and own property."

30 Compare art. 40(2) with arts. 40(3) and 69. *See* also *Kelo v. The City of New London*, 545 US 469 (2005); Rhuks Ako, *Nigeria's Land Use Act: An Antithesis in Environmental Justice*, 53 J. African L. 294–304 (2009).

31 *See* Minerals and Mining Act of 2006, sec. 1.

32 The "stool" or "skin" is the shrine that embodies the soul and spirit of the family, community, or nation. It is also the symbol of the legality or accreditation of the chief or head of family or community. *See* Nii Amaah Ollenu, *Principles of Customary Land Law in Ghana* 6 (Sweet & Maxwell 1962). The stool is also regarded in Ghanaian jurisprudence as an artificial person, as in the case of business companies. In Ghanaian parlance, the stool is a traditional chair mainly made of wood. *See* Gordon Woodman, *Customary Land Law in Ghanaian Courts* (Ghana U. Press 1996); Gordon Woodman, *Ollenu's Principles of Customary Land Law in Ghana* (Carl Press 1985).

33 Minerals and Mining Act of 2006, secs. 5(2), 2.

The South Sudan constitutional provisions on natural resources include land rights, parliamentary or institutional involvement and accountability, environmental protection, and miscellaneous. Yet, as far as land rights are concerned, the South Sudan Constitution is quite different from those of Botswana, Kenya, and Ghana. Land is categorized into public, community, and private interests or ownership.[34]

Although the Kenya Constitution has a somewhat similar categorization of land,[35] Botswana and Ghana have the categorization in legislation rather than in their constitutions.[36] Public land is land owned or held by any level of government and includes all land that is not deemed community or private land. In South Sudan, community land is land traditionally held or used historically by local communities or their members. Private land is privately registered leasehold or land acquired from the government or community under a lease for social and economic development. Every person has the right to acquire or own property as prescribed by law. The South Sudan Constitution boldly proclaims that "[n]o private property may be expropriated save by law in the public interest and in consideration for prompt and fair compensation. No private property shall be confiscated save by an order of a court of law."[37]

Unlike the constitutions of Ghana and Kenya, the South Sudan Constitution does not discriminate in terms of who can own land. Nationals, foreigners, and corporate entities are all accorded the same status. Unlike in the Kenya Constitution, there is no distinction between direct state acquisition and acquisition by means of legislation. Note, however, that there is a distinction between expropriation by legislation and confiscation by court order.

Because South Sudan is a federal state, individual states are accorded powers identical to those of the federal government, including expropriation of land; in case of a contradiction between a state's laws and the federal constitution, the federal constitution prevails. In view of the constitution's emphasis on foreign investors and private business,[38] the state can be an agent of private companies by acquiring land in the public interest and transferring it to private companies for resource exploitation.

Parliamentary or Institutional Oversight and Accountability

Beyond property rights, the constitutions of Ghana, Kenya, and South Sudan make direct and express provisions for accountability and transparency in the administration of natural resources. There are two cardinal provisions on

---

34 Constitution of South Sudan, art. 170(2).

35 *See* Constitution of Kenya, art. 61.

36 In Ghana, e.g., the State Lands Act of 1962 covers state ownership, and the Administration of Lands Act of 1962 covers stool or community land.

37 Constitution of South Sudan, art. 28(2).

38 *Id.*, at art. 37, 168(2), 170(6)b.

resources in the Ghana Constitution. Article 268, Clause 1, provides for parliamentary ratification of any legal agreement on resource exploitation:

> Any transaction, contract or undertaking involving the grant of a right or concession by or on behalf of *any person* including the Government of Ghana, to any other person or body of persons howsoever described, for the exploitation of any mineral, water, or other natural resource of Ghana made or entered into after the coming into force of this Constitution shall be subject to ratification by Parliament. (emphasis added)

This is the most far-reaching provision on natural resources in any African constitution. It is broad enough to cover any conceivable natural resource, including genetic and solar resources. The purpose of this provision is to prevent a return to the situation in the chaotic colonial period when chiefs granted concessions to foreign companies for virtually nothing in return,[39] hence the "any person" formulation. More important, this provision ensures transparency in the granting of concessions and resource transactions, because the people's representatives may vet and approve the transactions. Despite this bold proclamation, the constitution derogates from the rigor of Article 268(1) by permitting Parliament to grant exemptions from the application of Clause 1.[40] Article 269(2) allows Parliament to cede the right of approval to a governmental agency. Thus, agencies are susceptible to regulatory capture that may not serve the interests of the people. Besides, if parties have to await parliamentary delegation of the approval function on each occasion, and if the procedures of the committee or council are not transparent and scientific, the cost of transacting natural resource business may increase.

One might argue that Article 268(1) is not strong enough on accountability. It involves Parliament only at the final stage of the transaction, when Parliament ratifies a transaction or undertaking already executed by the executive or any other person.[41] Even then, the constitution does not prescribe the method of ratification.[42] This is exacerbated by the fact that there is no strict separation of powers under the Ghana Constitution. The majority of cabinet

---

39 *See* Muna Ndulo, *Mining Rights in Zambia* (Kenneth Kaunda Foundation 1987); Paul Rosenblum, *The Gold Mining Industry in Ghana, 1874–1910* (unpublished Ph.D. thesis, Columbia U. 1972); C. W. Newberry, *British Policy towards Africa: Select Documents, 1875–1914* 583–95 (Clarendon 1971).

40 *See* Okidi, *supra* note 6.

41 *Id.*

42 Recently, the minister for mines said that parliamentary approval of resource transactions was not required. *See Minister Defends Legality of Newmont's Akyem Concession*, http://myjoyonline.com/business/2013/November-15th/minister-defends-legality-of-newmonts-akyem-concession.php?cmtx_sort=2?email=1.

ministers are also members of Parliament,[43] which explains why the Parliament of Ghana has routinely ratified resource deals.[44]

The weaknesses in Article 268 may be ameliorated by Article 181(5), which engages Parliament at an earlier stage of the process. Article 181 in general is about Parliament's role in the contraction of loans by the state. Parliament, by a majority resolution, authorizes the government to enter into agreements for the granting of a loan.[45] An agreement reached on the basis of parliamentary authorization is then forwarded to Parliament for approval.[46] Clause 5 provides that Article 181 "shall, with the necessary modifications by Parliament, apply to an international business or economic transaction to which the Government is a party as it applies to a loan."[47] This clause has proved very controversial given the issues it raises, including whether it applies to all international business transactions entered into by the government, and the consequences of a breach. If it does apply to all international business transactions, the machinery of government will grind to a halt—even the purchase of a foreign airline ticket by a government official would need parliamentary approval. The Supreme Court of Ghana described this situation as reductio ad absurdum in the Balkan Energy case.[48] If Article 181 does not apply to all international business transactions, then which transactions are subject to parliamentary approval? The provision calls on Parliament to prescribe necessary modifications by way of legislation. The Supreme Court has called on Parliament to perform this mandatory task, which Parliament has so far failed to perform. The Supreme Court requested the Attorney General to categorize international business transactions involving the government into major and minor categories, with transactions in the major category requiring parliamentary approval.[49] This request is unconstitutional, however, because it is not the duty of the Attorney General, who is a member of the executive branch of government, to implement the particular constitutional mandate. However, it is within the province of the legislature to effect the necessary modifications that will make the provision applicable to natural resource transactions.

In five cases that turned on the interpretation and enforcement of Article 181(5), the Supreme Court of Ghana has given some guidance on the

---

43 *See* Constitution of Ghana, art. 78.

44 For the comparative effectiveness of parliamentary committees in exercising oversight and accountability, *see* Ricardo Pelizzo & Frederick Stapenhurst, *Government Accountability and Legislative Oversight* (Routledge 2014).

45 Constitution of Ghana, art. 181(1).

46 *Id.*, at art. 181(2).

47 The "necessary modifications" is intended to be legislation on government contracting loans, which must be modified to apply to international business transactions.

48 *A.G. v. Balkan Energy Gh. Ltd.* (May 16, 2012).

49 *Id.*

applicability and/or reach of the provision.[50] The counterparty to the transaction with the government need not be a foreign company; it is enough if the transaction is denominated in foreign currency, the directors and key officers of the company are foreign nationals, or key elements of the transaction have substantial foreign components.[51] Agencies of the government are considered separate from the government and therefore not within the purview of Article 181(5), although if it is established that the government is using an agency as an alter ego in order to circumvent or avoid the rigors of the constitutional provision, the transaction will be stopped from the possible violation of the constitution.[52] The difficulty with Article 181(5) and its interpretation by the Ghana Supreme Court is that the article is largely ignored by international arbitral tribunals. In two cases before an International Chamber of Commerce tribunal and the Permanent Court of Arbitration tribunal (both cases featuring Stephen Schwebel as arbitrator),[53] the tribunals argued that Ghana cannot use its domestic constitutional requirements to obviate its contractual obligations.[54] The international regime therefore appears to have put breaks on the accountability provisions in the domestic legal system. It is difficult to argue, however, that the government should benefit from its own failure to seek and obtain the approval of Parliament for the international business transactions that it enters into. It will be interesting to see how similar provisions in other African constitutions will work.

The Kenya Constitution of 2010 is one of the most comprehensive on the continent. Similar to the Ghana Constitution, it provides that "a transaction is subject to ratification by Parliament if it (a) involves the grant of a right or concession by or on behalf of any person, including the national government, to another person for the exploitation of any natural resource of Kenya."[55] This provision makes any transaction regarding natural resources subject to parliamentary ratification. The article does not necessarily mandate parliamentary involvement in negotiations and other processes leading to the conclusion of a deal. It provides for Parliament to enact legislation providing for the classes of transactions that are subject to ratification.[56] This clause derogates from the rigor of the transparency ethos of the constitution and good governance because the spirit of the clause is to hold dealers in resource transactions to account to Parliament, the peoples' representatives. For the constitution to allow that sacred responsibility to be delegated to a governmental agency

---

50 *A.G. v. Faroe Atlantic Co. Ltd.* [2005–6] SCGLR 271; *A.G. v. Balkan Energy Gh. Ltd.* (May 16, 2012); *Amidu v. A.G., Westville and Others* (June 14, 2013); *Amidu v. A.G., ISOFOTON Ltd., and Others* (June 21, 2013); *African Automobile v. A.G* (June 6, 2012).

51 *A.G. v. Balkan Energy Gh. Ltd* (May 16, 2012).

52 *Felix Klomega v. A.G., GPHA, and Others* (July 9, 2013).

53 http://globalarbitrationreview.com/news/article/32551/panel-rejects-bulk-ghana-power-claim/; http://globalarbitrationreview.com/news/article/32613/hague-panel-rules-against-ghana/.

54 *Id.*

55 Constitution of Kenya, art. 71(1).

56 *Id.*, art. 71(2).

denies the people, through their representatives, voice in resource transactions. This is worsened by the fact that there is no provision in the Kenya Constitution for prior notification of steps toward the granting of concessions. In addition, the provision is limited to natural resources and does not apply to broader "international business transactions" as does Article 181(5) of the Ghana Constitution.

Yet the Kenya Constitution has other provisions that express the trustee status of the state and can be articulated as a basis for the advancement of the transparency of natural resource management. Under Chapter 5, Part 2, far-reaching provisions are made for the protection of the environment and sustainable development. The state is mandated to "ensure sustainable exploitation, utilization, management and conservation of the environment and natural resources, and ensure the equitable sharing of accruing benefits."[57] The constitution requires the state not only to encourage public participation in the management of the environment and to establish environmental impact assessment and audit systems, but also to "utilize the environment and natural resources for the benefit of the people of Kenya."[58] These provisions, which are absent from the Ghana, Botswana, and many other African constitutions, can be used to ask for a comprehensive assessment of any natural resource venture by virtually anybody in Kenya and, if deficiencies are found, to stop the undertaking altogether. Article 70 of the constitution confers the right to judicial redress to any person who alleges that his or her right to a clean and healthy environment is being or is likely to be violated or threatened.[59] An applicant for judicial redress does not have to demonstrate or show that he or any person has incurred loss or suffered injury. This overcomes standing challenges in the English and American legal systems.[60]

The newest African constitution appears to have made significant strides in the area of institutional oversight and accountability for resource exploitation. Unlike the Ghana and Kenya constitutions, the South Sudan Constitution

57 *Id.*, at art. 69(1)a.

58 *Id.*, at art. 69(1)h.

59 Article 70 states, "If a person alleges that a right to a clean and healthy environment recognized and protected under article 42 has been, is being or is likely to be, denied, violated, infringed or threatened, the person may apply to a court for redress in addition to any other legal remedies that are available in respect to the same matter." Article 70, Clause 3 reinforces its justiciability and standing to bring an action by providing that "for the purposes of this Article, an applicant does not have to demonstrate that any person has incurred loss or suffered injury."

60 *See Ex parte Rose Theatre Trust*, [1990] 1 ALL ER 754; *Ex parte Greenpeace*, [1994] ALL ER 329; *Ex parte World Development*, [1995] WLR 386; *Lujan v. Defenders of Wildlife*, 504 U.S. 555 (1992); *Sierra Club v. Morton* 405 U.S. 727, 92 S. Ct. 1361 (1972); *Summers v. Earth Island Institute*, 552 U.S., 128 S. Ct. 1118 (2008). *See* also Tumai Murombo, *Strengthening Locus Standi in Public Interest Litigation: Has Leadership Moved from the United States to South Africa?* LEAD J. 165–78 (2010); John Bonine, *Broadening Standing to Sue for Citizen Enforcement*, Proceedings of the Fifth International Conference on Environmental Compliance and Enforcement 249–60 (Monterey 1999), http://www.inece.org/5thvol2/bonine.pdf.

does not make room for direct parliamentary approval of natural resource contracts.[61] Instead, the constitution establishes a body—the National Petroleum and Gas Council, or the Oil and Gas Council—not very independent of the legislature and the executive arms of the government to, inter alia, make policies for petroleum and gas, monitor and assess the policies, and approve strategies for the oil and gas sector.[62] Its most important function, for the purpose of this chapter, is to "approve all oil contracts for the exploration and development of oil and ensure that they are consistent with its principles, policies and guidelines," as well as to "review environmental and social impact of existing and future oil developments."[63] Whereas the approval of oil and gas contracts applies to future transactions, the review of the environmental and social impact of existing projects could lead to a retrospective taking or diminution of the rights of the developers. More than that, this relatively small body is highly susceptible to capture by interest groups.

In terms of transparency, it is debatable whether this council is better suited than the Parliament for overseeing resource management. The council is made up of representatives of oil- and gas-producing regions and institutions. This is a bid to ensure that those who will most directly feel the impact of the exploitation of natural resources are involved in decisions regarding the resource exploitation and revenue distribution. This is a lesson learned from countries such as Nigeria and Angola. However, the independence of the council is compromised by the membership of "relevant national ministers" and the national government in the same capacity, and with the same rights as the representatives of the oil-producing states.[64] The representation and work of the council "shall be as regulated by law" and "in accordance with the law."[65] There is no prescription as to the number of ministers and representatives of the national government who will be on the council. The law that will regulate the membership and work of the council is made by Parliament. Although this is an indirect way to involve the peoples' representatives in the management of resources,[66] it severely compromises the independence of the council.

The delegation of such a crucial part of the country's national heritage to a quasi-governmental institution is laden with potential dangerous consequences.[67] First, the institution is more amenable to capture by powerful interest groups, as has been seen in the Minerals Commission of Ghana and

---

61 The minister for petroleum and gas, as in the case of all the ministers, can be summoned to Parliament to answer questions.

62 Constitution of South Sudan, art. 173.

63 *Id.*, at arts. 173(5)d, 173(5)e.

64 *See id.*, at art. 173.

65 *Id.*

66 Apart from arts. 57(f) and (g), which empower Parliament to call a minister to account for his or her stewardship of the ministry.

67 Compare Article 171(1), on the establishment of an "independent" lands commission, with Article 173, where the word "independent" is conspicuously absent.

elsewhere.[68] This is compounded by the lack of clear prescription for the open and transparent work of the council. There is no prescription for input by nongovernmental independent bodies and no prescription as to its legal standing. The Oil and Gas Council is accountable only to the council of ministers. The one mitigating factor is that the principles stated in the constitution regarding resources must be adhered to in any legislation relating to the work of the Oil and Gas Council.[69] Even then, the functions of the Oil and Gas Council appears to conflict with the powers of the ministry.[70] For example, although the Oil and Gas Council is assigned the role of policy formulation and the ministry is a policy-implementing institution, Article 174(2) confers on the ministry the power to negotiate all petroleum contracts and also initiate legislation and other rules on oil and gas. These must be consistent with the ministry's (not the council's) policies, principles, and guidelines. It is unclear how the two government bodies will coordinate their efforts efficaciously. Although the South Sudan Constitution goes much further than any other African constitution in incorporating resource management provisions, it falls short of incorporating into these provisions adequate safeguards on transparency, accountability, and space for institutional growth.

Environmental Provisions and Resource Regulation

One area where African constitutions appear to have made significant strides is in the articulation of provisions for the protection of the environment. This is where the social contract between the state and the people is most evident. Almost all the constitutions under discussion profess their commitment to protecting the environment for the present generation and posterity. They go beyond intergenerational equity to give voice for judicial redress for environmental damage. Admittedly, older constitutions, such as that of Botswana, do not incorporate environmental provisions in a direct way because of the lower level of environmental consciousness when they were written. Starting with the Ghana Constitution of 1992, there has been a progressive growth in the nature, content, and application of provisions relating to the environment. Article 36, Clause 9, of the Ghana Constitution states that "the State shall take appropriate measures needed to protect and safeguard the national environment for posterity; and shall seek co-operation with other states and bodies for purposes of protecting the wider international environment for mankind."[71] This is a general provision on the environment that is not specifically linked to resource exploitation. Although it mandates the state to act, it minimizes that

---

68 *See* Francis Botchway, *Privatisation and State Control: The Case of Ashanti Goldfields Company*, 22(3) J. En. & Nat. Resources L. 201 (2004). *See* also *Minister Defends Legality of Newmont's Akyem Concession, supra* note 42.

69 Constitution of South Sudan, arts. 172, 68, 37.

70 *See id.*, at arts. 173 and 174.

71 Article 41(k) requires every citizen of Ghana "to protect and safeguard the environment." This is even more vague than Article 36(9), which requires state action.

mandate by asking for "appropriate measures" necessary. Chapter 6, where the environmental clauses are located, is titled "Directive Principles of State Policy" and is crafted in ways that do not make the provisions immediately justiciable; there are no definitive ways to enforce them. In the case of *Ghana Lotto Operators Association v. National Lotteries*,[72] the Supreme Court held that there is a presumption of justiciability for all the constitutional provisions, including Chapter 6. Although this is a progressive step toward environmental accountability, it vests the discretion of presumption in the judiciary, which can be engaged only ex post facto environmental damage. One way that constitutional provisions on the environment can be utilized, however, is to read them with Article 33, Clause 5, which allows for rights not specifically mentioned in the fundamental human rights chapter, which entitles an aggrieved person to seek redress in the High Court.

The Kenya Constitution removes the ambiguity and doubts regarding environmental accountability by providing that "every person has the right to a clean and healthy environment."[73] The constitution makes this right enforceable and justiciable by providing in Article 70 that

> if a person alleges that a right to a clean and healthy environment recognized and protected under Article 42 has been, is being or is likely to be, denied, violated, infringed or threatened, the person may apply to a court for redress in addition to any other legal remedies that are available in respect of the same matter.

The court is empowered to "make any order, or give any directions, it considers appropriate" in the circumstances. The remedies may range from an injunction against the act complained of, or against public officers compelling them to discontinue the offending act or omission, and where necessary, to provide compensation to the victim of the violation of the right to a clean and healthy environment. To avoid any doubts as to the claimant's standing or capacity to bring the necessary action to ventilate the environmental right, the constitution protects the interests of such claimants by stating that "*an applicant does not have to demonstrate that*" he or she or "any person has incurred loss or suffered injury" (emphasis added).[74] "Any person" clearly includes the claimant himself or herself. He or she does not need to prove injury or loss in order to proceed with the action. Notably, where the Kenya Constitution states "principles" of state policy regarding the environment, it specifies numbers and/or details. For example, under Article 69, the state is obligated to work to achieve and maintain tree cover of at least 10 percent of the land area of Kenya.[75] Such provisions function as transparency and accountability

---

72 *Supreme Court of Ghana Law Rep* (2007–08), at 1106.

73 Constitution of Kenya, art. 42.

74 *Id.*, at art. 70(3).

75 In 2014, the forest covered 6 percent of Kenya. *See* http://data.worldbank.org/indicator/AG.LND.FRST.ZS. At independence, the forest covered more than 40 percent of the land surface of Ghana. Today, the forest cover is less than 10 percent. This is due mainly to surface mining or land stripping, wood fuel harvest, and farming. *See* FAO Report, http://www.fao

safeguards with respect to the state's efforts to conserve and protect the environment and are relatively more justiciable and/or legally enforceable.

The environmental provisions in the Kenya Constitution are very important to the natural resources sector because there is no resource exploitation without environmental consequences. The two are inextricably connected. Companies involved in resource exploitation must comply with the environmental provisions in the constitution and will be held accountable by way of suits and other actions if their actions affect the environment in an unsustainable manner. The rights enunciated in the constitution are both vertical and horizontal. The state has obligations, and private interests also have obligations that can be challenged inter se. An interesting question with respect to this is what will happen if Parliament approves a resource exploitation agreement that a private third party believes violates the right to a clean and healthy environment? It also remains to be seen whether the laws that will be passed by Parliament based on the constitution will be faithful to the spirit and letter of the accountability provisions in the constitution.

As far as constitutional provisions on the environment are concerned, it appears that South Sudan has taken a backward step. As with the Ghana Constitution, the provisions on the environment in the South Sudan Constitution are found in the chapter on objectives and guiding principles of state policy. Under Article 37(2), all levels of the South Sudan government shall "protect and ensure the sustainable management and utilization of natural resources including land, water, petroleum, minerals, fauna and flora for the benefit of the people." Apart from its anthropocentric focus, this provision is quite vague and not sufficiently prescriptive. Article 41 is comparatively a much clearer provision on the environment than Article 37(2). It mandates that "every person or community shall have the right to a clean and healthy environment." This is very similar to the Kenya provision on environmental rights. The difference is the inclusion of "community" in the South Sudan provision. This provision is somewhat strengthened by Article 41, Clause 2, which states that "every person shall have the obligation to protect the environment for the benefit of present and future generations."[76] However, the right and obligation in the previous clauses are weakened by Clause 3, which qualifies the right and obligation with "appropriate legislative action and other measures." The discretion embedded in appropriate legislative action is enhanced by Clause 4, which mandates that all levels of government promote

---

.org/forestry/12961-0e814dc5074e2841d89a76153d5897732.gif; and http://www.theguardian.com/environment/datablog/2009/sep/02/total-forest-area-by-country. *See* also Hlako Choma, *The Impact of Mining Rights on the Local Communities of the Limpopo Province, South Africa: A Comparative Study*, 6(2) U.S.-China L. Rev. 14–15 (2009).

76 Article 41 states: (1) "Every person or community shall have the right to a clean and healthy environment. (2) Every person shall have the obligation to protect the environment for the benefit of present and future generations. (3) Every person shall have the right to have the environment protected for the benefit of present and future generations, through appropriate legislative action and other measures." *See* also Article 46(h), which obligates every citizen to protect the environment and conserve natural resources.

energy policies that will ensure that the basic needs of the people are met while protecting and preserving the environment. These ambiguities would not be so bad if Article 44 of the constitution did not boldly proclaim:

> Unless this Constitution otherwise provides or a duly enacted law guarantees, the rights and liberties described and the provisions contained in this chapter are *not by themselves enforceable in a court of law*; however, the principles expressed herein are basic to governance and the state shall by guided by them, especially in making policies and laws. (emphasis added)

In many African constitutions, the location of environmental provisions in the preamble and/or in the directive principles of state policy is enough to ensure their nonjusticiability. The South Sudan Constitution makes it clear that environmental rights and obligations are not justiciable.[77] This is an unfortunate step backward in light of the progress made in South Africa and Kenya regarding the enforceability of their respective environmental rights.[78] However, Article 20 of the South Sudan Constitution provides that "the right to litigation shall be guaranteed for all persons; no person shall be denied the right to resort to courts of law to redress grievances whether against government or any individual or organization." The right to ventilate a claim in court in South Sudan is therefore guaranteed by Article 20 of the South Sudan Constitution, although the content of what to claim or litigate may be nonexistent or nonjusticiable per Article 44.

Miscellaneous Provisions

In addition to the three main categories of constitutional provisions on natural resource regulation in Africa discussed above, some provisions are not directly related to natural resources but are relevant for the transparent management of resources and the attainment of equity in the distribution of the returns of resource investments. These provisions also shore up the social contract and accountability ethic of the constitutions. They include provisions that vest resources in the state or government in trust for the people and provisions on sovereignty and adherence to international law.

Vesting Resource Ownership in the State

A number of African countries vest natural resources ownership in the state, including Ghana, South Sudan, and South Africa. Other countries, such as Botswana and Angola, prescribe state ownership by means of legislation. Critics have argued that the ownership and control provisions in these laws

---

77 *See* Article 44. This may contradict the provisions mandating environmental impact assessment of resource projects.

78 *See* Louis J. Kotze, *A Critical Survey of Domestic Constitutional Provisions relating to Environmental Protection in South Africa*, 14(23) Tilburg L. Rev. 299–337 (2008). Without making the environmental provisions in the constitution justiciable, those provisions become mere hortatory pronouncements.

are akin to colonial-era exploitative legislation and impose social and environmental costs on communities where resources are exploited without a corresponding equitable participatory benefits and accountability.[79] These critics advocate instead for vesting resource ownership in the communities so that they can manage the resources, generate revenues, and pay taxes, thereby contributing to the government's financial resource base. The benefits of such a model are demonstrated in the U.S. state of Alaska, where 110,000 shareholders of 12 for-profit corporations in 2010 saw collective revenue of $8 billion and paid $170 million in taxes.[80] This model could benefit Africa, assuming appropriate governance mechanisms are in place to ensure proper exploitation of the resources and equitable sharing of the revenues. The state ownership of these resources could be limited to cases where, for example, oil resources are offshore or onshore land is sparsely inhabited, as is the case in Canada and Norway.[81] However, this model was tried in the preindependence era, and it did not work. Community leaders gave the resources away in exchange for drinks, vehicles, and honorary titles.[82] In contemporary times, state institutions are weak and incompetent to the extent that foreigners mine resources with impunity and for the most part pay a pittance to the state or the local people.[83]

Domestication of International Law Obligations

Almost all the four aforementioned constitutions pledge their faith and allegiance to international law. There are, however, differences in the language used in pledging the state's fidelity to international law. There are also differences in the respective legal systems and how they address or relate to international law. The Ghana and South Sudan constitutions place respect for international law and upholding of the principles of the United Nations Charter, the African Union, and other relevant international bodies in the chapters on directive principles of state policy.[84] In other words, such provisions are not justiciable. The Kenya Constitution states that international law is a source of law in the domestic legal system.[85] The four countries discussed in this chapter practice the dualistic system of incorporating international law

---

79 Karol Boudreaux & Tiernan Mennen, *Reverse the Curse: How Can Oil Help the Poor?* Foreign Affairs 182 (Jan.–Feb. 2014).

80 *Id. See* also Jill Shankleman, *Imagine There Is No Resource Curse* 38(4) Envtl. Policy & L. 210 (2008), which advocates for a new paradigm for developing petroleum and mineral resources in poor countries that includes transparency.

81 Boudreaux and Mennen, *supra* note 79, at 182.

82 *See* Ndulo, *supra* note 39.

83 *See* Oxfam, *Lifting the Curse*, http://www.oxfam.org/sites/www.oxfam.org/files/bp134-lifting-the-resource-curse-011209.pdfl; and TWN, Christian Aid et al., *Breaking the Curse*, http://www.christianaid.org.uk/Images/breaking-the-curse.pdf.

84 *See* Constitution of Ghana, art. 40.

85 Constitution of Kenya, arts. 2(5) and 2(6).

by means of domestic ratification of treaties.[86] They are obliged to follow the tenets of international law and apply them in their administration and exploitation of their natural endowments. They do so by upholding the principles of sovereignty in their constitutions, engaging in membership in the comity of nations, signing bilateral investment treaties, and upholding the principles of the United Nations and the African Union, and/or the pronouncements of the superior courts in the respective African countries.

Honoring international law is put to the test—and observed—in these countries through the regulation of resources, particularly the taking of land and resources in the public interest or for public benefit and the acceptance of stabilization agreements. It is also witnessed in the respective acceptance of arbitration in foreign countries as a way to resolve disputes. There have been significant calls for the renegotiation of resource contracts entered into by various African countries. Some countries are advocating the review of contracts on better terms or renegotiating existing contracts on the grounds that (a) previous awards of concessions were shrouded in corruption and lack of transparency because the contracts were negotiated behind closed doors, undercutting public oversight and scrutiny; (b) the government lacked resources to exploit the resources, so it entered into partnerships that compromised its short- and long-term interests; (c) the governments lacked the capacity to negotiate the contracts; and (d) the uncertain political terrain compelled the companies willing to do business in the region to negotiate terms that allowed them to take a large proportion of the profits made.

Some countries, such as Guinea, Liberia, Tanzania, and Zambia, have renegotiated their natural resources/extractive resources contracts.

Liberia's Mineral Concessions

In 2005, the National Transitional Government of Liberia entered into a series of concession agreements, including the Mineral Development Agreement (MDA), which was signed for Liberia's largest iron ore deposit. It is alleged that no due diligence was carried out: some of the members of Parliament acknowledged relying only on a summary of the agreement prepared by the executive to arrive at their decision. There were also allegations of potential corruption. Renegotiation took place in 2006; in 2007, Parliament approved the amendments to the MDA.

Democratic Republic of Congo and Various Mineral Contracts

The Democratic Republic of Congo (DRC), which is well-known for its mineral wealth, has not escaped allegations of entering into contractual arrangements that are not favorable to its citizens. A number of contracts signed with foreign private entities, including those entered into by the state-owned min-

---

86 For more on the dualist and monist systems of incorporation of international treaties into domestic law, *see* Ademola Abass, *International Law: Text, Cases, and Materials* 160–62 (Oxford U. Press 2012).

ing company Gecamines, were the subject of a detailed review by the Revisitation Commission.[87] A report released by the Revisitation Commission in 2008 stated a number of areas of concern, including high rates of return for the private companies and low rates of return for the DRC, undervaluation of the contribution of the DRC and Gecamines, and weak obligations on investors.[88] Government efforts that commenced in 2008 seek to establish some equitable distribution of the DRC's natural resources.

Niger Government and Areva Uranium Contract

Niger, the world's fourth-largest producer of uranium, exports a substantial portion of its uranium to nuclear power plants in France that provide about 20 percent of France's energy. The business transactions are carried out through Areva, a French energy company. Despite the substantial production of uranium, only 5 percent of production contributes to Niger's GDP. It was alleged that the partnership between French state operators and the Niger government dating back to the colonial era was unfair to Niger. Under a renegotiated arrangement, a 2006 law increasing taxes would apply to the Somair and Cominak operations partly controlled by Areva. Under this new arrangement Areva would be exempt from the taxes. Some critics, such as Oxfam, were of the view that the arrangement was still unfavorable.[89]

The fact that governments are opting for renegotiation rather than outright nationalization is an indication of their sensitivity to the consequences of nationalization, particularly the expensive costs involved in international arbitration and compensation.

Conclusions

Despite the need to promote accountability in the prudent management of Africa's natural resources, a number of African countries have suffered from decades of bad governance and lack of transparency and accountability.[90] One country that is thought to have avoided this quagmire is Botswana. It has largely fulfilled its end of the social contract by managing its resources for its people's benefit. It is also the country with the oldest surviving constitution in Africa.

A comparative analysis of its constitutional regimes for natural resources shows that the constitutions of African countries have progressed from reliance on property rights as the framework of resource governance to more comprehensive and eclectic provisions on natural resources. This trend places

---

87 http://www.mineweb.com/mineweb/content/en/mineweb-company-releases?oid=49696&sn=Detail.

88 *Id.*

89 Alice Powell, *Niger Government to Renegotiate Contracts with Areva* (*Publish What You Pay*, February 15, 2013).

90 *See* World Bank, *Africa: From Crisis to Sustainable Growth* (World Bank 1989).

significant emphasis on horizontal accountability in ways that engage the people, mainly through their representatives in parliament as well as through judicial redress in the management of their natural resources. The objective of empowering and giving voice to the people through their representatives in parliament as well as through the judicial process is palpable and commendable. However, the option of delegating parliamentary supervision and accountability to governmental agencies minimizes the reach of the accountability provisions. Furthermore, the framing of environmental provisions in language and in chapters that make them nonjusticiable derogates from the expectations of the constitutions of countries such as South Sudan and Ghana.[91] This trend, in part, explains why African constitutions have not delivered economic development for their people.[92]

There are few options for changing natural resources contracts that do not yield significant revenues or development or are constrained by the international obligations of African countries to the multinational natural resource companies and their principals.[93] The governments are therefore left with two options: to nationalize or to renegotiate. Given African countries' pledge of faith in international law, given that compensation is accepted by the constitutions and international law for nationalization, and given the costs involved in litigation or arbitration, the only realistic option available to African governments in fulfilling their social contractual obligations is to renegotiate inequitable deals. The question is, what are the criteria for assessing the fairness of renegotiated contracts? The transparency of the process in terms of the contribution and the shares of the respective parties,[94] as well as genuine efforts to integrate the resource business into the larger national economy, will go a long way in determining the fairness of a transaction.

---

91 The rampant spillages and environmental damage caused by natural resource companies, as in the Newmont cyanide spillage and Kosmos toxic mud spillage in Ghana, attest to the failure of the legal regime to protect the environment. *See* https://www.google.co.uk/images?hl=en-GB&q=mining+spillage+in+ghana&gbv=2&sa=X&oi=image_result_group&ei=cKvfU822NKfO0QXUuYDoBA&ved=0CCAQsAQ; Cephas Egbefome, *Oil Spills in Ghana and Kosmos Energy Snub*, http://opinion.myjoyonline.com/pages/feature/201104/63635.php; and http://www.modernghana.com/news/244322/1/newmont-downplaying-extent-of-cyanide-spillage-wac.html.

The tragedy of the oil pollution in the Niger delta region of Nigeria is well-known and documented. For images, *see* https://www.google.com/images?hl=en&q=niger+delta+oil+spill&gbv=2&sa=X&oi=image_result_group&ei=jQPpU5KlCKOk0QX61YHYCQ&ved=0CBQQsAQ.

92 *See* Rugumeleza Nshala, *Dispossession through Liberalization: How Sub-Saharan African Countries Lost Sovereignty over Mineral Resources* (SJD diss., Harvard U. 2012).

93 *Id.*

94 http://www.globalwitness.org/library/scant-information-and-wheeler-dealing-undermine-congolese-contract-review.

7

Conceptualizing Regulatory Frameworks to Forge Citizen Roles to Deliver Sustainable Natural Resource Management in Kenya

ROBERT KIBUGI

Citizens' Roles in Natural Resource Management

Accountability in natural resources management forms only one end of the sustainability continuum; at the other end are the guarantee of voice to citizens and normative clarity in legal entitlements and obligations. Giving voice to citizens conceptually revolves around notions of public participation and clarity on what such participation entails. Such clarity can be provided through a well-defined social contract mechanism such as a constitutional framework. This approach is important for Kenya, which is working to overcome the challenges of poverty through the attainment of sustainable development. The quest for sustainable development is now a constitutional legal construct, set by the supreme law—the Constitution—as a binding national value of governance to be integrated into the design and implementation of law and public policy decisions.[1] Sustainable development aims to bring about equity and the elimination of poverty. In terms of Principle 10 of the Rio Declaration, this requires the active participation of people in governance over natural resources so that they can have a voice in choosing the options and influencing the outcomes of management.

In ideal policy terms, the eradication of poverty has been identified as an indispensable requirement for sustainable development, which is necessary both to undo disparities in standards of living and to meet the needs of more people.[2] The United Nations Economic and Social Council defines poverty as a human condition characterized by the sustained or chronic deprivation of resources, capabilities, or choices.[3] Poverty also includes deprivation of the power necessary for the enjoyment of an adequate standard of living

---

1 Kenyan Const., art. 10.

2 *Rio Declaration on Environment and Development*, in *Report of the United Nations Conference on Environment and Development*, UNGA OR, A/CONF.151/26 (Vol. I), Aug. 12, 1992, Principle 5.

3 UN Econ. & Soc. Council, *Poverty and the International Covenant on Economic, Social and Cultural Rights*, E/C.12/2001/10, CESCR, 25th Sess., UN Doc. 10/05/2001, para. 8 (Apr. 23–May 11, 2001), http://www.unhchr.ch/tbs/doc.nsf/(Symbol)/E.C.12.2001.10.En?Opendocument.

and other civil, cultural, economic, political, and social rights. This deprivation denies people the resources necessary for dignified livelihoods, including the lack of access to certain natural resources for water, food, and other basic necessities.[4] Giving voice to people in the governance architecture is therefore key to ensuring meaningful service delivery in addressing poverty and enhancing sustainability. A constitution, as the supreme national law, is a useful tool for setting the basic standards.

A Social Contract Basis for Public Participation

Participation of citizens in resource management has multiple facets, such as consultation, representation, access to information, and awareness. Working with consultation and representation, the specific problem of meaningful public contribution to decision making arises. This particularly regards how to ensure the design and outcomes of consultations that have impact on the threshold of decisions eventually made by public officers. Part of the problem here arises because the uptake of the consultation by government is not fully developed. It could also be caused by unclear manifestation of the social contract architecture for the concerned natural resource or for natural resources as a whole. Applying the legal system to enhance efforts against poverty is therefore critical, because it sets the normative framework for how and when people contribute in resource management.

A social contract is, in constitutional terms, the basis on which the Kenyan state exists today. This existence is in the context of a 2010 constitutional compact designed in the manner conceptualized by the French scholar Jean-Jacques Rousseau in his 1762 treatise. Rousseau defined this in a manner responsive to the dilemma of sustainability and natural resources management today, especially the challenge of accountability and space for peoples' voices. Arguing in favor of what he called a "social compact," Rousseau noted that

> men to have reached the point at which the obstacles in the way of their preservation in the state of nature show their power of resistance to be greater than the resources at the disposal of each individual for his maintenance in that state. That primitive condition can then subsist no longer; and the human race would perish unless it changed its manner of existence.[5]

Based on this contention, he urged humanity to find a form of association that defends and protects, with the whole common force, the person and goods of each associate.[6]

---

4 Charo Quesada, *Amartya Sen and the Thousand Faces of Poverty*, para. 5 (Inter-American Dev. Bank 2001), http://www.globalpolicy.org/socecon/develop/2001/1205sen.htm. *See* also Michael Lockwood, & Ashish Kothari, "Social Context," in *Managing Protected Areas: A Global Guide* 56 (Michael Lockwood, Graeme Worboys, & Ashish Kothari eds., Earthscan 2006).

5 Jean-Jacques Rousseau, *The Social Contract or Principles of Political Right*; G.D.H. Cole trans., 1782 (originally published 1762) (public domain, rendered into html & text by Jon Roland of the Constitution Society), http://www.constitution.org/jjr/socon_01.htm#006.

6 *Id.*

Perhaps inspired by the same thinking, the people of Kenya have clamored for a new constitution for nearly three decades, especially since the 1980s. Kenya went through a period of concerted authoritarian rule in the years after independence in 1963. Between 1964 and 1982, the country was largely a de facto one-party state, with the Kenya African National Union (KANU) as the ruling party. Following a failed military coup d'état in August 1982, Parliament, controlled by the ruling KANU, enacted Section 2A to the Constitution, which prohibits popular multiparty democratic activities by declaring the country to have only a single political party. KANU was thus the only legally permitted political party.

The reductionist approach to democracy was followed by protracted struggles waged by Kenyans demanding the resumption of multiparty activity in the country.[7] These struggles took various forms, including seminars, workshops, and at times demonstrations, which were sometimes crushed with excessive force by the police.[8] The most prominent of the demonstrations were those referred to as the *"Saba Saba"* uprisings of 1990. (The first uprising occurred on *saba saba,* or "seven-seven"—the seventh day of the seventh month, July 7.)[9] The protests continued on a regular basis with increased frequency (at times nearly monthly) in 1997–2002. Detention without trial and crackdowns on opposition groups and the free media became commonplace. For all intents and purposes, Kenya was a one-party dictatorship[10] during this period.

A new social contract was concluded in August 2010, when a new constitution was approved through a referendum and become the basic law.[11] The preamble is indicative of the spirit, commencing with a philosophical phrase, "We, the people of Kenya," and ending with "Adopt, Enact and give this Constitution to ourselves and to our future generations." Through this Constitution, sovereignty is clearly vested in the people,[12] to exercise "either directly or through their democratically elected representatives."[13] In addition, the people delegate sovereign power to state organs through the Constitution,[14] which binds all persons and all state organs.[15] The constitutional compact in Kenya has therefore been recently revisited, revised, and endorsed by the population,

---

7 Grace Maingi, *The Kenyan Constitutional Reform Process: A Case Study on the Work of FIDA Kenya in Securing Women's Rights,* 15 Feminist Africa 63, 65 (2011), agi.ac.za/.../fa_15_case_study_grace_maingi.pdf.

8 *Id.*

9 *Id.*

10 *Id.*

11 The final results of the referendum are published in *Kenya Gazette,* Notice No. 10019, Vol. CXII, No. 84, Aug. 23, 2010. The proposed new constitution was ratified by over 67 percent of the total valid votes cast and supported by at least 25 percent of the votes cast in all eight provinces of Kenya.

12 Kenyan Const., art. 1(1).

13 *Id.*, at art. 1(2).

14 *Id.*, at art. 2.

15 *Id.*

with a 67 percent majority as the binding basis for individual and collective governance.[16] It is thus a good time to explore how it sets a legal basis for the role of the citizen in governance, including over natural resources.

The Utility of Fundamental Rights in Framing Peoples' Voice

The 2010 Constitution internalized a binding normative framework of rights and duties through the Bill of Rights. Article 19 clearly states that the fundamental rights in the Constitution "belong to each individual and are not granted by the State," in order to protect "human rights . . . preserve the dignity of individuals and communities and to promote social justice and the realization of the potential of all human beings." These fundamental rights form a unified framework, such that none is superior to another. In specific terms, the Constitution provides a primary basis for the protection of natural resources and the environment by providing for a universal right to a clean and healthy environment.[17] The normative framework for fulfillment of this environmental right includes a set of obligations on the Kenyan state and a distinct obligation on every person in Kenya, as set out in Article 69. In the former instance, the obligations require the state to, among other actions, ensure sustainable utilization of resources and sharing of benefits; ensure there is a minimum 10 percent tree cover; and ensure public participation in natural resources management.

The positioning of public participation through legal instruments is amplified by the 2006 East African Protocol on Environment and Natural Resources Management. This protocol underscores the key principle of "public participation in the development of policies, plans, processes and activities."[18] The protocol requires state parties, in order to contribute to the protection of the rights of present and future generations to live in an environment adequate for their health and well-being, to

- *ensure that officials* and public authorities *assist the public,* and *facilitate their participation in environmental management.*
- promote environmental education and environmental awareness among the public.[19]

The Constitution, in Article 69(2), lays the ground for a proactive approach to public participation in natural resource management:

> *Every person* has a *duty to cooperate* with *State organs* and *other persons* to protect and conserve the environment and ensure ecologically sustainable development and use of natural resources. (Emphasis added)

---

16 *Kenya Gazette, supra* note 11.

17 Kenyan Const., art. 42.

18 *East African Protocol on Environment and Natural Resources Management, 2006,* art. 4(2)(e).

19 *Id.,* at art. 34(d).

A textual reading of this provision highlights several issues. The first is that, in mandatory terms, the Constitution has created a duty for every person. A person is defined by the Constitution to "'include a company, association or other body of persons whether incorporated or unincorporated."[20] The second is that, under this duty every person is required to cooperate with organs of state and with other persons. The third issue concerns the intended objects of the duty and the cooperation. The first intended object is to protect and conserve the environment. The second intended object, mutually reinforcing the first, is to ensure both ecologically sustainable development and the use of natural resources.

In a legal positivist jurisdiction such as Kenya, the Constitution is the supreme law and plays a central role in framing key issues such as the role of citizens in resource management. Nonetheless, constitutional provisions can remain aspirational, unless put in practice through legislative and policy frameworks. The frameworks are necessary to ensure implementation in a manner that guarantees a voice for the people, through arrangements where citizens can affect decision-making processes and outcomes. This chapter examines the application of the concepts of *social contract* and *voice* relative to the legislative frameworks that established community forestry and public roles in water resource management.

Public Participation in Sustainable Forest Management

The Forests Act of 2005 is the legislative framework created for the sustainable management of forests in Kenya, superseding the 1942 legal framework. This legislation contains particularly strong provisions on public participation, especially through community forest associations (CFAs). Prior to the 2005 forestry legislation, Kenyan forestry tenure and rules had evolved from precolonial days,[21] when land, including forests, was owned and used under indigenous land tenure. Colonial land and forest tenure and use policies resulted in the expropriation of land and the creation of protected forests that excluded local communities. This state of affairs, over time, resulted in a complex and challenging legal relationship between the state and local communities because of the latter's exclusion from forestry management. In recent years, statistics show that about 3–4 million people inhabit lands within five kilometers of protected forests.[22] As a consequence, forest conservation efforts may be undermined by short-term economic objectives of local people, including

---

20 Kenyan Const., art. 260.

21 The transformation of Kenya into a colony was effected through the Kenya (Annexation) Order-in-Council, 1920. *See* Yash Pal Ghai & J. P. W. B. McAuslan, *Public Law and Political Change in Kenya: A Study of the Legal Framework of Government from Colonial Times to the Present* 3, 50 (Oxford U. Press 1970).

22 Republic of Kenya, *Report of the Government's Task Force on the Conservation of the Mau Forests Complex* 64 (Office of the Prime Minister 2009).

searching for water, firewood, and charcoal, and illegal cultivation.[23] It is therefore important to examine the pre-2005 evolution of forest legislation and to establish the background that informs current forest law, especially the shift to community forestry.

A History of Exclusion of People through Legal Mechanisms

The first comprehensive forest legislation was enacted in 1942 by the colonial government and remained the main legislation until the new law was enacted in 2005. This law, just like its predecessors, conferred extensive forest tenure rights on the state, including the legal ability to make decisions on the management and use of forests. During the period that the 1942 forest law was in force, Kenya experienced high-level deforestation, forest degradation, illegal forest encroachment for pasture and farming, and the irregular excision of forests with allocation to the political elite.[24] This factual outcome notwithstanding, the 1942 forest law created a legal regime for the establishment, control, and regulation of central government forests, forest areas in the Nairobi area, and forests on unalienated government land.[25] This 1942 law granted the forests minister the power to determine which areas of the country would be subject to the provisions of the forest law. The minister was thus empowered to declare any unalienated government land[26] to be a forest area; to declare the boundaries of a forest and occasionally alter those boundaries; and to withdraw the forest status of an area.[27]

The forest law at the time did not require the minister to give any reasons for such declarations, or to consult with any interested member of the public or other stakeholder.[28] This provision was inimical to sustainable forest management because this decision making carried potentially negative environmental, socioeconomic, and cultural consequences for local populations. The only basic form of public communication that the minister used was to publish notices of intention to vary forest boundaries or to cease a forest area

---

23 *Id.*

24 World Bank, *Strategic Environmental Assessment of the Kenya Forest Act 2005* 2 (World Bank 2007). *See* also National Environment Management Authority (NEMA), *National Environmental Action Plan 2009–2013* 9 (NEMA 2009).

25 The objectives of that statute were captured in its short title. Central forests were vested in the central/national government and have now been renamed state forests under the 2005 forest law.

26 This was land held under the (now repealed) *Government Lands Act*, ch. 280 in the Laws of Kenya. It defined government land to mean land vested in the government for the time being. The 2010 Constitution, art. 62(1), in contrast, states that public land is, inter alia, "land which at the effective date was unalienated government." Sec. 62 extensively lists the lands that qualify as public land.

27 *Forests Act* (1942), at sec. 4.

28 Francis D. P. Situma, *Forestry Law and the Environment*, in *Environmental Governance in Kenya: Implementing the Framework Law* 236 (Charles Okidi, Patricia Kameri-Mbote, & Migai Akech eds., East African Educ. Publishers 2008).

in the official *Kenya Gazette* about four weeks prior to the official decision.[29] The law was silent on the expected impact of such notices; for example, would public representations be entertained, or would the minister listen? In fact, these *Gazette* notices were routinely issued quietly, perhaps with the expectation that not many members of the public would read the official gazette or take notice.

Problems with these provisions were evident. For example, in 1998, it became public that between 1996 and 1998 the government had allocated half of the 1,063-hectare Karura Forest, an urban forest just outside the capital city, Nairobi, to private developers.[30] The forest provides a vital refuge from urban life. Residents were thus concerned about the clearance of a forest important for water catchment and of great potential value for relaxation, recreation, and education.[31] The excision and allocation to private individuals was undertaken without public consultation and was only revealed to the general public by residents of neighboring areas who noticed construction crews and equipment moving into and clearing vast forest areas. The revelation resulted in public demonstrations, public prayer meetings, and violent encounters with developers, as the public demanded revocation of the allocations. The demonstrations, at times bloody and destructive, finally succeeded in halting the developments in 1999, and the government reviewed and rescinded its decision.[32] These events demonstrate that the decision-making authority of the minister was wrongly exercised in allocating forest land to private individuals with political connections for other economic uses[33] without considering the nonfiscal environmental benefits, such as recreational facilities, accruing to the public. There was also no voice for the public to participate or hold managers accountable in forestry governance.

In contrast to these events, the 1942 statute contained a very extensive system of sanctions and offenses that criminalized any unauthorized conduct that would compromise the nature of the forest or its produce.[34] These provisions

---

29 *Forests Act* (1942), at sec. 4(2).

30 Michael Gachanja, *Public Perception of Forests as a Motor for Change: The Case of Kenya* 55(213) Unasylva 59, 60 (2003).

31 *Id.*

32 *Id.*

33 As a case in point, the Kenyan government has, since 2008, been involved in a complicated legal and political process of repossessing a huge portion of the Mau Forests complex, one of five important water catchment aeas of Kenya. The allocated land went to farming communities and the political class. The latter included the president and senior ministers; other administrators have been found to own huge tracts of land. More information is available at www.kwta.go.ke.

34 Sec. 9 of the 1942 Forests Act made it an offense for any person without lawful authority to (a) mark any forest produce or affixes upon any forest produce a mark used by any forest officer to indicate that the forest produce is the property of the government or that it may be lawfully cut or removed; (b) alter, obliterate, remove, or deface any stamp, mark, sign, license, or other document lawfully issued under the authority of this Act, or removes or destroys any part of a tree bearing the stamp or other mark used by any forest officer; (c) cover any tree stump in any Central Forest or forest area or on any unalienated government land

would therefore be enforced against ordinary citizens who entered the forests in search of basic items such as food and firewood. The hallmark of the overall forestry law and policy strategy therefore involved the creation of state forests as protected areas that excluded local people from decision making on management, consumptive use, or conservation.[35] These methods, often termed "exclusionary," "fence and fine," "coercive conservation," and even "fortress conservation," have not been effective in achieving their objectives:[36] Kenya's forest canopy now stands at a low 1.7 percent.[37]

Earlier Forms of Community Forestry in Kenya

The now-repealed 1942 forest law restricted individuals without permits or user rights to engage in any forestry activities. This legal provision notwithstanding, colonial and postindependence Kenyan governments implemented a system of agroforestry in state-owned forests, commonly known as the *shamba* system. The word *shamba* means "garden" in the Swahili language. The *shamba* system involved the allocation of garden plots to individuals for cultivating food crops as they planted and looked after trees grown for timber production. The system was pursued in the forest plantation establishment from 1910 to produce wood for industries and domestic uses on lands that were not natural forests.[38] The participants involved in this practice included serving and retired forest workers, landless peasants, and people living within the immediate vicinity of the forest area.[39]

Under the *shamba* system, a resident worker would agree to work for the forest department for nine months each year clearing the cut-over indigenous bush cover from a specified area (from 0.5 to 0.6 of a hectare annually). The forest department would plant exotic trees in the cleared land within two years.[40] The farmers were allowed to cultivate the *shambas* allotted to them and grow diverse food crops, including maize and potatoes, for two or three years, and had the sole right to all such produce.[41] Various changes transformed the *shamba* system. First, the volunteer workers/farmers were hired on a full-time

---

with brushwood or earth or by any other means whatsoever conceals, destroys, or removes or attempts to conceal, destroy or remove such tree stump or any part thereof; or (d) wear any uniform or part of a uniform or any badge, or other mark issued by the Forest Department to be worn by forest officers or other employees of the Forest Department.

35 *Id.*

36 Michael Wells, *Biodiversity Conservation, Affluence and Poverty: Mismatched Costs and Benefits and Efforts to Remedy Them*, 21(3) Ambio 237, 238–39 (1992).

37 Republic of Kenya, *supra* note 22, at 15.

38 Joram Kagombe & James Gitonga, *Plantation Establishment in Kenya: A Case Study on Shamba System* 2 (Kenya Forestry Research Institute & Forest Department 2005). *See* also FAO, *Forestry for Local Community Development* App. 2, Case Study No. 8 (FAO Forestry Paper No. 7, 1978).

39 Peter Allan Oduol, *The Shamba System: An Indigenous System of Food Production from Forest Areas in Kenya*, 4 Agroforestry Systems 365, 366 (1986).

40 *Id.*

41 *Id.*

basis by the forest department. This resulted in high direct tree-establishment costs and inefficiency because, as civil servants, the farmers were not obliged to cultivate land because they had alternative income; they had to rent the land from the forest department.[42] With time, laxity in controls and oversight led to an influx of people, a higher demand for more forest land to set up *shambas,* poorly tended *shambas,* and low survival of planted trees.[43] The *shamba* system, in this form, perhaps due to unclear legal and policy positions on its nature, scope, and purpose, experienced much turbulence and is blamed for significant deforestation and forest degradation.

The system was suspended by a presidential decree in 1987,[44] resulting in stagnation of national reforestation because no arrangements were put in place to carry on with alternative forest plantation methods. Subsequently, all forest workers and other people living in forest villages were evicted in 1988. Participating farmers lost their social amenities, sources of food, and jobs.[45] A resulting lack of fast-growing, nonindigenous timber for industry, firewood, and other uses raised the risk, and indigenous forests were targeted instead. The system was reintroduced in 1994 as nonresident cultivation[46] in an attempt to reduce the risk of cultivators claiming squatter rights on forest land.[47] There was a marked shift in administrative supervision from the forest department to the central government.[48] The transfer to central government supervision exposed the system to strong partisan influence by politicians and provincial administrators. This resulted in total disregard of technical advice, as implementation paid no regard to either environmental or sustainability considerations, resulting in more indigenous forest areas being cleared for farming with no efforts at replanting. In 2003, shortly after the election of a new government to office, the *shamba* system was stopped through a directive by the Ministry of Environment and Natural Resources,[49] ostensibly to pave the way for the passage of a new forest law and policy.

Community Forestry as a Mechanism to Enhance People's Voice

The Food and Agriculture Organization of the United Nations (FAO) conceptualizes community forestry as "any situation which intimately involves local people in a forestry activity."[50] This FAO definition embraces a broad

---

42 *Id.*

43 World Bank, *supra* note 24, at 2.

44 Oduol, *supra* note 39, at 366.

45 *Id.*

46 Kagombe & Gitonga, *supra* note 38, at 2.

47 Lynette Obare & J. B. Wangwe, *Underlying Cause of Deforestation and Forest Degradation in Kenya*, para. 1.3, www.wrm.org.uy/deforestation/Africa/Kenya.html.

48 *Id.*

49 Joram Kagombe & James Gitonga, *Plantation Establishment in Kenya: The Shamba System Case Study* 8 (Kenya Forests Working Group 2005).

50 Food and Agriculture Organization of the United Nations (FAO), *Introduction*, in *Forestry for*

spectrum for community forestry activities, including woodlots and other forest products for local needs; growing trees at the farm level; artisanal forestry activities that generate employment and wages; the livelihood activities of forest-dwelling communities; and activities in public forests that enhance forestry activities at the community level for rural people. This broader conception of community forestry developed by the FAO is applied here, as it anticipates a proactive decision-making role for local people in forest management, including the integration of their socioeconomic targets with safeguarding forest vitality. However, the scope of this discussion is limited to community forestry activities within a forest where the Kenyan state holds the tenure rights, with participating communities holding derivative user rights set out by law. The question to answer here is whether this form of community forestry based on derivative user rights is sufficient to give voice to participating communities in the continuum of forestry decision making.

An argument can be made that community forestry, in the FAO context, aims to facilitate local communities to mitigate poverty by accessing additional food sources, fuel, or financial gain. Alistair Sarre argues that this community forestry aims to increase both the involvement and the reward for local people.[51] This increment is achieved by seeking a balance between the interests of forest vitality, local community socioeconomic interests, and increasing local responsibility and decision making in the management of a forest resource. The view is supported by the Convention on Biological Diversity's Programme of Work on Forest Biodiversity, which focuses on sustainable use of forest biodiversity, which aims to "enable indigenous and local communities to develop and implement adaptive community management systems to conserve and sustainably use forest biodiversity."[52] Sarre speaks of community forests as "increasing the involvement of local communities" and "increasing their responsibility" over the health and quality of the ecosystem. Arguments in favor of community forestry accordingly suggest that given voice, local communities will play individual and collective roles in decision making, with responsibilities over forest vitality and local social, economic, and cultural objectives.

The 1992 UN Forest Principles support the utility of community forestry, in the same context as defined by the FAO, in the furtherance of sustainable forest management and tackling rural poverty. Principle 2 calls on governments to "promote and provide opportunities for the participation of interested parties, including local communities, indigenous people, individuals, forest dwellers and women, in the development, implementation and planning

---

Local Community Development (FAO Forestry Paper No. 7, 1997), http://www.fao.org/docrep/t0692e/t0692e02.htm#INTRODUCTION.

51 Alistair Sarre, *What Is Community Forestry?*, 4(4) Tropical Forest Update (1994), http://www.rainforestinfo.org.au/good_wood/comm_fy.htm.

52 Secretariat of the Convention on Biological Diversity (CBD), *Expanded Programme of Work on Forest Biological Diversity* 10 (Goal 4) (CBD Programmes of Work 2004).

of national forest policies."[53] The forest principles further urge that national forest policies should recognize and support the identity, culture, and rights of indigenous and local communities, and the role of women.[54] The principles therefore demonstrate that broad parameters are sought in defining community forestry, in a manner that provides beneficial opportunities to tackle rural poverty; enhance intragenerational equity, especially for women and youth; and enhance sustainable forest management.

The concern with providing responsibilities and incentives to local communities to enhance sustainable forest management has been a major policy issue with regard to protected state forests in Kenya. The Kenyan government appointed a task force on the conservation of the Mau Forests complex, one of five principal catchment basins (also known as "water towers") in Kenya, to address the role of local communities in sustainable management of these protected state forests. The task force, in its 2009 report, noted that communities living within five kilometers of the Mau complex forests (forest-adjacent communities) depend on these protected forests for diverse basic needs such as water, firewood, pasturing, and vegetables.[55] The report also noted that these socioeconomic activities of local communities—such as firewood collection, overgrazing livestock, or illegal logging for timber and charcoal—have been associated with degradation of protected state forests.[56] To overcome these challenges, the 2009 task force report recommended that

> participatory forest management should be fast-tracked to enhance the livelihoods of the communities. In particular, community forest associations should be supported to actively participate in forest management.[57]

It was noted that these measures are "intended to ensure that the forests play the role that they can and should play in creating and sustaining employment and alternative livelihoods in and around the forests."[58] The overall recommendation is that people residing in areas adjacent to the protected forests should be involved in reforestation and afforestation activities.

Current Legal Tools for Application of Community Forestry in Kenya

The legal concept of community forestry in state forests is anchored in the 2005 Forests Act. Section 46 provides that "a member of forest community

---

53 UN General Assembly, *Non-Legally Binding Authoritative Statement of Principles for a Global Consensus on the Management, Conservation and Sustainable Development of All Types of Forests*, UNGA, A/Conf.151/26 (Vol. III) (Aug. 14, 1992), Principle 2(d), http://www.un.org/documents/ga/conf151/aconf15126-3annex3.htm.

54 *Id.*

55 Republic of Kenya, *supra* note 22, at 64.

56 *Id.*, at 65.

57 Republic of Kenya, *Rehabilitation of the Mau Forest Ecosystem: Executive Summary* 5 (Interim Coordinating Secretariat, Office of the Prime Minister, Apr. 2010).

58 *Id.*

may, together with other members or persons resident in the same area, register a community forest association" and "apply to the Director for permission to participate in the conservation and management of a state forest." Among other requirements, the application should include the proposals of the community forest association concerning use of forest resources; methods of conservation of biodiversity; and methods of monitoring and protecting wildlife and plant populations and enforcing such protection.

Implementation of these provisions is guided by the 2009 Forests (Participation in Sustainable Forest Management) Rules.[59] These Forests Rules, just like the substantive statute, classify community participation into two forms. The first form involves community forest management agreements whereby a local community is authorized to participate in forest conservation and management based on user rights assigned by the Forest Service.[60] The second form involves the issuance of permits to community forest associations, allowing its members to engage in nonresidential cultivation of degraded industrial forest plantations as they tend and grow tree seedlings.[61]

Participation commences with legal entitlement to take part in activities, and it is this entitlement that provides the desired voice for populations. In the case of community forestry, this commences with the legal definition of "forest community," which is then the basis on which communities (and individuals) can partake in community forestry activities. The Forests Act creates the term "forest community" as a legal concept with a definition that comprises two dimensions. In the first dimension, a forest community is defined as "a group of persons who have a traditional association with a forest for purposes of livelihood, culture or religion."[62] In the second dimension, a forest community is also defined as "a group of persons who are registered as an association or other organization engaged in forest conservation."[63] With a history of land tenure reform and internal migration patterns in postindependence Kenya, communities living adjacent to state forests may not necessarily share a traditional ethnocultural homogeneity. Instead, they may share contemporary socioeconomic, cultural, and environmental interests. The Constitution, in reference to community land and forests, thus includes a community identified on the basis of "similar community of interest."[64] The second legal dimension in the definition of forest community, highlighted above, can be interpreted as having a connection with this category of community. The category represents contemporary forest-adjacent communities for whom statutory legal associations based on "similar community of interest" would facilitate par-

---

59 Legal Notice No. 165 (Nov. 6, 2009) [hereinafter *Forests Rules*].

60 *Id.*, at R. 43.

61 *Id.*, at R. 50.

62 *Forests Act,* at sec. 3.

63 *Id.*

64 Kenyan Const., art. 63.

ticipation in sustainable management of forests. It is this category of forest community that is primarily served by community forest associations (CFAs).

Assessing the Utility of Community Forest Associations in Enhancing Peoples' Voice

Section 46(1) of the Forests Act specifies that the CFA should be registered as a society to obtain legal status. Thereafter, the forest community may apply to the director of the Forest Service for permission to participate in the conservation and management of a state forest.[65] Every person in a forest community is eligible to join a CFA and participate in the election of officials. The members of the CFA are then eligible to take part in conservation of the forests, including approved socioeconomic activities, such as removing animal feed and nontimber forest produce.

The Forests Rules set out details on the implementation process. Rule 45(2) provides that the Forest Service may facilitate the formation of a forest association based on existing community structures. This is a noble provision, and considering that the capacity to register forest associations may be limited among rural communities, the contribution of the Forest Service would be instrumental. A 2009 manual on forming and registering CFAs[66] and the 2007 "Participatory Forest Management Guidelines"[67] suggest that an external facilitator or a local community leader may initiate the process. While it is unclear who the external facilitator would be, that person could possibly represent the Forest Service, a nongovernmental organization (NGO), or donor agency.

Nonetheless, Rule 45(2) makes reference to a forest association "based on existing community structures." This contrasts with Section 46 of the Forests Act, which requires that the associations be registered under the Societies Act,[68] which imposes its own complex registration procedure.[69] The Forests Act and the Forests Rules are unclear on how to reconcile "existing community structures" with registration under statutory provisions. The Participatory Forest Management (PFM) guidelines suggest that a facilitator should "identify existing community structures (formal or informal) that can be transformed to form a community forest association."[70] Presumably, such structures may also include present-day methods of community mobilization and organization,

---

65 *Forests Act,* at sec. 46(2).

66 Kenya Forest Service, *Manual on Forming and Registering CFAs* (Kenya Forest Service, Kenya Forests Working Group, Mar. 2009).

67 *See* Kenya Forest Service, *Participatory Forest Management Guidelines* (Kenya Forest Service, Dec. 2007).

68 *Societies Act,* ch. 108, in *Laws of Kenya.*

69 *Id.* at sec. 9 requires that every society should apply for registration within twenty-eight days of formation. The application should be in the manner prescribed in the Societies rules. Notably, prior to making an application for registration, a society must develop and adopt a constitution, which should be attached to the application. The first schedule to the act specifies 16 matters that must be included in a constitution.

70 *Id.*

similar to how people elect a local school committee or cattle-dip committee. If that is not possible, the forest community should proceed to form a new CFA, for registration under the Societies Act.

The Societies Act requires all societies to comply with the provisions of this law, such as adopting a constitution[71] and filing periodic returns to the registrar of societies.[72] The registrar also has the power and the discretion to require mandatory changes to the constitution of a society[73] and to declare a society illegal or prohibited.[74] The registration of forest associations under the Societies Act therefore presents multiple challenges. First, the process is not the most straightforward or simple, especially in regard to drafting a constitution with a list of very specific provisions. These provisions are standardized, because the general category of societies includes church organizations and, until recently, political parties.[75] The community may need legal expertise if there is no facilitator or if the facilitator lacks the legal training required to prepare a proper constitution. This becomes an additional expense to the community. More importantly, because CFAs are involved in sustainable forest management and utilization, it would serve them better if the mandatory requirements addressed closely linked issues. Even though Section 46 requires the forest community to submit proposals on forest conservation, it is not specifically required that the constitution of the CFA, registered under the Societies Act, should reflect sustainable forest management as a primary objective.

Second, the administrative role of regulating these associations as societies principally falls to the registrar of societies,[76] to whom the associations must submit returns, or notify of elections. The requirement for these associations to additionally report to, register with, and comply with directions from the Forest Service just increases the operational costs for communities. These forest communities carry a double load of compliance with two statutes. It would be viable for amendments to be made to the Societies Act that would authorize the director of the Forest Service to receive annual returns or to monitor regular elections, youth and gender equity, and compliance with the objectives of sustainable forest management. This would consolidate the oversight role so that the Forest Service could ensure that forest communi-

---

71 *Id.*, at sec. 19(1).

72 *Id.*, at sec. 30.

73 *Id.*, at sec. 19(2).

74 *Id.*, at sec. 4(1).

75 *Id.*, at sec. 2 defines a society to include "any club, company, partnership or other association of ten or more persons, whatever its nature or object, established in Kenya or having its headquarters or chief place of business in Kenya." Political parties now enjoy distinctive legal status under the *Political Parties Act*, Act No. 7 of 2007.

76 The registrar is appointed under sec. 8; the substantive minister is the attorney general, which means that power to register and the function of registration, and hence regulation of community forest societies, as societies, is vested in another sectoral ministry; however, there are no legal mechanisms in place to reconcile the procedure.

ties upheld the values and responsibilities of governance, transparency, and accountability, which are pertinent to sustainable forest management.

The reference to "existing community structures" in the rules would be more effective if the Forests Act provided a generic form of association for which the Forests Act itself provided registration and the Forest Service served as administrator and regulator. However, such a stipulation has to distinguish that "existing community structures" are not necessarily traditional or culture-based mechanisms. The requirements for including youth and gender equity should therefore be highlighted as paramount to reflect the realities faced by the present generation as well as future ones, an important ingredient of sustainable development.

Procedure for CFAs to Commence Community Participation in Forestry

The principal legislation and the Forests Rules are contradictory regarding how CFAs should commence participating in sustainable forestry. Section 46 of the Forests Act anticipates a situation where registered forest associations *"may apply to the Director for permission"* to participate in the conservation and management of a state forest (emphasis added). Contrarily, the Forests Rules appear to reserve the authority to empower the Forest Service, "whenever circumstances make it necessary or appropriate to do so, *to invite forest associations* to participate in the sustainable management of state forests" (emphasis added). The Forests Rules appear to reverse the letter and spirit of the Forests Act, which grants a legal basis for any forest community to proactively apply for registration of its forest association. This contradiction can be problematic, inasmuch as the Forests Rules were enacted as guidelines and are most likely to be the operational guide available to most frontline forest officers. The wording of the rules gives the Forest Service an upper hand in determining which local communities will engage in state forest management and utilization. If the rules are followed as written, a community could be locked out simply because the Forest Service declined to extend an invitation to participate. If the substantive statute is followed, any CFA that applied for community participation and was denied permission could declare a dispute and, as provided for by the Forests Act,[77] appeal to the National Environment Tribunal (NET) to make a final determination. The NET is established under the framework Environmental Management and Coordination Act (EMCA).[78] The decisions from this tribunal have a final appeal at the High Court,[79] which provides an additional avenue for communities to access environmental justice for objective determination and for review of administrative decisions by forestry officials.

---

77 *Forests Act, supra* note 62, at sec. 63(2).

78 *Envntl. Mgt. & Coordination Act,* at sec. 125.

79 *Id.,* at sec. 130.

Is There a Sufficient Mechanism for Equitable Sharing of Benefits?

In terms of revenue, socioeconomic benefits are pertinent to the success of community forestry because the communities engage in sustainable forestry for purposes of livelihood. Clarity and accountability in the handling, sharing, and distribution of financial benefits are therefore central to achieving success. The Forests Act appears to assume that a forest association will internally provide for the sharing of financial benefits; hence, when they apply for registration, the CFAs should submit their financial regulations to the director.[80] Inequity in the sharing of benefits between members of a CFA could disorient the commitment of some members to sustainability, and undermine conservation or adherence to the management plan. Such inequity in distribution of financial benefits, which may have been derived from socioeconomic activities or payment for environmental services, manifests a failure in fulfilling intragenerational equity, a key pillar of sustainable development.[81] It may therefore be necessary to amend the Forests Rules in order to require that a CFA submit benefit-sharing criteria for approval by the Forest Service. The legal provisions are also silent on whether the community using the forest should pay any specific payments such as rates, rents, or taxes to the Forest Service or to the government. Additionally, it is unclear whether any portion of the income received by a CFA should be invested in the forest management unit under the CFA to finance or pay for any aspect of sustainable forest management.

Challenges with Rules for Termination of Community Forestry Agreements

Section 49 of the Forests Act empowers the director of the Forest Service to terminate a community forest management agreement or withdraw a user right from a forest association if there is a breach of any of the conditions of the agreement. According to the model forest management agreement, one obligation of a forest association is to protect, conserve, and manage the assigned forest based on the agreement and the community management plan.[82] Therefore, the failure to fulfill the responsibility to exercise forest conservation is a legal basis for termination of the agreement. Termination of the agreement may also be at the discretion of the Forest Service, where the director "considers such action as necessary for purposes of protecting and conserving biodiversity."[83]

When the process of termination or withdrawal of a user right is commenced, the Forest Service must give thirty days' notice to the forest association to show cause why the action should not be finalized. According to the

---

80 *Forests Act, supra* note 62, at sec. 45(3).

81 Edith Brown Weiss argues that the concept of intergenerational equity implies an intragenerational aspect that current generations should provide members with equitable access to planetary legacy and conserve the planet and its resources for future generations. *See* Edith Brown Weiss, *In Fairness to Future Generations*, 3 Env. 7, 10 (1990).

82 Cl. 12.

83 *Forests Act, supra* note 62, at Sec. 49(1)(b).

Forests Act, if a forest association is aggrieved with the decision at this point, it may appeal to the Board of the Forest Service.

One difficulty concerns a contradiction arising from the Forests Rules and the draft model agreement on community forestry management agreements, which is part of the Forests Rules. Clause 15 of the model agreement provides for termination of an agreement but fails to expressly stipulate that the forest association has additional recourse for a final appeal to the Board of the Forest Service, in the event of a dispute. This is a violation of Section 49 of the Forests Act, which outlines this appellate avenue to the Forest Service Board. Instead of complying with the principal legislation, Clause 14 of the model agreement sets out and directs that a different legal avenue should be followed, as detailed below:

a) When the Forest Service is dissatisfied, it should submit the dispute for arbitration in accordance with the Arbitration Act.[84]

b) In the case of the Forest Association being dissatisfied, it may in the first instance appeal to the Board. In this case, if the decision of the Board is not acceptable to both parties, the matter should be submitted for arbitration under the Arbitration Act.

This dispute settlement procedure set out by the Forests Rules through the model agreement is certainly in violation of the dispute settlement approach in the principal legislation, the Forests Act.

In contrast, if the procedure set out in the Forests Act is applied, any CFA that is aggrieved with a decision by the Board of the Forest Service, including on termination of agreements, can declare a dispute and refer this dispute for determination by the NET.[85] The NET has rules of procedure[86] that have simplified the rules of evidence and technicalities, making it possible for people to represent themselves without requiring a lawyer.[87]

A 2010 dispute between the Forest Service, the National Environment Management Authority (NEMA), and CFAs, which was filed before the NET, demonstrated the role the tribunal can play in resolving such disputes. It was an appeal of administrative review of a decision by the Kenya Forest Service, in *National Alliance of Community Forest Associations (NACOFA)*[88] *v. NEMA & Kenya Forest Service,*[89] filed at the tribunal on November 19, 2010. The appeal

---

84 *Arbitration Act,* Act No. 4 of 1995, *Laws of Kenya.*

85 *Forests Act, supra* note 62, at sec. 63(2).

86 The *Environmental Management (National Environmental Tribunal Procedure) Rules*, 2003 (Legis. Supp. No. 57, Kenya Gazette Supp. No. 92, Nov. 21, 2003).

87 See arguments by Donald Kaniaru, *Environmental Tribunals as a Mechanism for Settling Disputes,* 37(6) Envtl. Policy & L. 459–63 (2007).

88 NACOFA is a community alliance and a registered society; it acts as a focal point for all CFAs in Kenya. More information is available at http://www.fankenya.org/nacofa/.

89 *National Alliance of Community Forest Associations (NACOFA) v. NEMA & Kenya Forest Service* (Trib. App. No. NET 62, 2010).

arose after the Forest Service was served notice by NEMA under Section 12 of the framework environmental law EMCA, which empowers NEMA to issue instructions to any lead agency to perform a function that the lead agency is required by law to perform but which in NEMA's view the agency has not performed. In this case, NEMA instructed the Forest Service to secure state forests and stop further degradation and illegal human activities.[90]

Prior to the instruction from NEMA, the Forest Service had allowed forest-adjacent communities to exercise user rights for grazing for a monthly fee. However, at the end of October 2010, when community members went to make payments, the Forest Service informed them that the user rights would not be renewed for another month. There was no notice given; not even the thirty days required by the Forests Act.[91] When the matter came up for hearing, the tribunal was informed that NEMA did not specifically require the Forest Service to terminate grazing rights. Further, the Forest Service argued that it did not have to give notice to the communities because although community forest management agreements had been prepared, only one out of sixteen had been signed.[92] This implied that the agreements were not enforceable *inter partes,* as between the communities and the Forest Service. The tribunal declined to order the Forest Service to allow communities to resume grazing, but asked the Forest Service to issue a notice confirming whether the step was permanent or temporary. It is noteworthy that the tribunal highlighted with concern the fact that the Forest Service did not take preparation and signing of community forest management plans seriously, and noted that there was "potential for forest-adjacent communities to contribute meaningfully to forest management efforts."[93]

The tribunal is therefore accessible to CFAs that have a dispute with the Forest Service. It is a good, affordable legal avenue to resolve any disputes involving forest communities. The opportunity of an additional appellate avenue from the tribunal to the High Court is helpful in magnifying the voice of communities through access to justice mechanisms. Thus, introducing the provisions of the Arbitration Act through the Forests Rules is an outright affront to, and violation of the Forests Act. These difficulties notwithstanding, the legal nature and practice of community forestry within the Kenyan legal framework has undergone extensive evolution. There is now a social contract basis that sets a foundation for giving a voice to local communities in sustainable management of publicly owned forests in Kenya. Certainly, the attainment of sustainability in forests management is a tenuous process, but legal and policy modifications can enhance positive outcomes that benefit forest management and the socioeconomic needs of the people.

---

90 *NEMA Demands Action to Save,* http://www.kenyaforestservice.org/index.php?option=com_content&view=article&id=175:nema-demands-action-to-save-forests&catid=223:hict&Itemid=98.

91 *Supra* note 89, at 4.

92 *Id.,* at 5.

93 *Id.,* at 8.

Public Participation in Water Management

Kenya's need to promote sustainable management of water resources has been a central factor in water sector reforms. The country's water policy, *Sessional Paper No. 1 of 1999 on National Policy on Water Resource Management and Development,* developed a framework to introduce public participation in water resource management through involvement of the private sector and the communities to be implemented by the water legislation of 2002.

In general, Section 107 of the water legislation sets out a procedure with regard to public consultation. This provision, indicative of the expected threshold of public consultation, requires that in any case where public consultation is necessary, the concerned officer shall publish a notice in the *Kenya Gazette,* in at least one national newspaper circulating in the locality to which the application or proposed action relates, and with at least one Kenyan radio station broadcasting in that locality. The notice will set out a summary of the application or proposed action; state the premises at which the details of the application or proposed action may be inspected; invite written comments on or objections to the application or proposed action; specify the person or body to which any such comments are to be submitted; and specify a date by which any such comments are required to be received, not being a date earlier than 30 days after publication of the notice.

This water law also provides mechanisms for public participation through representation in the management boards of both the Water Resources Management Authority and the Water Services Regulatory Board. These are the water resources regulators and water services regulators, respectively. In this context, Rule 2(b) of the first schedule to the act, which deals with membership and procedures of boards and committees, contains a general provision that "in making the appointment to either the board or committee, the Minister shall have regard to the degree to which water users are represented on the board." The underlying objective of this provision appears intended to secure participation, through representation, of the various kinds of people who utilize water and therefore provides a meaningful voice. However, the wording of the provisions appears aspirational rather than binding. It is deficient on an actual procedure through which public participation (through representation) would be specifically implemented, whether through gender and age equity, socioeconomic equity, or the role of the concerned public in electing such representatives. Two mechanisms, reviewed below, provide direct avenues for public participation in water resource management.

Participation through Catchment Area Advisory Committees

The Water Act empowers the minister in consultation with the Water Management Resources Management Authority (WRMA) to appoint a catchment area advisory committee (CAAC) for each catchment area. The main function of a CAAC is to advise the WRMA on matters such as water resource conservation, use and apportionment, regulation of permits, and other matters pertinent to proper management of water resources.[94]

A CAAC constitutes not more than 15 members in respect to each catchment area. The members of a CAAC are formed from among various stakeholders including government officials, representatives of farmers or pastoralists within the catchment area, representatives of the business community operating within the catchment area, and representatives of the NGOs engaged in water resource management programs within the catchment area.[95] However, this law does not specify the proportion of members of the public vis-à-vis co-opted public officers, making it difficult to assess how the public representatives would impact the threshold of decision making in the mandate of the CAAC.

A 2012 research report on public participation in water resource management disclosed that there was no equality in the ratio of public representation in the CAAC relative to representation of the national government, regional development authorities, and local authorities.[96] In this case, representation of governmental stakeholders was higher.[97] The impact of this disparate representation of the public and the government is experienced in decision making, because public representation does not meet the threshold required to influence what is to be decided, especially regarding a matter that may require a decision through a voting process.[98]

The appointment of members of the CAAC by the minister should be done according to the procedure in the first schedule to the Water Act. In relation to accommodation of constructive public participation, the operative word here is "appoint," demonstrating that the public has no direct role in electing or in any way directly determining who represents their interests in the CAAC. The law does not offer any guidance on how to ensure that there is gender equity, as required by the 2010 Constitution, or youth representation. In addition, the first schedule is silent on the mechanism for initiating the process of appointment—how does the minister identify those farmer or pastoralist representatives?

Generally, CAACs have more public (government) officials than public representatives as members. This implies that the public representatives may not have a constructive or positive impact on the threshold of decision making due to lesser membership. Second, although the Constitution requires mandatory gender equity, this is not reflected in some of the older legislation, such as the 2002 Water Act. Third, although the CAACs have members termed as "public representatives" who represent various local interests such as farm-

---

94 *Water Act* (2002), at sec. 16.

95 *Id.*

96 Robert Kibugi, Kevin Mugenya, & Mary Ondiek, *Putting People at the Centre: Enhancing Public Participation in Decision Making* 46–47 (Inst. L. & Envrtl. Governance 2012).

97 *Id.*

98 *Id.*

ers, pastoralists, or businesses, these members are appointed by the minister. Their being appointed by the minister, rather than elected by the local community, vitiates the argument that they are representing the local community interest.

The Role of Water Resource Users Associations in Enhancing Public Participation

The Water Act provides a role for community groups in the management of water resources under the water resource users associations (WRUAs). Section 15(5) states that the catchment management strategy shall encourage and facilitate the establishment and operation of the WRUAs, which will act as forums for conflict resolution and cooperative management of water resources in catchment areas. The water rules define WRUAs as "an association of water users, riparian land owners, or other stakeholders who have formally and voluntarily associated for the purposes of cooperatively sharing, managing and conserving a common water resource." Ideally, the WRUAs provide a good platform for the public to participate in decision making regarding water resource management, working with the WRMA. Similar to the CAAC, Rule 6 of the Water Rules requires public information on vacancies in a WRUA to "consist of publication in the Kenya Gazette, at least one announcement in a national newspaper in circulation in the locality, at least one announcement in the radio broadcasting in the locality, and any other local means of communication."

In order for the WRMA to register an association as a WRUA for water resource management activities, the association must "be legally registered, have a Constitution conducive to collaborative management of the water resources of a particular resource, and promote public participation, conflict mitigation, gender main-streaming and environmental sustainability." Typically, such associations are registered as societies[99] and would have to align their constitutions with the objectives and norms expressed in Rule 10. Similar to the challenge facing CFAs, the process of registration as a society under the Societies Act is lengthy and complicated. Once a WRUA has been registered with the registrar of societies, it can register with the WRMA. The WRMA monitors WRUAs to ensure that they adhere to the Water Act and has the mandate to suspend or deregister those that violate any conditions. This linkage between the WRMA, as the regulator, and WRUAs and the participatory management body is intended to provide value-addition for sustainability in water resources utilization.

The WRUAs play an instrumental role with regard to approval of permits that are required for abstraction rights from any water resource. This is an important avenue because the Water Rules detail how WRUAs and their members can participate in actual decision making on the approval of the water permits. Therefore, the WRMA is required to provide the relevant WRUA with copies of every water-use application, and the WRUA must give

99 Through the *Societies Act, supra* note 68.

comments within 30 days. If the WRUA does not provide commentary, the WRMA may proceed without further reference to the WRUA. Section 29 of the Water Rules provides a mechanism for notification of every water permit application, which should be displayed at the local government offices. It is notable that no specific role is given to the WRUA, as the grassroots organization, to carry out the public notification and awareness process. In practice however, whenever a person proposes to abstract water from a resource for development activities, that proponent is required by the WRMA to register and become a member of the local WRUA.[100]

Although the CAAC and WRUAs have registered some success in water resource management, their impact is diminished by very low public awareness regarding the existence, roles, function, or utility of grass-roots avenues for public participation in water resource management such as the CAACs and WRUAs. This is in spite of the Water Rules requiring the WRMA to take steps to engage members of the public who may otherwise not be informed or aware of the issues being brought before them. However, the rules are silent on the specific nature and scope of these steps, and there is no mechanism to monitor whether the WRMA or the two statutory committees are complying with this requirement.

Two options can be pursued to assist in resolving this challenge. The first, based on law reform, is to put in place a regulatory framework that requires WRUAs and CAACs to undertake proactive disclosure of information that is pertinent to natural resource governance. This proactive disclosure is already anticipated by the social contract mechanism through Article 35 of the Constitution, which requires the Kenyan state (including statutory entities such as WRUAs and CAACs) to publish and disseminate any important information affecting the nation. Such an approach, implemented through sectoral natural resource laws and regulations, would provide an instrumental mechanism for dissemination of information, enabling local communities with the voice they require to constructively participate in governance.

The second option, a practical, nonlegal approach, is to implement mechanisms of public awareness through civic education. This approach can be deployed to raise public knowledge of participation mechanisms (e.g., WRUAs and CAACs). Civic education is critical in giving voice to the population and enhancing citizens' roles in governance because it raises public awareness on the existence of rights, avenues for service delivery, mechanisms for accountability, and avenues for actual participation by individual members of the public.

Since the 2013 general elections, Kenya has begun to implement a devolved system of government that was adopted through the 2010 Constitution.[101] Based on this basic law, the specific implementation of water conservation

---

100 Interview with WRMA staff, Siaya County, Kenya (Jan. 2012).

101 *See* Kenyan Const., *supra* note 1, at ch. 11.

laws and policies is a function of county governments. In addition, county governments are required to integrate public participation into all areas of administration. The 2002 water law is under reform and expected to be fully replaced by the end of 2014. The cascading implementation of water resource laws to devolved county governments has already expanded the space and voice that people need to participate in governance at the most local level, consistent with Principle 10 of the 1992 Rio Declaration. More specific challenges are how to provide room for constructive and direct choosing of representatives of local community interests and how to mainstream and sustain citizens' interest. Proactive disclosure, implemented with civic education, will provide a helpful way to safeguard the gains made since the last water sector regulatory reforms enacted in 2002.

Conclusion

There is an immutable link between the social contract and the basic rights that enhance the voice of the Kenyan people in governing and managing their natural resources. It is the social contract, in the form of constitutional order, that sets the tone and defines the voice, using fundamental rights as a mechanism. The link between the Constitution and enhanced voice for citizen participation in resource governance is critical for two reasons.

First, in a positivist system such as Kenya's, the Constitution is the *Grundnorm*, supreme to all other laws, and it sets the tone for the content of other laws. Consequently, when the Constitution of Kenya has underpinned public participation, devolution of government, and sustainable development as fundamental governance norms, no other law can deviate. If such deviation occurs, the offending law is deemed unconstitutional.

Second, the Constitution, in its nature of a social contract, is the mechanism through which citizens agree on the rules of engagement for their own governance. This is evident in Article 1, where the Constitution clearly indicates that citizens have delegated their governance to elected representatives and governments at national and county levels. In addition, it sets out a collective set of norms defining rights and obligations of all persons through the Bill of Rights. For this reason, the Constitution is an ideal model of how all people in Kenya are expected to behave and conduct themselves, especially in claiming and asserting their rights, and in observing attendant duties. It is therefore an ideal basis to set the norms for public and local community roles in governance as well as for natural resource laws such as those in forestry and water.

The laws reviewed here, on water and forestry, provide the rules through which citizens can have a role in resource management through mechanisms of public consultation and representation. It is an approach that primarily involves the creation of statutory organs of local governance that citizens can establish as communities and play distinctive roles. In the case of WRUAs and CFAs, which depend on concerned people for their establishment, the participatory governance resonates with the proactive conception of public participation in Article 69(2) of the Constitution. These sectoral legal frameworks were, however, enacted prior to the 2010 constitutional order. Therefore, although they provide the normative content to the basis set by the Constitution, they need to be reviewed for complete conformity in terms of providing a voice for citizens in resource governance. The review is necessary because the constitutional framework, recently renegotiated in 2010, has reinforced the space available for citizens by emphasizing that it is from the people that sovereignty flows, and their place in governance is a right.

Going forward, statutory mechanisms designed to give voice for public participation in resource governance will have to internalize tools to ensure that the participating communities actually impact decisions and the governance process. Elements such as how to utilize CFAs and WRUAs in enhancing the socioeconomic circumstances of participating local communities will need to be addressed carefully. This is necessary to ensure that the environmental conservation element is not neglected if no balance with socioeconomic activities is achieved. In addition, having these mechanisms in place can amount to naught where concerned local communities have insufficient or no knowledge on the roles that these participatory mechanisms play in providing a voice in resource governance. It is therefore useful to adopt legal and nonlegal mechanisms, such as requiring the adoption of proactive disclosure of information by entities such as WRUAs and mounting a concerted and purposeful effort to make civic education a valued resource for enhancing public awareness.

8

The Impact of the Legal Framework of Community Forestry on the Development of Rural Areas in Cameroon

EMMANUEL D. KAM YOGO

Two decades have passed since community forestry was introduced in Cameroon through Law No. 94/01 of January 20, 1994. That law instituted for the first time in Cameroon a new type of forest—the "community forest"—which is also an integral part of what are called "nonpermanent forests" in the country's forestry system.[1] The adoption of the law came about as a result of a series of demands made by the International Monetary Fund (IMF) and the World Bank, within the framework of the structural adjustment programs of the late 1980s.

The IMF and the World Bank wanted Cameroon to adopt a new forestry law that would enable the country to derive substantial revenue from its forests while halting the abusive exploitation of those forests. The drafting of the new law was also a prerequisite for the signing of a standby agreement between Cameroon and the IMF at the beginning of the 1990s.[2] Consequently, a large number of IMF and World Bank experts were called in to help draft the law on forestry, wildlife, and fisheries regulations. Given that the drafting of the law took place soon after the UN Conference on Environment and Development, also called the "Earth Summit," held in Rio de Janeiro, the ideas and programs proposed at that conference had to be taken into consideration. Thus, "the Rio spirit," influenced by the objectives of sustainable development that emanated from the Rio Declaration, Agenda 21, and the Statement of Forest Principles,[3] inspired the drafting of the 1994 forestry law in Cameroon. Consequently, this law abided by some of the recommendations made at the Earth Summit, such as taking into consideration the situations of local or indigenous peoples[4] when exploiting natural resources. It was in this light that community forestry was enshrined in the Cameroon forestry law.

---

1 Law No. 94/01, Jan. 20, 1994, sec. 37, also known as the Cameroonian forestry law, established forestry, wildlife, and fisheries regulations in Cameroon. "Nonpermanent forests" are unclassified forests without land certificates.

2 Samuel Nguiffo Tene, *La nouvelle législation forestière au Cameroun* 6 (Fondation Friedrich Ebert 1994).

3 The *Statement of Forest Principles* was officially known as the *Non-legally Binding Authoritative Statement of Principles for a Global Consensus on the Management, Conservation and Sustainable Development of All Types of Forests.*

4 *See* Principle 22 of the *Rio Declaration on Environment and Development*; ch. 26 of *Agenda 21*; the *Statement of Forest Principles.*

A community forest is defined as a nonpermanent forest (explained below) and is thus subject to a management agreement between a village community and the Ministry of Forestry. Management of a community forest is the responsibility of the village community that stands to benefit from developing the forest, with technical assistance coming from the state forestry services.[5] The Cameroonian forestry law designates two types of forests: permanent and nonpermanent.[6] Permanent forests include state forests and council forests.[7] Permanent forests are classified and are subject to land certificates in either the name of the state (for state forests) or of a local council (for council forests). Nonpermanent forests consist of communal forests, forests belonging to private individuals, and community forests.[8]

No village community can be awarded a land certificate for a community forest. Instead, the legal status of a community forest is created and subject to the management agreement signed between the state and the village community. When a village community is responsible for the management of a community forest, the village community can receive technical assistance from the state services in charge of forests. The main objective in creating a community forest is to enable a group within a rural population to actively participate in forest management and to help develop the local community with the resources derived from the exploitation of the forest.[9]

After twenty years of legal recognition of community forestry, how has each party played its role in implementing this phenomenon? Further, how have community forests contributed to local development in Cameroon? This chapter answers these questions by examining the legal conditions for creating a community forest, the terms of management agreements, and the assessment of revenues realized from community forests.

The Rights and Duties of Stakeholders of Community Forests in Cameroon

Community forest stakeholders—the state and the village community, that is, the forest owner and the beneficiary of the transfer of the right to use and manage a forest—have each, under the law, rights and duties pertaining to the process of the creation of the right for village communities to use and manage community forests.

---

5 Decree No. 95/531/PM, Aug. 23, 1995, art. 3(11).

6 Law No. 94/01, *supra* note 1, at sec. 20.

7 *Id.*, at sec. 21.

8 *Id.*, at sec. 35.

9 *See* Egbe S. Egbe, *The Concept of Community Forestry under Cameroonian Law,* 15 Revue africaine de droit international et comparé 278 (2000).

The Rights and Duties of Village Communities

The Rights of Village Communities

The rights of village communities are based on the Cameroonian Constitution. The preamble of the constitution states that the people of Cameroon are "resolved to harness the natural resources in order to ensure the well-being of every citizen without discrimination."[10]

The forest is one of the natural resources of Cameroon. The above quotation delineates that the exploitation of the forest should contribute to the well-being of the population. Inasmuch as the constitution encourages the exploitation of natural resources to ensure the well-being of the population, the creation of community forests for the benefit of village communities can be said to come from a constitutional stipulation. Furthermore, the constitution states that "the State shall ensure the protection of minorities and shall preserve the rights of indigenous populations in accordance with the law."[11] It is true that the expression "indigenous populations" has been a subject of controversy in Cameroon since the present constitution went into force;[12] however, it is important to note that the forestry law uses the expressions "indigenous populations," "local population,"[13] and "citizens living around the forest"[14] without distinction or discrimination, and these terms all refer to village communities.

Cameroonian forestry law makes provision for a series of rights in favor of village communities. Among these are logging rights[15] and the right of

---

10 *See* Cameroonian Const., pmbl., para. 3.

11 *See id.*, at para. 5.

12 On the controversy, *see* Luc Sindjoun, *Identité nationale et révision constitutionnelle: Comment constitutionnalise-t-on le nous au Cameroun post-unitaire?*, 1 Polis 10–24 (1996); Léopold Donfack Sokeng, *Existe-t-il une identité démocratique camerounaise? La spécificité camerounaise à l'épreuve de l'universalité des droits fondamentaux*, 1 Polis 25–44 (1996); Alain Didier Olinga, *La protection des minorités et des populations autochtones en droit public camerounais*, 10 Revue africaine de droit international et comparé 271–91 (1998); Ekambi Dibongue, *Autochtones et allogènes à Douala: Quête hégémonique exogène et résistance endogène dans une métropole africaine*, 1 Revue Camerounaise de droit et de science politique 69–80 (2005); James Mouangue Kobila, *La protection des minorités et des peuples autochtones au Cameroun: Entre reconnaissance interne contrastée et consécration universelle réaffirmée* 295 (Dianoïa 2009).

13 Sec. 26(1) & sec. 30(2) of the Cameroonian forestry law.

14 Sec. 36 of the Cameroonian forestry law.

15 Law No. 94/01 to establish forestry, wildlife, and fisheries regulations has provisions in favor of logging rights of populations. According to sec. 8(1), "Logging or customary right means the right which is recognized as being that of the local population to harvest all forest wildlife and fisheries products freely for their personal use, except the protected species." Section 26(1) stipulates that "the instrument classifying a State forest shall take into account the social environment of the local population who shall maintain their logging rights." And sec. 30(2) on council forests stipulates: "The classification instrument shall determine boundaries and the management objectives of such forest which may be the same as for State forest, as well as the exercise of logging rights by local population."

preemption.[16] The right of preemption, if exercised by a village, authorizes that village to create a community forest. This right of preemption is a way to implement the principle of participation articulated in Cameroonian law on the management of the environment. The principle of participation has been developed at the international level since the Conference on Environment and Development was held in Rio de Janeiro in 1992. The principle essentially stipulates that all citizens, regardless of their social status, should participate in the sustainable development of their states. Concerning indigenous populations, the Rio Declaration on Environment and Development affirms that "indigenous people and their communities and other local communities have a vital role in environmental management and development because of their knowledge and traditional practices. States should recognise and duly support their identity, culture and interests and enable their participation in the achievement of sustainable development."[17] Additionally, the UN Agenda 21 states that "governments should incorporate, in collaboration with the indigenous people affected, the rights and responsibilities of indigenous people and their communities in the legislation of each country, suitable to the country's specific situation."[18]

The right of preemption, which a village community can consider as the right to obtain a forest "in priority,"[19] is a mechanism that favors the implementation of the "right to environment"[20] and the "right to development"[21] in favor of the local population. In obtaining the right to manage a community forest, a village community takes on the responsibility of sustainably and ecologically managing its bordering forest. This is a way to ensure the right to a healthy environment and to self-fund local development with financial resources drawn from the use and exploitation of community forests. The right to development has also been consolidated by the provisions of the forestry law, according to which "forest products of all kinds resulting from the management of community forests shall belong solely to the village community concerned."[22] However, it must be noted that the creation of a community forest does not give the right of ownership to the beneficiary community of

16 Sec. 37(4) of the forestry law states: "Village communities shall have the right of pre-emption." The right of preemption is the right to obtain a forest in priority (to any other person).

17 Principle 22, *supra* note 4.

18 *See* ch. 26.8 of *Agenda 21*.

19 *See* Decree No. 95/531/PM, *supra* note 5, at art. 27(3).

20 The right to environment is a basic issue in the evolution of environmental law in francophone countries today. *See* Shouqiu Cai, *Résultats et perspectives des recherches théoriques du droit à l'environnement*, in *Du droit de l'environnement au droit à l'environnement: À la recherche du juste milieu* 17–38 (Anthony Chamboredon ed., L'Harmattan 2007); Bernard Poujade, *La protection du droit à l'environnement par le juge administratif: L'exemple du contrôle juridictionnel des grands équipements publics*, in *Du droit de l'environnement au droit à l'environnement* 39–50.

21 The right to development is officially recognized by the Cameroonian Constitution. It is considered as a collective and an individual right; on this opinion, *see* Robert Charvin, *L'investissement international et le droit au développement* 113 (L'Harmattan 2002).

22 Sec. 37(5) of the Cameroonian forestry law.

the forest concerned. Thus, no land title can be issued to a village community on a community forest.

The Duties of Village Communities in Matters of Community Forestry

The duties of a village community in relation to community forestry are declaring intent to obtain a community forest, establishing a legal entity, holding a conference to compile an application to request an attribution for a community forest, and submitting a simple management plan for presentation.

Declaring Intent to Obtain a Community Forest. Village communities have a duty to declare their intention to obtain a community forest through a letter addressed to the minister of forestry. The letter of intent,[23] to which is attached a map of the forest zone solicited, enables the reservation of the concerned forest area for the bordering village communities.[24] All applications for the attribution of a community forest are given priority over any other title for exploitation in the area concerned. The application empowers the Department of Forestry to issue for sale standing volumes of forest that have never been requested by a village community. Bearing this in mind, after three months following the collection of official receipts from the village communities that border the forests concerned, and on the basis of the declaration of intent forwarded by some of these villages, the Department of Forestry must draw up and publish two lists: one indicating forests that have been solicited by village communities, and one indicating other forests that are open for tender; standing volumes of such forests are for sale by the Ministry of Forestry for the next three years. Any sale of standing of any volume of forest that trespasses into an area designated as a community forest, whether still under "attribution" or that has already been "attributed" (i.e., legally allocated) to a bordering village community, is null and void.[25]

From the date of deposit of the letter of intent, the bordering village communities must forward to the minister of forestry progress reports on the ongoing process they are currently in with respect to their requested community forest being "attributed" to them. (A copy also must be forwarded to the appropriate divisional delegate for forestry.) This must be done every six months. Failure to do this will mean that the village community concerned will lose its right to obtain the solicited forest. In a similar manner, any bordering village community that does not deposit an application file for the attribution of a community forest in accordance with regulations laid down in the manual of procedure made by the Ministry of Forestry, and which requires compliance within a deadline of three months, shall lose its right to obtain the forest concerned.

---

23 The letter of intent is deposited at the subdepartment of community forestry; a copy of the letter is sent to the competent divisional delegate of forestry. A notice of delivery is given to the village community.

24 Art. 6(4) of the Order No. 0518/MINEF/CAB, Dec. 21, 2001, gives priority to village communities for attribution of any forest that may be developed into a community forest.

25 *Id.*, at art. 7(3).

Establishing a Legal Entity for the Village Community. Decree No. 95/531/PM of August 23, 1995 lays down applicable modalities on the forest regime, and it provides that any village community having the intent to benefit from natural resources derived from a forest must have the status of a corporate body in the form of a legal entity as provided for by the provisions of the current legislation in force.[26] According to the legal instruments in force, legal entities for this purpose are associations, cooperatives, common initiative groups (CIGs), and economic interest groups (EIGs). The chosen legal entity should represent all the social components of the village community in question. A legal entity may comprise people from many different villages if all of them share the same boundary with the same forest. The aforementioned legal entities are governed by different laws.

Associations are governed by Law No. 90/053 of December 19, 1990, on the freedom of associations. Associations are easy to create,[27] but they face many disadvantages, such as the legal prohibition of receiving gifts and legacies if they are not known to be of public utility.

Cooperative societies and common initiative groups[28] are governed by law No. 92/06 of August 14, 1992 and Decree No. 92/455/PM of November 23, 1992. The creation of and regulations governing these two types of legal entities are often complicated for citizens who are not used to heavy bureaucracy. However, the modalities of these two entities are subject to some transparency principles that can be attractive to many people.

Economic interest groups are governed by the Organization for the Harmonization of Business Law in Africa's Uniform Act on Commercial Companies and Economic Interest Groups, which has been in force since January 1998. This type of legal entity has the disadvantage of being very costly to legally establish,[29] relative to the small revenues of some village communities, which can be a source of frustration to such communities.

It is also possible for a traditional chief to qualify to manage a community forest. However, the risk in doing this is that it may not be as transparent in its management as is desirable, because a traditional ruler can never be dismissed of his function by the simple wish of the villagers, even if he is guilty of embezzlement.

Holding a Conference and Compiling an Application to Request an Attribution for a Community Forest. According to Decree No. 95/531/PM of August 23, 1995, which lays down regulatory procedures of forestry regimes, any community

---

26 *See* Decree No. 95/531/PM, *supra* note 5, at art. 28(3).

27 Only a formal declaration to the senior divisional officer (SDO), followed by a receipt delivered by the SDO, is sufficient to create an association.

28 According to some authors, common initiative groups are the most popular form of legal entity created by village communities. *See* Joseph Gabriel Elong, *Organisations paysannes des pouvoirs dans le Cameroun forestier* 37–48 (Presses Universitaires de Yaoundé 2005).

29 For example, the fees for registering a demand and the required documents to be attached are too high.

wishing to manage a community forest is obliged to hold a consultative meeting, at which all interested persons and groups of the community concerned choose a management officer, define objectives, and delimit the boundaries of the forest.[30] This meeting is supervised by a competent local administrative authority, with the assistance of local technical official, namely the divisional delegate for forestry and wildlife. Meeting sessions should be widely publicized to ensure participation by all interested groups and persons in the community concerned. In the event that not all interested groups and persons in the community participate, the administrative authority has the discretion to call off the meeting and propose another date for future sessions.

If the meeting is held in accordance with the provisions of the relevant regulations in force, the proceedings are signed on the spot by all participants, and the application file for the attribution of a community forest is constituted. In accordance with the decree of application on forest regimes, this file must comprise, among other things, a stamped application indicating the assigned objectives[31] of the forest solicited, a site plan of the forest, supporting documents on the official name of the concerned community village, and the address of the lead official. The file must also include a description of the activities to be carried out by the community within the periphery of the forest solicited, the curriculum vitae of the officer in charge of forestry operations, as well as the proceedings of the consultation meeting.[32] Following the revision of procedures for attribution and community forest management norms of 2009,[33] two new documents have been added to the file requirements: a community forest temporary management agreement form, duly signed by the lead official of the legal entity, and an attestation demarcating the boundaries of the surface area of the land.

Once the application file for a community has been constituted, it is forwarded to the minister of forestry through official channels. If, after 60 days of transmitting the application, the minister does not receive the required document, the requesting community may submit another copy directly to the minister. This copy, however, must be accompanied by the references of the file that was deposited at the Divisional Delegation of Forestry. The minister must reply within a deadline of 10 working days. If the minister does not reply by the deadline, the community may consider its application approved;[34] the

---

30 Decree No. 95/531/PM, *supra* note 5, at art. 28(1).

31 Generally, the objectives of community forests are production (e.g., of wood products and nonwood products), protection (e.g., of fauna and vegetables), and valorization (e.g., of forest products and ecotourism).

32 Decree No. 95/531/PM, *supra* note 5, at art. 29(1).

33 *See* Decision No. 098/D/MINFOF/SG/DF/SDFC, Feb. 12, 2009, which adopted the document *Manual of Procedure for the Attribution and Norms for the Management of Community Forests*.

34 Minister of Forestry & Wildlife, *Manual of Procedures for the Attribution and Norms for the Management of Community Forests* 22 (2009).

solicited forest may not be subject to other exploitation licenses, or be a classified forest.[35]

Submitting a Simple Management Plan and Signing a Management Agreement. The forestry law requires that every community forest have a simple management plan, duly approved by the state service in charge of forestry.[36] The plan is established under the care of the village community and should conform to all activities carried out in a community forest.

The simple management plan is a document specifying the manner in which a village community wishing to acquire a community forest intends to manage it. It must lay down all the activities to be carried out by the villagers in the different sectors of the management of the natural resources of the forests concerned. The simple management plan must contain the following:

a. Proper identification of the community (i.e., the name of the community and the legal entity, the date of the first constitutive general assembly, the name of the village, region, division, subdivision, and/or district, and information on the lead official).
b. Location of the community forest (i.e., the administrative location, region, and surface area).
c. Priority objectives of the community forest.
d. Description of the community forest.
e. Socioeconomic and environmental information.
f. Results of the inventory of resources.
g. Resources and revenue management plan of activities.
h. Commitments[37] and signatures.

The approval of a simple management plan by the forestry administration is followed by the signing of a final management agreement.[38] A management agreement of a community forest is a contract in which the state grants to a village community a portion of the forest of the nonpermanent state forest, for managing, conserving, and exploiting that forest, for the interest and benefit of the relevant community that has been granted such liberties.[39] The management agreement is revised at least once every five years. Every village community that is a signatory of a management agreement is obliged to respect

35 A forest subject to a land certificate for the state or a local council.

36 Law No. 94/01, *supra* note 1, at sec. 37(2).

37 The village community usually declares to have knowledge of forestry and environmental legislation and undertakes to respect the provisions of the simple management plan, to submit annual reports on the activities carried out in the community forest to the state, and to execute plans for the community micro-projects.

38 Decree No. 95/531/PM, at art. 27(3)(a)–(c), stipulates that a senior divisional officer, a governor, or the minister of forestry and wildlife is allowed, depending on the cases, to sign a management agreement on behalf of the state.

39 *Id.*, at art. 3(16).

the terms of the agreement as well as the relevant management plan for the forest that it has been allocated, and must protect its community forest.

The Rights and Duties of the State Regarding Community Forestry

The state has relatively fewer rights and duties than the village communities that have been allocated a community forest. However, each of the state's rights and duties is, in substance, weightier and more onerous relative to those of village communities.

The first duty of the state stems from the constitution, which stipulates that "the State shall preserve the rights of indigenous populations in accordance with the law."[40] Within the context of community forestry, this preservation of rights of indigenous populations is translated through free "technical assistance"[41] that the state should extend to all village communities requesting a community forest. The state should also facilitate the formal organization of village communities by supervising[42] consultation meetings, prior to applying for a community forest. Officials of the Ministry of Forestry must follow up and monitor activities carried out in the community forest.

The rights of the state are prerogatives that allow the state to intervene in cases where the law is violated. In such cases, when a village community does not respect the management agreement and forestry law in force, the state may suspend or annul the respective agreement[43] or carry out any necessary work at the expense of the community concerned to repair any damage that has been caused to the forest.[44] However, in cases where management rules of a community forest have been violated by a third party, the state may take legal action against the offender.[45] In any case, the ownership of community forests belongs to the state.

The Substantive Terms of Community Forest Management Agreements between the State and Village Communities

A community forest management agreement is a contract between the state and a village community through which the government grants a forest to the village community. This community is responsible for the management, conservation, and exploitation of the forest during a specific period. Generally, a management agreement contains about 10 articles, the provisions of which concern the identification of the community forest, the roles of both parties, and the settlement of disputes.

---

40 *See* Cameroonian Const., pmbl., *supra* note 10.

41 Sec. 37(1) of the Cameroonian forestry law.

42 Decree No. 95/531/PM, *supra* note 5, at art. 28(1).

43 Sec. 38 of the Cameroonian forestry law.

44 *Id.*

45 Decree No. 95/531/PM, *supra* note 5, at art. 32(3).

The Identification of the Community Forest

The first provisions of a management agreement aim at identifying the forest. They specify the name of the beneficiary village community and fix the boundaries of the concerned forest in the north, south, east, and west. Next, the surface area of the forest, which generally does not exceed 5,000 hectares, is delineated.[46] Subsequent to this, the objectives of the use and exploitation of the forest are specified; this must have a direct link with the content of the simple management plan submitted. Finally, the length of time that the agreement is in force is indicated.[47]

The Roles of Both Parties to the Agreement

The contracting village community plays an important role in the management of the community forest and in the renewal of the management agreement. The village community must ensure the proper performance of the agreement during the period covered and provide an annual report to the administration. Before the expiration of the agreement, the community must take necessary administrative measures in order to renew it. Accordingly, it must provide relevant documents to demonstrate, among other requirements, the continuing existence of the legal entity under which the village community operates, the number and type of forest exploitation permits to which the forest is subject, information relating to possible amendments or replacement of management leaders, and, finally, a five-year action program with a plan of operation.

Minor breaches of the simple management plan or of the management agreement by members of the beneficiary village community in the community forest are subject to censure by the community itself, in accordance with provisions specified in the rules and regulations of the agreement and plan. In the case of a subsequent offense or serious breaches of the management agreement by members of the village community, the community forest manager must refer the matter to the local services branch of the ministry of forestry.

The main role of the state consists in ensuring the effective implementation of the agreement and examining any application for the renewal of the term of this agreement. For example, the state may prosecute individuals if the management agreement or the simple management plan of the community forest is breached. In cases of serious or repeated breaches with the complicity of the village community, the state must issue a written warning to the community via the local representative of the Ministry of Forestry. This warning must clearly indicate the facts and the gravity of the matter and, additionally, may be followed by the suspension or annulment of the management agreement by the state. Moreover, if a community is not sensitive to the warning issued by the state within a reasonable deadline of nine months, the ministry in charge of forests may decide to charge the community for any

46 *See id.*, at art. 27(4).

47 The maximum length of time is five years, although these periods can be renewed. *See id.*, at art. 30(3).

losses incurred. On the whole, the state remains in a position of public authority within the framework of the implementation and the renewal of a management agreement; this position can, and generally does, lead to disputes with beneficiary village communities.

The Settlement of Disputes between the State and Village Communities in Regard to Community Forestry

If a dispute arises over the interpretation or the implementation of the agreement between the state and a village community managing a community forest, both parties must find a solution through negotiations. If negotiations fail, both parties may jointly or separately refer the matter to the authority who signed the management agreement. If the settlement proposed by this authority is not satisfactory, the aggrieved party must carry the matter to higher levels of dispute settlement. In any situation, the litigation is considered a closed matter if a solution originates from the minister of forestry. As a principle, it is not foreseen that the intervention of a judge will adjudicate and produce a settlement of any dispute between the state and village communities. However, there is nothing in the law to stop a village community that is dissatisfied with the decision of the minister to contact a judge and express its dissatisfaction, which may lead to judicial intervention in the matter. Lastly, any litigation or dispute between a private logging company and a village community may be settled directly by a judge.

Achievements and Outcomes: Projects Funded by Income Derived from the Exploitation of Community Forests

According to Cameroon's forestry law, village communities must be paid the selling price of the products[48] extracted from the forests that have been allocated to them.[49] Village communities utilizing community forests have directly implemented development projects in all the regions where those forests have been created. These projects earn income for the village communities that implement them and are predominantly social, economic, or cultural in character.

At the social level, outcomes have been produced in the health sector and in the field of education. Health sector projects include the building of health centers and accommodation for medical staff,[50] rehabilitation of water points[51] and drilling projects for water,[52] medical care for sick persons in the

---

48 For example, timber sold to timber companies.

49 *See* section 67(2) of the Cameroonian forestry law.

50 This project was realized at Belabo, in the East region, and at NgambeTikar and NkolMetet in the Central region. *See* the Ministry of Forestry's Community Forests Unit's *Report of the Follow up Mission for the Implementation of Simple Management Plans in Community Forests for the Top 10* (Dec. 2008).

51 In a village, a water point is a place where drinkable water is available.

52 These outcomes are present at Dimako, Angossas, Mbang, and Ndikinimeki.

community,[53] the purchase of drugs for the community health centers, and the payment of nurses' salaries.[54]

In the educational field, village community-funded projects have given rise to outcomes such as paying teachers' salaries, rebuilding classrooms,[55] purchasing desks for schools and teaching resources, awarding scholarships to school pupils[56] and to students in the wider locality,[57] and paying for capacity-building seminars in agro-forestry for elected village members.[58]

On an economic level, many village communities have funded projects that have generated outcomes. These include building sheds for markets, purchasing a power generator for lighting houses,[59] purchasing corrugated metal sheets for improving habitat of community members, purchasing grinding mills, creating palm oil plantations,[60] constructing roads, purchasing logging equipment,[61] providing electricity to villages,[62] creating community cocoa farms,[63] supplying computer equipment for a secretary, creating a shop,[64] rehabilitating bridges,[65] distributing oil palm plants to villagers, and purchasing pesticides.[66]

Many community-funded projects have realized outcomes on a cultural level, due to income derived from community forests. Examples include constructing a community rest home in Ngoro[67] and community halls in Belabo and Mvangan, rehabilitating a traditional chief's residence in Ngambe Tikar,[68] extending support to the traditional council of the Fundong chieftaincy in matters relating to dispute settlement,[69] providing care to the elderly at Dja,

---

53 Project realized at Ngoro, in the Central region.

54 Project realized at Dja, in the Haut Nyong division.

55 Project realized at Ntui, Deuk, Belabo, Lomié, Mvangan, Kribi, and Sangmelima.

56 Project realized at Ngoro and Ngambe Tikar in the Central region.

57 Project realized at Deuk, in the Central region.

58 Project realized at Dja, in the East region.

59 Project realized at Ngoro, in the Central region.

60 Project realized at Deuk and NkolMetet in the Central region, and Mvangan in the South region.

61 Project realized at Ngambe Tikar, in the Central region.

62 Project realized at NkolMetet.

63 Project realized at Belabo.

64 Project realized at Mvangan.

65 Project realized at Kribi.

66 Project realized at Sangmelima.

67 See *Report of the Follow up Mission, supra* note 50, at 15.

68 *Id.*, at 16.

69 *Id.*, at 9.

building churches in Lomie,[70] giving gifts to churches at Mvangan, and purchasing sports equipment for youths in Meyomessi.[71]

Conclusion

Community forestry is an excellent tool for the implementation of the right to development and the right to environment. It is also the most appropriate mechanism for the protection of indigenous populations in the forested regions of Cameroon. The assessment of community forestry under the Cameroonian forestry law has produced varied results. Communities where village populations are well organized have seen excellent results and successful projects; in less-organized communities, the success rate has been much lower and concrete, positive outcomes far fewer. In this light, the impact of community forestry on local development outcomes largely depends, first, on the seriousness with which the village community views its allocation of a community forest and the attendant use, management, and exploitation of such forests, and, second, on how well run and well organized the beneficiary communities are. Clearly, well-organized village communities are able to build health centers and schools, and successfully invest income earned from their community forests to achieve Cameroon's Millennium Development Goals. However, the state should follow up on and monitor the functioning of executive bodies elected by village communities to manage community forests. Such oversight is necessary to avoid mismanagement of projects, such as the embezzlement of community forest–generated funds by individuals.

---

70 *Id.*, at 22.

71 *Id.*, at 28.

PART III

Urban Law and Policy

9
Urban Law
A Key to Accountable Urban Government and Effective Urban Service Delivery

MATTHEW GLASSER AND STEPHEN BERRISFORD

Each year, the World Bank Group hosts Law, Justice and Development (LJD) Week, an event that brings together government officials, development practitioners, and legal scholars from around the world who are working at the intersection of law and development. LJD Week 2013 was notable for the multiple sessions that focused on legal frameworks for urban governance and urban development. Urban legislation plays a central role in determining the voice that residents have (and often do not have) in the management and planning of their cities; in the social contract between citizens and firms, on the one hand, and local government, on the other; and in the accountability of local government for the provision of services and infrastructure. Because cities are increasingly acknowledged as the locations in which countries make the greatest economic and social development advances, it matters more and more that they are governed well. Good urban governance is built on good urban law. Drawing on the four sessions at LJD Week 2013 with an urban focus, this chapter discusses some of the ideas that arose there as the basis for a new urban legal agenda. This chapter does not purport to identify or build any sort of theory of urban law in an international development context, nor does it claim to have discovered the field of urban law, which has existed for more than 20 years.[1] It does, however, draw attention to the four sessions at LJD Week 2013 that had an urban theme, an indicator of a growing interest in the field. The conclusion of this chapter considers some of the guidance provided in these sessions and how it can help establish a better understanding of the importance of urban law, some of its limitations, and ideas to stimulate further work, research, and innovation.

The sessions covered urban land rights and titling,[2] urban law for improved development delivery,[3] urban law in Sub-Saharan Africa,[4] and

---

1 The term *urban law* has been used in the Latin American context since the early 1990s.

2 The panelists for this session were Lionel Galliez, Union Internationale du Notariat, and Robin Rajack, the World Bank. The session was moderated by Stephen Berrisford, of the African Centre for Cities, University of Cape Town.

3 The panelists for this session were Maria Mousmouti, University of London; Edric Selous, the United Nations; Gianluca Crispi, UN-Habitat; and Jaap de Visser, University of the Western Cape. The moderator was Robert Lewis-Lettington, UN-Habitat.

4 The panelists for this session were Stephen Berrisford, African Centre for Cities, University of Cape Town; Patrick McAuslan, Birkbeck College, University of London; Stevan Do-

insolvency in subnational governments.[5] The range of issues covered in these sessions reflects the diversity of urban law and the common themes and principles that warrant further expansion and deepening.

What is "urban law"? It is the law that shapes cities, their land use, their institutions, and their finances. It determines whether a city is efficient or inefficient or, sometimes, whether it is more efficient for some residents than for others. It is the law that enables effective citizen participation in the planning and governance of a city and that helps ensure fairness, transparency, and inclusivity. Urban law encompasses laws governing city council meetings, city records, budgeting, accounting, and reporting. It reflects key areas of a country's constitutional law, particularly the division of powers between city (or local) government and national or regional/state/provincial government, as well as the content of important human rights such as the rights to property, to housing or shelter, and to a decent environment. Where these aspects of constitutional law are not actually incorporated in the country's constitutional texts, they are inevitably part of the political and legal discourse in the country, part of the struggles to change constitutional orders, struggles that invariably play themselves out in the urban context.

Urban law is changing and developing as fast as cities are. As cities grow ever bigger, the law strives to adapt to the challenges of governance that occur in large metropolitan areas: politicians and officials in cities across the world are wrestling with the problem of managing urban agglomerations that spill over jurisdictional boundaries and sometimes over international borders. The blogosphere has seen a buzz of excitement over plans for a new Beijing-centered megalopolis that would be "bigger than Uruguay and more populous than Germany."[6] Cities on this scale have never existed before, and the challenges of developing coherent legal frameworks to deal with urban services, urban planning, and urban governance on this scale are unprecedented. At the same time, Sub-Saharan African countries are increasingly seduced by "urban fantasies," cities that exist in the imagination of lawmakers and speculators but have little bearing on the reality of the countries' urban citizens.[7] The pursuit of these urban visions, with their accompanying legal requirements, stretches the resources and capacities of country and city governments to unsustainability and financial indebtedness.

---

brilovic, Millennium Challenge Corporation; and Jaap de Visser, University of the Western Cape. The moderator was Matthew Glasser.

5 The panelists for this session were Lili Liu, the World Bank; Michael A. De Angelis, University of Rhode Island; Steven B. Webb, a private consultant; and Leif M. Clark, a retired U.S. bankruptcy judge. The panel was moderated by Matthew Glasser.

6 Lily Kuo, *China's New Megalopolis Would Be Bigger than Uruguay and More Populous than Germany*, Quartz (Apr. 12, 2014), http://qz.com/198337/chinas-new-megalopolis-would-be-bigger-than-uruguay-and-more-populous-than-germany/#198337/chinas-new-megalopolis-would-be-bigger-than-uruguay-and-more-populous-than-germany/.

7 *See* Vanessa Watson, *African Urban Fantasies: Dreams or Nightmares*? 26(1) Env. & Urbanization 215–31 (2014), together with Allan Cain's response; Allan Cain, *African Urban Fantasies: Past Lessons and Emerging Realities*, 26(2) Env. & Urbanization 1–7 (2014).

Box 1: Living Illegally in Johannesburg

Joao Simoes sells counterfeit shoes on the streets of inner-city Johannesburg. He travels to and from Mozambique each month, returning with four pairs of shoes—the maximum he can afford—on each trip. His goods are illegal, and he trades outside the demarcated vendor stalls established by the municipality. The demand for trading space far exceeds the number of official stalls. Traders like Joao therefore trade in small items they can carry on their backs or in their arms and seek customers in areas with high foot traffic such as taxi ranks and busy sidewalks. These traders pack up their goods and move quickly when they spot police officers who might confiscate goods, issue a fine, or extract a bribe.

Joao's living arrangements in an overcrowded building are equally precarious. He rents a space that is just large enough to accommodate a mattress. The building has been illegally taken over and is in poor condition. Joao knows he is at the mercy of his landlord, his fellow tenants, and the law and that he could lose his space at any time. He is fearful of crime in the apartment and places his few belongings and his small stock of shoes under the mattress that he sleeps on. But for the R400 he can afford to pay for rent each month, there is no "legal" alternative in inner-city Johannesburg.

Source: Tanya Zack, from a forthcoming work on the Ethiopian quarter in Johannesburg.

Urban law must be concerned with ensuring equity, as well as with enabling sustained growth and economic development. The quest for impressive cities must consider the displacement of the poor and vulnerable without consent and without alternatives. It is not sustainable—politically, environmentally, or socially—for cities to grow without legal frameworks that accommodate the needs of all their citizens. Cities without workable urban legal systems give rise to urban pathologies that blight a country's economic and social development prospects. Box 1 illustrates the multiple levels of illegality facing an emerging entrepreneur in the struggle to establish a viable microenterprise in downtown Johannesburg.

In societies where urban developers provide financial support to politicians (a category that includes most countries in the world), can the legal framework help protect the poor? Land use and urban planning laws in developing countries have often been dysfunctional: restrictive legislation can make it impossible for the poor to live legally in the city, and there are many cities in which the majority of residents live or work "informally," that is to say, illegally. These conditions signal a legal framework that is inappropriate and unenforceable.

Mayors, legislators, and urban lawyers around the world are developing legislation that is more in tune with the way the majority of their constituents actually live and work. They are using urban law to help cities be more inclusive, providing fair and equitable access to the services, jobs, and educational and cultural opportunities that cities offer. Many other policy makers, however, remain trapped in a mind-set that sees urban law as a means only to control and police fast-growing cities, as a tool to preserve the material benefits of urbanization for an elite, through rent seeking, gerrymandering, and even outright repression. The urban legal terrain is thus contested. It brings into stark relief the inequalities, inefficiencies, and injustices that often manifest in cities, while demonstrating the extraordinary benefits that accrue to a society where towns and cities are governed, managed, and planned through laws that work and laws that citizens regard as fair and just.

All of this is part of the landscape of urban law. This chapter uses the four urban law sessions from LJD Week 2013 as a point of departure to explore this terrain and suggest some linkages that might help deliver on the promises and opportunities presented by the developing cities of the 21st century. The four sessions demonstrate the interconnectedness of the different elements of urban law. Fundamental to cities are the laws that govern how a city government can finance infrastructure and how access to and the holding of land is regulated. On this legal bedrock are built the governance and planning structures and functions, each created and shaped by law. The interplay of these structures and functions shapes a city's economic, social, and environmental outcomes. These then set the political environment and fiscal conditions that can make it possible for a country to reap the rewards of well-managed urbanization. Running through all these elements are tensions between the interests of city efficiency and those of social justice, between facilitating investment in the urban economy, on the one hand, and including the poorest urbanites in the city's package of opportunities, on the other hand. Urban law is at the heart of the resolution of these tensions, and the four sessions presented at LJD Week 2013 each illustrate different dimensions of the impact of urban law on the growth and development of cities around the world.

Urban Land Rights: Titling and Tenure in Urban Settings

As noted in the session on urban land rights and titling, people often think of land in two dimensions.[8] Agricultural crops, forests, and country homes are all built on horizontally separated parcels. Much of the development literature on land tenure and property rights has focused on rural and agricultural property.[9] The development community's experience with rural land tenure issues provides a solid base, exploring how the attributes of tenure (exclusivity, transferability, enforceability) play out in developing economies. Going forward, as urban development becomes the dominant paradigm, new dimensions become important in the property rights discussion. In the urban context, locational advantage is more relevant than agricultural productivity. As people seek out living space close to where they work and other urban opportunities, they crowd together. This crowding together on scarce land

---

8 *See* A. Square, *Flatland: A Romance of Many Dimensions* (Seeley & Company 1884).

9 *See*, for example, Gershon Feder, *Land Tenure and Property Rights: Theory and Implications for Development Policy*, 5(1) World Bank Econ. Rev. 135–53 (1991).

presents at least two important legal challenges: how to deal with tenure in three dimensions, taking into account the vertical dimension that characterizes urban land use and development, and how to provide secure tenure in informally settled parts of the city.

Before modern cities, buildings were typically sold and financed with the parcel on which they sit. But urban development is a three-dimensional phenomenon. It requires that one separate ownership vertically, not only horizontally. In many cases, developing countries have not updated their land rights systems to reflect this paradigm shift. Developing appropriate laws to govern the ownership of parcels in three dimensions is one way to allow more people to live, with secure tenure, on an urban lot. It is a key to providing affordable access to the city for both families seeking housing and enterprises seeking premises for production, trade, and offices.

The importance of a clear legal framework for land tenure as a foundation for efficient land markets and financing is as true of vertical development as it is of horizontal. Hernando de Soto's argument that flaws in legal systems for tenure make it difficult for the poor and their assets to participate in market economies is true if one envisions the densification of cities and housing substantial portions of the population in high-rise buildings.[10] During LJD Week 2013, Lionel Galliez of the Union Internationale du Notariat pointed out the need for a clear description of vertical rights, because multistory development can help avoid the inefficiency of low-level urban sprawl. With any given population, the more a city is spread out, the greater its environmental footprint, and the more competition there is for surrounding agricultural land. To accommodate more people on a given amount of urban land, cities grow upward. The legal framework for vertical development has co-evolved with taller buildings in industrialized countries, but often it has not done so in developing economies that are now experiencing intense urbanization.

Legal systems for allocating rights in three dimensions have evolved in both civil and common law systems in response to the need to describe, organize, and transfer space in a vertical environment. During the session, Maître Galliez traced the history of density in Paris, which has among the highest densities of population in any developed country. Because much of Paris's development predates the widespread use of passenger elevators, there are few high-rise buildings, a typical height being six or seven stories. As early as 1804, the Napoleonic Code allowed for vertical division of space, stipulating that properties could share a common building or plot, governed by a housing collective, with the air and floor space within the individual units being privately owned.[11] In the 1860s, as urban development continued in France, notaries developed improved techniques for conveyancing, and these were codified into law. The experience of these notaries and the French courts in

---

10 Hernando De Soto, *The Mystery of Capital: Why Capitalism Triumphs in the West and Fails Everywhere Else* (Basic 2000).

11 Art. 664.

resolving thousands of cases over more than a century provides a valuable point of reference when drafting urban land legislation, especially in countries with a civil law tradition.

Maître Galliez pointed out that the eight principles developed by Elinor Ostrom, whose Nobel Prize–winning work on collaborative management of common resources was developed in the context of forests and fisheries, also apply to this model of dividing urban space:[12]

- Group boundaries are clearly defined.
- Rules governing the use of common goods are matched to local conditions.
- Those affected by the rules can participate in modifying the rules.
- The rule making of community members is respected by outside authorities.
- There are systems, carried out by community members, for monitoring members' behavior.
- There are graduated sanctions for rule violators.
- Dispute resolution is accessible and low cost.
- Responsibility for governing the common resource is built from the lowest level up to the entire system.[13]

One can adapt and build on these principles to develop principles that are tailor-made for the urban legal context in general and most useful for the urban land sector specifically. To do so requires a deep understanding of how urban land legal interventions materialize in the context of the everyday calculations and contests that characterize households' and firms' participation in the urban land market. To provide an example of this, and to move from the challenges of allocating vertical space to the problems of regularizing horizontal, informal tenure, Robin Rajack presented an overview of Trinidad and Tobago's ongoing experiment with incremental land tenure. Informal settlement patterns began after the abolition of slavery in Trinidad in 1833, and today these settlements are home to some 50,000 households, or 23 percent of the population. Half of these homes are on state lands; the rest are on private property.

There had been three legislative attempts to enhance land tenure for the country's poor:

- The 1966 Agricultural Small Holdings Tenure Act sought to give greater security of tenure to farmers of small agricultural holdings by restricting the right of the landlord to recover possession of such holdings.

---

12 Elinor Ostrom, *Governing the Commons: The Evolution of Institutions for Collective Action* (Cambridge U. Press 1990).

13 *See* http://onthecommons.org/magazine/elinor-ostroms-8-principles-managing-commmons #sthash.wqr53E1K.dpuf.

- The 1981 Land Tenants Act gave tenants of rented land who had built a dwelling on the land before or up to the date of the act the right to purchase the land from the freeholder at a price not exceeding half the open market value.
- The 1986 Regularization of Tenure (State Lands) Act was intended to sell 30-year leases to squatters who had occupied public lands since December 2, 1977, and who individually applied before a tribunal.

Because none of these legislative attempts was especially effective, the government determined to take a new systems approach to reform that would incorporate several interconnected elements: a legislative framework, institutions for effective implementation, funding for the cost of implementation, the customs and policies by which people have allocated and defended their informal rights, and the location of settlements on public or private land. With this perspective, the government determined that there was a need to develop a new instrument, a "certificate of comfort," that would be a personal asset attached to a particular individual.

Legislatively, this new approach was grounded in the 1998 State Land Tenure Regularisation Act.[14] A key feature of this act is an incremental statutory process for tenure regularization. The incremental approach was developed to parallel the incremental physical development of homes—residents had the experience and necessity of paying for the construction of their housing a bit at a time. The law reflected the community's existing approach to solving its housing problems. Providing a legal path that would allow tenure to be upgraded in increments was a way to adapt the titling system to the economic and practical reality of the people's lives. Three incremental tenure steps were provided:

- **A certificate of comfort:** Confers a right, for the life of an individual, not to be deprived of a place to settle. Although the government could require relocation, the certificate holder would be guaranteed a site. This certificate was available to the widest possible group of beneficiaries, including informal immigrants and noncitizens, provided they were occupying state land before January 1, 1998.
- **A statutory lease:** Confers a 30-year leasehold interest, any remainder of which can be transferred to heirs upon the death of the individual leaseholder. It is automatically issued if the land is in a designated area and the applicant is a citizen at least 18 years old.
- **A deed of lease:** A 199-year leasehold issued only when the applicant has paid (at a subsidized rate) for the land and associated infrastructure. Although it is not quite a freehold interest, it was designed to be functionally similar.

In implementing its "squatter regularization" program, the government determined to prioritize person-to-person interactions over technical capacity

---

14 State Land (Regularisation of Tenure) Act, ch. 57:05; Laws of Trinidad and Tobago; Act 25 of 1998.

(though the program did make use of state-of-the-art geographic information and global positioning systems). Rather than assign implementation to an existing unit, the government created a semiautonomous body, the Land Settlement Agency, to implement the policy.[15] Staff members include community and social development workers whose mission is to interact with individual families. The program encompasses extensive public relations efforts, with messages aimed at both the national audience and particular communities.

In the first four years of implementation, through 2002, more than 23,000 applications for certificates of comfort were received—these accounted for nearly 90 percent of informal households, clear evidence of overwhelming public interest in tenure regularization. During this same period, 4,100 certificates of comfort were issued, along with 333 statutory leases and 9 deeds of lease. The pace slowed substantially from 2002 to 2010, after an opposition government was elected. During these eight years, only about 1,000 new certificates of comfort were issued, as the government focused on construction of new housing. In 2010, the government again changed hands, and work on the backlog of applications accelerated. By 2013, some 2,500 certificates of comfort had been issued after the elections.

Along with tenure regularization, the Land Settlement Agency is mandated to install or upgrade physical infrastructure in informal settlements by improving roads, drainage, and wastewater disposal and by providing water and other amenities.[16] The intention of the program is to incrementally upgrade both the legal tenure of residents and the physical infrastructure serving their communities. Because most applicants still do not have their certificates of comfort, it is too early to pronounce the experiment a complete success, but the reestablishment of the program has given hope to many families.

The lessons learned in Trinidad and Tobago over nearly fifty years show how important it is for new laws to be designed to work in the context of a country—ideas that might look worthy in theory can often collapse when confronted by reality. That reality is informed by both the institutional capacity of the implementing agency and the affordability thresholds of households that are intended to benefit from the new law. The example also demonstrates the political nature of urban legal interventions: when the 1998 act's objectives resonated with the political objectives of the party in power, implementation surged; when a different party took office, implementation dropped dramatically.

Practicable and Enforceable Urban Law for Improved Development Delivery

Although the strategy in Trinidad and Tobago reflects a conscious attempt to develop an incremental title approach adapted to the local economic real-

---

15 The Land Settlement Agency was established by the State Land (Regularization of Tenure) Act, chap. 57.05, Act No. 25 of 1998.

16 *See* Land Settlement Agency website, http://www.mphe.gov.tt/agenciesdivisions/lsa.html.

ity, legislation governing urban development in other countries is sometimes ill suited to the context. During LJD Week 2013, one panel discussed typical weaknesses in urban legal frameworks and explored ways to support more appropriate and implementable legislation. Maria Mousmouti and Gianluca Crispi discuss this further in their chapter "'Good' Legislation as a Means of Expressing Social Contracts and Ensuring Voice, Accountability, and the Delivery of Results in Urban Development."

The speakers at the panel explained that one test for "good" urban laws is whether the laws can be implemented and enforced, and the panelists proposed factors that contribute to that end: effectiveness, efficiency, and simplicity. Two suggestions that may be helpful to urban policy makers, their advisers, and legislative drafters are presented here.

The first suggestion is how to approach the common problem that urban legislation is not well aligned with the social and economic realities of the poor, which leads to widespread noncompliance and lack of credibility. This chapter offers a way to think through whether a law can potentially be effective and aligned with the local context. The second suggestion is a practical approach to improve the quality of urban legislation through formal or informal codification.[17]

The 85th Percentile Rule

Traffic engineers have much experience setting maximum speed limits for highways. Around the world, one accepted methodology is to conduct a speed zone study, inter alia, to determine the 85th percentile speed, that is, the speed that 85 percent of drivers naturally travel at or below. This threshold is based on the theory that most drivers are reasonable and prudent, do not want to crash, and want to reach their destination in the shortest possible time. The great majority (but not all) will find a reasonable balance between speed and prudence. Those traveling at or above the 85th percentile speed are potentially dangerous, and for the benefit of all, their nonconforming conduct should be regulated. If the speed limit is set lower than this 85 percent cutoff, a large percentage of reasonable drivers would be unnecessarily penalized.[18] Sometimes this penalty is intended: many drivers are familiar with small-town speed traps whose purpose may be more financial gain than traffic safety.

A similar 85th percentile screen could be applied to land use regulation. Beginning with an acknowledgement of the way most residents live and the balance they strike between size, location, and services is a good start. Just as with speed limits, legislation should not penalize or criminalize the reasonable choices of a large percentage of residents. What is reasonable in any given

---

17 As Maria Mousmouti, University of Athens, pointed out during the panel discussion, there is no absolute standard of quality. Economists, lawyers, and laypeople might all have different perspectives on whether a law is practicable and enforceable.

18 American Public Works Association, *85th Percentile Statistical Rationale*, http://www.apwa-wa.org/forums/85th%20Percentile%20Statistical%20Rationale.doc.

city's context will depend on the economy and the choices available to people, for example, in regard to housing. Poor people cannot reasonably be expected to comply with expensive floor area or minimum lot size standards that may be reasonable for rich people. Inappropriately high standards increase the cost of urban land, limit access to the city and to urban services, and ultimately divide the city.[19] From the perspective of equity and inclusion, these outcomes are as undesirable as it would be to set a 30 kilometers per hour speed limit on a road that could reasonably support 100 kph traffic. If enforced, such conservative speed limits would make highways inefficient; unreasonably expensive land use standards would make cities inefficient.

Among the most pernicious urban laws are those that, on their surface, appear fair and equal but in reality have the effect of penalizing only the poor. Anatole France speaks of "the majestic equality of laws, which forbid the rich and poor alike to sleep under bridges, to beg in the streets, and to steal bread."[20] Some urban laws in developing countries have this character—and because most residents are too poor to comply, they violate the law in the ways they live or the ways they earn their living or both. Although the laws apply to rich and poor alike, the rich can afford large lots and wide setbacks, while the poor cannot.

In developing countries, inappropriate legal standards often result in discretionary, arbitrary, and unpredictable enforcement. Sometimes these laws act like a speed trap in that enforcement (or the threat of enforcement) serves primarily to raise revenue, and perhaps for the benefit of the enforcing officer rather than the community.

Laws that are out of step with conditions on the ground set the stage for the corruption of institutions. By starting with the perspective that what 85 percent of the people already do is likely to be reasonable, attention is focused on the context—on the actual situation on the ground, as opposed to some ideal or imported standard. A regulation that makes the majority of existing conduct illegal invites corruption and informal arrangements to overlook violations, as well as effectively pricing the majority of citizens out of any chance of compliance. An 85th percentile screen in setting standards for land use, street vendors, and use of common spaces, for example, would improve institutional legitimacy by allowing behaviors that most people consider reasonable and prudent under the prevailing social and economic circumstances. Enforcement could then focus on the outliers, freeing government resources and improving alignment between social expectations and the legal framework.

---

19 Matthew Glasser, *Land Use Law and the City: Toward Inclusive Planning*, in *World Bank Legal Review*, vol. 5: *Fostering Development through Opportunity, Inclusion, and Equity* 351–64 (Hassane Cissé et al., eds., World Bank 2013).

20 "La majestueuse égalité des lois, qui interdit au riche comme au pauvre de coucher sous les ponts, de mendier dans les rues et de voler du pain." Anatole France, *Le Lys Rouge* 118 (Calmann-Levy 1906).

A proposed regulation that would require a change in behavior by more than 15 percent of land users is prima facie unreasonable and unworkable. Of course, the 85th percentile test should not be absolute. It is suggested as one way to test for whether the broad principle is being applied, that is, trying to fit the law to the capabilities of people. Just as with speed limits, other factors may exist that call for a different standard.

As with almost all regulatory interventions in a complex social and economic milieu, there will be outcomes that are difficult to anticipate. The advantage of using a benchmark like the 85 percent rule is that the margin for unanticipated consequences is greatly reduced; most of the consequences will be made visible at the outset. However, the mere act of inserting a rule into a web of human behavior affects that behavior in ways that are difficult to predict. It is thus important to supplement a test such as this one with filters that establish as much as possible the range of potential costs and benefits that will accrue both to households and to firms in their compliance and to the implementing authorities as they execute the new law. There are also other nonmaterial considerations to take into account. For example, even if discrimination on the basis of race, religion, or gender is common in a community, it is unacceptable in a civilized society and interferes with the efficiency and productivity of cities. In such cases, whether or not the law is wholly enforceable, it stands as a statement of moral principle. This is a different situation from land use or licensing standards where the primary barrier to compliance with a law is the economic reality of the majority of the population.

Box 2 presents the story of a small business owner in Johannesburg. Almost everything that she does to sustain her business contravenes applicable legislation. She represents the 85 percent—typical of so many small-scale entrepreneurs whose success depends on being in the city. This is how most people in the city actually live. She is not a dangerous exception against whom society must be protected. Her living and working arrangements are appropriate to her social and economic context. The existing regulations, originally developed as apartheid-era standards for the privileged minority, are neither realistic nor desirable.

Codification

A second proposal aimed at promoting sensible urban legislation is codification—the practice of compiling separately enacted local laws into a unified municipal code in which like subjects are grouped together and changes are made by amending relevant sections of the municipal code, rather than by adopting stand-alone legislation. This practice helps avoid the too common problem of missing or conflicting legislation on a given topic. And when a city's general legislation is consolidated by topic, it is more easily reviewed for duplications and inconsistencies and is more transparent and accessible—easier for people, including lawyers, to understand and to use. Codification tends to lessen the volume of local legislation and helps reduce the unintended conflicts, gaps, and overlaps that characterize piecemeal lawmaking.

Box 2: Small Businesses in Johannesburg

Geraldine Chipalo is Zambian. Her imports of beans, peanuts, cassava, dried fish, eggplant, and okra are much sought after in Johannesburg, Cape Town, Durban, and East London. She uses a network of delivery trucks that serve traders like herself across South Africa. She also works with individual suppliers and customers who transport bags of spices, creams, and vegetables on their backs. The trading network is organized by word of mouth, and transactions are recorded on scraps of paper or in notebooks. Through this low-end globalization, boxes of goods arrive from many countries and are funneled to backyards to be sorted and sent to stalls, shops, and restaurants across South Africa. Geraldine's business is part of the cross-border trade that brings billions of rands into Johannesburg's economy each year.

Some customers collect goods from Geraldine at the house where she lives and where she stores her stock in a corner of the backyard. The house is surrounded by a wall that houses a food shop and hairdresser. Painted signs advertise the services and goods offered. The entrepreneurs who run these businesses also live on the property.

None of these three businesses is authorized by the city, and none would pass the many town planning and health regulations. The rules prohibit the use of a dwelling unit for retail purposes and for industry (Geraldine's repackaging of goods likely falls into this category), and only 20 percent of the floor area can be used for a business (Geraldine requires more room for storage and sorting). Advertising restrictions, parking requirements, and bans on nonresidential structural modifications add to the list of regulations that Geraldine violates. The regulations also include discretionary provisions related to aesthetics and desirability.

Source: Tanya Zack & Mark Lewis, *Inside Out* (Fourthwall, 2014).

In a seminal article comparing codification in three different legal systems (dynastic Chinese law, European civil law, and North American common law), John Head concludes that three conditions must exist for successful codification: the written law must be regarded favorably as a means of ordering society; the political authority must be powerful enough to impose a code; and the political authority must be eager to champion the cause of codification.[21] He refers to the level of a sovereign code that is intended to cover most aspects of a major area of law within a legal system. However, even at the municipal level, it is clear that codification is not a merely bureaucratic or administrative exercise. To succeed, codification must be understood and supported by the top political leadership in a city.

Codification of municipal law is at least as useful at the national or state level as it is at the local level. The enabling legislation for urban local gov-

---

21 John Head, *Codes, Cultures, Chaos and Champions: Common Features of Legal Codification Experiences in China, Europe, and North America*, 13 Duke J. Comp. Intl. L. 1 (2003).

ernment in many cities is characterized by inconsistencies and ambiguities. One Russian commentator has called for the development and adoption of a municipal code for the Russian Federation, citing the uncertainties, inconsistencies, and practical problems with the current national legal framework for municipalities.[22]

In the session, Maria Mousmouti pointed out that although formal codes require significant effort, commitment, and resources, informal codification is a useful first step.[23] The informal codification process involves the simpler preliminary work of collecting, consolidating, organizing, and presenting relevant legislation into one (informal) code, which can exist in the form of a loose-leaf volume, a website, or even just a shelf in a library that is identified as such. This is a short- to medium-term solution, useful on its own, and can be a step along the way to formal codification. Just as title and tenure solutions can be incremental, and must be adapted to local context and capabilities, so too can the codification process.

Whether at the national or the local level, codification is, by itself, no guarantee of effective law or effective implementation, but it can be a tool that helps drafters deliver more coherent content in a more usable form. Depending on the country and the constitutional dispensation, the scope of local legislation can be broad, affecting many different kinds of behavior, from misdemeanor offenses through land use and zoning provisions, local taxation and property registration, building codes and alcoholic beverage controls, and tariff and fee-setting legislation. The national legal framework within which cities operate prescribes the ways in which cities are organized and enlarged, their powers and functions, their relationship to other local governments and to other tiers of government, their finances and fiscal powers, and other structures and systems of urban governance. Neither the local laws nor the national framework are mere technical tools of interest only to specialists; they are the embodiment of policy choices made by those with power and influence.

In contrasting civil and common law, a recent article concludes that it is most important to focus on a legal system's ability to identify efficient rules, restrain rent seeking in the formulation and application of rules, adapt rules to changed conditions, reveal the law to those affected by it, and enable contracting around inefficient rules.[24] Those criteria are as relevant for the law of cities, at the local or national level, as is any other field of law, and they apply as much to legal systems within the civil law tradition as they do to those coming from a common law background.

---

22 Sergey Gennadevich Solovev, *Municipal Code of the Russian Federation as a Tool for Solving a Number of Legal Problems of Local Self-Government*, 30(8) World Appl. Sci. J. 995–99 (2014).

23 *See* also Denis Tallon, *Codification and Consolidation of the Law at the Present Time*, 14 Isr. L. Rev. 1 (1979).

24 Nuno Garoupa & Andrew P. Morriss, *The Fable of the Codes: The Efficiency of the Common Law, Legal Origins, and Codification Movements*, U. Ill. L. Rev. 1443 (2012).

Urban Law in African Countries

For many years, development professionals have advised policy makers in Africa that they need new and better urban planning, land use controls, and building codes as prerequisites for sound urban development. Many laws have been written, and enacted, but they have had little effect on the way the built environment has actually evolved. Legal requirements have been disregarded or circumvented, not because of criminal intent but because the cost of compliance is too high for the economic reality of most African cities. Widespread noncompliance undermines the legitimacy of urban governance, while leaving the livelihoods and homes of millions of urban residents at risk. The result is that few of the benefits of the rule of law are realized, while most of the costs of lawlessness are. One session at LJD Week 2013 focused directly on the experience with urban law in African countries, not because the region's urban problems are any more important than those of other regions, but because the legal dimension has long been neglected despite the growing prominence of the "African urban question."[25]

Increasingly, urban legal thinkers are exploring new approaches to regulating the African city. But how practical are these ideas? How do they resonate with the decision-making authorities in countries, or private sector investors, let alone citizens (most of whom are very poor)—and what are some of the legal dimensions to these ideas? For this LJD Week 2013 panel, the African Centre for Cities (ACC) at the University of Cape Town convened a panel of experts working on new urban legal frameworks to discuss the complex but increasingly urgent challenge of finding new paradigms to guide urban legal reform. The steady, and often rapid, urbanization of Sub-Saharan Africa highlights the need for effective and appropriate legal and regulatory frameworks to manage and support urban development.

The panel discussion was launched with a discussion of the draft *Urban Legal Guide* being developed by the ACC with support from Cities Alliance, Urban LandMark, UN-Habitat, and the World Bank. The intention behind the guide is to provide decision makers, lawyers, and urbanists with practical and strategic guidance on how to shape urban legislation that usefully reflects the needs of Africa's cities and their citizens. The guide grew out of an abiding frustration that the terms of urban law "reform" have been primarily influenced by suggestions from the international development industry, which often come with the promise of grants or loans, without sufficient attention to the context of African cities. Many of these cities are characterized more by lawlessness than by lawfulness. The poor do not have a voice, and sometimes they are not even taken into account, in the formulation of policies and laws. Fragile and conflict-affected situations, as well as authoritarian rule, are too common.

The guide recommends that legislators, drafters, and their advisers take as their point of departure the context within which the laws and regulations are meant to operate. It is easy enough to make rules, but much harder to

25 *See, e.g., Africa's Urban Revolution* (Susan Parnell & Edgar Pieterse eds., Zed 2014).

make rules that can be enforced and that are recognized as reasonable by those affected. The context for legislation includes both the capacities of officials and institutions meant to implement the law and the attitudes and motivations of the population to which the law will apply. The observation was made that a law which is said to be well crafted but cannot be implemented is an oxymoron.[26] The quality of the law depends fundamentally on whether it is implementable.

Patrick McAuslan, a legal scholar whose career was devoted to cities, law, land, and development in Africa, gave one of his last public presentations at this session during LJD Week 2013. He started by observing that African cities are tremendously varied. From Dakar to Cape Town to Mogadishu to Mongu, the culture, land management, planning, fiscal, and financial systems vary. The legal frameworks are no less diverse: the formal systems have roots in the civil law, the common law, or some hybrid, but these are overlaid with informal urban rules and customary law.

In relation to urban land administration and urban planning, the legal framework defines the boundary between formal and informal land markets and land management systems. How it does so varies from city to city, and in each city, the legal framework creates security for some and vulnerability for others. It establishes urban development standards that may be respected or ignored. And the law prescribes and circumscribes the powers of government. The law is pervasive, yet its application and practical effects are uncertain and variable.

Why is this? Why do well-intentioned laws fail? McAuslan cited several factors:

- Underestimation of the political dimensions of legal reform
- Overestimation of the state's capacity to implement
- The dominant influence of elite interests
- An inadequate identification of the impacts of different legislative options
- Unrealistic expectations

The cost of failure, which includes widespread noncompliance, is high. African cities are often vulnerable to nonstate armed groups, street gangs, militias, and bandits. The urban soil in which these factions thrive is fertilized by authoritarian styles of urban governance, an aversion to devolving power to local authorities, and a lack of meaningful participation. McAuslan was deeply concerned about this challenge of organized urban violence, citing David Kilcullen's writings on urban violence.[27] Like Kilcullen, McAuslan believed that, in the future, the most important conflicts will be urban wars.

---

26 Ann Seidman & Robert B. Seidman, *Drafting Legislation for Development: Lessons from a Chinese Project*, 44(1) Am. J. Comp. L. 1, 27 (1996).

27 David Kilcullen, *Out of the Mountains: The Coming Age of the Urban Guerrilla* (Hurst & Co 2013).

Swamped by a population without adequate voice or services, neglected areas of African cities risk becoming breeding grounds for sustained irregular conflicts along the model of clan militias in Mogadishu and criminal gangs in Nairobi. Nonstate actors in this lawless environment are free to apply a range of capabilities from persuasion through administration to coercion. Often they provide more stability and relative security than the putative authorities, and their ability to do so wins over a critical mass of the population that shelters and supports them. Urban violence grows out of these situations: Al Shabab supporters in Nairobi's slums reportedly enabled the Westgate shopping center attack; gang-related activities in townships and xenophobic violence in South Africa have shocked the world; urban ethnic violence in Abidjan has left hundreds dead. To address these issues, McAuslan suggested contextual investigation: identifying competing interests and institutional capacity; building and supporting civil society's capacity to engage; focusing on what can be done as opposed to behaviors that must be stopped; identifying minimum standards and working toward them; and developing assessments of the potential impacts of reform in the context of the socio-economic and political situation. Finally, McAuslan called for continued efforts to build a community of urban law practitioners and a set of resources and tools to guide reform efforts. He identified a cycle in which urban violence begets a response characterized by military or police action, more socio-economic segregation, special areas cordoned off from the masses by restrictive planning tools, and enforcement techniques aimed at keeping things under control beyond gated areas. These approaches breed violence and resentment and prevent cities from functioning normally and effectively. Breaking this cycle is not easy, but it does require demonstrably fair laws grounded in radically simpler legal and administrative frameworks than may currently exist. This is a medium- to long-term target, one that will inevitably be resisted by those with a vested interest in maintaining the status quo.

Yet, there are examples of appropriate urban legal practice in the region: South African planners are making efforts to devolve planning and create well-integrated cities, and the country's constitutional court provides an example for the continent in the way that it tackles urban governance and urban land issues; there was widespread national participation in the creation of the new Tanzanian federal constitution; civil society groups and free press are strengthening and growing in most countries and so are better able to hold (urban) decision makers to account. But these are relatively minor advances, and there is still a need for the international community to support them.

Jaap de Visser spelled out the problems of cities that get caught up in political conflicts between the national government and local politicians. He pointed out that opposition to national policies often emerges in cities, and that the national polity tends to respond by subverting effective local governance. This is what happened in Zimbabwe after the 2002 Movement for Democratic Change victory in Harare; in South Africa after the 2006 Democratic Alliance victory in Cape Town; in Ethiopia after the 2005 Coalition for Unity and Democracy/United Ethiopian Democratic Forces victory in Addis Ababa; and in Uganda after the 2006 opposition victory in Kampala. Mayors may be suspended, cities may be put under central government administration, and formal and informal intergovernmental disputes may erupt.

Where cities have a clear constitutional role, they have some level of protection from such political disputes. In South Africa, each of the eight largest cities—called metropolitan municipalities—is its own unitary political and planning authority with constitutionally protected powers to plan and manage urban development. An independent Municipal Demarcation Board, using statutory criteria, has determined the boundaries of these entities. In these large cities, electricity revenues make up 30 to 40 percent of municipal income, with municipal property taxes making up another 20 percent. The surplus over cost is used to cross-subsidize other services. The cities' electricity distribution business is essential for all other debt collection. The constitutional status of cities, combined with their strong revenue base, has given cities considerable freedom to maneuver even where there is a political difference between the national government and the local government. Despite this constitutional clarity, South Africa has seen a battle for control of land use powers between the provincial and national authorities, a battle that transcends party political affiliations. With the recent invalidation of key chapters of the Development Facilitation Act,[28] planning power is now clearly located at the municipal level. Cities in South Africa are now unambiguously able to make land use decisions, supported where necessary by other government authorities. As the new legal order becomes more firmly entrenched, national political leaders have begun to realize the importance of collaborating with local governments to ensure a competitive economy based on more efficient and more equitable towns and cities.

Insolvency in Subnational Governments

The legal and regulatory framework can help deliver equitable outcomes and sustainable approaches to financing urban infrastructure and services. Good municipal finance legislation includes clarity about what is to be financed by which level of government. There is no one right answer, and it is important to take into account that different countries have different systems. One reasonable choice is to focus national efforts on income support programs such as Brazil's Bolsa Familia or on the provision of social services such as health and education that are clearly of national interest and beyond the comparative advantage of local government. This leaves cities to focus on urban services within their comparative advantage. But wherever the funds come from, cities require steady and significant flows of funds to deliver clean water, reliable electricity, efficient public transit, safe streets and street lighting, public sanitation services, and so forth. If these funds are wisely invested in the city, the

---

28 Development Facilitation Act No. 67 of 1995. *See* also *City of Johannesburg Metropolitan Municipality v. Gauteng Development Tribunal,* 2 S.A. 554 (2010).

urban economy and productivity grow, ultimately generating more funding for urban investment.

Economic activity is the ultimate source of most government revenues: in almost every country, the lion's share of national government tax collections originates from taxes on individuals and businesses in cities. Although many cities have obvious problems of poverty and deprivation, cities are also where the highest personal and corporate incomes are generated, where valuable property and other forms of wealth are concentrated, and where most consumption occurs. These are things that a government taxes: income, wealth, and consumption. So when a city government or urban residents receive transfers from the national government, they are actually receiving back money generated from sources in the city.

When a national government considers a legal framework for urban development, it faces a fundamental choice: should it collect money (largely) from city-based taxpayers and then allocate it back to urban local governments, or should it authorize cities to themselves collect meaningful local taxes? Experience shows that local tax collection is both more efficient and better received by citizens than national tax collection. And, predictably, revenue autonomy tends to go hand in hand with other kinds of autonomy. Equally predictably, the greater these other kinds of autonomy are, the greater the probability is of tension between the local and central state over urban decision making. Although greater autonomy provides the city with legal and constitutional protections, it can pose a threat to a national government, particularly in a context of rapid urbanization and its associated demographic shifts, which invariably create political flux.

Just as a national government needs to make a decision about the extent to which it plans to provide cities with transfers to support operations, as opposed to providing revenue authority, so it must also decide about where urban investment capital will come from: from local sources or from national treasuries? The world's cities require a phenomenal amount of capital investment to catch up and keep up with growing demand for infrastructure and services.

Things do not always go well for cities and their finances. Historically, municipal defaults are strongly correlated with the business cycle: at least in the U.S. municipal bond market, the worst rates of municipal default seem to occur during depressions and recessions.[29] No other market is as large or is studied as extensively, but the correlation makes sense. When people cannot afford to pay their taxes or utility bills, or when the assessed value of property drops, municipal revenues fall.

---

29 Natalie Cohen, *Municipal Default Patterns: An Historical Study*, 9(4) Pub. Budgeting & Finance 55–65 (Dec. 1989); Moody's Investors Service, *U.S. Municipal Bond Defaults and Recoveries, 1970–2011* (Mar. 7, 2012), http://www.nhhefa.com/documents/moodys MunicipalDefault Study1970-2011.pdf.

Given the ongoing international financial crisis and high-profile subnational defaults in the U.S. jurisdictions of Detroit, San Bernardino, Stockton, and Jefferson County, a highlight of LJD Week 2013 was a panel on insolvency in subnational governments. In this session, three authors discussed their recently launched book *Until Debt Do Us Part: Subnational Debt, Insolvency, and Markets,* which presents the experiences of emerging economies in subnational debt restructuring, the characteristics of formal insolvency systems at the subnational level, and the evolution of the market after restructuring in several developed and developing countries.[30]

The book highlights several key lessons. First, subnational credit risks are usually intertwined with macroeconomic policy. Intergovernmental fiscal policy makers should therefore pay close attention to incentive effects and consider *ex ante* and *ex post* constraints and resolution rules that reduce the possibilities for ad hoc bargaining for bailouts and national support by municipalities and their lenders.

Ex ante legislation includes fiscal responsibility laws that impose fiscal discipline at the subnational level. These include debt ceilings, deficit targets, requirements that borrowing be preapproved, and limits on expenditure increases. Some countries have legislation that includes credit rationing, capital requirements, and credit rating penalties.

Ex post legislation includes constitutional or statutory prohibitions on bailouts; intercept provisions that allow creditors to access inbound transfer payments to cities from other levels of government; effective liquidity and borrowing monitoring to provide early warning of potential problems; and legislative or constitutional bans on bailouts from other levels of government.

The South African law on resolution of financial problems in municipalities, which is probably the most comprehensive legislation on the subject, provides for a variety of provincial and national interventions, including the preparation of mandatory financial recovery plans.[31] Critically, the law also provides for extraordinary relief, including the termination of a municipal debt, if a court finds that three conditions have been met: that the municipality cannot meet its financial obligations and is not likely to be able to do so in the foreseeable future; that assets not needed for basic municipal services have been liquidated for the benefit of creditors; and that employees not needed for basic services have been discharged.[32]

The two aims of these provisions in the South African law are to provide certainty about exactly what will happen if a debt is not paid when due, reducing the risk premium for well-managed municipalities, and to sharpen

---

30 *Until Debt Do Us Part: Subnational Debt, Insolvency, and Markets* (Otaviano Canuto & Lili Liu eds., World Bank 2013). The authors are indebted to Alejandra Núñez, who acted as rapporteur, for her summary of the session.

31 Municipal Finance Management Act, No. 56 of 2003, ch. 13.

32 *Id.*, at sec. 155.

the potential lender's analysis so as to avoid overindebtedness by municipalities that do not have the finances or management to support borrowing. If lenders know that they cannot count on a national government bailout, the healthy interaction between borrower and lender tends to discipline the market, avoiding the problem of overextended municipalities. By contrast, where there is an actual or implicit promise of a sovereign guarantee, a lender will focus on the sovereign's default risk and be relatively indifferent to the financial condition of the municipality.

Until Debt Do Us Part includes a comprehensive review of Chapter 9 of the U.S. Bankruptcy Code, which allows insolvent municipalities to get protection from creditors' legal actions and prepare a plan for debt adjustment while they continue to provide essential services. This chapter of the Bankruptcy Code is important because the number of filings thereunder has surged in recent years, and courts are facing questions that will determine the relationship between bankruptcy and the U.S. federal system. It is important to note that most U.S. municipal defaults have not involved the Bankruptcy Code, since only about half the states have enacted legislation authorizing the use of the federal Bankruptcy Code. Historically, most defaults were handled by state law, and often in an ad hoc manner. Michael De Angelis discussed the constitutional constraints that shape Chapter 9, its main features, and the key cases that have arisen so far. The main lesson at this stage is that Chapter 9 can be useful in providing a fresh start for municipalities whose fundamentals are basically good, but whose debt service has become untenable in an economic downturn.

U.S. bankruptcy judge Leif Clark highlighted creative solutions being pursued in the Jefferson County bankruptcy proceeding by bondholders and their lawyers. If the municipality's proposed payment plan is approved, the bankruptcy court will have the authority to compel rate increases to ensure the payment of billions of dollars' worth of bonds issued while the county was already in bankruptcy. Although this is a fascinating development, Clark highlighted the importance of identifying the challenges subnational governments face and enacting clear rules on lending—how it should be done and what types of lending instruments should be available to municipalities.

This session showed how the legislative minutiae applicable to a city's powers to borrow, and the consequences of default, directly impact on the quality of life, the economic prospects, and the social conditions of the city's inhabitants. Outcomes that might seem inevitable to a layperson can actually be—it transpires after examining the legislation—avoided. Risks that city governments assume on behalf of their citizens can be spelled out in legislation, and it is the details of this legislation that determine the outcomes for those citizens. This principle of understanding risks before assuming long-term financial risk on behalf of a city's residents is universally applicable and important to understand in a range of contexts beyond the United States.

Conclusion

Taken as a whole, the thinking reflected in the four sessions at LJD Week 2013, and of parallel thinking taking place in other fora, form the foundation for an approach to urban practice, linking the legal and urban development fields, that can lead to more appropriate and effective urban law.

The drafting of urban laws is not a technical exercise for lawyers alone—it must be informed by conditions on the ground, by the local economy and political dispensation, and by the ordinary behavior of typical families and enterprises. When laws are routinely disregarded, it is not necessarily a signal that stricter enforcement is needed—it may be a signal that the law is wrong for the context or the time. The societal cost of laws that are widely disregarded is high. This cost is made up of a number of elements, including the undermining of efforts to build societies governed by law; the negation of the usefulness of officials and systems that are forced into implementing the unimplementable; the opportunity costs associated with pursuing an unworkable approach rather than one that can work; and the numerous opportunities for corrupt practices that are presented by an unstable, unpredictable, and dysfunctional urban legal system. A developing country's resource base, consisting of both human and financial resources, is typically thin. The cost of laws that are both disregarded and ineffective imposes a high, often unmanageable, burden for these towns and cities. This burden grows exponentially over time, further crippling future efforts to achieve better urban development outcomes.

Similarly, the regulation of land uses is not a technical exercise for urban planners alone. City planning must be informed by what is practical and implementable in the context of each community as it grows and changes over time. Master plans sitting unrealized on a shelf do not necessarily signal only the need for a new plan—they may be a sign that a more inclusive, flexible, and adapted approach to planning is called for.

Finally, the financing of urban infrastructure is not an accounting exercise for finance officials. The relationship between the urban economy and infrastructure finance is an intimate one—the two are codependent: without a healthy economy, there will be no money for infrastructure; without infrastructure, there cannot be a healthy economy. Without an urban legal framework that ensures effective financing of the infrastructure, there can be none of the urban development that creates the sustainable revenue flows that enable a city government to manage and govern.

Appropriate legal regulation, contextually grounded planning approaches, and well-crafted financial instruments can work synergistically to create a robust, humane urban framework that helps realize the potential of a global urban transformation. When lawyers, planners, and finance professionals work together with their community, its institutions, and its political leaders, they can grow a dynamic city—one that accommodates change and enables all residents to feel part of the joint enterprise.

The views that arose at four urban law sessions during LJD Week 2013 were rich in their diversity. This chapter certainly cannot do justice to them other than by drawing attention to the range and complexity of the issues and by drawing out two central lessons that must infuse future initiatives to improve urban laws. First, urban laws are too important to leave to lawyers or to sectoral experts in any particular aspect of urban development. Collaboration across disciplines is essential to the success of urban legal reform. Second, there is the issue of the context within which the new urban laws have to take root and grow. The process of growing a healthy city is more like gardening or farming than it is like manufacturing. The evolving legal and regulatory framework of a developing country may owe much to the common or civil law that is in its DNA, but it must also reflect the characteristics, society, and customs of the land in which it grows. It must be appropriate for the terroir, and it will inevitably take on a distinctive local character.

> **ter·roir** *noun,* \ter-ˈwär\ the combination of factors including soil, climate, and sunlight that gives wine grapes their distinctive character.[33]

33 http://www.merriam-webster.com/dictionary/terroir.

10

Confronting Complexity

Using Action-Research to Build Voice, Accountability, and Justice in Nairobi's Mukuru Informal Settlements

JANE WERU, WAIKWA WANYOIKE, AND ADRIAN DI GIOVANNI

Nairobi is the most populous city in East Africa and one of the fastest growing cities in the world. Yet more than half of its 4 million residents (an estimated 55 percent) are crammed into about 200 informal settlements (slums) that occupy 5 percent of the city's residential area, or just 1.62 percent of the city's total land area.[1] The residents of these slums live in conditions of considerable insecurity and indignity characterized by inadequate housing and little access to clean water, sanitation, health care, schools, and other essential public services. The weak basic services that do exist are often controlled by cartels that charge extortionate rates for access.

Mukuru Kwa Njenga and Mukuru Kwa Reuben are two densely populated and vibrant slum settlements in Nairobi. Spanning 450 acres, these two settlements are part of a larger stretch of settlements in an industrial section in the south of Nairobi. Together, they are home to an estimated 500,000 people served by more than 200 informal schools and countless informal businesses, health facilities, and other social services.[2] Perhaps most striking about the Mukuru settlements is that 92 percent of all inhabitants are tenants who pay rent to absentee landlords who often own the structures but not the land underneath. Because the Mukuru settlements are built on privately held lands, they have not benefited from slum-upgrading programs in the same way that, for example, the Kibera and Korogocho settlements, located on public lands, have.[3] In addition, the identity of the titleholders is largely unknown to residents and difficult to determine, and owners of both the lands and the

---

1 City Council of Nairobi, *City of Nairobi Environment Outlook* 24–25, 36, (2007), http://www.unep.org/geo/pdfs/NCEO_Report_FF_New_Text.pdf.

2 A lower number of 110,000 people was reported in Kenya National Bureau of Statistics, *The 2009 Kenya Population and Housing Census* (Government of Kenya 2010). The research drawn on in this chapter suggests the much higher figure.

3 *UN-Habitat and the Kenya Slum Upgrading Programme*(strategy document, UN-Habitat 2003), http://mirror.unhabitat.org/pmss/getElectronicVersion.aspx%3Fnr%3D2602%26alt%3D1&rct=j&frm=1&q=&esrc=s&sa=U&ei=6qCxU5rIEIq7uASLmoCgCQ&ved=0CCAQFjAC&usg=AFQjCNH0JBtuW8UV1A1BRlptEYWw7oUZLA; World Bank, *Kenya Informal Settlement Improvement Project (KISIP)* (2011), http://www-wds.worldbank.org/external/default/WDSContentServer/WDSP/IB/2011/03/07/000371432_20110307092557/Rendered/PDF/582670PAD0P1135420IDA1R20111004611.pdf; Government of Kenya, *National Housing Policy* (2004), http://www.mintoreal.com/policy-documents/kenya-national-housing-policy.

structures often hail from the Kenyan elite, including civil servants, government officials, and businessmen.[4] Residents live under a constant threat of eviction due to insecure land tenure and land use contestation.

How can Mukuru's inhabitants achieve security of tenure and protect their basic rights, when so often they live outside the law, and so many terms of the debate are contested? This chapter describes efforts to confront those challenges through a multidisciplinary, action-based research project. The aim of this research is to help the residents of Mukuru identify solutions to improve tenure security and gain access to safer and more affordable basic services and ultimately more dignified and just living conditions. The research is designed to support efforts to achieve positive change on a number of levels:

- To understand the nature of land tenure and basic services in Mukuru
- To understand the interaction between formal and informal institutions and practices, including state and nonstate actors in the settlements
- To look at how various provisions under Kenya's new Constitution, including those on land tenure, human rights—especially economic and social rights—and the protection of vulnerable groups can be used to advance the welfare of informal settlers
- To work with Mukuru residents to develop new legal, planning, and financing tools and strategies of engagement

In some situations, strategies will address existing technical and political obstacles through targeted engagement with public authorities. In others, the research aims to provide the evidentiary foundation for legal advocacy.

The research was initiated by the Akiba Mashinani Trust (AMT), building on long-term support that it has provided to Mukuru residents, and Muungano wa Wanavijiji (MWW), a community organization. The research represents an attempt to move beyond previous advocacy efforts, which tended to be reactive, case-by-case responses to emergencies. Initial research activities involved attempts to identify private owners and titleholders of the lands in Mukuru Kwa Reuben and Mukuru Kwa Njenga. The need for research took on added dimensions following a number of successful advocacy campaigns, including an injunction putting a halt to demolitions in 2012 in Mukuru, and support to help residents use community savings schemes in one neighborhood to secure a loan to buy a 23-acre plot of land.[5] Those developments raised questions about shifting dynamics in the settlements and how to improve conditions and regularize service delivery. In the background is a sense that existing government and donor slum-upgrading efforts, although showing some successes, have failed to live up to principles of participatory upgrading

4 Kipchumba Some, *Nairobi Slum Dwellers Plan to Sue Firms over Land,* Daily Nation (Sept. 9, 2012).

5 For international reporting on these and related efforts in Mukuru, *see,* for example, Daniel Howden, *Kenya Slum Dwellers versus the Elite,* Independent (Sept. 26, 2012); William Oeri, *Nairobi Slum Residents to Build Homes without Govt Help,* Daily Nation (Dec. 12, 2011).

and have been based on inadequate knowledge and false assumptions about the underlying realities and dynamics, particularly regarding ownership and control of land tenure, and interactions between state and nonstate actors and between formal and informal institutions.

To address those questions and provide support to residents on a settlement-wide level, AMT and MWW are collaborating with the University of Nairobi's School of Urban Planning, Strathmore University's School of Law and School of Finance, and the Katiba Institute.[6] The research is based on two premises: working with settlement dwellers to formalize tenure rights of the inhabitants is a key to overcoming other challenges, especially around basic services; and achieving justice and legal solutions requires multidisciplinary research (lawyers, urban planners, finance specialists, and community organizers) and a mix of legal and nonlegal interventions. The efforts described in this chapter are still under way. The goal of this chapter is to make a case for the approach as a model to address layers of complexity and interrelated legal gaps in an effort to support broader legal and community-led advocacy efforts.

The efforts described in this chapter are by no means unique. However, the combination of groups and activities described here, when taken together, provide a model for finding solutions to the layers of urgent and complex problems faced in contexts such as Mukuru.

The chapter situates efforts on behalf of Mukuru within three larger debates around the promotion of access to justice, voice, and accountability. First, the enshrinement of economic and social rights under Kenya's 2010 Constitution has given rise to potential clashes over rights similar to those seen in other countries. Second, the research process described here is an affirmation of the need for multidisciplinary evidence to feed into policy reforms and efforts to formulate and enforce social and economic rights remedies resulting from public interest litigation. Finally, the link between legal and nonlegal advocacy efforts and how building legal awareness among community members can enhance ongoing nonlegal advocacy efforts is discussed. Dominant threads throughout the three debates are the close interlinkages between security of tenure and better access to services and the challenges in building links between formal and informal structures related to land use and service delivery. The chapter concludes by highlighting the potential limits of legal interventions, as well as the potential power of legal interventions in confronting the layers of complexity found in Mukuru.

Mukuru Kwa Reuben and Mukuru Kwa Njenga: The Conditions and Players

Much like other settlements across Nairobi, Mukuru Kwa Njenga and Mukuru Kwa Reuben are an overcrowded, unplanned, sprawl of shanty dwellings

6 The International Development Research Centre in Canada is providing financial and technical support for the project.

and commercial premises. Understanding the challenges faced by residents requires a look at both the conditions they live in and the complex web of actors, both formal and informal, in the settlements. One set of actors, the residents, live in structures that have been built haphazardly, with insufficient roads or pathways, thus rendering access to basic water, sewer, drainage, and waste disposal services impossible. The situation deteriorates during rainy periods, when the roads and pathways, which are almost all unpaved, become untraversable stretches of mud.

Houses in the two settlements are mostly single-roomed dwellings (usually measuring 10 feet by 10 feet) built from rusted corrugated iron sheets and, in some cases, lacking paved floors. So congested are these settlements that almost all the homes are dark and airless with little light and insufficient ventilation. This situation is aggravated by smoke or fumes emitted by the wood fires, charcoal burners, and kerosene stoves used for cooking. A direct result of these intolerable housing conditions is a high rate of respiratory diseases—a frequent cause of death, especially among young children. Proper water and sanitation are also chronic challenges.

Most housing units are built around narrow courtyards, with 11 housing units per plot. Although some of these plots share a pit latrine and bathroom, many are built without any toilet facilities. Families without facilities either pay to use public toilets on a per use basis or use makeshift methods to dispose of waste. Those challenges are even worse at night, when the settlements are unlit. Women and children face serious threats of sexual violence and rape when they dare to venture outside to make use of public toilets or otherwise.

Another set of actors is the formal service providers, such as the Nairobi County government and other governmental utilities providers, which provide next to no municipal services in Mukuru Kwa Njenga and Mukuru Kwa Reuben. Garbage is not collected and is dumped indiscriminately around the settlements; there is little to no access to sewage services; public latrines are emptied manually, with the nearby rivers often serving as dumping grounds. The government-run water company provides water only up to the edge of the two settlements. Consequently, most residents have no other option but to buy water from water cartels. This is an additional set of actors who supply water into the settlements through a complex and chaotic system of pipes, popularly known as "spaghetti connections," that connect to taps in each neighborhood. This makeshift water infrastructure is often laid on the ground and is prone to breakage and contamination from overflows from pit latrines and drain leaks. The average price for residents to fill a 20-liter can of unsafe water from those taps ranges from two-thirds to six times more than the average rate charged by the water company in formal settlements.[7] Similar realities are seen with electricity. The large majority of households have access to elec-

7 Based on initial research. *See* also City Council of Nairobi, *supra* note 1, at 46.

tricity in Mukuru (86 percent in Kwa Reuben, 75 percent in Njenga), although almost entirely through informal *Sambaza* connections.[8]

An additional set of actors is the owners or titleholders of land in the Mukuru settlements. Many of the homes in the Mukuru settlements are built on private lands. These lands were allocated in the 1980s and 1990s by the state to private individuals and corporations for the development of light industry. At the time of the grants, most of the lands were already occupied; others were occupied at various dates after the issuance of title. The government, before allocating lands, and the private parties who subsequently received titles to the lands, however, failed or neglected to secure or take possession of the lands.

The research team has been able to obtain copies of several title deeds issued for the lands on which these settlements are located. Both people and companies hold title to the lands on a leasehold basis. Some of the land has been retained by the original allottees, while some has been transferred to others by sale, sometimes two or more times. In a number of cases, land has been used as security for loans from banks, and in cases of default on these loans, the banks have taken over possession of titles. Only a small portion of land has been developed by the allottees or later transferees, even though the government's primary requirement in granting land was that it be developed for light industry purposes within two years.

In recent years, land in Mukuru has seen a dramatic rise in value, which has led to a sharp increase in the threat of eviction for residents who, in some cases, have occupied the land for decades. After years of neglect, many of the titleholders now see the land as a prime area for redevelopment and want to obtain vacant possession of the land by evicting the residents and selling the land to the highest bidder.

Another group of actors is the numerous individuals known as structure owners who built shacks on the land. Structure owners rent their units to tenants, often as absentee landlords, employing local agents, often youth from the communities, to collect rents.

The conditions faced by the residents of Mukuru Kwa Njenga and Mukuru Kwa Reuben—threat of evictions, extortion by formal and informal actors while trying to access services, insecurity, lack of sanitation, and failure to access water and health services—are also challenges for ensuring access to justice and accountability. Evictions have arguably been the most debilitating justice issue in Mukuru because, quite simply, they negate the ability of residents to enjoy what meager rights they have. Evictions are often conducted in the most inhumane of manners, posing security risks to residents and sometimes resulting in death. Many evictions happen at night, when families are sleeping, and, worse, by setting fire to housing units. The inaccessibility of the area and the lack of basic infrastructure services make it almost impossible

8 *Sambaza* is a Swahili word that translates to "spread" but is often used to imply sharing of services or resources.

for fire services to put out fires. Determining where to lay blame and who is responsible for evictions is sometimes impossible, in part because of the complex and uncertain status of tenure. Even where the parties responsible for ordering or carrying out evictions can clearly be identified, they are almost never held to account because of challenges in accessing a functional formal justice system.

To illustrate, structure owners are so accustomed to evictions through fire or other means that they have a "rapid response" strategy to mitigate against evictions. Building materials and labor are always readily available to reconstruct structures, which can often be erected within hours of being razed by a fire, allowing residents to quickly resume their daily activities. However, structure owners or landowners in many cases carry out evictions because they intend to "replan" and reconstruct newer, more profitable structures. In such instances, it is not uncommon for the owners to hire gangs to carry out the evictions and guard the area until new structures are in place and, sometimes, until new tenants have moved in.

In terms of the formal police system, security officers often collude with landowners in effecting evictions. Residents report this happening in different ways. Sometimes the police stand guard to ensure that residents do not resist evictions. In other instances, police action takes the form of noninterference, that is, by allowing organized gangs to stand guard. In interviews, residents indicate that they have little if any regard for formal security systems, instead choosing to develop or acquiesce to informal security systems that control the area.

Building an Action-Research Process around New Laws and a Constitutional Challenge

The 2010 Constitution of Kenya has provided some hope and led to some concrete progress in confronting the challenges of evictions and access to justice faced by vulnerable groups such as the residents of Mukuru. The Constitution emphasizes human rights and the protection of the marginalized as a national value and principle, in addition to introducing the right to decent housing and other basic services in its Bill of Rights.[9] New jurisprudence has begun to emerge, addressing the human rights implications of evictions. Of note, in 2011 in the case of *Satrose Ayuma and 11 others v. Registered Trustees of the Kenya Railways Staff Retirement Benefits Scheme*, the High Court of Kenya determined that it was unconstitutional to carry out evictions without adhering to international guidelines for evictions.[10]

---

9 Constitution of Kenya (2010), subsecs. 10(2), 43(1).

10 Constitutional Petition no. 65 (2010). This requirement was articulated as part of an interlocutory order to stop evictions that Justice Lenaola later confirmed in his final judgment on that matter. Similar holdings were reached by the High Court in *Mitu-Bell Welfare Society v. The Attorney General, Kenya Airports Authority, and the Commissioner of Lands* and *Ibrahim Sangor Osman v. Minister of State for Provincial Administration & Internal Security & 3 Others.*

Buoyed by the new Constitution and the court's willingness to protect slum settlement dwellers, residents of Mukuru through MWW filed a petition in the High Court in 2012 requesting similar protections from arbitrary evictions. The petition came when Mukuru residents were experiencing increasing threats of evictions, and it was brought with the assistance of AMT and the Katiba Institute. In the petition, the Mukuru residents asked the court to clarify the tenure status of the land that they occupied. More specifically, the petition sought a declaration that the grants issued to titleholders were unlawfully obtained and should therefore be canceled. The petition seeks to take advantage of Kenya's 2010 Constitution, as well as implementing legislation creating a National Land Commission (NLC), which has the power to review unlawfully obtained titles.[11] The basic allegation is that many of the grants issued to the titleholders in Mukuru did not comply with basic procedures for allocating land under the law at the time, and most of the grantees did not comply with the conditions attached to the grant of title in most cases (i.e., requiring that the lands be developed for industrial purposes within two years of the grant). The court ordered a stop to evictions (by way of an injunction) in Mukuru Kwa Njenga and Mukuru Kwa Reuben, pending a final ruling on the issues raised in the petition.[12] A hearing on the issues raised by the petition was pending as of September 2014.

Although the court order did not eliminate the harassment faced by Mukuru residents, it did secure a moratorium on evictions. If the petition is successful, then many of the titles could be found to be unlawful and eventually canceled, meaning that the lands now home to the Mukuru settlements would revert to public lands. More generally, the case stands to help residents resolve tenure disputes, which will be important in providing direction to other justice issues in Mukuru.

The Kenyan Constitution also introduced a right to "accessible and adequate housing, and to reasonable standards of sanitation."[13] Beyond the courts, there has been a push on developing a regulatory framework that would entrench a human rights–based approach in dealing with eviction matters. A draft bill on evictions and resettlement has been developed and is due to be introduced in Parliament.[14] The technical experts who helped develop the bill include three members of the Mukuru research project.[15]

---

11 Art. 67 of the Constitution creates the NLC; subpart 14 of the National Land Commission Act gives the NLC the power to review all grants and dispositions of public land to establish propriety and legality.

12 *Muunganowa Wanavijiji and Others v. The Hon. Attorney General and Others*, Petition No. 403 2012, High Ct. of Kenya in Nairobi (Constitutional & Human Rights Division) (Sept. 12, 2012). *See* also Leonard Mutinda, *Judge Blocks Slums Evictions*, Daily Nation (Sept. 12, 2012).

13 Constitution of Kenya, art. 43(1)(b).

14 Evictions and Resettlement Procedure Bill (2013), http://www.lands.go.ke/index2.php?option=com_docman&task=doc_view&gid=246&Itemid=134.

15 The members were Patricia Kameri-Mbote (Strathmore and Nairobi Universities), Jane Weru (Akiba Mashinani Trust), and Korir Sing'Oei (Katiba Institute). Weru learned that she would be invited as a technical expert to the task force when she led Mukuru residents to deliver a memorandum to the cabinet minister of lands in regard to evictions in Mukuru.

The Constitution also put in place a new framework for land rights that affirms the principles of equitable access to land and security of land rights.[16] It is hoped that the combination of clear regulatory framework and progressive jurisprudence on evictions will help diminish arbitrary and inhumane evictions. Such an achievement would be critical for Mukuru residents given their vulnerability to illegal, arbitrary, and inhumane evictions.

To support the legal action and larger advocacy efforts in Mukuru Kwa Njenga and Mukuru Kwa Reuben, AMT, along with MWW, initiated an action-based research project. The project is based on the premise that the insecurity of tenure faced by Mukuru residents is at the root of many of [the] challenges to housing and access to services they face. This insight has been a driving policy strategy of the international community in confronting the challenges of the urban poor and informal settlements for some time.[17] The goal of the research in Mukuru is to move beyond general prescriptions about tenure security to address the layers of competing interests and rights and failures in governance that would likely persist even in the face of greater tenure security.

Greater security of tenure for the Mukuru inhabitants is only the first step in confronting a complex web of challenges related to voice, accountability, and justice. Even if the residents of Mukuru achieve more permanent security of tenure, two fundamental challenges will arise. Confronting both challenges requires a better evidence base. First, there will be the need to identify criteria to select legitimate beneficiaries of the efforts to regularize tenure and service delivery, for example, distinguishing between long-term residents and casual workers who arrive for short-term employment opportunities. Second, there will be a need to replan the area based on a better understanding of realities on the ground.

These two challenges are, in the first place, practical, although as discussed below, they also pose a series of legal questions. The project has started to answer these questions by undertaking a situational analysis to build a better understanding of realities on the ground. The research has been participatory from the start, with the researchers engaging with community members to gather information. The University of Nairobi Planning School and Strath-

---

16 Constitution of Kenya, arts. 60–68 generally.

17 *See*, for example, *Habitat II, Istanbul Declaration on Human Settlements*, UN Doc.A/Conf.165/14 (UNGA), at para. 75 (June 14, 1996) ("Access to land and legal security of tenure are strategic prerequisites for the provision of adequate shelter for all and for the development of sustainable human settlements affecting both urban and rural areas. It is also one way of breaking the vicious circle of poverty"); *Holding Their Ground: Secure Land Tenure for the Urban Poor in Developing Countries* (A. Durand-Lasserve & L. Royston eds., Earthscan 2002). A more fulsome discussion of the varying forms of security of tenure, de jure and de facto, formal and informal, is beyond the scope of this chapter. A helpful overview of debates regarding land tenure security issues and how they apply in Nairobi and Mukuru more specifically is provided by P. Kameri-Mbote, C. Odote, A. Meroka, & F. Kariuki, *Literature Review for "Moving beyond Understanding the Dynamics of Informal Settlement Land Tenure and Service Delivery" Project* (Strathmore U. 2014).

more University's School of Finance have played major roles in helping community members develop a better understanding of, for example, who lives where and owns what in Mukuru; the number of households and population in each settlement; how services such as security, water, sanitation, and electricity are provided; who controls their provision, including the interface between formal service providers such as the Nairobi City Water and Sewerage Company and the prevailing informal service providers; how much land is available in Mukuru and is suitable for housing development; and what the different income levels are across the settlements. The main role of the Katiba Institute and Strathmore University's School of Law has been to work closely with the community to investigate the different existing tenure arrangements in Mukuru to determine how the Constitution and land laws can be used to address challenges related to insecure land tenure.

As of September 2014, the situational analyses were being completed. They will provide information that was previously unavailable to policy makers due to bureaucratic inertia or political motivations not to address conditions in the Mukuru settlements. Anecdotally, policy makers in the Nairobi County government have remarked to research team leaders that conditions in Mukuru and in informal settlements generally have gone unaddressed because they are viewed as too complex.[18] The value of the situational analyses, thus, is to enable research teams to develop appropriate financial, planning, and legal models that will help demystify the complexity of the situation. The models will help the residents begin developing tentative plans for upgrading the Mukuru settlements.

Part of the challenge is technical. For example, when it comes to housing, the communities have made it a priority to minimize the displacement of residents; many of the people living in Mukuru have strong social ties and derive their livelihoods from the settlements. Given that the densities in Mukuru are very high, any replanning may call for the development of multistoried housing, which brings up major financing and technical design issues. Thus, based on the initial situational analyses, the urban planning and finance teams will work closely with the community to determine what kinds of housing will be

---

18 Daniel Brinks and Varun Gauri note that the lack of knowledge in such situations might be symptomatic of larger challenges in political will: "Particularly in developing countries, there exists a dissonance between shared, universalistic discourses supporting constitutional and political aspirations for 'social justice' or 'human dignity' on the one hand, and the clientelistic and particularistic exchanges used to construct and maintain the political order, on the other. Social and political actors are generally aware of these dissonances; but for any given claim they may not possess specific knowledge whether fulfillment of aspirations is economically, politically, and technically feasible. It is often in the interest of political elites, moreover, to hide the true cost of fulfilling universalistic commitments so that public expenditures can continue to be used for narrow partisan or sectarian agendas." *See A New Policy Landscape in Courting Social Justice: Judicial Enforcement of Social and Economic Rights in the Developing World* 348 (Varun Gauri & Daniel Brinks eds., Cambridge U. Press 2010). *See* also C. Rodriguez-Gravito, *Latin-American Constitutionalism: Social and Economic Rights: Beyond the Courtroom: The Impact of Judicial Activism on Socioeconomic Rights in Latin America,* 89 Tex. L. Review 1664 (2011): "One of the defining traits of systemic policy failures is the lack of reliable data on the conditions of the victimized population."

appropriate and affordable to the categories of people in Mukuru. The hope is that the plans will gain greater legitimacy and ownership among residents due to their involvement in developing them.

The challenges faced by the communities are not simply practical or technical, however. Research teams are interrogating the existing systems of service delivery with a view toward trying to unravel some of the underlying reasons that formal service provision has failed to reach the Mukuru settlements. The solution is not as simple as coming up with a plan to formalize and regularize service provision. Such action could risk displacing positive innovations that the informal service delivery systems have developed. In addition, formalizing service provision would likely mean upsetting entrenched power dynamics, for example, irregular (and highly lucrative) relationships between formal and informal providers.[19] Recommendations on how services can be provided in an efficient and affordable way will include strategies of engagement with public officials and utilities providers that target these "nontechnical" elements. To illustrate, the collection of sewage is often performed by youth, providing them a steady if modest income that might be lost if service provision were formalized without a clear alternative.[20] An intermediary arrangement between a purely formal and informal setup would help ease the potential loss of employment. By contrast, a strategy related to water and electricity providers might call for efforts to formalize service provision, but would need to focus on possible risks to residents due to displacing existing monopolies on service provision, in addition to confronting a possible reluctance to extend services into the settlements due to political inertia. A main obstacle for Mukuru residents in seeking formal service provision from public utilities has been the lack of security in tenure. Holding title is typically a requirement for being connected, which brings us back to the starting point of the research: the concept of the relationship between land tenure and service delivery.

Efforts to develop situational analyses and planning, finance, and legal models are being undertaken in an ever-changing environment. Due to the increase in tenure security in Mukuru, however temporary, that resulted from the 2012 injunction freezing evictions, structure owners have been erecting better constructed and equipped structures in order to charge higher rents.[21] This development has caused the research team to adjust its thinking: previously the main focus was on residents, titleholders, and service providers, but the structure owners are now emerging as important actors whose competing interests must be addressed in any plans. It is in confronting this overlay of entrenched and, at times, competing interests—between residents and title-

19 An informal system of tenure reported to operate as an overlay to the existing formal title system—along with the social and political structures underlying it—would also be displaced or disrupted through efforts to achieve greater tenure security for the residents.

20 A group of youth sewage collectors approached MWW to request financial assistance to purchase plastic gloves and masks to foster more hygienic working conditions.

21 Based on observations and focus group discussions with community members by the research teams.

holders, informal service providers and structure owners—that the law and legal solutions hold their greatest potential in helping to confront the challenges faced by Mukuru's residents. Here is also where the experiences in Mukuru raise larger questions about how to promote justice, voice, and accountability for vulnerable groups in the face of complex and colliding interests.

Access to Justice Issues in Mukuru

Looming in the background to the situational analyses and efforts to develop community-driven upgrading plans is the ongoing litigation, which has yet to go to trial. In other words, the research efforts are not simply geared to an optimistic vision of the case's outcome. Research findings are intended to target the access to justice, voice, and accountability challenges faced by the residents in Mukuru. The findings will in our view help improve both the quality and the outcome of any final judgment in the Mukuru case. More specifically, the research findings aim to inform the outcomes in terms of the court's findings on the merits of the case and the substantive scope of the rights at stake, as well as on any determination of the appropriate remedy and any subsequent monitoring of such a judgment by the court.

In terms of the substantive scope of the rights at stake, Article 43(1)(b) of the Kenya Constitution provides that everyone has a right "to accessible and adequate housing, and to reasonable standards of sanitation." Three critical elements of Article 43 rights are relevant to the Mukuru case: horizontal application of Article 43 rights, potential clashes between private property rights and Article 43 rights, and the principle of progressive realization.

In considering the application of Article 43 rights, the first challenge is in determining who should be responsible to whom. In Mukuru, the majority of actors are private individuals, especially in relation to housing. These actors are the titleholders and structure owners, who in many ways are in an agency relationship with the titleholders. In this context, then, the most straightforward outcome from the perspective of the Mukuru residents would be for the court to decide in their favor on the issues of title, that is, by canceling the titles of current titleholders. In that case, title would arguably revert to the state, and the remaining issues related to housing and sanitation would become more of a traditional state-citizen dispute resolution, with the state more clearly holding responsibility in relation to rights claims. In that situation, reference could be made to Article 43(1) cases such as *Mitu-Bell* and *Satrose Ayuma*, where the courts placed an obligation on the state to ensure that alternative accommodation is available to residents prior to conducting any evictions.[22]

22 Consistent with approaches in other countries, such as *Grootboom* (South Africa) and *Olga Telis* (India) and the need to develop reasonable plans, or at least to halt evictions until a plan is developed.

Horizontal Application of Rights

Should the court show a reluctance to cancel titles, issues would arise concerning the horizontal application of Article 43 rights. The horizontal application of a constitutional right denotes an obligation to fulfill a right can be applied to a private individual.[23] In the case of Mukuru, Article 43(1) on the right to housing and sanitation arguably applies horizontally to the titleholders and structure owners. In other words, those actors have a positive obligation to ensure that proper sanitation is available in relation to housing units that they rent out, even if there are good reasons to argue that the government should be largely responsible for developing sanitation infrastructure. On sanitation, given the relationship between informal and formal service providers, there might be a possibility to impute an obligation under Article 43(1) on the informal providers. The argument here would be that the informal providers have stepped in to perform a public function and thus should carry the obligations that normally accompany that role. There is also an argument that the Constitution obligates landlords to put sanitary facilities in rental units that meet a certain standard of decency. In fact, part of the argument being developed in the case is that failure to provide any or decent sanitary services is a violation of the right to human dignity provided for under Article 28 of the Constitution. Conversely, responsibility for the informal providers could be imputed on the government, given its active role in the irregular provision of services or its tacit role in allowing the informal-formal relationships to continue while failing to meet its own state obligations to provide reasonable standards of sanitation.

The issue of private actors' responsibility in relation to housing and sanitation was confirmed by Justice Lenaola in the High Court case of *Satrose Ayuma*. The respondents, Registered Trustees of the Kenya Railways Staff Retirement Benefits Scheme, argued that Article 43 rights could not be enforced against them because they were nonstate actors. Justice Lenaola rejected that defense and affirmed that the enforceability of the Bill of Rights was not limited to a state organ. What is yet to be clarified is whether private actors attract the same level of obligation as the state in the application of the Bill of Rights or a diminished level of responsibility, depending on the nature of the right, as is the case in South Africa.[24] Arguments that certain elements of Article 43 should apply to titleholders, structure owners, or informal services providers remain largely untested.

---

23 Constitution of Kenya, art. 20(1).

24 Unlike in Kenya, where the Bill of Rights does not provide for any qualification on the obligation on the applicability of a right either between private or state actor or on the basis of the nature of the right, sec. 8 of the South African Constitution makes a distinction on the basis of the nature of right. Sec. 8 reads: "(l) The Bill of Rights applies to all law, and binds the legislature, the executive, the judiciary and all organs of state; (2) A provision of the Bill of Rights binds a natural or a juristic person if, and to the extent that, it is applicable, taking into account the nature of the right and the nature of any duty imposed by the right."

Potential Clashes in Rights

The level of responsibility of structure or title owners horizontally could further be shaped by how the court seeks to resolve the clash in constitutional rights arising in Mukuru, namely, between the right to private property of the titleholders and the right to housing and sanitation asserted by the informal settlement residents.[25] Not only are titleholders likely to resist any claim that they owe positive, horizontal obligations under Article 43, they might assert that they are the victims in this context, having been denied the right to use their property by informal settlers who have "invaded" their land. A telling example is the case of *Orbit Chemicals Ltd.* in which a titleholder in Mukuru (Orbit Chemicals Ltd.) sued the government for loss of use on account that "squatters" had invaded the land and this prevented Orbit as titleholder from using the land.[26] Although the Orbit Chemical case predated the current Constitution, Orbit's property rights claim could now be framed in terms of property rights under Article 40 of the Constitution. When framed in this way, resolving Orbit Chemicals' claims regarding Mukuru lands becomes a question how best to balance its asserted property rights and residents' competing housing rights claims.

The issue of how to strike a balance between individual-based rights and the need to safeguard the legitimacy of the state through the protection of vulnerable communities was front and center in drafting of the recent Evictions and Resettlement Procedure Bill and proved quite contentious. Many stakeholders were concerned that the bill would undermine indefeasible rights to property and lead to massive encroachments and the breakdown of the rule of law. As of September 2014, the bill had yet to be enacted, suggesting possible continued reservations about how to balance the competing interests at stake.

Resolving these competing claims is a complex adjudicative exercise. In respect to publicly held lands, the High Court sought to balance property rights with the housing rights of informal settlers in the *Mitu-Bell* and *Satrose Ayuma* cases by providing the minimum steps to be undertaken before demolition and eviction can occur. In both cases, the court ruled that evictions could not be undertaken unless alternative accommodation is available to settlers—and placed the obligation on the state. This approach is analogous to the judgments of the South African Constitutional Court, which has grappled with similar clashes on a number of occasions. For example, in *Port Elizabeth Municipality v. Various Occupiers*, the court ruled that the property rights of a private landowner did not permit a municipality to evict squatters from private lands without finding suitable land for the squatters. The South African Constitutional Court resolved, on the one hand, that property rights are "defensive

25 The right to property is provided for in art. 40 of the Constitution.

26 Specifically, Orbit demanded that the government be held liable for the "loss of user, income, mesne profits and possession of the plaintiff's property." *See Orbit Chemical Industries Ltd v. Attorney General* (2012), eKLR, Civil Case 876 of 2004 (Oct. 12, 2012). Although the issue of loss of use was not tried, it formed the basis under which Orbit Chemical was awarded a settlement by the court.

rather than affirmative,"[27] whereas, on the other hand, the constitutional right to housing protections are not unlimited and expressly contemplate evictions of settlement dwellers, "even if it results in loss of a home."[28] The court also emphasized the "need to seek concrete and case-specific solutions to the difficult problems that arise."[29]

Another significant element from the *Port Elizabeth* case is that what began as essentially a dispute between private actors took on a public dimension because the state, as arbiter of whether housing rights of the squatters should give way to the property rights of the landowners, was ultimately required to help resolve the dispute. In other words, the state is under an obligation to ensure that alternative arrangements are available for squatters in case of eviction or that private property owners are compensated for the loss of their use of property if eviction is not possible. Indeed, land rights under the South African Constitution are conditioned by considerations of public interest, much as they are in the Constitution of Kenya, and both the Constitutional Court and the Supreme Court of Appeal in the *Port Elizabeth* case rejected the High Court's earlier finding that sought to uphold private property rights of landowners, and thus justify the eviction of squatters on public interest grounds.

In Kenya, a similar balancing approach is possible under the Constitution. First, in light of the emphasis that the Constitution places on human dignity and the protection of marginalized and vulnerable groups, the property rights of owners would likely yield to the housing rights of settlement residents in cases where eviction would mean leaving people homeless with no alternative. Any limit to the right to property is subject to a general limitation clause in Article 24 that requires that any such limits be enacted through the least restrictive means. Evictions, when they leave informal settlers homeless—and especially due to the violent manner in which they are carried out in Nairobi—engage the right of residents not to be subjected to cruel, inhuman, or degrading treatment. The Constitution provides for no limitation on that right, arguably tipping the balance in favor of Mukuru residents in weighing their rights against those of private property owners.

The South African Constitutional Court affirmed a role for the state in helping reach a solution in the face of competing rights in *Modderklip Boerdery*, which involved squatters on private lands. Indeed, that case perhaps best illustrates the dilemma of competing rights where the parties implicated are

---

27 "The land-owner cannot simply say: this is my land, I can do with it what I want, and then send in the bulldozers or sledgehammers." *See Port Elizabeth Municipality v. Various Occupiers*, Constitutional Ct. (2004) (12) BCLR 1268 (CC) (South Africa), at para. 20.

28 *Id.*, at para. 21, referencing subsec. 26(3) of the South African Constitution.

29 *Id.*, at para. 22. Additional considerations to ensure that any eviction is just and equitable include the circumstances under which the settlers occupied the lands in question, the duration of their stay, and the availability of alternative suitable accommodations or land. With respect to the duration of the stay, the court ruled that "a court should be reluctant to grant an eviction against relatively settled occupiers unless it is satisfied that a reasonable alternative is available, even if only as an interim measure," which would mirror the situation currently faced by most Mukuru residents. *Id.*, at para. 27.

all nonstate actors, as in Mukuru. *Modderklip Boerdery* is sometimes critiqued because, rather than make a substantive ruling on the squatters' right to housing, the Constitutional Court framed the issue in terms of the right to the rule of law and access to justice. The rule of law protection under the South African Constitution requires that the state "provide the necessary mechanisms for citizens to resolve disputes that arise between them."[30] In this case, the state was obliged to provide mechanisms to resolve the dispute between private parties that include "the legislative framework, as well as mechanisms and institutions such as the courts and an infrastructure created to facilitate the execution of court orders."[31]

With this judgment, the court sidestepped the issue of the horizontal application of the rights at stake (the private property owners had raised this argument vis-à-vis the squatters) and focused on the need to ensure that any actions to resolve the dispute between property owners and settlement residents minimized "large-scale disruptions in the social fabric" and prevented "social upheaval."[32]As a remedy, the court ordered the state to pay compensation to Modderklip for losses related to the invasion by squatters of his land and prevented any evictions of the squatters from the land until the state had found an alternative place to relocate them. In essence, the court protected Modderklip's loss of use while preserving the right to housing of the squatters. As noted earlier, the South African Constitution appears to place a lower responsibility on private actors than state actors, a distinction not explicitly made in the Kenyan Constitution. It is unclear whether the Kenyan courts would be so quick to sidestep the issue of the horizontal application of rights when considering the same clash in rights between private parties. Notwithstanding questions of the horizontal application of rights, the court's order in *Modderklip*—which placed the onus on the government to address both sets of rights—seems apposite to the Mukuru context in at least one respect. Specifically, such a ruling could help confront the lack of engagement and bureaucratic inertia by public officials seen by Mukuru residents in the face of threats of eviction from private actors. Indeed, as discussed below, the larger challenge may be in the enforcement of any judgment, on top of challenges in seeking a judgment to affirm the rights of Mukuru residents.

---

30 *President of the Republic of South Africa & Anor v. Modderklip Boerdery & Ors,* Constitutional Ct. of South Africa, Case CCT 20/04 (May 13, 2005), at para. 39 (applying subsec. 39 of the const.). *See* A. van der Walt, *The State's Duty to Protect Property Owners and the State's Duty to Provide Housing: Thoughts on the Modderklip Case* 21 South African J. Hum. Rights 144 (2005), on the public dimensions of the private law dispute.

31 *President of the Republic of South Africa & Anor v. Modderklip Boerdery & Ors.*, para. 41.

32 *Id.*, at paras. 31, 43, 46. *Occupiers of 51 Olivia Road, Bereas Township and 197 Main Street Johannesburg v. City of Johannesburg,* 2008(3) SA 208 (CC) and *Residents of Joe Slovo Community, Western Cape v. Thubelisha Homes and Others,* 2010(3) SA 454 (CC) also affirmed an obligation of the state of "meaningful engagement" with settlement dwellers who risked being left homeless by evictions. *See,* for example, Anashari Pillay, *Toward Effective Social and Economic Rights Adjudication: The Role of Meaningful Engagement,* 10(3) I-Con 732 (2012), for a more detailed discussion.

Progressive Realization

The third element relevant to Article 43 rights affecting Mukuru is the principle of progressive realization. Economic and social rights in Article 43 are qualified by Article 21(2), which requires the state to take legislative, policy, and other measures, including the setting of standards to achieve the progressive realization of those rights. The Supreme Court of Kenya has made attempts to elaborate what the concept of progressive realization means, which it explained in terms of a "phased-out attainment of an identified goal" in its opinion in Advisory No. 2 of 2012, *In the Matter of the Principle of Gender Representation in the National Assembly and the Senate.*[33] In determining Article 43 rights, including those of housing and sanitation, courts have required the state to show that it is putting in place mechanisms that help move toward the progressive realization of the rights. This approach is well developed in other jurisdictions with social and economic rights, such as South Africa and India, where courts often require the state or those with the obligation to facilitate a social economic right to show tangible and systematic efforts being made to progressively realize the right.[34]

It is less clear how the Kenyan court will apply progressive realization in light of the horizontal application of rights contemplated under the Kenyan Constitution. Who would bear this responsibility, in situations where the parties implicated are all nonstate actors as in Mukuru, needs to be determined. In the context of Mukuru, both the horizontal application of rights and progressive realization pose a number of evidentiary issues. Here is where research findings can feed into a substantive analysis of the case.

In respect to the horizontal application of rights, the structure owners as well as other service providers are in many ways amorphous, operating largely as cartels. Although Mukuru residents can often point to who supplies water with relative ease, as well as to any actual or putative agency relationship among structure owners, service providers, and titleholders, generating sufficient evidence to prove these relationships in a manner that leads to legal liability presents a challenge. It is precisely these types of dynamics—who is providing what to whom—that the situational analyses are trying to chart with more accuracy. Similarly, the current efforts to work with the communities to identify legal, financial, and planning models—that is, to define what is tangibly possible for residents in terms of establishing dignified and desired living arrangements—should go a long way to helping define, more concretely, what progressive realization of the right to access to housing and

---

33 *Orbit Chemical Industries Ltd v. Attorney General, supra* note 26.

34 *See*, for example, *Government of the Republic of South Africa and Others v. Grootboom and Others* (CCT11/00) (2000) ZACC 19, where the court established a "reasonableness" standard to be used in evaluating how the state is responding to the requirement of progressive realization of a right. The reasonableness standard was further developed in cases such as *Minister of Health and Others v. Treatment Action Campaign and Others* (No. 1) (CCT9/02) (2002) ZACC 16, and in *Khosa and Others v. Minister of Social Development and Others;* and *Mahlaule and Others v. Minister of Social Development and Others* (CCT 13/03 and 14/03) (2004) ZACC 11.

reasonable sanitation entails. The project has involved discussions with policy makers, especially from Nairobi County government and the NLC, in a proactive effort to feed into their thinking on any solutions that they are developing to address the challenges faced by residents of Mukuru, and in Nairobi's informal settlements more generally.

By providing a detailed analysis of conditions in Mukuru, the research thus aims to help the presiding judges apply emerging legal standards under the Constitution and craft an appropriate remedy—whether the courts opt for a remedy that follows a procedural *Modderklip* path or a more substantive application of housing rights to resolve competing claims in Mukuru.[35] The models being developed with residents will provide a practical roadmap for the state to engage meaningfully with the residents of Mukuru to find solutions to the many problems they face daily and preserve the social fabric of their communities. To be sure, the "state" or "government" has been treated somewhat amorphously to this point; in reality, a series of responsibilities can be distinguished between the national and county levels. The research has thus sought to bring clarity to the separate or overlapping responsibilities of the different public bodies—in terms of lands, service delivery, planning, and so on—both in deciphering the applicable legal frameworks and in undertaking related legal and public advocacy. Anecdotally, efforts to use research to feed into litigation materials are helping reinforce a nascent culture of using expert evidence and evidence-based pleadings by groups bringing public interest litigation under the recent Constitution.

Challenges in Crafting a Remedy and Monitoring Its Enforcement

The importance of using research to feed into the crafting of an appropriate remedy should not be underestimated. That exercise, in contexts of social and economic rights adjudication like Mukuru, might be the larger challenge for the court (larger, that is, than resolving issues related to competing rights, progressive realization, and so on). The challenge of remedies can be formulated in two ways, each associated with larger debates about social and economic rights litigation.

At one level are traditional critiques about the legitimacy of courts in respect to public interest litigation, namely, that they not be seen as overreaching their role by issuing overly prescriptive or expansive rulings, and thus usurping executive and legislative powers on questions of public policy that the courts might neither be well positioned nor have the expertise to handle.[36] Economic and social rights have been a particular target of such critiques

---

35 More generally, *see*, for example, Charles F. Sabel & William H. Simon, *Destabilization Rights: How Public Law Litigation Succeeds*, 117 Harv. L. Rev. 1085 (2004), on fact-finding challenges faced by courts confronted with polycentric problems with a myriad of actors.

36 *See*, for example, *id.*, for a summary of classic critiques, primarily in an American context, notably referencing Abram Chayes, *The Role of the Judge in Public Law Litigation*, 89 Harv. L. Rev. 1281 (1976). *See* also Gerald N. Rosenberg, *The Hollow Hope: Can Courts Bring about Social*

because, by their nature, they typically involve larger, contested political choices regarding the use and redistribution of resources.[37]

In the context of Mukuru, however, the concern is more with a second, more recent, focus on the effects of social and economic rights litigation. National courts in a number of countries have increasingly upheld economic and social rights protections, often relying on newer constitutions. Questions have arisen, in turn, as to whether this increased protection of rights has achieved the sought-after social change; in other words, to what degree has it helped solve the social and economic problems targeted by litigation? Questions about the effects of economic and social rights litigation take on an added dimension in developing-country contexts, where poverty is more widespread and endemic than in more economically well-developed countries. From this perspective, questions arise as to what role courts and legal processes can play in finding solutions to large-scale social and economic challenges, which likely have eluded existing poverty reduction interventions.[38]

Attempts to analyze the impacts of social and economic rights litigation, to date, have focused on remedies as well as on the related issue of what role courts have played in supervising the enforcement of orders. With respect to remedies, commentators have tried to understand, for example, the relative effects of judgments and whether the judgments target more directly private or state actors and how prescriptive, expansive, or flexible the judgments are in directing actors to remedy the right's violation in question.[39] Where a court crafts remedies that eventually are not enforced—whether because of the complexity of the remedies or a lack of a culture of respect for rule of law, or because the remedy was not effective in addressing the rights violation—this has the potential to bring the administration of justice into disrepute. The early experiences in Kenya with social and economic rights litigation have been sensitive to such concerns. The enforcement of remedies in Kenya has generally been problematic, which points to a culture of respect for the rule of law that remains largely elusive.[40] In this light, the strategy of the courts in cases such as *Mitu-Bell* and *Satrose Ayuma* has been to retain supervisory jurisdiction, thus requiring parties to report on progress in complying with the court's order. Yet another strategy, seen in the *Satrose Ayuma* case, is for the court to clarify general principles of law and require the parties to work out

Change? (U. of Chicago Press 1991).

37 For a discussion of these debates in the Indian context, where they have been somewhat pronounced, *see*, for example, P. B. Mehta, *The Rise of Judicial Sovereignty*, 18 J. Demo. 70 (2007); S. Shankar & P. B. Mehta, *Courts and Socioeconomic Rights in India*, in *Courting Social Justice*, *supra* note 18.

38 *See*, for example, Brinks & Gauri, *Introduction*, in *Courting Social Justice*, *supra* note 18, for a more detailed discussion of the possible role of courts and litigation.

39 Questions of legitimacy are related to questions of the impact of judgments, inasmuch as decisions that are viewed as illegitimate might stand a greater chance of not being followed and thus having less effect.

40 The new constitution was enacted, among other reasons, to strengthen the culture of rule of law.

the most appropriate course of action under the circumstances. In these ways, the courts might be heeding the advice of Irene Ndegwa, who has stated, "The nature of remedy sought and granted must therefore take into account the attitude of the government during the course of the litigation or its previous record of compliance with court orders on related issues."[41]

The remedial strategy in *Satrose Ayuma* appears consistent with the balanced approach that Yash Ghai and Jill Cottrell have recommended, where parties are encouraged to work out solutions in economic, social, and cultural rights disputes while the courts play a superintending role with the option to intervene when there is a deadlock.[42] To situate this approach within a broader body of literature, the initial experiences in economic and social rights litigation points to an approach that is "experimental" or "dialogical," emphasizing relatively open remedies, but strong supervision by courts.[43]

Studying the trend in the enforcement of judgments made by the Kenyan courts, especially those judgments for social economic rights, will foster a better strategy for the types of remedies that will be most appropriate in cases like Mukuru. Using research to guide what constitutes appropriate remedies also amplifies the role of experts in devising judicial remedies. As Brinks and Gauri note, "[l]itigation campaigns that demonstrate the feasibility of social action can redefine what is socially possible and transform what were utopian aspirations and barely articulated wishes, which could be dismissed or bought off with more tangible short-term benefits, into needs that *must* be met by governments."[44] Against this backdrop, the research experiences in Mukuru could shed light on larger questions regarding enforcement of social and economic rights remedies. For example, will providing detailed analysis on the situation in Mukuru and working with residents to identify possible solutions to housing and basic services needs leave the court more inclined to view parties as better placed to work out remedial options (viz. restricting its role to monitor compliance with its ruling)? The research project could offer clues as to whether the strategy of providing information on options to the court increases the likelihood of compliance with the court's judgment. Finally, there are questions regarding how the court, when armed with bet-

---

41 Irene Ndegwa, *A Roof over Wanjiku's Head: Judicial Enforcement of the Right to Housing under the Constitution of Kenya*, in *Judiciary Watch Report, Judicial Enforcement of Socio-Economic Rights under the New Constitution: Challenges and Opportunities*. 143, 175 (J. Biegon & G. Musila eds., Kenya Sec. of the Intl. Commn. Jurists 2011).

42 Jill Cotrell & Yash Ghai, *The Role of the Courts in Implementing Economic, Social, and Cultural Rights*, in *Economic, Social, and Cultural Rights in Practice: The Role of Judges in Implementing Economic, Social, and Cultural Rights* (Y. Ghai & J. Cotrell eds., Commonwealth Secretariat 2004). This approach is discussed in *Port Elizabeth Municipality v. Various Occupiers*, *supra* note 27, at paras. 39–47.

43 Rodriguez-Gravito, *supra* note 18, relies on notions of constitutional dialogue and cites related literature in more detail. *See* Sabel and Simon, *supra* note 35, for a discussion of the experimentalist approach.

44 Brinks and Gauri, *supra* note 18, at 25.

ter information, could help parties move beyond potential deadlocks as they arise.

Challenges posed by potential deadlocks point to questions of power dynamics between parties and challenges in overcoming political inertia and the lack of bureaucratic capacity to address problems on the scale of those faced by the Mukuru residents. Brinks and Gauri suggest that courts can play a role in social and economic rights litigation in imposing a "unifying body of law in exchange for intervening in otherwise unequal local relations of power, especially in cases involving local authorities."[45] The chapter by René Uruena in this volume points to experiences in Latin America where courts have been an important tool in overcoming analogous deadlocks, by empowering or compelling agencies to address large social problems faced by the poor and mediating intense divisions over redistribution of resources in the process.[46] In the case of *Port Elizabeth*, which affirms the importance of court-supervised mediation, Justice Sachs found that the opportunity for mediation between the parties had run its course.[47] The approach taken by the research team thus has been one that does not see the courts or the law as panaceas.[48] The Mukuru research project is premised on working with communities to identify solutions, which implicitly evinces a preference not to rely solely on courts or legal processes to resolve the challenges that the settlements face. The research team has tried to use the evidence generated from the research to strengthen engagement with public officials in an effort to increase policy windows outside judicial proceedings. Finally, as described in the next section, legal advocacy efforts are seeking, in part, to rely on administrative redress mechanisms outside the courts, which might prove to be an alternative, complementary venue to the courts. The approach is guided by the view that administrative redress mechanisms might be easier to access, and more responsive and flexible, than the courts and could guard against an overreliance on judicial pronouncements and constitutional challenges in addressing large-scale social problems.[49]

Combining Legal Advocacy with Community Mobilization Efforts

The challenges in enforcing court judgments and remedies point to possible limits of the law and legal solutions in solving the many layers of challenges faced by residents in Mukuru Kwa Njenga and Mukuru Kwa Reuben. Con-

45 Brinks & Gauri, *supra* note 18, at 347.

46 Chapter 4 in this volume, "Courts and Regulatory Governance in Latin America."

47 *Port Elizabeth Municipality v. Various Occupiers, supra* note 27, at para. 47.

48 In this regard, *see* Justice Markandey Katju's judgment in the Supreme Court of India, *Writ Petition (Civil) 580 of 2003*, para. 56, remarking that "the view that the judiciary can run the government and can solve all the problems of the people is not only unconstitutional, but also fallacious and creates a false impression that the judiciary is a panacea for ills in the society."

49 For a general discussion on these points, *see*, for example, Varun Gauri, *Redressing Grievances and Complaints regarding Basic Services*, 41 World Dev. 115 (2013), on overreliance on courts.

scious of these limits, the research team has tried to build links to ongoing community-level advocacy efforts in addition to efforts to support the legal challenge on behalf of residents. More specifically, through efforts to involve community members in data collection activities and to share findings with them, the research process aims to build awareness of physical and legal situations. Three examples illustrate how increased awareness has had an empowering effect and helped community members better target their advocacy efforts.

The women of Mukuru recently mobilized to see how they could best solve the appalling living and health conditions they face. Aware of their rights to health and sanitation under the Constitution, a group of about 20 women began a campaign in November 2013, with AMT's assistance, to collect 20,000 signatures to demonstrate the number of people who are aware of and willing to demand action relating to their sanitary plight. On August 21, 2014, and having collected 15,000 signatures, the women delivered a letter to the cabinet secretary for health formally requesting him to set up an inquiry under Section 11 of the Public Health Act of Kenya. The letter proposes that the inquiry investigate and make recommendations on how to address the public health conditions in the two settlements. It is hoped that the results of such an inquiry would put pressure on the government to address larger tenure and planning shortcomings that are at the root of poor services such as the water and sewage infrastructure and associated health risks in Mukuru. This strategy, which begins with community mobilization, is based on an awareness of basic constitutional rights and seeks a response from public officials by way of formal, statutory processes as well as through the broader processes of political pressure. These efforts, still under way, are an example of using administrative recourse mechanisms as an alternative to relying solely on constitutional litigation.[50]

In 2013, leaders of a youth empowerment organization called Wajukuu, from an informal settlement in Lunga, not far from Mukuru, approached MWW leaders. The Wajukuu youth leaders had heard about MWW's efforts to support the Mukuru communities against evictions and sought guidance against similar threats of demolition in their neighborhood. The youth reported that their area chief (a leader under the informal governance structures in the settlement) had issued notices to vacate the settlement. Apparently, the local chief and the district commissioner were working closely with the structure owners, who were trying to negotiate to buy the land where the settlement is situated—an example of the power dynamics and interplay between formal and informal governance structures in the settlements. The lands in question followed the typical pattern: a company had been allocated land titles—a 2.5-acre stretch in the settlement—on the condition (never fulfilled) that the lands be developed for light industry within six months. The structure owners had

50 For an earlier account, *see*, for example, Mark Anderson, *Kenyan Women Sue for Ownership of Nairobi Slum*, Guardian (Oct. 2, 2013).

also approached MWW to ask it to withdraw a case, similar to the one in Mukuru, seeking cancellation of the company's title.

MWW and Wajukuu's first step was to mobilize area residents to inform them of the risk of demolition. During two awareness-building meetings held in the settlement, which hundreds of residents attended, MWW informed the community about the land that they occupied. In particular, MWW explained that the company had failed to fulfill the conditions under which the land was allocated, meaning that the NLC had the power to cancel the title. As the next step, community leaders held two meetings with the NLC requesting a cancellation of title. The NLC's chair was not prepared to cancel title and recommended that the leaders negotiate with the landowners to purchase the land. The chair explained that the NLC had the power to cancel and reissue the title to the original grantee. After this meeting, the district administration handed out pamphlets to settlement residents informing them that the land would be sold. Surveyors began demarcating the land into plots, but residents chased them away before they could complete the task. After this incident, the residents gathered in large numbers for a peaceful demonstration at the district chief's office. A few days later, residents held a peaceful demonstration along Lunga Road, and the settlement has experienced no further threats since.

In July 2012, similar efforts were undertaken in Mukuru after MWW discovered, through an advertisement in a national newspaper, that lands that house the Maendeleo community primary and secondary schools were slated to be auctioned. Thanks to a similar mix of community awareness raising and peaceful demonstrations, the auction was called off. That case predates the research project and the injunction freezing evictions in Mukuru Kwa Reuben and Mukuru Kwa Njenga. These examples demonstrate how public advocacy efforts were successful in building the confidence of residents to confront and stem the threat of eviction and the actions of titleholders that fell outside the constitutional framework in place in Kenya. The experiences demonstrate that raising awareness about the contested legal status of the lands can be a powerful tool for mobilizing coordinated community action. Yet these efforts also demonstrate the need for better legal frameworks and more predictable processes to regulate disputes. Although guided by an awareness of legal rights and peaceful in their execution, those efforts were ultimately successful because residents succeeded in shifting power dynamics in their favor. Those dynamics are continually in flux, however, and increased clarity on the applicable legal frameworks would help ensure that disputes are resolved in a more orderly and predictable manner—as has been the case since the 2012 injunction put a halt to evictions in Mukuru.

Conclusion

In a recent right to health case, Justice Majanja of the Kenyan High Court noted that

> the success of our Constitution largely depends on the State delivering tangible benefits to the people particularly those who live at the margins of society. The incorporation of economic and social rights set out in Article 43 sums up the desire of Kenyans to deal with issues of poverty, unemployment, ignorance and disease. Failure to deal with these existing conditions will undermine the whole foundation of the Constitution.[51]

In an earlier case in South Africa, Justice Yacoob of the Constitutional Court remarked, "People in need of housing are not, and must not be regarded as a disempowered mass. They must be encouraged to be proactive and not purely defensive."[52] In many respects, these two complementary sentiments have served as the launching point for the research project described in this chapter. A challenge going forward will be to achieve balance between empowering citizens and engaging with public officials to bring about the tangible benefits that Justice Majanja evokes. A related challenge will be in managing the expectations of residents who are eager to see change after decades of living on the margins of society.

As of fall 2014, the project was just past its midway point, and the problems that it seeks to understand are likely to persist for some years beyond the project's lifespan. Some of the above experiences point to the limits of legal action in the face of such endemic problems, as well as to how the research team is trying to carve out opportunities in the face of them. The ultimate successes of the project in combining knowledge building from different disciplines (urban planning, finance, and legal) with different types of policy engagement and advocacy, legal or otherwise, remain to be seen. The hope is that this model of action-based research will be a valuable example for promoting greater voice, justice, and accountability for vulnerable groups faced with similarly complex contexts. For the time being, the efforts are ultimately about helping the residents of Mukuru find solutions to their living conditions and, in the process, achieve their human rights to dignity now firmly entrenched in the Constitution of Kenya.[53]

---

51 *Mathew Okwanda v. Minister of Health and Medical Services & 3 others,* Pet. No. 94 of 2012, High Ct. at Nairobi, at para. 13.

52 *Occupiers of 51 Olivia Road v. Johannesburg, supra* note 32, at para. 20.

53 Constitution of Kenya, art. 28.

11

"Good" Legislation as a Means of Ensuring Voice, Accountability, and the Delivery of Results in Urban Development

Maria Mousmouti and Gianluca Crispi

Urban legislation is a pillar of sustainable urban development. It is an important development tool that lays down, in binding rules, acceptable behaviors in society and the rights and obligations of parties and governance frameworks in different areas of life. The global urban population is expected to grow by 3 billion in the next 50 years, with 98 percent of this growth occurring in developing countries.[1] Such unprecedented growth could result in anarchy and increased inequalities if not underpinned by strong and coherent policy and legal, institutional, and governance frameworks that ensure a solid context for planning, dialogue among actors, and rights-based approaches to development.

Urban areas dominate economies, drive technological development, and provide shelter and livelihoods. The quality of human settlements and urban governance affects the quality of life for millions of individuals. In this context, urban legislation defines conditions for access to land, infrastructure, housing, and basic services; it lays out rules for planning, decision making, and participation; it guides the improvement of livelihoods and living conditions by setting requirements for urban development initiatives; and it sets the context within which urban authorities, local governments, and communities are expected to fulfill their mandates, react to emerging challenges, and be accountable. Urban law provides a framework in which to mediate and balance competing public and private interests, especially in relation to land use and development; to create a stable and predictable framework for public and private sector action; to guarantee the inclusion of the interests of vulnerable groups; and to provide a catalyst for local and national discourse.[2] In other words, legislation determines the context, conditions, and terms of the social contract for urban development. Legislation can set meaningful sustainable frameworks for development, give voice to affected people and communities, and set appropriate frameworks for accountability, or it can accentuate inequalities and exclusion.

1 U.N. Dept. Econ. & Soc. Affairs, *World Urbanization Prospects: 2011 Revision* (U.N. 2012).

2 UN-Habitat, *Global Report on Human Settlements* 215 (U.N. 2009).

The Challenge: The Definition of Good Urban Legislation

The mere existence of legislation does not ensure effective urban management and development. Legislation can generate more problems than it actually solves. Unclear or ambiguous provisions that are complex, overlapping, or leave gaps in protection, that are difficult to access or understand and poorly enforced and implemented, with high compliance costs and unwanted effects, will have a negative impact on competitiveness and economic growth. Outdated, complex, and rigid legislation has hindered development and compelled citizens and administrators to seek informal arrangements and corrupt means to access basic services. Businesses, citizens, professional groups, consumers, and other stakeholders often complain about the negative effects of bad or unnecessary legislation. If legislation lays down the terms of a social contract and determines the framework for social development, its quality is of primary importance. In other words, what is needed for sustainable development is not just legislation but *good* legislation.

Legislation often suffers from misguided assumptions or overambitious expectations, inadequate appraisal of costs and consequences, unrealistic expectations, and severe gaps between intention and reality, as has been the experience in many African countries.[3] Planning laws are often outdated, irrelevant, and inappropriate for the contexts within which they operate. Laws that fail to make land available in pace with rapid urbanization result in insufficient land supply, increases in land prices, and the formation of slums. Laws that are not in line with the needs of the people and local socioeconomic realities such as urban poverty result in noncompliance and a loss of credibility for the planning system, not to mention their selective application in favor of specific groups or elites. Other common problems include regulatory barriers that limit opportunities in formal land markets, exacerbate inequality, and discourage investments; laws with high compliance costs; and laws that are not enforced or implemented.[4] A result of failed planning laws is the predominance of informal structures and the prevalence of the interests of elites over large groups of the population:[5] legislation designed to protect the public from the negative aspects of urban land development may be used to enhance the value of land owned by the wealthy.

Whereas cities can be drivers of economic growth, dysfunctional cities cannot harness the economies derived from the agglomeration of population, common infrastructures, and the availability and diversity of labor and market size. Instead, they generate congestion and high costs for infrastructure and services and cannot support the creation of sufficient jobs and quality of life for their residents, with broad-ranging consequences, including social unrest and insecurity. If legislation is a prerequisite for urban governance,

---

3 Stephen Berrisford, *How to Make Planning Law Work for Africa* 3–4 (Africa Res. Inst. 2013).

4 *Id.*, at 2.

5 *Id.*

good urban legislation is a precondition for sustainable urban development. But what is a good law?

Although everyone may agree on the need for "good laws," the features of a good law are not obvious. When it comes to legislation, quality is a broad and vague term, perceptions of which differ depending on the viewpoints of different actors, legal traditions, and social and political contexts. Even when it comes to specific areas such as urban legislation, different professions have different opinions: planners, lawyers, and developers do not share the same language, views, or ideas or necessarily see eye to eye.[6]

Although there is no single understanding of quality in legislation, common values characterize good legislation: efficacy, effectiveness, efficiency, and simplicity.[7] Views differ on the values that should prevail: whereas lawyers tend to stress principles like legal certainty, economists tend to favor efficiency and political scientists tend to emphasize efficacy. One aspect of good legislation on which everyone agrees is the need for laws to be effective.[8] Effective legislation sets rules that address existing problems, takes into account the voice of affected people and communities, ensures accountability, and can deliver the results it promises. What makes a law effective?

The effectiveness of legislation is largely determined by its purpose, substantive content, legislative expression, overarching structure, and results.[9] Effective legislation needs to have a clear purpose; introduce consistent and well-thought-out rules and enforcement mechanisms that realistically address the targeted problems; introduce clear, precise, and unambiguous rules and obligations; and allow for systematic monitoring and evaluation of the results of legislation in real life.[10] If these elements are in place, the basic conditions for effective legislation are fulfilled. In the opposite situation, if legislation is unclear, poorly articulated, or suffers from internal tensions or imbalances, it has few chances to succeed.

Ineffective urban and planning laws reflect different pathologies of ineffective legislation: blurred or inconsistent choices, unclear or ambitious objectives, rules whose impact has not been considered, lack of consideration of enforcement and implementation issues, inconsistent or contradictory drafting choices, and limited, fragmented, or nonexistent information on the application

---

6 Patrick McAuslan, *Land, Law, and Planning* 12–30 (Weidenfeld & Nicolson 1975).

7 Helen Xanthaki, *On the Transferability of Legislative Solutions: The Functionality Test*, in *Drafting Legislation: A Modern Approach* 1–18 (Constantin Stefanou & Helen Xanthaki eds., Ashgate 2008).

8 Helen Xanthaki, *Quality of Legislation: An Achievable Universal Concept or An Utopia Pursuit?*, in *Quality of Legislation: Principles and Instruments* 75–85 (Luzius Mader & Mart Tavres de Almeida eds., Nomos 2011).

9 Maria Mousmouti, *Effectiveness as an Aid to Legislative Drafting,* 2 Loophole 15–25 (2014), http://www.opc.gov.au/CALC/docs/Loophole/Loophole_May14.pdf.

10 *Id.*, at 23.

and the results of legislation. If good urban legislation is what is needed, then it is necessary to address these pathologies.

Improving the Quality of Urban Legislation

Improving the quality of legislation is not an easy or straightforward matter. However, it is indispensable for ensuring delivery in a development context. Efforts have led to the development of strategies and tool kits to improve regulatory governance, support decision making, improve legislative drafting, and rationalize lawmaking. These efforts have focused on improving the content of legislation and its responsiveness to local realities, taking into account the voices of affected groups and communities, making legislation simple, clear, and accessible, and ensuring that it can deliver results. This section examines alternative ways to improve the quality of legislation.

Address the Incongruity between the Law and Urban Realities

Urban laws often fail because their content is detached from local realities. Laws are often overambitious, set unrealistic objectives, and are irrelevant to local needs and conditions. In other words, laws fail because they do not set a realistic and feasible context for development. For example, in the Nigerian state of Kogi, regulation on the size of plots determines an acceptable size that ranges from 900 to 1,350 square meters. These requirements are in discordance with the needs of dense urban centers, smaller cities, and urban areas in the country, and place plots out of reach of the majority of the low-income population.[11]

Building standards are often regulated without taking into account local incomes, climates, traditional building techniques, and locally available materials, resulting in urban dwellers who cannot afford to build in compliance with existing regulations. The building codes in Mozambique (derived from the Portuguese building codes) are an example of rules that fail to reflect the socioeconomic situation of the country, building materials, and construction capacities. In the aftermath of a fatal earthquake in 1755, Portugal adopted a building code with very restrictive rules for construction that was extended to the country's colonies in Africa. Today, more than 250 years later, Mozambique, with little history of tremors, retains one of the more stringent building codes in Africa; it requires brick or cement block walls and reinforced concrete beams, and in this way excludes all but the wealthiest households.[12]

Laws that are not harmonized with the reality they aim to regulate and are incongruent with existing socioeconomic conditions cannot be successful in setting out the terms of social contracts, and therefore they have little chance to deliver targeted or appropriate results. This fault can be addressed by strengthening the basis of evidence on which legislation is premised, taking into account the views of affected groups, and making it easy to comply with.

---

11 UN-Habitat, *Legal Assessment* (U.N. 2014).

12 *Id.*

Use Evidence-Based Lawmaking to Link Legislation with Reality

Evidence-based lawmaking is a way to make legislation responsive to specific social problems. The use of evidence in lawmaking strives to set out realistic terms for development, give affected people and communities a voice, allow for participation, and assess the delivery of results. Assessing the impact of legislation through an analysis of the problem to be addressed, the examination of available policy or legislative options, and the appraisal of their positive and negative impact can make institutions more accountable and legislative interventions more responsive, effective, efficient, coherent, and transparent.[13] When legislation is not built on a solid basis of evidence, or when impact assessments are used in a formalistic rather than a substantive way, legislation tends to demonstrate gaps with reality that severely affect not only its function but also its capacity to deliver results.

In Mozambique, land belongs to the state, and citizens can acquire only the "right of use and enjoyment" (*direito de uso e aproveitamento dos terras*; DUAT). Although a DUAT does not confer full ownership, it is a secure, renewable, and long-term user right comparable to a lease. According to the Urban Land Regulations,[14] DUATs in urban areas cannot be issued before the land is provided with urban basic services, and DUATs issued when an urban plan is not in place are invalid. Similarly, rights based on good-faith occupation can be recognized only if they do not conflict with an existing urban development plan. Given that such plans are generally absent or outdated, this provision condemns large numbers of low-income households to living in informal arrangements. A careful consideration of the impact of such provisions might significantly improve both their functionality and their effectiveness.

Evidence-based lawmaking can make legislation more focused and reduce overambitious aspirations that introduce radical changes to the existing system but fail to have real impact. It also facilitates the consideration of all possible alternatives to achieve a policy goal. Alternatives to regulation, such as performance-based and incentive approaches, co-regulation and self-regulation schemes, information and education, might be less costly, more effective, more flexible, and adaptable to situation and sector specificities.[15]

Give Affected People a Voice

Cities are entities where businesses and large groups of people live and work. Listening to the these people, taking into account their needs and their opinions with regard to the functionality of different proposals and solutions, is

13 Organisation for Economic Co-operation and Development (OECD), *Building an Institutional Framework for Regulatory Impact Analysis (RIA): Guidance for Policy Makers* 24–25 (OECD 2008).

14 Government of Mozambique (GOM) *Urban Land Regulations 2006*, Decree No. 60/2006 (Dec. 26, 2006).

15 David Driesen, *Alternatives to Regulation? Market Mechanisms and the Environment*, in *Oxford Handbook of Regulation* 206ff. (Robert Baldwin, Martin Cave, & Martin Lodge eds., Oxford University Press 2010).

a valuable investment: not only does it generate more targeted legislative solutions, but it improves compliance with existing rules. In Colombia, for example, neighborhood plans can be approved without the collaboration and agreement of landowners, whose consent is usually sought only when a law is implemented. This process leads to various failures or extreme delays in the implementation of the plans. Due to the lack of consultation with and participation of stakeholders, by 2011, only 44 percent of plans approved in the previous 10 years had been implemented.[16]

Laws affect people directly and indirectly. Talking to stakeholders and interested or affected parties and groups *before* decisions on legislation are made is not only an element of good governance but a practice that enables sociopolitical interaction, encourages partnerships and joint solutions to problems, and increases the efficiency and legitimacy of decisions.[17] Consultation is a "two-way relationship in which citizens provide feedback to [the] government,"[18] which enhances the legitimacy of legislation, allows groups and communities to be heard, and improves both the content of legislation (as a binding expression of social contracts) and its potential to deliver results. Consultation provides firsthand data and information on the situation on the ground and thus can link legislative initiatives with reality. Consultation can also prove useful for identifying the specificities and needs of local communities and population groups. Building consultation and participation procedures into the process of designing and implementing urban legislation can have a positive impact on the legislation's quality and its capacity to deliver results.

Make Legislation Simple and Easy to Comply With

Because legislation is a binding expression of existing social contracts and sets out the rights and obligations of all social actors, it should be simple, understandable, and easy to comply with. Complexity increases costs for citizens and public administration, hinders compliance, and ultimately undermines the social contract and the fair distribution of burdens and benefits of urban development. Institutions with unclear mandates and complex and overlapping frameworks and procedures for decision making leave high margins for discretion, limit accountability, and favor informality and corruption. However, complexity is a common problem with technical legislation. Standards are often difficult to understand, and procedures and requirements for compliance may be burdensome, time-consuming, and costly. Planning regulations in developing and transition are often too detailed, rigid, and inflexible, making compliance difficult and inevitably motivating people to bypass them.

---

16 Departamento Nacional de Planeación, Partial Plans Database compiled using data from municipal planning offices, Colombia (2011).

17 Daniela Obradovic & Jose Alonso Vizcaino, *Good Governance Requirements Concerning the Participation of Interest Groups in EU Consultations'* 43 Common Market L. Rev. 1050 (2006).

18 OECD, *Citizens as Partner: Information, Consultation, and Public Participation in Policy-Making* 22 (OECD 2001).

An example of complexity is the procedure to register the DUATs in Mozambique: it is lengthy and complicated, and involves an overlapping double registration with the national-level Deeds Registry (Registro Predial, under the jurisdiction of the Ministry of Justice) and the Cadastral Services (with offices at the provincial and national levels and under the jurisdiction of the Ministry of Agriculture and Rural Development).

Because the procedure is so cumbersome and bureaucratic, most transactions take place informally, making identification of the ownership status of a property difficult. Simplifying the registration process and promoting greater transparency would not only reduce the discretionary and nontransparent application of legal provisions but also eliminate factors that result in the existence of a parallel extralegal land market.[19]

Furthermore, procedures can be costly, which makes compliance difficult. Data from many developing countries show that procedures required to obtain construction and occupancy permits are complicated, not understood by laypeople, time-consuming, and costly, resulting in increased informality and lack of compliance. For example, the cost to build a warehouse, obtain necessary licenses and permits, complete notifications, conduct inspections, and obtain utility connections amount to 104 percent of income per capita in Asia and the Pacific, 327 percent in Europe and Central Asia, and 850 percent in South Asia.[20] Delays caused by complex and costly procedures are not only an obstacle for growth, entrepreneurship, investment, and economic development but also a discouragement for citizens and authorities to apply and respect the law.

Government organizations can reduce the complexity of legislation by reviewing it, reducing procedural steps and paperwork, and making it less burdensome. One-stop shops; unified or simplified permit and license procedures; time limits for decision making; assistance with compliance, organizational, and structural measures; and the use of IT contribute to this goal of simplification.[21] The 2014 World Bank *Doing Business* report notes that Rwanda improved its ranking by 118 positions in the overall index (from 150th in 2008 to 32nd in 2014) by reducing unnecessary regulations and establishing a business-friendly legal framework. Key reforms involved cutting costs and time required for obtaining construction permits and for registering property. One-stop centers brought all licensing offices and applications under one roof, thus reducing waiting time and administrative hassle for entrepreneurs.[22]

---

19 Rogier J. E. van den Brink, *Land Reform in Mozambique* (Agric. & Rural Dev. Notes No. 43, World Bank Dec. 2008).

20 World Bank, *Doing Business*, http://www.doingbusiness.org/data/exploretopics/dealing-with-construction-permits.

21 OECD, *From Red Tape to Smart Tape—Synthesis Report: Administrative Simplification in OECD Countries* 17 (OECD 2003).

22 World Bank, *supra* note 20.

Administrative burdens refer to costs incurred by enterprises, the voluntary sector, public authorities, and citizens in meeting legal obligations to provide information on their action or production, either to public authorities or to private parties. If administrative burdens are too high, compliance with legislation becomes unduly costly and resource consuming, economic activity is hampered, and administration is an irritant to business activity. The reduction of administrative burdens aims to reduce bureaucracy-related costs in the form of permits, forms, and reporting and notification requirements, and to improve the cost-efficiency of regulations.[23] When unnecessary burdens are reduced, employees can spend more time on core business activities rather than on paperwork. Programs to reduce administrative burdens can have impressive results: in 2004, the Dutch Bureau for Economic Policy Analysis estimated that reducing the administrative costs by 25 percent would eventually lead to an increase in EU GDP of 1.6 percent.[24] Measurements of administrative burdens, using different methodologies, can quantify compliance costs; highlight repeated obligations, "congestion" points, and "irritating" procedures; and showcase ways to cut unnecessary costs. Benefits from burdens reduction can be impressive, especially in systems with a lot of regulations. However, experience shows that administrative cost reductions need to go hand in hand with broader simplification programs.

Reducing costs and enhancing the ease of compliance, as well as enhancing the transparency of implementation and the enforcement of urban legislation, enables urban legislation to be a more meaningful expression of social contracts, not only in setting out the rights and obligations of all social actors, but also in allowing these rights and obligations to be enforced and honored.

Improve the Clarity and Accessibility of the Law

As a binding expression of the rights and obligations of all social actors, legislation should be clear, accessible, and understandable to all. Legislation that is incomprehensible, fragmented, and dispersed is inaccessible to laypersons and even to trained jurists. Understanding what the law prescribes is a fundamental premise of the rule of law; the opposite of this leads to confusion, informality, and lack of accountability. However, the constant introduction of new legislation makes efforts at ensuring the clarity and accessibility of the law a major challenge. For example, Nairobi City county's bylaws have been amended repeatedly since the city was established 80 years ago. The most recent overhaul of bylaws was not explicit, and even city officials are not aware of all bylaws in force. In addition, the current structure has resulted in the adoption of new legislation ostensibly repealing bylaws but creating great

---

23 OECD, *Cutting Red Tape: National Strategies for Administrative Simplification* 9 (OECD 2006); OECD, *Cutting Red Tape: Comparing Administrative Burdens across Countries* 15 (OECD 2007).

24 European Commn., *Measuring Administrative Costs and Reducing Administrative Burdens in the EU* (MEMO/06/425, Nov. 14, 2006), http://europa.eu/rapid/press-release_MEMO-06-425_en.htm?locale=en.

uncertainty about the hierarchy of laws governing the city.[25] The clarity and accessibility of legislation can be improved by making legislation easily accessible and improving its coherence and consistency.

Make Legislation Easily Accessible

Urban legislation concerns statutes dealing with matters as distinct as planning legislation, building standards, and management and governance issues. Adding to the volume and the complexity of this diverse subject matter are seemingly inherent fragmentation and dispersion. Legislative material is found in different statutes amended over and over again, leading to a chaotic result, not to mention regulations, circulars, and issuances of guidance that make the picture even more complex. In Kenya, different planning provisions coexist without a clear connection between them: the Physical Planning Act 1996 authorizes the director for physical planning to develop local physical development plans. The Constitution of Kenya 2010 gives the function of land planning to the national government and the coordination of planning to counties. The Urban Areas and Cities Act of 2011 provides that every municipality must have an integrated development plan, prepared by the municipal board and approved by the county assembly. These provisions introduce parallel procedures: the relationship or connection between local physical development plans and integrated development plans is not clear, coordination mechanisms for different levels of planning do not exist, constitutionally allocated roles are not adequately reflected in statutory provisions, and regulatory fragmentation is inevitably extended to planning institutions where two distinct ministries coexist with overlapping functions. This grim reality points to the difficulty involved in knowing with reasonable certainty which provisions apply, where to find them, and what they mean. The lack of legislative transparency and clarity not only makes implementation difficult; it makes accountability measures difficult to establish.

The accessibility of legislation, especially in broad and complex areas of law, can be improved through codification. Codification brings together all relevant rules on a subject into a single text with legally binding force. This solution is a drastic way to rationalize legislation, remove contradictions and inconsistencies, and make legislation accessible to all parties. However, it has beneficial effects on the clarity, accessibility, coherence, foreseeability, and volume of legislation, including legal certainty.[26] Codified legislation lays down the rules of the social contract in a systematic way, providing easy access to them. It also provides an improved framework for holding institutions accountable, reinforces rule of law, and facilitates access to justice. Urban codes, bringing together all laws, regulations, and decisions dealing with the urban environment in a structured and organized way, would make these rules clearer, more accessible, and more easily implementable.

---

25 UN-Habitat, Kenya Legal Assessment (U.N. 2014).

26 Eva Steiner, *Codification in England: The Need to Move from an Ideological to a Functional Approach —A Bridge Too Far?*, 25 Stat. L. Rev. 209 (2004).

Improve Coherence and Consistency of Legislation

Although codification can make legislation more easily accessible, the lack of clarity in legislation is a systemic problem that codification alone may not be able to solve. There are numerous examples of inconsistencies between laws, conflicting definitions, definitions used in different ways or not at all that make understanding and interpretation complicated.

Drafting guidelines can help standardize, simplify, and clarify the language of the texts, facilitating their understanding and application. Especially in areas like urban legislation, where many active actors and stakeholders have a technical and nonlegal background, yet they assume an active role in legislating or setting standards, guidelines, manuals, and checklists can support actors and stakeholders' efforts by concretizing rules and instructions on techniques and procedures for lawmaking. Such guidelines introduce consistent standards to improve the homogeneity of legislative texts, thus contributing to clearer and simpler legislation. However, drafting manuals can prove counterproductive if they are too detailed or instructive. They are useful if they combine the broad principles and aims of drafting legislation with specific conventions that ensure consistency. Clarity and consistency in the law means that the social contract is expressed clearly and transparently in law—and actors and stakeholders, including regulators, policy makers, and those implementing or enforcing the law, can be held accountable for their decisions and actions.

Improve the Capacity of Legislation to Deliver Results

A good law is clear, implementable, and enforceable. Planning laws often seek to achieve ambitious and radical reforms without considering the resources and infrastructure required for their implementation. Legislators may assume that the administration will automatically adapt to ambitious provisions even though institutional capacity and resources might be lacking. These create laws that become effectively unusable, cannot be properly implemented, and are incapable of delivering intended results. For example, a draft planning law in Uganda was designed in such a way that its enforcement and implementation would require 20,000 civil servants.[27] In the Arab Republic of Egypt, the law in force calls for detailed plans for cities and villages to be prepared by planning offices within local governments. However, because the central government does not provide the required financial and human resources to allow local authorities to perform this mandate, only 10 of the 228 participating cities in Egypt have approved detailed plans to date.[28]

Institutional and financial capacity, coordination mechanisms, roles, and functions need to be considered early in the process of lawmaking. Enforcement and implementation do not come about magically—they do so only

---

27 Patrick McAuslan, *Law Reform in East Africa: Traditional or Transformative?* 89 (Routledge 2013).

28 UN-Habitat, Mohamed Nada (U.N. 2014).

when they have been clearly considered in the planning, designing, and drafting of legislation. Enforcement is the process of imposing observance of the law through formal and/or informal techniques,[29] which can include sanctions, prosecution, or more subtle ways such as education, information dissemination, and persuasion.

Rules do not produce compliance on their own. Identifying appropriate and realistic enforcement mechanisms and strategies when designing legislation is an essential requirement for legislation that delivers intended results. Devising realistic and clear enforcement strategies that take into account existing capacity and resources is a fundamental task when designing legislation. Investing in responsive regulation strategies that build synergies between punishment and persuasion and escalate compliance methods and sanctions when less interventionist methods fail is particularly relevant to making legislation that can deliver results.[30]

Implementation of legislation is a complex process of mechanisms, funds, and actors that is often diverted by changes in facts, resources, deflection of goals, and resistance from stakeholders.[31] Legislation is a black hole if there is no information on its implementation, its results, and the ways in which it operates in real life. The need to monitor the implementation of the law and evaluate its results is a requirement linked not only to the principles of legality and legal certainty but also to the need to prevent adverse effects and appraise the responsiveness of the law to the regulated problems and phenomena. If legislation lays down the terms of the social contract, the people need to know what the results are: the transparency of results enhances accountability and enables modification and improvements to be made to urban laws and regulation that do not achieve their objectives.

Monitoring the application and implementation of legislation is important to identify progress and problems in legislation's design, enforcement, and implementation and to intervene in a timely manner. Legislation must be monitored consistently, and secondary regulations must be drafted in response.

The effects of legislation also must be monitored in order to identify changes potentially or actually attributable to legislation. Post-legislative scrutiny or ex-post impact assessment reports or other reports from state or independent authorities are common tools for measuring the results, effectiveness, efficacy, and efficiency of legislation with an eye toward introducing

---

29 Bridget Hutter, *The Reasonable Arm of the Law? The Law Enforcement Procedures of Environmental Health Officers* 5 (Clarendon 1988).

30 Ian Ayres & John Braithwaite, *Responsive Regulation: Transcending the Deregulation Debate* 475 (Oxford University Press 1992); John Braithwaite, *The Essence of Responsive Regulation,* 44 U. British Columbia L. Rev. 475 (2011).

31 Eugene Bardach, *The Implementation Game: What Happens after a Bill Becomes a Law* 36–37 (MIT Press 1977).

necessary changes.[32] Complaints-based data, perception data, or other statistical data are also important for monitoring how legislation is implemented. Review clauses in legislation and sunset clauses are other mechanisms that promote learning from the results of legislation.

Make Legislative Quality a Guiding Value in the Process of Developing and Implementing Legislation

This chapter has demonstrated that good legislation is essential for expressing social contracts and for achieving results. Good legislation can be achieved through evidence-based lawmaking, taking into account the voice of affected people, in conjunction with facilitating compliance by making legislation clear, simple, and accessible, and paying attention to enforcement and implementation in the planning stages. However, legislation that delivers results does not happen effortlessly. Practices and tools cannot be isolated but must work with each other, and consistency in achieving such cooperation among different practices and tools throughout the life cycle of designing and implementing legislation is essential. Legislation will not deliver intended results unless specialized outcomes remain a clear and consistent concern in the entire life cycle of policy making, lawmaking, and the implementation of the law.[33]

The challenges identified in this chapter cannot be addressed in an ad hoc way. Only by ensuring that consistent structures and procedures exist to achieve regulatory quality and governance can intended outcomes be achieved—in other words, creating legislation that is clear and of good quality must be part of the policy and lawmaking process and culture, and effective structures and procedures must be put in place in support of it.

Legislation that delivers results is the result of complex mechanics in the conceptualization, design, drafting, enforcement, and implementation of the law. Effective legislation has two—equally important—dimensions: a *prospective dimension* when the law is formulated and drafted and a *real-life dimension* when a law is implemented.[34] Both must come into play, in harmony, in order for legislation to deliver intended results. This requires processes and institutions for regulatory governance as well as tools to guide legislative design and drafting. The tools can be assisted by an effectiveness test, a logical exercise that examines the unique features of existing legislation and legislation being designed, considering how the purpose, the structure, the content, and the results of the future intended law are aligned with existing law. The effectiveness test views legislation as a continuum rather than as separate and unrelated phases of policy design, drafting, implementation, and evaluation. It allows identification of the relationship between the purpose of the legisla-

32 Luzius Mader, *Evaluating the Effects: A Contribution to the Quality of Legislation,* 22(2) Stat. L. Rev. 119 (2001).

33 Maria Mousmouti, *Effectiveness as an Aid to Legislative Drafting,* 2 Loophole 15–25 (2014).

34 *Id.*

tion, the appopriateness of the means used to achieve the purpose, and the results of the legislation.[35]

For legislation being drafted, the effectiveness test examines the existence of a clear purpose and a consistent content responsive to the purpose of the law, and whether adequate information on results achieved will become available. At a later stage, the effectiveness test examines whether the relationship between intended purposes and results correlates; it evaluates this correlation and/or the lack thereof and examines areas where the legislation can be improved. In summary, the effectiveness test allows a diagnosis of strengths as well as weaknesses in the conceptualization and design of legislation and can thereby prevent regulatory failures. It also allows identification at an early stage of ineffectiveness of content and design, as well as ineffectiveness of enforcement and drafting.

The effectiveness test is a neutral tool that does not promote specific legislative choices over others but looks at the content and the consistency of legislative texts and judges them objectively in relation to intended regulatory objectives. Taken as a whole, it is useful in assisting with the design, drafting, and implementation of urban legislation that enables social contracts to be meaningfully expressed and enforced and intended results to be delivered.

Conclusions and the Way Forward

The relationship between urban development and legislation is one of interdependence: sustainable urban development requires good urban legislation to achieve results. Good urban legislation[36] lays down meaningful and inclusive frameworks, has the potential to give rise to appropriate social change, mediates conflicting interests, and makes sustainable and desirable urban development possible. To achieve this, legislation must be evidence-based and harmonized with realities, must take into account the voice of urban dwellers — allowing for their meaningful participation and utilization of clear and transparent urban legislation — and must set out frameworks to hold accountable institutions, actors, and stakeholders in urban legislation. Good legislation is a challenge that needs to be addressed urgently to improve effective and efficient delivery in urban development.

---

35 Maria Mousmouti, *Operationalising Quality of Legislation through the Effectiveness Test,* 6(2) Legisprudence 201 (2012).

36 The meaning of "good law" is discussed in the section titled "The Challenge: The Definition of Good Urban Legislation."

PART IV

Sexual and Gender-Based Violence

12

Justice Sector Delivery of Services in the Context of Fragility and Conflict

What Is Being Done to Address Sexual and Gender-Based Violence?

WAAFAS OFOSU-AMAAH, REA ABADA CHIONGSON, AND CAMILLA GANDINI

[D]espite its repeated condemnation of violence against women and children in situations of armed conflict, including sexual violence in situations of armed conflict, and despite its calls addressed to all parties to armed conflict for the cessation of such acts with immediate effect, such acts continue to occur, and in some situations have become systematic and widespread, reaching appalling levels of brutality.
— UN Security Council Resolution 1820 (June 19, 2008)

Over the past two decades, sexual and gender-based violence (SGBV) within the international legal framework has come to refer to any violence directed against a person on account of gender and to any violence that affects one gender disproportionately. SBGV includes gender-based acts that result in, or are likely to result in, physical, sexual, or psychological harm or suffering, including threats of such acts, coercion, or arbitrary deprivation of liberty, whether occurring in public or private life.

Some of the earliest internationally agreed-on references to SGBV can be derived from international instruments addressing violence against women (VAW) such as the Convention on the Elimination of All Forms of Discrimination against Women (CEDAW), the 1994 Declaration on the Elimination of Violence against Women (DEVAW), and the Beijing Platform for Action (BPFA). CEDAW's General Recommendation No. 19 defines VAW as a form of gender-based discrimination that includes "violence that is directed against a woman because she is a woman or that affects women disproportionately. It includes acts that inflict physical, mental or sexual harm or suffering, threats of such acts, coercion and other deprivations of liberty." Both DEVAW and BPFA also state that violence against women encompasses, but is not limited to, physical, sexual, and psychological violence that occurs in the family or in the general community or that is perpetrated or condoned by the state.[1]

---

1 Both DEVAW and BPFA state that VAW encompasses "(a) physical, sexual, and psychological violence occurring in the family, including battering, sexual abuse of female children in the household, dowry-related violence, marital rape, female genital mutilation and other traditional practices harmful to women, non-spousal violence and violence related to exploitation; (b) physical, sexual, and psychological violence occurring within the general

The definition of SGBV, however, has evolved over the years to include all forms of gender-based violence so as to reflect the reality that men and boys also experience sexual violence. This chapter focuses on sexual violence that affects women, because of its prevalence.

A Brief Background to SGBV

Prevalence

SGBV is one of the most prevalent forms of abuse. Although no accurate figure on its global prevalence is available, it is estimated that at least 35 percent of the world's women experience some form of SGBV during their lives.[2] Global estimates for men and boys who experience SGBV are even more difficult to obtain.

In fragile and conflict situations (FCS), SGBV is a major challenge, but it is often difficult to obtain reliable figures for its incidence.[3] Nevertheless, a global study of 50 countries found that significant increases in SGBV occur following major wars.[4] SGBV has been widely reported in many FCS: in the former Yugoslavia in the mid-1990s; in the Rwandan genocide in 1994; in Somalia in the early 1990s; in the Kashmir conflict; and in the civil wars in Peru, Sudan, and Liberia.[5] The results of a population-based household survey in the Democratic Republic of Congo (DRC) indicated a high incidence of rape—an estimated four hundred thousand women had been raped in the 12 months prior to the survey—and showed that the most pervasive form of sexual violence was perpetrated by intimate partners.[6]

---

community, including rape, sexual abuse, sexual harassment and intimidation at work, in educational institutions and elsewhere, trafficking in women and forced prostitution; and (c) physical, sexual, and psychological violence perpetrated or condoned by the State, wherever it occurs." *See Beijing Declaration and Platform for Action* (Fourth World Conference on Women, Sept. 15, 1995), A/CONF.177/20 (1995) and A/CONF.177/20/Add.1 (1995), para. 113.

2 World Health Organization (WHO) et al., *Global and Regional Estimates of Violence against Women: Prevalence and Health Effects of Intimate Partner Violence and Non-Partner Sexual Violence*" 16 (WHO 2013).

3 Mayra Buvinic et al., *Violent Conflict and Gender Inequality: An Overview* 119 (World Bank) 119 policy research working paper, Feb. 2013), http://elibrary.worldbank.org/doi/book/10.1596/1813-9450-6371. *See* also Dara Kay Cohen et al., *Wartime Sexual Violence: Misconceptions, Implications, and Ways Forward* (U.S. Inst. Peace Special Rpt. No. 323, U.S. Inst. Peace, Feb. 2013), http://www.usip.org/sites/default/files/resources/SR323.pdf.

4 Megan Bastick, Karin Grimm, & Rahel Kunz, *Sexual Violence in Armed Conflict: Global Overview and Implications for the Security Sector* (Geneva Ctr. for Democratic Control of Armed Forces 2007), cited in *World Development Report 2011: Conflict, Security and Development*, 60.

5 *See* Buvinic et al., *supra* note 3, at 120.

6 *Id.*

Forms

SGBV is manifested in various forms depending on the context. SGBV includes rape, forced impregnation and miscarriages, kidnapping, trafficking, abduction, forced marriage, beatings, domestic abuse, and enslavement. Other prevalent forms of sexual abuse include strip searches, forced nudity, public sexual humiliation, gang rape, rape with foreign objects, and public rape.[7] There is also increasing evidence that sexual violence has been used to forcibly displace populations, both internally and across borders, in places such as Colombia, the DRC, Libya, Mali, and the Syrian Arab Republic.[8] Postconflict societies also continue to experience or bear the impact of SGBV.[9]

Causes

Several different lines of thought have emerged regarding what causes SGBV in conflict.

One view suggests that SGBV is intentionally used as a weapon of war. It is not simply a random act[10] but an "assertion of power or an attack against another military force," including individuals thought to be supporting the other force. Here SGBV is intended to torture, humiliate, demoralize, weaken, or discredit.[11] When claiming conquered territory, military units often view

---

7 Rashida Manjoo & Calleigh McRaith, *Gender-Based Violence and Justice in Conflict and Post-Conflict Areas*, 12 Cornell Intl. L.J. 12 (2011), http://www.lawschool.cornell.edu/research/ILJ/upload/Manjoo-McRaith-final.pdf.

8 *See*, for example, *Report of the Secretary-General*, U.N. Doc. A/67/792 – S/2013/149 (Mar. 14, 2013). Women and children have been targeted, both inside and outside camps and settlements for refugees and internally displaced persons, and in villages surrounding camps.

9 It is relatively common for postconflict societies to experience increased trafficking, forced prostitution, domestic violence, and rape following a major conflict. *See* Manjoo & McRaith, *supra* note 7, at 13). For example, numerous studies have consistently revealed a peacetime reality of extremely high prevalence of SGBV in Liberia. The Liberian Ministry of Gender and Development's figures show that 6,277 cases were reported from 2010 to 2012. In 2012, rape accounted for 55 percent of cases, with 68 percent involving victims from the ages of 3 months to 14 years (*Id.*). The postconflict rise of domestic violence, for example, has led to speculation of a relationship between forms of SGBV and the availability of small arms, increased tolerance of violence within society, head of household being engaged in military violence (*Id.*, at 14), and acquisition of "hyper-masculinities." The experiences in the Central African Republic, Côte d'Ivoire, the DRC, and South Sudan suggest a link between SGBV and disarmament, demobilization, and reintegration and security sector reform programs. For example, incidents of SGBV have occurred where improperly trained security forces or ex-combatants have been redeployed or cantoned in proximity to civilian centers. There have been instances of armed groups deserting the national army and perpetrating sexual violence following failed integration initiatives (*Report of the Secretary-General*, *supra* note 8, at para. 7.

10 Traditionally, SGBV was seen as an unfortunate and unavoidable part of war, and SGBV "acts were primarily random incidents of frustration and violence caused by individuals." *See* Manjoo & McRaith, *supra* note 7, at 14.

11 *Id.*, at 15.

women's bodies as "spoils of war" and rape as a standard practice of war to which the victorious army is entitled.[12]

The second view sees SGBV as a form of opportunistic violence. In situations of fragility and conflict, the erosion of societal networks, increased militarization, and breakdown of law and order can lead to individuals or groups taking advantage of vulnerable members of society.[13] Increased levels of impunity during conflict can often lead to a rise in sexual violence because perpetrators know that they are unlikely to be caught or punished. In some instances, law enforcers are also perpetrators of SGBV.[14]

The third view considers the prevalence of SGBV in FCS as an extension of already prevailing violent practices:[15] "extreme violence women suffer during conflict does not arise solely out of the conditions of war; it is directly related to the violence that exists in women's lives during peacetime."[16]

Consequences

SGBV, particularly when directed against women, "impairs or nullifies the enjoyment by women of human rights and fundamental freedoms under general international law or under human rights conventions" and is a form of discrimination.[17] SGBV impacts an individual's right to (a) life; (b) protection from torture or cruel, inhuman, or degrading treatment or punishment; (c) equal protection under the law and, according to humanitarian norms, in time of international or internal armed conflict; (d) liberty and security of person; (e) equality and freedom from discrimination; (g) the highest attainable standard of physical and mental health; and (h) just and favorable conditions of work, among others.[18] Development outcomes, such as in the areas of health, education, economic opportunities, good governance, and violence prevention, have been linked to SGBV.[19] Prioritizing SGBV during the postconflict

---

12 *Id.*, at 16, citing U.N. Econ. & Soc. Council, Commn. on Human Rights, Sub-Commission on the Promotion and Protection of Human Rights, *Contemporary Forms of Slavery: Systematic Rape, Sexual Slavery, and Slavery-like Practices during Armed Conflict*, U.N. Doc. E/CN.4/Sub.2/2000/21 (June 6, 2000), para. 20.

13 Buvinic et al., *supra* note 3, at 12; Manjoo & McRaith, *supra* note 7, at 15; *World Development Report 2011*, *supra* note 4, at 60.

14 Cohen et al., *supra* note 3.

15 Manjoo & McRaith, *supra* note 7, at 16.

16 Elisabeth Rehn & Ellen Johnson Sirleaf, *Women, War, and Peace: The Independent Experts' Assessment on the Impact of Armed Conflict on Women and Women's Role in Peace-Building* 10 (UNIFEM 2002).

17 UN Committee on the Elimination of Discrimination against Women (CEDAW), CEDAW General Recommendation No. 19, A/47/38 (1992).

18 *Id.*

19 Linkages have been drawn between preventing the incidence of violence and its impact on health indicators (such as HIV/AIDS and maternal mortality) and its costs against health care infrastructure, as SGBV survivors require medical, psychological, and other services. Insecurity often prevents girls from attending schools and women from participating in market activities and farming. SGBV also sometimes hinders good governance. SGBV

stage can provide an opportunity to design and implement transformative gender policies, just as the transitional period following conflict might provide an opportunity to change underlying inequalities.[20]

The Existing International Legal and Normative Framework against SGBV

Early attempts to address SGBV in conflict are found in military codes and treaties, such as the Lieber Instructions of 1863, which expressly prohibits rape, and the Geneva Convention Relative to the Protection of Civilian Persons in Time of War of 1949 and its additional protocols of 1977, which provide that "women be especially protected from any attack on their honor, in particular against rape, enforced prostitution and any form of indecent assault." The UN Special Rapporteur on Violence against Women states that although these efforts are noted, they focus on SGBV as a crime on the woman and family's honor or morality. This is problematic, because when "rape is perceived as a crime against honor or morality, shame commonly ensues for the victim," and this has serious implications on women's ability to report the violence and hold the perpetrators accountable.[21]

---

manifests itself as a sexualized form of corruption (also called "sextortion" or "transactional sex"). In Tanzania, many women were pressured into "transactional sex." *See* Damien de Walque et al., *Coping with Risk: The Effects of Shocks on Reproductive Health and Transactional Sex in Rural Tanzania*, Impact Evaluation Ser. (Policy Research Working Paper No. WPS 6751, World Bank Group 2014), http://documents.worldbank.org/curated/en/2014/01/18832582/coping-risk-effects-shocks-reproductive-health-transactional-sex-rural-tanzania. In situations of fragility, sextortion may be exacerbated through "petty" corruption (when basic public services are sold instead of provided by right), which affects poor women and girls in particular. In postearthquake Haiti, for example, many displaced women and girls were forced into "survival sex" by men in positions of power, such as administrators of cash-for-work-programs and men charged with organizing relief distributions. *See*, for example, *Haiti Women Face New Struggles to Survive*, http://blog.amnestyusa.org/americas/haitis-women-face-new-struggles-to-survive/. Addressing SGBV is crucial to violence prevention because, in some cases, it can have an inflammatory impact on existing tensions or perpetuate a cycle of violence, such as when women's bodies are used as "frontlines" in ideological and political struggles or as a strategic component of warfare or group violence. *See* Sanam Naraghi Anderlini, *WDR Gender Background Paper* (World Bank 2011), https://openknowledge.worldbank.org/handle/10986/9250.

20 This is particularly relevant when new rules are adopted, for example, when drafting a new constitution; setting up transitional, investigative, or accountability mechanisms; or creating better protection systems for SGBV. There is also evidence that FCS triggers more inclusive behaviors toward women and other groups that are largely excluded in civil and political life during peacetime. Furthermore, FCS can result in strengthened women's networks, increased representation in a variety of political spaces, and inclusive and gendered policies, which would show promise for more responsive and inclusive development policies and interventions in the challenging context of fragility.

21 Manjoo & McRaith, *supra* note 7, at 18. "Rape and other forms of sexual violence are used as instruments of violence and terror—as torture, punishment, intimidation, coercion, humiliation, and degradation. Nonetheless, it is only recently that the international human rights community has begun to recognize rape as violence rather than as an assault on honour or a crime against morality." *See* United Nations, *Report of the Special Rapporteur on Violence against Women, Its Causes and Consequences*, U.N. Doc. E/CN.4/1998/54 (Jan. 26, 1998), para. I(4).

Recent international standards—from a variety of international, human rights, and humanitarian law instruments—have moved away from the honor paradigm and base condemnation on the rights of women and girls. These treaties, commitments, and resolutions, described below, form the backbone of the international legal framework for protection against SGBV.

International Treaties and Declarations

The 1974 Declaration on the Protection of Women and Children in Emergency and Armed Conflict calls on UN member-states to take all necessary steps to ensure the prohibition of persecution, torture, degrading treatment, and violence against women and children who are part of the civilian population.

The landmark Convention on the Elimination of All Forms of Discrimination against Women was adopted in 1979 and has been ratified by 188 member-states. Article 1 prohibits all forms of discrimination against women.[22] Article 2 requires all states parties to CEDAW to adopt measures that prohibit discrimination, including modifying or abolishing discriminatory laws, customs, and practices. Although CEDAW does not specifically mention SGBV, its General Recommendation No. 19 on Violence against Women (1992) considers VAW as a form of discrimination under CEDAW. General Recommendation No. 19 highlights states' obligation to address VAW and specifically mentions the special risk of SGBV faced by different groups of women, including those living in the context of conflicts. More recently, states' obligation to eliminate this form of violence was further strengthened through CEDAW General Recommendation No. 30 on Women in Conflict Prevention, Conflict, and Post-Conflict Situations (2013).

In 1994, the Declaration on the Elimination of Violence against Women (DEVAW) contributed to the growing international legal framework by providing a definition of VAW and underscoring the obligation of the state to pursue without delay the elimination of all forms of VAW. In the same year, the UN Commission on Human Rights, in Resolution 1994/45, appointed a UN Special Rapporteur on violence against women, its causes, and consequences.[23] This mandate has been extended to the present.

Also in 1994, the Organization of American States adopted the Inter-American Convention on the Prevention, Punishment and Eradication of

---

22 Art. 1 of CEDAW defines discrimination as "any distinction, exclusion or restriction made on the basis of sex which has the effect or purpose of impairing or nullifying the recognition, enjoyment or exercise by women, irrespective of their marital status, on a basis of equality of men and women, of human rights and fundamental freedoms in the political, economic, social, cultural, civil or any other field."

23 The mandate of the Special Rapporteur is to (a) seek and receive information on VAW from various actors; (b) recommend measures to eliminate all forms of VAW and its causes and to remedy its consequences; (c) work closely with all special procedures, other human rights mechanisms, and the Commission on the Status of Women in the discharge of its functions; and (d) continue to adopt a comprehensive and universal approach to the elimination of VAW, its causes and consequences.

Violence against Women (Convention of Belém do Pará), a critical step, both regionally and globally, in acknowledging acts of SGBV as human rights violations. The convention broadly defines violence against women and requires states to undertake measures to combat violence.[24]

The Fourth World Conference on Women and the Beijing Platform for Action

The 1995 Beijing Platform for Action specifically included (i) violence against women and (ii) women and armed conflict as two of its 12 critical areas of concern. Among the actions it recommended to be undertaken by governments are to (a) "investigate and punish members of the police, security, and armed forces and others who perpetrate violence against women"; (b) "urge the identification and condemnation of systematic practice of rape and other forms of inhuman and degrading treatment of women as a deliberate instrument of war and ethnic cleansing and provide full assistance to victims of such abuse"; (c) reaffirm that rape is a war crime and a crime against humanity and an act of genocide and take measures to protect women and children from such acts and bring perpetrators to justice; and (d) "undertake a full investigation of all acts of violence against women committed during war . . . prosecute all criminals responsible for war crimes against women and provide full redress to women victims."[25]

International Criminal Courts

International courts such as the International Criminal Tribunal for the Former Yugoslavia (ICTY), the International Criminal Tribunal for Rwanda (ICTR), the Special Court for Sierra Leone (SCSL), and the International Criminal Court (ICC) further redefined rape more broadly based on experiences of women in situations of conflict. In the *Prosecutor v. Jean-Paul Akayesu* case, the ICTR defined rape broadly as "physical invasion of a sexual nature, committed on a person under circumstances that are coercive," which includes rape with an object, among other situations. The court in the Akayesu case also highlighted that rape is a form of torture used for the intimidation, degradation, humiliation, punishment, control, or destruction of a person.[26] The Rome Statute of the ICC, which came into force in 2002, states that rape, sexual slavery, enforced prostitution, forced pregnancy, enforced sterilization, or any other form of sexual violence of comparable gravity can constitute a crime against humanity or war crime.[27] The SGBV can also be considered genocide

---

24 The convention monitors states' compliance through periodic state reporting and individual complaints to the Inter-American Commission of Human Rights.

25 *Beijing Declaration and Platform for Action, supra* note 1, at para. 145.

26 *Prosecutor v. Jean-Paul Akayesu,* Case No. ICTR-96-4-T, Judm. (Sept. 2, 1998).

27 *Rome Statute of the International Criminal Court,* A/CONF.183/9 (July 17, 1998, corrected by process-verbaux of Nov. 10, 1998; July 12, 1999; Nov. 30, 1999; May 8, 2000; Jan. 17, 2001; and Jan. 16, 2002), arts. 7–8.

when "committed with the intent to destroy in whole or in part a national, ethnic, racial, or religious group."[28]

UN Security Council Resolutions

In 2000, the groundbreaking Resolution 1325 on Women, Peace and Security (SCR 1325) was adopted by the UN Security Council. SCR 1325 reaffirmed women's important role in the prevention and resolution of conflicts, peace negotiations, peacebuilding, peacekeeping, and humanitarian response in postconflict reconstruction and in the promotion of peace and security. Its key provisions include actions to increase participation of women at all levels of peace and security decision making, to take special measures for the protection of women from SGBV, end impunity and prosecute those responsible for SGBV, and to incorporate a gender perspective in peacekeeping operations.[29]

Security Council Resolution (SCR) 1820, with its specific focus on sexual violence in conflict, was unanimously adopted in 2008. Key provisions include (a) "immediate and complete cessation" by all parties to conflict of sexual violence; (b) protect all civilians from all forms of sexual violence and develop effective protection mechanisms; (c) exclude sexual violence from amnesty provisions in conflict resolution processes; (d) develop training programs for all peacekeeping and humanitarian personnel; (e) implement a "policy of zero-tolerance" for sexual violence in peacekeeping operations; and (f) develop effective guidelines and strategies to protect civilians from all forms of violence.[30]

In 2009, SCR 1888 strengthened SCR 1820 by providing concrete steps and mechanisms to address sexual violence in conflict, including (a) appointment of a special representative to provide strategic leadership in addressing sexual violence in conflict; (b) deployment of a team of experts to assist national authorities to respond to situations of sexual violence in conflict; and (c) identification of women protection advisers (WPAs) in each UN peacekeeping operation. Furthermore, SCR 1888 calls for sexual violence to be included in all UN-sponsored peace negotiation agendas from the outset of peace processes. In 2010, as mandated by SCR 1888, a UN special representative of the secretary-general on sexual violence in conflict was appointed.[31]

---

28 *Id.*, at art. 6.

29 This resolution also mandated that the secretary-general carry out a study on the impact of armed conflict on women, women's role in peacebuilding, and the gender dimensions of peace processes and conflict resolution.

30 S.C. Res. 1820, U.N. Doc. S/RES/1820 (June 19, 2008).

31 The UN Special Representative of the Secretary-General on Sexual Violence in Conflict (SRSG) functions as the UN's spokesperson and political advocate on conflict-related sexual violence. She is also chair of the UN Action against Sexual Violence in Conflict. The five priorities for the SRSG's mandate are (1) to end impunity for conflict-related sexual violence, (2) to empower women to seek redress, (3) to mobilize political ownership, (4) to increase recognition of rape, and (5) to harmonize the UN's response. For more information on the work of the SRSG, *see* http://www.stoprapenow.org/page/specialrepresentativeonsexualviolenceinconflict.

Other relevant Security Council resolutions include SCR 1889 (2009), SCR 1960 (2010), SCR 2106 (2013), and SCR 2122 (2013).[32]

Other International Commitments

Other international commitments highlight how situations of conflict and fragility can lead to heightened vulnerability to SGBV and demonstrate its negative impacts on development.[33] Countries affected by conflict are also paying increased attention to women's issues. For example, when the g7+ group of fragile states adopted the Dili Declaration in 2010, they affirmed that the major challenges to achieving their new vision for peacebuilding and state building include insufficient attention to the protection of women from armed conflict and to the participation of women in peacebuilding and state building.[34] Among development institutions, there is already increasing interest in the topic, including at the World Bank through its analytical and operational efforts on gender and FCS.[35] Despite these efforts, a recent review by the World Bank's Independent Evaluation Group indicated that "the Bank has not responded adequately or in a timely manner to conflict-related sexual violence against women."[36]

Law and Justice Institutions: Selected Challenges

State Inability

> There was an ongoing war . . . social conditions were terrible . . . rebels were marauding in the countryside. And we sat down to ask people

---

32 These resolutions, together with SCR 1325, SCR 1820, and SCR 1888, collectively form the UN framework for implementing the women, peace, and security agenda. For texts of these resolutions, *see* http://www.un.org/en/peacekeeping/issues/women/wps.shtml.

33 For development impacts of SGBV, *see* note 21.

34 For more information about the Dili Declaration, *see* http://www.g7plus.org/news-feed/2010/4/10/dili-declaration.html.

35 These efforts include (a) two recent *World Development Reports* on FCS (2011) and gender equality (2012); (b) both gender equality and FCS were key themes for International Development Association replenishment round 16 (FY12–FY14) and round 17 (FY14–FY16); (c) in implementing the *World Development Report 2012 on Gender Equality and Development*, SGBV was identified as one of the Bank's priority areas for gender work; (d) there is increasing recognition on the role for law and justice institutions in mitigating conflict stresses and preventing violence (*see* the World Bank's *New Directions in Justice Reform: A Companion Piece to the Updated Strategy and Implementation Plan on Strengthening Governance, Tackling Corruption* [May 2012], http://www-wds.worldbank.org/external/default/WDSContentServer/WDSP/IB/2012/09/06/000386194_20120906024506/Rendered/PDF/706400REPLACEM0Justice0Reform0Final.pdf); and (e) assessments on the World Bank's SGBV in FCS work are emerging (*see* Alys Willman & Crystal Corman, *Sexual and Gender-Based Violence: What Is the World Bank Doing and What Have We Learned? A Strategic Review* [Nov. 2013] at the World Bank's website, http://www.wds.worldbank.org/external/default/WDSContentServer/WDSP/IB/2013/12/09/000461832_20131209163906/Rendered/PDF/832090WP0sexua0Box0382076B00PUBLIC0.pdf.).

36 *See* Indep. Evaluation Group, *World Bank Group Assistance to Low-Income Fragile and Conflict-Affected States: An Independent Evaluation* (Dec. 2013), at the World Bank Group's website, https://ieg.worldbankgroup.org/evaluations/fcs.

> what do you do for justice in this situation? There were no courts. Courts were the first casualties of hostilities. Judges, normally middle class people, they leave . . . lawyers as well. So you leave a society that doesn't have the instruments for the administration of justice . . . very often in the most serious conflicts you are returning to a situation without the basic infrastructure to provide basic social services.[37]

Despite ongoing achievements at the international level, addressing SGBV continues to be a struggle for many states. Although law and justice institutions are expected to play a role in preventing and responding to SGBV, in conflict and fragile contexts they are often too weak, unable, or unwilling to address it. Conflict creates disruption in social order and the delivery of justice and basic services. Some institutions may have committed the atrocities themselves and hence do not have the legitimacy to address rights violations. This was the situation highlighted in a recent study of conflicts conducted by the Peace Research Institute of Oslo[38] that found that between 2000 and 2009 armed state actors were more likely to be reported as perpetrators of SGBV than either rebel groups or progovernment militias.[39] Of the government actors included in Sexual Violence in Armed Conflict (SVAC)-Africa data, 64 percent were reported as perpetrators of sexual violence at some point during the study period, as opposed to 31 percent of rebel groups and 29 percent of militias.[40]

Low Levels of Reporting and High Levels of Attrition: What Is happening to SGBV Cases?

Law-and-justice sector institutions do not appear to be making sustained efforts in addressing SGBV. Reporting of SGBV cases tends to be low.[41] Where reporting occurs, the formal justice chain for rape cases is characterized by high levels of attrition.[42] Most cases drop out of the justice system before they reach the court, and very few result in convictions.[43] The reasons given for low levels of reporting and high levels of attrition include the following:

---

37 Barney Afako, presentation at the *Delivering Justice: Sexual and Gender Based Violence in the Context of Fragility* (panel session, Nov. 19, 2013, during the Law, Justice and Development Week, sponsored by the World Bank), https://collaboration.worldbank.org.

38 Peace Research Inst. of Oslo, http://www.prio.org/.

39 Cohen et al., *supra* note 3, at 4.

40 SVAC-Africa data, cited in *id.*

41 Buvinic et al., *supra* note 3, at 13; UN Women, *Progress of the World's Women 2011–2012: In Pursuit of Justice* (report prepared for UN Women, 2011), 51.

42 UN Women, *supra* note 41, at 49.

43 *Id.*, at 49, 51. Globally, a closer look at how cases proceed through the system shows that nearly half of the cases had been dropped at the police stage because the perpetrator/s cannot be found. Descriptions of the perpetrator were absent in 75 percent of the complaints. One-fifth of the cases that reached prosecution were dropped. Of the cases that went to court, 63 percent were withdrawn by the victims, or the victims were untraceable; in 14 percent, evidence was lost or not obtained. In Gauteng Province, in South Africa, research on the progression of rape cases from police to prosecution to the court system shows that

- *Resource Constraints.* Chronic lack of human and financial resources is a concern.[44] Lack of experienced staff can lead to inefficiency and lack of professionalism, compromising confidentiality and survivor safety.[45] Lack of resources can sometimes obscure more complex realities, such as gender discrimination or institutional culture of corruption.
- *Social Norms and Gender Bias.* Women who experience SGBV encounter difficulties dealing with legal systems in which gender-biased norms or practices are part of the institutional culture. Cultural norms of preserving family unity and honor when dominant among justice actors prevent redress for SGBV. In Kiribati, for example, three out of 10 police officers state that it is never acceptable to hit a woman; the rest, however, support the view that a husband has a right to beat his wife based on her behavior.[46] In some places, it is believed that this should be settled within the family or the community. In Afghanistan, there is an institutional practice by the police, prosecutors, Department of Women's Affairs, and Afghanistan Independent Human Rights Commission of mediating SGBV cases, even if the law mandates a specific punishment.[47] Cultural norms also stigmatize and shame women who report, as in this case from Liberia:

> Olivia's perpetrator was never caught, because her perpetrator was her uncle. This is the difficulty. We relocated Olivia's mother because everyone in the village went against her. She had "shamed" the uncle. . . . In their community, the best person to side with was the perpetrator, the one who raped her so badly. He was arrested and taken to the magisterial court, but somehow he has never been put in prison. When Olivia died [of her injuries] nobody from the village came to attend the funeral.[48]

---

only 17 percent of cases reach the courts and only 4 percent end up in conviction. In response to these figures, the government of South Africa invested in the Thuthuzela Care Centres, which are one-stop facilities established to provide SGBV survivors with a range of integrated services to improve conviction rates and reduce time for finalizing cases.

44 Courts, police, and prosecutors have claimed to be unable to perform their functions effectively for such reasons as lack of paper to take statements, lack of vehicles to visit sites, and lack of cameras to take pictures for evidence.

45 For example, justice actors are unable to collect, analyze, or understand forensic evidence to be able to build a good case. Lack of good interpreters hinders survivors from testifying effectively and creates inconsistencies in statements or testimonies.

46 UNIFEM, *Ending Violence among Women and Girls: Evidence, Knowledge and Data in the Pacific Island Countries: Literature Review and Annotated Bibliography* 21 (Aug. 2010), http://www.unicef.org/pacificislands/evaw.pdf.

47 UN Assistance Mission in Afghanistan (UNAMA) and Office of the High Commissioner for Human Rights (OHCHR), *A Long Way to Go: Implementation of the Elimination of Violence against Women Law in Afghanistan* 21 (report, UNAMA Nov. 2011), http://www.ohchr.org/Documents/Countries/AF/UNAMA_Nov2011.pdf.

48 SGBV Coordinator, Ministry of Gender and Development, as cited in World Bank, *Liberia's Specialized Sexual Offenses Court: Lessons, Challenges, and Opportunities: A Case Study* 3 (World Bank 2014).

- *Limited Access to Justice.* Some survivors of SGBV are often unaware of their rights and have limited skills, resources, and support to access justice. In many cases, social and cultural expectations dictate that survivors suffer in silence or keep the violence they suffered within the family. Once the barriers of reporting or filing a case have been broken, delays have real financial, social, and psychological costs for SGBV survivors, who run the risk of revictimization, by going through stigmatization and further violence.[49] Legal aid organizations and paralegals provide services to SGBV survivors, but they sometimes do not have the specific skills to address SGBV, such as assessing survivor safety, identifying resources, and devising safety measures.

Tensions around Formal and Informal Justice Processes

Most individuals take their cases to local, traditional, or community dispute resolution systems, commonly referred to as informal justice institutions.[50] In developing countries, at least four out of five cases are resolved in informal courts.[51] These informal institutions are generally geographically, financially, and culturally accessible.

However, formal justice systems, including the police, prosecutors, and the courts, have more complicated procedures and are often geographically distant.[52] They are also perceived as adversarial and may likely have a built-in bias toward more educated individuals. They are also generally focused on retribution and may exacerbate existing tensions; informal institutions tend to prioritize community cohesion or reconciliation, rather than women's rights and needs.[53]

This tension between formal and informal systems can be illustrated by a case example from Liberia. Citizens prefer to resolve disputes through informal or alternative channels, which are seen as based on social harmony and reconciliation.[54] A rape case is often resolved through the chiefs, elders, or tribal governors, in a "discrete" manner to avoid shaming all parties involved, and often involves public apologies and fines. Their decisions are generally

---

49 International Development Legal Organization (IDLO), *Accessing Justice: Models, Strategies and Best Practices on Women's Empowerment* 11 (report, IDLO 2013). These burdens are even greater for women who are subject to multiple forms of discrimination on account of their ethnicity, race, and sexual orientation, among other personal characteristics.

50 Informal justice systems refer to those justice institutions whose authority is primarily derived from social and cultural embeddedness, for example, religious and customary systems.

51 IDLO, *supra* note 49, at 11.

52 Formal justice institutions are those justice institutions whose authority emanates primarily from the state.

53 World Bank, *supra* note 48, at 4.

54 *Id. See* also Deborah H. Isser, Stephen C. Lubkemann, & Saah N'Tow, *Looking for Justice: Liberian Experiences with and Perceptions of Local Justice Options* 4 (Peaceworks Rpt. No. 63, U.S. Inst. Peace 2004).

accepted by citizens.[55] In SGBV cases, adult women survivors very rarely report cases of rape because of perceived shame and other social factors. These cases are seen as "taboo" and, if ever discussed, should be kept within the family or community.[56] These challenges should also be viewed in light of Liberia's chronically weak formal system.[57]

Legal and Justice-Related Initiatives against SGBV: What Has Been and Is Being Done? What Are Promising Approaches and Pathways?

Law and justice SGBV initiatives continue to face chronic challenges in stemming the tide of violence. Nevertheless, there are several law and justice initiatives from both FCS and non-FCS that may be useful in drawing lessons and developing options for addressing SGBV in FCS.

Specialized Legal and Justice Initiatives

Specialized approaches are those that involve creating or supporting institutions that specifically target SGBV. Specialization is usually proposed because of its potential benefits, including greater efficiency and awareness, sensitivity to the context or concern, more responsive provisions and processes, higher-quality outputs, and better coordination or integration.

Specialized SGBV Courts

In a study on specialized family violence courts in Australia, the United States, and the United Kingdom, evidence of the benefits of specialization includes (a) greater sensitivity to survivor needs; (b) greater efficiency, such as better case tracking, improved interagency collaboration and referral systems, and greater consistency in handling violence cases; (c) better outcomes for victim satisfaction and safety; and (d) improved reporting, prosecution, and conviction rates.[58] UN Women highlighted that when specialized domestic violence courts have adequate resources, they can help ensure accountability and victim safety through streamlining, more-responsive processes, such as closed session hearings, and enhanced capacity of judges and other personnel.[59] The

---

55 World Bank, *supra* note 48, at 5.

56 *Id.*, at 5–6.

57 For example, (a) the police have little means to investigate crimes or provide protection to survivors; (b) court renovations and provision of court hardware and vehicles do not translate to better service delivery; (c) dockets are crowded in urban areas; (d) there is lack of affordable legal aid options; (e) corruption is found at all levels; and (f) public perception of the formal system is overwhelmingly negative (*see id.*, at 3–4).

58 Heike Gramckow & Barry Walsh, *Developing Specialized Court Services: International Experiences and Lessons Learned* 4 (Justice & Dev. Working Paper Ser. 24/2013, World Bank 2013).

59 UN Women, *supra* note 41, at 59. Experiences with court personnel in regular courts frequently suggest that personnel frequently do not have the necessary gender sensitivity or comprehensive understanding of laws and processes applicable to SGBV; may not be sensitive to SGBV survivors' ordeals or gender concerns; and may be overburdened by other cases and responsibilities.

experience with specialized domestic violence courts in Spain and Brazil[60] shows that by "streamlining and centralizing court processes, such integrated courts eliminate contradictory orders, improve complainant/survivor safety, and reduce the need for complainants/survivors to testify repeatedly."[61]

However, translating the promise of benefits from specialization is challenging. Specialized structures often mirror the limitations in capacity, administration, and accountability of the wider institutional context. For example, Liberia's Criminal Court E, the country's first specialized sexual offenses court, is struggling to deliver justice to SGBV survivors.[62] Detailed analysis by the United Nations Mission in Liberia (UNMIL) in 2011 shows that the specialized court has not heard significantly more sexual offense cases than other courts.[63] The court completed just 18 such trials between 2009 and 2012.[64] The vast majority of cases that the court considered (93 percent) were dropped or dismissed.[65] Although the in-camera element is largely viewed as positive by those working with SGBV survivors, especially because a majority of cases before the court involve rape of children, few felt confident about case confidentiality or victim safety.[66] Bringing cases to the court remains an expensive endeavor, and survivor endowment funds are insufficient.[67]

---

60 They were established by Title V of the *Organic Act on Integrated Protection Measures against Gender Violence* (2004) in Spain and the Maria da Penha Law (2006) in Brazil.

61 UN Division for the Advancement of Women, *Handbook for Legislation on Violence against Women* (UN 2010), at 20.

62 Criminal Court E was established in 2008 through an amendment of the Judiciary Law of 1972. The court has exclusive jurisdiction over all sexual offense cases in Liberia's most populous county, Montserrado. SGBV cases from other parts of the country go to regular circuit courts. The court was designed to make the justice process more victim-friendly for survivors of SGBV, to increase the efficiency of the justice system in dealing with SGBV cases, and to raise the visibility of SGBV. This was set up alongside a specialized prosecution unit (the SGBV Crimes Protection Unit, within the Ministry of Justice) and a specialized unit of the police (Women and Children Protection Service, or WACPS). This "specialized approach" was intended to insulate SGBV from the prevalent inefficiency and non-victim-friendly norms prevalent in the wider justice system. Supporting the court were also other gender-focused policy and legal efforts in the country, including a new rape law that mandated harsher penalties for the crime of rape, made rape a nonbailable offense and in-camera (in private) trials. Liberia also had national actions on SGBV as well as for the implementation of SCR 1325. About 245 WACPS investigators were trained to support SGBV cases that will eventually go to the court. The Ministry of Gender's GBV unit supports survivors through counseling and referral services. Over US$200,000 went to refurbish the court, including television sets for in-camera sessions (World Bank, *supra* note 48, at 7–11).

63 On average, a circuit court completes four trials a year, figures similar to what Criminal Court E completes in a year. UNMIL's court statistics show that in 2011, out of the 2,118 cases on the dockets of the 12 circuit courts, only 44 trials were completed.

64 "2012 Criminal Court E Data," as cited in World Bank, *supra* note 48, at 16.

65 *Id.*

66 There is, however, a lack of wider support from sections of the Liberian legal community that view in-camera trials as a violation of defendants' constitutional right to due process, despite a Supreme Court decision in 2012 for its constitutionality (*id.*, at 13).

67 *Id.*, at 14.

Specialized Police and Prosecution Units

Specialized police and prosecution units contribute to improved visibility of SGBV concerns and increased levels of reporting. In Afghanistan, the first VAW unit in the Attorney General's Office was established in Kabul in March 2010.[68] Preliminary findings of its performance show that, despite challenges,[69] the unit is having a positive impact on reporting of SGBV cases.[70] In 13 Latin American countries, the visibility of violence against women and levels of reporting have increased since the opening of women's police stations.[71] In Rwanda, the number of cases received has increased and the stigma associated with SGBV has been reduced since the establishment of a gender desk at the national police headquarters.[72]

Evidence is emerging of the positive correlation between female police officers and increased SGBV reporting.[73] Female-run police desks and specialized services for women were first introduced in Brazil and Peru, and they have improved access for women.[74] In addition to increased levels of reporting, 70 percent of users of Brazilian women's police stations (delegacias especiais de atendimentoa mulher) felt welcome, about 75 percent were provided information and guidance on the process, and most received referrals to other agencies for support.[75] In Tamil Nadu, India, the introduction of 188

---

68 The unit was mandated to investigate and prosecute cases of violence and to support victims through the process. It has 11 prosecutors and 11 other employees and is integrated into government staffing. Subsequently, other VAW units were established in other provinces in Afghanistan: Herat, Balkh, Parwan, Kapisa, Nangarhar, Badakhshan, and Bamyan. See IDLO, *supra* note 49; UNAMA & OHCHR, *Still a Long Way to Go: Implementation of the Law on Elimination of Violence against Women in Afghanistan* (report, UNAMA Dec. 2012); UNAMA & OHCHR, *A Ways to Go: An Update on Implementation of the Law on Elimination of Violence against Women in Afghanistan* (report, UNAMA Dec. 2013).

69 From March 2010 to March 2011, only 21 cases went to court in the Kabul VAW unit. Most cases were either withdrawn or abandoned by the victims or complainants. The Deputy Attorney General for Criminal Investigation stated that few cases were prosecuted because more than 70 percent of the cases (misdemeanors, not felonies) were closed, mediated, or archived. Of the cases remaining, a large number were divorces or other civil matters, which were referred to the family courts; a small percentage were VAW cases constituting serious crimes. The deputy attorney general attributed the high rate of mediation and case withdrawal to Afghan culture and traditions.

70 In its first year of operation, the VAW unit in Kabul received 300 cases from 15 different provinces in Afghanistan. In March 2012, after two years in operation, the total number of registered cases tripled. Two years later, it received almost four times the number of cases. *See* IDLO, *supra* note 49; UNAMA & OHCHR (2012), *supra* note 68; UNAMA & OHCHR (2013), *supra* note 68.

71 Nadine Jubb et al., *Regional Mapping Study of Women's Police Stations in Latin America* (report prepared for Centro de Planificacion y Estudios Sociales [CEPLAES], Quito, 2008).

72 UN Women, *supra* note 41, at 92.

73 *Id.*, at 59–60.

74 Nadine Jubb & Wania Pasinato Izumino, *Women and Policing in Latin America: A Revised Background Paper* (paper presented at the Latin American Studies Association conference, Dallas, Mar. 27–29, 2003).

75 In 1985, the first women's police station, Delegacias Especiaias de Atendimento a Mulher (DEAM), opened in São Paulo. There are about 450 DEAMs throughout the country. More

all-women police units, covering both rural and urban areas and focusing on crimes against women, increased women's comfort level in approaching the police, including reporting of domestic violence.[76]

Specialized Legislation

There has been a significant increase in SGBV legislation in the past few years, and some promising outcomes are becoming evident, albeit implementation challenges persist.[77] In Timor-Leste, for example, prior to the passage of the Law against Domestic Violence in 2010, intimate-partner SGBV could be prosecuted only under the Penal Code.[78] The specialized domestic violence legislation makes all offenses falling within the definition of domestic violence a public offense requiring investigation and prosecution. The impact has been an increasing number of cases of domestic violence before the courts and confirmation from victims that the police no longer turn them away.[79] In Afghanistan, UNAMA has examined the implementation of the EVAW law, which was enacted by the government in August 2009. The law was lauded as landmark legislation because, for the first time, it criminalized 22 SGBV acts.[80]

One-Stop Centers

SGBV survivors require a variety of services to overcome institutional, social, and financial barriers. One promising approach is the establishment of one-stop centers. These centers integrate medical, legal, and social services for SGBV survivors, reducing the number of steps needed for full redress. In turn,

---

DEAMs were established under the Maria da Penha Law on domestic and family violence in 2006. The law granted DEAMs broader responsibilities for putting protective measures in place, including providing immediate assistance, investigating, and steering cases through the criminal justice system. See UN Women, *supra* note 41, at 58.

76 M. Natarajan, *Women Police Stations as a Dispute Processing System: The Tamil Nadu Experience in Dealing with Dowry-Related Domestic Violence Cases*, 16(1–2) J. Women & Crim. Just. 87, 106 (2005).

77 The *Women, Business, and the Law* survey shows that 76 of the 100 economies covered have laws on domestic violence, and 78 economies formally protect women from sexual harassment in employment. *See* World Bank & Intl. Fin. Corp., *Women, Business, and the Law: Removing Restrictions to Enhance Gender Equality* (Bloomsbury Publg. 2013), 25–26. For implementation achievements and challenges, *see*, for example, UN Women, *supra* note 41, at 22–45.

78 As a result, most cases were charged as a semipublic crime, requiring the victim to make a complaint. Victims were often pressured to withdraw their complaint and many cases of reported intimate-partner SGBV did not proceed to a hearing. *See* Lilian Dang, *Online Discussion on Law, Justice, and Women's Rights: Sexual and Gender-Based Violence in the Context of Conflict and Fragility* ("Week 2" of the "Gender Issues in Fragile Situations Community of Practice," a community of practice hosted by the World Bank on its c4d platform, July 22–Aug. 11, 2013), https://collaboration.worldbank.org/thread/2190 (membership required for access).

79 *Id.*

80 UNAMA & OHCHR (2012), *supra* note 68; UNAMA & OHCHR (2013), *supra* note 68. Although progress has been documented in terms of increased awareness and reporting, obtaining accurate assessment is challenging absent system-wide data collection and tracking and analysis of cases as they progress from police to prosecution to the courts.

such centers reduce secondary trauma and victimization, and evidence shows reduced attrition and increased conviction rates.[81]

An example of this interdisciplinary approach is the Oficina de Violencia Domestica (OVD; Domestic Violence Office) established by the Supreme Court of Argentina. OVD has a team of legal, medical, psychological, and social-work professionals on duty 24 hours a day, 365 days a year. This initiative improved efficiency, as courts can now make injunction decisions within one or two days, instead of within four months, as in the past. In addition, judges now have adequate documentation of injuries, eliminating delays in determining injuries that had healed by the time an examination was made.[82]

Another example is Thuthuzela Care Centres, located in public hospitals and established to provide SGBV survivors with a range of services, such as medical treatment, counseling, and court support in an integrated manner.[83] The Soweto Thuthuzela Care Centre located in Gauteng Province works with about 165 survivors each month. The trial completion time for cases dealt with by the Centre is an estimated 7.5 months, compared with the national average of two years. The conviction rate is 89 percent.[84]

In many FCS contexts, however, setting up one-stop centers could be daunting, as health providers, social workers, lawyers, and police officers, among others, are few and concentrated in urban centers. One promising development in the DRC is being implemented through Panzi Hospital. The program focuses on three health zones in South Kivu that have a very high incidence of SGBV, insecurity, and inaccessibility. The program's holistic approach combines medical, psychosocial, legal, and economic support for survivors of violence and children born of rape. The program is gaining international attention as a model for community hospitals, especially for cases of SGBV in FCS contexts.[85]

---

81 UN Women, *supra* note 41, at 63.

82 *Gender Justice in the Argentine Context: Justice Highton de Nolasco Shares Her Views*, http://www.lawschool.cornell.edu/womenandjustice/Featured-Judges/Justice-Highton-de-Nolasco.cfm; UN Women, *supra* note 41, at 59; Nancy Hendry, *Online Discussion on Law, Justice, and Women's Rights: Sexual and Gender-Based Violence in the Context of Conflict and Fragility* ("Week 2" of the "Gender Issues in Fragile Situations Community of Practice," a community of practice hosted by the World Bank on its c4d platform, July 22–Aug. 11, 2013), https://collaboration.worldbank.org/thread/2190 (membership required for access).

83 A victim assistance officer helps the survivor through medical, legal, and other processes. A site coordinator ensures that all services are coordinated to prevent multiple interviews of the victim and assists the survivor through other processes that risk secondary victimization.

84 UN Women, *supra* note 41, at 57.

85 Panzi Foundation DRC (Apr. 29, 2014), http://www.panzihospital.org/projects/panzi-foundation-drc. Other activities are training of community leaders, health care providers, police and paralegals, social assistants and community mobilizers; microfinance services; and literacy trainings.

Specialized Coordination or Referral Systems

Another promising approach to delivering integrated support services is coordination, or referral, systems. In Timor-Leste, for example, an interministerial network between the office of the Secretary of State for the Promotion of Equality, which deals with policy and advocacy, and the Ministry of Social Solidarity, which handles service delivery, brings together relevant participants from ministries, NGOs, and service providers on a monthly basis. Their work has culminated in the development of the National Action Plan for Gender Based Violence. The network has improved referrals and information sharing and drives policy development and other initiatives.[86]

Specialized Legal Aid

In addition to states providing mostly general legal services, women's groups and NGOs are providing specialized interventions for SGBV survivors. In Liberia, for example, women's NGOs, such as the Association of Female Lawyers of Liberia, Women AID, and the Women in Peacebuilding Program (WIPNET), are currently aiding survivors by providing support in reporting cases to the police, following up cases with the prosecutors and courts, and relocating survivors to other communities to avoid stigmatization.[87] Since the establishment of the Victim Support Service—the first legal aid organization for women and children in Timor-Leste—the rate of reporting of SGBV, the number of court hearings on SGBV, and resolutions of SGBV cases have all increased.[88]

Strengthening Forensic Capacity

Medico-legal, or forensic, evidence is "at the intersection of medical and justice processes and appropriate implementation requires coordination between the range of actors and sectors involved in prevention of, and response to, sexual violence."[89] However, in many countries, there is a lack of capacity among SGBV service providers—police, lawyers, prosecutors, judges, and health personnel—on what evidence should be collected to support SGBV cases and how such evidence should be analyzed. In FCS, this capacity gap is further compounded by weakened (or almost nonexistent) health and justice deliv-

---

86 See Dang, *supra* note 78.

87 Peace Medie, *Online Discussion on Law, Justice, and Women's Rights: Sexual and Gender-Based Violence in the Context of Conflict and Fragility* ("Week 2" of the "Gender Issues in Fragile Situations Community of Practice," a community of practice hosted by the World Bank on its c4d platform, July 22–Aug. 11, 2013), https://collaboration.worldbank.org/thread/2190 (membership required for access).

88 A local NGO, the Judicial Systems Monitoring Programme (JSMP), established the Victim Support Service to assist women and children victims through every step of the legal process, including reporting their cases to police, transporting them to counseling and forensic examinations, meeting with prosecutors, and attending court hearings. Victim Support Service separated from JSMP in 2012.

89 *Building National System Capacity for Medico-Legal Evidence in Conflict-Affected States* is available at http://stoprapenow.org/uploads/advocacyresources/1386878154.pdf.

ery systems. In response, the World Health Organization and United Nations Office on Drugs and Crime launched a project called Strengthening Medico-Legal Services for Sexual Violence Cases in Conflict-Affected Settings. The project seeks to support national capacity in the collection and use of forensic evidence in sexual violence cases in FCS.[90]

Specialized Data Collection, Research, and Evaluations

There are very few efforts that focus on data collection, research, and evaluation on SGBV in FCS. The few examples include Learning on Gender in Conflict in Africa or LOGICA, a multidonor trust fund at the World Bank that targets research to improve knowledge and practices among development practitioners; and the Due Diligence Project, a multicountry study that aims to strengthen an accountability framework to assess and measure effective implementation of government measures to end VAW.[91] There is a big gap in knowledge relating to men and masculinities. One example that addresses this gap is the International Men and Gender Equality Survey (IMAGES), led by Promundo and the International Center for Research on Women. It is one of the comprehensive surveys on male practices and attitudes in relation to gender equality, household dynamics, intimate-partner violence, health, and economic stress.[92]

General Initiatives

General initiatives may complement the specialized approaches mentioned above. The list of approaches below is informative, although the extent of their impact is hard to gauge due to limited evidence.

Gender-Sensitive and -Responsive Justice Processes

Institutionalizing gender-sensitive processes can facilitate access to courts. Some good-practice examples on making courtrooms more friendly to survivors of SGBV include (a) ensuring confidentiality and safety for survivors inside and outside the courtroom; (b) arranging the times that the defen-

---

90 *Id.*

91 The Due Diligence Framework is organized around the "Five Ps": prevention, protection, prosecution, punishment, and provision of redress. *See* Zarizana Abdul Aziz & Janine Moussa, *Due Diligence Framework: State Accountability Framework for Eliminating Violence against Women* (Intl. Human Rights Initiative, Inc. Malaysia), www.duediligenceproject.org.

92 The Sonke Gender Justice Network and Promundo have created a new report, based on the IMAGES survey, on men, masculinities, and GBV in the eastern DRC. The report reveals alarming attitudes about rape among many men. Carried out in the DRC, it provides findings on the effects of conflict, the prevalence of factors associated with SGBV, and gender-related attitudes from 708 men and 754 women interviewed in Goma, North Kivu, and several focus group discussions. IMAGES was also conducted in nine other countries and will have more insights on men's use of violence, participation in caregiving, and reaction to the gender equality agenda, among other topics. *See New Sonke-Promundo Report on IMAGES Report on Men, Masculinities, and GBV in Eastern DRC Reveals Alarming Attitudes about Rape amongst Many Men,* http://www.genderjustice.org.za/updates/highlights/2001241-press-release-and-preliminary-results-from-sonkes-images-study-in-drc.html.

dant and SGBV survivor enter and leave the courtroom to reduce the risk of intimidation and violence; (c) in-camera trials; (d) reducing unnecessary and repeated postponements; (e) allowing a supporting person to be present; (f) better interpretation and translation services; (g) requiring court personnel to treat witnesses with respect and sensitivity; and (h) prohibiting victim-blaming or gender-biased language in court.[93]

Access to Justice Initiatives

Access to justice initiatives, such as mobile courts, legal aid services, and legal awareness and empowerment programs, aims to bring justice services to those without access. In Somaliland, for example, the Ministry of Justice established mobile courts in the five regional capitals. Judges reported a strong uptake from women and internally displaced persons. In Indonesia, the provision of legal empowerment measures, legal aid through paralegals, and court-fee waivers are increasing access to courts.[94] Nevertheless, when specialized knowledge and sensitivity about SGBV is not available, these initiatives may not benefit SGBV survivors.

Women's Participation as Justice Actors

There is limited but increasing evidence on the impact of women as justice actors on SGBV. For example, in Sri Lanka, deployment of female Tamil police officers led to decreased SGBV as well as increased trust in the police.[95] In Liberia, the deployment of an all-woman Indian police force of 130 women led to increased rates of reporting of GBV in the areas they patrolled. The

---

93 "It is important for language—which is the embodiment of one's thought process—not only to be free from gender bias, but also be gender-fair or gender-inclusive. Although it can be argued that a change in the use of language alone is not sufficient to bring about gender-sensitivity, it is an important aspect of it, and can facilitate in the widening of one's perspective concerning issues on gender equality. Conversely, it is also the most patent manifestation of gender bias, and its power as an effective medium of perpetuating stereotypes and stigma cannot be underestimated. This is especially true for the members of the Bench and Bar, for their profession entails a lot of articulation, both in oral and written form." *See* Amparita Sta. Maria, *CEDAW Interactive Benchbook* (2008), http://cedawbenchbook.org/.

94 In Indonesia, 9 out of 10 female heads of household surveyed were unable to access courts for divorce cases mainly due to financial costs, including court fees and transportation expenses. By failing to access the courts, many of these women also failed to benefit from pro-poor government programs. Of help in court processes was a network of community facilitators and trained paralegals who promoted legal literacy and provided legal consultation and practical support to enable women to access the religious courts to obtain legal documentation for themselves and their children. Also, a series of studies, ongoing dialogue between civil society organizations and government stakeholders, legal empowerment programs, and field visits to rural communities contributed to broader access to justice policy developments, including court-fee waivers, which led to an estimated 14-fold increase in the number of clients able to access the courts. *See* Cate Sumner, Matthew Zurstrassen, & Leisha Lister, *Increasing Access to Justice for Women, the Poor, and Those Living in Remote Areas: An Indonesian Case Study* (Justice for the Poor briefing note, Mar. 2011).

95 Sanam Anderlini, *Delivering Justice: Sexual and Gender Based Violence in the Context of Fragility* (presentation at the Law, Justice and Development Week forum, World Bank, Nov. 19, 2013).

recruitment of other women into the force has also increased.[96] In Bougainville, Papua New Guinea, women mediators dealt with gender-based violence better than male mediators and chiefs, because they had a better understanding of gender subordination and ways to navigate it. However, women justice actors face difficult challenges. In Afghanistan, for example, where there are about 1,551 female police officers—one for every 10,000 women, reports indicate that these officers are "often shunned by their communities and even their families, the stigma facing Afghanistan's police women has even led to women being killed because of their work."[97]

Training of Service Providers and Addressing Their Gender Biases

There are some promising approaches on addressing institutional and personal biases and making institutions and individuals more gender-responsive. Sakshi, an Indian NGO, developed an education program to change internalized myths and gender stereotypes.[98] It conducted workshops to bring together judges, NGOs, health care providers, and litigants to look at the social context and barriers that women face in accessing justice. Visits by judges to shelters and women's prisons were organized to enable better understanding of the challenges faced by SGBV survivors.[99] Similarly, in Tanzania, Jurisprudence on the Ground is convening dialogues between members of the judiciary and rural women.[100] The project emphasizes the notion that when judges' understanding improves, they become proponents for simple but effective recommendations to make the system responsive to women, such as waiving court fees, providing forms free of charge, and prioritizing sensitive cases.[101]

Technical guidance is also important in challenging institutional and personal biases. In the Philippines, a CEDAW benchbook was published by the Philippine Judicial Academy. It analyzed decisions of the Philippine Supreme Court on SGBV using both national and international legal standards. Using

---

96 UN Women, *supra* note 41, at 60.

97 OXFAM Intl., *Fighting the Stigma Facing Afghanistan's Women Police*, http://www.oxfam.org/en/development/afghanistan/women-police-fighting-stigma.

98 UN Women, *supra* note 41, at 61. This is in response to results of interviews conducted with 109 judges from district courts, high courts, and the Supreme Court as well as with female lawyers and litigants on judicial perceptions and its impact on women litigants. The interview results showed that around half of the judges interviewed stated that women are partly to blame for spousal abuse, while another 68 percent stated that provocative attire is an invitation to rape.

99 *Id.* In assessing the impact of its work, Sakshi tracked major SGBV cases in the region, including the landmark Vishaka case, which was decided by judges who participated in the workshops.

100 This is a project that brings together members of the International Association of Women's Judges, the Society for Women, Aids in Africa–Tanzania, and the Tanzania Women Judges Association.

101 *See* Intl. Assn. Women's JJ., Tanzania: Jurisprudence on the Ground, http://www.iawj.org/JOGProgram1.html; Tanzania Women Judges Association, The Jurisprudence on the Ground project, http://www.tawjatz.org/the-jurisprudence-on-the-ground-jog-project/; UN Women, *supra* note 41, at 62.

the benchbook as a resource, a team of Philippine Judicial Academy experts, including Supreme Court justices and renowned law professors, provide technical guidance to judges on how to decide SGBV cases.[102]

Local Justice Innovations

Work-around local and informal justice systems provide promising entry points for addressing SGBV. In northern Uganda, where access to formal justice systems is difficult, peace rings are used to solve local cases, including SGBV. Peace rings are mostly led by women, handpicked by local chiefs and trained in dispute resolution. In Kenya, Maasai elders vowed to uphold a new tradition of equal rights for women and incorporated this into the *katiba,* their local constitution.[103]

Lessons and Recommendations on Justice Sector Delivery in the Context of FCS

Lessons and Insights

Integrating Gender Concerns in Standard Setting and Peace Processes

There are potential gains from including gender issues in the drafting of constitutions, laws, and peace agreements. Integrating gender concerns can contribute to a visible and commonly agreed-on platform for reform and advocacy around gender in general and SGBV in particular.[104] Putting SGBV on the agenda, however, is more than a budgetary or technical exercise; it requires the ability to engage in and influence political settlements.[105] It also

102 Sta. Maria, *supra* note 93. Workshops were held for judges and their staff to publicize the benchbook and instill greater sensitivity in judges. Chapter subjects in the benchbook include stereotyping, double victimization, stigmatization, and paradigm shifts reflected in actual Supreme Court decisions.

103 Deborah Espinosa, *Maasai Elders Vow to Protect and Support Rights of Women and Girls* (blog entry, originally posted June 12, 2012), http://www.landesa.org/maasai-elders-vow-protect-support-rights-women-girls-blog//.

104 UN Women, *supra* note 41, at 57. For example, the Colombian Constitution provides for a *tutela,* which facilitates simple and fast access to local courts in cases of domestic violence. In Guatemala, as part of the 1996 peace agreement, the government committed to setting up an Indigenous Women's Legal Aid Office (Defensoria de la Mujer Indigena) to prevent violence and discrimination against indigenous women.

105 In talking about the tasks of mediators in integrating both gender and SGBV concerns in peace negotiations, Barney Afako points out that SGBV is often misunderstood and its prevalence underestimated or denied by parties to the negotiation, among others. Nevertheless, he highlights the necessity of engaging parties early to find durable solutions to SGBV and to prioritize holistic approaches beyond criminal prosecutions. He suggests strategies to facilitate inclusion, including promoting education on the mediation process; encouraging parties separately to confront issues around SGBV and take unilateral steps in addition to reflecting commitments in agreements; and promoting, in the text of agreements, broader accountability and prevention strategies. He also identifies some of the mediator's tasks: (a) secure cessation of violence, and a platform for finding lasting solutions; (b) educate himself/herself, and assist parties in understanding SGBV, especially their obligations; (c) tailor interaction

requires a political positioning that challenges war, violent conflict, and militarized masculinities. The main challenge is that often SGBV efforts are ad hoc and/or siloed.[106]

Improving Efficiency of Justice Institutions—Taking Context into Account

Context is particularly important in setting up specialized initiatives such as courts and police units. Experience with specialized courts demonstrates the difficulty of insulating a specialized structure from the deficiencies of the wider institutional backdrop within which it must function.[107] The decision for a specialized initiative should be informed by analysis of context, including the wider institutional justice sector constraints and social norms that prevent access to justice, among others.

Working with Formal and Informal Institutions

An understanding of SGBV, gender, law, justice, and development that considers the existence of multiple sources and systems of law is crucial to identifying interventions that can bring about real change. Unfortunately, the common understanding of legal systems has tended to focus on dichotomizing systems: formal and informal.[108] Many interventions fail to address the interplay between these systems and their potential to mutually influence and reinforce inequalities or be unresponsive and discriminate against women.[109] In the final analysis, both systems need to be enhanced to better deliver services to SGBV victims and survivors. Shifting the focus away from a choice between institutions (i.e., formal or informal) and toward how women experience SGBV and what they need would lead to forging practical and innovative interventions that can effectively address SGBV in FCS.

---

with state and nonstate actors; and (d) appreciate what is possible to achieve by mediators and within the text, and what is for other stages and actors to address. In conclusion, he states that fighting for accountability for SGBV is part of gender justice. Nevertheless, the mediation process should be realistic about the capacity of criminal justice systems, without tempering commitment to lasting solutions. He suggests using a multiplicity of approaches required to facilitate the structural societal changes to address SGBV. Lastly, he highlights that men must be a core part of the strategy to address SGBV. (*See* Afako, *supra* note 37.)

106 "The Missing Peace Symposium: Sexual Violence in Conflict and Post-Conflict Settings," available at http://www.usip.org/events/the-missing-peace-symposium-2013.

107 World Bank, *supra* note 48, at 23–24.

108 Rea Abada Chiongson et al., *The Role of Law and Justice in Achieving Gender Equality* (background paper prepared for the World Bank's *World Development Report 2012: Gender Equality and Development*, Sept. 2011), https://openknowledge.worldbank.org/bitstream/handle/10986/9194/WDR2012-0028.pdf?sequence=1. Conservative approaches have tended to focus on national state systems, with interventions addressing court reforms such as case management, court infrastructure, and training of justice actors. More recent forms have also engaged nonstate systems, often as a set of institutions only in need of efficiency and/or norm-based reforms.

109 *Id.*

The Importance of Building the Knowledge Base

Fragile and conflict situations present unique challenges due to security and accessibility concerns. Recently, a United States Institute of Peace special report on wartime sexual violence highlighted the assumptions and misconceptions around SGBV and the serious knowledge gaps that impinge on the capacity to craft effective policy recommendations, stating:

> Just as well-substantiated research findings carry implications for policymakers, knowing more about the gaps in the knowledge base can help policymakers avoid the pitfalls associated with incomplete data and highlight areas where greater efforts are needed.[110]

Working with and Supporting Men

Working with men is an integral part of addressing SGBV. Men are generally in positions of power and influence, and hence can be useful allies in combating SGBV. In addition, working with men is important so that they can better support women seeking justice and address any misconceptions and resentments that they may feel toward women and programs addressed to women. Men also need support because the violence they are exposed to during conflict is the same violence they perpetrate against women. Supporting and assisting men, and not just working with them, is thus crucial to breaking the violence continuum.

Moving beyond Victimhood

A priority for efforts against SGBV should be to adopt a holistic approach to justice—"moving beyond victimhood"—and, instead, to place SGBV survivors at the center.[111] This approach would emphasize that legal systems are only a small part of what is needed to fully respond to the needs of survivors. A promising holistic approach in Iran is being implemented by the Omid-e-Mehr Foundation, which supports about two hundred young girls who experience severe violence. It has an 86 percent success rate in moving these girls beyond victimhood.[112]

Recommendations

From the promising approaches and lessons discussed, the following options to address efficiency, sensitivity, and responsiveness in delivering justice to SGBV survivors in FCS can be proposed.[113]

---

110 Cohen, *supra* note 3.

111 Anderlini, *supra* note 95.

112 *Id.*

113 Adapted from the summary report of *Online Discussion on Law, Justice, and Women's Rights: Sexual and Gender-Based Violence in the Context of Conflict and Fragility* ("Week 2" of the "Gender Issues in Fragile Situations Community of Practice," hosted by the World Bank on its c4d platform, July 22–Aug. 11, 2013), https://collaboration.worldbank.org/thread/2190 (membership required for access).

Enhance performance and accountability of justice sector actors. This can be done through (a) providing technical guidance, such as developing bench books with court authorities and protocols for handling SGBV cases, to judges, prosecutors, police, and other justice actors on SGBV cases; (b) integrating SGBV as a priority for access to justice initiatives, such as free legal aid, help desks, and mobile courts; (c) setting up survivor-friendly processes, including using gender-sensitive language; (d) supporting justice sector professionals to engage in dialogue with SGBV advocates and undergo social context trainings on SGBV; and (e) ensuring institutional accountability, including through monitoring and evaluation strategies.[114]

Set up context-appropriate specialized institutions. Specialized institutions are more responsive when informed by context-specific analytical work that takes into account impacts of wider institutional (justice sector) and social norms and the cost-benefit of such an endeavor. Providing a clear mandate, responsibilities and accountability structures, resources (financial, staff, and influence), and evaluation mechanisms are critical for effective operations of these institutions.

Improve the capacity of informal justice systems. Promising efforts include (a) undertaking analytical work aimed at understanding the informal justice space and, in particular, understanding how SGBV survivors navigate both formal and informal spaces; (b) developing a coherent policy to address SGBV across formal and informal justice institutions that can inform multiple stakeholders; and (c) improving the capacity of informal justice institutions to address SGBV.

Strengthen supporting institutions. Legal and justice initiatives cannot respond to SGBV without the support of other relevant sectors, such as health and social welfare, education, and employment and livelihood. Among the promising intersectoral efforts to consider are (a) setting up one-stop centers and, where not possible, a referral network with clear mandates and responsibilities; (b) providing relevant sectors with adequate resources, skills, influence, and authority; (c) developing institutional skills for referral, coordination, and collaboration; (d) developing capacity of service providers from all relevant sectors, especially for collecting and analyzing medico-legal and forensic evidence; and (e) supporting new and ongoing work to identify and address norms that perpetuate SGBV.

Expand the knowledge base on SGBV in FCS. Such efforts should include (a) compiling context-specific and local knowledge on how women experience SGBV and how they navigate the justice system; (b) gathering evidence on the effectiveness of justice interventions and their impacts on women; and (c)

---

114 Monitoring, evaluation, and accountability strategies are important in identifying ways to create clarity, measuring effectiveness, and scaling up or replicating interventions, among other tasks. Adopting accountability frameworks is important in identifying indicators, assessing what contributes to their successes (or lack thereof), and using international standards and women's human rights framework in holding state and nonstate actors accountable for failing to adequately address SGBV.

building evidence on the impacts and influence of women justice sector actors on SGBV.

Expand work on men and SGBV. There is room to improve work on men and SGBV. Among them are (a) undertaking analytical work around masculinities and femininities in FCS; (b) developing and implementing programs for men that help them understand and support SGBV initiatives; and (c) ensuring that male victims of SGBV have adequate support and access to justice.

13
Sexual Violence in Conflict: Can There Be Justice?

Justice Teresa Doherty

I have been involved in three civil war or internal conflict situations: in Northern Ireland as a citizen and a lawyer, and in Bougainville, Papua New Guinea, and Sierra Leone as a judge.[1] Each conflict was precipitated by different events and had different causes, and each was handled differently by the government concerned. However, they all had one thing in common: the government did not, initially, fully appreciate the reason or reasons for the unrest that escalated into civil war and instead took draconian measures. In each of those conflicts, the civilian population, particularly women and children, suffered unduly. In Bougainville and Sierra Leone, the incidence of sexual violence was outrageous. The secretary-general of the United Nations, in preliminary reports leading to the establishment of the Special Court for Sierra Leone, referred to the "egregious practice of sexual violence against women and girls in Sierra Leone."[2] Sexual violence was not unique to those internal conflicts, however; it has long been used as a weapon of war and continues to occur.

Reflections on the History of Sexual Violence in War

To understand and appreciate why sexual violence persists in war, one must consider how women have historically been perceived in both war and peace. In many cultures, women were considered property under the ownership of men: fathers, husbands, slave owners. Because it could reduce a woman's work ability or value on the marriage market, rape was often considered a property crime, committed not against the woman but against her owner. Roy Porter observes:

> the crime [of rape] was principally that of stealing and abducting a woman from her rightful proprietors, normally her father or husband. Moreover, in the case of a maiden, rape destroyed her property value on the marriage market, and . . . heaped shame on her family. . . . Violated daughters might be given as offerings to nun-

---

1 The chapter is adapted from a paper given at the World Bank Law, Justice and Development Week, Nov. 18–23, 2013. Extracts of that paper were also published in *Sexual Violence and the Role of the International Courts,* 11(3) New Zealand J. Pub. & Intl. L. 693–705 (Dec. 2013).

2 *Report of the Secretary-General of the United Nations to the Security Council on the Establishment of the Special Court,* S/2000/915, Part 111 (Oct. 4, 2000), on the competence of the Special Court and the subject matter of jurisdiction.

> neries, and in many societies they were married off to the abductor or rapists.[3]

In war, women were perceived as the property of the defeated clans, towns, or countries. In other words, women were property the conqueror could take, in the same way that the conqueror might take gold and livestock, as the spoils of war. It also showed that the defeated men could not protect their women and children from the conquerors. It occurred in European and Asian conflicts. In the wars waged by Khubilai Khan against the Japanese in the 13th century, women were captured, held, and distributed among conquering troops.[4] A recent BBC documentary claimed that there are 23 million descendants of Genghis Khan.[5]

Kelly Askin, an expert on the history of sexual violence in conflict, writes that although "sexual assault has been increasingly outlawed through the years, this prohibition has rarely been enforced. Consequently, rape and other forms of sexual assault have thrived in wartime, progressing from a perceived incidental act of the conqueror, to a reward of the victor, to a discernible mighty weapon of war."[6]

Was the concept of women as a spoil of war ever codified? There is little evidence to determine if ancient wars were subject to written or universally accepted codes or laws; there certainly were traditions, but they did not necessarily deal with the status of civilians. The war code of the Saracens made clear that "[w]omen and minors of both sexes become the immediate property of the captors." Male prisoners of war could be ransomed, released, or exchanged. However, women could not.[7]

Some laws prohibited the violation of women. For example, Nicetas records that the Turks prohibited the violation of women, as did Totila the Goth during the sacking of Rome and Alexander the Great, although it has been opined that in the latter's case this may have been due more to Alexander's sexual orientation than to altruism.[8] Susan Brownmiller notes that to the ancient Greeks, rape was "socially acceptable behavior well within the rules of warfare," and "women were legitimate booty, useful as wives, concubines,

---

3 Roy Porter, *Rape: Does It Have a Historical Meaning?* in *Rape: An Historical and Social Enquiry* (Sylvana Tomaselli & Roy Porter eds., Basil Blackwell 1986), as cited by Kelly Askin, *War Crimes against Women: Prosecution in International War Crimes Tribunals* (Kluwer L. Intl. 1997).

4 *See* James P. Delgado, *Khubilai Khan's Lost Fleet: In Search of a Legendary Armada* (U. California Press 2008).

5 BBC, *Andrew Marr's History of the World*, www.bbc.co.uk. However, the presenter, Andrew Marr, did not explain how that assessment was made.

6 Askin, *supra* note 3, citing Donald Arthur Wells, *War Crimes and the Law of War* 93–94 (2d ed., U. Press of America 1991).

7 Percy Bordwell, *The Law of War between Belligerents* (Callaghan & Co. 1908).

8 Thomas Cowan, *Gay Men and Women Who Enriched the World* (Mulvey 1988), as cited in Askin, *supra* note 3.

slave labor, battle-camp trophy."[9] "To the victor go the spoils" has been a war cry for centuries, and Peter Karsten states that women and children were historically considered "fair prey as spoils."[10]

Civilian women were sometimes killed because of their ability to produce children of the enemy. During the French Revolution, General François Joseph Westermann massacred women so that they could "breed no more brigands."[11] During the recent Balkan wars, stories circulated that women were raped with the intent that they would give birth to children fathered by the enemy. Forced pregnancy is now a crime against humanity under the Rome Statute of the International Criminal Court and the Statute of the Special Court of Sierra Leone. However, no one has yet been prosecuted for that crime.

In 1646, Hugo Grotius, considered by many the father of international law, wrote:

> You may read in many places that the raping of women in time of war is permissible, and in many others that it is not permissible. Those who sanction rape have taken into account only the injury done to the person of another, and have judged that it is not inconsistent with the law of war that everything which belongs to the enemy [including the women] should be at the disposition of the victor.[12]

Have attitudes about sexual violence in war changed?

The answer is debatable. Some treaties have tried to formulate codes:

- The Treaty of Amity and Commerce of 1785 (between the King of Prussia and the United States of America) specified in Article 6 that, in case of war, "women and children . . . shall not be molested in their persons."
- Order No. 20 of 1847, a supplement to the Rules and Articles for War for the United States of America, listed rape as a severely punishable offense.
- The Declaration of Brussels of 1874 stated that the "honour and rights of the family . . . should be respected." (Note the use of the word "should," rather than "shall": the respect was not mandatory.)
- The *Oxford Manual of 1880* asserted that "human life, female honour . . . must be respected. Interference with family life is to be avoided."

Although in most cases the language is imprecise, authorities such as Askin and Brownmiller propose that the provisions were intended to protect women and children against sexual assault. Yet the term *family honor* does not

---

9 Susan Brownmiller, *Against Our Will: Men, Women, and Rape* (Simon & Schuster 1975), as cited in Askin, *supra* note 3.

10 Peter Karsten, *Law, Soldiers, and Combat* (Greenwood 1978).

11 Hoffman Nickerson, *The Armed Horde, 1793–1939* (G. P. Putnam, 1940), as cited in Askin, *supra* note 3.

12 Hugo Grotius, *De jure belli ac pacis Libri Tres,* Francis W. Kelsey trans., vol. 2 of *Classics of International Law* (James Brown Scott ed., Oxford U. Press 1925).

automatically acknowledge a woman's individual rights, including the right not to be assaulted or to suffer.

Askin and Theodor Meron note that the Lieber Instructions, passed in the United States in 1863, which outlawed rape and assault on women, was a foundation of the modern laws of war subsequently codified in the Geneva Conventions.[13] But even these conventions do not clearly spell out that there should be no rape of and no sexual assault against women. Article 46 of the 1907 Hague Convention stipulated that "[f]amily honour and rights, the lives of persons, and private property, as well as religious convictions and practices must be respected."[14] However, Article 46 did not say that the physical integrity of individual women and girls was to be protected and respected. Here again, "family honour and rights" were to be respected. It seems that the drafters had not moved away from the concept that women and children were the property of husbands or fathers.

Twice as many people were killed in World War I than had been killed in all the wars between 1790 and 1913, and invading soldiers raped women and massacred opponents by the thousands.[15] Sexual assault was not only an indiscriminate act committed by soldiers but also a weapon of terror, rage, and intimidation. In 1919, a war crimes commission reported that there had been "extensive violations of the laws of war."[16] Thirty-two offenses were identified, including rape and forced prostitution,[17] but the only recommendation of the commission that appeared in the draft of the Versailles Treaty was Article 229, which provided for the trial of war criminals.[18] There were no postwar initiatives to prevent future abuses.

There were no prosecutions of sexual violence during World War II. Various explanations have been put forward for this failure to prosecute: because sexual assault was seen as an entitlement allowed to vanquishing soldiers; because some Allied troops behaved as badly as other combatants; and because Stalin was reluctant to take action against his own troops.

The first modern postwar criminal tribunals were held in Nuremberg and Tokyo; no sexual crimes were prosecuted. Rape and other forms of sexual violence were not explicitly criminalized in the Charter of the Nuremberg Tribunal nor expressly mentioned in the judgments as war crimes or crimes

---

13 Askin, *supra* note 3, at 323, citing Theodor Meron, *Shakespeare's Henry the Fifth and the Law of War*, 86(1) Am. J. Intl. L. 34 (1992). Meron writes that despite the prohibition of "all rape" in the Lieber Instructions, the protection of women's rights was not a priority.

14 *Convention (IV) respecting the Laws and Customs of War on Land, and Annex: Regulations concerning the Laws and Customs of War on Land* (The Hague, Oct. 18, 1907), https://www.icrc.org/ihl/INTRO/195.

15 Askin, *supra* note 3, citing Telford Taylor, *The Anatomy of the Nuremberg Trials: A Personal Memoir* (Knopf Doubleday 1992).

16 Askin, *supra* note 3, at 42.

17 *Id.*, at 47.

18 *Id.*, at 44.

against humanity.[19] As Jennifer M. Green notes, although rape was recognized as a crime against humanity in Local Council Law No. 10, which governed the trials held by Allied military powers against lower-level Nazis, no one was charged with rape.[20] Rape was stated as a crime in the Tokyo statutes, but no one was prosecuted despite the fact that thousands of Korean women and girls had been held as sex slaves, euphemistically called "comfort women."[21] The use of sexual violence in World War II was rampant: thousands of women and girls were assaulted and raped as the Soviet army entered Berlin, to the extent that the Soviet War Memorial erected by the Soviet Union in Berlin as a monument to the unknown soldier has been referred to as the "tomb of the unknown rapist."[22]

In August 1949, Article (4)(2)(e) of the Second Protocol to the Geneva Convention spelled out the fundamental guarantee of humane treatment, including the prohibition of rape, enforced prostitution, and any form of indecent assault.[23] Under customary international law, detained women were to be separated from men and, while in detention, to be supervised by women.[24]

The belief that women are a spoil of war persists today. In *Prosecutor v. Charles Ghankay Taylor*, I heard evidence of rebel combatants' belief that rape was "an entitlement."[25] A witness testified that, when challenged about the treatment of captured women, a leader in the Revolutionary United Front (a rebel group fighting in the Sierra Leone conflict) told his troops, "Enjoy yourselves boys. This is your time." Describing her violent gang rape and subsequent abduction and detention, a young girl averred that her sister had told her, "If they capture [you], they have a right to rape you."

Has Justice Been Delivered?

In the wake of internal conflicts in the 1990s, several ad hoc and hybrid international war crimes tribunals were set up to deal with internal conflicts. They have jurisdiction to prosecute war crimes, crimes against humanity, and

---

19 *The Charter of the International Military Tribunal, Annex to the Agreement for the Prosecution and Punishment of the Major War Criminals of the European Axis* (entered into force Aug. 8, 1945), United Nations Treaty Series, vol. 82, 279.

20 Jennifer M. Green, *Litigating International Human Rights Claims of Sexual Violence in the U.S. Courts: A Brief Overview of Cases Brought under the Alien Tort Statute and Torture Victim Protection Act*, in *Violence and Gender in the Globalized World: The Intimate and the Extimate* 129 (Sanja Bahun-Raunovíc & V. G. Julie Rajan eds., Ashgate 2008).

21 *Id.*, at 129.

22 Frederick Taylor, *The Berlin Wall: A World Divided, 1961–1989* 32 (HarperCollins 2006).

23 *Protocol Additional to the Geneva Conventions of 12 August 1949, and relating to the Protection of Victims of Non-International Armed Conflicts (Protocol II), 8 June 1977,* https://www.icrc.org/applic/ihl/ihl.nsf/INTRO/475?OpenDocument.

24 Jean-Marie Henckaerts & Louise Doswald-Beck, *Customary International Humanitarian Law: Volume 1: Rules,* "Rule 119" 431–33 (Cambridge U. Press 2009).

25 *Prosecutor v. Charles Ghankay Taylor,* SCSL-03-01-T. The author was a judge in that trial.

breaches of customary international law. There are variations in the jurisdictions of the tribunals that reflect the conflict that each tribunal deals with. For example, the statute of the International Criminal Tribunal for the Former Yugoslavia (ICTY) vests jurisdiction to try the crime of genocide, but the statute of the Special Court for Sierra Leone (SCSL) does not.

The first international criminal tribunal was the ICTY, established in 1993. Its statute provides for rape as a crime against humanity (Article 5(g)). Rape was widespread during the civil war in the Balkans; women were detained in camps and used by their captors for sex; women of one ethnic group were deliberately impregnated by men of another to ensure that their children were of the other ethnicity.[26] The International Criminal Tribunal for Rwanda (ICTR), established in 1994, is a venue for the prosecution of war crimes and crimes against humanity. War crimes include rape and outrages upon personal dignity, in particular humiliating and degrading treatment, rape, enforced prostitution, and any form of indecent assault.[27]

Initially there were few prosecutions for sexual offenses in the ICTY or the ICTR. Justice Richard Goldstone, an early prosecutor at ICTY, conceded this fact.[28] It was not until a witness described the gang rape of her young daughter during evidence in a case against the town mayor, Jean Paul Akayesu, that ICTR judge Navenethem Pillay asked why the rape was not being prosecuted.[29] Akayesu had not been prosecuted for rape or any other sexual crime. A new indictment was laid, and Akayesu was convicted; rape was declared "an act of genocide," and a definition was given.[30] The decision was a landmark both for its definition and for showing that rape is as much a crime in war as it is in peace. Women are not automatically the spoils of war.

Other cases followed as more women investigators and prosecutors were appointed to the courts. However, the fact that crimes were committed did not mean that the perpetrators admitted that sexual violence happened; at least

---

26 *See* Danise Aydelott, *Mass Rape during War: Prosecuting Bosnian Rapists under International Law*, 7 Emory Intl. L. Rev. 598–99 (1993).

27 Statute of the ICTR, art. 4(e), www.icls.de/dokumente/ictr_statute.pdf.

28 *See* Courtney Ginn, *Ensuring Effective Prosecution of Sexually Violent Crimes in the Bosnian War Crimes Chamber: Applying Lessons from the ICTY*, 27 Emory Intl. L. Rev. 566 (2013). Goldstone developed a comprehensive gender strategy that was integral to the recognition of rape as a crime against humanity. Ginn comments that perhaps his most important contribution was the creation of a gender adviser in the Office of the Prosecutor; *see* 578.

29 *Prosecutor v. Akayesu*, ICTR-06-4 (Sept. 2, 1998). Justice Pillay was until September 2014 the UN High Commissioner for Human Rights.

30 The chamber stated: "With regard, particularly, to the acts described in paragraphs 12(A) and 12(B) of the Indictment, that is rape and sexual violence, the Chamber wishes to underscore the fact that in its opinion, they constitute genocide in the same way as any other act so long as they were committed with the specific intent to destroy, in whole or in part, a particular group, targeted as such. Indeed, rape and sexual violence certainly constitute infliction of serious bodily and mental harm on the victims and are even, according to the Chamber, one of the worst ways to inflict harm on the victim as he or she suffers both bodily and mental harm."

one claimed that the sexual relations were by consent.[31] A defense witness in *Prosecutor v. Charles Ghankay Taylor* stated that because captive women were grateful to their Revolutionary United Front captors for "protecting" them, they showed their gratitude by "loving" the leaders of the rebels.

The SCSL was set up at the request of the government of Sierra Leone after civil war raged for 10 years.[32] The war was noted for the brutality of the atrocities visited upon civilians, including killing by beating and burning; the chopping off of arms, hands, and legs; the abduction of people for forced labor, as sex slaves, and as child soldiers; the cutting open of pregnant women to settle bets about the sex of their unborn babies; and the deliberate destruction of homes, villages, and cities.[33] The modus operandi was to enter a village; round up people living there; burn their homes; publicly rape women, particularly young women; and take away able-bodied males, females, and children. Children, both boys and girls, were trained to be soldiers. Young girls were used as sex slaves and, according to evidence adduced in *Prosecutor v. Brima, Kamara, and Kanu*, were "given" to young boy soldiers (referred to as SBUs, a name derived from the term "Small Boy Units" used by the rebels of both the Revolutionary United Front and the Armed Forces Revolutionary Council).

The SCSL is noted for several landmark decisions in international law, including decisions on the nonimmunity from prosecution of a sitting head of state for war crimes and crimes against humanity,[34] the application of amnesties in peace treaties to crimes against humanity and war crimes,[35] and convictions for the crimes of the recruitment and use of children in war (commonly referred to as child soldiers),[36] sexual slavery, and forced marriage. UN reports referred to the egregious and widespread sexual violence toward women and girls in Sierra Leone,[37] and they recommended the retention of specialized staff experienced in gender-related crimes and juvenile justice by the court. The SCSL Statute and Rules of Procedure and Evidence provided that person-

---

31 ICTY Outreach Programme, *Sexual Violence and the Triumph of Justice* (2011), available at the ICTY website, http://www.icty.org/sid/10949.

32 Special Court for Sierra Leone, www.sc-sl.org. For more information about the court, *see* Teresa Doherty, *Jurisprudential Developments relating to Sexual Violence: The Legacy of the Special Court for Sierra Leone*, in *Sexual Violence as an International Crime: Interdisciplinary Approaches* 157 (Anne-Marie de Brouwer et al. eds., Intersentia 2013).

33 *Prosecutor v. Brima, Kamara, and Kanu*, SCSL-2004-16-T (June 20, 2007) (Trial Chamber II); and *Prosecutor v. Brima, Kamara, and Kanu*, SCSL-2004-16-A (Feb. 22, 2008) (Appeals Chamber).

34 *Prosecutor v. Taylor*, SCSL-2003-01-I (May 31, 2004) (Decision of Immunity from Jurisdiction).

35 *Prosecutor v. Kondewa*, SCSL-2004-14-AR72(E) (May 25, 2004) (Decision on Lack of Jurisdiction/Abuse of Process: Amnesty Provided by the Lomé Accord).

36 *Prosecutor v. Norman*, SCSL-2004-14-AR72(E) (May 31, 2004) (Decision on Preliminary Motion Based on Lack of Jurisdiction (Child Recruitment).

37 *Supra* note 2.

nel employed by Prosecutor[38] and by the Witnesses and Victims Section[39] must include such specialized persons, and appointments were made accordingly.

SCSL jurisprudence led to legal developments in the prosecution of gender-based violence. Its statute provided crimes against humanity (rape, sexual slavery, enforced prostitution, forced pregnancy, and any other form of sexual violence); war crimes (outrages upon personal dignity, in particular humiliating and degrading treatment, rape, enforced prostitution, and any form of indecent assault); and the recruitment, conscription, and use of children under 15 in conflict, and attacks on peacekeepers.

The SCSL trial chambers heard evidence from many victims of gender-based violence and admitted into evidence reports from UN personnel and nongovernmental organizations (NGOs) that documented widespread and systematic sexual violence. Convictions were returned on counts of rape, sexual slavery, forced marriage, outrages against personal dignity, and rape as an act of terror. In the words of Justice Pierre Boutet, the court acknowledged "the necessity for international criminal justice to highlight the high-profile nature of the emerging domain of gender offences with a view to bringing the alleged perpetrators to justice."[40]

As tribunals have recognized the many forms that sexual and gender-based violence takes, the law has expanded, and the suffering of victims as individual human beings has been recognized. The international community has moved away from the concept that sexual offenses against women and girls are offenses against the rights of ownership or property crimes or an entitlement of a successful soldier. Rape has been recognized as a weapon of war—as an act of torture in the ICTY, as an act of terror in the SCSL, and as an act of genocide in the ICTR. International law has acknowledged that women, girls, and boys are not an entitlement to conquering troops and that sexual violence is a war crime and a crime against humanity.[41]

---

38 Statute Article 15(4) provides: "Given the nature of the crimes committed and the particular sensitivities of girls, young women and children victims of rape, sexual assault, abduction and slavery of all kinds, due consideration should be given in the appointment of staff to the employment of prosecutors and investigators experienced in gender-related crimes and juvenile justice."

39 Rules of Procedure and Evidence R.34(B).

40 *Prosecutor v. Brima, Kamara and Kanu: Decision on Prosecution Request for Leave to Amend the Indictment*, para. 34, SCSL-04-16-PT. *See* also Dissenting Opinion of Justice Pierre Boutet, in *Decision of Prosecution Application for Leave to File an Interlocutuary Appeal against the Decision on the Prosecution's Request for Leave to Amend the Indictment against Norman, Fofana and Kondewa* (Aug. 5, 2004).

41 The UN Department of Peacekeeping Operations has made a review of the case law of the ICTY, ICTR, and SCSL regarding sexual violence in light of UN Security Council Resolution 1820 (2009). *See Review of the Sexual Violence Elements of the Judgments of the International Criminal Tribunal for the Former Yugoslavia, the International Criminal Tribunal for Rwanda, and the Special Court for Sierra Leone in the Light of Security Council Resolution 1820*, http://www.icty.org/x/file/Outreach/sv_files/DPKO_report_sexual_violence.pdf.

How Are Perpetrators Held Accountable?

Perpetrators must understand that they are not immune from prosecutions and punishment. Impunity must be eradicated—it is not enough to say "addressed." As a judge who has dealt with sexual violence in the domestic courts and as war crimes and crimes against humanity, I believe that impunity can be tackled by charging, indicting, and giving a fair trial to those who perpetrate abuse and those who permit, condone, or fail to punish people under their command or control who practice sexual and gender-based violence.

Why did prosecutions not happen earlier in the tribunals? Failure to prosecute sexual violence has evoked explanations that women do not want to give evidence or to relive trauma or embarrassment. In some societies and cultures, a woman does not want it known that she has been sexually molested. The knowledge of sexual abuse can lead to a woman being ostracized from her community; she may be unable to find a marriage partner or, if she is married, become divorced or otherwise alienated from her family. Certainly, some women and girls find it traumatic to admit that sexual abuse has happened and to relive the experience by giving evidence in court, particularly if they are subject to strenuous cross-examination that challenges their credibility and personal history. International tribunals, including the ICTY, ICTR, and SCSL, have rules of evidence and procedure that state that credibility or character cannot be inferred by reason of a victim or witness's prior or subsequent conduct.[42] But not all domestic jurisdictions have such evidentiary protection of victims or witnesses.

In my experience, a paternalist attitude—"we do not want to upset those poor women so we will not put them through evidence"—is not what women want to hear. Women victims want justice that includes seeing their assailants punished and reparations. Witnesses also appreciate the chance to speak out. A woman witness in *Prosecutor v. Brima et al.* spoke with feeling and dignity when thanking the SCSL for the opportunity that she had been given to tell "the world" of the cruel gang rape of herself and her daughter.[43] That statement was made after, and despite, a lengthy cross-examination.

Victims and representative groups have urged that charges involving sexual violence against women be preferred in criminal indictments. For example, in the International Criminal Court case of *Prosecutor v. Lubanga,* there was lobbying by victims' groups to have sexual violence counts added to the indictment. The effort was not successful, but it is indicative of the growing voices of victims. Likewise, in the Extraordinary Chambers of the Courts of Cambodia in Case 2 *Prosecutor v. Nuon Chea et al.,* victims' representatives sought to have the indictment amended to include counts of forced marriage as a crime against humanity.

---

42 Rule 96(iv) of Rules of Procedure and Evidence of SCSL provides: "Credibility, character or predisposition to sexual availability of a victim or witness cannot be inferred by reason of sexual nature of the prior or subsequent conduct of a victim or witness."

43 *Supra* note 33.

The argument that victims are reluctant to come forward because they are reluctant to acknowledge sexual abuse can also apply to sexual violence against men and boys in conflict. There have been no convictions for crimes of sexual violence against men in international war crimes tribunals, even though the statutes of the ad hoc and hybrid tribunals are gender neutral. The original indictment against Charles Taylor charged him with counts of sexual violence against men and women. It was amended to charge crimes of sexual violence (rape, sexual slavery, and outrages against personal dignity) against women and girls in several districts of Sierra Leone. However, in her final submission, the prosecutor asked the court to return verdicts for sexual violence against men. Given that the evidence had closed and that sexual violence against men was not charged in any of the counts for which Taylor was indicted, it would have been contrary to Taylor's fair trial rights to accede to that submission. However, if sexual violence against men and boys is acknowledged as a crime that arises in conflict, then there is no valid legal reason why indictments cannot be preferred against perpetrators. The explanation that witnesses do not want to relive the trauma can also apply to men and women who were victims of other forms of violence. The sight of male witnesses shouting and weeping as they described the abduction, mutilation, and abuse they suffered at the hands of rebels in Sierra Leone will haunt me forever.

To return convictions in criminal trials, convincing and relevant evidence must be adduced at the hearing. Evidence is the vital element in any trial and calls for investigators and prosecutors who are experienced in taking statements from victims, as well as interpreters who are sensitive to what is being said and who properly convey what the witness says. Failure to interpret properly and to adhere to the wording of the original statement can lead to a challenge to the credibility of a witness. Investigators, lawyers, and judges must be sensitive to the cultural backgrounds of the victims and witness. A witness may be precluded from using certain words because of a cultural taboo and therefore may avoid using such words altogether or may use another word that has a different meaning when interpreted. For example, in the SCSL, a victim of sexual violence said, "he used me as his wife" or "he used me" when questioned about what a rebel soldier did to her. A witness describing the violence perpetrated upon her used the word "anus" because (it was explained to the Trial Chamber) cultural attitudes precluded her from using the word "vagina." A word may be common in several languages but its meaning may vary depending on the language of the speaker—for example, in *Prosecutor v. Brima et al.,* the interpreter repeated the word "mate" used by a witness speaking Krio. In Krio, "mate" means a co-wife, not a friend or fellow worker, as it does in England. The witness was talking about another wife of her husband.

Medical evidence is also relevant and can be of corroborative evidentiary value in criminal trials. Forensic medical information that can be readily understood by the lawyers, the accused, and the judges can be persuasive in a trial. The SCSL has heard evidence from doctors retained by the Forum for African Women Educationalists (FAWE). They had compiled records of the injuries suffered by those victims of sexual violence whom they treated and an explanation of the cause of those injuries. The patients and doctors later agreed to allow some records to be adduced in evidence. FAWE devised forms to be completed by an examining medical professional that can be submitted as evidence in criminal trials of persons charged with sexual offenses in domestic courts. In the Democratic Republic of Congo, Physicians for Human Rights (PHR) devised a form that a medical practitioner can complete describing an injury and stating what caused it. PHR has also developed a dictionary of medical terms to help lawyers and judges to understand what has been recorded. The intention is to enable the mobile courts sitting where the sexual crimes were alleged to have occurred to have forensic evidence available at hearings.

Coupled with the belief in some fighting factions that sexual violence enacted on victims of conflict is an entitlement of vanquishing soldiers is a lack of respect for the status of women and girls in some societies and a disregard for their rights and the integrity of their person. This attitude was brought home to me in a trial in Papua New Guinea. Three young men were charged with the rape of a very young girl they saw working in her family's field. When asked why they raped her, one defendant shrugged disparagingly and said, "Because she was there."

Antiquated attitudes in the domestic courts must also change. I have heard rape described by a member of a judiciary (not my own) as "assault with a friendly weapon," an expression that he thought amusing. The perpetuation of myths such as "rape is easily alleged and hard to disprove" in national justice systems leads to a perception that proving the crime of rape requires a different standard of evidentiary proof than do other criminal offenses. Many domestic courts require that the prosecution produce a forensic medical report when rape or sexual abuse is alleged. This is not necessarily a statutory requirement but rather a practice that has been adopted and applied over so many years that it has become institutionalized and is considered vital if a prosecutrix's evidence is to be accepted.

Yet the issue should really be the credibility of the witness and the evidence. Decisions made by war crimes tribunals show that a witness's account of a sexual assault will not automatically be rejected if there is no contemporaneously recorded medical evidence or early complaint by the victim. War crime tribunals hear evidence from witnesses about events that happened years before, when there were no police to make a complaint to or doctors to provide an urgent forensic medical report.

There has been a slow erosion of discriminatory attitudes about evidence in sexual violence cases. In particular, the International Association of Women Judges (IAWJ) has done much to promote gender equality and raise awareness about discriminatory attitudes in Africa, the Pacific, Asia, and the Americas. With the Global Leadership for Women, the IAWJ has promoted gender equality before the courts by educating and raising awareness of international law decisions and their impact on domestic jurisdictions.

Prosecutions for sexual violence as war crimes and crimes against humanity will not solely eradicate a feeling of impunity among perpetrators. Combatants must be educated that women, girls, and men are not the spoils of war whom vanquishing troops can abduct or rape with impunity. Those who order and command soldiers must be held accountable and know that the laws of war, in particular the Geneva Conventions, mean that they could be held responsible for the actions of their troops. The doctrine of superior responsibility has been spelled out in the international criminal tribunals and in domestic courts. For example, in Sierra Leone the International Military Training Program undertook training in this regard, including education on the laws of war and the Geneva Conventions. This included laws prohibiting violence against civilians.

Likewise, peacekeepers must be trained. The defense counsel in *Prosecutor v. Charles Ghankay Taylor* adduced evidence (including video footage) of attacks on civilians by ECOMOG (Economic Community of West African States Monitoring Group) peacekeepers in Sierra Leone.

Conclusion

As long as combatants believe that they can abuse civilians, abuse will continue. However, there is growing acknowledgment that sexual violence in conflict zones or wartime cannot be condoned any more than sexual violence in peacetime is condoned. There are promising signs of improvement.

Trends include an increased awareness among the public, political leaders, and the legal profession of the importance of prosecuting leaders who permit or condone the criminal activity of the troops under their command. There is an increasing awareness of the importance of training judges, investigators, medical witnesses, and interpreters to deal with sexual violence crimes. It is vital to teach armies and peacekeepers to respect the laws of war and the Geneva Conventions. All participants in the justice system must be dedicated to ensuring that sexual violence in conflict is no longer condoned.

PART V

Improving Access to Justice

14
The Ministério Público of the State of Minas Gerais and the ADR Experience

Danielle de Guimarães Germano Arlé and Luciano Luz Badini Martins

A porta da verdade estava aberta,
mas só deixava passar meia pessoa de cada vez.

(The door of truth was open,
but, each time, only half a person could pass through it.)

— From "A Verdade Dividida" (The Divided Truth), by Carlos Drummond de Andrade, one of the greatest Brazilian poets, from the state of Minas Gerais

Although the use of alternative dispute resolution (ADR) methods may be familiar to many readers, the way in which ADR is employed in Brazil, most notably at the Ministério Público,[1] deserves to be spotlighted. In particular, the use of ADR by the Ministério Público of the State of Minas Gerais (MPMG) helps highlight one of the goals of the Global Forum on Law, Justice and Development: the implementation of the science of delivery.

The Regulation of ADR in Brazil

In the Federative Republic of Brazil, there are no laws that specifically treat or regulate ADR methods. There are some laws on arbitration; on conciliation, which in many cases is treated in the Code of Civil Procedures; and on specific negotiations, which can take place at the Administrative Council for Economic Defense,[2] between the federal government and companies that violate free market laws. Still, there are no laws clearly stating that ADR can be used in Brazil.

Notwithstanding this situation, it is important to note that in Brazil, as in many countries that observe the rule of law, while some people may think that

---

1 The authors have kept the name of the institution in Portuguese (the language of Brazil), instead of using a direct translation ("Public Ministry") to emphasize its unique and broader role in the Brazilian constitutional system in comparison with other countries. Although a public institution, it is totally independent of and unattached to any branch of the government and possesses an unusually diverse range of attributes in its role as "society's attorney." Its functions are explained throughout the text.

2 In Portuguese, Conselho Administrativo de Defesa Econômica (CADE).

the use of ADR is not legitimate, it is in fact strongly supported by principles contained in the Federal Constitution.[3]

One constitutional principle that upholds the possibility of the use of ADR methods in Brazil is access to justice. This constitutional guarantee should be understood as each person's right to have access to an effective solution for his or her problem. It should be interpreted as a guarantee of access not only to the established judicial system but also to any of the multiple ways to effectively resolve a conflict. To have access to justice is to have available all the possible ways to attain real justice. The use of ADR in other countries and in private institutions has produced so many positive results that Brazil's "Judicial Power," through a National Council of Justice regulatory act in 2010, established that every member-state of Brazil must have judicial mediation as one of the possible methods offered to parties in conflict resolution. (The independent functions of the Brazilian republican state are distinguished as "Powers," and they are here termed the "Executive Power," the "Legislative Power," and the "Judicial Power.") Also, in 2012, the federal government, through its Ministry of Justice, created a School of Mediation and Conciliation (ENAM, the acronym based on its Portuguese name, Escola Nacional de Mediação e Conciliação).

In short, although there is no specific law on ADR, the Judicial Power has determined that each of its tribunals has to offer judicial mediation and conciliation to parties that want to use those methods of conflict resolution.

The Name of the Rose

In the final years of the 16th century, Shakespeare's Juliet famously declared:

> What's in a name? That which we call a rose
> By any other name would smell as sweet.

Her observation remains as true today as it ever was.

The MPMG prefers to call the rose "tratamento adequado de conflitos" (adequate dispute treatment; ADT), but in essence, what the institution applies are the methods of ADR, albeit adapted to the local context.

What Distinguishes the Ministério Público's Rose?

Some characteristics of the Ministério Público and the way it, as an institution, uses ADR methods, are unique. This chapter explains this uniqueness and seeks to inspire those who face similar situations when dealing with conflicts in which ADR can be applied.

---

3 The authors call Brazil's Constitution "Federal" because each of the 27 member-states also has a constitution; these state-level constitutions are subordinated to the federal one.

The Ministério Público of Brazil

Functions. The Ministério Público is a public institution whose members are in charge of ensuring that the law is applied. It operates independently from the three powers of government. The institution comprises public prosecutors, called "members," and civil servants who assist the prosecutors and perform administrative functions but, because they are not prosecutors, are not referred to as "members." The prosecutors' main job is to uphold justice. Put simply, Brazilian prosecutors can be defined as society's attorneys. However, the Ministério Público functions not just in the area of criminal law; it also protects civil rights, including those concerning the environment, health, education, anticorruption, governance, and consumers.

The prosecutors' duty is to bring criminal charges and try criminal cases, but they also can request the acquittal of a charge if during a trial they become convinced of a defendant's innocence. Prosecutors have the last word on whether criminal charges are filed, except when Brazilian law permits civil prosecution. In those rare cases, the prosecutors act as *custos legis* (law supervisors) and ensure that justice is actually delivered.

Besides that important task, Article 129 of Brazil's Federal Constitution establishes that it is part of the Ministério Público's job to protect society in many of the cases in which collective rights are involved. Another of the institution's missions is to protect children, teenagers, elderly people, and any others who are unable to give genuine consent.

Article 127 of the constitution states that the Ministério Público "is a permanent institution, essential to the jurisdictional function of the State, and it is its duty to defend the juridical order, the democratic regime and the inalienable social and individual interests."[4]

The Ministério Público, an institution that has enormous popular credibility, is one of the institutions that generated the "Brazilian Spring" (a popular protest movement that reached its apex in June 2013), precisely because there was a bill whose objective was to change the Federal Constitution to reduce some of the functions of the Ministério Público. Millions of people throughout the country went to the streets in protest, and the bill was ultimately voted down by federal legislators.

The Various Ministérios Públicos. As in the United States, some Brazilian institutions are federal and others exist at the state level. The Ministério Público of Brazil consists of multiple branches: the federal Ministério Público, where all criminal and noncriminal matters involving the federation are treated, and the 27 state-level Ministérios Públicos (one for each of the federation's member-states), where all the other issues are dealt with (i.e., crimes that do not involve the national interest, as well as state-level civil matters).

---

4 Official translation by the Federal Supreme Court (Supremo Tribunal Federal; STF), http://www.stf.jus.br/repositorio/cms/portalStfInternacional/portalStfSobreCorte_en_us/anexo/constituicao_ingles_3ed2010.pdf.

The MPMG is one of these 27 state-level Ministérios Públicos. The state of Minas Gerais is located in the southeast of Brazil and has an estimated population of 20.5 million.[5] The state's main economic activity is mining (Minas Gerais, loosely translated, means "general mining"); its gross domestic product (GDP) in 2012 was US$199,726 million.[6]

An Independent Institution. The Ministério Público is considered by the Federal Constitution completely independent. It is not part of the Executive Power at the federal, state, or municipal levels. Nor is it part of the Legislative Power or the Judicial Power. So, in which of these three powers of the republic does it fit? The answer: in none of them. The Ministério Público, in its present form, emerged in 1988, the year in which the Federal Constitution was proclaimed. And it was created as an entirely autonomous body, so that it could protect all Brazilian citizens regardless of the identity of the violator of their rights. Members of the Ministério Público can file a lawsuit against any of the Powers of the republic if they violate (by acting or by being absent from their obligation to act) any civil right of a citizen.

At this point, Brazil's Ministério Público becomes different from other public prosecution services that exist in other countries. It is important to point out this feature because it is one of the reasons that, in Brazil, prosecutors believe that it is their duty to help people obtain access to justice in all possible ways, not just through the judicial system.

How Does One Become a Member of the Ministério Público? All members of the Ministério Público are public prosecutors. Individuals who want to join the Ministério Público must already have established themselves as legal professionals and must demonstrate their competence in a meritocratic selection process. Being a prosecutor is not a political decision. Prosecutors are not elected by the population. If a citizen wants to be a prosecutor, he or she has to earn a law degree and have at least three years of experience in a legal practice. Applying for the job means undergoing very demanding and competitive examinations, which include legal, medical, and psychological tests, both oral and written. Candidates with the best test results become prosecutors, following a period of rigorous training. This training is conducted by the Ministério Público and includes practical and theoretical classes. At the MPMG, for example, the process of selecting new prosecutors can last eight months. Of 3,523 applicants in 2013, only 33 were accepted; they then went through a two-month training course at the MPMG's institutional school. During this course, the new prosecutors are prepared to deal with the problems they will face in their work and in society. Upon completion, they go to offices in different parts of the state of Minas Gerais, where they put into practice what they

---

5 *See* Instituto Brasileiro De Geografia e Estatítica, http://www.ibge.gov.br/estadosat/perfil.php?sigla=mg.

6 *See* http://en.wikipedia.org/wiki/list_of_brazilian_federative_units_by_gross_domestic_product.

have learned. Their performance is periodically evaluated during their first two years of employment.

At the time of writing, the MPMG had 1,049 active prosecutors, 2,857 civil servants assisting them, and 1,919 interns, who also help with legal and administrative duties.

A member's career typically consists of two sequential steps: first, one serves as a "promotor de justiça," a public prosecutor who can act on criminal and noncriminal cases before a judge of the first degree; subsequently, one becomes a "procurador de justiça," a public prosecutor who can act on criminal and noncriminal cases before a court (judges of the second degree, or courts of appeal).

Members of the Ministério Público do not become judges or public defenders; in Brazil, these professions follow completely different and separate career paths.

Again, to ensure operational independence, the nomination of members to the Ministério Público does not depend in any way on any of the three Powers; neither the governor (of a member-state) nor the president (of Brazil) chooses the members of the Ministério Público.

What Is the Difference between ADT and ADR?

The right of access to justice is a right that is guaranteed in Brazil's Federal Constitution (i.e., it is one of the most important rights), and filing lawsuits through the Judicial Power is regarded as only one way to resolve conflicts. Hence Brazil's readiness to use ADR. But to avoid using the words "alternative" and "resolution" in the English-based ADR, "tratamento adequado de conflitos" (adequate dispute treatment; ADT) was born.

The word for "alternative" in Portuguese means that there is a choice between two or more options. But, in Portuguese, "alternative" can also mean one thing being chosen as a second option, a Plan B, and one of the Ministério Público's goals in applying ADT methods is to start generating new values, so that when a citizen has a problem, he or she does not think first about going to court. It is important to nurture the idea that a citizen faced with a conflict should not ask a stranger to decide the best way to resolve it. Instead, the person should first think about solving his or her own conflicts.

For these reasons, the authors of this chapter chose the word "adequate" to supersede the idea, already ingrained in society, that the use of dispute settlement methods is something that should be undertaken only when one does not have access to the judiciary. Our purpose is to promote the opposite logic. We want to clearly convey the idea that conflicts can be resolved without constantly knocking on the door of the Judicial Power.

"ADT" is the term being used in Brazil by many institutions, including the Judicial Power. Also, the word "treatment" was chosen based on the prosecutors' mission, which is to protect society. "To treat" can be something larger than "to resolve." And "treatment" can be different from "resolution." In the majority of cases, nonadversarial methods are effective in resolving a case, but when they are not, they still have done their job, because even when a settlement is not reached, the conflict has still been treated. And the treatment consists of making the conflict more bearable (until it can be presented for a judge's decision, if a lawsuit ultimately has to be filed) and of teaching the parties that respectful conversation is possible.

If a conflict is viewed as a process, the value of "treatment" becomes more apparent, because one treats the conflict in totality, rather than focusing on solving a crisis.

Nonetheless, the well-known English term "alternative dispute resolution" is used in this chapter instead of "adequate dispute treatment," so as not to confuse readers, most of whom are more familiar with "ADR" than "ADT."

The Use of ADR Methods

Within the MPMG, ADR is seen as one of the ways in which all citizens can be guaranteed the effective resolution of their conflicts. The use of ADR is not a way to sidestep the judiciary. It is a way to give citizens an opportunity to resolve their conflicts by agreement, by moving toward solutions that will meet the interests of all the parties involved, before asking a judge to decide, as a third person, who is right and who is wrong—the well-known win-lose sentence. (The Judicial Power of the state of Minas Gerais, it should be noted, is effective in solving matters that need to be resolved by a third, public party—the judge—an authority who will decide how the conflict will be resolved.) It is also a way to build a more pacific society, because the use of ADR methods has the implicit objective of teaching people how they can resolve their own conflicts at home, at work, with their neighbors, and with others.

With this purpose in mind, the MPMG has invested in training all of its members in ADR methods. Moreover, for the first time in the history of this institution, citizens who intend to apply for a career as a prosecutor will have to study the subject, because they will have to answer questions about it during the selection process. This is a way to privilege and encourage the study of such an important matter to the country.

Negotiation

Negotiation of Civil Matters, Including Environmental Issues.

The Federal Constitution and other laws allow prosecutors to use all possible ways to protect the many fundamental rights within the purview of the Ministério Público. Besides investigating violations of protected rights, a prosecutor can file a lawsuit to pursue either protection (asking the judge for a decision, if necessary) or negotiation with the violator of the right.

Scholars have made two arguments. One is that negotiation is not possible in Ministério Público cases because, as a public institution, the Ministério Público is not equal to the other party involved in the conflict. The second argument is that negotiations are not based on the will of the parties, because if an agreement is not reached, a lawsuit can still be filed.

Concerning the first of these arguments, the Ministério Público is indeed not equal to other parties because, as a public and special institution, it has some prerogatives that private entities and other institutions do not have. However, "not equal" does not mean "no balance." Not being equal does not mean that it is impossible to work together in a balanced way to consider the interests of everyone involved.

Concerning the second argument, filing a lawsuit is not a prerogative of the Ministério Público; a lawsuit can be filed by anyone who feels that his or her civil rights have been violated.

Members of the Ministério Público believe that knowing how to negotiate based on interests, not power, can lead to balanced negotiations and that through negotiation, legitimate, sustainable agreements can be reached.

The Brazilian Public Civil Action Law lists the Ministério Público as one of the qualified representative plaintiffs of these actions. However, before starting an action, the Ministério Público can try to reach an agreement with the offender (of an environmental right, for example). This agreement is called a "term of conduct adjustment" (TCA). The Public Civil Action Law does not mention the word "negotiation" itself, but as Shakespeare's Juliet might say, "TCA is just another name for a rose."

The Ministério Público cannot, as society's attorney, agree to "give away" the rights of the Brazilian people during the negotiation period. Giving away is not what good collaborative or integrative negotiation is about. However, as has been done in many cases, the Ministério Público can agree to the conditions under which these societal rights will be respected by the offender. Here again, negotiating does not mean giving away. It means finding ways to address all interests. For example, in a conflict between, say, society's interests and the interests of a mining company, what can be done is to find common or complementary interests of both parties and to work on them, bearing in mind that the company itself is clearly also part of society and the economy.

In the cases in which the Ministério Público can act, a settlement means (a) a faster solution for society, (b) a more effective solution, and (c) a solution that recognizes the importance of the interests of all parties of a conflict (whether persons or companies).

The MPMG tries to implement methods learned from the well-known Program on Negotiation,[7] as well as from transformative mediation[8] and narrative mediation.[9] These concepts are better applied to mediation than to negotiation, but they also can be very useful when sitting down at the negotiation table.

Civil Negotiation Cases

A TCA is a kind of out-of-court settlement whereby a party (a person or a company) that puts collective assets—environmental quality, for example—at risk or causes harm to them assumes an obligation to cease the unlawful activity, to adapt its conduct to the law, and to repair the damage.

The use of TCAs has contributed to removing the red tape from the usually complex processes of environmental conflict resolution. Court disputes can drag on for years, but TCAs offer speedier resolution of disputes and avoid contributing to the backlog of unresolved cases. (In 2013, 13.7 million lawsuits were filed, but only 12.2 million were concluded in courts of first instance, leaving a backlog of 1.5 million lawsuits.)[10] In the environmental area especially, the "effective problem-solving" role of the Ministério Público overshadows the "court demanding" role, and environmental conflicts are normally resolved without the intervention of the judiciary by defining terms and conditions that are consolidated in the TCA.

---

7 "The Program on Negotiation (PON) is a consortium program of Harvard University, the Massachusetts Institute of Technology, and Tufts University, and serves as an interdisciplinary research center dedicated to developing the theory and practice of negotiation and dispute resolution in a range of public and private settings. PON's mission includes nurturing the next generation of negotiation teachers and scholars, helping students become more effective negotiators, and providing a forum for the discussion of ideas." *See* the Harvard Law School's *Program on Negotiation* website, http://www.pon.harvard.edu/.

8 "Two main goals of transformative mediation are to empower the disputing parties, and to enhance each party's recognition of the other. Recognition and empowerment are then key concepts in the theory of transformative mediation. To empower the disputing parties, the mediator seeks to 'strengthen people's capacity to analyze situations and make effective decisions for themselves.'" These goals reflect two basic premises of transformative mediation theory. First, the authors claim that mediation is more than just a tool for settling disputes. Mediation has the potential to produce valuable transformations in the character of the participants. That is, participation in the mediation process has the potential to make individuals more empowered and responsive to others. Second, the authors claim that this transformative potential can best be realized by mediators who use certain attitudes and practices to guide the mediation process. *See* Joseph P. Folger & Robert A. Baruch Bush, *Transformative Mediation and Third-Party Intervention: Ten Hallmarks of a Transformative Approach to Practice*, 13(4) Mediation Q. 263–78 (Summer 1996), http://www.colorado.edu/conflict/transform/folger.htm.

9 "Cobb investigates and critiques current concepts of empowerment, and current mediation practices designed to empower parties. She then suggests a narrative understanding of empowerment, and describes several mediation practices which follow from the narrative approach." *See* Sara Cobb, *Empowerment and Mediation: A Narrative Perspective*, 9(3) Negotiation J. 245–55 (July 1993), http://www.colorado.edu/conflict/transform/cobb.htm. Summary by Tanya Glaser. Copyright ©1997 by the Conflict Research Consortium.

10 *See* http://www.cnj.jus.br/images/imprensa/apresentacao_secretario_geral.pdf.

To expand the MPMG's effective conflict-solving performance, which increases the institution's level of efficiency, emphasis has been placed on theoretical refinement and implementation of a set of techniques aimed specifically at the resolution of environmental conflicts involving the defense of collective ("meta-individual") rights and inalienable rights.

In practice, priority is given to remediation of the damaged environmental area in natura and in situ. In the event that a complete or partial remediation proves impossible, the resolution of the conflict is guided by the definition of in natura and ecological compensation, which involves repairing the environmental damage through restoration or improving another similar area.

Finally, if environmental remediation or the establishment of ecological compensation is impossible, financial compensation will be established as an indirect way to repair damage. In this context, methods of assessment of environmental damage in terms of money should be used just as a reference. It is important that the methods should not aim at generating direct profit for the environmental systems, in accordance with the determinations of the Brazilian Constitution and the National Environmental Policy.

Transforming the multiple, cumulative, and synergistic impacts of environmental damage into monetary values is difficult. This difficulty is not due to lack of valuation methods but to the variety and diversity of damage caused and of methods of quantifying it. This situation creates legal uncertainty, which hinders the adoption of agreements because of the frequent vagueness of the clauses of the settlement estimating financial compensation for the irreparable damaged caused.

In conclusion, giving priority to ecological compensation has proved to be the most appropriate way to resolve many socio-environmental conflicts. This method takes into account both the need to recover the damaged area and the interest of the party responsible for the damage in wanting to preserve its good institutional image.

Following this line of thought, the agreements in recent cases concluded by the MPMG have had ecological compensation as their priority, instead of exclusive financial compensation. This approach has enabled, for example, the creation of protected areas donated by the mining sector as compensation for irreparable environmental damages. This adjustment had the necessary official approval of the state government. Another good example, dealing with the urban environment, involved the construction of roads as compensation by real estate companies found to have impaired urban mobility in the building of a shopping center and multifamily dwelling units.

Another innovative form of ecological compensation, involving payment for environmental services (PES), has been given to farmers for the following actions: conserving areas of environmental significance within their rural farmland; recovering historical sites, assets, or works of irreplaceable cultural value; constructing roads that divert traffic away from a historic city center; creating private reserves of natural heritage; establishing wild animal sorting centers;[11] relocating a historic building from an area set apart for mining to another site within city boundaries to be transformed into a museum; and expanding the boundaries of permanent preservation areas and forest reserves within farms.

These initiatives, like many others throughout Brazil, deserve to be widely disclosed and discussed because they represent important innovations in fulfilling out-of-court resolutions of environmental conflicts.

Negotiations in Criminal Matters

In Brazil—unlike in the United States, for example—the Ministério Público has limited bargaining power when it comes to criminal offenses. It can engage in such bargaining only when criminal law permits or when a public prosecutor proposes the application of a penalty (which can never be imprisonment) prior to the criminal trial itself. The proposal is offered in the preliminary hearing and, if denied, can be repeated at the beginning of the trial hearing. If accepted by the defendant, it cannot be offered again in the event of a second infringement. This kind of proposal is not essentially a penal mediation, as in the American judicial system.

Mediation

As discussed earlier, the Ministério Público has many functions, all of which converge to protect the most important rights and interests of society. When defending these rights, the Ministério Público can act either as a party (filing a lawsuit as the legitimate plaintiff of the action) or as a custos legis. As a custos legis, the Ministério Público acts not as a party but as a surveyor and has to express an opinion about the case. This occurs only in judicial cases allowed by law, or where an incapable person is involved.

At the MPMG, there is an understanding that if, by law, some rights or interests require intervention, it is better if the institution intervenes before the conflict escalates to the point of going to the Judicial Power.

In many conflicts, the more promptly a prosecutor can intervene, the more promptly a solution can be found. That is why the Ministério Público treats some conflicts with mediation before the parties involved pursue a judicial resolution.

Mediation is one ADR method, and it can be defined as assisted negotiation, where a third-party neutral (the mediator) helps the parties involved in a conflict to generate options and choose the best solution for that conflict. Mediation in the Ministério Público is different from judicial mediation, which starts when a party goes to the Judicial Power looking for a solution

---

11 Wild animal sorting centers (Centros de Triagem de Animais) are places managed or supervised by public environmental institutions, with the goal of treating rescued wild animals and reintroducing them into the environment.

for the conflict. It bears repeating that the Ministério Público is not part of the Judicial Power.

In Brazil, the only act that regulates mediation is a resolution issued by the National Council of Justice that explains how a judicial mediation should be conducted. However, when it comes to out-of-court mediation, such as the type promoted by the Ministério Público, there is still no regulatory law or normative act. In the MPMG, the creation of a normative act is under discussion, but it has not yet been published. In the eyes of the Ministério Público, the use of either mediation or negotiation is based on the constitutional guarantee of access to justice, and as such, no other law or regulation is necessary.

When promoting mediation, the Ministério Público draws on global concepts and accepted procedures, applying internationally accepted techniques, including the Harvard, transformative, and narrative methods. All prosecutors at the MPMG are trained in mediation, which makes them more efficient in all their work, not only when working on mediation cases.

Conclusion

In a world of more than 7 billion people, the MPMG believes that the only way to achieve a peaceful society is to learn to respect all differences. Those who are not part of one's own community must still be recognized as human beings. By recognizing the existence of the other as a different person, one recognizes one's own identity. However, this recognition does not mean that the other should be discriminated against or segregated. It means, instead, that society is formed by a rich diversity of cultures and that all people can learn from one another.

15

ICT-Driven Strategies for Reforming Access to Justice Mechanisms in Developing Countries

KARIM BENYEKHLEF, EMMANUELLE AMAR, AND VALENTIN CALLIPEL

In the wake of an unprecedented period of mobile technology dissemination in developing countries, notably through the use of cell phones and other information and communication technology (ICT) innovations, it has become possible to use those technologies to eliminate or greatly reduce barriers to access to justice in those countries. This recent spread of mobile technology in developing countries has literally transformed communication habits. The World Bank estimates that there were 6.8 billion mobile cellular subscriptions worldwide in 2013.[1] When it comes to the justice system, one of the biggest challenges or barriers for people living in developing countries remains physically accessing the justice system. In this context, one has to reflect on the role played by mobile technologies and other ICT initiatives in providing a solution to the global problem of poor access to justice. For instance, with the mobile technologies available today, it is possible to use text messaging to inform clients of the date of their hearing because in some parts of the world people still have no postal address at which they can be reached, but they usually have access to a mobile phone. This chapter argues that the justice system should capitalize on this spread of mobile technologies and that cyberjustice, through the use of ICT, can reduce the costs and delays of the judicial process and provide better access to justice through the science of delivery.

Two concepts—"cyberjustice" and "science of delivery"—that are frequently used in this chapter should be defined at the outset "Cyberjustice," simply put, "refers both to the integration of information and communication technologies into dispute resolution processes and to the networking of all stakeholders in the informational chain for judicial cases."[2] With the networking of virtually all actors of the judiciary, cyberjustice contributes to an integrated justice system. Cyberjustice initiatives include a wide range of actions such as community radio, text messaging, videoconferencing, digitization, and networking. The "science of delivery" is a multidisciplinary approach aimed at gathering and distributing knowledge that countries can use to get

---

1 World Bank, *The Little Data Book on Information and Communication Technology* (World Bank 2013).

2 François Senécal & Karim Benyekhlef, *Groundwork for Assessing the Legal Risks of Cyberjustice,* 7(1) Can. J. L. & Tech. 41, 44 (2009).

delivery in a specific local context.[3] In the legal field, this approach explores "how law and justice concepts, tools and knowledge can be used to improve development delivery and help translate the values of voice, social contract and accountability into development impact."[4]

The first part of this chapter makes the case that by using a methodology based on two pillars, modularity and collaboration (both comprising many different elements, which are explained throughout this chapter), ICT innovations can play an important role in providing effective access to justice in developing countries. Since 2011, the Cyberjustice Laboratory, a nonprofit research center affiliated with the University of Montreal, has used this methodology to develop successful prototypes[5] in the fields of online dispute resolution and modernization of judicial proceedings. The second part of the chapter argues that the World Bank's Global Forum on Law, Justice and Development and its partners, as well as the Community of Practice on Alternative Dispute Resolution (which operates under the auspices of the Global Forum), through their multidisciplinary approach, are effective platforms for developing ICT-driven strategies to modernize and reform mechanisms for access to justice in developing countries. The second part also highlights how mobile technologies can have an impact on transitional justice,[6] thereby illustrating how ICT initiatives can effectively improve access to justice. This chapter thus provides food for thought about solutions to improve access to justice in developing countries and stimulate the use of ICT in the judicial process of those countries; this chapter does not try to offer precise solutions, because, as the modular and collaborative methodology points out, any solution must be tailored to the needs and circumstances of each country.

---

3 World Bank, *Law, Justice and Development Week 2013—Concept Note*, http://siteresources.worldbank.org/INTLAWJUSTICE/Resources/LJDWeek2013_ConceptNote.pdf.

4 *Id.*

5 These prototypes include an Online Dispute Resolution Platform; an Interface for courtroom management that allows the networking of all actors in the trial and allows them to control the courtroom; a digital agreement as to the conduct of the proceeding (Entente sur le déroulement de l'instance; EDI) in accordance with the rules of the Code of Civil Procedure of Quebec; the *Metadata Cyberjustice Management*, a tool that allows for the defining and categorizing of information being attached to files generated during a hearing for the purpose of indexing this information; and finally, a Moot Court application, a case management system designed to allow the electronic filing of memoranda during Moot Court activities hosted by the Université de Montréal's Faculty of Law. For more information about the Cyberjustice Laboratory and its ongoing projects, *see* Cyberjustice Laboratory, Software, available at http://www.cyberjustice.com/en/software-presentation/.

6 Transitional justice is used after situations of armed conflict or generalized violations of human rights in order to bridge the gap between peace and justice. "Transitional justice is a leading rite of modern political passage and draws upon both legal innovations and ritual acts that enable the passage between two orders—the predecessor and successor regimes." *See* Lisa J. Laplante & Kimberly Theidon, *Transitional Justice in Times of Conflicts: Colombia's Ley de Justicia y Paz*, 28 Mich. J. Intl. L. 49, 50 (2006–2007).

Using a Modular and Collaborative Methodology, the Model Chosen by the Cyberjustice Laboratory

Many of those involved in judicial processes and proceedings express deep dissatisfaction regarding costs and delays, which put the protection of the court system beyond the reach of many of who need access to it. These obstacles contribute to a lack of trust on the part of litigants in the judiciary as a whole.[7] This dissatisfaction provokes people to avoid formal justice and turn to alternative dispute resolution mechanisms. A recent survey, for example, asked people in France to identify cases in which they would prefer finding a negotiated solution or compromise rather than going to court. The results speak for themselves: 97 percent responded affirmatively in the case of troubles with their neighbors, 92 percent in the case of commercial disagreements, and 87 percent in the case of purchases made over the Internet;[8] a similar preference for negotiation and compromise over litigation was observed in Quebec.[9]

The computerization of judicial processes and the networking of stakeholders in the legal world, which constitute a vital part of the transition to cyberjustice and a more-integrated justice system, contribute to reducing the costs and delays of the judiciary process and hence improve access to justice as a whole. Activities such as using paper to present procedures, making multiple copies of documents to be sent to all parties, and requesting parties to be physically present in the courtroom all have a definite impact on the costs and delays of the judiciary process. Allowing for official documents to be sent to parties via e-mail, eliminating the need for parties to be physically present in the courtroom, and allowing testimony to be presented via videoconference, among other cyberjustice solutions, significantly contributes to improving access to justice by reducing delays and costs. However, successful cyberjustice initiatives remain the exception, and the attachment to paper and to parties' presence at all stages of a procedure remains the rule. In fact, some projects aim at developing technological solutions to make the judicial process more efficient and transparent, as was the case of "Courtroom 21," a project developed at the Center for Legal and Court Technology in the United States.[10] The aim of the project was to identify and evaluate technologies that would be useful to the judicial system. The Cyberjustice Laboratory goes farther; it tries to understand why some jurisdictions have successfully implemented high-tech case-management solutions,[11] while in other jurisdictions millions of dol-

---

7 E. Allan Lind & Tom R. Tyler, *The Social Psychology of Procedural Justice* (Plenum, 1988).

8 France, Ministère de la justice, Sous-direction de la statistique et des études—Secrétariat général, *Enquête: Opinions des Français sur la justice—2013*, 8 (2013).

9 The majority of average-income households in Québec (53 percent) said that they were in favor of finding alternative solutions to the courts. *See* Observatoire des services professionnels, *L'offre et la demande de services juridiques: Les besoins des ménages à revenus moyens* (2013).

10 For more information, *see* William & Mary Law School, Center for Legal and Court Technology, http://law.wm.edu/academics/intellectuallife/researchcenters/clct/.

11 For example, British Columbia's JUSTIN project. In 2004, British Columbia adopted electronic filing software—the Justice Information System, or JUSTIN—to manage records in

lars were invested without getting satisfactory results.[12] The failure of some ICT initiatives shows that implementing technological solutions for some of the judiciary's problems (such as costs and delays) is pointless if the parties refuse to use the technology.

The premise underlying the Cyberjustice Laboratory's research projects is that ICT solutions that respect and understand the human and sociolegal reasons for being apprehensive about using technologies will be implemented successfully, resulting in a reduction of costs and delays associated with the judiciary process. Accordingly, the Cyberjustice Laboratory is studying the legal parameters and sociocultural barriers to the adoption of technological solutions in the field of justice. In other words, it is important to understand that there are legal, cultural, psychological, and social reasons that can block the implementation of ICT solutions for reducing costs and delays. This chapter explains how using a modular and collaborative methodology can help surmount these obstacles.

This part of the chapter shows that ICT initiatives using a modular and collaborative methodology can contribute to the reduction of costs and delays in the judicial process, providing more effective access to justice[13] and a bona fide delivery of justice in emerging countries through the science of delivery.

The World Bank's conception of the science of delivery is composed of four basic features:

> First, delivery is about problem-solving with emphasis on context-specific solutions. Second, delivery is concerned with addressing social goals in complex and interpenetrating systems in a way that identifies capacity gaps as well as intervention points. Third, delivery is collaborative and interactive. Lastly, a future delivery science will necessarily be multidisciplinary and thus, will require expertise from various disciplines to measure results and triangulate data that will help discover what is driving success or failure.[14]

The modular and collaborative methodology advocated by the Cyberjustice Laboratory encompasses these four basic features of delivery described in the above quotation. Since 2011, the Cyberjustice Laboratory, with its team of 36 researchers and its international and multidisciplinary background, has been working on the identification of sociolegal barriers to the adoption of technological solutions in the justice system. The team has conducted many socio-legal observations, such as testing ICT tools and holding mock hearings, to evaluate new technologies that may be useful in modernizing the judicial

---

criminal matters. JUSTIN was later adapted to civil proceedings. *See* British Columbia Ministry of Justice, Integrated Corrections Operations Network (ICON) II Project, http://www.pssg.gov.bc.ca/corrections/about-us/technology.htm.

12 The Integrated Justice Project is discussed in the next section.

13 Nicolas Vermeys, *La cyberjustice et l'espace OHADA: Des outils virtuels pour une avancée réelle,* Journal Africain du droit des affaires, Numéro spécial 102, 104 (2013).

14 World Bank, *supra* note 3.

process and rethinking the justice system to meet the needs of individuals. The project's innovativeness lies in its capacity to make concrete socio-legal observations thanks to the development, in cooperation with the primary stakeholders in the justice community, of a new generation of open-code, interoperable software modules designed to facilitate dispute processing and resolution in ways that are adapted to the needs of users and legal actors. One of the main goals of the Cyberjustice Laboratory is to take advantage of technological advances to make the justice system more accessible and efficient.[15] To achieve this goal, the Cyberjustice Laboratory has chosen to use a modular and collaborative methodology. This methodology comprises many different elements, which are explained in the following sections after a brief clarification of why some past ICT initiatives have failed. This chapter thus sheds light on why this methodology, which is in the continuum of the science of delivery, would be effective for implementing ICT initiatives in developing countries.

Failure of Past Cyberjustice Initiatives

Before considering the development and implementation of new ICT initiatives in emerging countries, it is important to analyze and understand the reasons why some of the initiatives launched in North America have not been effective. Understanding the reasons behind these failures helps to ensure that the same mistakes will not be made again and that different methods will be used when implementing cyberjustice initiatives in developing countries.

With the growth of computer technology, many ICT initiatives have been launched to help courts ease the backlog of cases and improve access to justice for ordinary people. Unfortunately, many of these initiatives have failed, due mainly to high expectations, improper implementation of new technologies by the courts, and misidentification of the needs of stakeholders.

Prior ICT initiatives that were ineffective often used a technology-driven or top-down approach. In the context of cyberjustice, this approach refers to a complete overhaul of the system using new technologies. The approach requires a high initial investment and subsequent gap-filling measures. As many authors have stated, in a complete overhaul, there can be resistance from the main stakeholders because of a lack of willingness to learn a new system in a timely fashion.[16] This is exactly what happened with the Integrated Justice Project[17] in Ontario, where stakeholders and litigants were reluctant

---

15 Cyberjustice Laboratory, *The Project*, available at http://www.cyberjustice.ca/en/the-project.

16 Karim Benyekhlef & Nicolas Vermeys, *Buenas practicas en Applicaciones de Ciberjusticia*, in *Buenas practicas para la implementacion de soluciones tecnologicas en la administracion de justicia*, 29–49 (Antonio Caballero, Carlos Gregorio de Gracia, & Line Hammergren eds., IIJusticia 2011).

17 The Ontario project was launched in 1996 by the Ministry of the Attorney General and the Ministry of Public Safety and Security. "The objective of the Project was to improve the information flow in the justice system by streamlining existing processes and replacing older computer systems and paper-based information exchanges with new, compatible systems and technologies." *See* Office of the Provincial Auditor of Ontario, *Integrated Justice Project*,

to use the interesting technological solutions offered.[18] The reluctance of the main stakeholders was not due to an inability to develop appropriate technological solutions for the judicial process, but to psychological, social, political, and cultural barriers[19] that inhibited research, implementation, and the use of advanced ICT solutions. Thus, to get all parties on board, it is necessary to understand the barriers to the use of new technologies and find a way to circumvent them. Properly identifying the needs of the stakeholders to ensure the successful implementation of ICT initiatives is also essential.

The failure of some past ICT initiatives was also due in part to poor assessment of costs. This was especially true in cases involving complete system overhauls because, as with any project of significant size, the possibility of hidden costs always exists. When identifying costs, it is important to take into account not only the initial acquisition costs but also the potential costs in relation to expansion and upgrades. As new technology becomes available, it is crucial to take into account the hidden costs related to hardware and software upgrades.[20] Therefore, at the onset of a project, a significant cost-benefit analysis is helpful in avoiding any surprises, and contingency plans should be in place when finalizing a budget in order to alleviate any fears of future costs. Achieving a proper budget analysis is easier on smaller-scale projects or on pilot projects as advocated by the modular methodology.

In sum, the failure of cyberjustice initiatives implementing a technology-driven approach or undergoing a complete overhaul of the justice system occurred mainly because the stakeholders were not prepared for such huge changes and stakeholder needs were not properly identified. Furthermore, given the complexity of the justice system, finding an answer to the problems in a homogenous, simple manner is implausible. One of the answers to the complexity of the justice system can be found in modularity.

Modularity: A Definition

As previously discussed, past ICT initiatives failed because they tried to solve a complex situation using a single software solution in a technology-driven approach. For this reason, the Cyberjustice Laboratory advocates using an "incremental or modular approach where compatible and interconnecting technological solutions are found in order to address precise problems rather than to construct complex networks."[21] Another important aspect of the Cyberjustice Laboratory's work is that all the modules are developed in open-source code to facilitate the sharing and adaptability of those modules.

---

283 (Annual Rpt., 2003).

18 For more details, *see* Carl Baar, *Integrated Justice: Privatizing the Fundamentals*, 42(1) Can. Pub. Administration 42 (1999).

19 These aspects will be detailed later in this section.

20 Benyekhlef & Vermeys, *supra* note 16, at 12.

21 *Id.*, at 7.

The open-source code allows stakeholders to make the changes they consider necessary given their specific situations.[22]

The goal is to develop justice system–friendly software modules that will contribute to delivering better access to justice.[23] Therefore, it is important when developing those modules to make sure that they are compatible and complementary, ensuring a smooth transition to cyberjustice and avoiding overlapping issues.[24] To deliver better access to justice in developing countries, it would be useful to develop or use existing ICT solutions to create different modules or platforms that would allow, for example, the use of mobile phones for intake, referral, and case management.[25] Small-scale changes, made one at a time, enable ICT initiatives to be implemented effectively. Again, the purpose of this chapter is not to provide a precise ICT initiative for developing countries; rather, it suggests that the methodology used by the Cyberjustice Laboratory in the development of ICT initiatives in Canada could be used, where the context is found to be appropriate, in implementing and developing cyberjustice initiatives in these countries.

Nor is the purpose of this chapter to argue that the modular and collaborative methodology is a miracle solution to the problem of access to justice. The point is to take advantage of ICT innovations to improve access to justice everywhere, including in developing countries—and having a modular and collaborative tactic optimizes the implementation of those innovations. As Nicolas Vermeys argues in his article on cyberjustice and the Organization for the Harmonization in Africa of Business Law (OHADA), even in developed countries, few substantial investments have been made in the field of cyberjustice, which means that currently the gap between the North and the South is not significant.[26] It should be kept in mind that when implementing ICT initiatives in developing countries, attention must be focused on the specific context in which the initiatives are to be implemented, and that they must be adapted accordingly[27].

Identification of the Judiciary's Factual Needs

When developing a cyberjustice system or proposing an ICT initiative, it is essential to properly identify the needs of the stakeholders. Judiciary stakeholders have often been resistant to change; therefore, "the successful implementing of said change will necessarily require stakeholder approval. This approval

22 Cyberjustice Laboratory, *supra* note 15.

23 *Id.*

24 Benyekhlef & Vermeys, *supra* note 16, at 7.

25 Sean Martin McDonald, *Law in the Last Mile: The Potential of Mobile Integration into Legal Services* (blog entry, Leg. Info. Inst., Corn. U. L. Sch., Dec. 22, 2011), http://blog.law.cornell.edu/voxpop/2011/12/22/law-in-the-last-mile-the-potential-of-mobile-integration-into-legal-services/.

26 Vermeys, *supra* note 13, at 103.

27 Further explanations on the topic are found later in this section.

obviously hinges on whether or not the provided cyberjustice solution corresponds to the needs of each stakeholder."[28]

From the Cyberjustice Laboratory's point of view, implementation of a new technology should be done in a modular way to ensure that stakeholders are comfortable with the tool created for them. In this manner, wasteful technology and redundancy can be averted, and funds spent optimally.[29]

Generally speaking, ICT initiatives could help to meet some of the basic needs of the judicial system in Latin America and Africa. The Study Center for Justice in the Americas (Centro de Estudios de Justicia de las Américas; CEJA) has highlighted some of those general needs in developing countries in regard to ICT and how ICT initiatives could help improve the delivery of justice:

> ICT would bring a positive impact on improving levels of transparency in the operation of the institutions of the justice system, improving access to the justice system by the citizenry, improving efficiency and efficacy in the performance of multiple tasks, enabling and enhancing innovation processes in the delivery of justice and in judicial management, enabling citizenry scrutiny over the justice system, facilitating accountability of the judicial authorities by the citizenry, among others.[30]

When assessing the actual needs of the judiciary in developing countries, it is also important to determine the "ICT readiness" of the countries[31] for the implementation of technological innovations in the judicial or extrajudicial system. In recent years, developing countries have improved and increased their ICT capacities, but not all countries are at the same level. In order to evaluate the ICT capacity of a country, three sets of indicators must be considered. First, *infrastructure indicators* compute the number of personal computers, mainline and mobile subscribers, Internet users, and 3G subscribers in a country. This group of indicators also analyzes the broadband usage, the number of Internet hosts, and the security of the Internet servers available in the country. Second, *capacity indicators* focus on the education level in a country

---

28 Benyekhlef & Vermeys, *supra* note 16, at 10.

29 Cyberjustice Laboratory, *supra* note 15.

30 C. Hernández & R. Adelardi, *Perspectivas de uso e impacto de las TIC en la Administración de Justicia en América Latina* 5 (working paper, CEJA & Microsoft n.d.). Original text in Spanish: "Las TIC podrían tener un alto impacto en mejorar los niveles de transparencia en la operación de las instituciones del sistema de justicia, en mejorar el acceso de la ciudadanía al sistema de justicia, en aumentar los grados de eficiencia y eficacia en el desempeño de múltiples labores, en posibilitar y potenciar los procesos de innovación en la impartición de justicia y en la gestión judicial, en posibilitar la auditoria ciudadana sobre el sistema de justicia, en facilitar la rendición de cuentas de las autoridades judiciales a la ciudadanía, entre otros ámbitos." Cited in Gabriela R. Szlak, *Online Dispute Resolution in Latin America*, in *Online Dispute Resolution: Theory and Practice, A Treatise on Technology and Dispute Resolution*, 534 (Mohamed S. Abdel Wahab, Ethan Katsh, & Daniel Rainey eds., Eleven Intl. 2012).

31 Mohamed S. Abdel Wahab, *Online Dispute Resolution for Africa*, in *Online Dispute Resolution: Theory and Practice, A Treatise on Technology and Dispute Resolution*, 562 (Mohamed S. Abdel Wahab, Ethan Katsh, & Daniel Rainey, eds., Eleven Intl. 2012).

and analyze the illiteracy rate, public expenditure on education, and international Internet bandwidth. Third, *financial indicators* study the economy of the country (e.g., gross domestic product (GDP), foreign direct investment (FDI), and public and private investments in telecommunications).[32] Mohamed S. Abdel Wahab, who has elaborated on the topic of ICT readiness, explains that according to these indicators, African states' readiness to implement ICT initiatives can be described as falling into three different groups:

> (1) ICT ready States such as South Africa, Egypt, Morocco and Tunisia; (2) ICT progressing States such as Nigeria, Cameroon, Tanzania, Algeria, Seychelles, and Ghana and (3) ICT potentially progressing States such as Botswana, Malawi, Zambia, Central Africa, Chad, Niger, Guinea, Somalia, Ethiopia, Burkina Faso, Sierra Leone, Ivory Coast, Burundi, and Rwanda.[33]

ICT-ready states are states where all three groups of indicators are at high levels. For instance, most people in the country have access to a computer or have a mobile subscription; the illiteracy rate is very low, the education system good, and the financial situation satisfactory. Implementing an ICT pilot project in such a country should not be very difficult because everything is in place to facilitate implementation, given that the needs of the stakeholders are fully understood and the solution offered is tailored to the realities of the country. ICT–potentially progressing states are states that have the willingness to implement ICT initiatives but that are not yet ready in terms of all three sets of indicators. A good example would be Somalia, a country that experiences internal political conflict.[34] It would be very difficult to successfully implement an ICT initiative in such a context because the realities and conditions on the ground do not allow for it to happen. The country first needs to improve crucial areas such as peace, stability, health, and food security before beginning to consider implementing cyberjustice initiatives. As for ICT-progressing states, these lie somewhere in between the ICT-ready states and ICT–potentially progressing states. This means that in ICT-progressing states, the three groups of indicators are somewhat present, but further adjustments have to be made before implementing cyberjustice initiatives, and these initiatives might have to be more basic in design and implementation than in an ICT-ready state.

---

32 *Id.*, at 563.

33 *Id.*, at 567.

34 The country has been without a strong central government for many years and is facing regular attacks from an extremist group, Al Shabab. The World Bank classified the country as "low income" and indicates that only 29 percent of children are enrolled in primary school. The population is estimated at about 10 million people, of whom only 0.045 percent are connected to the Internet and 0.11 percent have a subscription to a mobile phone. *See* World Bank, *Data by Country*, "Somalia," available at http://data.worldbank.org/country/somalia; UN Somalia, *Fact Sheets*, available at http://www.unsomalia.net/infocenter/factsheets.htm; BBC News, *Who Are Somalia's al-Shabab?* (May, 16, 2014), available at http://www.bbc.com/news/world-africa-15336689.

Whether a developing country belongs in the first, second, or third group will have a definite impact on the needs and realistic goals of that country when it comes to improving access to justice through ICT initiatives. Thus it is important to be able to effectively identify the needs of the judiciary and to distinguish needs from wants. Involving the stakeholders in the development phase of a cyberjustice initiative is another aspect to consider when identifying the factual needs of the judiciary.

Collaboration: Involving Stakeholders

For ICT initiatives to reflect the reality and needs of the legal field, judiciary stakeholders must be involved in the projects from the beginning. The legal field includes many different actors, and to be faithful to their needs, they all have to be involved, not just lawyers. Judges, law clerks, Department of Justice professionals, lawyers, and court administrators, as well as civil society, all have different needs. Computer programmers, software and application developers, and other IT professionals must be able to establish the needs of the judiciary when developing cyberjustice solutions.[35]

Being involved from the beginning in cyberjustice projects minimizes stakeholders' resistance to technological changes and promotes their understanding and ownership of the project. Another way to limit resistance is to develop ICT initiatives that use tools people are familiar with. It follows that, given the huge number of cell phone subscribers worldwide, using mobile cellular technology-driven initiatives would help ensure that stakeholders in developing countries are on board and willing to collaborate.[36]

The online dispute resolution platform known as PARLe (Plateforme d'Aide au Règlement des Litiges en ligne; Online Dispute Resolution Platform) serves as a good example.[37] For this project, the Cyberjustice Laboratory team conducted consultations with mediators, representatives of Quebec's Consumer Protection Office, the Ministry of Justice, and Educaloi, a local nonprofit organization that aims to improve access to justice in Quebec. These consultations allowed the Cyberjustice Laboratory team to gather valuable information on what the actual needs of the stakeholders and actors were. PARLe uses ICT tools to improve the resolution of low-intensity disputes by reducing costs and delays. This web-based dispute resolution platform adapted to consumer disputes involves a three-step process. The first step is the negotiation stage, where the litigants try to solve the issue on their own. The second step is the mediation stage, which becomes available to the parties only if the first step is unsuccessful. The last step is employed if the litigants

---

35 Benyekhlef, & Vermeys, *supra* note 16, at 11.

36 McDonald, *supra* note 25.

37 It is interesting to note that this application was developed by the Cyberjustice Laboratory in consultation with stakeholders in order to get their opinions on what services the future platform should offer. Implicating the stakeholders from the beginning contributed to getting them on board with the project. *See* Cyberjustice Laboratory, ODR: *PARLe,* available at http://www.cyberjustice.ca/en/odr-parle.

cannot agree; it involves electronically transferring the case to a competent tribunal. A great advantage of PARLe is that "due to its numerous features, the platform can easily be adapted to the specific needs of administrative tribunals and mediation and arbitration bodies."[38] This means that this project could easily be adapted and implemented in other parts of the world, such as Latin America, as a way to improve the resolution of consumer disputes and other low-intensity disputes. PARLe has been successful in part because the stakeholders were involved from the beginning of the project's development, ensuring that the actual needs of the actors were clearly understood and that the stakeholders were on board with the project once it was implemented.

Understanding the Socioeconomic Context in which ICT Initiatives Are to Be Implemented

The effectiveness of the use of a technology depends on the technological resources available and the sociocultural context in which the technology is implemented. It is not sufficient to merely import existing technology that has been successful in other contexts; doing so could be described as digital colonialism. To use ICT initiatives effectively in the improvement of access to justice in developing countries, digital colonization must be avoided. To avoid this phenomenon, ICT initiatives have to reflect the socioeconomic situation of the country in which they are implemented. For an ICT initiative to be implemented effectively and contribute to improving access to justice, "the technology [used] has to be accessible from a physical, a philosophical as well as an economic stand point."[39] In other words, developing ICT solutions that use the most widely available technologies throughout the country and that people are willing to use is vital. For developing countries, this might mean focusing on ICT initiatives that involve using a mobile device as opposed to a computer, because many people may not have access to the latter. ICT initiatives are more likely to improve access to justice in developing countries if they use technological resources that are readily available on the ground and that take into consideration the socioeconomic context in which they are implemented.[40]

Implementing technologies that improve the justice system and society at large demands an understanding of the likely cultural, psychological, and social impact of a given technology, inasmuch as technologies can have a positive or a negative effect on human behavior.[41] For example, an ICT initia-

---

38 *Id.*

39 Vermeys, *supra* note 13, at 118 (translated by author). Original: "La technologie se doit d'être accessible tant du point de vue physique, que philosophique, qu'économique."

40 Karim Benyekhlef, *The Rise of Mobile Justice in Developing Regions* (address presented at the Law, Justice and Development Week 2013: "Towards a Science of Delivery in Development: How Can Law and Justice Help Translate Voice, Social Contract and Accountability into Development Impact?" [hereinafter Law, Justice and Development Week 2013], World Bank, Washington D.C., Nov. 18–22, 2013).

41 Benyekhlef & Vermeys, *supra* note 16, at 3.

tive that makes submitting certain documents to the court in electronic format mandatory would put those who did not have access to a computer at a disadvantage and contribute to reinforcing the pre-existing socioeconomic divide between the rich and the poor. This is why "we must carefully study how a given cyberjustice solution will cause our habits to change and if those changes are beneficial to the process and its stakeholders."[42]

To be effective, a cyberjustice initiative also needs to take into consideration the specific components of the target country's legal process. "As long as we have not clearly established why such and such a component of [a given] legal process works in a certain way, why people have accepted a certain method of doing things or rather why they are attached to it, we cannot hope to succeed in implementing technological solutions in order to make that component more efficient."[43] Therefore, to be widely accepted and used in the judicial process, ICT initiatives have to respect and adapt to the judicial rituals of the country.[44]

Implementing Pilot Projects

As previously explained, cyberjustice initiatives involving a technology-driven approach or complete overhauls of the justice system failed mainly because the stakeholders were unable to adapt to huge changes, and the initiatives offered a simple solution to a complex situation. To ensure that cyberjustice initiatives see the light of day and are sustainable, this chapter advocates a modular and collaborative methodology in line with the science of delivery approach. Part of this methodology involves the use of pilot projects and/or small-scale initiatives as a way that the actual needs of the stakeholders are met and that the ICT tools used are effective. Using pilot projects allows for the review of "the policies and practices relating to technology with respect to policies designed to foster the development of access to justice."[45] Pilot projects allow for the study of the impact of ICT initiatives on the justice system and of user satisfaction with the changes made. "This preliminary work will make it possible to adopt best practices and to share the findings with the stakeholders, as well as to conduct an analysis of future prospects so that new projects can be suggested."[46]

One concrete example illustrates the point about pilot projects. The Management and Follow-Up of Cases System (Sistema de Gestión y Seguimiento de Casos; SIGESSCA) pilot project aims to improve access to justice through an online platform offering better access to legal services provided by university legal clinics in El Salvador, Guatemala, and Uruguay.[47] The online

---

42 *Id.*, at 4.

43 *Id.*, at 5.

44 Vermeys, *supra* note 13, at 131.

45 Benyekhlef, *supra* note 40.

46 *Id.*

47 *Id.*

platform makes it possible to manage, monitor, and share administrative and court files. Because the platform is decentralized, it provides better support for members of vulnerable groups. The platform also provides automatic tracking of regulatory legal deadlines and can send notifications to users through e-mails or text messages (SMS, or short message service). The SIGESSCA project has inspired legal clinics throughout Latin America to provide free legal aid to underprivileged groups. "From this point of view, this project clearly illustrates the important role that technology, especially mobile technology, can be called upon to play in delivering legal services to members of underprivileged groups and thereby increasing their access to justice."[48]

The first part of this chapter has made the case that the modular methodology advocated by the Cyberjustice Laboratory, which uses open-source code to develop pilot projects such as PARLe, allows for wide dissemination of good practices that will be helpful in the development and implementation of ICT initiatives in developing countries. These good practices in the field of cyberjustice can then be used in emerging countries to develop ICT initiatives that provide better access to justice. The second part of the chapter advocates utilizing the infrastructure (the knowledge, partners, and multidisciplinary approach) of the Global Forum on Law, Justice and Development and the Community of Practice on Alternative Dispute Resolution as a starting point for developing effective ICT initiatives aimed at improving justice delivery in developing countries.

The Global Forum on Law, Justice and Development: A Project Incubator

Access to justice remains difficult in a number of developing countries for various reasons, but mainly because of fear of tribunals and state institutions, and technical and procedural difficulties. ICT initiatives can contribute to alleviating some of these difficulties, particularly in the reduction of costs and delays.

Using electronic communications in the judicial system would allow litigants to save money, thus improving access to justice for many who cannot normally afford it.[49] Cyberjustice also encompasses developing solutions that reduce travel expenses, by developing online dispute resolution platforms and by allowing for witness testimony via videoconferencing.[50] Regarding reduction of delays, part of the solution lies in finding ways for litigants to get access to justice without needing the intervention of a judge.[51] Thus, "the remedies may involve computerizing and providing online access to ADR (alternative dispute resolution) mechanisms as well as to traditional justice

---

48 *Id.*

49 Vermeys, *supra* note 13, at 105.

50 *Id.*, at 106.

51 *Id.*, at 107.

systems"[52] that have ancestral roots to decrease the number of cases for the formal justice system.

This section explains how the Global Forum on Law, Justice and Development (GFLJD) and its partners, including the Community of Practice on Alternative Dispute Resolution, using the modular and collaborative method in the science of delivery, can be an effective platform for developing ICT-driven strategies that modernize and reform mechanisms for better access to justice in developing countries. The multidisciplinary approach of the GFLJD, which brings together an impressive list of partners from all over the world, makes the forum a perfect project incubator. Developing pilot projects to bring together the methodology of the Cyberjustice Laboratory and GFLJD partners such as the World Bank is a good starting point for implementing new ICT initiatives and studying the impact of existing initiatives that offer better access to justice in developing countries.

Using GFLJD Partners to Modernize and Reform Access to Justice in Developing Countries

The GFLJD consists of a permanent forum and an ICT web-based platform that seeks to promote "a better understanding of the role of law and justice and strengthen and better integrate legal and judicial institutions in the development process, through selected capacity building initiatives and an open repository of knowledge."[53] The GFLJD offers a platform that allows its 148 partners[54] to join in improving justice delivery in developing countries. The forum consists of "a structured partnership, built on a broad network of development partners such as other International Financial Institutions, International Organizations, Central Banks, government agencies, judiciaries, universities, think tanks and civil society organizations."[55] Also, the fact that the partners are from both the North and the South, helps bridge the gap between the two and allow them to share one another's experiences and knowledge when developing ICT-driven access to justice initiatives. All this knowledge provides "practical legal contributions to development challenges and will improve the legal and judiciary systems which form the intangible infrastructure for sustainable development."[56]

---

52 Benyekhlef, *supra* note 40.

53 Global Forum on Law, Justice and Development, *10 Things about the Global Forum on Law, Justice and Development* (2011), available at http://globalforumljd.org/about/10_things.htm.

54 These partners include but are not limited to the African Development Bank (AfDB), Center for Research on Collaboratories and Technology Enhanced Learning Communities (COTELCO), Centre de recherche en droit public (CRDP), Centre for Mediation and Law, Instituto de Investigacion para la Justicia (Research Institute for Justice), and World Bank. *See* Global Forum on Law, Justice and Development, *Partners* (2014), http://globalforumljd.org/partners/index.htm.

55 Global Forum on Law, Justice and Development, *Generating Innovative Legal Solutions to Development Challenges—Overview,* 12 (Jan. 2012), http://globalforumljd.org/docs/about/gfld_ppt_light.pdf.

56 *Id.*

The work of the GFLJD can definitely contribute to providing more effective access to justice in emerging countries through the science of delivery. Indeed, the GFLJD approach is in line with the four basic features of delivery[57] as defined by the World Bank. Thus, the exchange and knowledge transfer of the web-based platform that connects all GFLJD partners to relevant research and practices will improve development outcomes,[58] which is in line with the third feature of delivery: collaboration and interaction. Furthermore, the GFLJD "provides targeted audiences a coherent, sustained program of collaborative research and technical assistance to accelerate knowledge translation and use,"[59] allowing for the development of solutions for poor access to justice that are context-specific, as the first feature of delivery prescribes. Last, the GFLJD has a multidisciplinary approach because it brings together experts from the economic, legal, and technical fields.[60] According to the World Bank, this multidisciplinary expertise will contribute to "measure results and triangulate data that will help discover what is driving success or failure" of ICT initiatives.[61]

The GFLJD, through thematic working groups of partners, will produce sample agreements, operational manuals, guidance notes, as well as legal and policy analysis. The forum and its partners will also collect data, such as laws, commentaries, and jurisprudence.[62] All this information will be invaluable when developing ICT initiatives for emerging countries. Another important actor providing effective access to justice is the Community of Practice on Alternative Dispute Resolution, which operates under the auspices of the GFLJD but is not part of a particular thematic working group, allowing it to have a cross-cutting approach.

The Work of the Community of Practice on Alternative Dispute Resolution

The Community of Practice (CoP) on ADR is a group that brings together institutions devoted to the improvement of alternative dispute resolution processes. The CoP on ADR is co-led by the Cyberjustice Laboratory and the Ministerio de Reforma do Judiciario, Ministério da Justiça of Brazil and operates under the auspices of the World Bank's Global Forum on Law, Justice and Development.[63] The group's research focuses partly on how ADR mechanisms, such as negotiation, mediation, and arbitration, can be used to support

---

57 For a definition of the four basic features of delivery, *see* note 14.

58 Global Forum on Law, Justice and Development, *Information Note* (2011), http://globalforum ljd.org/about/index.htm.

59 *Id.*

60 *Id.*

61 World Bank, *supra* note 3.

62 Global Forum on Law, Justice and Development, *supra* note 55.

63 Karim Benyekhlef & Valentin Callipel, *CoP on ADR* (address presented during the Law, Justice and Development Week 2013).

development policies related to access to justice. The CoP on ADR is interested in ADR initiatives operating within the margins of the courts and in extra-judicial processes.[64] The work of the CoP on ADR is divided into three distinct research dimensions: (a) development of ADR and justice, (b) online dispute resolution contributions to development policies, and (c) ADR contributions to transitional justice policies.[65]

The CoP on ADR, with its highly qualified, diverse partners, is a good starting point for developing new ICT initiatives as well as for studying the impact of existing access to justice initiatives in developing countries. Using a modular and collaborative methodology, the group is able to give "special attention to the role played by information technology in support of ADR practice."[66] ADR processes definitely are an important part of improving access to justice and delivery of justice in developing countries. Using a multidisciplinary approach, the CoP on ADR focuses its expertise on studying social changes taking place in conflict resolution using ICT tools. It can closely monitor the impact social change may have on policies of regional development. Also, the CoP on ADR is a very useful tool for promoting awareness of the development, local implementation, and improvement of ICT initiatives in emerging countries.[67] Furthermore, the CoP on ADR will study the impact of those ICT initiatives on access to the justice system and justice delivery, as well as on implemented development strategies and policies in developing countries.[68]

The CoP on ADR believes that as mobile technologies continue to spread in developing countries, access to the traditional justice system will improve, but use of those technologies will also lead to extrajudicial procedural innovations that provide new options and make up for the inadequacies of the traditional justice system. The use of these new technologies is transforming models of justice and the way justice is administered,[69] and developing countries need to take advantage of this fact. In regard to ADR, the CoP on ADR believes that "the remedies may involve computerizing and providing online access to ADR mechanisms as well as traditional justice systems that have most often taken root in the shade of courts that, for example, in the case of Africa, date back to colonial times."[70] For this reason, mobile technology can be used as a tool that will improve the classical justice system but that can also be used as a procedural innovation for alternative justice.[71]

---

64 Benyekhlef, *supra* note 40.

65 Benyekhlef & Callipel, *supra* note 63.

66 Benyekhlef, *supra* note 40.

67 Cyberjustice Laboratory, *Forum on Law, Justice and Development Proposition for a Community of Practice Regarding Alternative Dispute Resolution: Concept Note* (unpublished, Feb. 21, 2013).

68 *Id.*

69 *Id.*

70 *Id.*

71 *Id.*

Moreover, cyberjustice initiatives have the potential of bringing formal and informal justice closer together. In other words, incorporating ADR processes into a state's justice system through ICT tools can help improve access to justice.[72] If, for example, the legislator of a given country were to decide to incorporate a web-based mediation platform for solving commercial litigation problems into the judicial system by making it obligatory for litigants to go through it before going to court, the delays, costs, and difficulties of accessing the justice system would effectively be reduced. Pierre Meyer explains in an article on arbitration that this reasoning is particularly true for African countries:

> In African societies, the law has been essential to the search for an acceptable solution which does not break with the social balance. The practice of law aims at obtaining conciliation and reconciliation—rather than the rigid application of a predetermined standard that could disrupt the social equilibrium, increasing tensions within society.[73]

The next section discusses the CoP on ADR's argument that mobile technologies can have a particularly important impact in the context of transitional justice, which often takes a hybrid form, bringing formal and informal justice together.

The Use of ICT in the Context of Transitional Justice

One important topic to be examined by the CoP on ADR is how ADR processes contribute to transitional justice. ICT initiatives can help improve delivery of justice in the context of transitional justice just as they do in general access to justice. But what is transitional justice, exactly? According to a 2004 report by the UN secretary-general, the notion of transitional justice

> comprises the full range of processes and mechanisms associated with a society's attempts to come to terms with a legacy of large-scale past abuses, in order to ensure accountability, serve justice and achieve reconciliation. These may include both judicial and non-judicial mechanisms, with differing levels of international involvement (or none at all) and individual prosecutions, reparations, truth-seeking, institutional reform, vetting and dismissals, or a combination thereof.[74]

Transitional justice mechanisms are usually employed in the aftermath of armed conflicts or in the context of periods of transition from totalitarian or authoritarian regimes to more democratic regimes.[75] There are many benefits

---

72 Vermeys, *supra* note 13, at 111.

73 Pierre Meyer, *OHADA—Droit de l'arbitrage* (Bruylante 2002) (translation by the author).

74 United Nations, *The Rule of Law and Transitional Justice in Conflict and Post-Conflict Societies, Report of the Secretary-General*, U.N. Doc. S/2004/616 (23 Aug. 2004), at para. 8.

75 Philipp Kastner, *Cyberjustice in the Context of Transitional Justice*, 2 (Working Paper No. 9, Cyberjustice Laboratory, Nov. 2013), http://www.cyberjustice.ca/en/documents-en/.

to using ICT in a context of transitional justice, such as information sharing, cost efficiency, access to the court system, participation, and outreach.[76] This chapter focuses on the latter.

The criticism has often been made that when it comes to transitional justice, some institutions, particularly international criminal tribunals, have neglected to take into consideration the needs and concerns of local populations. Furthermore, people living in remote areas have often not been able to take part in proceedings that usually take place far away from where the abuses or crimes being tried were committed. Local populations also lack a clear understanding of the mandate and work of these institutions.[77] ICT initiatives could help improve this type of situation. "New technologies may . . . play an important role in increasing access to transitional justice institutions and in facilitating communication between the institutions and their constituencies. Especially communities with low literacy rates may benefit from visual—ideally live—representation of proceedings held in other areas."[78]

Given that a large part of the population in developing countries lives in rural areas, courtrooms are often located miles away and traveling conditions are often far from ideal.[79] Therefore, physically accessing the justice system and transitional justice institutions remains one of the biggest challenges for people living in developing countries. In this context, using ICT tools can help alleviate the difficulties of reaching places that are far away in unsafe areas after a conflict for such purposes as participating in inquiries or witness interviews. Also, increasing communication with local communities enhances ownership over transitional justice mechanisms. Using ICT tools can also lead to exchanges of information or dialogue between the different communities affected by the situation in the country, thus promoting social cohesion and national unity.[80] "It would, therefore, be useful to encourage decentralized, bottom-up approaches that give a greater voice to grassroots organizations, even in the planning phase of a particular mechanism. The result may be a more collective, and collectively-owned, perhaps even continuously evolving process, exactly what may be needed to deal with situations of massive trauma."[81]

Conclusion

The recent spread of mobile technologies worldwide has allowed people in developing countries to bypass the landline infrastructure phase and gain almost complete mobile access to networks from their phones. Nowadays, one

---

76 *Id.*, at 7–8.

77 *Id.*, at 8.

78 *Id.*

79 McDonald, *supra* note 25.

80 Kastner, *supra* note 75, at 9.

81 *Id.*

can easily access the Internet from a basic cellular phone, rendering obsolete the need to buy or get access to an expensive computer.[82] This chapter has thus argued that governments and other institutions in developing countries must take advantage of this spread of technologies to improve access to justice with ICT-driven strategies that will modernize and reform judicial and extrajudicial mechanisms.

This chapter has discussed the issues and challenges in relation to ICT-driven strategies and cyberjustice initiatives. It has been shown that by using a modular and collaborative methodology when implementing ICT initiatives, these initiatives can improve access to justice in developing countries. Adapting pilot projects such as PARLe and SIGESSCA to developing countries could be the beginning of a transition to an integrated justice system.

The Cyberjustice Laboratory advocates unleashing the potential of mobile technologies, through a modular and collaborative methodology, to improve access to justice in both the judicial and the extrajudicial processes. This chapter has proposed that combining the experience of the Cyberjustice Laboratory with the GFLJD's approach, which is in line with the four basic features of the science of delivery, would allow for the development of ICT initiatives that would effectively improve access to justice in emerging countries. Furthermore, the CoP on ADR is a good starting point for developing new ICT initiatives as well as for studying the impact of existing initiatives for better access to justice in developing countries. Using ICT tools to bring formal and informal justice closer together is yet another way to improve access to justice.

The object of this chapter has been less to provide specific solutions to specific problems in highly specialized contexts than to offer some broad and useful guidelines that may serve as the basis for further reflection on possible solutions to improving access to justice in developing countries, and to stimulating those countries to do so. In particular, this chapter has highlighted the use of a modular and collaborative methodology that is in line with the basic features of the science of delivery, so as to harness the potential of mobile technologies and ICT initiatives. In so doing, the goal is to improve access to justice in developing countries through mobile technologies and ICT initiatives, and by extension, to deliver more justice generally in those countries.

82 Benyekhlef, *supra* note 40.

16
Courts and Regulatory Governance in Latin America
Improving Delivery in Development by Managing Institutional Interplay

RENE URUEÑA

Courts and the Regulatory State in the South

Almost 25 years have passed since the first institutional reforms in Latin America were implemented, following a wide trend toward the privatization of public utilities and other basic services. Part of this deep transformation entailed the adoption of regulatory forms of governance, that is, the role of an interventionist state was reduced in favor of a state whose intervention in the economy was done mostly through rules and regulation instead of taxing and spending.[1] One common institutional feature of this transformation was the independent regulatory agency (IRA). The basic premise was that certain areas of the economy, such as public utilities, telecommunications, and banking, were better served if the regulator remained at arm's length from political pressures. The answer was to create law-based "agencies," acting mostly through administrative means on the basis of a particular kind of expertise. The independence of these agencies would foster "credible commitments" on behalf of the state and limit regulatory opportunism.[2] Moreover, in the context of privatization, such independence would also provide much-needed assurance to foreign investors that their sunk costs would not be affected by administrative expropriation or manipulation.[3]

Latin America was particularly fertile ground for the logic of "credible commitments."[4] During the 1990s, independent regulatory agencies proliferated in the region at a rate never before seen. Jacint Jordana and David Levi-Faur report that only 43 regulatory authorities (mostly in the financial sector)

---

1 *See* Giandomenico Majone, *From the Positive to the Regulatory State: Causes and Consequences of Changes in the Mode of Governance,* 17(2) J. Pub. Policy 139–67 (1997).

2 *See* Fabrizio Gilardi, *Policy Credibility and Delegation to Independent Regulatory Agencies: A Comparative Empirical Analysis,* 9(6) J. European Pub. Policy 873–93 (2002).

3 *See* Brian Levy & Pablo T. Spiller, *Institutional Foundations of Regulatory Commitment: A Comparative Analysis of Telecommunications Regulation,* 10 J. L. Econ. & Org. 201 (1994).

4 *See* Vivien Foster, *Ten Years of Water Service Reform in Latin America: Toward an Anglo-French Model* (Intl. Bank Reconstruction & Dev.; World Bank 2005).

existed in the region before 1979; by 2002 they had grown threefold to 138.[5] These numbers, though, do little to explain the impact that such proliferation has in the delivery of basic services in the region. Although the *form* of the IRA was widely adopted in Latin America (and elsewhere in the world), little is known about the actual *operation* of IRAs in their own contexts, and particularly their role in boosting (or hindering) the delivery of the essential services that they regulate.[6]

This gap seems to be particularly pressing in economies outside Europe and the United States, where the work of IRAs seemed to follow a different trajectory from that predicted by the "credible commitments" literature. This gap has been explored in recent literature through the lenses of the "Regulatory State in South."[7] From this perspective, certain shared contexts of countries in the "South" (e.g., the presence of powerful external pressures, especially from international financial institutions, the greater intensity of redistributive politics in settings where infrastructure services are of extremely poor quality, and limited state capacity) are crucial to understanding regulatory governance in poorer economies— a reality that simply is lost in the perspective of regulatory transfer and diffusion. Understanding the impact of these shared contexts in the regulatory state is important for advancing regulatory theory and understanding the possibilities (and limits) of regulation in the delivery of essential services to the poorest.

One key insight on the Regulatory State in the South project, which was led by Navroz K. Dubash and Bronwen Morgan and consisted of case studies of regulatory governance in countries outside the North Atlantic, was that courts are central actors in regulatory governance in developing countries. Traditional literature on the regulatory state situates the judiciary as protecting contract and property rights, thus limiting state action and curbing discretion.[8] In sharp contrast to this view, the experiences of the water sector in Colombia and Indonesia, and of telecommunications in India, show that the judiciary is a privileged site of regulatory governance where international pressures, distributive politics, and limited state capacity operate.[9]

---

5 *See* Jacint Jordana & David Levi-Faur, *The Diffusion of Regulatory Capitalism in Latin America: Sectoral and National Channels in the Making of a New Order*, 598(1) Annals Am. Acad. Pol. & Soc. Sci. 102–24 (2005).

6 *Id. See* also Jacint Jordana, David Levi-Faur, & Xavier Fernández i Marín, *The Global Diffusion of Regulatory Agencies Channels of Transfer and Stages of Diffusion*, 44(10) Comp. Pol. Stud. 1343–69 (2011); David Levi-Faur, *The Global Diffusion of Regulatory Capitalism*, 598(1) Annals Am. Acad. Pol. & Soc. Sci. 12–32 (2005).

7 *See* Navroz K. Dubash & Bronwen Morgan, *Understanding the Rise of the Regulatory State of the South*, 6(3) Regulation & Governance 261–81 (2012). The Regulatory State in the South project explores the possibility of finding particular characteristics in regulatory governance as applied in the global South that are different from the same type of governance in the North.

8 *Id.*

9 On Colombia, *see* Rene Urueña, *Expertise and Global Water Governance: How to Start Thinking about Power over Water Resources?*, 9 Anuario Mexicano de Derecho Internacional 117–52 (2012); on Indonesia, *see* Nai Rui Chng, *Regulatory Mobilization and Service Delivery at the Edge*

Much has been said about the importance of the judiciary to economic and social development, particularly in Latin America, where activist courts have engendered economic transformations.[10] Courts are, indeed, a crucial site of distributive politics in the region. However, current efforts have been either focused on the justiciability and enforcement of social and economic rights or taken place in the context of rule of law programs concerned with reducing court backlogs, enhancing judicial training programs, and eliminating judicial corruption. The Regulatory State in the South project brought forth a different perspective on this nexus: in these countries, courts became deeply immersed in formulating regulatory regimes or reforming regulatory agencies; they became crucial players in the delivery of essential services, both as actors in their own right and as an institutional forum in which other actors could interact.

This chapter further investigates the implications of this insight for the delivery of essential services in the region. Why do courts get involved in the regulatory process in Latin America? How is this involvement undertaken? What are the effects of courts' involvement in the regulatory process in Latin America in terms of accountability and participation? Who wins and who loses when courts intervene? To explore these questions, the chapter builds on research done by a group of early-career scholars on the ground in Brazil, Colombia, and Argentina who came together as questions on the role of the judiciary in regulatory politics became part of a wider project on interinstitutional interactions led by the Universidad de Los Andes (Colombia), with the support of the International Development Research Center.

The research on which this chapter is based focuses on health care, the environment, and public utilities. Carolina Moreno explored the intervention of the Colombian Constitutional Court in the regulation of waste disposal in Bogota and its impact on the human rights of informal waste pickers. Florencia Lebensohn investigated the role of environmental expertise and regulation by the judiciary, focusing on the Matanza-Riachuelo River basin case in Argentina. Maria Prada and Santiago Rojas researched the impact of the judiciary in the provision of health services in Colombia. One further set of case studies focusing on Brazil will be published in a separate volume edited by Mariana Mota Prado, of the University of Toronto. This latter set of cases is not discussed in this chapter.

While each of these case studies will be published soon, the goal of this chapter is to present some of the overall lessons that can be distilled in terms of voice and accountability in the delivery of essential services in the region. The overall point is that the interaction between institutions matters for improving

---

of the Regulatory State, 6(3) Regulation & Governance 344–61 (2012); on India, *see* Arun K. Thiruvengadam & Piyush Joshi, *Judiciaries as Crucial Actors in Southern Regulatory Systems: A Case Study of Indian Telecom Regulation,* 6(3) Regulation & Governance 327–43 (2012).

10 *See* Roberto Gargarella, Pilar Domingo & Theunis Roux, *Courts and Social Transformation in New Democracies: An Institutional Voice for the Poor?* (Ashgate 2006); David Landau, *Political Institutions and Judicial Role in Comparative Constitutional Law,* 51 Harv. Intl. L. J. 319 (2010).

delivery of development in Latin America—and courts are a crucial player in such dynamics. The research focuses on three central ideas: first, the notion of a "regulatory space" (both national and global), and its importance in improving delivery; second, the idea of institutional adaptation, and why deviating from "best practices" may not be such a bad thing after all; and, third, the importance of knowledge and experimentalist governance as a platform for fostering better governance. The final section concludes the chapter.

Interaction in a Regulatory Space: National and Global

Although the diffusion of IRAs is a well-established fact, their outcomes cannot be understood by focusing on agencies as discrete units acting in isolation of other institutions. The challenges that regulation poses to the delivery of essential services can be better understood if the analytical unit is the *space* where interaction between institutions takes place. In this regulatory space, institutions are dynamic; they change and adapt to their interactions, defining the regulatory framework that impacts delivery of essential services.

A National Regulatory Space

A good way to begin thinking about this regulatory space is to highlight that IRAs do not enter a regulatory vacuum when they are implemented locally. A national ecosystem of institutions and actors is already in place when IRAs are adopted (as they were, for example, in Latin America during the 1990s), and there is some sort of regulation that needs to be adopted, transformed, or replaced through the work of the IRAs. These agencies enter as actors in a space where regulation is *already* being adopted, discussed, implemented, and rejected. As time passes, some IRAs become the main player in the regulatory field, as seen in some of the countries examined herein. However, these dominant agencies do not completely crowd out the regulatory space; on the contrary, this space includes both the IRAs and other relevant actors, with whom IRAs interact.

The notion of a regulatory space was suggested as a reaction to the narrow reading of the regulatory process in terms of a conflict between public authority and private interests. Against this view, the regulatory process can be better understood as a "space," where it becomes possible to explore the "complex and shifting relationships between and within organizations at the heart of economic regulation."[11] The key is "to understand the nature of this shared space: the rules of admission, the relations between occupants, and the variations introduced by differences in markets and issue arenas."[12]

The image of a regulatory space aptly captures some of the dynamic interactions between IRAs and courts we observed in our research. Most of the

---

11 Leigh Hancher & Michael Moran, *Organizing Regulatory Space* in *Capitalism, Culture, and Economic Regulation,* 271 (Leigh Hancher & Michael Moran ed., Clarendon Press 1989).

12 *Id.*

regulatory outcomes we encountered (particularly pertaining to waste management and health regulation in Colombia and environmental regulation in Argentina) were not the product of an isolated IRA making a decision but the result of a set of actors that interacted and, through their interaction, determined the outcome. Understanding the impact of regulation in the delivery of development requires a focus not on IRAs alone but on the regulatory space they inhabit.

The notion of a space is useful to think about the way in which regulatory governance is undertaken and experienced in the cases we researched in Latin America. Delivery of essential services may be affected as IRAs compete with other actors or develop efforts to coordinate with or even co-opt competing agencies, a dynamic that has been observed in international relations, transnational business governance, environmental governance, and domestic regulation.[13]

With the exception of Leigh Hancher and Michael Moran's early insights, the interplay within regulatory spaces has been mostly overlooked by administrative law scholarship, which has focused on individual agencies and their procedures. Recently, some U.S. scholarship has explored interaction,[14] focusing on interagency interaction and coordination as a problem of overlapping legislative delegation.[15] In this line of scholarship, courts are outside the shared regulatory space and act through judicial review in order to hinder or foster cooperation.[16] Our approach is different; it considers courts not as external to the regulatory space but as actors within it, with the same standing as IRAs. This, of course, has implications for judicial review, which are explored in the last section of the chapter.

The Matanza-Riachuelo River basin case, researched by Florencia Delia Lebensohn in Argentina, provides a glimpse of the way in which interactions in the regulatory space may hinder the delivery of a healthy environment in Latin America. The Matanza-Riachuelo River basin is home to Argentina's largest concentrations of urban poor, housing almost eight million people who live mostly in shantytowns that lack basic infrastructure. The basin is horribly polluted; consequently, diarrhea, breathing problems, skin diseases, and

---

13 On international relations, *see* Kenneth W. Abbott, Jessica F. Green, & Robert O. Keohane, *Organizational Ecology and Organizational Strategies in World Politics,* 13–57 (Harv. Kennedy Sch. Govt. Discussion Papers 2013); on transnational business governance, *see* Burkard Eberlein et al., *Transnational Business Governance Interactions: Conceptualization and Framework for Analysis,* 8(1) Regulation & Governance 1–21 (2014); on environmental governance, *see* Sebastian Oberthür & Thomas Gehring, *Institutional Interaction: Ten Years of Scholarly Development* in *Managing Institutional Complexity: Regime Interplay and Global Environmental Change* 25–58 (Sebastian Oberthür & Olav Schram Stokke eds., MIT Press 2011).

14 *See* Keith Bradley, *The Design of Agency Interactions,* 111(4) Colum. L. Rev. 745–94 (2011); Jody Freeman & Jim Rossi, *Agency Coordination in Shared Regulatory Space,* 125 Harv. L. Rev. 1131 (2011).

15 *See* Jacob E. Gersen, *Overlapping and Underlapping Jurisdiction in Administrative Law,* 1 S. Ct. Rev. 201–47 (2006).

16 *See* Freeman & Rossi, *supra* note 14.

other health problems are common. Cleanup efforts have been undertaken since the 1960s to no avail, a situation that has been traditionally chalked up to a failure of governance and incoherent regulation. More than 50 sets of rules apply to the river basin, which is under the concurrent jurisdiction of the federal government, the government of the Autonomous City of Buenos Aires, the government of the Province of Buenos Aires, and the governments of 14 municipalities. The Inter-American Development Bank approved a US$250 million loan in the late 1990s that was never used because governance problems proved to be an insurmountable obstacle.[17]

Lebensohn reports that, in 2004, a group of neighbors filed a claim for damages based on conditions in the basin. The Supreme Court of Argentina adopted two wide-ranging decisions (in 2006 and 2008), which led to an integrated cleanup plan for the basin. The plan can be seen as an effort by the court to organize a regulatory space left in chaos by the historical failure of traditional agencies. It gave specific directions for the coordination of most of the concerned agencies, culminating in the creation of a new agency, the Autoridad de la Cuenca Matanza-Riachuelo (ACUMAR), something akin to a regulatory joint venture, with the participation of the federal government and the provincial and city governments of Buenos Aires.

ACUMAR was structured like an IRA and became the crucial player for implementing the cleanup effort. However, its role cannot be understood in isolation of the court's intervention, either before or after its establishment in 2006. ACUMAR is constantly in touch with the Supreme Court, which played a big role in its creation and whose stature boosts its legitimacy, and with the federal court, which oversees the implementation of the cleanup efforts and provides a forum for the enforcement of those efforts, imposing fines in cases of noncompliance.

This interaction opened new spaces for participation and accountability in Argentina's environmental regulatory process. The Supreme Court itself allowed for participation in its public sessions as it discussed the cleanup plan (thereby defining a procedure that has since been used in matters beyond this case). Moreover, the court also ordered the ombudsman to set up a commission, the Comision de Participacion Social, to receive suggestions in relation to the cleanup plan. This body is composed of local nongovernmental organizations (NGOs), which distribute updated information and have standing to file administrative challenges before ACUMAR in matters related to the plan. As discussed later, a similar pattern was found in the Colombian case of health care, where the Constitutional Court held public hearings, which were widely attended, and required other institutions involved to provide for

---

17 *See* Decree No. 145/98, by which the Executive Branch approved a model contract to be entered into between the National Bank of Argentina and the Inter-American Development Bank to receive the US$250 million loan to clean the Matanza-Riachuelo River basin. The contract was signed on Feb. 5, 1998, between the Argentine state and the Inter-American Development Bank. *See* Florencia Delia Lebensohn, *Regulatory Role of the Supreme Court of Argentina: The Matanza-Riachuelo River Basin Case* (on file with author).

spaces of participation and notice-and-comment procedures in their regulatory processes.

The Matanza-Riachuelo River basin case evidences the existence of a regulatory space where IRAs act and a possible role that courts could play in facilitating essential services. In Argentina, the regulatory space was densely populated by numerous institutions with overlapping mandates, which proved to be an obstacle for effectively solving the pollution problem. The Supreme Court thus entered to organize the regulatory space and, by doing so, it opened spaces of participation and accountability. The court, though, triggered the creation of a new agency. That is one more actor in the regulatory space that has to interact with existing agencies, which in turn will adapt their strategies, forcing ACUMAR to adapt its own. Interactions in the regulatory space are in this sense decidedly nonlinear: the shape of the regulatory space changes as interactions occur and creates loops that influence the actors, their behavior, and cognitive frameworks.

A Global Regulatory Space

The regulatory space that IRAs inhabit is mostly circumscribed by national borders; IRAs interact mostly with other national institutions, and their impacts are felt within nation-states. That was the case in Colombia, where domestic IRAs interacted with domestic courts in order to solve social problems, thus affecting the regulatory process. But some interactions may also involve international institutions, such as international development banks or international courts. These interactions are part of an emergent "global administrative space," which has been defined as "a space, distinct from the space of inter-state relations governed by international law and the domestic regulatory space governed by domestic administrative law, although encompassing elements of each."[18]

Some aspects of regulatory governance in Latin America have been situated in the global regulatory space, particularly in connection with investment arbitration and the human rights to water.[19] Our research confirms the importance of this space beyond the nation-state.

In the Matanza-Riachuelo River basin, the Supreme Court expressly tied the monitoring of ACUMAR's performance to the use of international

---

18 *See* Benedict Kingsbury, Richard B. Stewart, & Niko Krisch, *The Emergence of Global Administrative Law,* 68 L. & Contemporary Problems 15–61 (2005).

19 On investment arbitration, *see* Andréa Rocha Postiga, *A emergência do Direito Administrativo Global como ferramenta de regulação transnacional do investimento estrangeiro direito,* 10(1) Revista de Direito Internacional (2013), doi:10.5102/rdi.v10i1.2369; Nicolás M. Perrone, *Los tratados bilaterales de inversión y el arbitraje internacional: ¿En dirección al mejor funcionamiento de las instituciones domésticas?* 17 Revista de Derecho 63–88 (2012); Benedict Kingsbury & Stephan Schill, *Investor-State Arbitration as Governance: Fair and Equitable Treatment, Proportionality, and the Emerging Global Administrative Law* (N.Y.U. Pub. L. & Leg. Theory Working Papers, Sept. 2009), http://lsr.nellco.org/nyu_plltwp/146. On water rights, *see* Rene Urueña, *The Rise of the Constitutional Regulatory State in Colombia: The Case of Water Governance,* 6(3) Regulation & Governance 282–99 (2012).

indicators, which fostered the adoption of quantitative instruments developed by the United Nations Economic Commission for Latin America (ECLAC), which became crucial to ACUMAR's task. More important, though, was the role of the World Bank. Lebensohn writes that, soon after the 2008 decision, Argentina secured from the World Bank one of the largest loans to a Latin American country for environmental purposes: US$1 billion. The grant was directly geared to boosting the cleanup effort by ACUMAR and others. The role of the World Bank in shaping interactions in the emerging global regulatory space cannot be understated. One part of the story is, obviously, financial clout: the Bank is in a privileged position to steer resources to particular players, thus boosting one actor and not the other. In this case, the Bank supported the Supreme Court's role in organizing the Argentinean regulatory space and put its funds behind ACUMAR.

Perhaps as important as its financial muscle is the Bank's *epistemic* clout: its intervention lends expert authority to some of the players in the regulatory space. In this case, the Bank's expertise lent its aura of technocratic expertise to ACUMAR, which badly needed it in order to become an important player in an already populated regulatory space. Most crucially, the Bank helped define the "problem" to be tackled: the overall shape of the regulatory space, both domestic and global. The Bank's role here was to underscore that the problem was one of *governance* (and not of, say, availability of technology or of technical capacity), hence the strategy was to boost the institutional capacity of ACUMAR. This exercise of epistemic framing was important in the process of improving delivery of essential services in that it created the conceptual infrastructure that will guide the decision-making process in the future.

Policy Transfers, "Best Practices," and Deviations

IRAs are not merely "transplanted" or their policies "transferred" from their original site (usually the Anglo-Saxon world) into a new environment (in this case, Latin America). The trajectory of independent regulatory agencies examined suggests that institutions that are "transplanted" are then transformed by contextual interactions, creating doubt as to whether, over time, the very idea of "transfer" is still useful.

The Matanza-Riachuelo River basin case is a clear example of this dynamic. ACUMAR was created with the sole purpose of regulating and managing the cleanup project, but it had an unclear policy goal (beyond, of course, the general objective of cleaning up the basin). Its ideological and technical bent remained unclear as it started operating: was it a strong proenvironment agency that would use its legitimacy to prioritize the cleanup effort over all other (economic) interests? Or was it an agency more akin to a public utilities regulator, concerned with economic efficiency and cost recovery?

As it turned out, ACUMAR was neither. Its emphasis changed as it interacted with other actors in the regulatory space—from focusing on the environment, to considering costs, and then back to the environment. This finding differs from the idea of policy transfer, which implies that the "policy" remains for the most part unchanged as it is transferred.[20] To be sure, the idea of "transfer" does acknowledge that the policy must "take root" and deal with its context, but it frames this as a problem of effectiveness; the policy's internal rationale remains untouched. The same can be said of literature on transplants and "legal origins," and the prescriptive agenda attached thereto,[21] which has had some influence on thinking within multilateral institutions working in the development field.[22] The concept of transplant assumes that law is an instrument that can be used to solve certain kinds of problems in varying contexts. Again, the most sophisticated versions of this literature acknowledge that the effectiveness of these transplants may require that the context be considered, but the instrument itself is not transformed as it is used. The focus remains on the IRA as an isolated and static actor that adopts regulation based on its expertise and that is required to consider the impact of its regulation on the wider context but remains oblivious of the effects of the wider context on itself.

In contrast, our research suggests that the internal rationale of some IRAs does change as their policies are implemented over the years, and courts have an important role in this process. The case of waste management in Bogotá, researched by Carolina Moreno, provides an example. Colombia is a standard case of expertise-based regulation for public utilities, adopted by IRAs established in the 1990s. In the case of Bogotá, waste management was arranged, also in the 1990s, through the concession of exclusive service areas to private providers. The creation of these exclusive areas required the approval of the national IRA; once approved, the municipality's independent agency signed the concession contracts with private providers and set the tariff structure through the contract. In doing this, both the national IRA and the municipality's agency followed an efficiency-based rationale, in which the main considerations were cost recovery and universal coverage.

As Moreno reports, this regulatory framework overlapped with the human rights of informal waste pickers *(recicladores)*, who traditionally have earned a living by going through the city's garbage containers. The tariff structure failed to recognize a cost associated with their work. Moreover, it established a duty on consumers: to dispose of waste using private concessionaries (mainly through closed garbage containers, which could be picked up by trucks), thus putting waste pickers out of business. This conflict ended up before the Constitutional Court, which ordered that the tariff structure both take into consideration the human rights of waste pickers and, eventually, strike down the whole bidding process—not because of disputes related

20 David P. Dolowitz & David Marsh, *Learning from Abroad: The Role of Policy Transfer in Contemporary Policy-Making,* 13(1) Governance 5–23 (2000).

21 Rafael La Porta, Florencio Lopez-de-Silanes, & Andrei Shleifer, *The Economic Consequences of Legal Origins,* 46(2) J. Econ. Lit. 285–332 (2008).

22 Alvaro Santos, *The World Bank's Uses of the "Rule of Law" Promise in Economic Development,* in *The New Law and Economic Development: A Critical Appraisal* 253–300 (David M. Trubek & Alvaro Santos ed., Cambridge U. Press 2006).

to the contract but because the tariff structure underlying the bidding process failed to consider the human rights of informal waste pickers.[23]

The trajectory of the regulatory agency in this case suffered important changes. As it interacted with the Constitutional Court for almost a decade, both the national and the municipal IRAs struggled to include the language of human rights in their decision making. The Constitutional Court spoke in deontological terms, requiring the regulator to consider the right to work of waste pickers and, even more complex, their right to a "vital minimum," that is, a constitutional construct that imposes on the state the duty to provide for the minimum material needs of its citizens so as to guarantee their dignity. The regulatory agencies, in contrast, had a fairly functionalist view of rights and the law; their role was to create a predictable and stable environment for the investor and to respect property and contractual rights.

The clash of rationalities was imminent, but it did not lead to paralysis. The independent agencies shifted their discourse and developed a different kind of regulation but still maintained the overall structure of privatization and concessions. Interestingly, even after the recent political upheaval in Bogotá concerning waste management, when a left-wing mayor tried to terminate the concession contracts, the basic tariff structure remained in place. The deep grammar of regulation that resulted from the interaction between the IRAs and the Constitutional Court, which mixed elements of both standard efficiency-seeking regulatory practice and human rights, became the new regulatory common sense in the country.

The fact that an institution (in this case, IRAs) needs to adapt to its context seems intuitive enough. However, the dynamics of change and adaptation seem foreign to the traditional reading of IRAs and their role in the delivery of essential services, as they continue to be portrayed as static actors with univocal rationality that "travels" across the world. Part of the problem is the idea of deviation from what are termed "best practices." As seen earlier, the logic underlying IRAs is one of credible commitments, which in turn requires a certain level of independence from political pressures.

Interactions of the kind described here can be read as a deviation from these best practices. The fact that a Constitutional Court intervenes in the regulatory process can be read not as an exercise in adaptation but as a deviation from the required independence that makes for good regulation. There is a specific meaning attached to a "good" regulatory system, which can be easily consulted in the World Bank's *Handbook for Evaluating Infrastructure Regulatory Systems*.[24] If a regulatory framework deviates from this standard, it is "wrong" and needs to be "fixed."

---

23 Corte Constitucional Colombia, *Sentencia T-724*, M.P. Jaime Araujo Renteria (2003), http://corte-constitucional.vlex.com.co/vid/-43620288;] Corte Constitucional Colombia; *Auto 275*, M.P. Juan Carlos Henao (2011), http://www.corteconstitucional.gov.co/relatoria/2010/T-616-10.htm.

24 Ashley C. Brown, Jon Stern, & Bernard William Tenenbaum, *Handbook for Evaluating Infrastructure Regulatory Systems* (World Bank 2006).

This prescriptive mode is often problematic, because there is the possibility of normative disagreement with the model of the state that underlies regulatory good practices, as embodied in instruments such as the *Handbook,* that is, the idea of the state as an interest-driven actor that should remain in the background as regulator rather than play an active role as service provider.[25] If such disagreement occurs, then best practices become impositions of multilateral institutions, which then trigger a political debate well known in Latin America.

Interestingly, though, the Colombian case study suggests that, in the case of regulatory governance, the disagreement seldom occurs at that level of "hot" ideological politics. Perhaps due to the amazing expansion of IRAs in Latin America, both defenders of best practices and those who resist them assume that the rationale underlying IRAs remains unchanged as time passes. Their rationale is seen as a "fact," which one embraces or rejects but never tries to change. However, our research suggests that this is not necessarily the case. Even the basic (and admittedly debatable) understanding of the state changes as IRAs live out their lives in their national context. Sometimes it changes toward recognizing a more active role for the state, as was the case in the Colombian example, or it could change otherwise. As IRAs adapt to their environment, their inner rationale also adapts, and this transforms regulatory governance.

The same could be observed in the Matanza-Riachuelo River basin case, where there is clear agreement on the overall goal of environmental improvement. However, this goal triggered ever-changing regulatory strategies on behalf of ACUMAR, some of which reflect diverging ideological commitments, some more market-oriented than others. But this is hardly a case of mere deviation from best practices. It implies a complex process of interaction and adaptation that may lead to different courses of action to achieve the goal of an appropriate delivery of essential services, such as appropriate waste management or a clean environment. From this perspective, the experience of judiciary involvement in the cases researched in Colombia and Argentina suggests that there is a wide range of experimentation that is possible in regulatory governance, where institutions are players that repeatedly shape each other. Beyond the top-down approach of best practices, the trajectory of IRAs seems also to involve adaptation and learning from other institutions following a different rationale. This may suggest that a way to improve delivery of services is to go beyond best practices, and to gear the interaction and adaptation that is already occurring to a more purposeful process of experimentation.

Experimentalism, Expertise, and Interactions

Much of the dynamic described in the previous two sections can be thought of as instances of experimentalist governance, where an ultimate goal is set and autonomy is given to relatively independent agents to use different means

25 Megan Donaldson & Benedict Kingsbury, *Ersatz Normativity or Public Law in Global Governance: The Hard Case of International Prescriptions for National Infrastructure Regulation,* 14(1) Chi. J. Intl. L. 1–51 (2013).

to achieve that goal, subject to constant review and deliberation.[26] Confirming the need to go beyond best practices, our research suggests that this is an important angle when thinking about regulatory governance in Latin America. However, it still seems unclear whether this is an actual emergence of experimentalist governance in the region.

In this respect, the case of waste management in Bogotá stands in sharp contrast with the Matanza-Riachuelo River experience. Interaction between the Colombian judiciary and IRAs seems ill-suited for an experimentalist description; while the interaction indeed occurred and had impacts, it was not part of a purposive process of adaptation and experimentation toward an ultimate goal. Rather, it seemed to be an ad hoc process, with no clear ultimate goal and no organized system of review and deliberation. In this sense, while the waste management case does evidence a process of IRA adaptation triggered by interaction with a court, this process was not crucially driven by iterative sharing of knowledge. Instead, the injection of deontological values (such as human rights) into the functional contractual framework of concessions seems more an instance of *bricolage,* that is, the tinkering with the deep grammar of neoliberal regulatory governance to achieve new norms, without a notion of the causal pathways that would lead these new legal utterances to achieve the overall policy goal of a better waste management.[27] In contrast, the Argentinean case suggests a more structured process of experimentalist governance, where interaction in the regulatory space seems geared to better knowledge, which would enhance ACUMAR's effectiveness. The process implies the adoption of a broad goal (the cleanup), and of specific metrics (the UN's ECLAC indicators), under which the performance of the "autonomous" entity (ACUMAR) would be monitored in consultation with relevant stakeholders, who participated through the spaces opened by the ombudsman, following orders by the Supreme Court.

Even if the cases investigated provide uncertain evidence of an actual turn in Latin America toward experimentalist governance, such examples do underscore the importance of knowledge production and diffusion in regulatory governance in the region. Cognitive pathways develop, as knowledge flows between IRAs and other institutions that populate the regulatory space, transforming the way in which issues are framed and understood. To be sure, cognitive frameworks are important in general political processes,[28] but they seem particularly relevant in the case of regulatory governance, where techni-

---

26 Charles F. Sabel & Jonathan Zeitlin, *Learning from Difference: The New Architecture of Experimentalist Governance in the EU,* 14(3) European L. J. 271–327 (2008); Charles F. Sabel & Jonathan Zeitlin, *Experimentalist Governance,* in *The Oxford Handbook of Governance,* 169–86 (David Levi-Faur ed., Oxford U. Press 2012).

27 Claude Lévi-Strauss, *The Savage Mind,* Nature of Human Society Series (Weidenfeld & Nicolson 1966).

28 Robert D. Benford & David A. Snow, *Framing Processes and Social Movements: An Overview and Assessment,* 26(1) Annual Rev. Sociology 611–39 (2000).

cal expertise plays a key role in shaping the issues, suggesting causal relations, and providing legitimacy for IRAs and other actors in the regulatory space.

The important role of knowledge can be seen in the case study on Colombian health care developed by Maria Prada and Santiago Rojas. In 2006, after several years of massive failure in the implementation of a new health care system by regulators, the Colombian Constitutional Court stepped in, adopting an ambitious decision aimed at solving some of the system's structural problems. The problem, however, was that the court stepped into a regulatory space with a steep learning curve; health care is a very technical field that had been dominated by economists since liberalization occurred in the early1990s. The complexities of the health care system were not lost to the court, which adopted a mammoth four-hundred-page decision that tried to find strategic bottlenecks in the system and gave specific orders to dozens of governmental institutions to fix them.

Foreseeing difficulties with the implementation of such a wide-ranging decision, the court implemented a complex monitoring procedure, where agencies constantly had to report back to the court on their improvements. During this process, the court oscillated between judicial activism in the form of direct regulation (mainly in the 2006 decision) and a more restrained tone, adopted during the monitoring process, deferent to the expertise of more-established players in the regulatory space. The institutional form of this dynamic mirrors that of the Matanza-Riachuelo case, as the Colombia court tried here to establish a structure of agency autonomy and monitoring, closely resembling ideas of experimentalist governance. The court would thus rely on the expertise of other agencies in the regulatory space to find the most appropriate means to achieve a given goal, but it still defined the goals to be achieved.

This structure required a reliable system of monitoring, which the court tried to develop by establishing the parameters for acceptable indicators, which would in turn be adopted by the regulatory agencies themselves, and then reported back to the court. Highlighting the global dimension of this process, the standard that the court adopted for this purpose was not national but international: the basic framework of health indicators developed by the Inter-American Commission of Human Rights, which became part of the health care regulatory space where the Colombian court acted. As noted earlier, a similar pattern was observed in the Argentinean case, where the Supreme Court used international indicators (in that case, the UN's ECLAC) to structure a credible system of monitoring.

The role of knowledge and expertise in the process of monitoring is remarkable. In sharp contrast with its strong ("activist") original decision, the follow-up process shows a court open to learn from the agencies it interacts with, a move that may point both to a more deferential attitude toward the technical expertise of these agencies and to the relative lack of political power of the court. Moreover, this attitude also applied to "experts" in civil society. The court held open hearings, where it invited NGOs to participate, but, more interestingly, it also created an Expert Commission: a standing committee of about 30 people, chosen by the court, consisting mainly of NGO and private insurers' representatives as well as some academics. The commission's task was to enhance the court's technical knowledge by discussing the challenges faced by the health care system in implementing the court's structural injunctions and possible alternative means to comply. The commission met in Constitutional Court building, with court law clerks setting the agenda and moderating the discussion among the experts. Afterward, a summary of the debate and the conclusions were sent to the justices in charge of the monitoring process.

An interesting development occurred during this process, triggered by the interaction of courts and regulatory agencies. Much of the legitimacy of IRAs is derived from their "expert" status, as opposed to the "political" opportunism of nonindependent institutions and of Congress. The court's intervention seems also to place the onus on the "technical" side of the equation, this time, though, based on a different technical expertise: law. However, the court also creates mechanisms to draw from *other* technical knowledge and tries to include it in its own process of monitoring—not as a binding order, to be sure, but as a general framework of discussion.

The goal of this "expert" consultation seems different from public hearings, which the court also held. The idea here seems less to provide voice to stakeholders than to tap into expertise that the court seems to lack. This layout points to a form of participation in regulatory governance that is different from notice-and-comment procedures and other similar participatory arrangements.

It is hard to estimate the exact influence of this process in the final outcome. The court did not refer to this process in its further decisions, and the "Commission of Experts" was not convened again. The very existence of this process, however, underscores the importance of informal expert consensus in the delivery of essential services in Latin America. In much the same way that best practices are often the result of a technocratic consensus among experts who define the vocabulary being deployed by IRAs in domestic settings, the interaction of such agencies with courts seems also influenced by the role of expert knowledge.

The flow of such knowledge can be better understood in terms of the global regulatory space. It is developed in sites beyond a particular nation-state, such as the World Bank in the case of the *Handbook for Evaluating Infrastructure Regulatory Systems,* or the Inter-American Commission of Human Rights in the case of health indicators, and is then deployed transnationally in different domestic settings. Improving voice and accountability, especially in regard to this specific aspect of the global regulatory space and its impact on the delivery of essential services, remains challenging despite its importance.[29] Recent scholarship has tried to frame similar exercises of power through information as expressions of "international public authority," thus subject

29 Megan Donaldson & Benedict Kingsbury, *Ersatz Normativity or Public Law in Global Governance: The Hard Case of International Prescriptions for National Infrastructure Regulation,* 14(1) Chi. J. Intl. L. 1–51 (2013).

to requirements of public law or of global administrative law.[30] Opening new spaces of participation in the regulatory process risks expanding the influence of experts, whose opinions could outweigh the opinion of nonexperts; in the Colombian case, the "Commission of Experts" seemed to have more direct access to the decision-making process. Moreover, the question of accountability also poses challenges: should scholars think of expertise as a source of authority in the global regulatory space? How can they start thinking about accountability in that context?[31]

Conclusion: Courts and Agencies as Institutions, Actors, and Spaces of Deliberation

Our research posits a regulatory space where different institutions interact. This interaction occurs at three different levels.

On a first level, private parties (e.g., consumers and service providers) are actors that are regulated by these institutions; they have exogenous preferences, and courts and IRAs are constraints to their interactions; they are "institutions" in the sense that they embody and enact rules of the game that private actors must follow.[32] This is the standard view of regulation and was observed in our research. For instance, in the waste disposal case, the central point was to create regulatory incentives so that informal waste pickers could continue doing their job. The IRA first had to adopt some command-and-control regulation in order to lead private suppliers to open a space for this to happen; it then had to force the discussion on certain contractual clauses to achieve this goal.

At this level, interinstitutional interaction presents certain kinds of challenges and opportunities for both private actors and institutions. For private actors, institutional interplay opens a wide range of possible strategic behaviors by adopting cross-institutional political strategies. Forum shopping is a possibility, as was the case in Bogotá, where waste pickers went to the Constitutional Court to get what the IRA was denying. Private parties may also engage in fostering the creation of a *new* institution (such as ACUMAR, in Argentina) to trigger interaction with existing institutions that may benefit the private actor. Moreover, private actors may seek to trigger internal insti-

---

30 On public law, *see* Armin von Bogdandy & Matthias Goldmann, *Taming and Framing Indicators: A Legal Reconstruction of the OECD's Programme for International Student Assessment (PISA)* in *Governance by Indicators: Global Power through Quantification and Rankings*, 52–85 (Benedict Kingsbury ed., Oxford U. Pr. 2012); on global administrative law, see Sabino Cassese & Lorenzo Casini. 2012. *Public Regulation of Global Indicators* in *Governance by Indicators: Global Power through Quantification and Rankings* 465–74 (Benedict Kingsbury et al. ed., Oxford U. Press).

31 *See* Rene Urueña, *The Rise of the Constitutional Regulatory State in Colombia: The Case of Water Governance,* 6(3) Regulation & Governance 282–99 (2010); David Kennedy, *Challenging Expert Rule: The Politics of Global Governance,* 27 Sydney L. Rev. 5 (2005).

32 Douglass C. North, *Institutions Matter,* Econ. History (1994), http://128.118.178.162/eps/eh/papers/9411/9411004.pdf.

tutional change by using interaction, as when Colombian health care patients used litigation in order to change internal procedures of health regulatory agencies. Finally, though we did not observe this, it is possible to expect that private actors may also seek to create strategic inconsistency, by seeking interaction between institutions that lead to inconsistent results.

For institutions, the main challenge at this level is effectiveness. Interinstitutional interplay may hinder the effectiveness of regulation directed toward private actors. In the waste management example, the IRA adopted a set of rules whose impact was undermined by the intervention of a court. However, interaction could also bolster effectiveness, by lending legitimacy to a weak institution (as was the case of health care in Colombia) or by providing an enforcement mechanism that the IRA lacked, as the example of ACUMAR in Argentina shows.

At a second level, institutions themselves are actors. As such, their interactions can be driven by strategic behavior as well: institutions can compete with each other, cooperate, or end up co-opting or dominating other institutions in the regulatory space. Our research suggests at least two ways to think about this scenario. First, IRAs behave as actors, and courts set the rules for their interaction. That was the case in Argentina, where several institutions with overlapping mandates behaved strategically and failed to solve an environmental challenge. The Supreme Court consequently stepped in to develop rules of coordination. Second, a court can also be one of the actors behaving strategically: the Colombian Constitutional Court competed with other agencies in the health care case, successfully leading many of them in following its regulatory scheme.

This latter situation brings up the question of the role of judicial review in the global regulatory space. As seen earlier, most literature in regulatory governance situates courts either as enforcers of property and contract rights or as a limit to the power of independent agencies. The case studies examined in this chapter suggest a different landscape. Courts seem not to be external to the regulatory space; rather, they appear to be actors within it. They develop specific regulations, compete with other regulatory agencies, and seem to be in need of legitimacy. This need for legitimacy may have implications on the institutional design of judicial review in Latin America, which has been traditionally expansive. Possible normative outcomes could include creating constitutional frameworks that restrain courts in their new regulatory role, or the exact opposite: embracing the role of courts as actors in the regulatory space, and developing constitutional frameworks that set the conditions for a wholly new form of regulation resulting from the interaction between courts and independent agencies. How would regulatory reform and judicial review be transformed if the rule (and not the exception) was active involvement of the judiciary in regulation?

At this second level, where institutions behave as actors, interaction also triggers interesting processes of learning and adaptation. The rationale of IRAs does not remain unchanged, as the waste management case showed.

Interaction can be structured in such a way as to take advantage of this learning process: some of the efforts discussed in this chapter (in Argentina, for instance, and in the health care case in Colombia) seem close to experimentalist views of governance. Such possible influence of experimentalist governance is in stark contrast when the focus is on best practices, but it may suggest an interesting range of possibilities to enhance delivery of essential services to the poorest. Instead of focusing on IRAs as stand-alone units and on the ways that things should be done, scholars could think in terms of interaction and how it triggers learning and experimentation. One way to make this approach operational is to think about institutional design that opens spaces for interactional learning. Some of the examples explored here, though, seem to do that on an ad hoc basis, without purposefully highlighting the learning aspect of the regulatory interaction.

From this perspective, multilateral financial institutions may have an important contribution to make. As seen, much of adapting and learning is based on knowledge. In fact, the very definition of the problems that need to be solved is influenced by issues of framing and cognitive path dependencies. While funds for institutional functioning are crucial (e.g., the World Bank's involvement with ACUMAR), much of the regulatory heavy lifting is done under the form of informal expert networks, often influenced by state-of-the-art knowledge produced by multilateral institutions. This is an angle of the delivery of essential services that seems important to explore, both in its promises and in its challenges of accountability and participation.

At the third level, regulatory regimes may also interact. Although this idea may seem peculiar from the perspective of law and development scholarship, it has proved fruitful in international law and international relations.[33] Global regimes, featuring a specialized set of norms, a distinct institutional architecture (including courts), a distinct epistemic community, and a particular rationale, can be seen as independent enough to "collide" with other specialized global regimes.[34] We observed some hints of this possibility. The waste management experience can be seen as part of Colombian institutional politics, but also as a Colombian expression of a more global interaction between international human rights and the rules of investment protection. While this approach is less conducive to specific proposals of domestic institutional reform, it would seem that improving delivery of essential services to the poor requires that scholars, activists, and development experts widen their angle to think also of delivery in terms of global governance.

---

33 *See* Martti Koskenniemi, *Hegemonic Regimes*, in *Regime Interaction in International Law: Facing Fragmentation*, 305–23 (Margaret Young ed., Cambridge U. Press 2012); Gunther Teubner & Peter Korth, *Two Kinds of Legal Pluralism: Collision of Transnational in the Double Fragmentation of the World Society*, in *Regime Interaction in International Law: Facing Fragmentation* (Margaret Young ed., Cambridge U. Press 2012); Robert O. Keohane & David G. Victor, *The Regime Complex for Climate Change*, 9(1) Perspectives Pol. 7–23 (2011).

34 Gunther Teubner & Andreas Fischer-Lescano, *Regime-Collisions: The Vain Search for Legal Unity in the Fragmentation of Global Law*, Mich. J. Intl. L. 999 (2004).

PART VI

Anticorruption and Stolen Assets Recovery

17
The New Brazilian Anticorruption Law
Federation Challenges and Institutional Roles

William Coelho and Letícia Barbabela

After a long period of military dictatorship, Brazil's democracy established a new constitutional order. The 1988 Constitution laid the foundation for governance and anticorruption strategies that could achieve the objectives specified in Article 3: to build a free, just, and solidaristic society; to guarantee national development; to eradicate poverty and substandard living conditions; to reduce social and regional inequalities; and to promote the well-being of all, without prejudice as to origin, race, sex, color, age, or any other form of discrimination.

Corruption has plagued society since the earliest of times, and as history has advanced, corruption seems to have become more resistant to preventive measures. Today, corruption is a billion-dollar business that consumes funds intended for health care, education, and infrastructure, and impedes the realization of Brazil's constitutional objectives. A study conducted in 2010 by the Federation of Industries of São Paulo State calculated that the cost of corruption in Brazil in 2008 was between 1.38 percent and 2.3 percent of the country's GDP, or between R$41.5 billion and R$69.1 billion.[1]

Over the past decade, the Brazilian Congress has undertaken a series of legislative reforms and promulgated new laws enhancing Brazil's anticorruption legal framework. Even the Organisation for Economic Co-operation and Development's (OECD's) Working Group on Bribery[2] recognized Brazil's efforts to implement the International Anti-Bribery Convention and recommendations. Nevertheless, Brazil still scores very low in anticorruption rankings such as the Transparency International Corruption Perceptions Index and the World Bank Worldwide Governance Indicators.

This chapter first explains the national context in which the new anticorruption laws have appeared, focusing on the peculiarities of the Brazilian Federation model and the existing anticorruption legal framework, including the features of the new Anticorruption Law, Act 12,846/2013. The chapter then clarifies the roles of the private sector, the Office of the Comptroller General, and the Ministério Público. The chapter concludes that the Anticorruption

---

1 *See* the Federation of Industries of São Paulo State website at http://www.fiesp.com.br/indices-pesquisas-e-publicacoes/relatorio-corrupcao-custos-economicos-e-propostas-de-combate/.

2 *See* OECD Working Group on Bribery, *Brazil: Phase 2. Follow-up Report on the Implementation of the Phase 2 Recommendations* 3 (2010), http://www.oecd.org/daf/anti-bribery/anti-briberyconvention/45518279.pdf.

Law is a major paradigm shift in addressing corruption in Brazil, not least because it demands changes in the way that both the public and the private sectors deal with anticorruption challenges.

The Challenges of the Brazilian Federation Model

Dynamic political and institutional arrangements shape the use of power; understanding federalism as a way to share power and responsibility is critical to comprehending the roles of national institutions.

It is not possible to advocate a pure or authentic model of federalism. Research shows a broad range of federation frameworks and meanings, creating a colorful kaleidoscope of experiences and structures for each and every federalized nation, based on geopolitical factors, political leadership, and diverse historical legacies. Contextual and circumstantial flexibility is inherent to a federal system, and historically the pendulum has swung between more centralized and, at times, decentralized governance.

The complex influence of factors on the formation of federations is summarized in James Bryce's[3] notions of centrifugal and centripetal forces on political constitutions. Centripetal forces act on independent states, which merge to form one large sovereign state through an agreement or a treaty after partially giving up their sovereignty (segregative formation). In the United States,[4] for example, the township was organized before the county, the county before the state, the state before the union. Conversely, centrifugal pressures impel unitary states to break down and disperse into several states linked by a federation (aggregative formation). Moreover, scholars generally recognize two levels of federal government: national and state.[5]

On February 24, 1891, the day of the promulgation of the first republican constitution in Brazil, political institutions were modeled on the American federal system, based on the "compound republic" ideas of Alexander Hamilton, James Madison, and John Jay.[6] But unlike the U.S. experience, Brazil's federalism was the result of centripetal forces (segregative formation) that,

---

3 James Bryce, *Studies in History and Jurisprudence* (Clarendon 1901).

4 *See* Alexis de Tocqueville, *Democracy in America,* vol. 1, 61–81 (Henry Reeve Henry transl., J. C. Spencer ed., J. & H. G. Langley 1841).

5 C. Friederich, *Trends of Federalism in Theory and Practice* (Pall Mall 1998); M. Burgess, *Comparative Federalism: Theory and Practice* (Routledge 2006); D. Elazar, *Federalism: An Overview* (HSRC 1995); E. L. Gibson, *Federalism and Democracy in Latin America* (Johns Hopkins U. Press 2004); V. A. Earle, *Federalism: Infinite Variety in Theory and Practice* (F. E. Peacock 1968); Ivo D. Duchacek, *Comparative Federalism: The Territorial Dimension of Politics* (U. Press Am. 1987).

6 A. Hamilton, J. Madison, & J. Jay, *The Federalist: A Collection of Essays Written in Favor of The New Constitution, as Agreed upon by The Federal Convention* (H. B. Dawson ed., Morrisania 1864).

exceptionally, recognized three levels within a symmetrical federal government: the union, the states, and the municipalities.[7]

In short, the municipalities, together with the states, the Federal District (Brasília), and the union,[8] compose the federal entities in Brazil. Each municipality has administrative and political autonomy and its own executive and legislative branches; the municipal taxes, laws, and institutions tend to vary.[9]

Municipalities occupy a unique position in the Brazilian Federation.[10] According to Anwar Shah, a World Bank specialist in fiscal federalism, "municipal governments in Brazil . . . should be the envy of all governments in [the] developing (or even advanced nations) world." Similarly, another Brazilian scholar, J. A. de O. Baracho, states that the "municipalism, with its strong prestige in Constitutional order, strengthens the ties between state and community, enhancing planning and applying social policies to foster greater interaction between federal and local government."[11]

The Brazilian federal model shaped the internalization of international anticorruption mechanisms. Because municipalities are considered federal entities in Brazil, each municipal branch has the same authority as a state or the union to use anticorruption mechanisms. Thus, all of these federal entities have the power to apply fines to companies or strike deferred prosecution agreements, for example. Therefore, unifying the agenda of the numerous colegitimates is a challenge to the implementation of the new Anticorruption Law.

Taking Regulation Seriously

Before examining the perspectives of the new anticorruption law itself, a brief look at Brazilian history in terms of anticorruption legislation is in order.

During President Getúlio Vargas's administration, Brazil's 1940 Penal Code (Decree-Law 2,848/1940) dedicated a full chapter to offenses against public administration, with a range of situations envisaged, including 14

---

7 According to Article 1 of the Brazilian Constitution:

> The Federative Republic of Brazil, formed by the indissoluble union of the states and municipalities and of the federal district, is a legal democratic state and is founded on: I – sovereignty; II – citizenship; III – the dignity of the human person; IV – the social values of labor and of the free enterprise; and V – political pluralism.

8 The federal district has both municipality and state competences; therefore, it is not considered a federation-level entity here.

9 Otherwise, municipalities would have no judiciary power and no public prosecutors. For municipal matters, state's judges and public prosecutors are entitled to act.

10 *See* J. A. L. Sampaio, *O Município no Direito Comparado*, in *Vinte Anos da Constituição Federal de 1988* 661–87 (Cláudio Pereira de Souza Neto, Daniel Sarmento, & Gustavo Binenbojm eds., Lumen Juris 2009).

11 A. Shah, *The New Federalism in Brazil* 14 (PRE Working Paper Series, World Bank 1990); J. A. de O. Baracho, *O Principio da Subsidiariedade: Conceito e Evolucao*, 200 Revista de Direito Administrativo 25 (Apr.–June 1995).

articles[12] for public officials' misconduct[13] and 10 articles[14] for ordinary citizen's corrupt acts.

Articles 316, 317 and 333[15] define specific corruption offenses in the Penal Code, including official misconduct, where a public official demands an unlawful advantage[16] or practices active or passive bribery.[17] In general, any payment or advantage requested, solicited, or received by a public official, whether promised or offered, is against the law, regardless of the value of the payment or advantage.

During the 1960s, the Tax Evasion Law (Act 4,729/1965) established the falsification of accounting documents as a criminal offense, and Decree-Law 201/1967 defined a series of acts related to abuse of office by mayors and council members as misconduct and established sanctions for those acts.

At the very end of the dictatorial regime, Act 7,492/1986, which regulates crimes against the Brazilian financial system, came into force.

Other than these rules, most of the relevant anticorruption legislation was passed under the new constitution.

---

12 Arts. 312–36 of the Penal Code.

13 Brazil adopted a broad concept of "public official" for criminal law purposes:

> Art. 327: For the purposes of criminal law, anyone who, even though temporarily or unpaid, performs a public job, position or function is considered to be a public official.
>
> Para. 1. Anyone who performs a public job, or holds a function in a para-state body or who works for a service-providing company hired or contracted to carry out any typical activity in the Public Administration is also considered to be a public official.
>
> Para. 2. The penalty is increased by 1/3 (one third) if the offender on the crimes established at this Chapter holds a function in a committee, steering board or advisory organ of a governmental entity or of an entity owned by the government.

14 Arts. 328–37 of the Penal Code.

15 "*Concussão,*" according to art. 316: "Demanding an improper advantage, for oneself or for another, directly or indirectly, even when out of his/her duties (functions) or before assuming his/her duties (functions) but because of them. Penalty – deprivation of liberty from 2 (two) to 8 (eight) years and fine."

"Passive corruption," according to art. 317: "Requesting or receiving an improper advantage for oneself or for another person, directly or indirectly, even if outside or prior to assuming the public office, but due to such function, or accepting a promise of such an advantage. Penalty – deprivation of liberty from 2 (two) up to 8 (eight) years and fine."

"Active corruption," according to art. 333: "Offering or promising an improper advantage to a public official, in order for him to conduct, to omit or to delay an official act. Penalty – deprivation of liberty from 2 (two) to 12 (twelve) years and fine.

Sole Paragraph – The sentence is increased by 1/3 (one third) if in order to get the advantage or to follow the promise, the public official holds back or omits an official act or practices that act breaking his official duties."

16 In the Brazilian Penal Code, this criminal offense is called "*concussão.*"

17 In the Brazilian Penal Code, this criminal offense is called "active" and "passive" corruption, the former being the demanding side and the latter the supplying side.

The "Law on Administrative Improbity" (Act 8,429/1992) is an important piece of anticorruption legislation, regulating both civil and administrative infractions. This law describes in Articles 9, 10, and 11 a series of actions that, if practiced by public officials, are subject to penalties. These articles are divided among acts concerning illicit enrichment of public officials, squandering of public assets, and offenses against the principles of public administration.

Anyone who induces or contributes to an act of improbity or who benefits from such an act, directly or indirectly, is subject to punishment under the law, regardless of whether an individual or a legal entity committed the act. Even if the public official is the recipient of the money, anyone who took part in the official's enrichment is also liable. Inasmuch as this law has a civil nature and provides civil sanctions, it may be applied to both individuals and legal entities.

The Public Procurement Act (Act 8,666/1993) established rules about public procurement and contains provisions on both criminal and civil penalties regarding procurement and bidding fraud.

Complementary Act 135/2010, which amends Complementary Act 34/1990 (the "Law of Ineligibilities"), was the result of a people's initiative. This was a bill signed by over 1 million voters to increase the anticorruption liability of political candidates. Pursuant to the so-called Clean Record Law, any politician who has been impeached or who has resigned to avoid impeachment, or any politician who has been convicted by a judicial courts will be disqualified as a potential candidate for political office for any level of government for eight years.

In this legal context, Brazil signed the Inter-American Convention against Corruption (1996), ratifying it in 2002 (Decree 4,410/2002); the OECD's Convention on Combating Bribery of Foreign Public Officials in International Business Transactions (1997), ratifying it in 2000 (Decree 3,678/2000); and the UN Convention against Corruption (2004), ratifying it in 2006 (Decree 5,687/2006).[18]

Even considering that most provisions related to corruption offenses and the relevant penalties had already been laid down in the Brazilian legal framework or were under legislative discussion before the three above-mentioned conventions were signed, their ratification had a significant political impact. Accordingly, some legislative innovations for antimoney laundering crimes and tools, the introduction of a broad legal concept of foreign public officials, and preventive access to information mechanisms are highlighted below.

---

18 According to a recent study conducted by the National Secretariat of Judicial Reform, the legislative process to internalize international treaties and conventions in Brazil took between five and seven years. *See* Ministério da Justiça, *O Impacto no Sistema Processual dos Tratados Internacionais* 166 (José Luis Bolzan de Morais coord., Ministério da Justiça, Secretaria de Reforma do Judiciário 2013).

Act 9,613/1998, known as the Money Laundering Act, was created through compromises made at the Vienna Convention in 1988 to promote accountability in multiple sectors of the economy. Identifying clients and keeping records of operations and suspicious communications make people and companies subject to it. In 2012, it was amended by Act 12,683, resulting in considerable progress in preventing and combating money laundering by raising the fine to as much as R$20 million, securing goods against deterioration and devaluation, admitting any criminal offense as the origin of illicitly obtained money, and including new agents subject to the law.

In accordance with the Organization of American States (OAS) and OECD Conventions, Act 10,467/2002 amended the Brazilian Penal Code, adding Articles 337-B and 337-C, which established criminal liability for acts of corruption and bribery committed by foreign public officials and institutions. Article 337-D was added to provide a legal definition of "foreign public officials" for criminal prosecution purposes.

Besides investigative and repressive legislation, transparency has become more evident in Brazil. The Information Access Act (Act 12,527/2011) enhances prevention policies to promote transparency and to open government recognition. An important gain for community empowerment and civil society monitoring was made by impelling public entities to process information requests, ensure proactive disclosure, and guarantee full online access to official information of all branches at the local, regional, and federal levels.

As the scope of fraud and corruption varies, legislation also has to develop in order to serve as a starting point to conquer corruption. Brazil has shown, by its commitments made internationally and effective regulation implemented nationally, that fighting corruption is a prominent item on its political agenda and that the new Anticorruption Law is the step that was missing.

Act 12,846/2013: Overcoming the Liability of the Legal-Entity Loophole

Although public officials and corrupt agents could be prosecuted under the existing law, the lack of liability of legal entities for corrupt practices constituted a dangerous regulatory gap.

The regulation loophole was spotlighted by the OECD Working Group on Bribery in a 2007 report, which recommended[19] taking urgent steps.

> Brazil has not taken the necessary measures to establish the liability of legal entities for the bribery of a foreign public official. The Work-

---

19 Other OECD recommendations were raising awareness and providing training for applying the foreign bribery offense on society stakeholders, public institutions, and diplomatic representatives; and putting in place the due diligence process to verify that applicants were engaging in acts of bribery, protect whistleblowers, encourage Brazilian business activities in foreign markets, and ensure that law enforcement authorities were provided with sufficient resources. Some clauses related to tax offenses were also introduced.

> ing Group has determined that the current statutory regime for the liability of legal entities is inconsistent with Article 2 of the Convention. As a consequence legal entities are not punishable in Brazil for foreign bribery by effective, proportionate or dissuasive sanctions as required by Article 3 of the Convention. The Group recommends that this serious gap in the law be urgently addressed, and welcomes recent initiatives taken by Brazil in this regard.
>
> . . .
>
> With respect to the liability of legal entities, the Working Group acknowledges the recent initiatives taken by Brazil in this area and recommends that Brazil (i) take urgent steps to establish the direct liability of legal entities for the bribery of a foreign public official; (ii) put in place sanctions that are effective, proportionate and dissuasive, including monetary sanctions and confiscation; and (iii) ensure that, in relation to establishing jurisdiction over legal entities, a broad interpretation of the nationality of legal entities is adopted.[20]

In a similar vein, during the third round (2011) of review in the implementation of the Inter-American Convention against Corruption, when serious concerns were raised about the gap in legal entities' liability, the Committee of Experts suggested the following recommendation:

> Adopt measures to allow application of the appropriate penalties, subject to its constitution and the fundamental principles of its legal order, to companies domiciled in its territory that engage in the conduct described in article VIII of the Convention, regardless of the penalties that may be applicable to the persons linked to those companies who may be involved in the commission of acts constituting such conduct.[21]

Unlike other countries' legal systems, there were no specific provisions directed at anticorruption compliance in Brazil. There was, for instance, no analogue to the internal controls requirement of the U.S. Foreign Corrupt Practices Act (FCPA). Therefore, Brazilian law did not punish corporate corruption properly.

Indeed, most cases of grand corruption have at least one thing in common: the use of companies and structures established through legal means to hide illegal acts. A 2011 World Bank study reviewed over 200 cases of corruption and concluded that shelf companies were an active and often-used means of concealing corruption.[22]

---

20 OECD Working Group on Bribery, *supra* note 2, at 4.

21 The recommendations were made in the *Final Report* that was adopted by the committee, in accordance with the provisions of arts. 3(g) and 25 of its *Rules of Procedure and Other Provisions*, at the plenary session held on Sept. 16, 2011, at its 19th meeting, held at OAS Headquarters, Sept. 12–16.

22 The *Stolen Assets Recovery Initiative* report reviewed grand corruption investigations from 80 different countries and found that almost 70 percent of these cases involved corporate vehicles that concealed, at least in part, beneficial ownership information. *See* E. van der D.

In 2010, the Office of the Comptroller General (Controladoria-Geral da União; CGU) prepared the long-awaited draft bill in cooperation with the Ministry of Justice and the Federal Attorney General's Office (Advocacia Geral da União; AGU) establishing the direct liability of legal entities for acts of corruption committed against the national and foreign public administration. The bill (Bill 6,826/2010), which was inspired by the FCPA Act (1977) and the United Kingdom's Bribery Act (2010), was submitted to the Chamber of Deputies in February 2010.

At the Chamber of Deputies, apart from the existing Committees on Work, Administration, and Public Service; Taxation and Finances; Industrial, Commercial, and Economic Development; Justice, Constitution, and Citizenship, a special committee was created to inform the Chamber of Deputies on the matter. That special committee began its work in October 2011.

The special committee was given a great number of tasks, and it was by far the most active committee, and the one that took longest to give its opinion. Among those who took part in the discussion, apart from representatives, were many interest groups, including the CGU; civil society organizations representing companies and entities dealing with compliance, such as the Federation of Industries of São Paulo State, Comitê Anticorrupção e Compliance do Instituto Brasileiro de Direito Empresarial, Instituto Ethos de Empresas e Responsabilidade Social, Instituto de Estudos Sócio Econômicos, and PATRI Políticas Públicas e Relações Institucionais & Comerciais; as well as lawyers, law professors, and agencies involved in anticorruption and governance endeavors. There were organized seminars and forums outside the Congress, in São Paulo, Curitiba, and Recife, and capitals of member-states situated in the southern, southeastern, and northeastern regions of Brazil.

There were push-backs on various points and discussions on penalties, whether they should be mitigated, and if so, how it would be achieved. The special committee's final official opinion was given in April 2013. The other committees gave their opinions in June 2013.

Due to the legislative process of the bicameral Congress, after approval by the Chamber of Deputies was given, the bill was forwarded to the Senate. Plenary sessions and discussions ended in the Senate in July 2013. Back at the Chamber of Deputies, the draft law was sent to President Dilma Rousseff, who rejected three provisions: (a) the limitation of the fine, which would not exceed the value of the good or service provided for in the public contract; (b) the necessity and legal requirement of proving intention or fault for some sanctions, as opposed to civil strict liability; and (c) the provision that the extent of involvement of public officials in the corrupt act must be considered a circumstance for applying the sanctions. After that, the draft law was transformed into the law, Act 12,846/2013, in August 2013.

---

de Willebois et al., *The Puppet Master: How the Corrupt Use Legal Structures to Hide Stolen Assets and What to Do about It* (World Bank 2011).

The draft law was debated at a turbulent time, when government expenses on contracts linked to the 2014 FIFA World Cup tournament and the 2016 Summer Olympic Games generated dissatisfaction throughout the population. Consequently, in June 2013, people went to the streets demanding more public spending on public health, education, and transportation. During the year leading up to the World Cup, Brazil experienced an extensive anticorruption campaign largely motivated by citizens through social media. The online mobilization followed large investigations conducted by traditional media outlets. Alongside the protests was the trial, Criminal Case No. 470, in the Supreme Court, well known as the "Mensalão case,"[23] which made corruption policies and issues a matter of popular discussion. The public sentiment of growing intolerance for corruption and the scene of the economic crisis in Brazil created an environment for the new Anticorruption Law's easy approval.[24]

---

23 Criminal Case No. 470 began as a political scandal, known as "Mensalão," that took place during President Luiz Inácio Lula da Silva's government. Since 2004, the Brazilian Press had been writing on an alliance between the Worker's Party and the Brazilian Labor Party (PTB) involving bribery. In 2005, a congressional committee of inquiry began investigating a bribery scheme involving the Brazilian Post Office ("CPI dos Correios"). In this context PTB's president, Representative Roberto Jefferson, first brought up the term "Mensalão" (meaning, roughly, "big monthly payment"), insinuating that there was a bribery procedure organized by important people in the Worker's Party involving a monthly, expensive payment to congressmen in exchange for political support inside Congress. There was a complex plot, involving advertising agencies, high-ranking political figures, financial institutions, and public companies. The Ministério Público Federal filed Criminal Case No. 470 before the Brazilian Supreme Court in November 2007, accusing 40 people, among them the former presidential chief of staff minister in Lula's government, the former president of the Worker's Party, and the former treasurer of the Worker's Party. The trial, broadcast on a public television channel, began in 2012. The criminal offenses described involved money laundering, bribery (active and passive corruption), tax evasion, fraudulent management of a financial institution, conspiracy, and embezzlement. In 2013, 25 defendants were accused of different criminal offenses, and 11 were arrested. In November 2013 the Supreme Court president ordered the imprisonment of the authorities. In February 2014, after a close vote among justices of the Supreme Court (6 to 5), 8 defendants, including some of those already arrested, were absolved of the crime of conspiracy, which altered their term of imprisonment. Pursuant to the Brazilian Constitution, justices of the Brazilian Supreme Court are chosen by the president and must be approved by the Senate. At the time of the trial of Criminal Case No. 470, 8 out of the 11 justices had been appointed by Worker's Party presidents, 6 by President Lula, and 2 by President Rousseff. Despite the criticism directed at the trial and the positions held by the justices, Criminal Case No. 470 is considered an unprecedented event in Brazilian history and a victory for democracy.

Another high-profile political scandal was the Sanguessugas (leeches) scandal, also known as ambulance's mafia, that took place in 2006. It was a conspiracy among congressional representatives involved in the purchase of ambulances. These representatives acted together in embezzling public funds consisting of federal transfers for public health care. There were administrative procedures taken to revoke 72 representatives' terms in office.

24 In addition to the popular display of discontentment, Brazil, with the sixth-largest GDP in the world, has faced economic challenges over the past few years. Since 2010, when economic growth was at 7.5 percent, the Brazilian economy has steadily decreased. In 2011, growth was at 2.7 percent, in 2012 at 1 percent, and in 2013 there was a slight improvement, to 2.3 percent, according to the Brazilian Institute of Geography and Statistics. According to the Worldwide Governance Indicators, the "control of corruption" and "voice and accountability" indicators dropped by one percentile from 2011 to 2012. In Transparency International's International Corruption Perception Index, Brazil lost three positions from 2012 to 2013, going from 69th place to 72nd place. Aside from that, in March 2014 Standard & Poor's

The draft law was discussed in the Chamber of Deputies' special committee for over two years; it was then sent to other committees, to the Senate, back to the House, and finally to the president, which took less than four months. That this accelerated legislative process took place during the period of intense popular demonstrations against corruption was no coincidence. It is clear that popular dissatisfaction, expressed at this relevant time, overcame lobbyists' interests in freezing the legislative process of the Anticorruption Law.

International recommendations for Brazil to close the loophole became stronger, as did institutional[25] pressure, as well as pressure from the press and civil society. By signing international conventions against corruption such as those of the OAS, OECD, and the United Nations, Brazil committed to the implementation of such a law. The fight against corruption is a global matter, and the liability of legal entities is especially relevant to this issue. Domestically, Brazil had effective legal dispositions on bribing public officials, but corporate corruption was still hard to combat effectively in the existing legal framework.

Act 12,846 was approved on August 1, 2013, and pursuant to its influence on the drafting of the law, apart from the president, the minister of justice, the AGU, and the CGU signed the law. The law was promulgated on August 2 and, after a 180-day period of *vacatio legis*, came into force on January 29, 2014.

The Main Features of the New Brazilian Anticorruption Law

Act 12,846/2013, the so-called new Anticorruption Law,[26] established a comprehensive system to fight domestic and international corporate corruption in Brazil. The new law created liability for legal entities committing illicit acts against foreign public officials or national public administration, that is, in the three branches of government and at all levels of the Brazilian

---

downgraded Brazil's credit rating, creating concerns about foreign investment. Expectedly, the Brazilian government is concerned about maintaining those investments. It was an auspicious time to approve a law such as the Clean Companies Act.

25 The National Strategy for Combating Corruption and Money Laundering (Estratégia Nacional de Combate à Corrupção e Lavagem de Dinheiro; ENCCLA) was created in 2003 by an initiative taken by the Ministry of Justice as a way to contribute to the systematic fight against money laundering in Brazil. It is an articulation of agencies from the three branches of government, the Ministérios Públicos, and society that, directly or indirectly, prevent and combat corruption and money laundering and identify and recommend measures of improvement. Currently, around 60 agencies take part in ENCCLA, including the police, the judiciary, the CGU, the Federal Court of Accountability (TCU), and the Securities and Exchange Commission.

26 Strictly speaking, Act 12,486 should not be called the "Anticorruption Law," because it is really just the missing ,part of the anticorruption legal puzzle; there are other laws directed at curbing corruption. The term "Clean Companies Law" is more appropriate in the sense that it points out the specific innovation implemented by that law. However, inasmuch as the term "Anticorruption Law" has already become widespread among lawyers, public officials, and the juridical community in Brazil, it would not be worthwhile to semantically "swim against the stream."

Federation. A recent comparative study concluded that the "Brazilian law either meets or exceeds all OECD Convention requirements, except those on Enforcement."[27]

Administrative and Civil Strict Liability

According to the Brazilian Constitution—just as in the German and Italian constitutions—only individuals can be held criminally liable for corruption offenses. These individuals may face criminal, civil, and administrative sanctions. A legal entity, however, can face only civil and administrative proceedings.[28]

Nicola Bonucci, the director of legal affairs at the OECD, predicted that one of the issues the OECD would "vigorously debate" while reviewing the Brazilian Act 12,846 in June 2014 was that, while the OECD gives preference to criminal liability for the offense of bribery of foreign public officials, the Brazilian Anticorruption Act creates only civil and administrative liability for such offenses.[29]

To consider social interests and comply with international conventions, without neglecting constitutional boundaries, the new Brazilian Anticorruption Law establishes administrative and civil mechanisms to curb corporate corruption. Criminal liability for legal entities, however, depends on constitutional amendments, which require a qualified majority in Congress. Proper implementation of an administrative and civil sanctioning system can enhance the fight against corruption.

Another change in Brazilian law is the incorporation of "strict liability"[30] for corrupt acts, which means that legal entities are held liable without requiring legal proof or verification of actual fault or prior penalties. It is sufficient to prove the existence and practice of the corrupt act, the resulting consequences, and the casual connection between them. Strict liability sets aside difficulties of demonstrating subjective elements of the acts of the legal entity's manager, required in criminal proceedings.

Who Is Subject to the New Anticorruption Law?

In that corrupt acts have both a supply and a demand side, seeking only the public official's accountability for corrupt acts is not enough. Thus

---

27 Sonia Zaheer, *Brazil's Landmark Clean Companies Act: Comparison to the OECD Anti-Bribery Convention and Issues,* Pacific McGeorge Global Business & Dev. L.J. (2014).

28 An exception is art. 225, para. 3, which allows criminal liability for legal entities only for environmental crimes.

29 *See* Stella Dawson, *Brazil's Corporate Bribery Law Is a Step Forward but Faces Tough Scrutiny* (2013), http://www.trust.org/item/20131122222839-uqg1w/.

30 The use of the strict liability model for corruption acts is innovative. The standard of strict liability (or objective liability) is used in other areas of the Brazilian legal system; for example, in consumer issues, environmental damage, and state liability.

Act 12,846/2013 includes the liability of other relevant actors in corruption schemes: the companies themselves.

In the general provisions, Article 1 establishes the target of the Anticorruption Law, clarifying that the object of the law targets any type of company under Brazilian regulation, whether incorporated or not, and regardless of the form of organization or corporate model adopted for it. The law also governs any foundation, association, or foreign company that has a registered office, branch, or representation in Brazilian territory (even if the registration is temporary).

This broad concept embraces all types of enterprises and also oversees companies' transformation, incorporation, merges, and splits. It also contemplates joint liability cases of controlling or controlled companies, joint ventures, and economic groups that have engaged in corrupt practices.

Typology of Corruption Conduct

Article 5 describes in five items corrupt acts that threaten national and foreign public assets, principles of public administration,[31] and international commitments made by Brazil.

> Article 5 For the purposes of this law, all acts committed by legal entities mentioned in Article 1's sole paragraph are injurious to the domestic or to the foreign Public Administration, if they threaten the national or foreign public assets, the principles of public administration or the international commitments assumed by Brazil, by:
>
> I – Promising, offering or giving, directly or indirectly, a public agent or third part related to him an improper advantage;
>
> II – Financing, funding, sponsoring or otherwise subsidizing, the practice of any illicit acts established in this Law;
>
> III – Using a person or an entity to hide or conceal the identity or the intention of the one who benefits from the acts performed;
>
> IV – Regarding bids and contracts:
>
> a) Frustrating or defrauding, by combination or any other way, the competitive nature of the public bidding procedure;
>
> b) Preventing, hindering or defrauding the performance of any act of public bidding procedure;
>
> c) Chasing away or trying to chase away any bidder, by fraud or otherwise by offering him an advantage of any kind;
>
> d) Defrauding a public bidding or a public procurement;

31 Art. 37 of the Brazilian Constitution defines the principles of public administration as legality, impersonality, morality, publicity, and efficiency.

> e) Creating, fraudulently or irregularly, an entity to participate in public biddings or to conclude public procurements;
>
> f) Obtaining advantage or improper advantage by deception, modifications or extensions of contracts with the government, without authorization by law, convening public bidding or its contractual arrangements; or
>
> g) Manipulating or defrauding the public procurement arrangement's economic and financial balance;
>
> V – Hindering government's research or supervisory activities or intervening in its operations, especially regarding regulatory agencies or any of the National Financial System's supervisory bodies.[32]

Congress members wisely adopted the strategy of using descriptions of offenses pertaining to individual criminal, administrative, and civil liability that had already been consolidated in Brazilian jurisprudence and by scholars, mostly from the Penal Code, the Law on Administrative Probity (Act 8,429/1992), and the Public Procurement Act (Act 8,666/1993).

Sanctions, Regulation, and Sentencing

The Anticorruption Law sanctioning system comprises administrative and judicial sanctions.

The principle of *audi altera partem,* as well as the right of due process, must be observed to enforce the sanctions, provided in Article 6:

> I – Fine in the amount of 0.1% (one-tenth percent) to 20% (twenty percent) of the gross revenues[33] of the year previous to the initiation of administrative proceedings, excluding taxes, which will never be less than the advantage earned when possible to estimate; and
>
> II – Special publication of the conviction.

Article 6 is one of the most controversial articles in the Anticorruption Law, because it sets the amount of the fine that can be applied to companies that are accountable for detrimental acts against Brazil's public administration.

Article 7 lists factors to consider when a sentence is about to be passed, namely: the seriousness of the violation; the benefit that the offender could or would have gotten from the infraction; the nature of the commission of the crime; the severity of damage or the risk of damage, whichever is relevant under the circumstances; the negative effects of the act; the offender's economic situation; the company's cooperation in bringing to light the infractions; the existence of internal mechanisms or procedures toward promoting

---

32 *See* the original text in Portuguese at http://www.planalto.gov.br/ccivil_03/_ato2011-2014/2013/lei/l12846.htm.

33 If it is not possible to determine the company's annual gross revenue as a reference, the fine will be any amount from R$6,000 (approximately US$2,500) to R$60,000,000 (approximately US$25,000). *See* art. 6, para. 4.

integrity (compliance); audit and whistle-blowing triggers of accountability; the effectiveness of a code of conduct and ethics applied within the company; and the value of the contracts established.

Article 7 could be considered harsh because it states that acts can produce liability without proof of intention and knowledge on the part of company directors.

The "name and shame" sanctioning strategy,[34] another interesting stipulation in Article 7, refers to the level of publicity that the court's conviction receives, at the relevant company's expense, in widely disseminated media. In many commercial markets, upholding a reputation of trustworthiness is crucial for a company's success and business performance. This legal provision targets the company image, producing a sort of reputation-shaming effect, through the extensive disclosure of the corrupt practice. In the same vein, Article 22 creates the National Registry of Punished Companies (Cadastro Nacional de Empresas Punidas), which gathers all the sanctions applied at all levels of the federation and makes them public.

The enforcement of legal stipulations on administrative matters does not rule out further enforcement on judiciary terms. The judicial sanctions, described in Article 19, regard (a) the forfeiture of property, rights, or goods that represent advantage or profit directly or indirectly obtained from the corrupt act; (b) the cessation or suspension of activities; (c) the compulsory legal entity's dissolution in Brazil; and (d) the prohibition from receiving public incentives, grants, donations, or loans from public or publicly controlled financial institutions for one to five years.

Deferred Prosecution Agreement

Article 16 provides a sort of deferred prosecution agreement (DPA) that already exists in Brazil as a leniency agreement in Brazil's Economic Law. Article 17 allows the DPA to be used in Brazil under not just the new Anticorruption Law but also the Public Procurement Act.

According to the new Anticorruption Law, the highest authorities of each branch of government can strike an agreement with companies if the latter collaborate with investigations and are cooperative throughout the administrative process, which would result in the identification of other companies involved and in quicker access to documents and information. Therefore, the DPA can be an enforcement tool to address offenses by legal entities. The DPA is intended to encourage self-reporting by companies, as opposed to being

---

34 *See* J. G. van Erp, *Naming and Shaming in Regulatory Enforcement* (2012), http://hdl.handle.net/1765/31662, which "identifies three aspects of firms' reputations that can motivate compliance. First, a reputation is a financial asset, because it enables firms to increase their market share, share value or business opportunities. Second, entrepreneurs do not only strive for a good reputation because it pays off financially, but also because they value being regarded as respectful, credible and reliable, and want to act in accordance with social norms. Third, a reputation defines duties and obligations and thus increases firms' awareness about normative expectations of its stakeholders."

faced with the inconvenience of waiting and then fighting an administrative or a civil prosecution. For that matter, an important prerequisite to reaching the agreement is the company's corporate compliance program.

To benefit from the DPA, the company must observe certain requirements. It has to take the initiative to show interest in cooperating, and it has to cease completely its involvement in the infracting or offending acts. Also, it is necessary that the company admit its participation in the wrongdoing and completely cooperate with investigations.

This behavior can lead to a reduction of up to two-thirds of the amount fined and can also exempt companies from the aforementioned shaming sanctions. Still, the company will not be exempt from making good any damage caused. After the DPA's conclusion, if the requirements are not fulfilled, the company will be prevented from striking another DPA for three years.

Authorities Entitled to Investigate

The new Brazilian Anticorruption Law establishes that the liability of legal entities for acts of national and foreign bribery falls to each body and entity in the three branches of government (executive, legislative, and judicial) at every level of the federation (union, member-states, the Federal District, and municipalities). The OECD Working Group on Bribery, in analyzing the draft bill,[35] observed that it provided "mechanisms to establish liability and a uniform system throughout the country, with a view to strengthening the fight against corruption in accordance with the unique features of the Brazilian federal system."

Although there are decentralization benefits, there is also a major challenge for coordinating and implementing the Anticorruption Law system throughout the huge number of federal legal entities. There are 5,561 municipalities in Brazil, 26 states, the Federal District, and the union itself, totaling 5,589 federal entities, each one empowered to act under the rules of the Anticorruption Law.

The main authorities of each branch of all federal entities can investigate, conduct an administrative procedure (Article 8), propose DPAs (Article 16), and file lawsuits (Article 19).

Brazil's scattered form of federalism can lead to conflicting decisions. Because there is no central administrative mechanism for implementing uniform procedures and interpreting such matters, imbroglios that arise from administrative procedures will increase or encourage the judicialization of administrative proceedings so that legitimate final decisions can be arrived at. Keeping in mind that the Brazilian judicial system operates less than efficiently, it will be some time before courts can start ruling on cases involving the Anticorruption Law.

---

35 OECD Working Group on Bribery, *supra* note 2, at 36.

This environment of uncertainty could have a negative impact on international companies that do business in Brazil. Due to the way the judicial system works, and the fact that all federal entities enjoy a large degree of autonomy, the CGU, the federal government, and higher courts currently cannot impose a completely uniform procedure for the implementation and practice of the new law.

Another issue related to the thousands of public authorities empowered to apply the Anticorruption Law is the possibility of the inadequate use of the DPA standard, especially in small municipalities.

According to Article 16, the authorities that represent each branch within a federal entity are entitled to adopt a DPA with companies involved in wrongdoing that effectively collaborate with investigation and administrative procedures. For this to happen, the company has to identify other companies that took part in the corrupt act or acts and provide relevant information and documents quickly. So the DPA is a way to accelerate and improve investigations from the government's perspective, and to mitigate penalties or legal consequences from the company's perspective.

There are many municipalities that have a deficient or incipient administrative structure, a lack of resources, or an insufficiently trained staff. Despite the formal and symmetrical federation autonomy (which the Anticorruption Law provides for), some municipalities have a very low Human Development Index (HDI) ranking and are likely to have difficulty in applying the Anticorruption Law, especially when complex cases arise. This difficulty may cause opacity on the details of a DPA's terms and duration, and on how companies meet such agreement terms. Even worse, the lack of structure and expertise in small and poor municipalities can create a situation where the effect is contrary to that intended by the law. The empowerment of local authorities can be turned into a tool for corrupt agents to bribe businesspeople.

In 2013, Transparency International classified[36] Brazil as a country engaged in "Little or No Enforcement" of the OECD Anti-Bribery Convention.[37] Enforcement is not just a challenge related to the Anticorruption Law. Specifically, it is a problem in the Brazilian judicial system. Among the causes of difficulties in enforcement are the great number of judicial actions, the excessive opportunities to appeal, and the lack of modernization. These problems are frequently brought to the public's attention. But the main concern is not just the lack of judicial decisions; the small number of investigations opened into potentially corrupt activities is also troubling. In this light, nonjudicial ways of resolution become an interesting tool for dealing with corruption offenses.

---

36 F. Heinmann et al., *Exporting Corruption Progress Report 2013: Assessing Enforcement of the OECD Convention on Combating Foreign Bribery* (Transparency Intl. 2013).

37 The lack of enforcement is not just a Brazilian issue. According to the Transparency International 2013 study, 30 of 38 countries that signed the OECD Anti-Bribery Convention, which represents 38.2 percent of world exports, are barely investigating and prosecuting foreign bribery.

Countries should make efforts to curb corruption among institutions and public officials to achieve social and economic development and to attract international investments. But it is certain that there will be no good governance without consistent legal regulation, an engaged society, and accountable institutions.

Meanwhile, Brazil has a large number of interconnected oversight bodies that constitute a national network with the institutional mission of fostering mechanisms for preventing, detecting, punishing, and eradicating corrupt acts. This network includes the CGU and state and municipalities comptroller systems, the federal and state courts of accountability, the Federal Police Department, the State Judiciary Police, the federal and state-level Ministério Públicos, the Supreme Court, the Superior Court of Justice, the state courts, the National Council of Justice, the National Council of the Federal Prosecutor, the AGU and state and municipalities attorneys' offices, the Public Ethics Commission, and the Ministry of Justice.[38]

Facing the above concerns gives rise to institutional challenges that need to be resolved. According to the cooperative federalism model, all federal entities share responsibilities in achieving constitutional objectives and improving skills of governance; further, they must work in partnership (federal statehood) to put forward an integrative exercise of authority to curb corruption. The importance of the CGU and the Ministério Público in this matter is highlighted next.

Federal Cases and Standards: The Crucial Role of the CGU

The CGU[39] is the agency of federal government created in 2003 to assist the president of the republic in eliminating corruption, having within its structure the Secretariat for Prevention of Corruption and Strategic Information. Assistance from the CGU is provided for matters that, within the executive branch, are related to defending public assets and enhancing management transparency through internal control activities, public audits, corrective and disciplinary measures, corruption prevention, and coordinating ombudsman's activities.

---

38 The Ministry of Justice's Secretariat of Judiciary Reform (Secretaria de Reforma do Judiciário do Ministério da Justiça) constitutes an innovative approach to enhance cooperative federalism. Although it is linked with the executive branch, it has the institutional goal of articulating stakeholders, directly and indirectly, to find solutions for the Brazilian judicial system. It was created to promote, coordinate, systematize, and receive proposals regarding judiciary reform. Its main role is to articulate the executive, judiciary, and legislative branches, Ministérios Públicos, state governments, and organized civil society and international organizations. All this aims at modernizing the judiciary's management through constitutional reform and legislative changes currently underway in Congress.

39 The CGU portfolio is available at http://www.cgu.gov.br/Publicacoes/balancas/arquivos/_cgu.pdf.

In other words, at the federal level, the CGU is in charge of initiatives to curb and prevent corruption, and also to educate individuals, the public, and companies on anticorruption issues. Recently, the CGU has faced new challenges, working with matters directly related to the Information Access Act and the Anticorruption Law.

At the federal executive branch level, Article 9 of the Anticorruption Law is clear in indicating that the CGU is responsible for investigating, conducting administrative proceedings, and imposing sanctions for acts of corruption. And Article 8, Paragraph 2 reserves the right for the CGU to use any federal executive branch agency procedure that has been filed under the Anticorruption Law.

The CGU, as a federal institution, can directly act when federal matters are involved. However, at the state and municipal levels of implementing laws, the CGU occupies a cornerstone position. Foreseeing the new challenges of the Anticorruption Law and the strengthening of the cooperative federation model, the CGU acts like a mirror that reflects good technical practices for state and municipal governments, so as to unburden conflicting decisions and inefficiency arising from DPAs.

The CGU regularly issues publications,[40] such as booklets, brochures, and instruction manuals, which are published in an easy-to-read format and written in a clear and objective way that dissects legal provisions, which at first blush may seem complicated to the legally untrained eye. This pedagogical work[41] is especially relevant when dealing with the effectiveness of the law's stipulations, because it serves as orientation for public officials and policy makers, and also for civil society.

The empowerment of civil society through access to easy-to-use, high-quality information has the potential to create a stakeholder committed to the observance of the law. Particularly at the local level, if citizens become engaged in promoting accountability and making their voices heard, law enforcement can be improved.

Because the Information Access Act is enforced at the state and municipal levels, the CGU already has a consistent record of collaborative work, for example, publishing the *Manual for Law of Access to Information in States and Municipalities*[42] and *Technical Guidance for Municipalities' Local Regulation of the Information Access Act and Checklist*.[43] Even though the manuals are not mandatory and do not have to be observed by states and municipalities, in con-

---

40 The CGU's guidelines and booklets are available at http://www.cgu.gov.br/Publicacoes/.

41 Two CGU initiatives on civil society education should be highlighted: (a) Portalzinho da CGU is an educational website designed for children (http://www.portalzinho.cgu.gov.br), and (b) the "Say No to Petty Corruption Campaign" (http://www.cgu.gov.br/redes/diga-nao.

42 Available at http://www.cgu.gov.br/Publicacoes/transparencia-publica/brasil-transparente/arquivos/manuall_lai_estadosmunicipios.pdf.

43 Available at http://www.cgu.gov.br/Publicacoes/transparencia-publica/brasil-transparente/arquivos/guia_checklist.pdf.

nection with federal principles of autonomy, they have had a positive impact on the implementation of transparency web portals, an online system that citizens can check to find the amount and destination of public money that has been spent by the Brazilian government, on the federal, state, and local levels.

It is a known fact that corruption is not an isolated phenomenon. It is a global bane that affects all countries and institutions. In 2007, before the anticorruption draft bill was presented, the CGU, in compliance with Brazil's ratification of the OECD Anti-Bribery Convention and with the support of the United Kingdom's embassy in Brazil, launched a booklet about the convention's terms, objectives, and legal implications that was addressed to judges, prosecutors, lawyers, policy makers, legal practitioners, and entrepreneurs. Aligned with the trend of international cooperation on anticorruption issues, Brazil's internal federal cooperation must be fortified and must become more uniform in approach. The CGU can strongly contribute to the Anticorruption Law's implementation, by defining standards on administrative procedures and the imposition of sanctions, as well as providing technical notes and developing capacity-building programs for the benefit of municipalities' administrative staffs.

CGU leadership should mitigate the omission or misuse of the new Anticorruption Law tools, which is a great concern among the companies subject to the law.

Toward Anticorruption Enforcement: The Ministério Público's Role

The 1988 Constitution is the historical milestone of a new era of the Brazilian republic, and, without a doubt, the Ministério Público[44] occupies a prominent position in the constitutional order, having an institutional mission that is both noble and arduous.

Aside from its role in criminal prosecution, the Ministério Público also plays a large part in representing collective rights of all kinds. Just as society struck back against the lack of a voice during the dictatorial regime,[45] the Constituent Assembly wisely empowered the Ministério Público to be a legitimate representative of society's voice in the public sector, in order to defend democracy and human rights. But instead of working as criminal investigators, the prosecutors became political agents of social transformation, standing at the

44 The Portuguese version of the institutional name is used—instead of using "Prosecutor's Office," "General Attorney's Office," or a free translation (e.g., "Public Ministry")—to emphasize the unique and broader institutional role in the Brazilian constitutional system in comparison with other countries. The Ministério Público's autonomy and institutional independence led to arguments that it could have become a "fourth branch of government" in Brazil.

45 The authoritarian military government ruled Brazil from 1964 to 1985.

forefront of the fight against corruption in Brazil. Hence there are innovative prerogatives[46] for Brazilian public prosecutors.

In terms of implementing the Anticorruption Law under the constitutional rules, the Ministério Público faces two challenges: to investigate and curb corporate corruption, and to articulate the clockwork of Anticorruption Law implementation in order to develop and disseminate policies and good practices among the different federal entities.

According to Article 19 of the law, the Ministério Público, like the union, the states, the Federal District, and the municipalities, is entitled to file lawsuits against legal entities that have engaged in corrupt acts.

Acting as a law enforcement authority on administrative, civil, and criminal law, the Ministério Público investigates and files civil and criminal actions. It is also one of the institutions entitled to file public civil actions, but recent studies have shown that it files a greater number of actions than other co-legitimates. This extensive experience with criminal and administrative improbity investigations demonstrates that the Ministério Público has a more robust and suitable background to deal with such matters[47] compared with other co-legitimates. Apart from this, the extensive reach and influence[48] of the Ministério Público, being an institution that has a presence in all federation entities, is well posited to strategically and effectively carry out its mission, which is to improve effective cooperation among federal agencies, organizations, and entities that have a role in combating and minimizing corruption in Brazil.

If, on the one hand, the federalist model leads to uncoordinated authorities, each applying the law as it sees fit, the Ministério Público on the other hand, works closely with municipalities' matters to avoid dispersed efforts against corruption. It is clear that the work done by the Ministério Público on a domestic scale has a positive effect on coordinating anticorruption initiatives at the local, regional, and national levels.

But what if the local authority does nothing about corporate bribery that takes place in a state or municipal public procurement? The Ministério Público can do something about it, because it is empowered by the constitution to make individuals and legal entities accountable for their actions.

---

46 The Ministério Público in Brazil upholds a prerogative based on administrative and political autonomy, an autonomous budgetary initiative, and functional independence (arts. 127 and 128 of the Brazilian Const.).

47 Among all institutions with legal standing, the Ministério Público filed about 95 percent of civil lawsuits to protect collective rights. *See RT informa*, 6(37) Editora Revista dos Tribunais 5 (May–June 2005).

48 According to a 2012 publication produced by the National Council of the Public Prosecutor (Conselho Nacional do Ministério Público; CNMP), there were 10,663 public prosecutors in Brazil and 34,954 Ministério Público clerks and interns spread throughout the Brazilian states and municipalities. *See* CNMP, *Ministério Público: Um retrato—ano 2: Dados de 2012* 45 (CNMP 2013).

Besides the direct legal standing for bringing anticorruption cases into courts, when administrative omission is observed (e.g., if a mayor or a council makes no effort to hold a corrupt agent or company accountable for corrupt actions), the Ministério Público is entitled by Article 20 of the Anticorruption Law to act in place of absent local authorities, and may judicially propose even administrative sanctions against the corrupt actors.

Apart from its investigative mission, the Ministério Público is a catalyst and an agent in strengthening state and municipal anticorruption investigative bodies.

The Anticorruption Law reaffirms the duty to adequately structure the federal comptroller system. Some states already have a more advanced structure, following the path led by the CGU, but a great many entities, especially in the poorest municipalities, do not have agencies prepared to investigate corruption, conduct administrative procedures, create or establish DPAs, or impose adequate penalties. At the local level, the public prosecutor can propose agreements[49] to local authorities to engage them in investigating and applying sanctions by implementing certain administrative structures. If a local government does not adequately develop its internal control systems under the new Anticorruption Law, the Ministério Público, on behalf of the people, can file actions against that municipality and oblige it to do so.

Thus, the public prosecutor can work together with the local government to promote good governance practices and implement the requisite administrative structures to investigate and apply sanctions, as well as promote accountability under the Anticorruption Law.

Besides seeking to strengthen good governance practices at the local governmental level, the Ministério Público works with civil society and the public at large to understand anticorruption issues.[50] Brazilian citizens have already demonstrated their dissatisfaction with the effects of corruption, and the Ministério Público can enhance the opportunity for the people's voices to be heard. In this sense, nonrepressive ways to implement the law, through education for instance, is an innovative tactic.

---

49 The Conduct Adjustment Commitment (*Termo de Ajustamento de Conduta;* TAC) is an alternative way to implement the effectiveness of an extrajudicial procedure. The TAC consists of a commitment meant to adjust the offender's conduct to legal requirements through penalties or in a way to make up for the damage caused. It represents a possibility for building a nonjudiciary solution to a conflict of interests, for example. Although designed to be used by public entities, TACs are more commonly used by the Ministério Público in matters of environmental law, consumer law, administrative law, civil law, and the like. If the requirements of the commitment are not fulfilled, lawsuits can be filed based on the commitment alone. For further information about the TAC's main features, *see* G. de A. Rodrigues, *Ação Civil Pública e Termo de Ajustamento de Conduta. Teoria e Prática* (Forense 2006).

50 The campaigns "What Do You Have to Do with Corruption?" (http://www.oquevocetemavercomacorrupcao.com/conteudo/home/index.asp?cod=0), "Conscious Vote" (http://www.facebook.com/votoconscientempmg), and "Everybody against Impunity" (http://www.facebook.com/Todos ContraAImpunidade?fref=nf) are examples of the Ministério Público's work on developing social awareness related to corruption.

People are close to the government in the municipalities, especially the smaller ones. Education can empower civil society to demand accountability and compel the government to undertake correct acts and actions to benefit the public. Civil society is thus an important stakeholder in ensuring the law's enforcement, demanding accountability, and supervising government actions. Once the public is well informed through the effective establishment of transparency web portals, the Ministério Público will become an effective conduit for local citizens to be heard. Because the voice of citizens has become increasingly influential, and with the mega sporting projects continuing through the 2016 Summer Olympic Games, this popular engagement and public pressure may create a conducive environment for the Anticorruption Law to be enforced.

Compliance Mind-set: The Private Sector's Role

In countries where there is weak rule of law and where bribery is necessary to do business, there is a high risk of corruption. The lack of legal certainty, which ensures the functioning of the market and which companies need to make long-term investments, is not the only problem in such environments. Corrupt practices also diminish the quality of the services offered, harm free competition, reduce institutional morale, and affect company images, among other things.

Globalization has strengthened the private sector's role in the fight against corruption, a role increasingly recognized as internationally important. This movement is in line with the UN Global Compact's 10th principle against corruption, on the private sector's shared responsibility and willingness to play its part in eliminating corruption.[51]

In Brazil, the new Anticorruption Law addresses both repressive and preventive measures affecting the way companies do business. The repressive approach brings the feared high fines, strict liability impositions, and bad publicity. As prevention measures, Article 7 of the law introduces concepts such as internal mechanisms of integrity, auditing, whistle-blowing, and company observance of ethics codes as issues to be taken into account for sanction mitigation.

All these dispositions attempt to change the Brazilian business mentality by raising the risks on taking some shortcuts often preferred by companies. The short-term benefits brought by corruption cannot be better than the long-term ones of making a clean deal. The main idea is to stimulate the adoption of preventive measures by creating structures that are not just formal but also have a practical impact on identifying fraud and overcoming fragilities.

---

51 For further information, *see* http://www.unglobalcompact.org/aboutthegc/thetenprinciples/principle10.html.

In the past, the employee who worked in accord with the Bribery Act was often the only one found guilty, because it was hard to prove whom that employee answered to inside the company. Nowadays, the greater implication of corruption placed on the company by strict liability can make being less susceptible to bribery a major advantage. Hence the importance of investments aimed at implementing preventive measures.

In Brazil, the "Corporate Pact for Integrity against Corruption," launched in 2006, included private institutions, the UN Office on Drugs and Crime, and the UN Development Programme.[52] The pact provides guidelines and procedures to be followed in the marketplace by signatory companies. Also, the work implemented by Transparency International, whose approach is focused on three pillars—business integrity, financial integrity, and research and reporting[53]—can serve as a guideline for conducting business properly and safely.

Companies with anticorruption programs and ethical guidelines were found to have up to 50 percent fewer incidents of corruption, and be less likely to lose opportunities than companies without such programs. Companies with superior performances as corporate citizens were shown not only to match but often to outperform their peers. Better corporate governance in companies located in emerging economies is associated with better performance and market valuation.[54]

Apart from promoting an open and accountable business environment and building corporate social responsibility, companies should consider Brazilian federation challenges and be aware of local dynamics before doing business. This demands that companies invest money and time training employees and creating internal integrity mechanisms, but it is also important to identify peculiarities implemented by municipal decrees and to analyze previous procurement in the municipality.

The Anticorruption Law's harsh dispositions and the possibilities of mitigation are different ways to engage companies in the fight against corruption. Corporate governance is best achieved by routine and permanent functions that can be measured and improved, and therefore should be the focus of companies.

The Anticorruption Law will be successful if companies are encouraged to internalize compliance benefits and abandon corruption as a profitable solution in fear of the consequences. The "clean companies" concept will certainly have a positive impact on business, not just in mitigating penalties, but most importantly in earning the confidence of all stakeholders, including civil society and the public sector.

---

52 Further information is available at http://www.empresalimpa.org.br/.

53 Further information is available at http://www.transparency.org/whatwedo/activity/engaging_the_private_sector_in_the_fight_against_corruption.

54 Transparency Intl., *Global Corruption Report 2009: Corruption and the Private Sector* (Cambridge U. Press 2009), http://www.transparency.org/whatwedo/publications/doc/gcr/.

Conclusion

Brazil is experiencing a paradigm shift in combating corruption, moving from a domestic point of view to a more progressive, international one. Ensuring observance of the law on all federal levels is a matter of investing in the enforcement capacities of agencies and the training of personnel, because a uniform judicial or administrative interpretation and implementation demands time and coordination. Cases will take time to get to the courts. And the administrative dispositions are more likely to be implemented than the judicial ones.

In complying with international obligations and community wishes, the new Brazilian Anticorruption Law fills a loophole in the national legal framework against corruption by establishing the administrative and civil liability of corrupt acts committed by a legal entity, and not just an individual.

Due to the Brazilian federation model, there are 5,589 federal entities empowered to enforce sanctions against corrupt acts. On the one hand, empowering local governments by raising municipalities to federal entity status can be considered a strategic advantage. But on the other hand, the abundant number of colegitimates empowered to apply the Anticorruption Law and its penalties could lead to inconveniently conflicting decisions, and could undermine deferred prosecution agreements. Or worse, the lack of proper institutional structures and expertise, especially in the smaller and poorer municipalities, could have the effect of not curbing corruption at the local level. Instead, ineffective institutions could create opportunities for further corruption.

The challenge ahead is to build a comprehensive and unified agenda of cooperative anticorruption enforcement that orchestrates different contexts, needs, and policies. This would create an atmosphere of overarching unity, linking diverse actors within the Brazilian federal system in the enforcement of the anticorruption legal regime. Envisaged as a federal network that composes and, in a unified way, governs the wide array of political and administrative interests among the federal entities, and balances and coordinates the different developmental stages of each federal entity as it undertakes this journey of anticorruption enforcement.

At the federal level, the CGU occupies a central position in implementing the Anticorruption Law. Through federal cases and standards to be followed by other federal entities, the CGU currently has an important pedagogical role to perform. It bears noting that, additionally, the CGU can further contribute by providing technical training to staff working at the state and local levels.

The Ministério Público can continue its important work of developing awareness of the law and providing support for the appropriate implementation of it by coordinating its efforts with local authorities. Such a position is a consequence of its unique institutional situation and characteristics, its constitutional functions, and its rootedness in the Brazilian territory.

As the ultimate target of corruption efforts, the private sector has a major role to play in the law's effective implementation. That is why it is so important to change business mentality. By making repressive measures tougher than they used to be, the law encourages companies to adopt preventive practices against corruption.

As Carlos Drummond de Andrade, one of Brazil's most influential poets, put it, "Laws are not enough. Lilies do not arise from the laws." In the same vein, although anticorruption laws are already on the books, a huge effort on several fronts is crucial if corruption, with its deep historical roots, is to be diminished and eventually eradicated. As the 2013 public demonstrations on anticorruption made apparent to all, Brazil as a country needs—and has through the public voice asked for—political mobilization at the highest levels for this new legal framework, based on widely shared ideals, to be implemented effectively, and consistently, thereby enabling Brazil's anticorruption goals to be met.

18

Voice and Accountability

Improving the Delivery of Anticorruption and Anti-Money Laundering Strategies in Brazil

FAUSTO MARTIN DE SANCTIS

In Brazil, public institutions historically have been used for and by a variety of private interests, permitting numerous corrupt schemes to take place, in a constant exchange of favors and neglect of public resources. During the past few decades, Brazil has experienced moments of deep unease with the many scandals that have involved corruption in the political environment—and that have precipitated popular street protests. The most important of these protests were the demonstrations during the impeachment of President Fernando Collor de Mello in 1992[1] and demonstrations in June and July 2013.

Certainly, the historical importance of an event is determined by what succeeds it. It is therefore too early to evaluate the complete results of the demonstrations that occurred in June and July 2013, which were fueled by discontent with inadequate public services and recurring corruption scandals.[2] However, some conclusions can be drawn even just a year later.

The demands from the demonstrators were many, and loudly expressed. They first demanded a halt to an increase of bus fares in the state capitals of Paraná, São Paulo, and Rio de Janeiro. Startled by the impressive number of people who went to the streets to protest, local and state governments quickly backed down from the proposed fare increase.

---

1 A popular campaign demanded the impeachment of President Fernando Collor de Mello, who took office in 1990. Charged with corruption, influence peddling, and illegal schemes within his government, he was targeted by the "Get out Collor" (*Fora Collor*) campaign, which mobilized thousands of students to go to the streets with their faces painted in protest. On September 29, 1992, the National Congress impeached President Collor.

2 "In Brazil, there are many words for corruption: *cervejinha, molhar a mão, lubrificar, lambileda, mata-bicho, jabaculê, jabá, capilê, conto-do-paco, conto-do-vigário, jeitinho, mamata, negociata, por fora, taxa de urgência, propina, rolo, esquema, peita, falcatrua, maracutaia*, etc. There seems to be more words in Brazil and in other countries where corruption occurs daily. Originally, the word corruption (*corrupção*) comes from Latin *corruptione* and it means: disruption, decomposition, debauchery, depravity, bribery, perversion, subornation." (*"Existem no Brasil muitas palavras para caracterizar a corrupção: cervejinha, molhar a mão, lubrificar, lambileda, mata-bicho, jabaculê, jabá, capilê, conto-do-paco, conto-do-vigário, jeitinho, mamata, negociata, por fora, taxa de urgência, propina, rolo, esquema, peita, falcatrua, maracutaia, etc. A quantidade de palavras disponíveis parece ser maior no Brasil e em países onde a corrupção é visualizada cotidianamente. Originalmente, a palavra corrupção provém do latim Corruptione e significa corrompimento, decomposição, devassidão, depravação, suborno, perversão, peita."*) Antônio Inácio Andrioli, *Causas estruturais da corrupção no Brasil* [Structural causes for corruption in Brazil], 64 Revista Espaço Acadêmico (Sept. 2006), http://www.espacoacademico.com.br/064/64andrioli.htm.

Following these demonstrations, Constitutional Amendment Bill No. 37/2011 (Projeto de Emenda à Constituição; PEC no. 37/2011), also known as the "impunity proposal" (*PEC da impunidade*), was abandoned on June 25, 2013. The bill had been an attempt to add a paragraph to Article 144 of the federal constitution to remove the investigative powers of the federal and state public prosecutors and grant exclusive authority for criminal investigations to federal, federal district, and state police officers.

In addition to the decrease in urban bus fares and the demise of Bill No. 37/2011, other demands included free public transportation passes for students; regulation of the "Clean Record Act" (*ficha limpa*), which prohibits convicted politicians from assuming public positions; the addition of corruption to a list of serious crimes with enhanced punishments; and the termination of salaries for administratively punished judges and prosecutors.

After the initial popular groundswell, the demonstrations weakened because of the recurring acts of vandalism promoted by groups known as "black blocs" in the two main Brazilian cities, São Paulo and Rio de Janeiro.[3] These groups relied on black masks for anonymity and used radical methods such as attacks on police officers, banks, stores, and car dealerships. This radicalization perverted the greater movement's legitimacy and undermined the peaceful efforts of the majority of protestors. As a result, the initial agenda of popular demands evaporated, as did the possibility of using the movement's propelling strength to spark greater discussion and provide new perspectives for political action in Brazil.[4]

---

3 As described by André Takahashi, the black bloc tactics were a response to police violence. The black bloc is composed of small affinity groups created during demonstrations that act independently within protests. But, unlike the Free Pass Movement (Movimento Passe-Livre, or MPL) and its peers, the black bloc is not an organization or a collective group; it is an idea, a tactic of self-defense against police violence, as well as an aesthetic form of protest based in the depredation of symbols of the state and capitalism. The black bloc looks more like a decentralized network, such as the Anonymous, than an organic and cohesive movement. André Takahashi, *O black bloc e a resposta à violência sócia* [Black bloc and the response to social violence], http://www.cartacapital.com.br/sociedade/o-black-bloc-e-a-resposta-a-violencia-policial-1690.html.

4 As highlighted in the article *Os projetos da pauta prioritária ainda não votados*, these are the bills presented or entered as part of the agenda at the National Congress as a response to the call of the streets; voting on these bills is likely to occur in 2015. These are the highlights: (1) Senate: (a) Bill 248/2013 institutes a national free pass for students in public transportation; (b) Bill of Constitutional Amendment 10/2013 ends privileged jurisdiction for common crimes committed by high authorities; (c) Bill of Constitutional Amendment 33/2013 ends social benefits for prisoners' families. (2) House of Representatives: (a) Bill 6,953/2002 establishes rules for defending and protecting public service users; (b) Bill 204/2011 includes corruption in the legal hall of serious crimes; (c) Bill of Constitutional Amendment 6/2012 requires a clean slate for government employees; (d) Bill of Constitutional Amendment 11/2003 reduces from two to one the number of senator substitutes; (e) Bill 8,035/2010, National Education Plan; (f) Bill 8,039/2012 creates the Educational Responsibility Act; (g) Bill for Complimentary Act 202/89 implements taxes for great fortunes; (h) Bill for Complimentary Act 123/12 reserves 10 percent of the GDP for public health; (i) Bill for Complimentary Act 92/07 authorizes the government to institute nonprofitable state foundations; (j) Bill 5,141/2013 exempts public transportation companies from paying CIDE (Portuguese acronym for intervention in the economic domain contribution) taxes; (k) Bill 4,881/2012 creates the Urban Mobility Pact;

In spite of their outcome, the popular demonstrations did raise questions about the need for political change. José Eduardo Cardozo, head of the Brazilian Department of Justice, observed the following:

> [I]n spite of the diversity of the agenda of demands, a very clear axis was pointed out by the demonstrations: the demand for quality public services in areas as diverse as health, education, and transportation. Thus, the corruption topic is deeply connected to the reasons that led people to attend these demonstrations. Every cent misused deteriorates the quality of public services.[5]

At the core of the Brazilian population's dissatisfaction is the habitual misappropriation of public resources. Employment in public positions is routinely used as a means of private enrichment and influence peddling. This trend has fostered the perception that impunity is almost always the rule and that the welfare state is constantly being undermined by powerful private interests.

The diversion of public funds weakens a series of measures, including the implementation of policies that reduce child mortality rates, provide quality public health and education services, ensure the supply of potable water, and improve access to sewer systems, urban sanitation, and other forms of infrastructure.

Corruption not only directly affects public administration but also indirectly affects the entire population, preventing the needs of a vast number of people from being met. Corruption also creates unfair competition for companies that adopt fair practices in their transactions, undermines the possibility of foreign companies investing in the country, and consequently slows Brazilian economic growth, leaving a trail of misery and inequality.

As highlighted by UN secretary-general Ban Ki-Moon during a 2013 message regarding International Anticorruption Day,[6] corruption is a hidden cost that raises prices and lowers quality without benefits for producers or consumers. Ban noted that crimes of corruption stifle economic growth and undermine sustainable management of countries' natural resources, thus

---

(l) Bill 1,151/1995 regulates same-sex civil unions; (m) Bill 478/07 institutes the Unborn Child Statute; (n) Bill 5,139/2009 regulates public civil lawsuits for protecting diffuse, collective, or homogenous individual rights; (o) Bill 3,465/2012 grants priority for the adjudication of corruption crimes; (p) Bill of Constitutional Amendment 11/2011 prohibits ineligible people from being appointed as ministers or to similar commissioned positions. *See* Congresso em Foco, *Os projetos da pauta prioritária ainda não votados* [The still-unpassed bills of the priority agenda], http://congressoemfoco.uol.com.br/noticias/os-projetos-da-pauta-prioritaria-ainda-nao-votados.

5 Ministry of Justice (Ministério da Justiça), *Reivindicações Sociais Pautam Metas Para a Enccla Combater a Corrupção* (Nov. 29, 2013), http://portal.mj.gov.br.

6 Ban Ki-Moon, *Mensagem do Secretário-Geral da ONU, Ban Ki-Moon* [Message from the UN Secretary-General, Ban Ki-Moon], Centro de Informações das Nações Unidas—Rio de Janeiro (Dec. 2013), http://www.unicrio.org.br/dia-internacional-contra-a-corrupcao-%E2%80%93-9-de-dezembro-de-2010-2/. On December, 9, 2003, Brazil and 110 other countries gathered in Mérida, Mexico, to sign the UN Convention against Corruption. The date has since been celebrated as International Anticorruption Day.

negatively affecting billions of people around the globe.[7] The UN Office on Drugs and Crime (UNODC) estimates that developing countries lose about US$40 billion to corruption every year.[8]

In the 1970s, Brazil saw the emergence of the so-called Gérson's law (*Lei de Gérson*), which alluded to the behavior of pursuing advantages at any cost, assuming that people should gain as many benefits as possible without worrying about the means employed to obtain them.[9] Eliana Calmon cautions that society should not lose its moral compass in the face of the behavior of the "Brazilian way of being" (*jeitinho brasileiro*) and Gérson's law. Such behavior, Calmon explains, "helps people to survive, makes some even smarter and, little by little, creates marginal rules to circumvent obstacles, including legal ones."[10]

This attitude is so ingrained in the collective unconscious of Brazil that one could say that Brazilian civil society's inaction in the face of the innumerable acts of corruption that have occurred in the past decades is caused by the acceptance of this thesis: people keep silent because they believe that it is perfectly natural for politicians to be dishonest.

Corruption has reached alarming levels in Brazil. Recent history is replete with acts of corruption in the federal government, municipalities, public hospitals, education boards, medicine distribution programs, agencies responsible for environmental supervision, and social security. Brazilians demand repressive as well as preventive state actions to promote integrity and deter improbity, misuse of funds, and corruption.

The Brazilian government has been considered too weak to clearly establish the limits between what is public and what is private.[11] But there are a

---

7 Mônica Villela Grayley, *ONU diz que Corrupção Piora Situação de Pobreza e Desigualdade no Mundo* [UN says that corruption worsens poverty and inequality situations in the world], Notícias e Mídia Rádio ONU (Dec. 2013), http://www.unmultimedia.org/radio/portuguese/2013/12/onu-diz-que-corrupcao-piora-situacao-de-pobreza-e-desigualdade-no-mundo/.

8 United Nations in Brazil, *Corrupção tira 40 bilhões de dólares de países em desenvolvimento, afirma ONU* [Corruption takes away US$40 billion from developing countries, UN states], Nações Unidas no Brasil (July 2012), http://www.onu.org.br/corrupcao-tira-40-bilhoes-de-dolares-de-paises-em-desenvolvimento-todo-ano-afirma-onu/.

9 It started out as a TV commercial in 1976, in which Brazilian midfielder Gérson, from the Brazilian national football (soccer) squad that won the 1970 World Cup, announced a brand of cigarettes by saying: *"Por que pagar mais caro se o Vila me dá tudo aquilo que eu quero de um bom cigarro? Gosto de levar vantagem em tudo, certo? Leve vantagem você também, leve Vila Rica"* ("Why pay more if Vila gives me everything I want from a good cigarette? I like taking advantage of everything, right? Take advantage yourself too, take Vila Rica.") This message was infused into Brazilian culture as a principle by which people should take advantage at any cost. Hélio Gurovitz, *Viva a Lei de Gérson!* Superinteressante (Feb. 2004), http://super.abril.com.br/superarquivo/2004/conteudo_313516.shtml.

10 Eliana Calmon, *O jeitinho brasileiro* [The Brazilian way of being], 10(20) Revista ETCO: Instituto Brasileiro de Ética Concorrencial 24–25 (Apr. 2013).

11 Leonardo Avritzer clarifies recent measures taken by the Brazilian government and its effects on the community. *See* Leonardo Avritzer, *A Realidade Política Brasileira* [The Brazilian political reality], Revista Carta Capital (June 1, 2011), http://www.cartacapital.com.br/sociedade/a-realidade-politica-brasileira.

number of ways in which this perception can be changed (and in the process reducing the level of bureaucracy in public services and improving the Brazilian economy's competitiveness), including creating transparency with respect to public services, providing high-quality education, undertaking political reform (especially campaign finance reform), modifying the punitive system (particularly regarding punishment for crimes committed by politicians), and reforming the tax system.

Because public resources designated for the electoral campaign system are insufficient, there is a need for reform to guarantee government sustainability at the federal, state, and local levels. A sense of impunity bred by a slow and inefficient judiciary and judicial system also hinders the reduction of corruption. The presumption of innocence and the legal possibility for an accused person to launch numerous appeals permits the perpetuation of corrupt acts, because criminal prosecution of corruption hardly ever obtains final results with final judgments, and very rarely leads to the imprisonment of those found guilty.

Although they do not necessarily indicate the practice of corruption, the presence of some factors should invoke special attention, such as those recorded by the Brazilian nongovernmental organization (NGO) Brazil Transparency (Transparência Brasil):[12] lack of transparency in governmental administrative actions, absence of administrative and financial controls, subservience of the legislative and municipal councils to the executive branch, low levels of employees' technical capabilities, absence of training for government employees, and alienation of the public regarding the budgeting process. Dedicated exclusively to fighting corruption, Brazil Transparency has been working for years on what demonstrators are now demanding in an attempt to make their voices heard.

Following this introduction, the second section of this chapter describes the collaborative efforts, targeted recommendations, and results of the National Strategy for Combating Corruption and Money Laundering. The third section summarizes the robust anticorruption legislation in Brazil, including the new Anticorruption Act. The fourth section discusses how courts specializing in financial crimes and money laundering improve accountability in Brazil. The fifth section, the conclusion, offers recommendations on how to continue to improve the delivery of anticorruption and anti–money laundering strategies in Brazil.

---

12 Brazil Transparency develops a wide range of programs to improve prevention mechanisms, strengthen civil organizations' supervision and control of state actions, and systematize knowledge on corruption in Brazil. *See* Antonio Chizzotti, José Chizzotti, João Alberto Ianhez, Antoninho Marmo Trevisan, & Josmar Verillo, *O Combate à Corrupção nas Prefeituras do Brasil* [Combating corruption in Brazilian municipalities], http://www.transparencia.org.br/docs/Cartilha.html.

The National Strategy for Combating Corruption and Money Laundering (ENCCLA)

The Voice and Collaborative Involvement of Multiple Stakeholders

In 2002, the Federal Justice Council's Studies Committee, a Brazilian federal justice administrative office, elaborated concrete recommendations to improve investigation and prosecution of money laundering crimes through the cooperation of many sectors, from government and civil society, including representatives from federal courts, federal public prosecution offices, federal police, and the Brazilian Federation of Banks. This committee is considered the embryo of ENCLA, the Brazilian acronym for what in English would be National Strategy for Combating Money Laundering and Recovering Assets, which was later renamed Estratégia Nacional de Combate à Corrupção e à Lavagem de Dinheiro (ENCCLA), or National Strategy for Combating Corruption and Money Laundering.

ENCCLA aims to be the central government's voice in articulating and promoting joint actions among Brazilian public enforcement agencies to perfect the systematic prevention and repression of corruption and money laundering. ENCCLA is composed of 60 agencies and entities, including the following: public prosecution offices, police services, the judiciary, the Office of the Comptroller General (Controladoria-Geral da União), the Federal Court of Accountability (Tribunal de Contas da União), the Securities Commission of Brazil (Comissão de Valores Mobiliários), the intelligence unit of the Council for Financial Activities Control (Conselho de Controle de Atividades Financeiras), the National Superintendence for Pension Funds (Superintendência Nacional de Previdência Complementar), the Superintendence for Private Insurance (Superintendência de Seguros Privados; SUSEP), the Brazilian Federal Reserve (Banco Central do Brasil), the Brazilian Intelligence Agency (Agência Brasileira de Inteligência), the Office of the Federal Attorney General (Advocacia-Geral da União), and the Brazilian Federation of Banks (Federação Brasileira de Bancos).

The topic of corruption was added to ENCCLA after the Federal Court of Accountability in its 2000 annual report suggested organizing a national strategy aimed at combating corruption modeled after the strategy against money laundering that had been created earlier.

Brazil followed the international trend that attempts to halt this very deleterious practice. The European Commission, responsible for combating organized crime, human trafficking, and corruption, believes that "corruption is one of the particularly serious crimes with a cross-border dimension. It is often linked to other forms of serious crime, such as trafficking in drugs and human beings, and cannot be adequately addressed by EU States alone."[13]

---

13 *See Corruption: Boosting Anti-Corruption Policy at EU Level,* at the European Commission, Home Affairs website, http://ec.europa.eu/dgs/home-affairs/what-we-do/policies/organized-crime-and-human-trafficking/corruption/index-eu.

Two topics are constantly covered by ENCCLA's agenda: corrupt practices, defined as that which implies the obtainment of unjust advantages or the misuse of public funds by government employees or other third parties, and which are considered offenses in the Criminal Code and in other special legislation; and public policies capable of combating these crimes and others, including money laundering.

The risks of corruption in public procurements and contracts involving services and construction related to the 2014 World Cup and 2016 Olympic Games have been the subject of particular attention. Accurate examinations have been demanded, and many people are concerned by the risks that corrupt actions pose for the international community's perception of Brazil. Thus, detecting areas, markets, and economic sectors that demand operational, regulatory, and legislative adjustments is among ENCCLA's main actions.

Other actions undertaken by ENCCLA members in recent years have shown that the collaboration of institutions from the executive, legislative, and judicial branches is very effective. Corruption and ethical deviations in the public sector—and in private corporations—are under constant vigilance. There is a serious commitment to perfecting Brazilian institutions amid a wider and inspiring social trend toward further development of public safety policies.

Delivering Recommendations and Results

In its eleventh annual plenary meeting, held November 25–28, 2013, ENCCLA issued many recommendations and pronouncements, with a special emphasis on the following:

1. ENCCLA recommends that control, supervision, and criminal prosecution activities, especially those related to combating corruption and money laundering, should be considered priorities and should be preserved in their efficiency even in the face of needs of adjusting budgets;
2. ENCCLA recommends the creation of a data repository that allows the identification of companies supervised by SUSEP (Superintendence for Private Insurance), and which is modeled after the Registry of Financial System Clients (Cadastro de Clientes do Sistema Financeiro; CCS). Such a data repository should address the need to provide precise and quick information in order to identify policyholders, participants, and beneficiaries who are relevant for investigation and adjudication;
3. ENCCLA recommends the creation and strengthening—within federal, state, and local public attorney offices—of groups that specialize in combating corruption and administrative improbity, especially in connection with activities related to adjudicating and accompanying administrative improbity lawsuits, enforcement of Audit Courts decisions, civil cases involving the recovery of assets, the enforcement of civil and criminal decisions and civil cases *ex delicto,* as well as possible interventions as assistant prosecutor

in criminal cases. It is also recommended that, whenever possible, the groups should act in partnership with other Public Administration agencies and Public Prosecution offices;

4. ENCCLA recommends immediate approval by the National Congress of legislation that criminalizes government employees' unjust enrichment;
5. ENCCLA recommends that bills, approved by ENCCLA in 2011 and 2012, regarding (a) regulation of aspects related to apprehension, custody, transport, conversion, and destination of funds in cash withheld for noncompliance with legislation and (b) property extinction, should be sent to the National Congress;
6. ENCCLA salutes the efforts of the São Paulo Municipality's Office of the Comptroller General as a good practice and a reference for combating corruption in large Brazilian cities;
7. ENCCLA demonstrates its support of National Goal 4, set forth by the National Justice Council (Conselho Nacional de Justiça), which gives priority to producing judgments that concern administrative improbity-related and corruption cases, in order that such judgments may consolidate into a clear pattern that combats the problem of impunity;
8. ENCCLA emphasizes the necessity that Act No. 9,613/1998 (Money Laundering Act) should be enforced by those responsible for enforcement of regulation on new subjects.[14]

The 2003 creation of criminal courts that specialize in financial and money laundering crimes was a result of ENCCLA's recommended actions. ENCCLA obtained other results in combating corruption and money laundering, including

1. Deploying, up to 2012, approximately 11,000 agents in all regions of the country, due to the creation of the National Program for Capacitating and Training to Combat Corruption and Money Laundering (Programa Nacional de Capacitação e Treinamento para o Combate à Corrupção e à Lavagem de Dinheiro).
2. Cementing its place as one of the most advanced countries for preventing money laundering with the implementation of the Registry of the Financial System Clients, managed by the Brazilian Federal Reserve.
3. Enhancing speed and economy in investigations and criminal prosecution by implementing standardization for requesting and responding to bank secrecy breach requests and the respective tracking, as well as the development of the Bank Operations Investigation System (Sistema de Investigação de Movimentações Bancárias).

---

14 ENCCLA, *Ações: ENCCLA 2014, Recomendações e Declarações*, http://www.cgu.gov.br/Imprensa/Arquivos/2013/Propostas%20de%20Acoes%20ENCCLA%202014%20Plenaria%20Final.pdf.

4. Optimizing investigation and criminal prosecution, simplifying the analysis of great volumes of data with the creation of the Laboratory for Technology against Money Laundering and the replication of this model in other parts of the country, creating an integrated technology network oriented toward combating corruption and money laundering.
5. Gaining greater control over corruption with a draft for patrimonial inquiry to discipline filing assets that are part of government employees' private property. This draft culminated in Decree No. 5,483/2005.
6. Gaining greater transparency and control over corruption with the regulation of government agencies' access to accounting documents on entities hired by the public administration, culminating in Interministerial Ordinance No. 127/2008.
7. Enhancing modernization and greater border control with the registry of national territory entering/exiting activity.
8. Enhancing effectiveness in cutting criminal organizations' financial fluxes with the creation of the National System for Seized Goods (Sistema Nacional de Bens Apreendidos), managed by the National Justice Council, and the promotion of "anticipated alienation" of these assets before final decisions, later modified by Act No. 12,683/2012 and Act No. 12,694/2012.
9. Computerizing the judiciary's access to the Internal Revenue Service branch thanks to the creation of the System for Supplying Information to the Judicial Branch (Sistema de Fornecimento de Informações ao Poder Judiciário; INFOJUD).
10. Enhancing publicity, transparency, and social control with the creation of the Registry of Nonreputable and Suspect Entities (Cadastro de Entidades Inidôneas e Suspeitas), maintained by the Office of the Federal Comptroller General.
11. Enhancing publicity, transparency, and control with the creation of the National Registry of Social Entities (Cadastro Nacional de Entidades Sociais), managed by the Department of Justice.
12. Enhancing effectiveness in investigating and prosecuting financial crimes with the creation of police departments that specialize in financial crimes, within the federal police service.
13. Increasing the specialization of Brazilian authorities in combating organized crime by assembling the National Group for Combating Criminal Organizations (Grupo Nacional de Combate às Organizações Criminosas), at the state public prosecution level.
14. Increasing effectiveness in controlling cross-border money operations with the computerization of documents regarding the inflow and outflow of assets in the country.
15. Providing greater transparency and control with the creation of an electronic list of people convicted by federal courts and a National Justice

Council recommendation for the creation of a similar list at the state justice level.

16. Enhancing Brazil's adherence to international standards for the prevention of money laundering with the definition of "politically exposed people" (Pessoas Politicamente Expostas) and the regulation of the financial system's obligation regarding them.
17. Providing greater effectiveness of justice with the possibility of searching for evidence in other countries with the consolidation of a central authority for international legal cooperation.
18. Enabling greater control of a sector susceptible to criminality with the regulation of the acquisition and use of prepaid bankcards and similar tools, in order to prevent offenses and identify suspicious bank operations.
19. Diffusing knowledge with the creation of WICCLA, a Wiki encyclopedia for combating money laundering and corruption with information on such topics as action patterns used by criminals when committing crimes, legislation regarding these topics, and databases available to government agencies.
20. Improving the legal system with the elaboration of many bills and proposals of changes in ongoing bills on such topics as criminal organizations, money laundering (Act No. 12,683/2012), loss of ownership of property acquired with illicit money, statutes of limitation, lobbying, bank and tax secrecy, administrative improbity, and legal persons' liability.[15]

Delivering Anticorruption Legislation to Increase Accountability

Because corruption has a cross-border reach, the international community has adopted many treatises and conventions related to it. Brazil is a signatory to the UN Convention against Corruption (Mérida Convention), enacted in 2006. The Mérida Convention was a legal milestone in the fight against corruption. Within the Organization of American States, Brazil is a signatory to the Inter-American Convention against Corruption of 2002, and to the Convention on Combating Bribery of Foreign Public Officials in International Business Transactions (OECD Convention) of 2000.

The Brazilian government's efforts to combat corruption led to the extension of an invitation to join the Open Government Partnership (OGP). The OGP is an international initiative launched in 2010 by U.S. president Barack Obama that aims to secure concrete government commitments in the areas of promoting transparency, fighting corruption, and developing new technologies capable of making governments more open, effective, and responsible.[16]

---

15 Department of Justice, http://portal.mj.gov.br/main.asp.

16 *See* Office of the Comptroller General (Controladoria-Geral da União), *Prevenção da Corrupção* [Preventing corruption], http://www.cgu.gov.br/PrevencaodaCorrupcao/CompromissosInternacionais/index.asp.

In the legislative field, the Anticorruption Act (No. 12,846) of August 1, 2013, was partly motivated by the popular demonstrations starting in June 2013 that evidenced society's rejection of corrupt practices and its distrust of the country's institutions. The act originated in the Chamber of Deputies in 2001; although it was analyzed by Congress for years, it was sent to the Senate in 2013 as a matter of urgency because of these demonstrations. The act, which became effective in January 2014, intends to halt corruption and other practices that harm the public sector. The legislature heard the population's voice regarding anticorruption.

The Anticorruption Act is based on international instruments for combating corruption, such as the U.S. Foreign Corrupt Practices Act (FCPA). In effect since 1977, the FCPA is an innovative legislation that prohibits American companies from offering bribes to foreign government employees. The British equivalent is the 2011 UK Bribery Act.

The Brazilian Anticorruption Act is aimed at complying with international commitments assumed by Brazil. Its main characteristic is the adoption of strict liability (civil and administrative) for legal entities involved in practices against national or international public administrations. This legislation does not exempt managers, directors, or any other individuals who act as accomplices in any unlawful action from their individual liability. It penalizes companies for acts against public administration committed by employees. Companies are now responsible for the payment of any bribes to government employees made by their employees, thus dissuading company agents from engaging in such actions.

The statute has mechanisms for recovering public goods. It imposes sanctions that affect companies' revenues and possibly allow for the loss of some goods, thus signaling a greater possibility of recovering public assets. There is the possibility of implementing a fine of 20 percent of a company's annual gross revenue, which may never be less than the net profit. If the gross revenue criterion is somehow inapplicable, the fine may reach a limit of R$60 million (around US$30 million). Moreover, these sanctions do not exempt any obligation to compensate for any damage caused under the act.

Another highlight of the legislation is the possibility for public entities (the Office of the Comptroller General, the Office of State Inspectors, Public Prosecutors, the Administrative Council for Economic Defense, and other state and local public agencies) to sign leniency agreements with companies responsible for harmful acts, as long as they effectively collaborate with investigations.

Even though leniency agreements do not exempt transgressors from their obligation of completely compensating for damage, they offer such advantages as reducing fines by two-thirds, exempting impeached companies from publication of their conviction, and exempting such companies from the prohibition of incentives, subsidies, and loans from public institutions.

Leniency agreements should be handled with confidentiality so no harm is generated against the presumed innocence of any persons involved. The confidentiality of companies' contributions is a determining characteristic of these agreements, under penalty of causing them great damage. Leniency agreements are conditioned on the immediate cessation of an accused person's participation in the violation, as well as the admission of the person's guilt in being involved in the legal transgression. The agreements are also based on the assumption of effective cooperation with investigations and administrative procedures, identification of other transgressors, and timely delivery of information and documents that demonstrate criminal conduct.

Some aspects of the Anticorruption Act, which went into effect in January 2014, deserve examination even at this early juncture. These include the severe sanctions contained in Article 19 that are supposed to be applied to offending legal entities (such as the loss of assets that constitute benefits obtained, directly or indirectly, from the offense); the compulsory dissolution of legal entities; prohibition on receiving any incentives, subsidies, subventions, donations, or government loans; the absence of technical and legal criteria for administrative decisions; the regulation of the statute; the parameters for evaluating such mechanisms and procedures; the harmonization of the act with guidelines adopted by other countries; and the ways in which small and medium-sized companies can adopt compliance measures.

Sanctions are important measures used in halting the commission of offenses, but they should encompass a greater set of activities involved in the field of risk prevention. Effective compliance programs can mitigate sanctions imposed when the legal entity is able to demonstrate "the existence of mechanisms and internal procedures of integrity, audit and incentive for filing complaints about irregularities and the effective application of ethics and conduct codes within the legal entity."[17]

This rule on internal audits, which is one of the act's best reforms, stimulates the implementation or the strengthening of business compliance programs whose main goal is to act according to the law. It is a legal improvement that will use companies' internal procedures and policies as mechanisms to minimize punishment.

The Anticorruption Act creates, at the federal executive branch level, the National Registry of Punished Companies (Cadastro Nacional de Empresas Punidas), which publicizes convicted companies, making it easier for people to verify sanctions applied to those companies. The act also provides extraterritorial coverage as demonstrated in Article 28, which states that the act is applicable to "harmful actions committed by Brazilian legal entities against foreign public administrations, even when committed in foreign lands."

By creating instruments that make it easier for people to identify those responsible for infractions, organize information about the investigations, and promote whistle-blowing as well as mechanisms for companies to incorporate ethical practices, the act should be effective in the prevention and repression

17 Art. 7, ch. VIII, Act No. 12,846/2013.

of criminal actions involving public administrators and private entities, which should have been eradicated long ago.

Transparency and access to information—both guaranteed as rights of the citizen and duties of the state in the Brazilian constitution—aim at repelling corrupt practices and are inserted in many laws, including the Tax Responsibility Complimentary Act (Lei Complementar de Responsabilidade Fiscal; Act No. 101, of May 4, 2000), which regulates how public expenses should be used primarily on social programs and in the maintenance and development of health, security, and education services; the Transparency Complimentary Act (Lei Complementar da Transparência; Act No. 131, of May 27, 2009); and the Information Access Act (Lei de Acesso à Informação; Act No. 12,527, of November 18, 2011).

Brazil also has Act No. 8,429, of June 2, 1992, which concerns acts of administrative improbity and emphasizes sanctions that should be applied to government employees in cases that involve their unjust enrichment while performing a mandate, post, job, or a function within the public administration (directly or indirectly). The act can, by extension, punish legal entities involved in such situations. It directly reaches all agents that have contact with public funds—even though their activity may be strictly private—as well as holders of elected office. The act does not remove other responsibilities within the criminal, administrative, and political spheres, allowing judges with civil jurisdiction to apply the requisite sanctions against transgressors.

The Public Procurement Act (No. 8,666, of June 21, 1993) defines crimes against the public administration by public managers and employees in cases of government procurements and contracts.

The Clean Record Complimentary Act (Lei Complementar da Ficha Limpa; Act No. 135, of June 4, 2010) can also be considered a landmark for democracy and the fight against corruption and impunity. It renders ineligible for eight years any candidate with a revoked mandate or a conviction by a collegiate organ (even when there is still the possibility of an appeal), or who has resigned in order to avoid revocation.

The Brazilian Criminal Procedure Code, amended by Act No. 12,403, of May 4, 2011, established that government employees may be removed from their duties as an alternative to preventive arrest. However, this modification, combined with an appeals system that allows a multiplicity of judicial reviews, in addition to the possibility of filing habeas corpus petitions against any decision—even when the defendant is not imprisoned—deserves new reflection in the face of the need for a quick, effective system against corruption.

Brazil has also advanced in combating money laundering. Among the many measures undertaken to repress this kind of crime is the mapping and identification of the mechanisms that transform criminally acquired funds from criminal organizations into "lawful" funds.

Act No. 12,683/2012, of July 9, 2012, which amended Act No. 9,613, of March 3, 1998 (criminalizing money laundering), removed its list of predicate crimes and categorized the acts of money laundering and concealment of the illicit origin of funds derived from any criminal activity as separate and apart from the acts constituting other offenses. The new rules, inserted by the legislative change that occurred in July 2012, aimed at increasing state efficiency as an important tool against organized crime.

Act No. 12,850, of August 2, 2013, which defines criminal organization and regulates criminal investigation, the means for obtaining evidence, related infractions, and criminal procedure, also constitutes a great advancement in Brazilian legislation.

In addition to these legal statutes, principles and programs concerned with institutional and legal reform have been the subject of discussions in many countries that are signatories of international agreements. These agreements seek to obtain a set of institutional arrangements, management roles, controls, and regulations that may create opportunities to develop integrity and transparency, and reduce the risk of behaviors that violate ethical principles.

The Office of the Federal Comptroller General (CGU) created the program Transparent Brazil (Brasil Transparente) to aid states and municipalities in the implementation of government transparency policies required by the Information Access Act. The Federal Government Transparency Portal, launched in November 2004, is a CGU initiative created to secure the correct use of public resources. Its goal is to increase public management transparency, allowing citizens to monitor the use of public funds and help with supervision.[18] This initiative considers transparency to be the best antidote to corruption; it is a mechanism that induces public managers to act responsibly and allows citizens to collaborate in controlling government officials' actions by enabling them to check whether public resources are being employed as they should.

Transparency's strength is greatly relevant for the improvement of state policies, as highlighted by the considerations of Jorge Hage, chief minister of the Office of the Federal Comptroller General, who listed the following advances experienced in Brazil:

> The emphasis in opening public actions and expenses to broad public scrutiny, by means of concrete and even radical measures (considering our centuries-old secrecy tradition and obscurity within Public Administration), such as the Transparency Portal; the construction of a System of Internal Affairs Services in all sectors of the federal government, which is entombing the sense of impunity that had always prevailed, and now accounts for more than four thousand government employees expelled from the Administration for unacceptable behavior; and the articulation among organs responsible for the internal control of the Executive Branch, police authorities

18 *See* http://www.portaltransparencia.gov.br/sobre.

and Public Prosecution, which has resulted in thousands of lawsuits for improbity or other criminal behaviors.[19]

Improving Accountability: Specialized Courts for Financial Crimes and Money Laundering

In considering current legal statutes and governmental initiatives aimed at combating corruption, the specialization of trial courts in financial crimes and money laundering—created in 2003 by Resolution No. 314/2003 of the Federal Justice Council (Conselho da Justiça Federal)—brought great contributions that positively enhanced the agility and flexibility of criminal prosecution. Resolution No. 517/2006 broadened this jurisdiction, allowing the inclusion of crimes committed by criminal organizations.

Such specialization represented an improvement in the quality of decisions, information exchange among many investigative agencies, and greater interaction in the use of control mechanisms in financial and bank activities. Crimes within these specialized jurisdictions are usually transnational and demand a greater specialization of the authorities involved.

Legal cooperation among law enforcement agencies is frequently undertaken and involves the recovery of public assets, the breach the bank and tax privacies, and the seizure and forfeiture of goods and assets involved. Furthermore, anticipatory alienation of assets determined by federal courts before the issuing of final decisions occurs with greater frequency. This is because it is usually impracticable to preserve seized assets for years, because significant deterioration occurs due to the slowness or inefficiency of the judicial proceedings. Moreover, funds budgeted for preserving seized assets are usually lacking. In the case of an acquittal, the defendant receives a compensatory amount (which results from the former anticipatory alienation of goods) instead of an asset that has deteriorated in quality or value.

Criminal investigations and procedures involving these crimes generate an enormous amount of paper (or electronic files) that require increased attention and demand correct and careful classification. Yet there is also a need for flexibility and agility—arguably a true answer to the anxiety of the wider community—as well as a need for rapid productivity that corresponds to the volume of cases that have commenced ("mass magistracy"), despite the need for a step-by-step verification during the process. The maxim that "anything goes in order to reach production rates" can be true only if it is accompanied by effective work, seriousness, honesty, and supportive conditions.

The anxiety level of judges immersed in this scenario is heightened because they are torn between the demands for fast and speedy decision making and their consideration of well-established values. Clearly, judges currently work

---

19 Jorge Hage, *A força da Transparência,* 10(20) Revista ETCO: Instituto Brasileiro de Ética Concorrencial 22–23 (April 2013).

under high expectations that there will be greater efficiency in obtaining evidence and adjudicating cases under more stringent time constraints.

One should not forget the concept of legal interests, intended, according to Claus Roxin, as an unalienable requirement "for a peaceful conviviality among men, founded on liberty and equality." Meanwhile, another requirement, the subsidiarity of criminal law, is defined by the same German professor as "a preference for less restrictive socio-political measures."[20]

What comes into question here is not a mere symbolic criminal norm—presumably ineffective—but the real recognition of the indispensability of state intervention, expressed in and through the protection of an authentic legal interest. When considered in this light, it becomes apparent that one can thus avoid any primary legal damage from being perpetuated in the public perception that authorities are vested with the power to repress and prevent certain unlawful acts, and that this power is further legitimized and bulwarked by evident social support and, further, is resonant and in alignment with commonly and widely held social values. In this light, therefore, the claim of intangible abstraction does not properly fit into the analysis, since a rejection of such corrupt or unlawful practices is clearly found within the conscience of the common citizen, on both an individual and a societal level. The line of reasoning here weakens and invalidates the notion that civil and administrative compensatory claims would suffice in combating the crime.

Specialized financial courts improve accountability—in terms of both upholding criminal financial accountability and holding the judiciary also accountable for effectively adjudicating financial crimes. Without specialized financial courts, it would be difficult to have any form of accurate familiarity with financial operations that must inform judicial outcomes and decisions. Financial transactions and operations are barely taught during the undergraduate years of law school, which reveals a significant need to constantly update legal education and the court system in order to legally address the kind of financial transactional creativity that surrounds the practice of money laundering, crime, and corruption.

It is indispensable that the various authorities charged with the suppression of these crimes come together, thereby making possible the exchange and acquisition of know-how that enables all of them (chiefs of police, prosecutors, and federal judges) to encounter, combat, and address this kind of criminality in a proper and unified way.

One of the political impacts of the implementation of such courts is the motivation of formal institutions of power (e.g., the police, federal prosecutors, and the Council for Financial Intelligence Unit) to combat such crimes, making them take up sound and adequate measures to effect this end, includ-

---

20 *Cf.* Luiz Greco, *Que comportamentos pode o Estado proibir sob ameaça de pena? Sobre a legitimação das proibições penais* [Which behaviors can the state prohibit with criminal sanctions? A study about the legitimacy of criminal punishments] 2 (Luiz Greco trans., Financial Criminal Law Seminar March 2004).

ing the relocation of members interested in the suppression of these crimes, as well as greater focus and cooperation of everyone.

It is important to keep in mind that the coordination of the above-mentioned institutions contributes to a growing number of government employees with knowledge in the field of anticorruption and money laundering, which helps enable solutions to even the greatest difficulties or problems associated with money laundering crimes—particularly, the difficulties that arise in tracing and uncovering the linkages between illegal assets and the crime that gave rise to them. Developing such a coordinated specialization in the difficult task of tracing linkages between assets and criminal activity enables the avoidance of parallel, and often conflicting, investigations by different authorities. Coordination also lends clarity to the process by allowing everyone to know to whom and where a request should be made. This stands in contrast to a situation without coordination and specialization in linking assets to criminal activity, where all processes would surely be extremely different, and inefficiently diffuse.

The social panorama has changed as well; there is now a common societal consciousness of the need to repress money laundering and financial crimes. Recent federal police operations demonstrate that some crimes, especially money laundering, have enabled criminal organizations to commit such serious offenses as capital flight, corruption, and fraud, and the general public is aware of this.

To combat criminality, there is some need for the invasion of privacy. However, so as not to surrender to the parallel power represented by organized crime, the state should be armed with appropriate means for investigation.[21]

There is no shortage of difficulties for judges adjudicating the voluminous cases for which the judiciary is responsible. There are voluminous amounts of paper, files, and documents that must be organized and numbered for subsequent judicial decisions to be made in a reasonable amount of time. Personal meetings with lawyers, prosecutors, and police chiefs have increased greatly in recent years, demanding a greater amount of judges' time in carrying out these activities. To demonstrate all of the different phases of money laundering schemes, most legal proceedings are necessarily confidential. This situation generates considerable discussion associated with frequent requests made by lawyers who want access to investigation-related documents. Judges are also constantly being asked to issue decisions with urgency despite having to preside over complex court hearings.

Regarding the economic environment, specialization aims at allowing illegally acquired assets to be recovered by the judiciary so that the assets will not be tradable in the market. For the protection of investors, this should always be effected through transparent processes. The efforts of the Brazilian

---

21 *See* Mário de Magalhães Papaterra Limongi, *Mudança de postura* [Change of attitude], O Estado de S. Paulo, Jan. 14, 2013.

Department of Justice's Office for Recovering Assets and International Legal Cooperation (Departamento de Recuperação de Ativos e Cooperação Jurídica Internacional) are instrumental in tracking down, freezing, and recovering assets acquired through criminal acts.

All things considered, there is a clear demand for assembling adequate structures to properly equip specialized courts to deal with specialized criminal activities. Without these courts, society would continue to feel unequally treated in white-collar crimes and money laundering, generating more skepticism toward the work and effectiveness of enforcement agencies.

The idea of discrimination in criminal courts, however, assumes an unjustifiably unequal treatment for similar situations. The peculiarities inherent to money laundering and financial crimes themselves demonstrate how difficult it is to reveal, investigate, prosecute, and adjudicate (in a reasonable amount of time) these cases. Nevertheless, the feeling that criminal decisions are arbitrary and subjective—a sentiment already widely expressed in Brazil—would hardly abate if the state was not capable of effectively addressing such difficulties. Failure to do so would, in the eyes of society, delegitimize criminal prosecution, which in turn would enhance risks to institutional security, especially if society develops a paramount sense of skepticism toward the legitimacy of criminal prosecution in the courts and by authorities.

Criminal justice faces serious risks if it is not able to mitigate or eradicate historical inequalities that exist within its system. As an example, those who possess a degree, are financially well-off, and do not have a criminal record would receive privileged treatment during criminal prosecution, especially in its initial phases of prosecution.[22]

Such political, social, and economic landscapes demand the assembling of a structure compatible with public expectations generated by the creation of specialized courts. Such courts are under pressure to evaluate a great number of secrecy breaches (tax and bank secrecy), communication intercepts, and seizure and forfeiture procedures—all of which demand constant and immediate action by the judge in extremely delicate cases that cannot be solved with hurried readings.

It should be noted that, because these procedures are mostly confidential, lawyers must justify their requests to verify and access all documents and files associated with such cases. Such requests, together with lawyers' legal

---

22 In spite of the enormous exposition reached by the Declaration of the Rights of Man and Citizen of 1789, which read *"les hommes naissent et demeurent libres et égaux en droits,"* the first legal document to prescribe them was the Virginia Bill of Rights of 1776, affirming that "all men by nature are equally free and independent and have certain rights." Such formulations were conceived in an abstract manner. Even during the medieval period, there were reflections about the importance of equality, namely, in the work of Saint Thomas Aquinas and, in general, in the whole Aristotelian thought, in which one could equate justice with equality (i.e., they were synonyms). To be just, or to be fair, is to be equal, and to be unjust is to be unequal.

rights and prerogatives, have caused frequent debates and discussions that have halted or delayed judicial proceedings.

Legal proceedings undertaken by court employees have become voluminous and complex, and require detailed analyses of procedures to rectify irregularities and allow removal of matters unrelated to the courts' jurisdiction. The number of court staff assigned to common criminal courts is inadequate and needs to be increased. Also needed is adequate physical space to store the volumes of confidential documents generated by these cases and proceedings.

Thus, specialized courts, despite their benefits, are hindered by obstacles that inhibit quick adjudication. This situation would greatly improve, and normalcy be established, if future specialized courts were created based on statistically verified needs, a detailed consideration of the jurisdiction, and the number of judges and employees needed.

Recommendation No. 31 of the Financial Action Task Force on Money Laundering (FATF) clearly states that all FATF member-states must provide authorities involved in combating money laundering and the financing of terrorism with adequate financial, technical, and human resources to guarantee the functionality of the crime prevention and repression system.[23] This applies to the federal police, federal prosecutors, and superior courts, so they can avoid the application of statutes of limitation.

To keep specialization from constituting a frustrated attempt to suppress and prevent financial/economic criminality, specialized courts' needs must be addressed. Otherwise, the initiative could be delegitimized, despite the solid and valid arguments in its favor. Specialized courts give hope for improvement in public safety by making it more difficult to carry out organized crime and, consequently, discouraging criminal practice.

Further, by running efficiently and fighting crime adequately, specialized courts would create the sense that the law applies to everyone and that the

---

23 "When conducting investigations of money laundering, associated predicate offences and terrorist financing, competent authorities should be able to obtain access to all necessary documents and information for use in those investigations, and in prosecutions and related actions. This should include powers to use compulsory measures for the production of records held by financial institutions, DNFBPs and other natural or legal persons, for the search of persons and premises, for taking witness statements, and for the seizure and obtaining of evidence. Countries should ensure that competent authorities conducting investigations are able to use a wide range of investigative techniques suitable for the investigation of money laundering, associated predicate offences and terrorist financing. These investigative techniques include: undercover operations, intercepting communications, accessing computer systems and controlled delivery. In addition, countries should have effective mechanisms in place to identify, in a timely manner, whether natural or legal persons hold or control accounts. They should also have mechanisms to ensure that competent authorities have a process to identify assets without prior notification to the owner. When conducting investigations of money laundering, associated predicate offences and terrorist financing, competent authorities should be able to ask for all relevant information held by the FIU." *See* FATF Recommendations, No. 31, http://www.fatf-gafi.org/media/fatf/documents/recommendations/pdfs/FATF_Recommendations.pdf.

utility and legitimacy of legal statutes exist. Specialized courts allow nations to recover their credibility, strengthening the democratic institutions that support and generate the rule of law.

If specialized courts function effectively, the well-being of society improves and social and economic benefits are generated, thanks to the strengthened sense that national issues are being efficiently resolved. The Brazilian experience in implementing specialized courts has proved successful, generating hope that criminal law can be an effective instrument that finds workable solutions to social conflicts.

A 2010 report by the FATF demonstrates that Brazil significantly improved its ability to prosecute money laundering and financial crimes (including crimes of corruption) by implementing a system of federal specialized courts. Currently, according to the Brazilian Department of Justice's Recovering Assets and International Legal Cooperation Office, Brazil has had US$3 billion seized in other countries, of which US$40 million has already been brought back to Brazil.[24]

Even if Brazil has not advanced enough in adjudicating legal proceedings—as evidenced by the low number of final decisions—foreign states should still authorize the liberation of blocked assets, for it should be noted that ENCCLA issued its "Recommendation 3"[25] endorsing such specialized courts as indispensable and recommending their continuance.

Currently, Brazil has 25 criminal courts in 15 states that are dedicated to adjudicating financial crimes and money laundering. In 2012, the Brazilian judiciary commenced 1,763 new cases involving corruption and money laundering, and 3,742 new cases related to the practice of administrative improbity.[26] There were 1,637 verdicts handed down in 2012, resulting in 205 unappealable convictions. The total number of active corruption, money laundering, and improbity cases in the Brazilian courts reached 25,799 by the end of 2012.[27]

Actions undertaken by the National Justice Council that established "Goal 18"—which resolved that 76,793 cases related to corruption, administrative improbity, and crimes against public administration should be adjudicated by

---

24 Rafania Almeida, *O mais luxuoso dos crimes: Legislação avança no combate à lavagem de dinheiro, mas criminosos inovam nas formas de omitir os ganhos e de explicar o enriquecimento ilícito* [The most luxurious crime: Law improves the fight against money laundering, but criminals create new ways of concealing ill-gotten resources and justifying unjust enrichment], 3(8) A República: Associação Nacional dos Procuradores da República 10–13 (Dec. 2013).

25 *See* Department of Justice, http://portal.mj.gov.br/main.asp.

26 Jorge Vasconcellos & Gilson Luiz Euzébio, *Justiça condena 205 por corrupção, lavagem e improbidade em 2012* [Judiciary convicts 205 for corruption, laundering, and improbity in 2012], http://www.cnj.jus.br/noticias/cnj/24270:justica-condena-205-por-corrupcao-lavagem-e-improbidade-em-2012.

27 At the time of writing this chapter, the National Council of Justice still had not consolidated statistical data for 2013 regarding crimes of corruption and money laundering, even though they were sent by the courts of the country.

the end of 2013 (as indeed, they were)[28]—signify that the trials related to those crimes are now a high priority. Celerity in investigating and judging processes will bring positive results; the quicker the actions of authorities, the greater the effect on stifling crime.

Conclusions

Reducing corruption in Brazil is an issue of necessity and practical significance. Productivity and national development are intrinsically connected to the country's ability to demonstrate that it can overcome its limitations. In the words of Marilza M. Benevides:

> Let us remember, once again, that organizations are made of people and that there are no rules of conduct that can take head-on the human condition that enables moral and other more complex weaknesses to surface. The need for legislators and regulators to intervene and for organized society to mobilize is a means to mitigate the risks posed by such moral and complex weaknesses that surface through human creativity. From legislators, we should expect clear regulations, in addition to adequate monitoring, supervision, and a consistent system of punishment. From market players, we should expect mobilization and activism. When all these parts come together, the light at the end of the tunnel starts to shine.[29]

Encouraging ethical behavior is essential: "In a world where almost everything is public, ethics is an often overlooked or hidden asset, which allows crises to be overcome like no other. It is as if there was magic: even where there is only a slight presence of ethical sensibilities, much can be achieved. Ethical sensibility and behavior should be managed with the same dedication used to manage our best assets, because it is capital."[30]

Brazil's sustainable development must be linked to the consolidation of society, where ethics and transparency set the tone and where civil society—here taken to mean the actions of each and every citizen—and state agencies are united in a common desire to build a society committed to collective welfare.

There is no doubt that Brazil has enough legislative tools and public policies to tackle corruption, money laundering, and financial crimes. Many

---

28 Márcio Pacelli, *Maior Cooperação Internacional Ajuda Brasil a "Combater Crimes de Corrupção, Afirma Conselheiro* [Greater international cooperation helps Brazil face corruption crimes, counselor states], *CNJ* July 9, 2013, http://cnj.jus.br/noticias/cnj/25375-maior-cooperacao-internacional-ajuda-brasil-a.

29 Marilza M. Benevides, *É a ética do mercado! Que ética? Há enormes desafios a serem enfrentados até que o Brasil avance no combate à corrupção"* [It is the ethic of the market! What ethic? There are huge challenges facing Brazil in the fight against corruption], (http://www.jornalda paulista.com.br/site/page.

30 Ricardo Young, *A mágica oculta* [The occult magic] 10(20) ETCO: Instituto Brasileiro de Ética *Concorrencial* 29–29 (Apr. 2013).

governmental agencies have joined forces in the attempt to create measures to confront bold criminality.

The actions of the task force created in the state of São Paulo to reduce organized crime serve as an example that should be recognized and emulated. A 2013 pronouncement by ENCCLA stated that it gave its "unconditional support for the actions of the Task Force [which was] created in order to identify, track down, block, and seize assets of illegal origin that have been financing violent criminal organizations in the State of São Paulo."[31]

The judgment of Criminal Case No. 470 (the Mensalão case) in 2012 by the Brazilian Supreme Federal Court was a landmark case in Brazil's investigation and adjudication of corruption and money laundering cases. The Supreme Federal Court found that there was a scheme of illegal funding that was intended to distribute money to congressmen of the governing coalition during the government of former president Luiz Inácio Lula da Silva. This money was supposedly used to generate a slush fund used in electoral campaigns and for bribes to congressmen for their support of the federal government's agenda.

The recent imprisonment of those convicted demonstrated publicly that actions were being taken by the federal police, public prosecution, and judiciary, suggesting that the country is acting to correct its course. The revelation that public funds had been diverted to supply the "Mensalão" scheme, with spurious payments made to many congressmen, left no one in any doubt that the public interest had been brazenly neglected.[32]

The Brazilian judicial criminal system's sluggishness and inefficiency is recognized by its citizens and the international community. These problems need to be reviewed in order to better enforce penalties for crimes, including corruption, practiced against public administration. There is a need for new reflections on the multiple tiers of judicial review that exist before decisions against corrupt acts and crimes can be made final. It is important to strengthen the work of federal criminal specialized courts in financial crimes and money laundering, given that those courts have secured good results in combating corruption.

Brazilian legislation needs to be reviewed—specifically the areas of criminal law and criminal procedure, and especially with respect to criminal penalties, requirements for provisional release, and the appeals system. In this light, civil society, the judiciary, prosecutors, and government agencies should collectively and cooperatively be engaged in addressing these legislative matters so as to diminish the country's high levels of corruption.

---

31 Department of Justice, *ENCCLA*, http://portal.mj.gov.br/main.asp?View={7AE041E8-8FD4-472C-9C08-68DD0FB0A795}&BrowserType=IE&params=itemID%3D%7B70EFA623%2D3CEA%2D4B8D%2DAA9C%2D160F6EB41BA9%7D%3B&UIPartUID=%7B2868BA3C%2D1C72%2D4347%2DBE11%2DA26F70F4CB26%7D.

32 These events occurred between 2003 and 2005, during the government of former president Lula.

One area of legislation that is currently being improved is the criminalization of government employees' unjust enrichment from corruption. As discussed earlier, Brazil has undertaken international commitments (with the United Nations and the Organization of the American States) to combat unjust enrichment, but the lack of clear legal definitions makes it difficult for the country to comply with these treaties. Bill No. 236, of 2012, which will amend the Criminal Code,[33] intends to criminalize the unjust enrichment of government employees, enabling punishment of those who acquire, sell, lend, rent, receive, give, utilize, or benefit from goods and assets—movable or immovable—and which value is proportionately incompatible with the employee's earnings as is generated by his or her job and any other lawful means (Article 277).

Thus, the popular demonstrations experienced in recent decades in Brazil, most notably the demonstrations in June and July 2013, reflect Brazilian society's rejection and intolerance of corruption. The institutionalization of ENCCLA also reflects this popular feeling, as does the recent enactment of important laws to prevent and combat corruption and money laundering, including the creation of specialized courts in financial and money laundering crimes. These actions are indicative of significant improvements in the capacity and political will to diminish and eradicate corruption that has long existed in Brazil. Yet systemic deficiencies and vulnerabilities mentioned throughout this chapter must be corrected to ensure that corruption and money laundering are effectively fought and that the fight is conducted in full harmony with the specific strategies undertaken by, first, ENCCLA's proposals and, second, the wider concerns of the Brazilian population.

33 The Criminal Code is undergoing legislative procedures and waiting for amendments to be presented.

19

Development-Oriented Alternatives to Debarment as an Anticorruption Accountability Tool

FRANK A. FARIELLO JR. AND GIOVANNI BO

The sanctions system is one of the World Bank's primary tools for imposing accountability for fraud and corruption by private sector actors in connection with its operations.[1] The system originated in 1996 in response to World Bank President James Wolfensohn's determination to proceed forcefully against corruption in Bank-supported operations.[2] The system was operationalized in 1998 as an internal administrative process, designed to assist the World Bank in upholding its fiduciary duty under the Articles of Agreement to ensure that the funds entrusted to it are used for the purposes intended, by providing a way for the Bank to exclude corrupt actors from Bank-financed procurement—a step commonly referred to as "debarment." More precisely, debarment is a declaration that a firm or individual is ineligible for the award of Bank-financed contracts or further participation in the implementation of Bank-financed operations.

The authors wish to thank Christopher R. Yukins, professor of government contract law and codirector of the Government Procurement Law Program, The George Washington University Law School; Yasutomo Morigiwa, professor of jurisprudence, Nagoya University Graduate School of Law; Tina Søreide, economist at the Faculty of Law, University of Bergen and Chr. Michelsen Institute; M. Rohil Hafeez, manager in the Integrity and AML/CTF unit of IFC's Risk Management and Portfolio Vice Presidency; and Roman Majtan, procurement analyst in the World Bank's General Services Department, who acted as peer reviewers for this chapter and provided us with invaluable insights. The views expressed in this chapter are, nevertheless, solely those of the authors, as are any remaining defects or inaccuracies.

1 An analysis of the broader World Bank Group sanctions system as it works at the Bank's sister institutions, International Finance Corporation (IFC) and Multilateral Investment Guarantee Agency (MIGA), is beyond the scope of this chapter; as of this writing, only the Bank has seen actual sanctions cases. Nevertheless, many of the same considerations apply to those institutions.

2 At the beginning of the Wolfensohn presidency, corruption was rarely mentioned in international development circles as a major obstacle to development. One year into his tenure, Wolfensohn gave a groundbreaking "cancer of corruption" speech to the World Bank/International Monetary Fund (IMF) annual meeting, citing corruption as a "major barrier to sound and equitable development." *See* James D. Wolfensohn, *Annual Meetings Address* (Oct. 1, 1996), http://go.worldbank.org/PUC5BB8060. Since then, corruption has become widely recognized as a major obstacle to development that the Bank has tackled aggressively by supporting hundreds of anticorruption programs in its client countries and sanctioning more than 650 companies and individuals on grounds of fraud or corrupt activity. *See* World Bank Off. Suspension & Debarment, *Report on Functions, Data, and Lessons Learned, 2007–2013* 4 (World Bank 2014), http://siteresources.worldbank.org/EXTOFFEVASUS/Resources/OSD Report.pdf.

Since 1998, the system has evolved toward a quasi-judicial model, with increasing transparency and due process protections, while retaining its administrative nature. As a result of reforms approved by the World Bank's Board of Executive Directors in 2004 and 2006,[3] the sanctions system now consists of a two-tier adjudicative process, with a first level of review carried out by a Bank officer and, in contested cases, a second level of review by the World Bank Group Sanctions Board, an independent body composed of three Bank staff and four non-Bank staff members who consider the case de novo and make a final, nonappealable decision.

The reforms in 2006 added a range of additional possible sanctions: debarment with conditional release, conditional non-debarment,[4] letters of reprimand,[5] and restitution.[6] In 2010, the "baseline," or default, sanction was changed to debarment with conditional release. Yet a recent review of the sanctions system found that debarment (with or without conditions for release) remains far and away the most commonly imposed sanction, accounting for 93 percent of all sanctions imposed by the system.[7]

---

3 The Bank's sanctions procedures are based on recommendations made by Dick Thornburgh in his *Report concerning the Debarment Processes of the World Bank* (hereinafter Thornburgh Report). *See* Dick Thornburgh et al., *Report concerning the Debarment Processes of the World Bank* 5–6 (World Bank 2002), http://siteresources.worldbank.org/PROCUREMENT/Resources/thornburghreport.pdf.

4 A party that is sanctioned with conditional non-debarment remains eligible to be awarded Bank-financed contracts provided that compliance with certain defined conditions within a set time frame is met. However, failure to comply with the conditions for release results in the party's debarment for a defined period of time. Compliance is determined by the World Bank integrity compliance officer (ICO) and is subject to the same procedure as for conditions for release from debarment. Conditional non-debarment is normally applied in cases where the respondent has already taken comprehensive voluntary corrective measures, and the circumstances otherwise indicate that the respondent need not be debarred. Conditional non-debarment may also be applied to parents and other affiliates of respondents in cases where they were not engaged in misconduct but when a systemic failure to supervise made the misconduct possible. *See* World Bank, *Sanctioning Guidelines* (Jan. 1, 2011), http://go.worldbank.org/CVUUIS7HZ0 (hereinafter, Sanctioning Guidelines).

5 Letters of reprimand are generally imposed when debarment and conditional non-debarment are disproportionate to the offense. In such cases, the Bank issues a letter of reprimand to the sanctioned party. Examples include cases where an affiliate of the respondent has been found to share responsibility for the misconduct because of an isolated lapse in supervision, but the affiliate was not in any way complicit in the misconduct. *See id.*

6 Restitution, as well as financial and other remedies, may be used in exceptional circumstances, including those involving fraud in contract execution where there is a quantifiable amount to be restored to the client country or project. *See* Sanctioning Guidelines, *supra* note 4.

7 Of the 177 sanctions imposed through fiscal year (FY) 2012, only 5 deviated from the baseline sanction of either fixed-term or debarment with conditional release: three conditional non-debarments (one of which was accompanied by a letter of reprimand) and two letters of reprimand; all of these were imposed in the context of a negotiated resolution of the case (also referred to as a settlement). Similarly, restitution has been imposed only five times; four times in the context of settlements and by the Sanctions Board in one case. *See infra* note 41 and *Review of the World Bank Group Sanctions Regime, 2011–2014, Phase I Review: Stock-Taking, Initiating Discussion Brief*, http://consultations.worldbank.org/consultation/sanctions-reviews.

Recently, the Bank has begun to reflect on the underlying objectives that it has set for the sanctions system. Although the traditional legal basis for sanctions lies in the fiduciary duty to protect the proper use of Bank financing, one can argue that the fiduciary duty is itself merely a means to an end—and that end is the Bank's development mandate as set out in its Articles of Agreement. Indeed, the articles provide that "the Bank shall be guided in *all its decisions*" by its mandate[8]—and, although it is rarely pointed out, those decisions include sanctions decisions. As this chapter discusses, a sanctions system that is expressly aimed at supporting the Bank's development mandate could look quite different than the system that exists today.[9]

Debarment: The Good, the Bad, and the Ugly

For the World Bank, debarment has served a vital function in upholding the Bank's fiduciary duty by excluding corrupt actors from Bank financing. Other international financial institutions, including the other major multilateral development banks, have analogous sanctions systems aimed at tackling fraud and corruption in the operations they finance.[10] National administrative systems, including the United States[11] and the European Union[12] and a growing

8 *See* International Bank for Reconstruction and Development (IBRD) Articles of Agreement, art. I, and International Development Association (IDA) Articles of Agreement, art. I.

9 Sanctions also serve a de facto purpose, not expressly stated in sanctions policy, of protecting the Bank's reputation from harm by association with corrupt actors. Although some commentators consider avoidance of reputational risk to be an illegitimate objective for a public institution, we disagree. *See* Hans-Joachim Priess, *Questionable Assumptions: The Case for Updating the Suspension and Debarment Regimes at the Multilateral Development Banks*, 45 Geo. Wash. Intl. L. Rev. 271, 278 (2013) (arguing that reputation "cannot be regarded as a valid aim for a sanctions and debarment regime because it is in conflict with the application of the strict rule of law"). An international organization like the World Bank depends on the goodwill and consequent financial support of its membership, without which it could not pursue its development mandate.

10 In addition to the World Bank, all other major multilateral development banks (MDBs), namely, the European Bank for Reconstruction and Development (EBRD), the Inter-American Development Bank (IDB), the Asian Development Bank (ADB), and the African Development Bank (AfDB), have adopted internal mechanisms for addressing and sanctioning violations of their respective anticorruption policies. In September 2006, the MDBs, together with the European Investment Bank Group and the IMF, established a Joint International Institution Anti-Corruption Task Force and agreed on four prohibited practices: corruption, fraud, coercion, and collusion. See *International Financial Institutions: Anti-Corruption Task Force, Uniform Framework for Preventing and Combating Fraud and Corruption* 1 (2006), http://siteresources.worldbank.org/INTDOII/Resources/FinalIFITaskForceFramework&Gdlines.pdf. *See* also Stephen S. Zimmermann & Frank A. Fariello, Jr., *Coordinating the Fight against Corruption: Agreement on Cross Debarment among Multilateral Development Banks*, in *The World Bank Legal Review*, vol. 3, 189 (World Bank 2012).

11 *See* Federal Acquisition Regulation (FAR) 48 C.F.R. subpart 9.4 (2005) (containing the regulations that control how federal agencies can administratively suspend or debar).

12 The EU procurement regime is primarily governed by Directive 2004/17/EC (the "Utilities Directive") and Directive 2004/18/EC (the "Public Sector Directive"), which institute mandatory obligations to exclude possible contracting parties for past convictions of specified corruption offenses and the option of states excluding parties not meeting certain other criteria that involve the trustworthiness and reliability of the economic operators. *See* Directive

number of developing countries, including India,[13] Colombia,[14] Nigeria,[15] and Tanzania,[16] to name a few, have adopted debarment as an anticorruption tool in public procurement.

The original vision for the Bank's sanction system was ambitious indeed. Thornburgh sets out his vision for the system thusly: "With regard to effectiveness, we believe that the goal should be to employ procedures that would have the promise of ensuring detection and debarment of virtually all firms that in fact have engaged in fraudulent or corrupt activities."[17]

It has become clear over time that the system has not been able to achieve Thornburgh's vision as a comprehensive mechanism for excluding bad actors from Bank-financed operations. The Bank imposes roughly 40 to 50 sanctions per year; it finances about 20,000 to 30,000 contracts per year. Although, one hopes, only a small percentage of those contracts are tainted by corruption,[18] the system would need to take a quantum leap in reach to fulfill its original exclusionary ambitions.

In addition to the direct protective impact of excluding corrupt actors from Bank-financed operations, the sanctions system is intended to serve as

---

2004/17/EC of the European Parliament and of the Council, *Official Journal of the European Union: Legislation* (O.J. L) 134, 30.4.2004, p. 1, and Directive 2004/18/EC of the European Parliament and of the Council, O.J. L 134, 30.4.2004, p. 114, art. 45(1). In December 2011, the European Commission proposed a revision as well as the adoption of a directive on concession contracts. Under the new rules, the grounds for exclusion are extended to include undue influence in the decision-making process leading to the award of a contract, false statements in connection with the procedure for the award of a public contract, and agreements to distort competition. *See* Directive 2014/24/EU of the European Parliament and of the Council of Feb. 26, 2014, on public procurement and repealing Directive 2004/18/EC, O.J. L 94, 28.03.2014, p. 65; Directive 2014/25/EU of the European Parliament and of the Council of Feb. 26, 2014, on procurement by entities operating in the water, energy, transport, and postal services sectors and repealing Directive 2004/17/EC, O.J. L 94, 28.03.2014, p. 450; and Directive 2014/23/EU of the European Parliament and of the Council of Feb. 26, 2014, on the award of concession contracts, O.J. L 94, 28.03.2014, p. 1.

13 Sandeep Verma, *Debarment and Suspension in Public Procurement: A Quick Survey of Associated Government Regulations and Practice in India* (Dec. 5, 2012), http://ssrn.com/abstract=2185219.

14 *Estatuto anticorrupción por la cual se dictan normas orientadas a fortalecer los mecanismos de prevención, investigación y sanción de actos de corrupción y la efectividad del control de la gestión pública,* http://www.contraloriagen.gov.co/documents/10136/49245504/cartilla-estatuto-anti corrupcion.pdf/.

15 *See* Nigeria Pub. Procurement Act of 2007, part II, sec. 6.

16 *See* Tanzania Pub. Procurement Act No. 21 of 2004, sec. 57, which mandates the Public Procurement Regulatory Authority to debar a supplier, contractor, or consultant who has been declared ineligible by a foreign country, international organization, or other foreign institutions from participating in public procurement.

17 Thornburgh Report, *supra* note 3, at 8.

18 However, a 2007 report of the Stolen Asset Recovery (StAR) Initiative estimates that corrupt money associated with bribes received by public officials from developing and transition countries is US$20 billion to $40 billion per year—a figure equivalent to 20 to 40 percent of flows of official development assistance. United Nations Office on Drug and Crime and the World Bank, *Stolen Asset Recovery (StAR) Initiative: Challenges, Opportunities, and Action Plan* 1 (World Bank 2007).

a disincentive against corrupt behavior, that is, in legal terms, to act as both a specific deterrent for the sanctioned party and a general deterrent for others who participate in Bank-supported operations.[19] More broadly, the system aspires to contribute, however modestly, to the global fight against corruption through direct means but also through cross-debarment and referral of the Bank's investigative findings with national authorities.[20]

The notion that debarment provides a deterrent is widely accepted in the legal literature.[21] In theory, a rational actor who is prone to corrupt behavior will refrain from that behavior if its "cost" in likely penalties exceeds its likely benefits.[22] Of course, this seemingly commonsense calculation hinges on an unknowable—the likelihood of getting caught or, more to the point, the actor's perception of that likelihood. Moreover, the "cost" of engaging in corruption includes subjective factors such as the moral cost in the mind of the actor, which in turns depends on a complex set of social, cultural, and psychological factors.

---

19 *See* Thornburgh Report, *supra* note 3, at 60 (stating that "[c]ompliance is achieved, in broad terms, through incapacitation in the form of debarment, and through deterrence in the form of publicizing the risk of future debarment"). Compare Priess, *supra* note 9, at 280 (arguing that these aspects of the current sanctions and debarment systems, which Priess views as punitive, should be eliminated).

20 In April 2010, the heads of five leading MDBs—the AfDB, the ADB, the EBRD, the IDB, and the World Bank Group—signed the Agreement for Mutual Enforcement of Debarment Decisions. *See* Intl. Fin. Institutions Anti-Corruption Task Force, *Uniform Framework for Preventing and Combating Fraud and Corruption* (Sept. 2006). *See*, generally, Stephen S. Zimmermann & Frank A. Fariello, Jr., *Coordinating the Fight against Fraud and Corruption: Agreement on Cross-Debarment among Multilateral Development Banks*, in *International Financial Institutions and Global Legal Governance* (World Bank 2011).

21 Debarment in national systems is generally not meant to be a punishment for misconduct. Rather, debarment is the consequence that the law attaches to the government's lack of trust in a given player. In the U.S. context, *see* FAR, Section 9.402 (b). *See* also Jessica Tillipman, *A House of Cards Falls: Why "Too Big to Debar" Is All Slogan and Little Substance*, Res Gestae Paper 7 (2012) (arguing that debarment as a "nuclear sanction" should not be utilized simply because it is politically popular), http://ir.lawnet.fordham.edu/res_gestae/7. In economic terms, however, debarment is a cost in a firm's cost-benefit analysis. *See* James C. Nobles, Jr., & Christina Maistrellis, *The Foreign Corrupt Practices Act: A Systematic Solution for the U.S. Multinational*, L. & Bus. Rev. Am. 5, 11 (Spring 1995) (submitting that "[f]or large defense contractors, disbarment from U.S. government contracts could well be the most significant deterrent to engaging in conduct proscribed under the FCPA"); Drury D. Stevenson & Nicholas J. Wagoner, *FCPA Sanctions: Too Big to Debar?*, 80 Fordham L. Rev. 775, 803 (2011) (arguing that FCPA fines have little if any deterrent effect when the benefits derived from the sanctionable conduct largely outweigh the cost of getting caught). *See* also J. Kelly Strader, *White Collar Crime and Punishment: Reflections on Michael, Martha, and Milberg Weiss*, 15 Geo. Mason L. Rev. 45, 102 (2007) ("There is substantial evidence that white collar defendants are strongly deterred by civil/administrative sanctions, including debarment). For a discussion of the various objectives of procurement systems, *see*, generally, Steven Schooner, *Desiderata: Objectives for a System of Government Contract Law*, 11 Pub. Proc. L. Rev. 103 (2002).

22 *See, for example*, John Coffee, *No Soul to Damn, No Body to Kick: An Unscandalized Inquiry into the Problem of Corporate Punishment*, 79 Mich. L. Rev. 386, 389 (1981) (quoting Gary S. Becker, *Crime and Punishment: An Economic Approach*, 76 J. Pol. Econ. 169 [1968] and R. Posner, *Economic Analysis of Law* 165–67 [Aspen 1977]).

Another problem with the debarment-deterrence equation is that debarments have an unpredictable economic impact on the debarred party. Debarment periods are calculated against a baseline that is common to all sanctionable practices, adjusted for aggravating and mitigating factors relating to the respondent's culpability or responsibility, not on the debarment's impact on the respondent or others. So if a debarred party does a great deal of Bank Group or multilateral development bank (MDB)–financed business, it may suffer severe loss of business or even corporate death as a consequence of debarment. On the other hand, a debarred party that does little Bank Group business may suffer very little direct loss of business from the debarment.[23] So the same debarment may impose wildly different economic costs on the debarred party, and therefore create different degrees of specific deterrence; such disparate impact also raises questions of fairness and proportionality.

To the authors' knowledge, there have been no empirical studies that prove or disprove the widely held belief that debarments and other such penalties have a strong deterrent effect.[24] Some research suggests that the severity of the penalty is less important to deterrence than the mere fact that there is a credible reaction, coupled with the legal costs of defending oneself against the charge and the reputational cost of the penalty.[25] In the Bank context, this latter view suggests that all Bank sanctions, not just debarment, could provide a degree of deterrence. Indeed, private sector stakeholders often say that they fear the cost in reputation and goodwill occasioned by the public nature of sanctions more than the sanction itself.[26] Moreover, because Bank sanctions are part of a larger enforcement architecture, including the sanctions systems of other MDBs and national enforcement measures, Bank sanctions need not, in and of themselves, provide perfect deterrence.

Although the deterrent effect of debarment remains unclear, we do know that debarment can come at a significant cost to the Bank and its borrowers

---

23 Indirect loss of business may ensue from loss of reputation and the fact that Bank sanctions are being used, by an increasing number of external parties, for due diligence purposes.

24 On the issue of corporate punishment, research has primarily focused on the doctrine of corporate criminal liability, with some scholars submitting that harsh corporate penalties provide deterrence on a massive scale. *See*, for example, Brent Fisse, *Reconstructing Corporate Criminal Law: Deterrence, Retribution, Fault, and Sanctions*, 56 S. Cal. L. Rev. 1141 (1982–83) (arguing that the nature of deterrence and retribution as applied to corporations implies the need for criminal as well as civil liability); and Christopher A. Wray & Robert K. Hur, *Corporate Criminal Prosecution in a Post-Enron World: The Thompson Memo in Theory and Practice*, 43 Am. Crim. L. Rev. 1095, 1097 (2006). In contrast, other commentators believe that harsh penalties might distort firms' incentives to monitor for misconduct and undermine the deterrence of professional firms' members. *See*, for example, Assaf Hamdani & Alon Klement, *Corporate Crime and Deterrence*, 61 Stan. L. Rev. 271–310 (2008) (also calling for greater reliance on purely financial corporate penalties).

25 *See*, for example, Erling Eide, Paul H. Rubin, & Joanna M. Shepard, *Economics of Crime*, in *Foundations and Trends in Microeconomics* 205–79 (Now Publg. 2006); and Alon Harel, *Economic Analysis of Criminal Law: A Survey*, in *Research Handbook on the Economics of Criminal Law* (Edward Elgar 2012).

26 Anne-Marie Leroy & Frank Fariello, *The World Bank Group Sanctions Process and Its Recent Reforms*, 74–75 (World Bank 2012).

in the delivery of development results. A debarred company is excluded from Bank-financed public procurement, which, in markets where willing qualified bidders are few and far between, can have an anticompetitive effect and impede the delivery of development results, at least in the immediate term.[27] In such cases, debarments may (or may not) fulfill the system's fiduciary objective, but they arguably come into conflict with the broader objective of promoting the Bank's development mandate. The problem is particularly acute because debarments are applied in a way that is arguably overbroad in cases where the system's putative fiduciary objectives may not be served. The sanctions system operates on a *respondeat superior* basis,[28] which is to say that a corrupt act by any agent or employee is attributed to the principal, whether or not it can be shown that the legal entity as a whole poses a fiduciary risk to Bank operations.

Debarment may have other possible negative side effects, although these remain to be studied empirically. By reducing the number of market actors, for example, depending on the conditions of a given market, including the number of competing actors, debarment may have the effect of facilitating collusive practices among the remaining market actors, at least in smaller markets.

One problem with the system's wider aspiration to reduce overall levels of corruption through deterrence is that corruption, broadly defined, is not subject to consistent legal standards; enforcement is similarly uneven. Similar to what has been recently argued in regard to enforcement of the Foreign Corrupt Practices Act (FCPA),[29] because of this uneven playing field, debarments

---

27 *See*, for example, Danielle Brian, *Contractor Debarment and Suspension: A Broken System*, 13 Pub. Procurement L. Rev. 235, 236–38 (2004) (calling for contract unbundling as a way to favor competition); John S. Pachter, *The New Era of Corporate Governance and Ethics: The Extreme Sport of Government Contracting*, 13 Pub. Proc. L. Rev. 247 (2004) (suggesting that "the suspension and debarment arena has become a virtual bid protest forum for companies seeking to eliminate competition"); and Johann Graf Lambsdorff, *Deterrence and Constrained Enforcement: Alternative Regimes to Deal with Bribery*, Passauer Diskussionspapiere: Volkswirtschaftliche Reihe, No. V-60-10 (2010), http://hdl.handle.net/10419/55014 (stating that debarment is a less effective sanction than fines because the costs of debarment, like those of imprisonment, are higher than those of fines, in that debarment hurts both the company and the public by limiting competition). *See* Stevenson & Wagoner, *supra* note 21, at 816 (arguing that debarment reduces competition for future bidding on new projects).

The Thornburgh Report recognized the importance of protecting respondents against inaccurate or unjust determinations because of the Bank's "special economic interest and responsibility" and because of the adverse significant impact of debarments on both contractors and the Bank. In fact, debarment not only cuts contractors off from a major source of funding that is available in the country but can adversely affect future competitions and the Bank's ability to obtain needed goods or services because the number of qualified contractors may be limited. Hence, in excluding a firm from future business, the Bank "may be eliminating from future contention one of the very few firms with the characteristics required by the Bank for important projects." Thornburgh Report, *supra* note 3, at 7.

28 *See*, for example, Sanctions Board Decisions, nos. 36, 37, 39, and 44, as cited in the *World Bank Group Sanctions Board Law Digest* (Dec. 2011), at 37 et seq. The Sanctions Board has recognized a possible "'rogue employee'" defense but, to the authors' knowledge, that defense has never been successfully asserted. *See* Sanctions Board Decision no. 39.

29 Andrew B. Spalding, *Restorative Justice for Multinational Corporations* (2014), http://papers.ssrn.com/sol3/papers.cfm?abstract_id=2403930; *see* also Andrew B. Spalding, *Unwit-*

and other deterrence-based enforcement approaches may simply drive some of the Bank's client countries (and the private sector) toward projects financed by donors with fewer legal constraints (so-called black knights). With less scrupulous actors on both the demand and the supply sides of the equation, this uneven enforcement picture could paradoxically result in an increase in corruption levels in certain countries. This dilemma should be addressed through better and more harmonized enforcement, but that is a long-term goal.

Beyond the issue of whether debarments provide deterrence, or more deterrence than other sanctions, the authors would argue that Bank sanctions need not always be designed to deter. Given how few sanctions the Bank imposes relative to the volume of the operations it finances, sanctions need to have a demonstration effect with general impact beyond the particular case or respondent. But that demonstration effect need not always come in the form of a negative incentive like debarment; it could provide a positive incentive, for example, for self-cleaning or other comprehensive corrective actions, including—as this chapter discusses—remedial actions that mitigate the harm occasioned by the corrupt act. This approach to sanctions might not only avoid the negative consequences for development effectiveness that debarment can sometimes inflict but could also be designed in a way that actively contributes to the Bank's development mandate.

Notwithstanding the collateral consequences and other drawbacks of debarment, the authors do not intend to argue that debarment should be done away with. For one thing, its immediate purpose—the exclusion of bad actors—remains vital. Even if the system cannot hope to catch and exclude all bad actors from Bank financing operations, that is not a reason not to exclude those that it does manage to catch. Debarment also plays an indispensable role as a "backup" sanction; given that the Bank is a non sovereign, debarment remains the only effective tool for the enforcement of alternative forms of sanction such as restitution. And although robust empirical evidence for the deterrence value of debarment appears to be lacking, one may reasonably infer that debarment does deter corrupt behavior; it should do so in principle, and, as the aphorism goes, absence of evidence is not evidence of absence.

The collateral consequences of debarment vary widely, depending on the markets impacted, the nature of the debarred party, and the length of the debarment period. If a debarred firm as an enterprise (rather than a few individuals within a firm) constitutes a corrupt actor, it can be persuasively argued that its presence distorts the market and, on balance, it is better to remove that actor even if its removal reduces competition. While debarments may have short-term negative consequences, they may well, in the longer term,

---

ting Sanctions: Understanding Anti-bribery Legislation as Economic Sanctions against Emerging Markets, 62 Fla. L. Rev. 351, 355–56 (2010) (arguing that companies subject to antibribery legislation are investing less in countries where bribery is perceived to be more prevalent).

help clean markets dominated by corrupt actors (who may, through collusive behavior, freeze out other actors) and improve competitive conditions.[30]

The authors would posit, however, that the ambiguities surrounding debarment suggest that a more proportionate and nuanced approach to sanctions is not only possible but desirable, and the sanctions system's current, almost exclusive, reliance on debarment as the sanction of choice deserves reconsideration.

Alternatives to Debarment

Against this background, the time may be ripe for study and reflection on possible alternative approaches to debarment. Debarment, whether for a defined or indefinite period, with or without conditional release, is not the exclusive reaction available to the Bank when faced with corrupt behavior by a private sector actor. The Bank may also impose conditional non-debarment (usually involving an integrity compliance program), restitution or financial remedy, and letters of reprimand, with the last being a "slap on the wrist" reserved for responsibility cases and very minor forms of misconduct (principally in the settlement context). Outside the sanctions system *stricto sensu*, the Bank maintains a Voluntary Disclosure Program (VDP) that allows participants to avoid debarment or other sanctions entirely; it also refers most cases of corruption to appropriate national authorities.[31] Unfortunately, up to now, none of these alternatives has lived up to its full potential, leaving debarment in a dominant position in the system.

Integrity Compliance Programs

Integrity compliance was introduced into the Bank sanctions system as part of the 2009–10 round of reforms; these reforms were definitively incorporated into the sanctions process through the issuance of new sanctions procedures and related internal guidance in January 2011.[32] The reform was intended, first and foremost, to address the risk of recidivism by debarred parties by imposing integrity compliance as a condition for release. Integrity compliance is

---

30 But *see* Tina Søreide, *Drivers of Corruption: A Brief Review* (World Bank forthcoming), where she argues that selective leniency is a better strategy for disrupting cartel behavior.

31 Although the sanctions system targets the so-called supply side of corruption, the Bank has the discretion to exercise contractual remedies to address the demand side of corruption. *See* IBRD General Conditions for Loans, secs. 7.02(c) and 7.03(c) (2012) (providing that the Bank may suspend and terminate in whole or in part the right of the borrower to make withdrawals from the loan account if it determines that any representative of the borrower has engaged in a sanctionable practice in connection with the use of loan proceeds, without the borrower having taken timely and appropriate action satisfactory to the Bank to address such practices when they occur). Additionally, the World Bank regularly refers its investigative findings to national governments and law enforcement agencies in member countries. *See* Integrity Vice Presidency (INT), Annual Reports [hereinafter INT Annual Reports], http://go.worldbank.org/T40HHT3RF0.

32 *See* Leroy & Fariello, *supra* note 26.

also a feature of conditional non-debarment, under which a sanctioned party may avoid debarment altogether if it adopts and implements a robust integrity compliance program. This secondary function, which could be an alternative to the current heavy reliance on debarment, has been used in only five reported cases, all but one in the context of settlements.[33]

So far, the Bank's Integrity Compliance Officer (ICO), a position that was established to determine whether a debarred party has met the conditions for release from debarment or non-debarment, has seen limited engagement by respondents, in particular small and medium-size entities (SMEs), raising the prospect that, contrary to intentions, debarment with conditional release will become, de facto, a road to indefinite debarment.[34]

The reasons for this lack of engagement are various, but one possible explanation is the potentially heavy cost that integrity compliance places on sanctioned parties. For some firms, this cost may outweigh the benefits of Bank-related business. Walmart, for example, has spent US$109 million in the past two years to enhance its global compliance program.[35] Walmart, of course, is a giant multinational corporate group, but even for moderately sized multinational firms, the average cost of a compliance program has been estimated at US$3.5 million.[36] Although compliance programs are widely believed to bring important benefits to firms in preventing future corruption, like debarment, robust empirical evidence for this belief is largely lacking.[37] By contrast, it is

---

33 As of FY 2013, the only case of conditional non-debarment outside the settlement context was sanctions case no. 112, decided by the Sanctions Board in decision no. 53. *See supra* note 7.

34 For a discussion of the pattern of nonengagement of small and medium-size enterprises in the sanctions system, *see* Giovanni Bo & Frank Fariello, *The World Bank Group Sanctions System and Access to Justice for Small and Medium-Sized Enterprises;* and Bart Stevens & Robert Delonis, *Leveling the Playing Field: A Race to the Top,* in *Fostering Development through Opportunity, Inclusion, and Equity,* both in *The World Bank Legal Review* vol. 5 (World Bank 2014), which also describes the steps that the Bank is taking to ameliorate these issues.

35 Walmart, *2014 Annual Report,* 56, http://cdn.corporate.walmart.com/66/e5/9ff9a87445949173fde56316ac5f/2014-annual-report.pdf.

36 In this study, the average cost of a compliance program includes the full cost of an organization's compliance efforts, including the cost of noncompliance with laws, regulations, and policies. *See The True Cost of Compliance: A Benchmark Study of Multinational Organizations* (Ponemon Inst. 2011), http://www.tripwire.com/tripwire/assets/File/ponemon/True_Cost_of_Compliance_Report.pdf (estimating that the average cost of compliance among the organizations in the study was US$3.5 million compared with the nearly US$9.4 million for organizations that experience noncompliance-related problems).

37 *See,* for example, Nicole Sandford & Donna Epps, *Compliance Program: On Everyone's Agenda,* 29(6) Financial Executive 59 (July 2013); Katharina Wulf, *Ethics and Compliance Programs in Multinational Organizations* 403 (Springer Gabler 2012); and Dove Izraeli & Mark Schwartz, *What Can We Learn from the U.S. Federal Sentencing Guidelines for Organizational Ethics?,* 17 J. Bus. Ethics 1045 (1998) (referring to a 1994 survey of the Ethics Resource Center, indicating that ethics programs appear to improve ethical behavior, and to a study by the Council of Ethical Organizations finding that "[e]mployees of companies that had implemented or fortified comprehensive ethics compliance programs in response to the guidelines . . . reported that they were less likely to violate laws and policies"). This notwithstanding, one of the major challenges with measuring compliance program effectiveness lies in the interpretation of the data obtained from the multiplicity of indicators and metrics that may be used (e.g., compli-

not uncommon for large multinational corporations that have robust compliance programs in place to face corruption scandals by corporate officers.[38]

Financial Restitution and Other Remedies

The Bank's sanctions system also embraces restitution and other financial remedies as a possible sanction. The term "restitution" is an ambiguous one, with legal sources and scholars often using the word in ways that conflate at least three distinguishable concepts:

- *True restitution*, or what is known in U.S. law as the disgorgement of illicit profits. True restitution is based on the idea that a person(s) who engages in misconduct such as corruption to make a profit (the "wrongdoer") has been unjustly enriched. Justice demands that a wrongdoer not be allowed to gain from his or her misconduct and therefore must give up those illicit profits.
- *Damages or compensation*. This can be seen as the flip side of the true restitution coin, with a focus on the person(s) who were harmed by the misconduct (i.e., the "victim") rather than the wrongdoer.[39] The victim is made whole by the wrongdoer with payment or action adequate to undo harm he or she has suffered. "Damages" is the term used in national tort and contract law; "compensation" is the term generally used in international law.
- *Fines*. Although often lumped together as part of restitution, fines in most legal systems are not considered restitution at all, but rather a form of punish-

---

ance audit results, incidents, training data, risk assessment results, hotline data, and employee disclosures). *See* Jaclyn Jaeger, *Measuring Compliance Program Effectiveness*, Compliance Week (July 19, 2011), http://www.complianceweek.com/news/news-bulletin/measuring-compliance-program-effectiveness (also arguing that the answers as to whether compliance programs are effective "are still elusive"); Jaclyn Jaeger, *The Metrics System: Measuring Compliance Effectiveness*, Compliance Week (June 12, 2012), http://www.complianceweek.com/news/news-bulletin/the-metrics-system-measuring-compliance-effectiveness; Steve Koslow, *Why Measuring Compliance Effectiveness Is So Difficult*, Compliance Week (May 1, 2012), http://www.complianceweek.com/news/news-bulletin/why-measuring-compliance-effectiveness-is-so-difficult.

38 *See* Roberta Holland, *Bribery Probe Ends with Charges against Former GSK China Top Executive*, Compliance Week (May 21, 2014), http://www.complianceweek.com/bribery-probe-ends-with-charges-against-former-gsk-china-top-executive/article/347876/ (reporting that the investigation into pharmaceutical giant GlaxoSmithKline's operations in China resulted in bribery charges against the former head of GSK China and prompted GSK to conduct a "rigorous review" of its compliance procedures in China); Michael Scher, *Walmart: It's Not the Company, It's the Compliance System*, The FCPA Blog (May 13, 2014), http://www.fcpablog.com/blog/2014/5/13/walmart-its-not-the-company-its-the-compliance-system.html#sthash.sCu4NPTj.dpuf (reporting that the compliance program that Walmart had in place at the time of the alleged misconduct of certain executives was "good for its time").

39 *See* Directive 2014/24/EU, *supra* note 12, art. 57 (listing payment of compensation in respect of any damage caused by the criminal offense or misconduct as one of the elements evidencing the firm's reliability); and U.S. Sentencing Guidelines, *Guidelines Manual*, ch. 8, sec. B1.1, Restitution—Organizations (Nov. 1, 2013) (stating the general principle requiring an organization to take all appropriate steps to provide compensation to victims and otherwise remedy the harm caused or threatened).

ment that is unrelated to restoring the status quo ante of the parties involved in the wrongdoing, but related rather to the harm to the public good.[40]

The legislative history of the Bank's sanctions process indicates support, at one time or another, for all three forms of restitution, particularly the first two. However, restitution has been used sparingly—in only five reported cases.[41] The reasons for this relative nonuse of restitution, whether under a true restitution or damages concept, has to do with the inherent difficulties of calculating the quantum to be restituted and identification of the appropriate beneficiary.

In cases of true restitution under national law, the amount to be paid in restitution equals the amount that the court (or other decision maker) determines to be the value of the illicit gain to the wrongdoer, as measured, for example, by the amount of a tainted contract (plus any ancillary quantifiable benefits to the respondent arising from the misconduct) less the contractor's costs. In practice, calculating these amounts with precision can be extremely challenging, in particular, outside the settlements context.

In cases involving damages under national law, the amount to be paid is equal to the damage done to those harmed by the misconduct. The main issue in determining the quantum of damages tends to be the extent to which "indirect" harm can be attributed to the wrongdoing, with the usual test being articulated as "proximate cause"—that is, whether it was reasonably foreseeable that the wrongful act would cause the harm. In a typical case involving a tainted contract in the Bank context, a minimum measure of damages could be calculated as the contract value less the reasonable value of any goods, works, or services received by the victim.[42] In many cases, the secondary effects of the poor or subpar performance of the contract would clearly be a legitimate factor—but calculating and proving these secondary effects is very challenging.[43]

In theory, fines could provide a way out of these difficulties of calculation. Typically, no attempt is made to peg the amount to a restoration of the status quo ante, with respect to the respondent or the victim. Instead, the quantum of a fine is a notional amount determined by what is needed to act as an effective deterrence against future wrongdoing and is usually graduated according to the seriousness of the wrongdoing. The idea of imposing fines for sanctionable practices has, from time to time, been floated within the

---

40 *See,* generally, Graham Virgo, *The Principles of the Law of Restitution* (Oxford U. Press 2006).

41 *See* Integrity Vice Presidency, Press Release 2011/279/INT (re C. Lotti & Associati Societa' di Ingegneria S.p.A.); Press Release 2013/003/INT (re Oxford U. Press East Africa Ltd. and Oxford U. Press Tanzania Ltd.); Press Release 2009/168/EXC (re Limited Liability Company Siemens); Press Release 2012/282/INT (re Alstom Hydro France and Alstom Network Schweiz AG) and Sanctions Board Decision no. 53.

42 The U.S. Court of Appeals for the Federal Circuit in *Hansen* thus provided additional guidance on the computation of damages (although, confusingly, it referred in this case to "restitution" instead of "damages").

43 Various ways have been devised under national and international systems to get around these difficulties.

Bank—indeed, the idea goes back to Thornburgh[44]—but the Bank has never formally embraced fines.[45] Among other things, doubts have been expressed about the Bank's legal authority to levy fines, given that it is not a sovereign power, although, arguably, payment of a notional amount as a condition for release from debarment or non-debarment could circumvent this objection. More fundamental are the objections that fines would create the perception, if not the reality, that corrupt actors could view fines as simply another cost of doing business, allowing them to pay their way out of trouble.[46] Fines would tend to favor larger firms with deep pockets over SMEs. Fines also would tend to contradict the Bank's traditional assertion that its sanctions system is not meant to be punitive but protective in nature.[47]

Besides difficulties of calculation, restitution has posed challenges for the Bank in identifying the suitable beneficiary of restituted funds. Traditionally, at least under a damages concept of restitution, funds are returned to the party harmed. In cases where the victims of the wrongdoing are clearly identifiable, there is a strong argument that financial penalties should be passed on or otherwise used for the benefit of those persons. But in the context of Bank sanctions, the harm done to development effectiveness through corruption in connection with a Bank-financed operation may be widespread, and identification of a specific victim or victims practically impossible.

More recently, the Bank has taken the view that the proceeds of restitution belong to the government concerned, as the most direct victim of corruption. This was the Bank's commitment in its 2010 settlement with Lotti Ingenieria S.p.A., where the Bank imposed the restitution of US$350,000 to the government of Indonesia for unjustified payments received by Lotti and its partners as a result of fraudulent invoicing.[48] But this approach raises its own concerns. In some cases, government officials have been complicit in the sanctionable practice at some level, so returning money to the implicated government agency may not always seem to be the most prudent course of action.

The current guidance in the Sanctioning Guidelines recognizes these difficulties when it provides that financial remedies should be used only in

---

44 *See* Thornburgh Report, *supra* note 3, at 59–60.

45 One exception was the US$100 million Siemens Integrity Initiative (SII), which was created as part of the 2009 settlement agreement between the Bank and the Siemens Group. The US$100 million figure was deemed a kind of restitution, but the payment was not calculated based on an estimate of illicit profits or damage done, nor was there any requirement that the SII be directed to the "victims" of Siemens' wrongdoing. *See* World Bank, Press Release 2009/001/EXT.

46 *See* Stevenson & Wagoner, *supra* note 21, at 795–96.

47 Notwithstanding this assertion, even without fines, some stakeholders see the sanctions system as punitive in nature.

48 In one case, notwithstanding the respondent's intent to comply with its obligation, restitution has not been paid yet because of the inability to determine which government agency is entitled to receive the funds.

"exceptional circumstances."[49] Nor is it surprising that four out of the five reported cases where restitution has been imposed as a sanction came in the context of a negotiated resolution of the case. Settlement negotiations allow for an exchange between the Integrity Vice Presidency (INT) and the respondent to sort out the relevant facts and, in appropriate cases, identify and agree on reasonable proxies where precise facts are lacking. By contrast, in the absence of clear criteria by which to assess the funds to be restituted or, in most cases, clear evidence on which to base such an assessment, the Suspension and Debarment Officer (SDO) and the Sanctions Board have been quite understandably reluctant (or perhaps simply unable) to move into this delicate area. However, there has been one case to date where restitution was imposed by the Sanctions Board as a condition for non-debarment of the respondent based on the sufficiency of the evidence produced by INT on charges of overbilling.[50]

Letters of Reprimand

The Sanctions Committee, which predated the Sanctions Board, imposed letters of reprimand on a fairly regular basis. It did so when a sanctionable practice was deemed minor enough for this proverbial slap on the wrist or, interestingly, in cases where the committee did not find that the respondent's conduct amounted to a sanctionable practice but evidenced an ethical failure that merited some censure.[51] Under the current system, letters of reprimand have been used only occasionally in the context of settlements.[52] Letters of reprimand could be used more frequently, and their customary use as censure for unethical but nonsanctionable conduct could also be revived. It does not seem likely, however, that letters of reprimand could function as a mainstream alternative to debarments; the principle of proportionality demands that the use of such a light sanction should be limited to minor forms of misconduct.

Voluntary Disclosure Program (VDP)

The VDP provides another possible alternative to debarment. Under the VDP, firms not already under investigation may be spared sanction if they meet certain conditions, including self-investigation, implementation of integrity compliance, and a firm commitment to avoid sanctionable practices in the future.[53] In the course of public consultations, private sector actors expressed dissatisfaction with what they perceived to be onerous terms and conditions, in particular the 10-year mandatory debarment for breach of VDP terms.[54] As a result, firms' participation in the VDP has so far not met initial expectations

---

49 *See* Sanctioning Guidelines, *supra* note 4, at sec. II.F.

50 *See supra* note 41.

51 *See* Leroy & Fariello, *supra* note 26, at 10.

52 As of FY 2013, three letters of reprimand have been issued, all of them in the context of settlement.

53 *See* World Bank, *Voluntary Disclosure Program Guidelines for Participants* (2011), http://go.worldbank.org/T3PD4EE550. *See* also Stevens & Delonis, *supra* note 34, at 406–7, which allows that "[t]he VDP is not an appropriate fit for everyone."

54 *See supra* note 7.

and—for the moment at least—cannot be seen as a viable mainstream alternative to debarment.[55]

Referral to National Authorities

Although the Bank's sanctions system aims at preventing bad actors from participating in future projects through its sanctions, criminal investigations remain within the jurisdiction of member-states. The Bank has had a longstanding practice of referring investigative findings to national authorities when an investigation leads INT to believe that the laws of a member country have been broken. Following a 2009 recommendation by a panel led by Paul Volcker,[56] the Bank undertook to make these referrals on a routine basis.

In theory, the deterrent component of sanctions could be served by this kind of referral. Indeed, the prospect of action (typically of a criminal nature) by national law enforcement could be a far more potent deterrent than the economic and reputational price exacted by a Bank sanction. However, this assumes that a referral is likely to lead to real consequences; the track record so far in terms of follow-up by national authorities is not very encouraging. In FY 2012, the World Bank made 46 referrals of findings to agencies and authorities in more than 30 countries. In FY 2013, only 10 referrals prompted national authorities to launch their own investigations.[57]

Community Service as Restitution

Despite its drawbacks, debarment continues to dominate the Bank's sanctions system, partly because the Bank's Sanctioning Guidelines enshrine it as the baseline sanction, partly because the potential alternatives to debarment have faced their own sets of issues.

One promising and innovative idea for an alternative (or complement) to debarment is the adoption of various forms of community service. For the purposes of this chapter, the term "community service" is used broadly, with a meaning that captures the provision of goods, works, or services to a community of stakeholders, preferably those who were affected by the corrupt behavior that gave rise to the sanction.

Community Service in National Law

Community service as a form of penalty for individuals has a long history in penal law. In its earliest days, it took the form of penal servitude and, later,

---

55 In fairness, it should be noted that these kinds of results appear to plague leniency programs generally, including in the FCPA context. *See,* generally, Søreide, *supra* note 30.

56 Paul A. Volcker et al., *Independent Panel Review of the World Bank Group Department of Institutional Integrity,* paras. 81 et seq. (Sept. 13, 2007), http://go.worldbank.org/VVY6KYS720.

57 *See* 2012 and 2013 INT Annual Reports, *supra* note 31.

as a formal sentencing option in lieu of incarceration.[58] Discussions about the adaptation of this form of sentence for use against corporate offenders have occurred only recently. The assumption is that imposing community service orders on corporate respondents would be superior to imposing fines in regards to the five major aims of corporate criminal law: deterrence, direction, instruction, retribution, and redress.[59] In the United States, sentencing guidelines provide that community service may be ordered as a condition of probation where the service is reasonably designed to repair the harm caused by the offense, provided that the organization performs the service only by employing its resources or paying its employees or others to do so. An order that an organization perform community service is viewed as "an indirect monetary sanction [. . .] generally less desirable than a direct monetary sanction" and is warranted where "the convicted organization possesses knowledge, facilities, or skills that uniquely qualify it to repair damage caused by the offense."[60]

Community Service in the World Bank Sanctions Context

Although community service comes out of penal law traditions, the authors would argue that it can find a place in the World Bank's administrative system and—perhaps paradoxically—help shift the system away from its current focus on negative incentives toward more positive ones.

A firm found to have engaged in corrupt acts could undertake to "give back" to the community affected by its misconduct, either by undoing the harm caused by the misconduct or, if that is impractical, engaging more generally in the provision of goods, works, or services to benefit that community. To take a straightforward case, a firm that "cut corners" on a road it built by

---

58 Malcolm M. Feeley, Richard Berk, & Alec Campbell, *Between Two Extremes: An Examination of the Efficiency and Effectiveness of Community Service Orders and Their Implications for the U.S. Sentencing Guidelines*, 66 S. Cal. L. Rev. 155, 156 (1992) (examining community service as a form of sentencing in light of the relative severity of the sanctions, the issues surrounding implementation, and the question of deterrence). *See* also Gordon Bazemore & Dennis Maloney, *Rehabilitating Community Service toward Restorative Service Sanctions in a Balanced Justice System*, 58 Fed. Probation 24 (1994); and David C. Anderson, *Sensible Justice: Alternatives to Prison* (New Press 1998). For a comparative analysis and use of community service in Europe, *see* Gill McIvor, Kristel Beyens, Ester Blay, & Miranda Boone, *Community Service in Belgium, the Netherlands, Scotland, and Spain: A Comparative Perspective*, 2 Eur. J. Probation 82, 83 (2010) (submitting that community service should be regarded as "one of the most successful late modern punishments" that evolved from a purely rehabilitative "measure" to a punishing community "penalty").

59 Brent Fisse, *Community Service as a Sanction against Corporations*, 1981 Wis. L. Rev. 970, 1004 (1981) (also submitting that community services orders on corporate offenders should be formal sanctions, rather than conditions of probation, mitigation of sentence, or nonprosecution). *See* also Peter J. Henning, *Corporate Criminal Liability and the Potential for Rehabilitation*, 46 Am. Crim. L. Rev. 1417 (2009); and Marti Flacks, *Combining Retribution and Reconciliation: The Role of Community Service Sentencing in Transitional Justice*, 1 Interdisc. J. Hum. Rights L. 1 (2006) (arguing that community service sentencing could complement or replace prosecution in that "it falls in the unique position of being a mechanism of both retributive and restorative justice").

60 U.S. Sentencing Guidelines, *Guidelines Manual*, ch. 8, sec. B1.3., "Community Service: Organizations (Policy Statement)" (Nov. 1, 2013).

building the road to only 75 percent of its intended width would repair or reconstruct the road to the original specifications, even in the absence of contractual remedies available to the borrower to demand full performance. In the alternative, if the road was built to specifications but its price was inflated, community service could return to the intended beneficiaries the value of that excess cost. In less straightforward cases, where the nexus between the corrupt act and harm is more attenuated due to the lapse of time or the widespread nature of the corruption, the community service could be aimed more broadly at the project beneficiaries where the corruption took place or to the broader community, region, or country(ies) affected.

Within the existing set of Bank sanctions, satisfactory performance of this sort of community service could be deemed either a form of in-kind restitution or simply a condition for non-debarment.[61] Farther upstream, an offer of community service could be considered as cooperation in mitigation or avoidance of debarment.

Advantages of Community Service

The concept of community service is particularly attractive to a development institution such as the World Bank because the concept holds a sanctioned party to account in a way that directly addresses the harm that corruption does to development effectiveness, thus contributing directly to the Bank's mandate. And it avoids collateral consequences for Bank procurement and for the markets in which the sanctioned party operates.

Direct engagement with the affected communities could potentially give communities greater voice on the governance challenges affecting them and enhance accountability for the corrupt actor. The communities could, for example, be consulted on the extent of the harm suffered and on how that harm could be put right, as a key input into designing an appropriate community service action plan. The sanctioned party, for its part, could be called on to explain and apologize for its actions, thus holding it to account more powerfully than any mere financial penalty could. This, in turn, may open up a broader dialogue on the conditions that made the corruption possible—and what could be done about them.[62]

---

61 While well within the spirit of the language, to be used as a form of restitution, the Bank's Sanctioning Guidelines should probably be adjusted to allow explicitly for nonmonetary forms of restitution. The current language, which talks about "financial remedies" and "amounts to be restituted," appears to assume that restitution will come in the form of a payment.

62 In an effort to promote a culture of compliance, a proposal by external stakeholders as part of the sanctions review was made to include as a sanction the obligation to finance collective actions to prevent corruption (e.g., conferences, forums, business associations, school programs) in the country where the corrupt act took place and with the active participation of the administration that was involved in the corrupt act. *See* Review of the World Bank Group Sanctions System, *Submission of the French Council of Investors in Africa*, Paris (Oct. 28, 2013), http://siteresources.worldbank.org/INTLAWJUSTICE/Resources/SanctionsReview_CIAN.pdf.

Community service may also be a way to overcome a number of the challenges posed by financial forms of restitution discussed in this chapter. Community service does not require a precise calculation of illicit profit or damages or the precise identification of a victim or victims, which can be slippery concepts. And it avoids the need to return funds to a government agency that may have been complicit in the original wrongdoing.

More broadly, the introduction of community service into the system could help shift the system away from its current focus on negative incentives toward a system that rewards good behavior while promoting the delivery of development results. The need to revisit the balance between the negative and positive incentives in the system was raised during recent external consultations, where a number of stakeholders advocated a shift to encouraging or rewarding integrity; rehabilitation, including self-cleaning; and other corrective measures. More broadly, many external stakeholders maintained that the system is too punitive, too focused on negative incentives like debarment, and too little focused on positive incentives like rewarding integrity, rehabilitation, and self-cleaning.[63]

Challenges of Community Service

Community service as a form of restitution comes with its own set of challenges. As a threshold issue, the Bank would need to consider what forms of service would be appropriate, presumably with corrective actions that restore the status quo ante as the preferred option. The Bank would agree with the sanctioned party on an action plan, including activities and a timetable, which would then need to be monitored and assessed. Triggers and consequences would need to be articulated for late, poor, or nonperformance, with the ultimate consequence presumably being debarment, with some flexibility for force majeure and other justifying circumstances. Indeed, this form of sanction would, in essence, require a new contract, albeit one that provides goods, works, or services free of charge, with all the usual complexities attendant to contracts, beginning with the threshold issue of who the parties to the contract should be: the Bank, the relevant borrower, the affected line agency, or the community(ies) impacted—or a combination of these.

The legalities of the arrangement under local law would have to be confirmed. For example, nonpayment notwithstanding, the arrangement could be seen as a form of public procurement, with all the concomitant constraints.

---

63 World Bank, *Review of the World Bank Group Sanctions System, Global Multi-Stakeholder Consultations, Phase I: July–October 2013, Feedback Summary*, http://siteresources.worldbank.org/INTLAWJUSTICE/Resources/FeedbackSummaryPhaseI.pdf. For a discussion on the self-cleaning concept, *see* Sue Arrowsmith et al., *Self-Cleaning: An Emerging Concept in EC Public Procurement Law?*, in *Self-Cleaning in Public Procurement Law* (Carl Heymanns 2009) (arguing that contractors adopting certain self-cleaning measures should be allowed to participate in public procurement and avoid debarment); and Roman Majtan, *The Self-Cleaning Dilemma: Reconciling Competing Objectives of Procurement Processes*, 45 Geo. Wash. Intl. L. Rev. 291 (2013) (arguing that it is possible to improve integrity while increasing competition through a more flexible approach toward debarment that uses restitution and other means).

Short of legal constraints, the willingness and ownership of the initiative by local authorities would be a sine qua non.

The idea also carries some risks. Like any other contract, there is a possibility that the community service itself might become the subject of corrupt practice, which would not only defeat the putative purpose of the sanction but also create significant reputational risks for the Bank. And the arrangement might create reputational risks if the Bank were seen as merely providing a public relations opportunity for a corrupt actor, making communication of the Bank's intentions and objectives—and those of the sanctioned party—of paramount importance. Any public airing of the underlying corruption would need to be carefully managed to ensure a candid and constructive dialogue with the affected communities, not an opportunity for the sanctioned party to engage in self-justification.

In terms of sanctions policy, the Bank would need to grapple with a number of additional issues. Perhaps most important, the Bank would need to consider whether community service could or should replace debarment entirely, or serve merely as a form of corrective action in mitigation or as a condition for a reduced debarment period.

The Bank would also need to consider in what circumstances this form of sanction would be appropriate, in particular, if it is to be limited to less serious sanctionable practices or to a certain class of sanctioned parties. This chapter does not argue for limiting the use of community service to less serious sanctionable practices—rather, the cost of the service could be scaled to the seriousness of the underlying misconduct or, better still, the damage done by that misconduct. (If the service were aimed directly at undoing that damage, the scaling would occur automatically.)

We would argue that the possibility of community service should be limited to a particular class of eligible respondents. Potential eligibility criteria include the following:

- Respondents must be willing and able to perform the community service. Willingness could be demonstrated by requiring the respondent to offer to engage in community service as an alternative to debarment. The respondent should be required to demonstrate that it possesses the knowledge, facilities, and skills to undertake the services proposed. Cases where the respondent misrepresented its qualifications or experience (a not uncommon scenario), or any other case where the sanctioned party's ability to perform is in doubt, would not be ripe for community service.
- If a respondent continues to pose a fiduciary risk, then the exclusionary rationale for its debarment remains strong, and alternatives like community service should not be entertained, except perhaps as a mitigating factor. Whether or not current management was implicated in the underlying wrongdoing would be a key indicator of a persisting fiduciary risk for the Bank.

- The respondent must manifest sincere intent to reform—and not just those who wish to take advantage of community service, either as another opportunity for corrupt behavior or simply as a public relations exercise. Although an otherwise subjective quality like sincerity would be problematic given the system's current setup, reasonable proxies could be found in the mitigating factors that are currently listed in the Sanctioning Guidelines, namely, whether the firm has begun to take voluntary, convincing corrective actions to remedy the situation, has launched an internal investigation, and/or is cooperating with the Bank in its investigation of the misconduct. (Indeed, one can argue that community service itself is a kind of further corrective action.)

To put the community service idea into practice, the Bank would need to determine how this form of sanction would work procedurally. Like monetary forms of restitution, community service seems more adaptable to the settlement context, where direct negotiations between the Bank and the respondent allow for the ironing out of the fairly complex attending issues.

The bodies that conduct sanctions proceedings—the SDO and the Sanctions Board—were set up to determine the facts of a case and to make a fairly straightforward assessment of an appropriate sanction based on those facts. Under their current configuration, they are not well positioned to negotiate the terms and conditions of community service, either with the respondent or with governments or local populations. One way around this would be to allow decision makers to make debarment decisions either reducible or convertible to conditional non-debarment, by which the respondent, within some reasonable time after a debarment is imposed, could approach the Bank (either the ICO or some other appropriate Bank official) with a proposal to reduce the debarment period or to convert the debarment into a conditional non-debarment on terms and conditions to be proposed by the respondent and acceptable to the Bank, with the principal condition being the satisfactory performance of appropriate community service in accordance with an action plan agreed to with the Bank.

To limit transaction costs, it may be preferable that community service be undertaken as a supplemental activity under an existing Bank Group operation—presumably the one that was affected by the corruption. If that is not feasible—because corruption often comes to light long after the fact, when the relevant operation is already complete—then some other project may serve as host. As a last option, the community service might be undertaken as a standalone miniproject. Although the full panoply of Bank project preparation cycle should be avoided, the Bank's operational policies, including appropriate consultation with prospective beneficiaries and country ownership principles, as well the Bank's safeguards and anticorruption policies, could be applied, mutatis mutandis.

Conclusion

Community service is an attractive alternative to the Bank's almost exclusive current reliance on debarment as the sanction of choice for corrupt behavior by private sector actors in the projects that it finances. Although the Bank would need to address a number of practical, policy, and procedural issues to make the idea work, the effort would be worthwhile. Community service, as a sanction or as a complementary mitigation measure in appropriate cases, would avoid or mitigate the potential anticompetitive impacts of debarment while providing a way to compensate for, if not eliminate, the direct harms done by the sanctionable practice to development effectiveness.

Perhaps most significant, by engaging with the affected project beneficiaries, community service has the potential to provide a teaching moment on the causes and consequences of corruption while giving voice and compensation to those who, all too often, are left "out of the bargain" in sanctions cases: the populations that the Bank is ostensibly striving to help.[64]

---

64 Jacinta Anyango et al., *Left out of the Bargain: Settlements in Foreign Bribery Cases and Implications for Asset Recovery* (World Bank 2014).

20

Making Delivery a Priority

A Philosophical Perspective on Corruption and a Strategy for Remedy

MORIGIWA YASUTOMO

That corruption is a major obstacle to delivery in development is now widely accepted. However, the concept of corruption is not as clear as one might suppose. Corruption must be the corruption of something, but of what? We speak of a "corrupt person" and of a "corrupt society." Transparency International and others have developed the standard definition of corruption: the abuse of public office for personal gain. However, this definition raises some crucial questions: Who is the corrupt actor? Is the object of the corruption a person (or persons), a society, a public office, or, perhaps, all of them? Are there more candidates?

A corrupt person is typically a public official who takes bribes. But is it the person who is corrupt, or is it the office that the person holds that is corrupted? In a corrupt society, no one seriously expects people to refrain from giving or taking bribes, even if everyone knows there are norms that prohibit bribery and that it is wrong to engage in such acts. In this case, is the society corrupt? Or, are the public offices of such societies corrupt?

The term "corrupt" is ambiguous. It can be modified to characterize a person or a society, but the crux of corruption is in the violation of the norm addressed to those in whom public power is entrusted. The norm dictates that the competence and discretion of the official be used for the sake of public interest, but if these powers are used for the benefit of the official's personal interest at the cost of the public, then corruption exists. It may exist in the persons who hold public office, or in the society in which actions that may be called "corrupt" are prevalent, but ultimately, it is the function of the public office that is compromised. The standard definition is thus quite accurate on this point. The abuse of public office constitutes corruption in the precise sense.

What is "abuse" in this context? It is the use of discretion given to the official based not on impersonal and universal, or *public*, reasons but on personal and particular, or *private*, reasons. The public character of the office is

---

The text is a much-revised version, if not a different paper, of the author's presentation on February 2, 2014, at the International Conference on Institutional Design for Conflict Resolution and Negotiation, held at Nagoya University. The author wishes to express his appreciation to Hassane Cissé and Elise Wei Tan for encouragement and excellent review of earlier drafts and to Satoru Kobayashi for help in conducting research.

compromised when corruption occurs. Why is the compromise of the public character of the office detrimental? What does it destroy? These are the important questions.

The short answer to these questions is this: Corruption destroys the expectation that justice will be done, and if the extent of destruction crosses a threshold, the sense of justice of the members of the society will in turn be destroyed. The practical basis of justice—the public trust in the powers that execute justice—is destroyed. What is justice in this context? It is justice in the sense given in *Corpus Juris Civilis,* the summa of Roman law: *Justitia est constans et perpetua voluntas ius suum cuique tribuendi.* Justice is the constant and perpetual will to distribute to each, one's own. Put into modern parlance, justice is the sustainable effort to give each person his or her rights. A longer response is in order.

Why Justice Is Good and Corruption Is Bad

A real-life anecdote serves to illustrate these points more clearly. On a field trip with my seminar students, I visited the Kyoto University Primate Research Institute in 2013. We observed a colony of chimpanzees led by the alpha male, Akira. Akira was getting on in years and was no longer very confident of his authority to rule. He would cry out almost every 20 minutes, demanding a response from all the members of his clan. Failure to respond meant defiance. Thus, the chimpanzees had no choice but to respond and cry out every 20 minutes all day. I interpreted Akira's behavior as his compensation strategy for the decrease in his authority, geared also to alleviate his uncertainty and to discover any sign of revolt at an early stage.

Akira's actions demonstrated the essence of spontaneous political power, where "might is right" and the "law of the jungle" prevails. In order for a chimpanzee to survive and, to thrive, he or she must lead a life that pleases and appeases the alpha male. Akira had no obligation to protect the others, much less to protect every individual equally. He would protect those he found it in his interest to protect, namely, those who obeyed and served him, and he would give special favors and privileges to those he found to be of good use to him or very pleasing. The same norms of governance, in principle, ruled humans in all quarters of life until a few centuries ago; where rule of law is not a reality, it is still the norm today.

In 18th-century Western Europe, a new way of governance arose that would develop into the liberal democratic polity, where the law of the jungle and the evolutionary law of "the survival of the fittest" need not apply. In this new society, people have human rights; they are not subject to the whims of the ruler. Citizens are free to choose a life of their own, with their own values and the freedom to live according to their own principles. The sovereign must respect and protect the freedom of the citizens, who live under the "rule of law" and are treated as equals, having the equal right to be free. The little guy can stand up to the big guy. In the event the big guy does not, for example, pay what he owes, the little guy himself cannot do much about it, but the government can, and the little guy will be paid. Political power is used to enforce this system of equality, where everyone is equal under the law. The liberal democratic state has the duty of "the sustainable effort to give each person his or her rights." The state has the obligation to provide justice, although it may not always be able to live up to its promise.

The equal right to be free is what is attained in this universal, impersonal state. Of the polities known so far, liberal democracy has been the best bet for safeguarding the equal right to be free. It is important to ensure that those in power rule for the sake of the public interest, that is, the common interest of the people, those citizens who make up the polity, the individuals who are free and have the equal right to live a life of their choice.

In this type of polity, those in power are public servants, or the servants of the people, rather than their masters. They serve the public interest, not their personal interests. Although their personal interest is not unimportant—civil servants are citizens, too—the personal interest of the civil servant should never get in the way of performing the duty to seek and enhance the public interest. Public institutions, therefore, should be designed so that the legitimate personal interests of the civil servant do not get in the way and the common interest of the public and private interests of the civil servant coincide. For example, a higher salary should be paid to those who better serve the public interest.

This leads to the question: What is the critical difference between a liberal democratic state and the types of governance prevalent before this system? The difference resides in the answer to the question: Who is the master? In other words, in whose interest is the state run? A liberal democratic state is run for the benefit of its citizens, while the older type of rule is essentially the same as the colony of the chimpanzees cited earlier; the primary beneficiary is the alpha male. In a liberal democracy, the citizen does not have to cater to the wishes of the alpha male in order to survive or placate the alpha in order to enjoy freedom. Instead, the state has the obligation to protect the equal right to be free of all its citizens. No matter how much the public official may dislike you, she or he cannot act against you for personal reasons. The public official, who is bound to enforce justice, must honor your rights of citizenship, your equal right to be free.

How does one bring about justice? Is it not a daydream to posit that those in power willingly use their competence for the public good as a matter of duty? Can such a psychological state be imagined? If imagined, is it rational? These and other questions naturally arise.

What does it take to ensure that public officials will use their power not for personal gain but for justice? It cannot be accomplished simply through moral reflection and the conviction that it is good to have justice. Justice needs not only morality but also real-life advantage on the part of those with political power. For justice and other public goods to become a reality, they should exist not simply for normative reasons; they should also be compatible with the personal interests of those in power.

At this point, another difficult question must be asked: Which justice, which conception of justice, should be implemented? Justice cannot be a personal conviction, let alone a whim, of an official. In many cases, it should be in tune with the sense of justice of the populace, although there may be situations when this does not apply (e.g., when the people are entrenched in a tradition of class, gender, or racial bias). How do those entrusted with power free themselves from jaundiced views? The short answer is: reason and procedure.

The public conception of justice should be developed through public discussion and due process. Such a conception must be a product of public reason as well as an act of will on the part of representatives of the sovereign following procedural or natural justice. What form does such an amalgam of reason and will take? It takes the form of law. To be accurate, law should be a product of such reasoned, public, and procedurally correct will.

The laws under discussion here are the laws of a liberal democratic state. Whereas the laws of, say, the Mongol Empire are essentially the same as those of the chimp Akira's reign, the laws of a constitutional democracy are geared to meeting the public interest of the sovereign people. They protect the rights of the citizen. Therefore, such law constrains the power of the sovereign; it doesn't just render it legitimate.

Justice is "good" because it provides equal freedom to all. Corruption is "bad" because it destroys the system that can provide equal freedom for all. Corruption replaces a system of equal freedom with the only alternative available, the rule of the alpha male, where the law of the jungle prevails.

The Public/Private Distinction, or the Parable of Village X and the Big River

Thus far, political power has been seen as something that can bring about justice if it remains free from abuse. However, there is an even greater positive and extraordinary aspect of political power. It gives a unique and legitimate solution to problems of collective decision making that cannot be solved in the absence of public authority.[1]

An illustration of this concept is the story of Village X and the Big River. Village X was located next to a wide, deep, and fast-running river. Village X was an impoverished but peaceful and egalitarian village. There were no bullies and everyone was equal. The villagers cooperated to overcome hardship and barely managed to survive harsh winters. Village X produced a product, *x*, which, when combined with *y*, a product found only in Village Y, located on the other side of the river, created *xyyx*, a commodity sought by everyone in the world. To carry *x* from Village X to Village Y, one had to walk upstream for six hours to cross the river, where it was shallow enough to do so, and

1 This section of the chapter is based on Yasutomo Morigiwa, *Die philosophischen Grundlagen der Richterethik*, C6117E Schleswig-Holsteinische Anzeigen 110–15 (2009).

then walk back downstream on the other bank, which took another six hours, to Village Y. If a bridge were built between Villages X and Y, crossing the Big River would take only 10 minutes.

One day, the people of Village X got together to discuss their future. They concluded that building a bridge between Villages X and Y would not only make everyone's lives easier but would hold great potential for the future. The people of Village X unanimously agreed to build a bridge between Villages X and Y. For the very same reason, the people of village Y also agreed unanimously.

Life in Village X and Village Y was harmonious until the Big Question arose: Where should we build the bridge? Every head of household in Village X, rational beings that they were, wanted the bridge to be built at a site that brought the highest utility to his household. The upshot was that there were as many site proposals as there were households in Village X. Their proposals were equal in value because everyone was equal, and to the Big Question, each gave essentially the same answer: Wherever it is to my greatest benefit.

There was no rational way of choosing one site over another. One might have proposed the democratic way: take a vote. But because everyone had an equal say, there was no way of choosing on which site to vote.

How did the village solve this problem? The residents became political. They chose someone to be responsible for the enforcement of the demands of the public interest and endowed him with the necessary political authority. His duties included forcing people to do things against their will as long as this political authority did not infringe on the basic rights of each citizen. This authority also had the obligation to justify an authoritative decision with reasons that any rational being could not but admit as being fair and reasonable, that is, public reasons that are by definition universally valid.

For example, citizen A and citizen B of Village X both wanted the bridge to connect directly to the road in front of their houses, which were located in different parts of Village X. Before the age of political authority, there was no just way of choosing between the two sites; this was an egalitarian village, so the one could not be favored over the other without being unfair. However, once political authority existed, with the obligation to choose in favor of the public interest, something magical happened. New reasons, called "public reasons," were presented:

- Public Reason 1 (from a civil engineering standpoint): The bridge should be built on a solid foundation. As it happened, the site that B wanted had a sandy bank, whereas the site that A wanted had solid footing.
- Public Reason 2 (from a socioeconomic standpoint): The bridge should be built at the point closest to the locale where product *x* is produced. As it happened, the site proposed by A was closer than the site proposed by B.
- Public Reason 3 (from a geopolitical standpoint): The bridge should be close to the most densely populated areas. As it happened, more people lived closer to the site that A wanted than to the site that B wanted.

Based on these public reasons, the political authority decided to build the bridge at a point near where citizen A wanted it. The political authority enforced the decision, something citizen B did not like. However, because the decision was in the interest of the public, citizen B could not complain.

Compare this solution with the situation before political authority existed, where there was no solution, only solutions. A consensus might have been reached after a rational discussion among the citizens of the egalitarian Village X. However, such a discussion of public reasons would have gone against the personal interest of any villager not living near A's property, which was the majority of the villagers. Hence, it is unlikely that such a conclusion would have been reached voluntarily. Even if that were the case, it is even more unlikely that the villagers would voluntarily abide by their decision. Therefore, the establishment of a political authority that could force the villagers to decide in terms of public reasons and then enforce the implementation of the public decision would be in the interest of all those who wanted the bridge, which is everyone. Finding himself in a "you'll thank me later" circumstance, the political authority found it in his interest, as well as duty, to force citizens into considering public reasons and to abide by the outcome whether they liked it or not.

How could the political authority justify its decision to build the bridge near A's house, over other equal private claims? Because the decision was now a public decision, justified not by a particular private reason but by public reasons, and public reasons override private reasons. This type of decision did not exist before the distinction between the public and the private became a reality.

Public reasons apply to all, and hence are valid for all, whereas private reasons can be good reasons for only a certain person or group of persons. Public reasons are reasons that private entities cannot reject without being selfish. The democratic authority justified its decision by means of public reasons that demonstrated that building the bridge at the site chosen was in the public interest, thus rendering this a public decision, or a collective decision supplying the community with a public or common good.

It was natural that the public authority came up with public reasons against which both A and B found it difficult to argue (although in this particular case, A had little reason to disagree). The search for public reasons is essential for the survival of public authorities. Reasons given in terms of civil engineering, economics, and geopolitics are examples of public reasons. Ideally, they are valid for all, anytime, anywhere. They help identify our common interest, not my personal interest. It brings into existence things that are ours and never mine: *res publica*. The search for such reasons is not only ethically and politically correct but also necessary for the political survival of those who are responsible for the running and development of the republic.

There is a happy coincidence, or to be exact, an orchestrated harmonization, between the private interests of those who run the public system and the interests of the public at large. A unique solution is found for an insurmountable problem, thanks to a rational and public political authority with power such that no one can say no, if the contention against the public decision is a raw assertion of private interest. By definition, a political power deprives citizens of the freedom to say no (on matters over which they have a mandate). However, or because of this power to coerce, public authorities provide the citizenry with new possibilities. Intuitively, coercive power keeps at bay the bad guy. It gives legitimacy and security to the good guy, publicly acknowledging that the good guy is doing the right thing and ensuring it will do what it can to make sure that the rights of good citizens are protected. It gives the citizenry a new reality, where they can avail themselves of a newly entitled, secured freedom and other public goods (derived from the public decision, via the economic benefit brought about by the bridge in the case of Village X), which, without political authority, would have been virtually impossible.

In sum, there are two kinds of political power: that which does not distinguish between private and public reasons for action, and the more developed political power that does. The more primitive form may provide for the interest of the public if the authority in power happens to be good-natured and benevolent or decides playing the good guy would be to his benefit. The advanced form of power, however, has no choice but to serve the public interest: the only way it can validate its existence is to use its power for the benefit of the public, enforcing its public decisions (justified by public reasons). Only the latter form of political power may be called "public" in its proper sense. This is a political power that is not inimical to the people. Instead, its raison d'être is in protecting the rights of the people. Therefore, it is in the interest of the citizens to establish and maintain such a form of power, just as it is in the interest of the political authority in power to serve such a public. This democratic power came into being in modern Europe and has since been theoretically purified into the political model of liberal democracy.

The Rationality of Corruption

Justice is good because it provides equal freedom for all. Corruption is bad because it destroys the system that can provide justice, in other words, equal freedom for all. Corruption replaces justice with the rule of the alpha male, where might is right, and the law of the jungle prevails. Corruption erodes and destroys the public system of a constitutional democracy, which enables justice, or equal freedom for all. Corruption destroys justice by replacing public action geared to enhancing the public interest with public action benefiting the personal interest of a public official. It unbuttons all that the public/private distinction is designed to keep intact. This is comparable to slowly burning the bridge in the parable of Village X and the Big River. This section illuminates the rational and irrational aspects of corruption by connecting arguments from social choice theory to the political philosophy of liberalism. This in turn provides a framework for understanding and justifying anticorruption policies generally.

From the macro, objective, collective view, corrupt behavior is irrational: it destroys the institutional mechanism that makes a just, free, and sustainable society possible. However, sadly, there may be rationality if one takes a micro, subjective, personal view, namely, the viewpoint of the public official with a personal agenda. This is what might be called *situational rationality*. One situation where corrupt behavior becomes rational is when the public official is severely underpaid and has a family to support. If the amount of the bribe is such that it is worth taking the risk of being detected, or even if the price of the bribe is not quite right but the risk of detection is negligible, then it is possible to argue for situational rationality in favor of corruption. These are situations where corruption is morally reprehensible but rationally understandable.

An important element is missing in the description of the typical drivers of corruption mentioned in the above paragraph. There is no hint of whether there is a practice of corruption or whether this is a unique act of corruption within a context of impeccable moral standards pervading the society in question. The strength of the drivers is relative to what is mistakenly called the culture or tradition of corruption. The degree of systemic or endemic corruption is the important context in which the rationality of corruption must be described and understood.

To better understand the significance of this environmental condition, compare it with a society that in essence is no different from a colony of chimpanzees. Here, there can be no corruption. Not because there is no bribery or horse-trading, but because the public/private distinction does not make sense in this context. The alpha male is the state. The public interest of the state and the personal interest of the alpha male cannot be distinguished. It is the same coffer. Corruption exists only in the context of a polity that distinguishes the public from the private, and corruption that is illegal exists only where the nature and limits of power is specified by the law.

Bo Rothstein, in his inspiring paper, cites Alina Mungiu-Pippidi:

> Mungiu-Pippidi argues that the root of systemic corruption is a particularistic political culture, which is defined as a system in which the government's treatment of citizens "depends on their status or position in society, and people do not even expect to be treated fairly by the state; what they expect is similar treatment to everybody with the same status."[2]
>
> Both North et al. and Mungiu-Pippidi argue convincingly that corruption and similar practices are rooted in deeply held beliefs about the proper order of exchange in a society—personal-particularistic versus impersonal-universalistic. The implication is that to effectively curb corruption and establish "good governance," the whole political culture has to move from the "limited access" or "particu-

---

2 Bo Rothstein, *Corruption and Risks. Anti-corruption: The Indirect "Big Bang" Approach* 18(2) Rev. Intl. Pol. Eco. 228, 237–38 (2011) quoting Alina Mungiu-Pippidi, *Corruption: Diagnosis and Treatment* 17(3) J. of Democracy 88 (July 2006).

> laristic" equilibrium to the very different equilibrium characterized by "impersonal" and/or "universal" forms of exchange.[3]

The personal-particularistic society mentioned is in essence the chimpanzee colony, and the impersonal-universalistic society is constitutional democracy. To be more accurate, the personal-particularistic society does not know of the distinction between the personal and the public. An individual chimpanzee would not distinguish personal interest from public interest because, even if chimpanzees had the intellectual capacity to conceptualize the public as distinct from the private, there is no institution to protect the public interest. The political machine exists for the benefit of the alpha male. The machine protects the life and interest of others only insofar as doing so benefits the personal interest of the alpha male.

Great minds such as Thomas Hobbes,[4] Jean-Jacques Rousseau,[5] John Locke,[6] and Immanuel Kant[7] developed the idea that such a machine can be reinterpreted and tweaked into a mechanism to protect the public interest, especially the protection of the right to be free and equal. The principles governing such a free and egalitarian society and the mechanism for providing such a just and stable society have since been developed by political philosophers of liberalism, notably John Rawls.[8]

The gist of the argument is to *distinguish* the public role of the ruler from her private life. The public duty of those charged with governance is to provide public goods that only political power can provide (as symbolized by the free and equal character of Village X and the wealth brought about by the building of the bridge). The grasping and implementation of the concept of the public (i.e., the universe of public reasons for action), distinguished from the private, is the key to understanding the environmental conditions that make equal liberty possible.

To render public discourse based on public reasons effective, by giving it the status of an overriding or exclusive reason for action, political authority is needed, an authority that declares and enforces the superiority of a public reason for action on matters mandated to the authority.

Although such implementation is the collective responsibility of the citizens of the society, in reality it is primarily up to the representatives of the

---

3 Rothstein, *supra* note 2, at 238.

4 Thomas Hobbes, *Leviathan* (Richard Tuck ed., Cambridge U. Press 1996).

5 Jean-Jacques Rousseau, *Du contrat social* in *Œuvres complètes,* vol. 3 (Bernard Gagnebin & Marcel Raymond eds., Gallimard 1964).

6 John Locke, *The Second Treatise of Government,* in *Two Treatises of Government* (Peter Laslett ed., Cambridge U. Press 1988).

7 Immanuel Kant, *Die Metaphysik der Sitten,* in *Werkausgabe,* vol. 8 (Wilhelm Weischedel ed., Suhrkamp 1997).

8 John Rawls, *A Theory of Justice* (Harvard U. Press 1971); Rawls, *Political Liberalism* (Columbia U. Press 1993); Rawls, *Law of Peoples: With "The Idea of Public Reason Revisited"* (Harvard U. Press 1999); Rawls, *Collected Papers* (Samuel Freeman ed., Harvard U. Press 2001).

people—and the persons running the government—to develop, run, and improve the system. Hence, when discussing the environmental conditions needed for liberty, special attention needs to be given to government personnel. The personal obligation and the rights of those in charge of governance are the same as those of any other citizen: security, freedom, and welfare of oneself and one's family. These personal interests are not to be neglected, but they should never take precedence over the enhancement of the public interest with which the official is charged. When the priority of interests changes, the doors to corruption open. Corruption destroys a just and stable society through the corrosion of the society's foundational institutions.

The situational rationality of corruption and, hence, the measures necessary for combating corruption should be apparent. Society must make corruption irrational to combat it. To make corruption irrational, society must structure and restructure the political institutions so that there is little room for the situational rationality of corruption. What defines such a structure? A constitution. What is the means by which to bring this about? The rule of law. More specifically, the implementation of a type of rule of law fit for constitutional democracy. Law in a constitutional democracy is the means by which people are treated as equals, that is, they are equally free.

A society where such law is in action is a just society, where everyone is equal under the law: citizens are abstracted from their personal traits and treated as right holders, as citizens who are equally free. Only in the context of such an impersonal-universalistic society can corruption be suppressed. Otherwise, rational beings will continue the strategy ingrained in them through natural selection, of surviving in the world of the chimpanzee: befriend the alpha male or get out of his way and keep a low profile. Given that the typical method of demonstrating friendship and trust in this milieu is mutual grooming, or "I'll scratch your back if you scratch mine," this strategy translates into corrupt behavior.

Again, there is nothing wrong with this behavior in a world where the public/private distinction does not exist. In that world, equal freedom cannot exist. Corruption can happen only when there is an entity that can be corrupted: a public office, an institution constituted by laws to ensure equal freedom. Corruption happens only in a legal system where the public and private are distinguished and a rational agent in office is charged with protecting the public interest but institutional safeguards and professional ethics are faulty or missing. In such social conditions, the official may perceive prioritizing personal interests as rational. If the conditions necessary for civic virtue to pay off are nonexistent, it would be irrational for the public servant to muster his esprit de corps and refrain from corruptive behavior.

Public institutions are designed and trusted on the assumption that the officials are using their power or competence to enhance the public interest, not their personal interest. Thus, drivers of corruption can be identified as the conditions that enable the official to believe that it makes more sense to prioritize personal interest rather than the public interest. When making the enhancement of personal interest the main driver for official action becomes rational, then corruption is almost inevitable.

Effective anticorruption policies must make such drivers for action among public officials irrational. To attain this goal, an economic, political, and ethical milieu embodied in the basic institutions of a just society must be built, such that engaging in corrupt acts would be irrational. To curb the motivational drive, anticorruption policies should recognize the need for establishing the environmental conditions discussed above, as well as the immediate objectives of the particular policy in question. The values the society stands for must be made abundantly clear through its laws and other measures.

The Goal of Strategies for Meeting the Delivery Challenge

The "delivery challenge" is the challenge of delivering intended results and outcomes that derive from anticorruption policies. In other words, it is the challenge of identifying, clarifying, and making operational the set of reasons on which the players in society—especially the public officials—are rationally induced or impelled to base their actions and decisions, which ideally are consistently in full alignment with, and conducive to prioritizing the attainment of, the public interest, not their own private benefit.

Solutions to this delivery challenge comprise measures that render acting on legitimate private reasons, such as looking after one's family, consonant with or indistinguishable from acting in the public interest. This means the measures will affect public officials in such a way that their behavior would seem as if they were acting on public reasons that justify or lead to the attainment of the public interest, in other words, greater social utility in terms of wealth, justice, or any other public good.

The usual method for such alignment of the public and the private is suppressing reasons for corrupt acts and decisions under the threat of certain and severe sanction. This seems to be the straightforward remedy. However, when the ethos and nature of corruption are seen in the light of the argument of this chapter, the very limited focus and command of such threat of sanction, if operating alone, should be apparent. As long as the matrix that makes corruption rational continues to exist, there will be attempts at rent-seeking, or to bypass such sanctions, from many quarters. When there is enough apathy, if not antipathy, a sanction becomes ineffective. This fact has long been recognized as the reason why corruption endures and is endemic in societies.

Besides the strategy of making the pursuit of personal interest irrational, the possibility of making the pursuit of the civil servant's personal interest compatible with her duty to pursue the public interest should be considered. The goal is to make the attainment of public interest *not irrational*. Instead of making the pursuit of personal interest irrational the primary goal, society should seek ways of making the pursuit of the public interest compatible with the official's private concerns.

The implementation of this strategy will be difficult as long as one thinks of public and private interests as being in a zero-sum game relationship. Societies must reconsider the situation and look for ways to understand the situation such that win-win and other types of games are possible. If they are successful, then the strategy will translate itself into a matter of designing and tweaking the rules so that the public interest and the personal concerns of officials become compatible. Ideally, the architecture of the system allows the two types of interest to coexist in a win-win relationship with each other. This is the optimal solution to the delivery challenge.

However, if such an arrangement is not practically attainable, as is often the case, the policy maker can strive for the second-best solution: designing and running the system so that reasons that motivate action to increase one's personal utility or benefit *overlap* with reasons for serving the public interest. For example, a highly probable and gratifying reward—tangible or intangible—might be given to an agent or public official when he or she complies with measures satisfying the public interest. Conventionally, this tactic could take the raw form of higher pay and bonuses. However, from the viewpoint of institutional stability, a more subtle form of comparative advantage to corruptive behavior should be devised. This second solution may well be up to the delivery challenge.

Recall that there are only three methods that will make rational persons choose to cooperate in a public scheme:[9]

- Making a severe sanction highly probable in the event of noncooperation
- Making a gratifying reward highly probable in the event of cooperation
- Making the acts involved into a repeated game, that is, make the players play the same game over and over again ad infinitum.

To illustrate the third method, assume a rational actor in a prisoner's dilemma. He would calculate, under condition of uncertainty, the payoff of his move to either confess or not, in relation to the move that his counterpart makes. It is well known that confessing will always be the rational move to make, because the least-severe sanction will be handed down in case the other party betrays as well, which he or she will, because it is rational to do so. However, if the same game is repeated many times, and the actors become aware of this, the matrix changes.[10] Further, if the actors are not only rational but also

---

9 Acts of self-sacrifice, with complete disregard for one's personal interest (and the welfare of the family), are possible, and sometimes even laudable, but are hardly sustainable.

10 Whereas Friedrich Nietzsche's interpretation of eternal recurrence results in humanity's going beyond good and evil, the outlook here is constructive. If the realm of the public remains undiscovered, what Nietzsche says in *Gay Science* and *Will to Power* is comprehensible. However, if the potential of a just institution is understood and recognized, then rationality should demand another view, a turn for the ethical. *See* Friedrich Nietzsche, *Die fröhliche Wissenschaft*, in *Sämtliche Werke: Kritische Studienausgabe*, vol. 3 (2nd ed., Giorgio Colli & Mazzino

creative and reasonable, they would opt for institutional safeguards that warrant one's trust in the other actor to live up to his promise. In other words, he would opt for an institution that would allow the highest payoff if both kept their mouths shut. We now have a new ball game.

The second strategy, making the private overlap with the public, tries to make the most of the third method, repetition. What would an institution fitting the bill look like? Don't all institutions assume repetition? Isn't that what we are assuming when we say, you know the drill? For such a repeated game to become possible, the sanction involved cannot be years of incarceration. It cannot be long, or the idea of the game being repeated over a lifetime becomes nonsensical. Further, the actors' actions are to be open to the public and remembered by the other player. Otherwise, the fact of repetition, the acknowledgment that this is a repeated game, is not possible.

Now consider the issue not as a two-person prisoner's dilemma but as that of an institution involving many people. Take the residents of Village X before the bridge is built. There was no system of governance enforced by a legitimate democratic power. Each villager was busy making *xyyx*s as efficiently as possible. For a time, everyone produced *xyyx*s the same way, making the six-hour walk up the river and then back down to Village Y, with a backpack full of *x*s to exchange for *y*s. They would then make another 12-hour walk back to their Village X and combine the *y*s with the *x*s to make *xyyx*s. They repeat the work involved in the production of *xyyx*s day after day. This means that the matrix involved in deciding how to produce *xyyz*s does not change.

If an initiative to innovate had been implemented, to make more *xyyx*s with less labor, the situation would have changed and the matrix would have fluctuated. For instance, to shorten the time needed to fetch *y*s from Village Y, each person might have tried to find the closest point possible for crossing the river and kept it a secret to gain comparative advantage. Some people might have drowned in the process, being too daring or greedy. Others might have formed a group to build a small bridge upstream that allowed them to reach Village Y in, say, nine hours instead of twelve. Although initially the group might have monopolized the use of the bridge, eventually, its members would decide to allow others to use it for a toll. The members of the group, if successful, would gain more wealth than others and establish a new class, with power over others. Village X is no longer a community of equals.

Through this process, the improved system of production—using the bridge—would become the normal mode of production; it would become the system. The matrix involved in production would settle down. This is what the repeated game sequence would bring about. It is no longer a utility-maximizing game among equals. Although the players are still in a

---

Montinari eds., Walter de Gruyter 1988); Nietzsche, *The Gay Science: With a Prelude of Rhymes and an Appendix of Songs* (Walter Kaufmann trans., Random House 1974); Nietzsche, *Der Wille zur Macht: Versuch einer Umwertung aller Werte* (13th ed., Kröner 1996); Nietzsche, *The Will to Power* (W. Kaufmann & R. J. Hollingdale trans., Vintage 1968).

utility-maximizing game with others, they no longer play under the same rules, with the same roles. The games would be repeated almost every day. However, it is no longer the original game alluded to as a ball game. It is becoming a new kind of game: the production of *xyyxs*.

After a while, a slightly more efficient system of production might develop, with the accompanying fluctuation in the matrix. Then, again, things would settle down into a system of repeated games. This time, it is a new version of the same kind of game. New versions of this game would continually arise, with accompanying fluctuation in the matrix resulting in a complex system of division of labor.

Throughout this process, there would be a concentration of wealth and power into a group and within the group. Thus a spontaneous system of political power is established. It is the rule of the alpha male of the group. Justice is what the alpha male determines. The rational actors that wished to become friends or agents of the alpha male would take on managerial tasks instead of doing the hours-long round-trip hike, with a loaded backpack of *x* or *y*s.

Those who could not join the clique are left working to produce *xyyxs*. Let's put ourselves in the shoes of one of these players. What choice would I have to enhance utility in this game? If there were no real options, it would be a repeated game, a life of eternal recurrence. Let's assume there are no new bridges, no other changes that bring about a new set of repeated games. Then, is there no room to innovate on an individual basis? Or would there be attempts to do something about the situation?

Someone might have tried to improvise, perhaps a villager who presented the toll taker at the bridge with a gift in exchange for a discount. This looks like the primordial form of a bribe. However, it isn't. The toll taker is not taking a bribe; he is merely embezzling or cheating the alpha male out of what belongs to him. The public/private distinction does not yet exist, hence a bribe, an incentive to induce abuse of public office for private gain, cannot exist. The monitoring that the toll taker does is for securing the alpha male's gain, not the public interest. The alpha male now has a principal-agent problem on his hands. However, since there is no such thing as we, the people, we do not have a corruption problem.

This example is a humane and developed form of the rule of the alpha male; although the bridge is used to provide benefits to the alpha male and his group, the fact that there is demand, that many wish to use the bridge, demonstrates that the use of the bridge is indeed in the public interest, even if, like much in the marketplace, it was not meant to be.[11] Accordingly, rent seeking by users brings about phenomena that resemble corruption. What is missing here is the

11 However, the bridge is not a public good in the economic sense, because there is no problem in keeping free riders out. Public goods in economics are defined by nonexcludability and nonexclusivity. Because there is effective monitoring at the tollbooth, free riding is not a problem. Hence the first condition of nonexcludability is not satisfied.

distinction between the public and the private. There is no abuse of public office for private gain. What we see is the abuse of a job in a business for private gain.

Why is the public/private distinction important? Without the distinction, there is little room for justice as we in the modern world understand it: equal freedom for all. The alpha male, the toll taker, and the worker are not equals. Those days are gone. This has become a class society, where class is defined in terms of wealth and power. The villagers are now divided by rank. There is no such thing as common cause or civic duty. Unless a class consciousness can be brewed only personal gain and personal motives exist. Although this is a system that may appear to the modern eye to be unfairly advantageous to the alpha male, the worker has no reason to cooperate with the toll taker to oust the alpha male, unless he is involved in a coup d'état plot, to replace the present alpha male. This is life in the "particularistic political culture" referred to by Rothstein. Remember, in this world, where equality is lost, living a life without justice is not morally reprehensible, it is merely rational.

The modern mind might cry out for a revolution, changing the system into one where everyone is equally free in the public sphere. For there to be a revolution, the missing link must be reintroduced. The worker and the toll taker must see each other as equals in the public sphere, or as citizens. For people who see each other as one of "we, the people," bringing about such a classless, egalitarian society is a common cause worth fighting for.

For the cause to become a spring for action, the individual must be able to see himself or herself as a public being, as a citizen, as well as a private being with personal relationships. Such vision must become reality, not false-consciousness. In other words, the possibility of the constitution of a liberal democratic state must become a reality. Thinkers such as Hobbes, Locke, Rousseau, and Kant were needed for the conceptual awakening. A French and an American revolution and the constitutions they brought about were needed to make it into a political reality.

Once the conceptual and political reality is in place, the building of a real bridge, a bridge that allows a 10-minute crossing connecting Villages X and Y instead of the makeshift ones upstream, is no longer a daydream. Political power dedicated to serving the public interest, supported by citizens, will give the impetus for the building of the bridge, as well as developing other public goods.

For such dynamic development of consciousness, the mind of the villager must be able to contemplate the possibility of a lifelong repetition of the work he does daily. He must also be able to see that some of his fellow men can end the routine and make a better living for themselves with much less work required. The rational villager will then recognize that the matrix for the repeated game changes as he realizes that there are alternatives and will act accordingly, trying to make life easier for himself.

If independence of the self is not an issue, the villager will try to gain the favor of the person in power, the counterpart of the alpha male in the chimpanzee world. He will not attempt to change, and probably not even be aware of the changes in, the institution in which he labors to raise his quality of life. Only when his endeavor fails and only when the probability of establishing a democracy is realistic will he risk working for a world of equal freedom. When he does act, and perhaps fight, for the common cause of equal liberty, he is not only rational but also reasonable and perhaps ethical. Whether he realizes it or not, he has become a public being, a citizen, as well as a private person vying for personal gain. He is a game changer.

This is the mind-set we want to develop, especially in the civil servants of the developing world. Hence, the goal of all strategy is to maintain, and if possible, enhance the conditions that make it rational for one to have hope for a humane world of equals. Anticorruption laws, regulations, and policies should seek to align individual personal interests with overarching public interests, not neglect the personal. In other words, laws, regulations, and policies should enhance conditions whereby individuals can envisage—and ideally, experience—themselves as being part of a world of equals in which such individuals perceive the desirability (and the feasibility) of realizing public goods, the benefit of which is enjoyed by all, and further, that such public benefit is distributed as equally as possible.

Relative to a simple system of sanctions for corruptive behavior and rewards for the opposite, this is a more complex and holistic approach, and a more practical conduit of understanding that may inform the design and formulation of effective anticorruption policies. This should give us the big picture, a framework within which we can understand corruption as situationally rational and gauge the circumstances in ways that can provide effective policy making.

The Significance of the Rule of Law

At this juncture, it is crucial to ask if it is realistic to expect most, if not all, civil servants to voluntarily enlighten themselves and to reach a stage where they can perpetually act for the public interest. If the answer is not an immediate, unequivocal yes, a strategy must be devised that will bring about civic-minded action without the need for genuine and complete recognition of the public/private distinction, without full awareness of the public sphere and sense of civic duty. Is such a feat possible? Yes, through the rule of law.

Instead of an idealistic condition where each person must come to realize the reality of the public sphere, imagine there is a set of rules that mandates public officials to act in a certain way. These rules should, in the real world, be embodied in a constitution and the laws or bylaws that implement and enforce the constitution. There can be different sets of public reasons justifying the norms. Further, and perhaps more importantly, there may be differences in the reasons that drive public officials to observe these rules. The reason for observance can be very personal. The point is that public officials behave *as if* they understand the significance of the public interest and work for the public good.

How can it be rational for a public official to abide by these laws without requiring an understanding of the reasoning behind them? That is the beauty of law. Existence of a statute provides an exclusionary reason for leaving behind responsibility to provide one's personal interpretation of the norm, culminating in a set of practical reasons for the official action in question.[12] Law mediates between the two elements of moral reasoning, considered reasons for action and the act itself, by providing a reason that preempts the set of reasons that usually support consummating the act. This is what the *authority of law* means.

In other words, the authority of law provides the public reason that mandates an official to no longer consider the merits of a case, once it is determined that the legal norm applies to the case. Law makes personal moral reasoning redundant and renders local, short-term calculation of subjective utility based on first-order reasons useless. The existence of law creates a whole new game, or better, mode of existence.

Once such law is in place and functioning, it is in the best interest of the public official to do what the law mandates. Why? Because in the standard case, there are two reasons that together make possible a matrix that makes it both rational and reasonable for the official to forgo personal accounting of the merits of the case. These reasons depend on the factual condition that there exist on the whole a just and stable institution of norms backed up by a supreme public official with sufficient power of sanction to keep myopic and selfish behavior at bay.

What are the two reasons? First, the law can be substantiated by the right reasons for the action. Second, the law is backed up by sanctions that are effective and just in its application. These reasons together function as assurance for the trust that the official places in the law. As long as these standard conditions for the functioning of law exist, and public officials behave accordingly, law provides the same assurance for all other members of society, thus creating a situation where the prisoner's dilemma on a societal scale is averted.

Of course, when there is corruption, the standard conditions for the efficacy of law usually do not fully apply. When corruption is endemic, much of the conditions necessary are not in place. Note that the inapplicability of the conditions is not an inherent weakness of the law itself, but rather the problem of the politics behind the law. To further discuss this issue, investigation of the relationship between the politics of a constitutional democracy and the rule of law is in order. However, this goes beyond the scope of this chapter.

Recall the mediating function of law. Law provides a practical reason for officials to act in the public interest, to perform their duty to the people, not

---

12 On the concept of an exclusionary reason, *see* Joseph Raz, *Practical Reason and Norms* (3rd ed., Oxford U. Press 1999).

necessarily through internalization of the standards of public morality and accurate comprehension of the public interest but through fidelity to law and a minimal understanding that fidelity to law pays.[13] This notion highlights the importance of the rule of law as the method of choice for bypassing the arduous task of a complete education of each public official necessary for a constitutional democracy, which depends on the official's putting public interest before her personal gain. A constitutional democracy can be destroyed by losing a war; it can also be destroyed by losing the war against corruption. Corruption attacks democracy internally, whereas war destroys democracy externally. There is good reason to hate corruption as much as we do war. Anticorruption policies should be designed and implemented with the goal of keeping a constitutional democracy from disintegrating.

Conclusion

Focusing on the philosophy behind the delivery challenge—as a general approach to the problem of corruption, present in a plethora of societies—has hopefully brought to light, in the minds of policy makers seeking to solve the problem, familiar but vexing situations from a perspective not fully considered before, illuminating the same situations in a new light. What has been presented is a generalized outlook and methodology for finding a solution to an old problem.

Whereas the first two methods of sanction and reward treat the players as merely rational and not necessarily reasonable or ethical, the third method brings out the presupposition behind the two approaches, treating the actions the two methods prescribe as rounds in repeating games. The third method appeals to longer-term interests and sophisticated rationality, and ultimately to the morality of the players. Note that being moral does not mean self-sacrifice: in the third method, the personal interest of the players is never neglected; we took the strategy of aligning it with the public interest. As the first two methods took the strategy of appealing to personal interest with no mention of the public, the difference in the methods can also be understood as a change in methodology: the third introduces the public/private distinction.

All three methods can provide ways of designing systems and institutions to persuade or impel players toward noncorrupt acts and decisions. If this outcome is achieved, then anticorruption policies will have delivered the intended outcome. The designing of a general "method of choice" should make good use of the third method, which appropriately incorporates the first two.

13 The same reasoning applies to the citizen when law functions as a norm for behavior, that is, when law addresses the subjects of government. This chapter focuses on the function of legal norms when they address governing leaders and their agents, namely, as norms for adjudication when addressing officials of the judiciary and as norms for execution of official duty when addressing officials of the executive.

The existence of the rule of law, with its mandate over the players and control of their social functions, is essential if such a comprehensive policy is to work effectively. Through the rule of law, moral deliberation, as well as local and short-term calculation of subjective utility, based on first-order reasons, is rendered senseless for the public official. Contrary to intuition, this is not to be abhorred. Admitting the fact that the benefits of establishing, safeguarding, and developing the public sphere are not universally acknowledged by the very officials in whom we entrust the governance of the public sphere has allowed us to focus on the salutary effect of the dynamic and preemptive function of law in practical reasoning.

Put straightforwardly, an efficient constitutional legal system provides a matrix for the public official, such that abiding by the law brings about greater personal utility in the long run. Hence, even if the public official does not see the big picture, which makes clear that serving the public interest provides greater social utility and will result in personal returns unimaginable without the procurement of the public good in which the public official takes part (visualize the copious gains from the sale of mass-produced *xyyx*, which would have been impossible without the bridge directly connecting Villages X and Y), the action taken by the public official, acting as the law mandates, will be the same as if she understood the big picture.

The task of the designer of the legal system, of administrative officials, and of those who serve in the judiciary, is to endeavor to legislate, apply, and adjust the components of the legal system so that this important functional equivalence is maintained (although in the case of the attorney, this would be a constraint to his activity rather than the goal). Each of the three branches of government must deal with law in its own way to make all laws and regulations—that is, the public and private means of creating legal norms—understandable and operable. Doing so would induce a change in the rational decision making and planning of both citizens and public officials, impelling them to abide by the law for their own interests, thus acting *as if* they had changed their priorities and decided to serve the public interest.

This chapter has clarified what it is that corruption destroys by explaining the rule of law in a way in which law is seen as an instrument by which public reason is unified and maintains its functionality in a constitutional democracy. It is crucial that constitutional democracy, when regarded from a functional point of view, be a system of repetitive games for gaining legitimacy played by actors in democratic politics who demonstrate their competence and accountability through their fidelity to law. This system works in tandem with the actors' legitimate concerns for their own personal interests. It is hoped that the outlook provided herein enables policy builders to better understand and organize their mission as it relates to the delivery challenge. This chapter, hopefully, has demonstrated what philosophical critique of real-world problems can do.

21

Measures for Asset Recovery

A Multiactor Global Fund for Recovered Stolen Assets

STEPHEN KINGAH

For citizens living in developing countries where democratic culture is still nascent, finding a voice to shape the future can be harrowing. Citizens who struggle to educate their children and ensure their good health are often taken aback by the opulence exhibited by some of their political leaders. Embezzlement through corrupt practices is a serious problem in the developing world, and the transfer of illicit proceeds siphoned or directed away from serving the public interest is a vexing problem. The starting point in any durable and fruitful debate on financing development must be a frank discussion at the national, regional, and global levels on how to arrest the slippage of public money and assets stolen from poor countries by powerful elites and saved in bank accounts in rich countries and tax havens. A discussion of the tracing, recovery, and return of stolen assets from poor countries cannot be separated from discussions on development finance. Since 2000, and especially after 2007, the World Bank and the United Nations have made an effort to ensure that stolen assets are traced, recovered, and returned to the countries they were stolen from.

Identifying how and where stolen financial and physical assets are concealed can be a Herculean task because the assets are often layered via money laundering and the use of trusts, foundations, and shell companies. Recovery entails domestic and international legal cooperation to retrieve the stolen assets, which may imply a protracted effort in locating, confiscating, freezing, and releasing assets. This chapter focuses on stolen assets as defined by the United Nations Convention against Corruption (UNCAC). Its remit pertains to the funds misappropriated by powerful economic and political elites who take assets intended for public use and misdirect them toward private ends. Poor countries lose close to US$40 billion annually from such actions.[1] The issue is global, as evidenced by examples found in Haiti,[2] Iraq,[3]

The author is grateful to reviewers and for insights from Elise Wei Tan. All opinions and arguments expressed in the chapter are the author's.

1 UNODC & World Bank, *Stolen Assets Recovery Initiative: Challenges, Opportunities, and Action Plan* (World Bank June 2007).

2 Siri Schubert, *Haiti: The Long Road to Recovery*, Frontline World PBS (May 22, 2009).

3 Missy Ryan & Khalid Al Ansary, *Iraqi Official Calls for More Action against Corruption*, Reuters (Sept. 6, 2009); Jomana Karadsheh & Phil Black, *Corruption Sting Nabs Iraqi Deputy Minister*, Cable News Network (Sept. 7, 2009).

Kenya,[4] Nigeria,[5] Peru,[6] and the Philippines.[7] In most cases, political leaders simply instructed their central bankers to credit specific foreign bank accounts directly (Mobutu in the Democratic Republic of Congo, Marcos in the Philippines) or gained illicit kickbacks from overpriced procurement contracts (Abacha in Nigeria, Fujimori in Peru, Boigny in Côte d'Ivoire).[8] A motive for these leaders and other political elites to misappropriate assets and store them abroad is to hide illegally accumulated wealth.[9] UNCAC is the international legal cornerstone of anticorruption and plays an important role in tracing the recovery and return of stolen assets. This chapter presents the international, regional, and national normative and institutional architecture in place to address corruption and secure the recovery and return of stolen assets. It proposes a multilevel approach to asset recovery.

To ensure that recovery and return actions are effective, legitimate, and sustainable, a confluence of actors must be engaged in the process. The chapter considers the importance of efforts to trace, recover, and return stolen assets to developing countries. It elucidates the existing international, regional, and national normative and institutional architectures that address the issue. It then pulls together insights on problems faced by those involved in asset tracing, recovery, and return, suggesting ways to mitigate these problems through a stronger partnership among states, companies, civil society groups, and the World Bank through an international financial institution with experience monitoring how returned assets are used.

Why Tracing the Recovery and Return of Stolen Assets Is Important

Stealing public assets is not only perverse; it is an action that is bereft of any sense of equity, justice, and fairness. The depravity and perversity of looting state assets is aligned to the amoral character of diverting public assets for private gain or personal use. Besides this lack of moral compunction, stealing such assets is illegal in many jurisdictions—public officials cannot lawfully engage in the blatant theft of public assets. In addition, stealing public funds through corrupt acts locks developing countries in a cycle of poverty that breeds further poverty.[10] There are many arguments to support the state-

---

4 Daniel Howden, *Kenya's Decline and Fall*, The Independent (July 1, 2009).

5 A. Abubakar & Y. Hassan, *Nigeria: Rule of Law Frustrates Anti-corruption War*, Daily Trust (June 3, 2009), at http://allafrica.com/stories/200906030377.html.

6 UNODC & World Bank, *supra* note 1.

7 *Id.*

8 Raymond Baker, *The Biggest Loophole in the Free-Market System*, 22(4) Wash. Q. 29, 33 (Autumn 1999); UNODC & World Bank, *supra* note 1.

9 Dev Kar & Devon Cartwright-Smith, *Illicit Financial Flows from Developing Countries, 2002–2006* (Global Financial Integrity Dec. 2008).

10 Mark Robinson, *Corruption and Development: An Introduction*, in *Corruption and Development* 2 (Mark Robinson ed., Frank Cass 1998).

ment that the recovery and return of stolen assets is important for the health of developing countries.

The first argument is contingent on justice. Public assets belong to the people. Public funds and physical assets are intended to satisfy public needs and serve the common good of the people. Taxpayers' money or funds gained through aid and grants are meant to provide for public services and basic infrastructure, including education, health care, sanitation, nutrition, and public housing. In many countries where the majority of the people live under the poverty line, political elites enjoy opulent lifestyles. In Nigeria, for instance, where more than 100 million people live on less than US$2 a day,[11] more than US$400 billion is estimated to have been stolen from state coffers by corrupt officials since independence in 1960.[12] The World Bank and the United Nations estimate that for every US$100 million of stolen assets, the world loses the chance to immunize 4 million children from diseases or the opportunity to connect 250,000 people to potable drinking water.[13] Tracing, recovering, and returning stolen assets to the people are just actions because the loot is often the result of unjust enrichment at the expense of the public.

Closely linked to this argument of justice is one of fairness. It is unfair that for every dollar lent to Africa, 60 cents flows back to the rich world.[14] Such debts incurred by leaders on behalf of their states are imputed to the public, which is expected to pay for what the political leaders diverted from the intended targets of the resources. In certain cases, loans contracted with foreign institutions are negotiated by individuals who eventually misdirect the resources for private purposes. However, because the loans are taken on behalf of countries, the cost of both the principal and the interest is eventually imputed to the public. This situation is even more egregious when funds and equity companies procure the debt at prices inferior to the initial principal and then sue the debtor nations for the full amount.

Another argument is one of accountability, and it relates to official development assistance (ODA). This argument is directly linked to the element of transparency. For example, it is estimated that about 85 percent of the aid that has gone to Africa ends up not being used for the originally intended goal.[15] One explanation is the looting of such funds by political and economic elites. Tracing, recovery, and return are often the tripod of an arduous and protracted process whereby officials or elites accused of stealing funds are

---

11 Raymond Baker & Eva Joly, *Illicit Money: Can It Be Stopped?* N. Y. Rev. of Books (Dec. 3, 2009).

12 Alan Bacarese, *Advancing International Understanding and Cooperation in Combating Fraud and Corruption: Recovering Stolen Assets—a New Issue?* 10 Acad. Eur. L. Forum 421, 422 (2009).

13 UNODC & World Bank, *supra* note 1, at 2.

14 Leonce Ndikumana, *Capital Flight from Sub-Saharan Africa: Linkages with External Borrowing and Policy Options*, 25(2) Intl. Rev. Applied Eco. 149 (Mar. 2011).

15 Dambisa Moyo, *Dead Aid: Why Aid Is Not Working and How There Is Another Way for Africa* 39 (Allen Lane 2009); Johannes Dieterich, *Ban Development Aid? A Zambian Economist's Hard-Hitting Book Polarizes Opinion*, German Times 7 (Sept. 2009).

exposed and publicly grilled. In countries where democracy is tenuous and the rule of law weak, such processes may be used for political vendettas.

Closely linked to accountability is the deterrence argument. Deterrence is also a basis that can be used to justify the importance of tracing, recovery, and return of stolen assets.[16] Shaming potential culprits is so powerful that it signals to them that the price of looting public funds and stealing public assets is high. The process of tracing, recovery, and return of stolen assets highlights the dangers of engaging in illicit enrichment at the expense of taxpayers. Efforts to recover assets show that bad deeds do not pay and that they will be forcefully prosecuted.[17]

When foreign constituencies or external actors such as international development partners understand that states and corporate and social actors in poor countries are serious about tracing, recovering, and returning stolen assets, they will be encouraged to assist these countries in checking slippage. This is the effectiveness argument, which is particularly important when international development partners need to justify to skeptical taxpayers in the global North that aid serves a purpose. If leaders in developed countries and other willing external partners are aware that local officials have the commitment and capacity to prevent embezzlement and to recover stolen assets, they will be encouraged to maintain engagement. Given that most of the funds that came from development partners have been stolen in the Democratic Republic of Congo (DRC), Indonesia, Nigeria, and the Philippines,[18] there is a strong sense that such crimes need to be prevented in the future.

International Rules and Institutions Focused on Asset Recovery

Global Rules and Institutions

At the international level, UNCAC plays a major role in asset recovery and return.[19] A number of important resolutions preceded the adoption of the convention, including UN General Assembly (UNGA) Resolution 55/61 (Dec. 20, 2000), in which the UNGA authorized the secretary-general to convene an ad

---

16 *Chair's Statement by the Kingdom of Morocco and the United Kingdom on the Second Meeting of the Arab Forum on Asset Recovery* (Oct. 28, 2013), at https://star.worldbank.org/star/sites/star/files/chairs_statement_uk_morocco_at_afar_ii_conculsion.pdf

17 Gerard Byam, *Opening Statement by Director of Strategy and Operations, MENA Region, World Bank*, Arab Forum on Asset Recovery (AFAR II) (Oct. 2013), available at https://star.worldbank.org/star/sites/star/files/opening_statement_from_the_the_director_of_strategy_operations_mena_region_the_world_bank.pdf.

18 Raymond Baker & Jennifer Nordin, *How Dirty Money Binds the Poor*, Financial Times (Oct. 13, 2004).

19 The United Nations Convention against Transnational Organized Crime (2000) proscribes corruption in Art. 9 but does not go into details on aspects of asset recovery. For an insightful history of the international efforts before and after the Cold War that led up to the UNCAC, *see* Alejandro Posadas, *Combating Corruption under International Law*, 10 Duke J. Comp. & Intl. L. 345–414 (2000).

hoc group of experts to deal with the question of returning illicit money. UNGA Resolution 56/181 (Dec. 20, 2002) directed that stolen money be returned to countries of origin. UN Economic and Social Council (ECOSOC) Resolution 2001/13 (July 24, 2001) strengthened international cooperation on the issue. In the Monterrey Consensus of March 2002, corruption was regarded as an impediment to development; it was also held as such in the World Summit on Sustainable Development (WSSD) in September 2002. UNCAC was signed in 2003 and entered into force in December 2005. It comprises 171 states parties, including the European Union. How does the UNCAC address issues pertaining to asset recovery and associated matters such as implementation, mutual legal assistance, and participation of civil society and the private sector?

UNCAC provisions on asset recovery marked an important first in international treaties. The section on asset recovery (Chapter V) is regarded as one of the main reasons that so many developing countries quickly signed the UNCAC. Article 1(b) states, inter alia, that the goal of the convention is "to promote, facilitate and support international cooperation and technical assistance in the prevention of and the fight against corruption, including in asset recovery." The negotiations that led to the inclusion of Chapter V were intense. There was marked resistance from countries of the North with concerns that such provisions not be used to encroach on or violate the rights of individuals through the pretext of asset recovery. The provisions on asset recovery are expansive and contain elements such as asset freezing and confiscation of assets acquired through corrupt means. Articles 43–50 cover a litany of related aspects such as joint investigations and mutual legal assistance in recovery efforts. Since the adoption of UNCAC, the provisions on asset recovery have been welcomed,[20] especially because many adopters hope that UNCAC will be especially useful for developing countries.[21]

Implementation of the convention is the remit of the Conference of the States Parties (COSP). The COSP comprises the Implementation Review Working Group, the Working Group on Prevention, the Working Group on Asset Recovery, the Working Group on Technical Assistance, and expert groups that handle international cooperation between the sessions of the COSP.[22] The

---

20 Bacarese, *supra* note 12; Mark Vlasic & Jenae Noell, *Fighting Impunity: Recent International Asset Recovery Efforts to Combat Corruption*, Cayman Fin. Rev. (Jan. 5, 2010).

21 Tim Daniel, *UN Convention against Corruption*, in *The Global Corruption Report* 106 (Robin Hodess, Tania Inowlocki, Diana Rodriguez, & Tony Wolfe eds., Pluto Press 2004).

22 The first COSP was held in Jordan in Dec. 2006, when an intergovernmental working group was created to address issues related to the implementation mechanisms. Parties also created the Working Group on Technical Assistance and Asset Recovery. The second COSP took place in Bali in Jan. 2008. During this meeting, there was a deliberate decision to avoid an adversarial approach to the issues of anticorruption, especially because the parties were keen to move toward universal adherence of the UNCAC. Other subjects covered during the meeting included technical assistance tools and the bribery of officials of international organizations. The third and thus far most important COSP was held in Doha, Qatar, in Nov. 2009. States parties adopted Resolution 3/1 on the terms of reference of the IRM. The UNCAC Civil Society Coalition took issue with the fact that COSP did not make the involvement of CSOs obligatory in the reviews and called for full publication of the reviews: *see* TPI, *UN*

secretariat of the COSP is housed in the UN Office on Drugs and Crime (UNODC). An important aspect of implementation was discussed at the third session of the COSP, held in Doha in 2009.[23] There it was agreed that implementation be handled through the Implementation Review Mechanism (IRM). Reviews are contemplated in two tranches or cycles of five years. The first cycle relates to the implementation of Chapter III (criminalization and law enforcement) and Chapter IV (international cooperation) of the UNCAC; the second cycle covers Chapter II (prevention) and Chapter V (asset recovery). Because the second cycle is to be rolled out in 2015, it is hard to assess the effectiveness of the mechanism. COSP IV, in Marrakesh in 2011, adopted many important resolutions, including increased assistance to the Working Group on Asset Recovery.[24] It also made decisions on technical assistance aspects of the review mechanism. Resolution 4/1 of COSP IV expressed concern about the unresponsiveness of several states parties in the conduct of country reviews. COSP V, in Panama in 2013, focused on the effectiveness of law enforcement cooperation in detecting corruption offenses (Resolution 5/1).[25] The conference also issued a resolution on cooperation in the area of asset recovery (Resolution 5/3). Resolution 5/5 contained a novel element on the promotion of the contribution of young people and children in preventing corruption and fostering a culture of respect for the law and integrity.

Mutual legal assistance (MLA) is a fundamental element of UNCAC. Chapter IV is dedicated to ways to enhance international cooperation and covers MLA. One of the longest provisions of UNCAC, Article 46(1), stipulates that "States Parties shall afford one another the widest measure of mutual legal assistance in investigations, prosecutions and judicial proceedings in relation to the offences covered by this Convention." MLA that may be requested includes taking evidence; effectively serving judicial writs; executing searches, seizures, and freezes; and examining objects and sites.

In terms of the involvement of civil society, Article 13 makes clear that the role of civil society participation is salient in realizing the goals of the UNCAC. The UNCAC Civil Society Coalition, created in 2006, is an umbrella organization that brings together more than 300 civil society groups working toward big-tent participation and transparency in the implementation of UNCAC. Also important is that the review process of UNCAC envisages a strong role for civil society entities. NGOs active in this area include Transparency International, Global Witness, and Open Society. Resolution 4/6 of COSP IV, on the role of NGOs in the mechanism of the review of implementation of UNCAC, pro-

---

Convention against Corruption Review Mechanism: A Flawed Step Forward, Transparency Int. (Nov. 2009). The fourth COSP was held in Marrakesh in 2011; the fifth was held in Panama in 2013. Conferences are planned for 2015 in the Russian Federation and 2017 in Austria.

23 COSP, *Report of the Conference of the States Parties to the United Nations Convention against Corruption on Its Third Session,* Doha, CAC/COSP/2009/15, 9–13 (Nov. 2009).

24 Resolutions and decisions adopted by COSP of UNCAC, CAC/COSP/2011/4 (Oct. 28, 2011).

25 Resolutions and decisions adopted by COSP of UNCAC, CAC/COSP/EG.1/2013/3 (Nov. 28, 2013).

vides for briefings with NGOs on the outcome of the review process, including aspects such as technical assistance. Article 12 of UNCAC covers the provisions related to the private sector. Specifically, Article 12(1) calls on states to take actions to prevent corruption involving the private sector. Some of the acts that are proscribed include making off-the-book accounts; making inadequately identified transactions; using false documents; and destroying bookkeeping documents earlier than foreseen by the law. Article 12(1) was inspired by the Organisation for Economic Co-operation and Development (OECD) system of combating bribery and corruption in international business transactions.[26]

The main institutions at the international level that address issues of asset recovery are UNODC and the World Bank. The entities partnered in 2007 to create the Stolen Asset Recovery Initiative (StAR). It is both a platform that facilitates cooperation between countries involved in asset recovery and an initiative that disseminates best practices on asset recovery experiences around the world. StAR has developed a user-friendly database that tracks ongoing and completed examples of asset recovery cases launched in various jurisdictions. StAR has also developed a strong training and capacity building package and course that have been dispensed in partner countries, and the organization is helping regional networks facilitate communication and cooperation in asset recovery.[27]

In addition to these formal initiatives at the international level, Interpol plays a vital role in asset recovery. Equally significant are G8 and G20 efforts to combat dirty money.[28] The dialogue between high-level G20 government officials and business leaders (B20) alongside major civil society groups (C20), especially on coordinated actions to enhance asset recovery, is significant. The Asset Recovery Expert Network is run by the International Centre for Asset Recovery (ICAR), housed at the Basel Institute of Governance.[29]

Regional and Multilateral Rules and Institutions

The first regional entity to adopt a convention against corruption was the Organization of American States (OAS) when it endorsed the Inter-American Convention against Corruption in Caracas in March 1996 (entered into force in 1997). Article XV, pertaining to measures regarding property, provides for the

---

26 OECD Working Group on Bribery in International Business Transactions, Recommendation 10(i). *Recommendation of the Council for Further Combating Bribery of Foreign Public Officials in International Business Transactions* (Nov. 2009).

27 StAR, *Stolen Asset Recovery Progress Report* (Oct. 2009). StAR has also published *Guide to Non-Conviction Based Forfeiture* (Apr. 2009); *Management of Returned Assets: Policy Considerations* (Oct. 2009); *Towards a Global Architecture for Asset Recovery* (2009); *Income and Asset Declarations: Tools and Trade-Offs* (2009); and *Barriers to Asset Recovery: An Analysis of the Key Barriers and Recommendations for Action* (2011).

28 *See, e.g.*, G20, *Leaders' Statement: The Pittsburgh Summit* para. 15 (Sept. 24–25, 2009).

29 Anne Lugon-Moulin, *History, Experience, and Workings of the Basel Institute of Governance*, Cayman Fin. Rev. (Jan. 5, 2010).

tracing, freezing, seizure, and forfeiture of property or proceeds gained from committing a crime proscribed under the convention. In the European Union, the Treaty on the Functioning of the European Union (TFEU) addresses issues of fraud in Article 325. In the specific area of asset recovery, an important communication in 2003 from the EU Commission on corruption included topics such as confiscation but did not include asset recovery.[30] Council Framework Decision on Asset Recovery Cooperation, backed mainly by Austria, Belgium, and Finland, does cover aspects of asset recovery.[31] In 2011, the EU Commission adopted an important communication on antifraud,[32] which states that the goal of the text is to improve prevention, detection, conditions of investigation, and reparation and deterrence.[33] Swift recovery of money that has been the subject of fraud and paid from the EU budget is an important component of the strategy.[34] Member-states are responsible for making investigations pertaining to irregularities and fraud and for recovery of funds that are wrongly paid out. Such wrongful payment can also be a result of investigations of the commission's Anti-Fraud Office (OLAF). In the case of direct budget management, commission services are required to issue recovery orders following OLAF investigations.[35] In 2012, the commission adopted another important communication on the matter,[36] noting that fraud costs EU taxpayers at least €600 million per year.[37] Divergence of rules in member-states has diluted hopes of reaching complete deterrence in dealing with the problem. The key is to aim for equivalence in protection across EU member-states so that individuals with malevolent intentions do not forum shop for jurisdictions with lower standards.[38]

The African Convention on the Prevention and Combating of Corruption (CPCC), adopted in Maputo in 2003 and celebrated as taking a human rights-based approach to combating corruption,[39] makes provision for asset recovery in Article 16. Article 16 encapsulates important elements such as confisca-

---

30 EU Commission, *Communication from the Commission to the Council, the European Parliament and the European Economic and Social Committee: On a Comprehensive EU Policy against Corruption,* COM(2003) 317 final, Brussels 10 (May 28, 2003).

31 Council decision concerning cooperation between asset recovery offices of member-states in the field of tracing and identification of proceeds from, or other property related to, crime, 2007/845/JHA (Dec. 6, 2007).

32 European Commission, *On the Commission Anti-Fraud Strategy,* COM(2011) 376, final, Brussels (June 24, 2011).

33 *Id.*, at 3.

34 *Id.*, at 4.

35 *Id.*, at 16.

36 EU Commission, *Proposal for a Directive of the European Parliament and of the Council on the Fight against Fraud to the European Union's Financial Interests by Means of Criminal Law,* COM(2012) 363 final, Brussels (July 11, 2012).

37 *Id.*, at 2.

38 *Id.*, at 4.

39 Thomas R. Snider & Won Kidane, *Combating Corruption through International Law in Africa: A Comparative Analysis,* 40 Cornell Intl. L.J. 691, 748 (2007).

tion, seizure, and repatriation. A crucial feature of asset recovery in Africa is that it is pursued through quasi-judicial human rights bodies; thus, recovery efforts as encoded in the CPCC are not novel. In 2001, 11 African countries adopted the Nyanja Declaration on the Recovery and Repatriation of Africa's Wealth.[40] In *Asociación pro Derechos Humanos de España (APDHE) v. Equatorial Guinea* (2007), the government of President Obiang Nguema was brought before the African Commission on Human and Peoples' Rights to respond specifically to the motion that the president, his family, and his government had used proceeds from natural wealth to illicitly enrich themselves. The case was brought by the Spanish NGO APDHE and the U.S. rights-based organization EG Justice and Open Society Justice Initiative. They based their actions on spoliation of the natural resources of Equatorial Guinea by President Obiang and the Mongomo ethnic group. They also based their case on corruption, a corrupt judiciary, and the crackdown on dissent. The case was dismissed on the grounds that national remedies had not been exhausted in Equatorial Guinea. The U.S. Department of Justice subsequently opened a case against the son of President Obiang, and there is a pending case in France against specific African leaders brought by a civil society organization (CSO) on grounds of *bien mal acquis*.

In the Middle East, although there is no formal convention covering corruption and asset recovery, the Arab Forum on Asset Recovery (AFAR) was launched in 2012.[41] AFAR aims to provide regional training for practitioners involved in the tracing, freezing, recovery, and repatriation of stolen assets in Arab countries in transition following the Arab Spring. It represents a collective effort to recover assets for citizens in countries that have been subject to the callous dictates of exploitative and corrupt leaders. AFAR is unique because it brings together policy makers and practitioners, including the G8 Deauville Partnership and Arab countries, in efforts to recover stolen assets. AFAR provides information on stolen assets and training on best practices. It also focuses on regional and international awareness training on the issue. Between 2011 and 2012, through AFAR, US$100 million in financial and physical assets were frozen or returned to these countries.[42] For example, US$29 million from a bank account in Lebanon was returned to Tunisia. Efforts are being made to recover and return Sw F60 million of Ben Ali funds from Switzerland back to Tunisia, and an MLA has been reached in this respect. Physical assets have been recovered as well: for example, airplanes and yachts belonging to former president Ben Ali and his family have been sent back to Tunisia from Spain, France, and

---

40 Daniel Scher, *Asset Recovery: Repatriating Africa's Looted Billions*, 14(4) African Sec. Rev. (2005).

41 *Arab Forum on Asset Recovery* 2012, Doha Qatar, http://star.worldbank.org/star/ArabForum/arab-forum-2012.

42 Jean Pesme, *Understanding the Arab Forum on Asset Recovery: Questions Answered by Jean Pesme, StAR Coordinator* (Oct. 28, 2013), available at http://star.worldbank.org/star/sites/star/files/the_arab_forum_and_asset_recovery_-_questions_and_answers_final.pdf.

Italy.[43] The AFAR demonstrates that mobilization and collective action work, even if slower than expected or desired.

In Asia, the Asia Pacific Economic Cooperation (APEC) Forum member-states follow the Santiago Commitment, the APEC Course of Action, and APEC Transparency Standards. The APEC Forum promotes cooperation in extradition, legal assistance, and recovery. Members agree to promote regional cooperation in areas of the extradition, recovery, and return of stolen assets.[44] The APEC senior officials met in September 2004 and resolved to adhere to UNCAC standards on asset recovery and return.[45] In November 2013, APEC member-states agreed to create an informal network of law enforcement officials and practitioners who are experts on asset tracing, freezing, and confiscation in the Asia-Pacific region. The Asset Recovery Interagency Network of Asia and the Pacific (ARIN-AP) is modeled on Europe's Camden Asset Recovery Inter-Agency Network (CARIN).[46] It encompasses members from twenty-one jurisdictions in Asia-Pacific and six international organizations. Its mission statement notes that "the aim of ARIN-AP is to increase the effectiveness of members' efforts in depriving criminals of their illicit profits in a multi-agency basis by establishing itself as the center of professionals' network in tackling the proceeds of crime."[47] ARIN-AP targets the creation of national contact points that exchange experiences on asset recovery.

The aspect of implementation of the anticorruption treaty provisions in the inter-American system is handled by the OAS Secretariat under the auspices of the Permanent Council. In Africa, the task of implementation is under the aegis of the Executive Council of the African Union, which has the power to appoint an 11-member advisory board charged with the implementation of the CPCC and its specific provisions (Art. 22). In the Middle East, AFAR II, in Morocco in 2013, set the agenda and objectives of the forum in terms of future goals. It was attended by 200 delegates from all over the world (25 countries), mainly law enforcement and prosecution officials. Work continues throughout the year in sessions on matters such as financial investigations, MLA, and the role of civil society in asset recovery.[48] Within Asia, cooperation on such matters is very loose and voluntary. The Asian Development

---

43 Gerard Byam, *Opening Statement by Director of Strategy and Operations, MENA Region, World Bank*, AFAR II (Oct. 26, 2013).

44 APEC, *Santiago Commitment to Fight Corruption and Ensure Transparency*, 2004/AMM/032 rev1 Agenda Item XXII, 16 APEC Ministerial Meeting, Santiago, Chile 1 (Nov. 17–18, 2004).

45 APEC, *APEC Course on Fighting Corruption, APEC Course of Action on Fighting Corruption and Ensuring Transparency*, 2004/AMM/033 rev2 Agenda Item XXII, 16 APEC Ministerial Meeting, Santiago, Chile 1 (Nov. 17–18, 2004).

46 APG News, *Launch of the Asset Recovery Inter-Agency Network for Asia Pacific* (Jan. 7, 2014) http://www.apgml.org/news/details.aspx?n=28.

47 *See* ARIN-AP website, http://www.arin-ap.org/about/mission.

48 *Arab Forum on Asset Recovery*, Marrakesh (Oct. 26–28, 2013), http://star.worldbank.org/star/ArabForum/About.

Bank has sought to play an active role.[49] The APEC Forum's Anti-Corruption Transparency Working Group was constituted as a task force in 2005 and was upgraded to a working group in March 2011. The working group coordinates the implementation of the Santiago Commitment, the APEC Course of Action, and APEC Transparency Standards. It is open to APEC observers, including the Association of South East Asian Nations (ASEAN) and the Pacific Island Forum (PIF).[50] China organized an asset recovery event as chair of APEC in February 2014 in Ningbo.[51]

MLA is envisaged in the Inter-American Convention, which provides that bank secrecy norms cannot be used to forestall cooperation (Article XVI). This provision is similar to the one in the AU CPCC that aims to avert the use of bank secrecy as a decoy to elude cooperation (Article 17). The Inter-American Convention also provides for MLA in processing requests (Article XIV). Clauses on MLA are included in the Council of Europe's Criminal Law Convention (Article 26) and the OECD 1999 Convention on Combating Bribery of Foreign Public Officials in International Business Transactions (Article 9(1)). MLA issues have been discussed in the intersessional meetings of AFAR and in the APEC Forum.

On civil society involvement, Article III of the Inter-American Convention is explicit that in addition to NGOs, community-based groups must be engaged fully in preventive efforts. Civil society involvement is weaker in the African system but sharper in the European Union, where the commission consulted with taxpayer groups and academics before adopting its proposal on a directive to criminalize fraud. In Asia, the APEC Forum has highlighted the importance of the partnership of CSOs, companies, and governments to work together to dismantle the illicit networks of financial flows.[52] In the framework of AFAR, intersessional expert dialogues have been organized on the role of civil society in asset recovery, and AFAR has developed a guide for CSO involvement in asset recovery activities that is hosted on its website.

Problems in Asset Tracing, Recovery, and Return

In discussions of efforts to deal with asset recovery, attention is often given to what specific developed countries (regarded as popular destinations of stolen assets) are doing to curb the practice and to retrieve and return stolen assets. Some examples of national experiences are presented here to indicate some of

49 ADB/OECD Anti Corruption Initiative for Asia and the Pacific, Combating Corruption in the New Millennium, Tokyo (Nov. 30, 2001).

50 APEC, http://m.apec.org/Groups/SOM-Steering-Committee-on-Economic-and-Technical-Cooperation/Working-Groups/Anti-Corruption-and-Transparency.aspx.

51 *See* APEC, APEC Network of Anti-Corruption Authorities and Law Enforcement Agencies (ACT-NET), 18th Anti-corruption and Transparency Working Group (ACTWG), Ningbo, China.

52 APEC, *Chair's Summary, APEC Pathfinder Dialogue with ASEAN and PIF Partners, Combating Corruption and Illicit Trade across the Asia-Pacific Region, Bangkok, Thailand* 2 (Sept. 23–25, 2013).

the challenges entailed in asset recovery. The examples cited at the national level are those that have attracted extensive media attention. In the United States, the main law that addresses matters related to graft does not specifically deal with asset recovery but targets entities that bribe foreign officials. The U.S. Foreign Corrupt Practices Act (FCPA) makes it illegal to bribe foreign public officials, but says nothing about the corruption of foreign private individuals.[53] In the wake of the 2008 global financial crisis, Congress adopted the Dodd-Frank Act, which seeks to sharpen prudential standards and check flows of illicit assets. Institutionally, the Department of Justice (DoJ) has been vigorous in implementing the FCPA,[54] and has taken steps to ensure that stolen assets are recovered and returned to requesting countries. Attorney General Eric Holder established a special unit for this purpose. The DoJ also operates the Kleptocracy Asset Recovery Initiative, and further efforts in asset recovery are channeled through stringent antimoney laundering legislation.

Another jurisdiction where important legal and institutional efforts have been made to improve standards of recovery and return is Switzerland. Some of the impetus for these efforts emanated from judicial proceedings on the recovery and return of money stolen from Haiti by Jean-Claude Duvalier. In the absence of a local conviction order in Haiti and with the expiry of the statute of limitation forfeiting conviction in Switzerland (15 years), it was hard to freeze and recover the funds there. Despite a court's decision to reject efforts to recover assets allegedly stolen by Duvalier, Swiss officials were able to use administrative discretion to retain the frozen assets.[55] Eventually, Swiss legislators changed the law waiving the local conviction requirement through the 2010 Restitution of Illicit Assets Act (RIAA), or *lex Duvalier,* which requires the Swiss government to show that assets held could not have been acquired legally in office by the accused and to prove that the originating country is known to be corrupt. Once this occurs, the burden of proof shifts to the respondent.[56] Another important development in Switzerland occurred in 2009, when a Swiss judge ordered the confiscation of assets belonging to the

---

53 Foreign Corrupt Practices Act of 1977, Pub. L. No. 95-213, 91 Stat. 1494 (codified as amended at 15 USC secs. 78dd-1 & 78dd-2 (1994)). The act was subsequently modified by the Omnibus Trade and Competitiveness Act of 1988, Pub. L. No. 100-418, 102 Stat. 1107; International Anti-Bribery and Fair Competition Act of 1998, Pub. L. No. 105-306, 112 Stat. 3302. *See* Alejandro Posadas, *Combating Corruption under International Law,* 10 Duke J. Comp. & Intl. L. 345–414 (2000).

54 Sasha Kalb, *Foreign Corrupt Practices Act: Developments in 2009 and Expectations for 2010,* Cayman Fin. Rev. (Jan. 5, 2010).

55 ICAR, *Duvalier Asset Cannot (Yet) Be Returned to Haiti: Swiss Federal Court Decision,* Basel Institute of Governance (Feb. 3, 2010). Because of similar considerations, especially the aspect of expunged statute of limitation, another court in Switzerland ordered the release of funds owned by the former leader of the DRC (Mobutu) to his family, but this was challenged by Mark Pieth; *see Court Agrees to Release Mobutu Assets,* Swiss Info (July 14, 2009).

56 *See* Mark V. Vlassic & Gregory Cooper, *Beyond the Duvalier Legacy: What New Arab Spring Governments Can Learn from Haiti and the Benefits of Asset Recovery,* 10(1) Nw. J. Intl. Hum. Rights 19, 24 (Fall 2011).

Abacha family—not in Switzerland but in Luxembourg and in the Bahamas. This was a legal first.[57]

In the United Kingdom, there have been court orders on the recovery and return of stolen assets to Nigeria and Zambia. In the case relating to Nigeria, the United Kingdom's Serious Organized Crimes Agency made a decision to repatriate £43 million in stolen assets from offshore accounts to Nigeria.[58] In the case relating to Zambia, a London court ordered former president Frederick Chiluba to pay back to the Zambian state the sum of £23 million in looted funds.[59] In the context of AFAR, the United Kingdom has worked with Arab countries to recover stolen assets.[60] In 2012, the British government established the Cross-Government Task Force on Asset Recovery. Its goal is to accelerate efforts in tracing stolen assets from the Arab Republic of Egypt, Libya, and Tunisia. The main tasks have included gathering evidence and instituting court cases. Led by the Home Office minister, the task force is a multiagency team of 10 investigators from the National Crime Agency, the Metropolitan Police, the Crown Prosecution Services, the UK Central Authority, and Her Majesty's Treasury. The task force cooperates with Egyptian officials on asset recovery, and court orders have been issued allowing for intrusive financial investigations.[61]

In some examples of recovery efforts (Haiti, the Philippines), the first challenge relates to the requirement in some jurisdictions that petitioners secure a local conviction order as a precondition for asset tracing and recovery in the *lex situs* where the stolen assets are concealed or in a preselected remedial jurisdiction. This is a difficult requirement to satisfy because many of the requesting states have weak judicial systems and, given the patronage maintained by political elites, it is often hard to ensure that there will be a local conviction order. Such was the case in the efforts to trace and recover the stolen assets of Abacha of Nigeria.[62] In a welcome recent development, following a court order from the constitutional court in Liechtenstein, the government there agreed to release US$167 million stolen by Abacha to be returned to Nigeria.[63] An outstanding US$1.1 billion tied to Abacha's stolen assets is still wrapped in legal proceedings in the United Kingdom, France, and Luxembourg. As a practical

---

57 Frances Williams, *Swiss Judge Sets Precedent in Global Graft Fight*, Financial Times (Nov. 23, 2009).

58 Yemi Akinsuyi, *UK to Repatriate 43 Pounds Stolen Money to Nigeria*, This Day—African Views on Global News (2010).

59 David Smith, *Former Zambian President Faces Jail in Unprecedented Corruption Trial*, Guardian (Aug. 13, 2009); Jonathan Clayton, *Frederick Chiluba Likely to Avoid Jail after Zambian Corruption Trial*, Times (Aug. 17, 2009). It is noteworthy that in the Zambia case, local conviction failed; *see* Cecilia Dugger, *Former President of Zambia Is Acquitted*, N.Y. Times (Aug. 17, 2009).

60 Dominic Jermey, *How the UK Is Working to Return Stolen Assets to the Arab World*, Foreign and Commonwealth Office (Oct. 23, 2013).

61 *Id.*

62 Boco Ede, *Nigeria: Corruption—EFCC Blames Judiciary for Slow Impact*, Daily Trust (July 6, 2009).

63 William Wallis, *Liechtenstein Agrees to Return Abacha's Stolen 167 Million to Nigeria*, Financial Times (June 18, 2014).

matter, local conviction is challenging to secure because, in many instances, those who are accused of stealing state assets leave the country, as happened in Haiti. However, there are other ways to recover assets than secure a conviction and seek enforcement elsewhere, including a foreign jurisdiction opening its own investigation, nonconviction-based recovery proceedings, plea agreements, and civil remedies.

Even where there is local conviction, the process can be difficult because a tracing and recovery order must be implemented. Strong bank secrecy laws can render the process arduous and complicated.[64] Even if there are waivers or legal changes with respect to bank secrecy laws, and agreements on mutual legal assistance are in place, it may be difficult to change the culture and practice within foreign banks and financial houses that are inclined to protect the confidentiality of their clients and maintain tight control on access to information. It is important to note, however, that the issue of bank secrecy laws is greatly tempered in most jurisdictions, which do have norms and mechanisms in place to allow bank secrecy practices to be lifted for cooperation on combating crimes, including acts of corruption. So, whereas bank secrecy posed a considerable challenge in the past, increased cooperation within and between jurisdictions has reduced the problem.

There is no guarantee that, when funds are recovered and returned, they will serve the people and the public. Monitoring mechanisms to ensure that returned proceeds are properly used to address poverty are vital.[65] If funds are returned to countries with dubious political and economic elites and where institutions are weak, there is a chance that the assets will again be the object of graft and abuse. To mitigate this problem, third parties such as development agencies and the World Bank have the responsibility to ensure that funds are used for the benefit of the public.

Cost can be a prohibitive factor in asset tracing, recovery, and return. Successful efforts are characterized by protracted and costly court proceedings that may entail hiring lawyers, accountants, economic experts, and investigators to trace, recover, and return stolen assets. Given that many countries are hard-pressed to pay for such services, tracing and recovery efforts are often aborted even before they start. When private firms are experienced and have trained experts in asset recovery, the cost of their services can be prohibitive for governments in developing countries. In Pakistan's asset recovery effort, for instance, the firm Broadsheet was hired to help authorities track and recover assets stolen by Asif Zardari and the Bhutto family. Broadsheet requested US$1 million up front and 20 percent of the recovered proceeds.[66] In addition to the issue of cost is the task of identifying the modalities and tools

---

64 Khadija Sharife, *Africa's Missing Billions*, Foreign Policy (May 11, 2009).

65 Ignacio Jimu, *Managing Proceeds of Asset Recovery: The Case of Nigeria, the Philippines, Peru, and Kazahkstan*, 6 ICAR Working Paper Series (2008).

66 Samina Ibrahim, *On the Billion-Dollar Trail* (International Centre for Asset Recovery Sept. 1, 2002).

that allow experts to work together given the complexities entailed in asset recovery processes.

Asset recovery can be a dangerous business. Entrenched interests are at stake, and those who are affected often wield enormous wealth and power and may make efforts to silence those who are determined to combat graft and to trace, recover, and return looted assets. For example, officials involved in asset recovery processes in Burundi and in the Democratic Republic of Congo have been killed.[67] In many cases, it is clear that the families of those accused of illicit enrichment are willing to do everything possible to retain their loot.[68]

Furthermore, asset recovery can be a long process.[69] As indicated by Pakistan's experience, the time between the freezing of assets and return is anything but short.[70] In the Nigerian effort to retrieve funds stolen by Abacha concealed in Swiss banks, the entire process lasted five years.[71] It took eighteen years for closure in the process of recovering identified stolen assets of Ferdinand Marcos of the Philippines.[72] The longer a process takes, the more likely the funds will be moved to other concealed jurisdictions.

The task is further complicated by the fact that different jurisdictions may have different legal systems or belong to different legal families (e.g., common law as opposed to the continental European civil law families), meaning that time must be spent to align procedures and practices. All this enhances the opportunity for culprits to move their assets.[73] There is the additional challenge of working across many languages and navigating different legal and social cultures when multiple jurisdictions are involved.

Asset tracing and recovery can succeed only if there is strong political will in both the requesting and the requested state to ensure that norms and institutions are put in place to guarantee the successful tracing, recovery, and return of stolen assets. In many developing countries, those accused of stealing public assets may have powerful networks in the administration and in the judiciary, thereby complicating the process of asset tracing and recovery. There may be a persistent problem of double standards, whereby leaders

---

67 Celia W. Dugger, *Grand Larceny in Africa*, N.Y. Times (June 16, 2009).

68 Jack Smith, Mark Pieth, & Guillermo Jorge, *The Recovery of Stolen Assets: A Fundamental Principle of the UN Convention against Corruption*, 2 CMI U4 Brief 2 (Feb. 2007).

69 Eric Holder, *Remarks Delivered at the Arab Forum on Asset Recovery* (Oct. 28, 2013), http://star.worldbank.org/star/sites/star/files/speech_of_us_attorney-general_eric_holder_to_afar_ii.pdf.

70 Jeremy Carver, *The Hunt for Looted State Assets: The Case of Benazir Bhutto*, in *The Global Corruption Report* 102, 103 (Robin Hodess, Tania Inowlocki, Diana Rodriguez, & Tony Wolfe eds., Pluto Press 2004).

71 UNODC & World Bank, *Stolen Assets Recovery Initiative: Challenges, Opportunities, and Action Plan* 19 (World Bank June 2007).

72 *Id.*, at 20.

73 Alan Bacarese, *Tracing, Freezing, Confiscating, and Repatriating the Proceeds of Corruption* (paper presented at the Annual Asia-Pacific Regional Seminar for the ADB/OECD, Bali Indonesia 3 Sept. 5–7, 2007).

express the desire to combat illicit transfers but tacitly condone the acceptance of dirty money in financial houses located in their own countries.[74] Political will is clearly needed to change or harmonize relevant laws in support of international or cross-border efforts regarding asset tracing and recovery, including bank secrecy laws. Strong political will is also required for mitigating some of the stringent preconditions or procedures that must be fulfilled before a legal process of asset tracing and recovery can come full cycle (including implementing a local criminal conviction order).

A Multiactor Approach to the Problem

Are there ways in which a wider pool of actors can combine their efforts to ensure that stolen assets are traced, recovered, and returned to poor countries in a better coordinated, more effective, and expedited manner? Given that asset recovery can be uncoordinated and very slow, what can be done to obviate these limitations?

The answer to these questions may lie in the creation of a global fund for asset recovery, referred to here as the Global Stolen Asset Recovery Fund (GSARF). But before addressing the nature of such a fund, the author requests that the reader bear in mind two important caveats. First, the proposal for such a fund, which will function according to specific terms and conditions that govern its operation, is likely to run at cross-purposes with one of the main principles behind UNCAC's asset recovery approach—namely, that asset recovery is unconditional. Second, according to the author's understanding, some of the multilateral institutions that may be important for the effectiveness of such a fund, such as the World Bank, have yet to indicate their support for such a proposal. This proposal is a solution to the problems of asset recovery highlighted in this chapter. It originates solely from the author. Nonetheless, even if current realities are not yet conducive for or supportive of the creation of such a fund, it could be a solution to consider in the future.

The GSARF ideally would be run similarly to the Global Fund to Fight AIDS, Tuberculosis and Malaria (GF). The GF model, which includes the World Bank as a monitor, uses a network of local coordinators, accepts the contributions of the private sector and civil society, and is vital for a sustainable approach to asset recovery. All the actors in the GSARF would agree on what percentage of funds recovered through the fund would be contributed to the GSARF. This money could then be used to help governments that want to institute asset recovery proceedings but lack the funds to do so. The World Bank would play an important role in assessing the needs of the requesting states and disbursing the funds. The GSARF could also be used to support the StAR initiative.

---

74 Raymond Baker, *The Biggest Loophole in the Free-Market System,* 22(4) Wash. Q. 29, 30 (Autumn 1999).

Given that the GSARF would mainly target asset recovery cases pertaining to flows from developed to developing countries, a more customized approach could also focus on South/South asset recovery efforts. It is wrong to assume that stolen assets from developing countries are concealed only in rich countries. A GSARF-like body at the regional level could be aligned with the respective regional development banks. The regional development banks in Africa, Latin America, Asia, and Europe already play important roles in combating graft in the projects they finance, and they have schemes to address the issue in their local shareholder member-states. Given that these institutions have experience in the operation of the financial infrastructure in their respective regions, they could act as trustees or guarantors for region-wide GSARF-like bodies that would work closely with state officials, the private sector, and civil society to ensure that stolen assets are used for the benefit of the populations they serve. The World Bank could play a coordinating role among the various regional development banks.

At the national level, it makes sense to consider the creation of asset recovery focal points that would work closely with the GSARF at both the regional and the global levels. Similar proposals have been made in the past.[75] Such national focal points could form a broad umbrella that includes representatives from the national government, the private sector, and civil society.

It is not enough to say that many actors should be involved in the GSARF. Their competence would be a vital factor. States parties and local authorities would be central players because they hold the power to make sovereign requests and grants. They also can shape national and international institutions to meet specific tasks in the area of asset recovery. Successful asset recovery also needs ethical and strong leadership.[76] It would be hard to achieve success if public officials who are supposed to be doing the recovery are the ones looting.[77] But even if public officials are decent and positively driven, they cannot work alone. The involvement of the private sector would be salient. For the requesting states, the use of private investigating firms with accountants and lawyers specialized in asset tracing and recovery is important, as evidenced in recovery efforts in Kenya, Nigeria, and Pakistan. Their input or participation should be cost-free or pegged at relatively marginal rates.[78] Civil society also would be central in advocacy and awareness efforts.

Finally, there is room in this proposal for the expansion of the European-led CARIN.[79] The network was officially initiated in 2004 in The Hague and

---

75 Ian King, *Banks Accused of Aiding Corrupt Regimes,* Sunday Times Online (Mar. 11, 2009).

76 Stephen Riley, *The Political Economy of Anti-Corruption Strategies in Africa,* in *Corruption and Development* 155 (Mark Robinson ed., Frank Cass 1998).

77 Scher, *supra* note 40.

78 Scher, *supra* note 40, proposes that in the case of Africa, the African Union should develop a unit that specializes in asset recovery rather than relying on the expensive services of private companies. However, until such a unit is created, these experts will be needed.

79 Bacarese, *supra* note 12, at 432.

brings together practitioners and experts of law enforcement and the judiciary from 53 member jurisdictions, including EU member-states. The initiative is focused on identifying, freezing, seizing, and confiscating proceeds of crime. It is aimed at transborder cooperation in closing loopholes used by criminals to move proceeds acquired illegally. Some of the many members and observers of CARIN include the UNODC, the International Criminal Court, Interpol, Israel, the Russian Federation, and South Africa. The World Bank is an associate member of the network. This model has been replicated in Southern Africa with the creation of the Asset Recovery Inter-Agency Network of Southern Africa (ARINSA). Affiliated with CARIN, ARINSA brings together investigators and prosecutors to share their experiences recovering funds that are proceeds from crime. The Asset Recovery Unit in South Africa provides secretariat support services for ARINSA. ARIN-AP is also modeled on CARIN. The UNODC is helping put in place a similar mechanism in West Africa. In the Americas, the Asset Recovery Expert Network operates within the framework of the OAS. The CARIN model is worth replicating because it is targeted in its goals and flexible thanks to the use of select national focal points.

Conclusion

Many developing countries are caught in a situation of persistent poverty while leaders amass enormous wealth through illegal means. In many cases, the assets taken from public coffers or acquired illegally from the state are siphoned off without the local population benefiting at all. The gravity of the situation is compounded when the looted funds are sourced from external funders as loans that must be repaid by citizens. The assets that are stolen from developing countries are often hidden abroad in distant safe havens, and citizens in developing countries often lack the means to bring their deceitful leaders to account. A multiactor approach to addressing some of the problems associated with asset tracing and recovery through the creation of a global fund for asset recovery, as described in this chapter, could resolve some of the attendant issues. Such a fund could provide technical assistance to countries that need better capacity in preventing corruption and recovering looted assets. The multiactor model would ideally be activated at the national, regional, and global levels. In any case, efforts to create interagency networks on asset recovery on regional bases should continue. In due course, it would be useful for regional interagency networks on asset recovery to cooperate on an interregional basis; some have already started. As this chapter has demonstrated, major challenges and limitations exist in connection with the proposed transnational and global fund. But such challenges must not serve as a pretext to avoid debates on solutions.

PART VII

Perspectives on the World Bank Inspection Panel

22

Improving Service Delivery through Voice and Accountability

The Experience of the World Bank Inspection Panel

DILEK BARLAS AND TATIANA TASSONI

Pressure for more accountability and internal concerns about the performance of its portfolio led the World Bank to establish, in 1993, an unprecedented mechanism to investigate complaints related to specific projects, so as to provide its Board of Executive Directors with a source of independent judgment on projects facing severe implementation problems.[1] The Bank Inspection Panel is the first accountability mechanism with the mandate to investigate an international financial institution's compliance with its own operational policies and procedures for the design, appraisal, and implementation of the projects it finances.[2] International review mechanisms prior to the Inspection Panel were concerned exclusively with the activities of states, rather than of international organizations, and the existing review mechanisms of international

---

1 *See* World Bank Inspection Panel, *Accountability at the World Bank: The Inspection Panel at 15 Years* 3–5 (World Bank 2009), for a history of events leading to the creation of the Inspection Panel. *See* also Ibrahim F. I. Shihata, *The World Bank Inspection Panel: In Practice* 1–8 (2nd ed., Oxford U. Press 2000); and Dana Clark, Jonathan Fox & Kay Treakle, *Demanding Accountability: Civil-Society Claims and the World Bank Inspection Panel* 1–9 (Rowman & Littlefield 2003). The Inspection Panel was created in the aftermath of the 1992 UN Conference on Environment and Development. Principle 10 of the Rio Declaration on Environment and Development calls for greater transparency and participation, for the right of citizens to hold their governments accountable for the impacts of environmental policies, and for a citizen's right to redress and remedy. United Nations Conference on Environment and Development: Rio Declaration on Environment and Development (adopted June 14, 1992), U.N. Doc. A/CONF.151/5/Rev.1, 31 I.L.M. 874, 878, http://www.un.org/documents/ga/conf151/aconf15126-1annex1.htm.

2 The panel model was replicated in other international financial organizations. Today, almost all international financial institutions have accountability mechanisms similar to the Inspection Panel, but, unlike the Panel, along with the compliance function, these mechanisms also have a formal grievance redress and problem-solving role. Such accountability mechanisms can be found at the International Finance Corporation (IFC) and the Multilateral Guarantee Agency of the World Bank Group, the African Development Bank (AfDB), the Asian Development Bank, the European Bank for Reconstruction and Development (EBRD), the Inter-American Development Bank (ASDB), and the Japan Bank for International Corporation, among others. The Inspection Panel spearheads the annual meeting of accountability mechanisms, which provides a forum to exchange ideas, challenges, and lessons learned. Members and staff of these accountability mechanisms belong to the Independent Accountability Mechanisms Network (IAMs Network). *See* Kristin Lewis, *Citizen-Driven Accountability for Sustainable Development Giving Affected People a Greater Voice: 20 Years On* (2012), www.inspectionpanel.org.

organizations were limited to the institution's internal activities. The Inspection Panel's creation reflected the need to look beyond the existing state-based accountability systems on the premise that actions of institutions such as the World Bank can have significant impacts on local communities and their environments.[3]

The Inspection Panel is a three-member body that provides an independent forum for private individuals and communities that believe that their rights or interests have been or could be harmed by a project financed by the World Bank as a result of a failure to follow Bank operational policies and procedures.[4] It is an accountability mechanism for Bank operations to respond to people who feel harmed by Bank-financed projects.

This chapter argues that the Inspection Panel (hereafter "the Panel") has improved and increased the sustainability and effectiveness of Bank operations, including service delivery. The Panel has positively affected not only the people who have resorted to the Panel but also the Bank's application of its operational policies and procedures. The chapter illustrates through case studies how the Panel has become an instrument that gives voice to people affected by Bank projects, and how its accountability actions have clarified and strengthened the Bank's operational policy framework, particularly safeguard policies, an environmental and social framework that the Bank created to ensure the sustainability of the development projects it finances.

The chapter briefly introduces the Panel and its function and procedures and describes the policy framework within which the Panel operates. It then presents cases studies illustrating how voice and accountability are expressed through the Panel's work and how they have had an impact on Bank operations. Concluding remarks follow.

The Inspection Panel and the Bank's Operational Framework

The Inspection Panel is an investigative body tasked with responding to complaints known as "requests for inspection." Requests are lodged by two or more individuals or communities that feel affected by a Bank-financed project or program and believe that they or the environment in which they live has been or will be harmed as a result of the Bank's noncompliance with the policies and procedures applicable to Bank operations. The Panel is an internal body of the Bank; it is functionally independent from Bank Management, whose actions it investigates, and reports directly to the Board that created it. The Panel process is designed to deal with issues of policy compliance on the part of the Bank and harm, if any, resulting from noncompliance.

---

3 Robert Lloyd, Jeffrey Oatham, & Michael Hammer, *Global Accountability Report* (One World Trust 2007).

4 *The World Bank Inspection Panel Resolution,* resolution no. IBRD 93-10 & resolution no. IDA 93-6.

A request for inspection that meets certain admissibility and eligibility criteria may warrant investigation by the Panel.[5] As of May 2014, the Panel had received 94 requests for inspection, 30 of which proceeded to a full investigation. In a number of cases, an investigation was not needed due to early resolution of the requesters' concerns.[6]

The investigation is a fact-finding process by which the Panel determines facts relevant to the claims included in the request and assesses whether there was compliance by the Bank with the policies applicable to the design, appraisal, and implementation of the project in question. In practice, the scope of the Panel's mandate is confined to situations where there may be linkages between the harm alleged by the requesters and Bank policy violations; the operational policies, as they stand and are in force at a given time, are the only standard of compliance for an investigation.[7] The Panel does not recommend, nor can it implement, steps to remedy the harm that may have been identified with an investigation. The responsibility to formulate an action plan that addresses the harm and compliance rests on Bank Management, in collaboration with the member government and in consultation with requesters. Moreover, the founding resolution gives the Panel no formal role with respect to the implementation or monitoring of progress in implementation of these action plans.

From a narrow lens, the Panel may seem to be simply an investigative body with a limited mandate and no power to propose remedies or changes to policies. It could be regarded as yet another oversight body that may slow down, create obstacles, and dramatically increase costs for Bank operations. This is indeed a limited view: in more than 20 years of operations, the Panel has demonstrated that it is an important change agent, contributing to better development outcomes for the Bank and acting as a promoter of the rule of law within the institution.[8]

Operational Policies and Procedures: The Creation of a Social Contract

Operational policies and procedures are instructions from Management to its staff on how to design, appraise, and implement a project the Bank finances;

---

5 Inspection Panel, *Operating Procedures* at paras. 25, 42, 43 (Apr. 2014), www.inspectionpanel .org; *see* also World Bank, *BP 17.55, Review of the Resolution Establishing the Inspection Panel: Clarification of Certain Aspects of the Resolution,* at para. 9 (1999). The Inspection Panel Resolution was reviewed for the first time in 1996.

6 *See,* e.g., *Inspection Panel Report and Recommendation, India Mumbai Urban Transport Project,* Request No. 58, received in 2009 (Aug. 7, 2009). Earlier requests related to the same project were the subject of another Panel investigation.

7 *See* Shihata, *supra* note 1, at 33, for a discussion of the scope of the Panel's mandate.

8 Sabine Schlemmer-Shulte, *Sustainable Development Principles in World Bank Inspection Panel Decisions,* in *Sustainable Development Principles in the Decisions of International Courts and Tribunals 1992–2012* 2 (Marie-Claire Cordonier Segger, Duncan French, & Nico Shrijver eds., Cambridge University Press 2012).

and they may be viewed as "operational codes" that may apply in different situations.[9] They are not instructions to borrower countries,[10] but they reflect standards that borrowers must meet to qualify for Bank financing.[11] These policies provide standards that are applicable to Bank-financed operations and that are intended to assist the Bank in fulfilling its purpose of combating poverty and promoting the sustainable economic and social development of its member countries.[12]

The policies and procedures most raised in requests for inspection are the so-called safeguard policies, which cover environmental and social aspects of Bank projects and ensure, primarily, that projects do "no harm" to people and the environment in the development process.[13] These policies generally reflect best practices for sustainable development purposes.[14] Among others, safeguard policies include the policies on environmental assessment, involuntary resettlement and indigenous peoples, issues of particular relevance in the Panel's case record.[15] Safeguard policies generally establish higher standards than most of the borrowing countries' legislation,[16] and their application in projects often faces some resistance and challenges. Nevertheless, safeguards have often provided a platform for the participation of stakeholders in project design and have been an important instrument for creating a sense of ownership among local populations and delivering better development results.[17]

The operational policy framework, including safeguard policies, can be considered an expression of a social contract that goes beyond the framework of formal financing agreements and includes the people affected by the projects

---

9 Shihata, *supra* note 1, at 43.

10 Borrower countries here included countries acting as guarantors of loans made to other entities.

11 Shihata, *supra* note 1, at 47. *See* also David Freestone, *Environmental and Social Safeguard Policies of the World Bank and the Evolving Role of the Inspection Panel*, in *The World Bank and Sustainable Development Legal Essays* 48 (Nijhoff 2003).

12 Schlemmer-Shulte, *supra* note 8, at 2.

13 The Bank is undertaking a review and update of its safeguard policies that "will lead to a new integrated framework that builds on the existing core principles of the safeguard policies, and may include several components, such as principles, policies, procedures, and guidance." *See The World Bank's Safeguard Policies Proposed Review and Update Approach Paper* (Oct. 10, 2012) [hereinafter *Approach Paper*].

14 It is important to note that the operational policies become binding on the borrowing country only when they are reflected in loan agreements, which are international agreements between a state and the Bank. The Bank's responsibility under its supervision policy is to ensure that borrowers' obligations are complied with.

15 The ten safeguard policies are available at http://web.worldbank.org/WBSITE/EXTERNAL/PROJECTS/EXTPOLICIES/EXTSAFEPOL.

16 Sabine Schlemmer-Shulte, *The World Bank, Its Operations, and Its Inspection Panel*, 3 Recht der Internationalen Wirtschaft 181 (1999).

17 *Approach Paper*, *supra* note 13, at 1.

that the Bank finances.[18] It is through its environmental and social framework that the Bank has committed itself to finance operations that promote its member countries' sustainable development and ultimately ensure economic and social benefits to these countries' citizens. Although in strict legal terms, one cannot regard the Bank's relationship with affected people as a formal contract, the social and developmental role of the Bank has generated a relationship with affected people that has created de facto obligations toward them. These obligations in turn led to the establishment of an enforcement mechanism such as the Panel that has had a profound impact not only on the Bank and its operations but also in empowering local communities to make their voices heard and to demand timely and meaningful access to information, participation, and Bank accountability in projects and programs that affect them.[19]

By creating the Panel, the Bank agreed to be held accountable to private citizens and individuals for complying with the standards that govern its operations. It bound itself to adhere to specific rules of engagement (rules created through an internal decision-making process)[20] and to address failures in following such rules when that failure has caused, or may cause, harm to people or the environment. In this context, the Panel's role and function provide the opportunity for affected people to ensure that the Bank honors the social contract expressed through its operational policy framework.[21] By giving voice to affected people and promoting clarification in the application of policies and bridging policies' lacunae through its accountability function, the Panel contributes to reaffirming as well as strengthening such social contracts.

---

18 Clark et al., *supra* note 1, at 1, mention a social contract embodied in the operational policy framework. For an overview of the history of social contract thinking in relation to international development, *see* Sam Hickey, *The Politics of Social Protection: What Do We Get from a Social Contract Approach?* (Inst. Dev. Policy & Man., U. Manchester, Chronic Poverty Res. Ctr. July 2011), which traces the history of social contract thinking, pointing to the work of John Rawls as the most important contribution to social contract theories in relation to international development. In this context, there are two approaches to social contract thinking. The first, known as the social or rights-based approach, where a social contract is an expression of the rights and obligations of individuals vis-à-vis each other and the state, was first theorized by Jean-Jacques Rousseau and later adopted by Rawls. The second, known as the liberal interest-based approach, found its first proponent in Thomas Hobbes. Both approaches take the idea of reciprocity (social cooperation is to mutual advantage), but they differ in the basic idea: the social approach is based on the desire to treat people fairly and to reach equality, while the liberal approach presumes that in the social contract context, individuals aim to maximize their advantage.

19 Daniel Bradlow argues that the executive directors' decision to establish the Inspection Panel constitutes the first formal acknowledgment that international organizations have a legally significant noncontractual relationship with private parties that is independent of either the organization's or the private actor's relationship with a member-state. *See* Daniel Bradlow, *International Organizations and Private Complaints: The Case of the World Bank Inspection Panel,* 34 Va. J. Intl. L 553, 160 (1994).

20 Shihata, *supra* note 1, at 41.

21 Clark et al., *supra* note 1.

Voice and Accountability in Practice

The role of voice and accountability in effective service delivery has increased in the international development discourse. Accountability and voice, which includes access to information and the right to participation, are critical aspects of effective service delivery.[22] Increasingly, accountability is regarded as an instrument not only for adherence to procedures but also for delivery of outcomes.[23] Accountability provided by a mechanism such as the Inspection Panel has improved the way that the Bank conducts its operations because the compliance investigation promotes respect of obligations contained in the policies, and it plays a key role in clarifying the application of these policies, leading to improved and more sustainable outcomes. In giving voice and exercising the accountability function, the Panel is an internal governance tool that enhances institutional development effectiveness.[24]

The sections below illustrate these points in practice, with examples of actual cases. One section shows how the Panel process provides an opportunity for project-affected people and communities to voice their concerns and engage in a dialogue with Bank Management at several stages of the process. The section on the impacts of the Panel's accountability function presents specific findings that brought clarity to some aspects of the operational policy framework of the Bank.

Voice

One of the most important characteristics of the Inspection Panel is that it provides a forum for community-led, "bottom-up," accountability. Its creation opened a direct channel of communication between affected people and the World Bank's highest level of decision making, the Board of Executive Directors. The findings of Panel investigations are made public and become available to a wide set of stakeholders, producing a "sunshine effect" and putting a public spotlight on people's problems and the Bank's reactions.[25]

---

22 *See* Samuel Paul, *Does Voice Matter? For Public Accountability, Yes* 9 (Policy Res. Working Paper No. 1388, World Bank 1994). Paul argues that service outcomes are created through actions taken by providers who have the resources and skills to carry them out and that the public has no direct means to improve service outcomes. Therefore, he assumes that enhanced accountability is the mediating variable that induces providers to generate improved outcomes. This implies that an increase in provider responsiveness and compliance, and the reinforcement of these behaviors through changed agency structures, monitoring, and incentives, are conditions required for service outcomes to improve.

23 Anne Marie Goetz & Rob Jenkins, *Voice and Accountability in Service Delivery* 3 (Birkbeck College, U. London 2004).

24 Suresh Nanwani, *Accountability Mechanism of Multilateral Development Banks: Power Complications Enhancement*, in *Law in the Pursuit of Development* 115 (Amanda Perry-Kessaris ed., Routledge-Cavendish 2009). He speaks of "empowerment through access." *See* also Shihata, *supra* note 1, at v, where World Bank President Louis Preston states that the "Panel is part of the Bank's evolving policy of improving its effectiveness, strengthening accountability and increasing openness."

25 Edith Brown Weiss & Harold K. Jacobson, *Engaging Countries: Strengthening Compliance with International Environmental Accords* (MIT Press 2000).

The Bank has immunity from national courts, and there is almost no judicial recourse for third parties affected by Bank-financed projects because of the Bank's status as an international organization and the immunities provided in its Articles of Agreement, which are signed and ratified by all member countries. Because communities affected by Bank-financed projects were not a party to loan agreements and contracts with the Bank, prior to the Panel, they had no opportunity in any forum to seek an adjudication of their rights and interests.[26]

The Panel's creation reflected a growing interest in giving individuals and private groups more formal legal recognition, with rights and obligations under international law. This interest went beyond the traditional approach of international law governing relations between sovereign states. The Panel process recognizes the rights of the affected communities and nongovernmental organizations (NGOs) in areas of social and economic development and environment, and significantly contributes to the growing reality of public participation.[27]

According to the resolution that established the Panel, concerns of affected people must be brought to Bank Management's attention before being brought to the Panel to give Management an opportunity to address these concerns.[28] This early window of discussions, with the possibility of an impending Inspection Panel process, can create an important opportunity and incentive for Management to take early action to address problems. A recent complaint submitted by an NGO in Nepal on behalf of the lesbian, gay, bisexual, transgender, and intersex (LGBTI) community related to the Nepal Enhanced Vocational Education and Training Project is an example of this window of opportunity.

In September 2013, the Panel received a request for inspection from the Blue Diamond Society, an NGO, on behalf of the LGBTI community of Nepal. The Blue Diamond Society stated that the project invited only men and women to apply for offered trainings, thus discriminating against the LGBTI community and those who prefer to choose a "third gender" or "other." The Blue Diamond Society feared that some people in the LGBTI community would be deterred from applying for training and that discrimination, marginalization, and a pattern of possible exclusion might result, thereby possibly hindering

---

26 David Hunter, *Using the World Bank Inspection Panel to Defend the Interests of Project-Affected People*, 4(1) Chi. J. Intl. L. 201–11 (2003).

27 Laurence Boisson de Chazournes, *Public Participation in Decision Making: The World Bank Inspection Panel*, 31 Studies Transnatl. Leg. Policy 84 (1999).

28 Inspection Panel Resolution, *supra* note 4, at para. 16. No data are available to show how many complaints are resolved before coming to the Panel through Management interventions. The World Bank Independent Evaluation Group's *Safeguards and Sustainability Policies in a Changing World* report notes that "the Bank does not yet have a system for receiving or resolving such complaints and continues to deal with such issues on an ad hoc basis." World Bank Group, *Safeguards and Sustainability Policies in a Changing World* (2010), http://siteresources.world bank.org/EXTSAFANDSUS/Resources/Safeguards_eval.pdf. The Bank is in the process of developing a more systematic approach to deal with complaints received.

their future empowerment. Following the receipt of the request, representatives from the Bank, the Blue Diamond Society, and the Ministry of Education and Sports met to discuss the concerns raised in the request, and the ministry agreed that subsequent calls for applications related to vocational training delivered under the project would be revised to address the requesters' concerns. The Panel decided not to register the request, taking into account Management's swift actions to meet with the requesters and propose steps to address and resolve their concerns.[29]

The procedure to present a request for inspection is relatively easy and user friendly. It ensures that any affected people and community, even those in remote locations, can access the Panel. Requests for inspection need not be long and detailed, can be submitted as a simple letter in any language, and do not have to reference specific Bank policies in describing the complaint.

People who come to the Panel are often the poorest or in some way most vulnerable and lack voice or influence in the political process. They may fear that raising their concerns against a World Bank–financed project might put them at risk of retaliation or losing project benefits. For this reason, the Panel developed strict provisions to maintain the confidentiality of the requesters' identities when they so request. Panel procedures also allow affected people to submit a request through a local representative, that is, a civil society organization or, in exceptional cases, a foreign representative, when the executive director agrees that the party submitting the request does not have access to appropriate local representation. In several Panel cases, requesters have relied on representatives to submit a claim. The Panel procedures also provide that an executive director may, on his or her own initiative, request an inspection.

The 94 requests for inspection received by the Panel by May 2014 came from 45 countries from all regions of the world. The requests were filed by a mix of local, national, and international civil society organizations on behalf of project-affected people, or by community members acting on their own behalf without the support or representation of another organization. During the 20 years of its operation, the Panel has received 40 percent of its requests directly from affected communities. Indigenous communities in different countries brought 22 requests to the Panel.[30]

Over the years, requesters have brought to the attention of the Panel many different types of harm or potential harm to people or their environment and issues of compliance regarding a wide range of operational policies. These include harms arising from displacement and resettlement of project-affected people; project impacts on indigenous peoples, their culture, traditions, and

---

29 Inspection Panel, *Nepal Enhanced Vocational Education and Training Project: Notice of Non-Registration* (2013), http://www.inspectionpanel.org.

30 They include Adivasi from India (belonging to the Jenu, Kurubas, Yeranas, and Soligas communities), Pygmies from Democratic Republic of Congo, Garífuna from Honduras, Pueblo Naso and Ngobe-Bugles from Panama, Kuoy from Cambodia, Pehuenche from Chile, Anuak from Ethiopia, Cherangany-Sengwer from Kenya, and Adivasi from Nepal.

land tenure; impacts on cultural property, including sacred places, natural habitats, and the environment (e.g., wetlands, forests, fisheries, protected areas); harm resulting from lack of adequate consultation, participation, and disclosure; and impacts of economic and social reform programs.

Once the Panel registers a request, Bank Management has 21 working days to develop a formal response, and the Panel has 21 working days from receiving the Management response to decide whether or not to recommend an investigation.[31] This phase, known as "eligibility," provides important additional opportunities for affected people and the Bank to resolve their differences. Once a request has been filed and the eligibility phase has begun, Bank Management has a strong incentive to address problems and alleged violations of Bank policies and avoid the need for an investigation.

In several Panel cases, in its response, Management indicated that it was taking, or was planning to take, steps to address the requesters' concerns. In such cases, if the Panel is satisfied that the process will not be detrimental to the interests of the requesters and that both Bank Management and the requesters are interested in pursuing this course of action, the Panel may recommend deferring a decision on whether an investigation should take place. The Panel stays in regular contact with the requesters to foster such opportunities. Interactions between requesters, Bank Management, and the Panel during this phase have resulted in resolution of a number of concerns brought to the Panel.

For example, in April 2009, the Panel received a request claiming that the Bank failed to comply with the principles of transparency, disclosure of information, and consultation in respect to the Republic of Yemen Institutional Reform Development Policy Grant Program, which the requesters contended would produce negative effects on wages and employment. In its eligibility report, the Panel recommended an investigation into the issues of consultation and participation. A Board discussion on the Panel's recommendation was requested, and, in advance of this discussion, Management submitted an enhanced action plan to address the issues that the Panel had recommended for investigation. Based on this action plan and the requesters' expressed interest in its implementation, the Panel proposed, and the Board agreed, to defer its recommendation for a year in order to provide an opportunity for the Bank to address these concerns. During this time, the requesters confirmed many positive developments in the Bank's interactions with civil society organizations in the Republic of Yemen, including the translation of documents into Arabic, transparency and disclosure of information, and consultation with respect to projects and policy issues. In September 2010, the Panel sent the Board its final report and noted that an investigation was not warranted.[32]

---

31 *Inspection Panel Resolution, supra* note 4, at paras. 18–19.

32 Inspection Panel, *Yemen: Institutional Reform Development Policy Grant—Final Report and Recommendation on Request for Inspection* 8 (2008), http://www.inspectionpanel.org.

In cases where the Panel does carry out an investigation, Bank Management is required to develop actions to address Panel findings of noncompliance and harm. These actions are normally included in an action plan submitted for Board approval. The Panel process, over the years, has led to substantial benefits for affected people and their environment. Types of positive impacts include a range of remedial actions to ensure that affected people obtain the benefits set forth under the Bank's policy on involuntary resettlement, such as increased compensation, livelihood restoration, inclusion of all those eligible for benefits and compensation, and improved conditions and resettlement sites; strengthening of the rights and protections for indigenous peoples and traditional communities affected by Bank projects, such as rights of full participation and representation; respect for traditional practices and means of representation of the community; rights to land tenure, including collective title; adherence to requirements under Bank policies relating to the environment and natural habitat, such as analysis of environmental impacts and of alternatives to proposed projects and minimization and avoidance of adverse environmental impacts; and protection of cultural resources, including places recognized as protected by traditional local communities.

According to the 1999 Clarification to the Panel Resolution, Management needs to consult with requesters and affected people when preparing an action plan to address Panel findings.[33] Management is required to reach out to the requesters for meaningful consultations during the preparation of the action plan and to take the results of those consultations into account in its discussions with the borrower to finalize the action plan. These consultations ensure that the voices of affected people, which are heard during the investigation process, are also listened to in the preparation of the final action plan so that the agreement between the Bank and the borrower takes into account the concerns of the requesters and affected parties.

However, a structural asymmetry occurs in this process because the Panel's investigation report is not made available to requesters and the public until after the development of the Management action plan and the subsequent Board meeting. As a result, although Management is required to consult with requesters in developing an action plan and has access to the Panel's investigation report, the requesters do not have access to the Panel's findings during this consultation process. This asymmetry may prevent requesters from playing a meaningful role in the consultation. In this context, the Panel has the authority to submit a report to the Board on the adequacy of these consultations.[34]

In April 2014, the Panel updated its operating procedures (OPs) to make the review process more efficient and effective.[35] This was the first update of the OPs since they were drafted in 1994. The updated OPs reflect the governing framework of the Panel and changes in Panel practices that evolved over time.

---

33 World Bank, *supra* note 5, at para. 15.

34 *Id.*, at para. 16. The Panel has not used this authority thus far.

35 Inspection Panel, *supra* note 5.

During the course of updating the OPs, in order to enhance opportunities to obtain early solutions to affected people's concerns, a pilot approach was launched to allow Management and the requesters to address concerns without immediately triggering the full Panel process.[36] This approach is now considered in cases where the issues of alleged harm are clear, limited in scope, and amenable to early resolution. It applies in cases where Management has initiated or planned to address the alleged harm and confirms that it is able to do so, and when the requesters support a postponement of a decision on registration to explore this opportunity. It is within the requesters' prerogative to return to the regular Panel process at any time. An independent assessment of the experience of this pilot project is planned for 2015, when the appropriate lessons will be drawn.

The Panel is piloting this approach for a request received regarding the Nigeria: Lagos Metropolitan Development and Governance Project. The request was sent by the Social and Economic Rights Action Center on behalf of individuals, families, and groups living in the Badia area of Lagos state. The requesters, a vulnerable slum community in Lagos, allege that the project has worsened their impoverishment and insecurity as a result of evictions that have occurred under the project. The requesters and Management are engaged in addressing the affected communities' concerns under the pilot approach. The Panel will inform the Bank's Board of its recommendation on how to proceed.[37]

The Panel's Accountability Function

The following Panel cases illustrate some impacts of the Panel's findings on the application of the standards in the Bank's operational policies and procedures. They show how the Panel has "used its competencies to sharpen the operational policies' teeth," as noted by one author, by clarifying the scope of application of certain policies and by helping identify some policies' lacunae.[38] These are cases where the voice of affected communities and the Panel's investigation and findings led the Bank to reflect on lessons learned and to corresponding actions. By promoting the Bank's learning experience, the Panel process has led to greater attention in the Bank to project quality and effectiveness and increased Bank awareness about the policies and their application and of problems in projects that Management may not always be fully aware of.

Ultimately, the effectiveness of the Panel process depends on Bank Management, which addresses the harms and learns lessons to apply to future operations. The action plans that Management prepares in response to the

---

36 *Id.*, at annex 1.

37 Inspection Panel, *Nigeria: Lagos Metropolitan Development and Governance Project—Pilot Approach to Support Early Solutions for Request for Inspection Interim Note* (Mar. 20, 2014). , http://www.inspectionpanel.org.

38 Schlemmer-Shulte, *supra* note 8, at 3.

Panel's findings, as well as actions taken throughout the process, lead to outcomes of the Panel process. Although the relationship between the Panel and Management has not been easy over the years—becoming at times adversarial—and even with a mandate only focused on compliance with policies and procedures, the Panel has become a small but key part of the development landscape in which the Bank operates. Decisions have been made and concrete changes have occurred on the ground and in the Bank's implementation of its operations. These are positive changes that should be embraced as key achievements of the World Bank as well as of the Panel.

Bridging the Gaps: Legacy Issues

Over the years, the Inspection Panel has reviewed a number of projects where the Bank has become involved in financing either in late stages of a project cycle or after project preparation or implementation has been suspended for a significant period of time. These projects normally include some legacy issues regarding possible social and environmental impacts, the attainment of their objectives, or even justification of the best possible alternative for attaining such objectives. Legacy issues are also associated with the economic, social, and environmental impacts related to the closure of mines, factories, or other similar businesses or enterprises.

Other than the general OPs applicable to all projects and programs financed by the Bank, there is no specific OP dealing with situations of this nature where most of the preparatory work has been done or has become to a certain extent obsolete, or where damage already done by previous undertakings must be dealt with when Bank financing is considered.

The two Panel cases described below provide examples of this situation and how the Bank addressed it as a result of the requests for inspection.

In 2007, the Panel received a request related to the Uganda: Private Power Generation Project (the Bujagali project). The Bujagali project consisted of a 250-megawatt, run-of-the-river hydropower project developed by a private sector company (Bujagali Energy Ltd., BEL) on Dumbbell Island on the Nile River, Uganda.[39] This was the second attempt to carry out this undertaking, aimed at meeting Uganda's growing electricity needs. About seven years earlier, in December 2001, the Board of Executive Directors approved an International Development Association (IDA) guarantee to support an earlier proposal for the Bujagali hydropower project. Due to difficulties encountered by the former project sponsor, however, the earlier Bujagali project was terminated by the government in September 2003, and the IDA guarantee was canceled. At that time, construction of the power plant had not begun, but the sponsor had completed the economic, social, and environmental assessments of the project and some resulting activities, and the Resettlement and Community Development Action Plan was under implementation. As a result of the resettlement plan,

---

39 The original project included a separate associated project for the construction of transmission lines, substations, and related works.

approximately 8,700 people were either resettled or lost assets for which they were entitled to compensation under the project. By the time the (first) Bujagali project was terminated, neither the affected people nor all the affected villages had received all the compensation and/or assistance under the action plan agreed to with the Bank.

People affected by the construction of the dam and the resettlement operations submitted a request in 2007,[40] shortly before the Board discussion of a new IDA guarantee to support the (second) Bujagali project. The Panel carried out an investigation and found that many of the affected people had been left in limbo after the first attempt at the project halted, and key elements of the resettlement process to which they were entitled under Bank policy, such as livelihood and income restoration or community development initiatives, had not been provided. The Board discussion of the Panel's investigation report and Management's response resulted, among other things, in an agreement that Management would "develop guidance for staff on how to address environmental and social safeguard issues in legacy projects that suffer significant interruptions in implementation, to avoid situations such as the one described by the Panel in the Bujagali project."[41]

A similar situation occurred in the Ghana: Second Urban Environment Sanitation Project (UESP II), a component of which was a proposed sanitary landfill at Kwabenya, a township located in the Accra metropolitan area. In 2007, the Panel received a request for inspection submitted by a local NGO on behalf of the Agyemankata community, which lives in the Kwabenya area. The requesters claimed that the Kwabenya landfill, if constructed, would result in the involuntary displacement of much of the Agyemankata community and leave those who are outside the area of displacement but in proximity to the landfill at grave risk to their health. According to the requesters, the site for the Kwabenya landfill was based on a 1990 United Nations Development Programme (UNDP) strategic plan for the greater Accra metropolitan area; although circumstances on the ground had substantially changed since 1990, the analytical studies underpinning the project and the related action plans had not reflected such changes.

The Inspection Panel investigation report, dated 2009, noted that one of the Panel's concerns related to legacy issues and the impacts of changing circumstances on the ground. The Panel found that the Kwabenya 2003 environmental and social assessment relied heavily on a siting study and environmental assessment from many years earlier sponsored by another financier, without properly taking into account the social and environmental reality in the

---

40 This was the second request related to the Bujagali project. The first request was submitted in 2002; the Panel investigated that complaint. That investigation report is available at http://www.inspectionpanel.org.

41 News Release no. 2009/166/AFR, *World Bank Board Discusses Investigation by the Independent Inspection Panel of Power Project in Uganda,* http://siteresources.worldbank.org/EXTINSPECTIONPANEL/Resources/Bujagali_Press_Release_Final_121208_Clean.pdf.

proposed landfill area resulting from an influx of people with corresponding investments in physical structures and commercial activities.

Following the investigation related to the Ghana landfill project and as recommended in the context of the Uganda Bujagali project investigation, Management prepared Interim Guidelines for Addressing Legacy Issues in World Bank Projects to provide Bank project teams and Management with guidance on how to address legacy challenges related to safeguard issues when the Bank restarts engagement in projects.

Clarifying the Scope of Policy Application

In some instances, the Panel's investigation and compliance findings have identified the need to clarify the scope of a policy application or some of its provisions. The case of the Cambodia Forest Concession Management and Control Pilot Project (FCMCPP) provides an example of this with respect to the policy on environmental assessment, particularly the provisions related to the environmental classification of projects. Depending on the type and magnitude of their impacts, projects are categorized as A, B, C, or FI, with category A reflecting the highest degree of impacts.[42]

In early 2005, the Panel received a request for inspection concerning the FCMCPP submitted on behalf of affected local communities, mainly indigenous peoples. The project was a technical assistance (TA) operation aimed at demonstrating and improving the effectiveness of a comprehensive set of forest management and operational guidelines and control procedures in forest concession areas. The request claimed that through this project, the Bank was supporting and promoting a flawed and corrupt forest concession system and the interests of logging concessionaires with track records of illegal logging and human rights abuses. In its investigation report, the Panel commended the World Bank's willingness to become involved in the forestry sector in Cambodia at a time when others would not, but also found that the Bank did not put sufficient emphasis on the environmental and social impacts of the concession system. The Panel noted that, "given the very serious potential impacts, and the close association of the Project with these impacts, the Project should have been placed in Category A and a full Environmental Assessment carried out."[43]

In response to the investigation report, Management stated that it drew significant lessons from the process that would be important for the Bank's future dialogue with the government of Cambodia on natural resources management and for future operations in the region and across the Bank. Actions

---

42 OP/BP 4.01 assigns proposed projects to one of four categories. A project is assigned category A if it "is likely to have significant adverse environmental impacts that are sensitive, diverse, or unprecedented." A project is classified as B if its potential impacts "are less adverse than those of Category A projects." Category A projects require a much more extensive environmental assessment.

43 Inspection Panel, *Investigation Report Cambodia: Forest Concession Management and Control Pilot Project*, "Executive Summary" xxi (Mar. 30, 2006).

proposed by Management following the investigation included a review and update of the Guidelines for Environmental Screening and Classification to provide guidance to Bank staff on the classification and methods to undertake environmental and social safeguard–related actions in TA projects, including approaches in natural resource management (NRM) projects and the proposed wider use of strategic environmental assessments to support the preparation and implementation of NRM projects. The Panel has indeed taken into consideration the new guidelines for the classification of projects in other investigations.[44]

A Key Issue: Land Administration and Management Projects

Increasingly, the Panel has received complaints concerning land use, land administration, and management projects or complaints where land rights issues figure prominently in the complaint whether or not the project is tasked specifically with regularizing land titles or with land management activities.[45] In its investigation reports on projects dealing with land administration and land use management,[46] the Panel has generally found (a) inadequate assessment of social, political, institutional, and legal risks during project preparation; (b) the impact of such projects may warrant application of the policies on involuntary resettlement and indigenous peoples; (c) projects involving indigenous peoples should carefully assess the social and legal importance of collective titles for certain groups; (d) longer-term impacts of land titling for tenure security of poor and marginal communities need careful consideration; and (e) the importance of paying greater attention to changing social, political, institutional, and legal circumstances in land-related projects.

Panel cases have also revealed a policy lacuna with respect to impacts from land management projects. Because the Bank's safeguards framework does not clearly specify how to address consequences for people and communities from changes in rights to land and land-based resources, the Bank has issued guidance documents clarifying the application of existing policies in the aftermath of Panel investigations. One notable example is the investigation

---

44 Inspection Panel, *Management Report and Recommendation in Response to the Inspection Panel Investigation Report Cambodia Forest Concession Management and Control Pilot Project* (May 16, 2006), www.inspectionpanel.org.

45 In 2013, the Panel received a complaint from the Cherangany-Sengwer indigenous peoples related to Component 2 of the Kenya: Natural Resource Management Project dealing with the management of forest resources. Notably, although the objectives of the project are not strictly related to land administration and land management activities per se, the issue of recognition and regularization of ancestral land rights is at the root of the complaint and of implementation challenges that the project has encountered since the early stages. The request, management response, and the Panel's report and recommendation are available on the Panel's website.

46 Other Panel investigations related to land administration and management projects have concerned the Honduras: Land Administration Project, the Panama: Land Administration Project, and the Cambodia: Land Management and Administration Project. The related investigation reports are available on the Panel's website.

related to the Albania: Integrated Coastal Zone Management and Clean-up Project (Albania Coastal Management project).[47]

In July 2007, a number of families from the small community of Jale, on the Adriatic coast, filed two requests for inspection concerning the Albania Coastal Management project. The requesters stated that the local construction police demolished their residences as part of the implementation of the World Bank Southern Coastal Development Plan because residents did not possess building permits. They believed that their displacement—they claimed human rights violations, inhumane actions, and violence during the demolitions—occurred as a result of the Bank project and that the Bank did not consider their rights and their well-being. Given that no resettlement was planned for people whose houses were demolished, the requesters also alleged that the Bank failed to comply with its policy on involuntary resettlement.

Bank Management argued that the project was not linked to the demolitions and, therefore, that the families in Jale were not entitled to benefits and rights under the policy on involuntary resettlement.[48] In its investigation report, the Panel argued that a claimed "agreement" with the government to suspend demolitions in the project area (stated in the project appraisal document) had given the impression that a safeguard was in place to protect potentially affected people, and the Bank, against the critical project risk of demolitions. During its investigation, the Panel found that the government had not made such a commitment and that, without such alleged agreement or without applying the policy on involuntary resettlement to ongoing demolitions, Management failed to safeguard people potentially affected by project-related activities. The Panel investigation concluded that the involuntary resettlement policy should have been applied to the demolitions related to the project.[49]

Acknowledging lack of clarity in the application of the policy on involuntary resettlement, Management indicated that it would review the application of safeguard policies in projects that support land use planning to issue guidance to address environmental and social issues.[50] As a result of the investigation, Bank Management indicated that it had undertaken a Bank-wide review of more than one thousand projects in the portfolio and quality control arrangements in all regions. Following discussion of the Board, two guidance

---

47 For analyses from different angles of this investigation, *see* Andria Naudé Fourie, *The World Bank Inspection Panel and Quasi-Judicial Oversight* 208 (Eleven Intl. Publg. 2009); *see* also Alberto Ninio, *Accountability and Environmental and Social Safeguards: Postscript and Update* (response to David Freestone's article in *The World Bank and Sustainable Development Legal Essays, supra* note 11, at 69.

48 Inspection Panel, *Bank Management Response Inspection Panel Review of Albania: Integrated Coastal Zone Management and Clean Up Project* 10 (Sept. 17, 2007), www.inspectionpanel.org.

49 Inspection Panel, *Investigation Report Albania: Integrated Coastal Zone Management and Clean Up Project* (Nov. 24, 2008), www.inspectionpanel.org.

50 Inspection Panel, *Management Report and Recommendations on Response to the Inspection Panel Investigation Report Albania: Integrated Coastal Zone Management and Clean Up Project* 8 (Feb.18, 2009), www.inspectionpanel.org.

documents were issued for Bank staff. The first was a clarification of the policy on involuntary resettlement, regarding an application for land use planning projects; the second was an Interim Guidance Note on Land Use Planning. The latter is intended to clarify risks intrinsic in land use planning projects, the application of safeguards during project implementation, measures available to mitigate risks, and recommended actions in supervisions.

Conclusions

By responding to concerns raised by people and communities affected by Bank projects, the Panel has offered an opportunity to affected people to make their voices heard with respect to projects and programs that may affect their lives, and it has given them additional means of participation in the decision-making process. At the same time, the Panel's compliance function has contributed to strengthening the OP framework, clarifying the scope of application of its rules, and promoting, as a result, the rule of law within the World Bank.

Although a mandate focused exclusively on compliance with policies and procedures, which does not allow other formal avenues to address the issues raised by the complainants, may constrain the process of achieving redress of harm suffered by affected communities as well as the learning of the institution, the cases presented in this chapter show that the underlying concepts that led to the Panel's creation are as valid today as they were 20 years ago. The Panel process has led, in many cases, to positive actions on the ground as well as within the institution, thus becoming valuable to both complainants and Bank staff. At the same time, the updating of the OPs, the introduction of differentiated ways to evaluate complaints at their point of entry, and the increased attention on learning from past cases are reflections of the need to ensure the delivery of better results in fulfilling the accountability mandate.

The pioneer establishment of the Panel was a forceful, credible, and effective commitment of the Bank to the implementation of the social contract embodied in its operational policies and procedures. The Panel—through its process and investigations—has been an effective conduit both to address the concerns of affected communities and civil society and to improve the World Bank's service delivery and support for sustainable development.

23
The World Bank's Inspection Panel
A Tool for Accountability?

YVONNE WONG AND BENOIT MAYER

The World Bank needs no introduction. Since it commenced operations on June 25, 1946, it has approved billions of dollars of loans, provided millions of hours of technical assistance, and published countless papers about development economics. Its first loan, to France for postwar reconstruction, was for $250 million.[1] Today, the World Bank, through its two development institutions, the International Bank for Reconstruction and Development (IBRD) and the International Development Association (IDA),[2] provides public sector loans and grants to developing countries for human development (education and health projects), infrastructure, communications, and many other purposes.

As an institution managing public funds and influencing public policies, the World Bank raises queries with respect to accountability. Accountability is a broad concept with several meanings. It generally refers to the responsibility, answerability, or blameworthiness of a party that performs a duty or works in an official capacity. As a social or political concept, *accountability* extends beyond the scope of the legal concepts of *responsibility* (i.e., the legal consequences of a breach of an international obligation, particularly the obligation to make reparation)[3] or *liability*; however, its content, although vaguely defined, often stops short of an obligation to make full reparation. Intergovernmental organizations, such as the Bank, are not generally held directly legally responsible or politically accountable for individuals affected by their conduct. Rather, the dominant perspective is that such organizations are accountable only to states, which are then charged with the responsibility of exercising public power over individuals.

---

1 World Bank Group Archives, *World Bank Group Historical Chronology*, 12 (last updated Sept. 2005), http://siteresources.worldbank.org/EXTARCHIVES/Resources/World_Bank_Group_Historical_Chronology_19944_2005_.pdf.

2 Each institution plays a different but supportive role in the Bank's mission of global poverty reduction and the improvement of living standards. The IBRD focuses on middle-income and creditworthy poor countries, while the IDA focuses on the poorest countries in the world. IBRD loans are made with favorable interest rates and rather long repayment schedules, whereas IDA credits are extended to the poorest of the poor countries with no interest and very relaxed loan repayment schedules. The IBRD and IDA also provide loans and guarantees in support of private sector projects. However, the majority of Bank financing for private sector operations is done through the International Finance Corporation and the Multilateral Investment Guarantee Agency.

3 *See*, in particular, as applicable to international organizations such as the World Bank, the draft articles on the responsibility of international organizations adopted by the International Law Commission in 2011, in *Y.B. Intl. L. Commn.*, 2011, vol. II, pt. 2.

In public sector Bank-financed projects, the borrowing government, not the Bank, generally implements the project. However, the conditions under which these loans are made generally have significant bearing on the design and implementation of the project. Consequently, the Bank, by requiring certain conditions for its loans, can have a direct effect on the economic and political decisions of borrowing states and thereby affect individuals and communities in borrowing states. That the Bank's imposed conditions influence key policy strategies (particularly in fiscal, monetary, and development policies) of the borrowing states by effectively changing the public decision-making power of those states has prompted various commentators to demand greater accountability from the Bank.[4] The Bank's response to date has been to adopt various policies addressing socio-environmental concerns and to create an institutional review mechanism, the World Bank Inspection Panel, in 1993.

This chapter examines the general functioning of the World Bank Inspection Panel (hereafter "the Panel") during its first two decades of operation (1994–2014) to assess whether it really is a vehicle through which individuals can hold the World Bank accountable. In making this assessment, the chapter considers (a) the history of the Panel's creation; (b) the novelty of the Panel as a mechanism for implementing the accountability of an international organization; (c) the legal framework of the Panel; (d) the accessibility of the Panel to the people whom it seeks to help; (e) the transparency, independence, and public accountability of the Panel; and (f) the direct and indirect outcomes of the Panel mechanism. The chapter suggests that, while not providing affected persons a legal avenue for redress, the Inspection Panel, if used strategically as part of larger advocacy strategies, particularly by increasing media coverage on problematic projects, can nevertheless serve as a useful tool in helping redress wrongs committed as a result of the Bank's failure to comply with its own policies. More generally, the Panel can also push for a cultural change toward greater consideration of the unintended consequences of development projects.

Background to the Panel's Creation

Concerns grew in the early 1970s that the Bank was administering loans and supporting projects without due regard to a variety of environmental and social impacts. In response to these concerns, the Bank began developing social and environmental policies—which came to be known as the "safeguard policies"—as a guide for its projects. Inherent in this development was the assumption that Bank projects would be negotiated only with borrowing governments that supported socially and environmentally

---

4 *See*, for example, Namita Wahi, *Human Rights Accountability of the IMF and the World Bank: A Critique of Existing Mechanisms and Articulation of a Theory of Horizontal Accountability*, 12 U.C. Davis J. Intl. L. & Policy 331, 333–34 (2006); Benoit Mayer, *Development Is No Excuse for Human Rights Abuses: Framing the Responsibility of International Development Agencies*, 5(2) Trade, L. & Dev. 286–343 (2014).

responsible development investments. However, the Bank's safeguard policies were often more rigorous than the actual practices of most borrowing governments, and during the late 1980s and early 1990s these policies were routinely ignored by Bank staff. This disregard of Bank policies finally came to a head in the Bank's funding of the Sardar Sarovar Dam on the Narmada River in India, a project that required the resettlement of 120,000 people. As a result of a broad grassroots and international campaign against the project, the Bank commissioned an independent review of its role. This review, known as the 1992 Morse Commission report, found clear violations of Bank policies and denounced their devastating human and environmental consequences.[5] The Morse Commission found that the Bank largely disregarded its social and environmental policies and tolerated its borrowers' violations of its safeguard policies. Furthermore, the follow-up report on the Morse Commission report found that the violations identified in the Narmada River case were not an aberration but a systemic part of the Bank's culture. The same year, a devastating internal report, authored by Bank vice president Willi Wapenhans, criticized the Bank's pervasive "culture of approval," in which the incentive structure encouraged staff to move large amounts of money quickly, without adequate attention to the social and environmental implications of projects.[6]

On September 1, 1993, the Bank's Board of Executive Directors[7] heeded the call for greater public accountability in relation to World Bank lending, passing a resolution creating the World Bank Inspection Panel.[8] The Panel was established to provide people directly and adversely affected by a Bank-financed project with an independent forum through which they could request the Bank to act in accordance with its own policies and procedures.[9] The Panel's creation, heralded by many observers as groundbreaking because it envisaged a mechanism for individuals to hold an international organization accountable, inspired the establishment of comparable mechanisms in other multilateral development banks and development agencies.

---

5 Bradford Morse & Thomas R. Berger, *Sardar Sarovar: Report of the Independent Review* (Resource Futures Intl. 1992).

6 World Bank, *Accountability at the World Bank: The Inspection Panel 10 Years On* 2 (World Bank 2003) [hereinafter *10 Years On*].

7 The Board of Executive Directors is responsible for oversight and day-to-day decision making at the Bank. All loans and projects supported by the Bank are approved by the Board of Executive Directors. There are 24 executive directors representing 184 member governments. The president of the World Bank, the most senior member of Bank Management, is also the chairman of the Board of Executive Directors.

8 Two separate resolutions (IBRD Res. 93-10 and IDA Res. 93-6) were actually passed, but they have identical content and so are referred to as "the resolution."

9 As stated in the paragraph subheaded "Purpose in the Operating Procedures" as adopted by the Panel on August 19, 1994, in *10 Years On*, *supra* note 6, at 147.

International Law and the Law of International Organizations

The Inspection Panel's agenda is somewhat novel. International organizations like the Bank have rarely granted standing to individuals. The funds lent by the Bank are provided by states to states, according to terms specified in a loan agreement by the government of the borrowing state. These agreements are entered into in accordance with the World Bank's Articles of Agreement (the IBRD and IDA each have their own Articles of Agreement) and the Bank's General Conditions Applicable to Loans and Guarantee Regulations.[10] The General Conditions provide that the rights and obligations of the Bank under such agreements "shall be valid and enforceable in accordance with their terms notwithstanding the law of any State or political subdivision thereof to the contrary."[11] Individuals are not parties to the loan agreement, and they are rarely consulted or even informed when such agreements are reached. The Bank's General Conditions provide for arbitration in the event of a dispute between the Bank and a state, but arbitration is not accessible to individuals because the Bank's objective of fostering economic development may not always coincide with the protection of individual rights. Utilitarian ends may be achieved at the cost of individuals' interests, or projects may simply be misconceived or misconducted. In such cases, individuals do not always have access to effective administrative law remedies in the borrowing state. There is clearly a need, then, for a mechanism allowing individual claims against the Bank.

Although the Bank has a legal personality in domestic and international law, it is generally impossible for individuals to bring legal claims against the Bank in domestic or international forums. An important obstacle is the doctrine of jurisdictional immunity of international organizations. This theory rests on the assumption that an international organization can truly operate in the common interest of all member-states participating in it only if it is not subject to the control or jurisdiction of any individual member-state. This immunity, however, is limited to those acts that are necessary for the Bank's functions or achievement of its purposes, and the Bank may in principle waive its immunity.[12] Bank employees, for example, have succeeded in bringing discrimination suits; however, the exception to immunity has not extended to affected individuals in borrowing countries.[13] The legal and political ramifications of law and practice are such that, should affected individuals attempt to bring an action against the Bank, that action is unlikely to be successful, inasmuch as domestic courts are hesitant to diminish the scope of immunity available to international organizations.[14]

---

10 These documents are available at the World Bank website, http://www.worldbank.org.

11 IBRD, *General Conditions for Loans*, sec. 8.01 (Mar. 12, 2012).

12 *See Broadbent v. Org. Am. States*, 628 F.2d 27 (D.C. Cir. 1980). *See* also Wahi, *supra* note 4, at 368–69; art. 7, sec. 3 of the IBRD's and the IDA's Articles of Agreement.

13 Wahi, *supra* note 4, at 370.

14 *Id.*

Even if it is assumed that opportunities exist for individuals to bring a claim before domestic courts, perhaps through a tort claim, such actions are likely to have limited success in borrowing countries because a large number of them have illiberal regimes that deny the standards envisaged by the safeguard policies or, more generally, a duty of care to its people, a necessary element for a tort claim. Moreover, a tort-based claim would posit that the state (as the sole actor implementing various policy measures) is the primary violator of the rights of the persons affected, with the Bank responsible only as an aider or abettor. Political obstacles may prevent such claims from succeeding in illiberal regimes,[15] or there might simply be little incentive for claimants to look beyond the responsibility of the state, except in exceptional circumstances relating to a change in government, for example, following the independence of a former colony.[16]

Likewise, claims are equally improbable before international jurisdictions. Individuals generally do not have any standing before international courts or tribunals, especially against international organizations.[17] In principle, individuals could appeal to their state to seek redress for wrongs resulting from Bank projects. However, diplomatic protection is not a right for affected individuals, and a borrowing state is likely to be reluctant to seek redress from the Bank for funding a project that the same state has itself implemented. Thus, before the creation of the Panel, if a citizen's government, on its own behalf, chose not to bring a claim against the Bank, affected individuals traditionally had little or no recourse against the Bank.

The Panel's creation challenges these traditional relationships between the Bank, its member-states, and affected individuals, in that it allows any affected individual in a country where Bank-financed projects are in place to request a review of the compliance of the Bank with its internal rules. Although the government of the borrowing state remains represented on the Bank's Board of Executive Directors, which retains ultimate authority,[18] the Panel's creation contributes to a certain shift of power in the traditional roles allowed to individuals in international relations. This shift is explained by some commentators as part of a reflection on a nascent global administrative law, whereby individuals tend to play a more prominent role by invoking

---

15 *Id.*, at 371.

16 *See*, by analogy, the case of Certain Phosphate Lands in Nauru (*Nauru v. Australia*) before the Intl. Ct. J, judm., June 26, 1992, ICJ Rep. 240 (1992).

17 Exceptions exist, particularly in international human rights law, through regional courts and other international mechanisms, but such mechanisms do not allow individuals to bring claims against international organizations. Other nonjurisdictional mechanisms have been established to receive individual claims in highly specific circumstances. *See* Simon Chesterman, Thomas Franck & David Malone, *Law and Practice of the United Nations* 504–64 (Oxford University Press 2008).

18 Jonathan A. Fox, *The World Bank Inspection Panel: Lessons from the First Five Years*, 6 Global Governance 279–318 (2000), http://repositories.cdlib.org/reprint/CGIRS-Reprint-2005-7.

general administrative standards against institutions that were previously unaccountable to them.[19]

The Legal Framework of the Panel

Since 1993, the resolution that created the Panel (hereinafter the Resolution) has been supplemented by two "clarifications" adopted by the Board of Executive Directors. The Panel has also issued its own operating procedures and administrative procedures to add details to the procedural and administrative aspects of the Resolution. The original operating procedures of 1994 were fully refurbished in 2014. Hence, the Panel's operations are now governed by the following documents:

I. The resolutions establishing the inspection Panel dated September 22, 1993 (IBRD 93-10 and IDA 93-6, called together "the Resolution");

II. The clarifications adopted by the Board of Executive Directors in 1996 and 1999;

III. The operating procedures as adopted by the Panel on August 19, 1994 and revised in April 2014;

IV. The administrative procedures adopted by the Panel.

Pursuant to the Resolution, the Panel is charged with investigating claims of noncompliance with Bank policies in the design and implementation of Bank projects. The Panel's mandate extends only to projects undertaken by the IBRD and the IDA: it does not extend to the activities of the private sector lending arms of the World Bank Group, that is, the International Finance Corporation (IFC) and the Multilateral International Guarantee Agency (MIGA).[20]

Panel Composition

As set out in the establishing Resolution, the Panel consists of "three members of different nationalities from Bank member countries,"[21] appointed by the Board of Executive Directors for three years. The Panel has generally been composed of two nationals from developed countries and one from a develop-

---

19 Benedict Kingsbury et al., *Foreword: Global Governance as Administration—National and Transnational Approaches to Global Administrative Law*, 68 AUT L. & Contemporary Problems 1, 3 (2005).

20 The IFC provides financing for private enterprises without government guarantee; the MIGA encourages the flow of foreign private investment, mainly by offering guarantees against noncommercial risks. Although the Inspection Panel cannot consider claims involving the IFC and MIGA, complaints relating to the projects of these institutions may now be addressed to the Compliance Advisor/Ombudsman.

21 *Resolution Establishing the Inspection Panel, Resolutions IBRD 93-10 and IDA 93-6, Sept. 22, 1993*, para. 2, http://ewebapps.worldbank.org/apps/ip/Pages/Panel-Mandate.aspx.

ing country. The chairperson is more often from a developed country.[22] At the time of writing, the Panel was chaired by Eimi Watanabe (a Japanese national and former assistant secretary-general and director of the UNDP's Bureau for Development Policy), with members Zeinab Bashir El Bakri (a Sudanese national and former vice president of operations at the African Development Bank) and Gonzalo Castro de la Mata (a U.S. and Peruvian national and former chair of an independent advisory panel for the Export-Import Bank of the United States).[23]

Mandate

The establishing Resolution provides that the Panel has the power to receive requests and to investigate claims where the Bank is alleged to have failed to comply with its operational policies and procedures. These operational policies and procedures currently include the operational policies (OPs),[24] Bank procedures (BPs),[25] the former operational directives (ODs),[26] and similar documents. The mandate of the Panel does not extend to verifying that the Bank has complied with its "Guidelines and Best Practices and similar documents or statements."[27] The Panel cannot consider claims that extend to an evaluation of these policies or that are based on the domestic law of the borrowing country or on international law (such as international human rights law). However, in the application of the Pilot Program on the Use of Borrower Systems to Address Environmental and Social Safeguard Issues in Bank-Supported Projects, the Bank may, under certain circumstances, adopt a borrower's own safeguards in place of its own.[28] In this context, the borrower's safeguards replace the Bank's own safeguards as the frame of reference for the Panel's mandate, but the Panel may also "examine Management's assessment of the equivalence of the relevant Bank policies and procedures with the country system."[29] Therefore, the Panel not only can assert a project's (non)

---

22 There have been two exceptions: the chair of the Panel was Alvaro Umaña-Quesada (Costa Rica) from 1997 to 1998, and Edward S. Ayensu (Ghana) from 2002 to 2003.

23 The 11 former Panel members are Richard E. Bissell, Alvaro Umaña-Quesada, Ernst Günther Bröder, Jim MacNeill, Edward S. Ayensu, Maartje van Putten, Edith Brown Weiss, Tongroj Onchan, Werner Kiene, Roberto Lenton, and Alf Jerve.

24 Operational policies are short, focused statements that follow from the Bank's Articles of Agreement, the general conditions, and policies approved by the Board. OPs establish the parameters for the conduct of operations; they also describe the circumstances under which exceptions to policy are admissible and spell out who authorizes exceptions.

25 Bank procedures explain how Bank staff carry out the policies set out in the OPs. They spell out the procedures and documentation required to ensure Bank-wide consistency and quality.

26 Operational directives contain a mixture of policies, procedures, and guidance. The ODs are gradually being replaced by OPs/BPs/GPs, which present policies, procedures, and guidance separately.

27 *Resolution Establishing the Inspection Panel, supra* note 21, at para. 12.

28 See OP 4.00, *Piloting the Use of Borrower Systems to Address Environmental and Social Safeguard Issues in Bank-Supported Projects*, March 2005.

29 Edith Brown Weiss and Roberto Danino, *Joint Statement on the Use of the Country System,*

compliance with the borrower's safeguards but also can decide on the validity of adopting those safeguards by Management itself.

As of early June 2014, 94 cases had been brought before the Panel (see the annex). Most of these cases pertain to the Bank's social and environmental safeguard policies or to procedural rules related to project supervision. The claims often allege violations of the Bank's policies on involuntary resettlement (OP/BP 4.12), environmental assessment (OP/BP 4.01), natural habitats (OP/BP 4.04), pest management (OP 4.09), forestry (OP/BP 4.36), projects on international waterways (OP/BP 7.50), indigenous peoples (OD 4.10), poverty reduction (OP 1.00), and cultural property (OP/BP 4/11). More than a dozen cases concern hydroelectric projects.

Filing a Claim (Who Has Standing)

The Resolution provides several options for filing a claim with the Inspection Panel:

1. As affected parties, two or more individuals who are directly affected by the alleged violations of Bank policies and who allege that they have been or could be harmed by those violations can bring a claim on their own behalf.
2. A local representative, such as a nongovernmental organization, can submit the claim on behalf of directly affected persons with proper proof of authorization.
3. In exceptional circumstances where local representation is not available (which can include countries where local NGOs are not allowed to operate or where there is a risk of retaliation), a nonlocal representative with proper proof of authorization can file the claim on behalf of local affected parties. In this case, evidence must be provided that local representation is not available.
4. An Executive Director may, "in special cases of serious alleged violations of such policies and procedures, ask the Panel for an investigation."
5. The "Executive Directors, acting as a Board, may at any time instruct the Panel to conduct an investigation."[30]

Most of the cases were presented to the Panel by affected parties or local representatives. The identity of individual claimants was sometimes kept confidential at their request.[31]

Chairperson of the Inspection Panel and Senior Vice President and General Counsel, in Mexico Decentralized Infrastructure Reform and Development Project (R2004-0077, 0077/3) (Inspection Panel and World Bank, June 8, 2004).

30 *Resolution Establishing the Inspection Panel, supra* note 21, at para. 12.

31 For example, in case 84, Kenya: Natural Resource Management Project; case 83, Afghanistan: Sustainable Development of Natural Resources—Additional Financing, and Sustainable Development of Natural Resources II; and case 82, Ethiopia: Protection of Basic Services Program Phase II Additional Financing and Promoting Basic Services Phase III Project.

A nonlocal representative, the U.S.-based NGO International Campaign for Tibet (ICT), once attempted to lodge a claim using option 3, in case 16, China: Western Poverty Reduction Project. Per option 3, if a nonlocal representative files a claim, the Board must agree that "appropriate representation is not locally available" at the time that it considers the request for the inspection. In case 16, China objected to ICT's representational authority. However, the Board sidestepped this objection by utilizing option 5, adopting all the elements of ICT's claim and requesting the Panel to investigate the alleged policy violations, thereby avoiding the need to evaluate the lack of locally available representation.[32] The Panel's use of option 5 was applauded by some commentators, who saw it as an indication that the Board was dedicated to ensuring access to the Panel by the largest possible number of potential claimants and to using option 5 where the risk of reprisals against vulnerable complainants was high.[33]

Option 4 (request by an individual executive director) has apparently never been implemented.

Eligibility of a Claim

Eligibility of a claim necessitates that specific conditions be met with regard to

I. standing (as described above);

II. object: it is alleged that the Bank has violated its policies and procedures, and that the rights or interests of specific individuals have been consequently affected;

III. consultation: individual claimants have attempted to raise their concerns with Bank Management without satisfaction;

IV. cause: the project is under consideration or has been approved by the Bank, and the loan has not yet been substantially disbursed.[34]

The Panel is specifically prohibited from hearing complaints about

a. actions that do not involve any action or omission on the part of the Bank;[35]

b. claims by suppliers (actual or potential) of products or services relating to procurement;[36]

---

32 Friends of the Earth Intl. & Intl. Acctg. Project, *Strategic Guide for Filing Complaints with International Financial Institutions*, 7 (Apr. 2004) [hereinafter Friends of the Earth], http://www.foei.org/publications/pdfs/strategic_guide.pdf.

33 Stefanie Ricarda Roos, *The World Bank Inspection Panel in Its Seventh Year: An Analysis of Its Process, Mandate, and Desirability, with Special Reference to the China (Tibet) Case* vol. 5, 493–94 (Max Planck Y.B. U.N. L. 2001).

34 *See*, in particular, *1999 Clarification of the Board's Second Review of the Inspection Panel*, para. 9, http://siteresources.worldbank.org/EXTINSPECTIONPANEL/Resources/1999ClarificationoftheBoard.pdf.

35 *Resolution Establishing the Inspection Panel*, *supra* note 21, at cl. 14(a).

36 *Id.*, at cl. 14(b); *1996 Clarifications (Eligibility and Access)*, http://ewebapps.worldbank.org

c. requests filed after the closing date of the loan financing the project or after the loan financing the project has been 95 percent disbursed;[37]

d. claims into matters that have already come before the Panel if no evidence of changed circumstances has been presented;[38] and

e. claims involving projects financed by the IFC or the MIGA.

The Panel Process

The Panel process starts at the reception of a request. The process consists of seven stages, as follows:

1. The Panel receives a request and registers it, unless the request is considered ineligible.
2. Management (those persons responsible for the design, appraisal, planning, and implementation of the project) responds to the claim, either by disputing the alleged policy violations or by acknowledging the concerns raised by the requesters and proposing appropriate measures.
3. The Panel reports to the Board on eligibility and recommends either the initiation of an investigation of all or part of the request or the rejection of the request. The operating procedures establish clearly that the Panel "may decide not to recommend an investigation even if it confirms that the technical eligibility criteria for an investigation are met,"[39] particularly with regard to the seriousness of the harm alleged.
4. The Board decides whether to request an investigation by the Panel.[40]
5. If an investigation is initiated, the Panel investigates and reports to the Board and Management.
6. Management proposes appropriate measures in response to the investigation findings.
7. The Board makes a final decision on whether to take action, and both the Panel's report and Management's response are made public.

Practice

Relatively few cases make it all the way from registration to investigation. Out of 77 cases or joint cases completed by early June 2014,[41] 66 were registered, but only 27 were investigated by the Panel. Several reasons can be identified for cases that do not make it through the entire process. Some cases

---

/apps/ip/PanelMandateDocuments/ReviewResolution1966.pdf.

37 *Id.*, at cl. 14(c).

38 *Id.*, at cl. 14(d).

39 *2014 Updated Operating Procedures*, para. 41.

40 *Id.*, at para. 49.

41 Ten other cases are still pending: cases 65, 81, 82, 84, 87, 89, 91–94. Some cases were joined: 72/75; 54/55/63; 53/56; 42/43; 32/33.

appear as inadmissible; thus, 10 cases were not registered (stage 1),[42] and 10 others were dismissed by the Board on the recommendation of the Panel's eligibility report (stage 4)[43] on the ground of eligibility criteria. The causes of ineligibility are diverse. One request was not registered because it was submitted by a single person (eligibility criterion I: standing, requiring at least two individuals).[44] Eight cases were dismissed on the ground of eligibility criterion II (object), including five cases where there was no apparent nexus between a Bank project and the harm alleged[45] and one case regarding a project funded by the International Financial Corporation, hence beyond the mandate of the Panel.[46] Five cases were dismissed following an eligibility report based on eligibility criterion III (consultation), because the requesters failed to raise their concerns to Management.[47] Eligibility criterion IV (cause) also justified the rejection of six cases: four decisions not to register requests related to projects that had been closed or where funds had been almost entirely disbursed,[48] one decision by the Board on the recommendation of the Panel regarding a program that had not yet been adopted, and one request regarding a matter that had already been investigated in a previous case.[49] Lastly, the registration of a request concerning procurement was refused in application of exclusion b.[50]

Other cases were discontinued by the Board, at stage 4, on the grounds of possibility for resolution between Management and requesters. In 12 cases (nine times during the Panel's second decade), the Panel recommended not investigating despite recognizing that all eligibility criteria had been met.[51] These recommendations were based on a large range of considerations, including the goodwill and reactivity of Management, the engagement of a fruitful dialogue between Management and the requesters, the seriousness of the harm alleged, the likelihood of a violation of the Bank's policies, and the clarity of the causal link between the violation and the harm alleged. Moreover, political considerations were sometimes put forward, for example, when the Panel recommended against initiating investigations on a delicate project involving the cooperation of Israel, Jordan, the West Bank, and Gaza, on the

42 Cases 88, 86, 77, 68, 59, 50, 35, 21, 5, 2.

43 Cases 70, 52, 42/43, 29, 28, 25, 18, 15, 12, 3.

44 Case 29.

45 Cases 68, 25, 15, 12, 3.

46 Case 5.

47 Cases 52, 42/43, 29, 28, 18.

48 Cases 88, 50, 21 (project closed); case 77 (more than 95 percent disbursed).

49 Respectively, cases 86 & 29.

50 Case 35.

51 Cases 85, 83, 80, 79, 78, 76, 73, 72/75, 45, 17, 14, 13. In other cases during the first decade, eligibility reports did not clearly distinguish considerations on the eligibility criteria and other considerations on the opportunity of an investigation.

basis of the "special circumstances surrounding this unprecedented regional collaborative effort."[52]

The Panel has consistently preferred negotiated solutions agreed on by Management and the requesters of investigations, in line with the reputational interests of the Bank and, arguably, the interest of the claimants in a speedy resolution of the case. Thus, no formal investigation was initiated in the last 21 cases completed by the Panel.[53] In cases that became more frequent during its second decade, the Panel postponed a recommendation after finding that a case was eligible to allow an opportunity for Management to adopt corrective measures.[54] In ,more recent cases, the Panel favored consultations between Management and the requesters before the registration of the request. Case 90, Nepal: Enhanced Vocational Education and Training Project, was not registered because Management could quickly reach an agreement with the requesters. Likewise, registration of case 91, Nigeria: Lagos Metropolitan Development and Governance Project, was postponed to allow consultation. A pilot approach to support early solutions in the Inspection Panel process, adopted as part of new operating procedures, aims at encouraging negotiations between Management and requesters by deferring registration of complaints. This pilot program seeks rapid remediation for the benefit of requesters and avoids the dismissal of requests on the ground of eligibility criterion III (requesters have not previously communicated their concerns to Management).

Investigations were initiated only in cases where the eligibility report clearly highlighted problematic elements. As a consequence, all investigations have identified some violations of an operational policy or procedure. Yet less emphasis has been put on the remedial measures, and the Board of Executive Directors has generally accepted the action plan proposed by Management. In some cases, however, the Board has called either for more mitigating measures (e.g., case 24, Uganda: Third Power Project, Fourth Power Project, and Proposed Bujagali Hydropower Project) or for a more detailed action plan (e.g., case 37, Democratic Republic of Congo: Transitional Support for Economic Recovery and Emergency Economic and Social Reunification Support Project), or has directly added some measures to the action plan (e.g., case 34, Pakistan: National Drainage Program Project).[55] The legal framework of the Panel's process does not require any follow-up after the decision of the Board on an action plan or any prior arrangement by Management. Such follow-up was nevertheless requested by the Board in certain cases, requiring Management to report on the implementation of the action plan (21 cases)[56] and the

52 Inspection Panel, Report and Recommendation, in case 76, Israel / Jordan / West Bank and Gaza: Red Sea–Dead Sea Water Conveyance Study Program, Feb. 15, 2012, para. 92.

53 Cases 90, 88, 86, 85, 83, 80, 79, 78, 77, 76, 74, 73, 72/75, 71, 70, 69, 68, 67, 66, 64.

54 E.g., cases 89, 71, 67, 60, 57, 54/55/63, 41, 40.

55 World Bank, *Accountability at the World Bank: The Inspection Panel at 15 Years* 43 (World Bank 2009) [hereinafter *Inspection Panel at 15 Years*].

56 Cases 62, 60, 53/56, 51, 49, 47/48, 46, 44, 40, 38, 37, 36, 34, 32/33, 31, 27, 26, 23, 8, 7, 4.

Panel to assess effective compliance (five cases).[57] It is not clear what the real consequences of noncompliance are, though they seem limited to the project, and perhaps the employment prospects of Bank administrators. The Panel has also developed a practice of visiting the project location one last time, following the final decision of the Board or any other form of arrangement with Management, in order to explain the remedy to the requesters.

During its second decade, the Panel developed the practice of deferring its decision on eligibility as a way to exert pressure on Management and to ensure the effective implementation of remedial measures. In such cases, a first eligibility report confirms the eligibility of a request but postpones the recommendation to the Board; a second or third eligibility report, taking into account Management's actions, adopts a recommendation as to the opportunity of investigation. Going forward, the pilot program on a new approach to support early solutions adopted in April 2014 indicates that the Panel may also defer registration in order to promote an early constructive dialogue between Management and requesters. In one recent case, a request was withdrawn before registration because an early agreement could be reached between Management and the requesters.[58]

Impediments to Access: Why Claims May Not Be Filed

The Inspection Panel has received 94 requests in 20 years of operation. Given the scope of the Bank's activities, this might be considered relatively few compared with the number and scope of projects approved by the Bank every year. The Panel's limited mandate may contribute to explaining why such a small number of cases have been filed to date. Several other obstacles can also be identified.

Insufficient Awareness

Although the Panel's purpose is to be a forum in which aggrieved individuals may bring their complaints regarding the Bank's failure to conform to its own policies, in reality the Panel may be underutilized because individuals affected by Bank projects remain unaware of the availability of this mechanism. Civil society actors may lack information about the Panel and even fail to realize that the project adversely affecting them receives financial support from the Bank. Bank investment projects blend easily with nation-state projects. The advent of the Panel might incentivize governments to conceal the role of the Bank so as to avoid review.

Even when affected individuals are aware that a specific project implemented by their government is funded by the Bank, and that they may request an inspection by the Panel, these individuals may not be sufficiently aware of the Bank's operational policies and procedures, particularly its social and

57 Cases 32/33, 26, 8, 7, 4.

58 Case 90, Nepal: Enhanced Vocational Education and Training Project.

environmental safeguard policies, to identify issues of compliance.[59] Development projects often affect vulnerable individuals with limited education and little political resources. This, compounded by the fact that information is usually not readily disseminated, means that affected groups are unlikely to know whether and how the Bank's safeguard policies can help them. The Panel has, however, evidenced some flexibility when claimants did not specify any particular policy. The Panel itself verifies whether a policy that appears contrary to principles of justice indeed infringes on some of the Bank's operational policies and procedures, thus assuming "the responsibility to identify all policies relevant to the investigated cases and examine the issues in their light."[60] Yet, for requesters to make the decision to utilize the Panel at all, they need to have a broad understanding of the Bank's operational policies and procedures, technical documents that remain relatively unknown outside the specialist community.

Linguistic and Cultural Barriers

Understanding the Panel's procedures and the Bank's policy language requires a command of English. Although requests can be addressed in the language of the requesters, acquiring access to Bank policies is often difficult for locally affected people because the Bank does not provide copies of Bank policies in local languages.[61] At most, the Inspection Panel's website (which is available only in English) contains an eight-page brochure titled "Panel in Brief," translated into 12 languages other than English. Nevertheless, a large majority of cases come from countries where English is not the main language.

In addition to language, culture can also be an impediment to understanding Panel procedures. In some borrowing countries, filing a complaint may be at odds with local cultural norms and perspectives. Requesting an investigation to remedy a project requires a certain degree of internalization of Western legal and political values, including that of political participation. If formally filing a claim against a public authority is not accepted within a certain culture, requests are unlikely to be sent to the Panel. While many requests were sent from Africa (28), Latin America (23), and South Asia (20), only three requests have originated from Southeast Asia (two in Cambodia and one in the Philippines), and one from Northeast Asia. Also, the Panel members are composed of three different nationalities, and mostly educated in Western institutions, usually in either the United Kingdom or the United States.

The passing of time may contribute to increased awareness. Encouraging media attention for current and past claims will be useful in this regard, although it may also be at odds with the World Bank's reputational strategy.

---

59 Fox, *supra* note 18.

60 *Inspection Panel at 15 Years, supra* note 55, at 40.

61 Dana L. Clark, *A Citizen's Guide to the World Bank Inspection Panel*, 2d ed., 12 (Ctr. Intl. Envtl. L. Oct. 1999), http://www.ciel.org/Publications/citizensguide.pdf.

To address these issues, the Panel and Management are encouraged to disseminate information regarding the existence and accessibility of the Panel.[62]

Knowing that claimants are at times unable to recognize Bank-financed projects, international NGOs and Bank staff can communicate with local civil society actors regarding where Bank projects are taking place. The diffusion of information on the existence of the Panel mechanism should be a component of any Bank project. NGOs can be instrumental in helping disseminate Bank policies and providing translations to locally affected communities. The translation of Panel documents into local languages is also an indispensable step for the dissemination of information. Further, the Panel members themselves, with their diverse nationalities, work experience, and academic connections, can facilitate the marketing and advertising of the Panel by writing and publishing widely in respect of the Panel process. This not only spreads news of the Panel but also highlights the diversity and expertise of the Panel members for potential claimants. This enhanced communication can help build trust in the Panel and thereby increase its use.

Costs (Financial and Other)

Even in cases where affected people are informed about the Panel and the Bank's safeguard policies, and their concerns fit the Panel's mandate, the costs and risks of filing a claim can be prohibitive. Specifically, the claim process is highly technical, expensive, and time consuming. For a claim to be valid, it must include a description of the project; an explanation of how Bank policies, procedures, or contractual documents were violated; a description of the claimant's interests harmed by the violation of the policies; and a description of the steps taken to have Bank staff resolve the violations. The office of the Inspection Panel offers advice on the preparation of requests, and the Panel may ask for additional information before deciding on registration. The length and depth of analysis varies based on the request; some requests are written by domestic lawyers but generally do not involve specialist lawyers. Requests represent a certain investment of time and monies, resources that could be invested in other political or legal strategies. The Panel procedure is free of charge, but there is no financial assistance provided for requesters to meet their costs.

Even more than the financial costs, requesters may fear reprisal for filing a claim. For instance, in the China Western case, the risk of reprisal was so intense that outside representation was required for a claim to be made. Indeed, when the Panel traveled to the project area, its members recognized a "climate of fear" among local affected people.[63] Likewise, in case 10, India: NTPC Power Generation Project in Singrauli, the representative of the claimants was attacked by contracting agents working for the borrower, the National Thermal Power Corporation (NTPC), in the presence of the company's

---

62 *See,* in particular, *2014 Updated Operating Procedures, supra* note 39, at para. 76.

63 Friends of the Earth, *supra* note 32, at 9.

officials.[64] Pressure was also evidenced in other cases, particularly in case 69, Liberia: Development Forestry Sector Management Project, where the Panel's eligibility report noted, as "a matter of serious concern," that it had received information indicating that claimants had "been put under pressure and intimidation since bringing their complaint to the Panel." The Panel duly recognized the "potentially deterring effect on the ability of people to bring their concerns to the Inspection Panel without fear of reprisal, thus undermining the integrity of the Inspection Panel process and ultimately the Bank's accountability."[65] Similar concerns arose in several other cases.[66] With such risks of reprisals, it is no wonder that some claims never make it to the Panel.

While the Panel allows a claim to be filed by a nonlocal representative to avoid the fear of reprisals from hindering the claim's relevance, the operating procedures of the Panel require that the representative demonstrate that it has explicit authorization to act as the agent of the adversely affected people. This calls for specific affected individuals to authorize representatives and, although their identities can be kept confidential at their requests, authorization to do so is contingent on a certain degree of trust of the Panel. This condition should perhaps be put aside, at least when large international NGOs submit a claim that appears very plausibly to reflect the concern of an affected community, a condition that Panel members could confirm through a field visit and informal consultation with this community.

Rejection of the Panel

Although the Panel seeks to provide a forum for individuals affected by Bank projects, and for greater transparency and accountability, the motivation to use an institutional mechanism like the Panel cannot be taken for granted. Some people may find the Panel an inappropriate tool because it requires a certain amount of engagement with the World Bank. Located within the World Bank's headquarters in Washington, DC, the Inspection Panel certainly does not appear as a forum where requesters and Management are on equal footing.[67] It arguably serves as a legitimized channel of dissent, bringing outsiders' critiques within the World Bank's own structure. Despite the guarantees of independence of the members, the Panel remains largely dependent on the support of the Board of Executive Directors. Some potential claimants may view the system as so fundamentally flawed as to feel politically uncomfortable with proceeding in the Panel process. Similarly, where individual grievances are

---

64 *Id.*

65 Inspection Panel, *Eligibility Report*, in case 69, Liberia: Development Forestry Sector Management Project, Feb. 7, 2011, para. 116.

66 E.g., cases 41 (Brazil: Parana Biodiversity Project), 32/33 (India: Mumbai Urban Transport Project), 24 (Uganda: Third Power Project, Fourth Power Project, and proposed Bujagali Hydropower Project). *See* also *Inspection Panel at 15 Years, supra* note 55, at 49.

67 *See*, for example, the recount of Pacifique Mukumbu-Isumbisho as to how his community has decided to address the Inspection Panel, even though it "was divided: some thought the Panel could not be independent because it was a part of the Bank" (*Inspection Panel at 15 Years, supra* note 55, at 48).

primarily with the government rather than with the Bank, potential claimants may view the Panel as an inappropriate forum in which to express themselves.

The Attractiveness of the Panel Process

In addition to obstacles that limit access to the Panel, other elements reduce its attractiveness for possible requesters. This section identifies some of the issues affecting the transparency, independence, and accountability of the Panel process, as well as its ability to remedy the violations that it identifies.

The Control of the Board of Executive Directors

The Panel makes a recommendation as to whether an investigation should take place, but the decision is ultimately that of the Board of Executive Directors. The Board also decides on appropriate remedial measures, if any are to be taken. This process has been criticized for being unduly restrictive on the Panel and for obstructing its independence. In practice, the Board has historically used this mechanism to prevent inspections in borrowing countries on the basis of political considerations. The 1999 Clarification sought to remedy this situation by providing guidelines as to when the Board should approve a recommendation for inspection by the Panel. Specifically, this document aims to avoid confrontation between the Panel and the borrowing government before the Board's decision by insisting that the Board approve the conduct of an investigation "without making a judgment on the merits of the claimants' request, and without discussion" except as to technical eligibility criteria.[68] It is interesting to note that the 1999 Clarification also prohibits the Panel from doing preliminary in-country investigations of any depth. It also restricts the Panel's right to comment on a borrowing government's responsibility for problems related to a project. Not surprisingly, the 1999 Clarification attempts to curb the politicization of the Panel process prior to Board approval of a Panel recommendation for investigation.

A review of the cases before the Panel to date shows that the 1999 Clarification has been favorable in relation to Board approval for Panel recommendations for inspections. Prior to the 1999 Clarification, of the six investigations recommended by the Panel, only two were approved by the Board: in the first case, Nepal: Arun III Hydroelectric Project, the Board approved a full inspection; in case 10, India: NTPC Power Generation Project in Singrauli, it approved only a desk review (a report not based on direct field research), given the tense situation in the project area.[69] In four other cases, the Board rejected the Panel's recommendation for an investigation. Thus, in case 4, Brazil: Rondonia Natural Resources Management Project, the requesters argued that the demarcation and protection of lands for indigenous peoples and rubber tappers were being impeded by the Bank project, which was designed to allow

68 *1999 Clarification, supra* note 34, at para. 9.

69 Clark, *supra* note 61, at 16.

some extension of roads into the Amazon region. While the Panel recommended a full investigation, the Board was not satisfied with the evidence of harm, even in the face of detailed evidence from the Panel, and rejected an investigation in favor of a Management-generated action plan.[70] Likewise, in case 7, Argentina/Paraguay: Yacyretá Hydroelectric Project, the executive director representing Brazil objected to the Panel recommendation and continuously challenged the eligibility of the claimants. The process became highly politicized, and the Board denied the Panel's recommendation for an investigation, accepting instead Brazil's assurances that it had developed an action plan and would implement it; the Board approved the action plan without seeing or evaluating it.[71]

Following the 1999 Clarification, however, the Board has never directly rejected a Panel's recommendation for investigation, and 21 investigations have been carried out since then.[72] However, this does not mean that the Board has ceased all pressure on the Panel. While this greater independence of the Panel is encouraging, the fact remains that under the formal framework, the Board maintains the ability to reject the Panel's recommendations for inspection. In order to fulfill its role, the Panel requires a high degree of independence from the Board. If the Board has any capacity to short-circuit the Panel's information-gathering process, the Panel clearly cannot function as effectively as if it were free from any Board interventions. A better approach may be to modify the Resolution so as to eliminate the Board's authority to approve an investigation altogether. This would avoid the risk of intervention from the Board and reduce the politicization of the Panel process. Such a procedure would ensure the Panel's full ability to report completely and independently about Bank policy failures.

Input from Requesters

Another serious defect in the Panel process is the lack of participation by the claimants and the lack of transparency in the recommendations by Management to the Board. Without adequate participation and transparency, Management recommendations for remedial actions may fail to address the concerns of the claimants. Thus, Management has an opportunity to consult and respond to the investigation report before the final decision of the Board. However, this report is not communicated to requesters before the Board

---

70 In January 1997, the Inspection Panel was asked to review the 18-month progress on Management's action plan and in April 1997 submitted the report to the Board. The Panel's report found that deforestation continues at an alarming rate, nearly 450,000 hectares annually, and emphasized the need for stronger mechanisms to protect the borders of protected areas. The report also found little progress in the implementation of the promised health program for the indigenous people.

71 Clark, *supra* note 61, at 16. The Panel was asked to assist the Board in evaluating implementation of the action plan in 12 months, although this Board evaluation never took place.

72 In case 71, Lebanon: Greater Beirut Water Supply Project, the Board postponed a recommended decision to initiate an investigation into the outcome of a study commissioned by Management; a second eligibility report, based on the result of this study, did not recommend further investigation.

decision has been made, which deprives requesters the opportunity to communicate their observations. The requesters are similarly unable to make any observations on the plan of action that Management proposes in response to any breaches identified in the investigation report. While there is nothing preventing Management from consulting with requesters, there may be little incentive to do so. There is consequently a risk that the plan of action does not fully address the concerns raised by the requesters.

The 1999 Clarification partly addresses this issue. In particular, Management must now consult with the requesters when conceiving the Management Report and Recommendation in Response to the Inspection Panel (MRR), and, under the 2014 operating procedures, it must "communicate to the Panel the nature and the outcomes of the consultations with the affected parties on the action plan."[73] Moreover, the Panel may report "on the adequacy of these consultations," including on the basis of a field visit.[74] These measures constitute an important step forward from the previous operating procedure, where claimants' views were represented in the approved action plan only if Management approved. However, more work may be required. In particular, "the possibility of a constructive dialogue is hampered by the fact that the Panel's Resolution does not allow the disclosure of its Investigation Report at this stage," which limits the ability of the requesters "to engage meaningfully with Management in the preparation of remedial steps."[75] Thus, the Panel recognizes that, "in several cases, . . . Requesters have expressed to the Panel strong concerns about the lack of consultations during this phase of the process, or that the consultation[s] have been far from adequate."[76]

No Appeals Mechanism

Furthermore, the Panel process does not include a mechanism for the claimants to appeal the Panel's or the Board's approved action plans. Consequently, where Panel reports or action plans do not align with claimants' concerns, there seems to be little that the claimants can do. This was the scenario in case 25, Papua New Guinea: Governance Promotion Adjustment Loan, where the requesters felt that their process rights were not fully respected by the Panel, but had no legal recourse available.[77]

Panel Composition

It is recognized that the Panel does not achieve the degree of independence expected from a juridical mechanism, so attempts to enhance its independence can only promote its credibility and effectiveness. It follows that reforms directed toward greater independence of the Panel vis-à-vis the Board and

73 *2014 Updated Operating Procedures, supra* note 39, at para. 70.

74 *Id.*

75 *Inspection Panel at 15 Years, supra* note 55, at 41.

76 *Id.*, at 56.

77 Friends of the Earth, *supra* note 32, at 8.

Management should be pursued. This reasoning underlies the provisions in the Resolution that attempt to safeguard the independence and integrity of the Panel members from Management influence through sanctions or safeguards. The provisions exclude the nomination of anyone who has worked for the World Bank Group as a staff member, an executive director, or an alternate or adviser to an executive director for at least two years after the person's term of service has ended.[78] The provisions also specify that Panel members "may be removed from office only by decision of the Executive Directors for cause,"[79] and that Panel members may not be employed by the Bank Group following the end of their service on the Panel.[80] Yet Panel members are elected by the Executive Directors on the recommendation of the Bank's President. This method does not reflect the principles of transparency, public participation, and public accountability that are at the core of the Panel's mandate.

Nature of the Panel

Fundamentally, the very nature of the Panel—as essentially a fact-finding mechanism—falls short of what many actual or potential requesters expect: a reparation. The function of the Panel is to bring Bank projects into compliance with the internal rules of the Bank, not to repair the wrongs caused by violations of international law (e.g., human rights and environmental protection). Thus, the dismissal of four cases on projects that were completed or near completion suggests that some requesters had broader expectations of the Panel (including a more restorative function);[81] and many other cases with similar expectations do not file a request in the first place. Some of the remedies provided as a result of Panel investigations evidencing clear cases of noncompliance do not provide answers to requesters; "a significant number of findings of non-compliance still go unanswered in action plans."[82] The lack of follow-up on remedial actions has been identified by requesters as "[o]ne of the main concerns expressed by affected people and civil society organizations about the Panel process."[83]

If the Panel does not overcome the image that it works largely for the benefit of the Bank itself, it may be seen as more akin to an internal audit procedure than a legal process. This view will remain as long as compensation is not provided for past damage (as opposed to a plan of action to avoid future damage) and as long as the costs suffered by the requesters are not covered by the Panel where a breach has been identified.

---

78 *Resolution Establishing the Inspection Panel, supra* note 21, at cl. 4.

79 *Id.*, at cl. 8.

80 *Id.*, at cl. 10.

81 *Supra* note 48.

82 Natalie Bridgeman & David Hunter, *Narrowing the Accountability Gap: Toward a New Foreign Investor Accountability Mechanism*, 20 Geo. Intl. Envtl. L. Rev. 187–236 (2007).

83 *Inspection Panel at 15 Years, supra* note 55, at 44.

The Consequences of Inspection Panel Investigations and Recommendations

Regardless of the Panel's problems, the fact that 94 claims have been filed reflects the growing relevance of the Panel process over the last 20 years. What, then, has been the practical experience of claimants who have engaged the Panel? Has the Panel met its objective of improving the Bank's compliance with its operational policies and procedures, particularly its safeguard policies, and alleviating harm associated with policy violations? Has the Panel process improved project quality, given the important lessons learned about why projects fail, and provided a measure of accountability?

According to its constituting documents, the Panel is neither an enforcement nor a judicial mechanism. It cannot provide compensation, nor can it issue an injunction against further work on a project or rule that the project should be canceled. The Panel has an investigatory and advisory role: it reports its findings to the Board, which ultimately must make a determination of how to respond to the Panel's report. Claimants can generally expect an action plan leading to improvements over the long term, even though it is often difficult to assess the impact of these action plans.

There have been instances where action plans have clearly failed to provide the remedial action that requesters expected. For instance, the action plan developed in response to a Panel claim challenging violations of environmental and social policies in case 10, India: NTPC Power Generation Project in Singrauli, resulted in increased compensation for about 1,200 families affected by forced evictions, but this payment did not succeed in restoring livelihoods, left unresolved the plight of thousands of other families, and ignored the devastating environmental, health, and food security issues at stake in the region.[84]

In some cases, the Panel proceedings led to the cancellation of or withdrawal from an offer of funding. The cancellation of the Bank support to Arun III Hydroelectric Project (Nepal) as a result of the first case before the Panel was largely celebrated as "an extraordinary success which illustrated both the significance and the necessity of the Panel."[85] The consequences of the Bank's withdrawal were not only financial but also symbolic, bringing international opprobrium on the project of the borrowing state. As Handl argues, this withdrawal "may well, and indeed should, discourage other potential lenders, be they private or public entities, from going ahead with an investment project that has been found wanting in light of the environmental and social development criteria that the bank is obliged to follow as a matter of public international law and policy."[86] Indeed, Nepal's project was halted for good.

---

84 Friends of the Earth, *supra* note 32, at 8.

85 Roos, *supra* note 33, at 516.

86 G. Handl, *The Legal Mandate of Multilateral Development Banks as Agents for Change toward Sustainable Development*, 92 Am. J. Intl. L. 642, 665 (1998).

By contrast, other states have been able to carry out their projects after the World Bank withdrew its support on the basis of Panel proceedings. For example, in case 16, China: Western Poverty Reduction Project, the opposition of the Panel did not "discourage other potential lenders . . . from going ahead with the investment project."[87] The government of China withdrew its loan application and carried out the project, essentially unaltered, with purely domestic funds. In this case at least, the withdrawal of the Bank did not prevent the project but may have even further reduced the degree of international oversight on the project. Without funding, the Bank is unable to provide input on the design or implementation of a project, and affected individuals lose an avenue to advance the protection of their rights and interests.

The China: Western Poverty Reduction Project case highlights an important dilemma for the Bank: should it continue funding projects and try to mitigate their important unintended consequences, or should it withdraw from such projects and run the risk that the state carries it out with unmitigated social or environmental costs?

In other cases, without discontinuing the involvement of the Bank, the Panel has been able to trigger action by Management. Some results have been obtained without investigation and, in at least one case, even before the registration of the case.[88] Thus, the success of the Panel mechanism should perhaps be measured not in terms of whether an investigation is initiated but in terms of whether the requesters recognize that their grievances have been addressed. The Panel's eligibility report in case 74, Kazakhstan: South-West Roads, noted that "the Requesters, who highlighted to the Panel team that the engagement of the Panel has brought more attention to their grievances, are satisfied with the fact that their concerns were either resolved or about to be resolved."[89] Management had taken or promised remedial action before the Panel could make any recommendation on an investigation.

Nevertheless, given the relatively small number of cases (compared with the number of Bank projects) and their sometimes ambivalent outcomes, the Panel's greatest overall impact to date has perhaps been indirect and diffuse, although this impact is naturally more difficult to measure. The Panel itself highlights, as part of its outcomes, its possible "influences on projects similar to those subject to a request for inspection," its "influence at the broader institutional level," and, last but not least, its role as a "model for similar institutions in other organizations."[90]

The very existence of the Panel puts pressure on the Bank's staff to be more conscious in complying with the safeguard policies and to supervise

---

87 *Id.*

88 Case 90, Nepal: Enhanced Vocational Education and Training Project.

89 Inspection Panel, *Report and Recommendation*, case 74, Kazakhstan: South-West Roads Western Europe–Western China International Transit Corridor (CAREC 1b & 6b) (IBRD Loan No. 7681-KZ), Oct. 18, 2011, para. 66.

90 *Inspection Panel at 15 Years, supra* note 55, at 90–92.

projects more closely. The Panel may have fostered a cultural change within the Bank's Management, from the long-criticized "culture of approval" to greater consideration of the negative consequences of its projects—although the Panel does face, at times, the hostility of the Bank's staff.[91] As one commentator noted, "[T]he panel clearly has had some impact on promoting a sustainable development agenda with the Bank, but the degree of its impact remains a matter of speculation."[92] Although not perfect, the Panel process envisages a forum where individuals affected by Bank projects can raise concerns that have in many cases remained unaddressed for years. Regardless of the ultimate outcome of the Panel process, this forum raises awareness of the problems at the highest levels in the Bank and in the borrowing country. This agenda-setting dimension is one of the greatest benefits of the Panel process, because an international organization such as the World Bank, leading the way for other multilateral development banks and development agencies, may finally become more systematically attentive to the unintended impacts of its projects.

Another indirect effect is the increased media attention and support from international NGOs interested in Bank activities. International attention has so far played a critical role in pressuring the Board of Executive Directors to take action. In addition, the time and effort involved in launching an Inspection Panel claim may increase solidarity among claimants, empower them to have a dialogue with government officials and project authorities, increase awareness within the country, and strengthen the networks of support at the local, national, and international levels.[93]

Concluding Remarks

The struggle for accountability and responsibility continues. At present, the World Bank Inspection Panel is the only platform through which people can raise their concerns with the Bank and have them evaluated by a somewhat independent institution, thus initiating a process that may trigger a remedy or contribute to a policy change. The Panel is not yet mature. It must continue its efforts to increase awareness of its role and to ensure that its light caseload is not due to claimant access issues.

Yet, if claimants go into the process aware of the Panel's limitations and pursue an Inspection Panel claim as part of a broader strategy for voicing their discontent, the Panel can be a useful tool to help increase accountability at the World Bank and promote more sustainable aid to development. The Panel process can contribute to drawing attention to the problems generated by lending decisions and to promoting respect for human rights and environmental protection. By allowing individuals to play a role in international

91 *Id.*, at 37.

92 Fox, *supra* note 18.

93 Clark, *supra* note 61, at 47.

relations mechanisms, the Panel can also help empower and organize local communities, giving them valuable mechanisms to advance their rights under the emerging normative framework applicable to Bank projects. This can have real impacts, both in particular projects and in promoting institutional learning for sustainable development.

The Panel's creation signifies a door opening, if only a crack, to the accountability of international financial institutions vis-à-vis the individuals adversely affected by aid's unintended consequences. The Panel reflects a growing recognition of participation rights as well as a march toward the responsibilities of international organizations.[94] While the door is far from being wide open, at least it is no longer locked. The challenge, going forward, is to remove the door from its hinges, so it stays open and can never be closed again. While this may constitute a dramatic shift in power in respect to states and their citizens, the growth of the Bank's public decision-making power, and therefore its ability to affect individuals' livelihoods, makes this shift not only justifiable but also clearly necessary. Traditional roles ascribed to international organizations, states, and individuals no longer make sense when international organizations such as the Bank wield so much influence over states and their citizens. It seems unlikely that the influence of the Bank will diminish in the foreseeable future, so the Panel is a necessary first step toward greater accountability of multilateral development banks.

---

94 *See* Mayer, *supra* note 4.

Annex: Summary of Requests for Inspection (as of June 2014)

No.	Name of Case	Date Received	Registration	Panel Recommendation	Approved by Board	Panel's Activity	Final Outcome
94	Armenia: Education Improvement Project	16 May 2014	Pending				Case pending
93	Tajikistan / Kyrgyz Republic / Afghanistan / Pakistan: Central Asia South Asia Electricity Transmission and Trade Project (CASA-1000)	21 Apr. 2014	Pending				Case pending
92	Sri Lanka: Road Sector Assistance Project–Second Additional Financing	24 Mar. 2014	Pending				Case pending
91	Nigeria: Lagos Metropolitan Development and Governance Project	30 Sept. 2013	Deferred decision, in implementation of the pilot approach to support early solutions in the Inspection Panel process				Case pending
90	Nepal: Enhanced Vocational Education and Training Project	25 Sept. 2013	No				Management immediately agreed to take action
89	Uzbekistan: Second Rural Enterprise Support Project	5 Sept. 2013	Yes	Deferred its decision, pending			Case pending
88	Romania: Mine Closure, Environment and Socio-Economic Regeneration Project	2 July 2013	No				Ineligibility (IV)
87	Nepal: Power Development Project	20 July 2013	Yes	Investigation	Yes	Eligibility Report	Investigation pending

86	Malawi: Second National Water Development Project–Additional Financing	22 May 2013	No				Ineligibility (IV)
85	Arab Republic of Egypt: Giza North Power Project	21 Feb. 2013	Yes	No investigation	Yes	Eligibility Report	
84	Kenya: Natural Resource Management Project	14 Jan. and 28 June 2013	Yes	Investigation	Yes	Eligibility Report and Initial Investigation Plan	Investigation pending
83	Afghanistan: Sustainable Development of Natural Resources–Additional Financing, and Sustainable Development of Natural Resources II	3 and 6 Dec. 2012	Yes	No investigation	Yes	Eligibility Report	
82	Ethiopia: Protection of Basic Services Program Phase II Additional Financing and Promoting Basic Services Phase III Project	24 Sept. 2012	Yes	Investigation	Yes	Eligibility Report and Investigation Plan	Investigation pending
81	India: Vishnugad Pipalkoti Hydro Electric Project	23 July 2012	Yes	Investigation	Yes	Eligibility Report and Initial Investigation Plan	Investigation pending
80	India: Improving Rural Livelihoods through Carbon Sequestration Project	23 Apr. 2012	Yes	No investigation	Yes	Eligibility Report	
79	Kenya: Energy Sector Recovery Project	10 May 2012	Yes	No investigation	Yes	Eligibility Report	
78	Kosovo: Kosovo Power Project (Proposed)	29 Mar. 2012	Yes	No investigation	Yes	Eligibility Report	

77	Argentina: Santa Fe Infrastructure Project and Provincial Road Infrastructure Project	2 Sept. 2011	No				Ineligibility (IV)
76	Israel / Jordan / West Bank and Gaza: Red Sea–Dead Sea Water Conveyance Study Program	24 June 2011	Yes	No investigation	Yes	Eligibility Report	
74	Kazakhstan: South-West Roads: Western Europe–Western China International Transit Corridor (CAREC-1b & 6b) (2011) (Second Request)	15 June 2011	Yes	No investigation	Yes	Eligibility Report	Arrangement between Management and the requesters
73	Argentina: Second Norte Grande Water Infrastructure Project	4 May 2011	Yes	No investigation	Yes	Eligibility Report	
72/ 75	India: Madhya Pradesh Water Sector Restructuring Project (2010) (First Request)	31 Aug. 2010	Yes	No investigation	Yes	Eligibility Report	
71	Lebanon: Greater Beirut Water Supply Project	4 Nov. 2010 and 16 July 2011	Yes	Investigation (first eligibility report), no investigation (second eligibility report)	No (calls for additional consideration of a study commissioned by Management)	Two Eligibility Reports	Additional actions by Management following the first Eligibility Report
70	Tajikistan: Energy Loss Reduction Project (Request from Uzbekistan)	8 Oct. 2010	Yes	No investigation	Yes	Eligibility Report	Ineligibility (II)
69	Liberia: Development Forestry Sector Management Project	24 Sept. 2010	Yes	No investigation	Yes	Eligibility Report	Arrangement between Management and the requesters

68	Poland: Third Employment, Entrepreneurship and Human Capital Development Policy Loan	14 June 2010	No				Ineligibility (II)
67	Chile: Quilleco Hydropower Project	21 Apr. 2010	Yes	No investigation	Yes	Two Eligibility Reports	Management revised its program
66	Kazakhstan: South-West Roads: Western Europe–Western China International Transit Corridor (CAREC-1b & 6b) (2010) (First Request)	24 Apr. 2010	Yes	No investigation	Yes	Eligibility Report	The initial program was slightly modified
65	South Africa: Eskom Investment Support Project	6 Apr. 2010	Yes	Investigation	Yes	Eligibility Report and Investigation Report	Board approves a set of measures agreed to by Management and the borrowing government, case pending
64	Pakistan: Tax Administration Reform Project	22 Dec. 2009	Yes	No investigation	Yes	Eligibility Report	Arrangement between Management and the requesters (19 March 2010)
62	Papua New Guinea: Smallholder Agriculture Development Project	8 Dec. 2009	Yes	Investigation	Yes	Eligibility Report and Investigation Report	Board approves Management Action Plan (13 Dec. 2011
61	Peru: Lima Urban Transport Project	1 Oct. 2009	Yes	Investigation	Yes	Eligibility Report and Investigation Report	Board approves Management Action Plan (16 June 2011)

60	Cambodia: Land Management and Administration Project	4 Sept. 2009	Yes	Investigation	Yes	Two Eligibility Reports and Investigation Report	Board approves Management Action Plan (8 March 2011)
59	Kenya: Export Development Project	21 Apr. 2009	No				
58	India: Mumbai Urban Transport Project (Third Request)	29 May 2009	Yes	No investigation	Yes	Eligibility Report	Arrangement between Management and the requesters (27 June 2009)
57	Republic of Yemen: Institutional Reform Development Policy Financing	13 Apr. 2009	Yes	No investigation	Yes	Two Eligibility Reports and Statement of the Panel Chairman to the Board	Management revises its program (consultations)
54/55/63	Democratic Republic of Congo: Private Sector Development and Competitiveness Project	25 Feb., 13 March, and 15 Dec. 2009	Yes	No investigation	Yes	Three Eligibility Reports	Management revises its program
53/56	Panama: Land Administration Project	25 Feb. and 17 March 2009	Yes	Investigation	Yes	Eligibility Report and Investigation Report	Board approves Management Action Plan (3 Feb. 2011)
52	Colombia: Bogota Urban Services Project	30 Oct. 2007	Yes	No investigation	Yes	Eligibility Report	Ineligibility (III)
51	Argentina: Santa Fe Road Infrastructure Project and Provincial Road Infrastructure Project (Third Request)	13 Sept. 2007	Yes	Investigation	Yes	Eligibility Report and Investigation Report	Board approves Management Action Plan (20 Oct. 2009)

50	Cameroon: Urban Development Project and Douala Infrastructure Development Project	5 Sept. 2007	No				Ineligibility (IV)
49	Ghana: Second Urban Environment Sanitation Project	16 Aug. 2007	Yes	Investigation	Yes	Eligibility Report and Investigation Report	Board approves Management Action Plan (18 June 2009)
47 /48	Albania: Integrated Coastal Zone Management and Clean-Up Project	30 July and 13 Aug. 2007	Yes	Investigation on the matters raised by the first request	Yes	Eligibility Report and Investigation Report	Board approves Management Action Plan (17 Feb. 2009)
46	Albania: Power Sector Generation and Restructuring Project	30 Apr. 2007	Yes	Investigation	Yes	Eligibility Report and Investigation Report	Revised set of Management actions (19 Nov. 2009)
45	India: Uttaranchal Decentralized Watershed Development Project	7 Mar. 2007	Yes	No investigation	Yes	Eligibility Report	
44	Uganda: Private Power Generation Project	5 Mar. 2007	Yes	Investigation	Yes	Eligibility Report and Investigation Report	Board approves Management Action Plan (4 Dec. 2008)
42/ 43	Argentina: Santa Fe Road Infrastructure Project (Proposed) and Provincial Road Infrastructure Project	28 Aug. and 21 Sept. 2006	Yes	No investigation	Yes	Eligibility Report	
41	Brazil: Parana Biodiversity Project (2006)	10 July 2006	Yes	No investigation	Yes	Two Eligibility Reports	Amendment of the Grant Agreement (2 Feb. 2007)
40	Nigeria: West African Gas Pipeline Project (2006)	27 Apr. 2006	Yes	Investigation	Yes	Two Eligibility Reports and Investigation Report	An action plan is implemented by the Bank with several local actors (5 Aug. 2008)

39	Romania: Mine Closure and Social Mitigation Project (2006)	6 Jan. 2006	Yes	No investigation	Yes	Eligibility Report	An action plan is implemented by the Bank with several local actors (26 Jan. 2006)
38	Honduras: Land Administration Project (2006)	3 Jan. 2006	Yes	Investigation	Yes	Eligibility Report and Investigation Report	Board approves Management Action Plan (4 Oct. 2007)
37	Democratic Republic of Congo: Transitional Support for Economic Recovery and Emergency Economic and Social Reunification Support Project	19 Nov. 2005	Yes	Investigation	Yes	Eligibility Report and Investigation Report	Board approves Management Action Plan (9 Jan. 2008)
36	Cambodia: Forest Concession Management and Control Pilot Project	28 Jan. 2005	Yes	Investigation	Yes	Eligibility Report and Investigation Report	Board approves Management Action Plan (30 June 2006)
35	Burundi: Public Works and Employment Creation Project	17 Sept. 2004	No				
34	Pakistan: National Drainage Program Project	10 Sept. 2004	Yes	Investigation	Yes	Eligibility Report and Investigation Report	Board approves Management Action Plan (31 Oct. 2006)
32/ 33	India: Mumbai Urban Transport Project	28 Apr. and 29 June 2004	Yes	Investigation	Yes	Eligibility Report, Investigation Report, and Progress Report	Board approves Management Action Plan (28 March 2006)
31	Colombia: Cartagena Water Supply, Sewerage and Environmental Management Project	20 Apr. 2004	Yes	Investigation	Yes	Eligibility Report and Investigation Report	Board approves Management Action Plan (Nov. 2005)

30	Mexico: Indigenous and Community Biodiversity Project (COINBIO)	26 Jan. 2006	Yes	No investigation	Yes	Eligibility Report	
29	Cameroon: Petroleum Development and Pipeline Project	26 Nov. 2003	No				Ineligibility (I, III, IV)
28	Philippines: Manila Second Sewerage Project (MSSP)	26 Sept. 2003	Yes	No investigation	Yes	Eligibility Report	Ineligibility (III)
27	Cameroon: Petroleum Development and Pipeline Project, and Petroleum Environment Capacity Enhancement Project	25 Sept. 2003	Yes	Investigation	Yes	Eligibility Report and Investigation Report	Board approved Management Report and Recommendation in response to the Panel Investigation Report (May 2004)
26	Paraguay/ Argentina: Reform Project for the Water and Telecommunication Sectors, SEGBA V Power Distribution Project (Yacyretá 2002—second request)	17 May 2002	Yes	Investigation	Yes	Eligibility Report, Investigation Report, and Progress Report	Board approved Management Report and Recommendation in response to the Panel Investigation Report
25	Papua New Guinea: Governance Promotion Adjustment Loan	6 Dec. 2001	Yes	No investigation	Yes	Eligibility Report	Ineligibility (II)
24	Uganda: Third Power Project, Fourth Power Project, and proposed Bujagali Hydropower Project	27 July 2001	Yes	Investigation	Yes	Eligibility Report and Investigation Report	Board received Management Report and Recommendation in response to the Panel Investigation Report (June 2002)

23	India: Coal Sector Environmental and Social Mitigation Project and Coal Sector Rehabilitation Project	21 June 2001	Yes	Investigation	Yes	Eligibility Report and Investigation Report	Board approved Management Report and Recommendation in response to the Panel Investigation Report (July 2003)
22	Chad: Petroleum Development and Pipeline Project, Management of the Petroleum Economy Project, and Petroleum Sector Management Capacity Building Project	22 March 2001	Yes	Investigation	Yes	Eligibility Report and Investigation Report	Board received Management Report and Recommendation in response to the Panel Investigation Report (Aug. 2002)
21	India: NTPC Power Generation Project in Singrauli (Second Request)	27 Nov. 2000	No				Ineligibility (IV)
20	Ecuador: Mining Development and Environmental Control Technical Assistance Project	13 Dec. 1999	Yes	Investigation	Yes	Eligibility Report and Investigation Report	Board approved Management Report and Recommendation in response to the Panel Investigation Report (Apr. 2001)
19	Kenya: Lake Victoria Environmental Management Project	12 Oct. 1999	Yes	Investigation	Yes	Eligibility Report and Investigation Report	Board approved Management Report and Recommendation in response to the Panel Investigation Report (May 2001)

18	Brazil: Land Reform and Poverty Alleviation Project (Second Request)	14 Sept. 1999	Yes	No investigation	Yes	Eligibility Report	Ineligibility (III)
17	Argentina: Special Structural Adjustment Loan	26 July 1999	Yes	No investigation	Yes	Eligibility Report	
16	China: Western Poverty Reduction Project	18 June 1999	Yes	Investigation	Yes	Eligibility Report and Investigation Report	The beneficiary state continues the project with its own resources (July 2000)
15	Lesotho: Lesotho Highlands Water Project	26 Apr. 1999	Yes	No investigation	Yes	Eligibility Report	Ineligibility (II)
14	Brazil: Land Reform and Poverty Alleviation Pilot Project	14 Dec. 1998	Yes	No investigation	Yes	Eligibility Report	
13	Nigeria: Lagos Drainage and Sanitation Project	17 June 1998	Yes	No investigation	Yes	Eligibility Report	
12	Lesotho–South Africa: Proposed Phase 1B of Lesotho Highlands Water Project	6 May 1998	Yes	No investigation	Yes	Eligibility Report	Ineligibility (II)
11	India: Ecodevelopment Project	2 Apr. 1998	Yes	Investigation	No	Eligibility Report	
10	India: NTPC Power Generation Project in Singrauli	1 May 1997	Yes	Investigation	Partly approved a limited investigation (a desk study in Wash., DC) after reviewing a remedial Action Plan submitted by Management	Eligibility Report and Report on Desk Investigation	Management Action Plan approved by the Board

9	Brazil: Itaparica Resettlement and Irrigation Project	12 Mar. 1997	Yes	Investigation	No	Eligibility Report	Approval of Government of Brazil Action Plan (to complete project with its own funding with continued Bank supervision for two more years)
8	Bangladesh: Jute Sector Adjust-ment Credit	13 Nov. 1996	Yes	No investigation	Yes	Eligibility Report and Progress Report	Project revised
7	Argentina / Paraguay: Yacyretá Hydroelectric Project	30 Sept. 1996	Yes	Investigation	No	Eligibility Report and Progress Report	The Board approved two Action Plans agreed to between the Bor-rowers and the Bank Management (Feb. 1997)
6	Bangladesh: Jamuna Multipurpose Bridge Project	23 Aug. 1996	Yes	No investigation	Yes	Eligibility Report	Project revised to respond to claim
5	Chile: Financing of Hydroelectric Dams in the Bio Bio River	17 Nov. 1995	No (project financed by IFC–outside of Panel's mandate)				Ineligibility (II). Bank's President appointed external consultant to review the project
4	Brazil: Rondonia Natural Resources Management Project	16 June 1995	Yes	Investigation	No	Eligibility Report, Addi-tional Review Report, and Progress Report	Partial concession to affected people; limited Panel role in monitoring implementa-tion
3	Tanzania: Power VI Project	16 May 1995	Yes	No investigation	Yes	Eligibility Report	Ineligibility (II)

2	Ethiopia: Compensation for Expropriation and Extension of IDA Credits to Ethiopia	2 May 1995	No				Ineligibility (II)
1	Nepal: Arun III Hydroelectric Project	24 Oct. 1994	Yes	Investigation	Yes	Eligibility Report and Investigation Report	On the basis of a study commissioned to independent experts, the Bank's President decides to withdraw financing for the Project (Aug. 1995)

Source: World Bank Inspection Panel website, http://ewebapps.worldbank.org/apps/ip/Pages/Panel_Cases.aspx (accessed June 6, 2014).

24

The Inspection Panel of the World Bank

An Effective Extrajudicial Complaint Mechanism?

KARIN LUKAS

The World Bank's Inspection Panel was established by a resolution of the Bank's Board of Executive Directors in 1999[1] in response to external demands for greater transparency and accountability, as well as Bank Management's efforts to improve the efficiency of World Bank projects.[2] The Inspection Panel's mandate is to carry out independent investigations of Bank-financed projects[3] to verify that the projects comply with the Bank's policies and procedures. These investigations are triggered by requests of claimants that demonstrate that the claimants have been, or are likely to be, harmed as a result of noncompliance.

The Inspection Panel (hereafter "the Panel") is an investigatory body without decision-making powers. Thus, its "decisions" are not binding for the parties involved and must be seen as recommendations. For a complaint to be eligible for an investigation, it must demonstrate that the claimant's rights or interests have been or are likely to be directly affected by an action or omission of the Bank resulting from a failure to follow its policies and procedures, that the failure has or is likely to have material adverse effects on the claimant, and that no more than 95 percent of the project's funding has been disbursed. Other than persons affected by Bank operations, only an Executive Director or the Board may file a complaint. To investigate the matter, the Panel may visit the project site, conduct public hearings, and hire independent experts. However, an on-site visit requires the consent of the government concerned, which, in some cases, has been an obstacle.[4] The Panel investigates the case based on relevant policies and procedures,[5] and presents its findings in a

---

1 Intl. Bank Reconstruction & Dev. & Intl. Dev. Assn., *The World Bank Inspection Panel* (IBRD Res. No. 93-10; IDA Res. 93-6, adopted by the World Bank Board Exec. Directors, Sept. 22, 1993) [hereinafter Inspection Panel Resolution].

2 Ibrahim Shihata, *The World Bank Inspection Panel* 5 (World Bank 1994); Inspection Panel Resolution, *supra* note 1.

3 These are projects supported by the International Bank for Reconstruction and Development (IBDR), the International Development Association (IDA), or the Global Environment Facility.

4 *See,* for example, the NTPC Power Generation Project, Singrauli, where the Indian government refused consent, and the Panel was restricted to a desk study (Inspection Panel Report and Recommendation, July 24, 1997).

5 These include the following (which are relevant from a human rights perspective): operational policy (OP) & bank procedure (BP) on development cooperation and conflict; operational directive (OD) on indigenous peoples; OD 4.15, on poverty reduction; OD 4.30, on involuntary resettlement; OP 4.20 & BP 4.20, on gender and development. For a complete list, *see* http://web.worldbank.org/WBSITE/EXTERNAL/PROJECTS/EXTPOLICIES/EXTOPMANUAL/0,,menuPK:64701637~pagePK:51628525~piPK:64857279~theSitePK:502184,00.html.

report presented to the Board, the president, and Management. The report includes the Panel's conclusion as to whether the Bank was in compliance with its policies and procedures. The Board makes the final decision on any action to be taken. When the Panel was established, it was a unique complaint mechanism among international organizations; since its creation, other development banks have installed similar mechanisms.[6]

The Panel complaint procedure is a three-phase process. It is set into motion by a decision of the Panel on the admissibility of the request (the admissibility phase). Next, Bank Management responds, for example, by proposing an action plan (the Management phase). Last, the Bank's Board of Executive Directors either approves or rejects the request (the Board phase). Approval authorizes the Panel to conduct an investigation. Each of these phases is discussed in the following section.

The Complaint Process

Requests made to the Panel are accepted only when they are filed by "two or more persons who share some common interests or concerns."[7] Only in exceptional cases and with prior consent of the Board may an international NGO file a complaint as a representative of an individual or community. In such cases, formal proof of representation is mandatory.

Requests are submitted to the World Bank office in the country where the requester resides or to the office nearest the country of residence. If the Bank office response does not meet the concerns of the requester, a "request for inspection"[8] may be submitted to the Panel. These requests are accepted by the Panel only if an adverse effect (material or imminent) has arisen directly through an action of the Bank or an omission on the part of the Bank to follow its operational policies and procedures; examples might include environmental damage, involuntary resettlement, or impinging on the rights of indigenous peoples.[9] A request can be submitted before or after a project has been approved by the Bank.

---

6 *See,* for example, the Accountability Mechanism of the Asian Development Bank, the Independent Consultation and Investigation Mechanism of the Inter-American Development Bank, the Independent Review Mechanism of the African Development Bank, and the Project Complaint Mechanism of the European Bank for Reconstruction and Development. On the latter, *see* http://www.ebrd.com/pages/project/pcm.shtml.

7 *Review of the Resolution Establishing the Inspection Panel, 1996 Clarification of Certain Aspects of the Resolution* (World Bank 1996), http://ewebapps.worldbank.org/apps/ip/PanelMandateDocuments/ReviewResolution1966.pdf.

8 World Bank Inspection Panel, *Suggested Format for a Request for Inspection* (brochure), http://siteresources.worldbank.org/EXTINSPECTIONPANEL/Resources/BrochureEnglishwhole.pdf.

9 World Bank, *Processing a Request* (Inspection Panel page at the World Bank's website), http://web.worldbank.org/WBSITE/EXTERNAL/EXTINSPECTIONPANEL/0,,contentMDK:20173251~menuPK:64129467~pagePK:64129751~piPK:64128378~theSitePK:380794,00.html (March 8, 2013).

There are three possible outcomes of a request for inspection. First, before submitting a request, affected persons must approach the Bank's Management to see if the parties can resolve their concerns directly. When a resolution is not reached, the Panel registers the request and encourages dialogue between the requester and Bank Management. Second, Bank Management responds to "some of the Requester's concerns" with proposed action.[10] In such cases, the Panel postpones its recommendations to give Management and the requester more time to resolve their differences.[11] If a dialogue is established, the Panel may act as a mediator and facilitate a resolution. Third, a full investigation by the Panel is granted to the requesters. During an investigation, Bank Management can develop "action plans" to address any findings of noncompliance by the Panel.[12]

As soon as the Panel determines the eligibility of a request, Bank Management responds to the Panel's initial assessment. At this stage, the Panel may decide whether to collect additional facts with a field visit. By doing so, the Panel may recommend that the Board open the investigation process. The Board is the only body that can authorize this phase. When donor-country directors support a recommendation but the borrower country opposes it, decisions about authorization are postponed or denied.[13] If the Board does not approve an investigation phase, it may authorize the Panel to undertake a review of the existing problems.[14] By doing so, the Panel can decide to collect additional facts with a field visit, which usually includes meetings with affected persons and their organization(s). When no investigation is approved, only an eligibility report (or a final eligibility report, in cases where field visits were conducted) is issued.[15]

In the event of an investigation, the Panel reviews relevant documents, conducts interviews with Bank staff, and visits the borrowing country (which includes having meetings with the requester and other relevant stakeholders). Once the investigation has been completed, the Panel sends an investigation report to the Board and to Bank Management. Management then has six weeks to submit to the Board its own report and recommendations in response to the Panel's findings. The Board makes the final decision on whether to approve Management's and/or the Panel's recommendations. Management

---

10 World Bank, *Message from the Panel*, in *The Inspection Panel Annual Report July 1, 2009 to June 30, 2010* xiv (World Bank 2010).

11 *See* World Bank, *supra* note 9.

12 *Id.*, at xiv.

13 That was the case in the Yacyreta Hydroelectric Project in Argentina and Paraguay in 1996. *See* Kay Treakle & Elías Díaz Peña, *Accountability at the World Bank: What Does It Take? Lessons from the Yacyretá Hydroelectric Project, Argentina/Paraguay*, in *Demanding Accountability: Civil-Society Claims and the World Bank Inspection Panel* 75 (Dana Clark, Jonathan Fox, & Kay Treakle eds., Rowman & Littlefield 2003).

14 *Id.*, at 76.

15 The eligibility report consists of the registration of the request, its eligibility and a case description, and Panel recommendations and annexes.

recommendations are intended to bring the project into compliance with the Bank's policies and procedures. At this stage, the Board may ask the Panel whether the consultations between Management and the requester, as well as other affected persons, were conducted appropriately prior to approving Management's recommendations for remedial measures.[16] It should be noted here that once a request has been filed, the requester largely loses any option to participate in further dialogue. Nor can the requester comment on Management's response or have access to information before decisions are made about the claim.[17]

The Panel procedure does not include an appeals mechanism or a follow-up mechanism.[18] The reports do not contain information on monitoring or on follow-up activities concerning the Panel's recommendations. There have been instances where the Board has endorsed Management's suggestion to monitor a project to ensure that outstanding issues relating to resettlement are substantially resolved and to report to the Board on these issues at regular intervals;[19] however, the Panel does not participate in this monitoring phase.[20] Hence, in the author's view, the likelihood that remedial actions or action plans may fall short of successful and effective implementation is increased. Moreover, the Panel does not have the power to impose any sanctions to enforce Bank policies. It is the Board's role to consider the findings and to decide what actions should be taken to enforce Bank policies.

Reforming the Bank's Safeguard Policies

In response to the changing global context, the Bank has undertaken a review of its environmental and social safeguard policies. The Bank's review is part of an operational policy reform process that will affect the future design of development projects. Following the October 2012 release of an "approach paper"[21] for the safeguard policies review process, the Bank began a three-

---

16 *See* World Bank, *supra* note 9.

17 See Dana Clark, Jonathan Fox, & Kay Treakle, *Lessons Learned*, in *Demanding Accountability: Civil-Society Claims and the World Bank Inspection Panel* 267 (Dana Clark, Jonathan Fox, & Kay Treakle eds., Rowman & Littlefield 2003).

18 On very rare occasions, the Board has invited the Panel to review Management's action plan, usually instead of endorsing a full investigation, but this can certainly not be seen as a regular follow-up procedure. *See*, for example, the case of Argentina/Paraguay, Yacyretá Hydroelectric Project, INSP/R96-2).

19 This was, for example, the case in the Coal Sector Mitigation Project and Coal Sector Rehabilitation Project, India, in 2001. *See* Elvira Nurmukhametova, *Problems in Connection with the Efficiency of the World Bank Inspection Panel* vol. 10, 405 (Max Planck Y.B. U.N. L. 2006).

20 For a list of Management follow-up measures after Panel investigations as of April 2011, *see Status of Follow-up Progress Reports by Management to Panel Investigations* (Apr. 2011) at the Bank's website, http://siteresources.worldbank.org/EXTINSPECTIONPANEL/Resources/Post_Investigation_IPN_Cases_April_2011.pdf.

21 Http://siteresources.worldbank.org/EXTSAFEPOL/Resources/584434-1306431390058/SafeguardsReviewApproachPaper.pdf.

stage consultation process that will run at least through early 2015.[22] Civil society organizations (CSOs) from various countries and regions will participate in the review.[23]

In 2010, the World Bank's Independent Evaluation Group (IEG) undertook an evaluation of the Bank's safeguard policies.[24] According to this evaluation, the safeguard policies have been effective in avoiding or mitigating adverse impacts, particularly in high-risk projects. The IEG also found that the quality of the safeguards during design and appraisal improved during the review period (1999–2008). However, the IEG also identified a need to adapt the safeguard policies to reflect the changing context in which the Bank operates, including a rapidly changing business environment, new lending modalities and financing instruments, and evolving best practices and borrower needs. Also recommended was a stronger focus on using the safeguard polices to support environmentally and socially sustainable development and to assess a wider range of potential social risks and impacts.

Some stakeholders have requested that the Bank consider in the review process a number of areas that are not addressed under the current set of safeguard policies. These include human rights; occupational health and safety; gender; disability; the free, prior, and informed consent of indigenous peoples; land tenure; natural resources; and climate change.

The examination of these areas, and if and how they can best be addressed by the Bank, will be part of the review process. The Bank will undertake an internal dialogue on these issues, followed by consultations with shareholders and external experts.

The core policies under review are the eight environmental and social safeguard policies: Operational Policy (OP) 4.01, Environmental Assessment; OP 4.04, Natural Habitats; OP 4.09, Pest Management; OP 4.10, Indigenous Peoples; OP 4.11, Physical Cultural Resources; OP 4.12, Involuntary Resettlement; OP 4.36, Forests; and OP 4.37, Safety of Dams. Also under review is OP 4.00, the Policy on Piloting the Use of Borrower Systems for Environmental and Social Safeguards ("Use of Country Systems"), which is more process- and less content-oriented.

CSOs demand that the safeguard policies must continue to be based on mandatory, enforceable, time-bound requirements and that the Bank must maintain its responsibility to ensure that the borrower complies with these policies. The same CSOs criticize the approach of the International Finance

---

22 For more information on the review process, see World Bank, *The World Bank Safeguard Policies: Proposed Review and Update* 14 (approach paper, World Bank 2012), http://consultations.worldbank.org/Data/hub/files/consultation-template/review-and-update-world-bank-safeguard-policies/en/phases/safeguardsreviewapproachpaper.pdf.

23 Bank Info. Ctr., *World Bank Safeguards Review*, http://www.bicusa.org/issues/safeguards/.

24 World Bank, *Safeguards and Sustainability in a Changing World: An Independent Evaluation of World Bank Group Experience* (IEG Study Series, World Bank 2010), http://go.worldbank.org/ZA4YFV9OL0.

Corporation, which relies on self-reporting by borrowers, and the Bank's recent Investment Lending Reform, which relegated many requirements to nonbinding guidance.[25]

This safeguard policies reform process is likely to have a decisive impact on social and environmental considerations in future Bank projects.[26] Its outcome is still unclear, but the Bank is aware of the risk that a change of the current system might be viewed by CSOs as a dilution of the existing standards. The review process envisaged by the Bank therefore includes broad external stakeholder consultations. A first draft of the revised safeguard framework is under way and planned for submission to the Executive Board's Committee on Development Effectiveness.[27]

The Strengths and Weaknesses of the Complaint Mechanism: A Review of Relevant Cases

This section analyzes Inspection Panel cases that include both the eligibility and the investigation phase, and touch on issues with human rights relevance. These issues are involuntary resettlement, consultations with project-affected persons, rights of indigenous people, compensation, and poverty reduction. In total, 26 cases[28] were analyzed. The section does not discuss each case in detail, but the chapter's concluding remarks are based on the case analyses,[29] outlining the strengths and weaknesses of the Panel process.

---

25 *See*, for example, *Forest Peoples, Forwards or Backwards? The World Bank's Safeguard Review and Update* (Apr. 29, 2013), http://www.forestpeoples.org/topics/safeguard-accountablility-issues/news/2013/04/forwards-or-backwards-world-bank-s-safeguard--0.

26 *See* also Jochen von Bernstorff & Philipp Dann, *Reforming the World Bank's Safeguards: A Comparative Legal Analysis* (report, German Fed. Ministry Econ. Cooperation Dev., 2013), http://www.jura.uni-tuebingen.de/professoren_und_dozenten/vonbernstorff/projekte /World Banks Safeguardsacomparativelegalanalysis.pdf.

27 *See* http://www.bicusa.org/world-bank-spring-meeting-safeguards-setting-standards-for-sustainable-development/.

28 These are Nepal, Arun III: India, NTPC Power Project; China, Western Poverty Reduction Project; Kenya, Lake Victoria Environmental Project; Ecuador, Mining Development and Environmental Control Technical Assistance Project; Chad, Petroleum Development and Pipeline Project; India, Coal Sector Environmental and Social Mitigation Project; Uganda, Third Power Project, Paraguay/Argentina, Reform Project for the Water and Telecommunication Sectors (Yacyretá 2002); Cameroon, Petroleum Development and Pipeline Project; Colombia, Cartagena Water Supply Project; India, Mumbai Urban Transport Project; Cambodia, Forest Concession Management and Control Pilot Project; Democratic Republic of Congo, Transitional Support for Economic Recovery Grant Project; Honduras, Land Administration Project; Nigeria, West African Gas Pipeline Project; Uganda, Private Power Generation Project; Albania, Power Sector Generation and Restructuring Project; Albania, Integrated Coastal Zone Project; Ghana, Second Urban Environment Sanitation Project (UESP II); Argentina, Santa Fe Infrastructure Project; Panama, Land Administration Project; Cambodia, Management and Administration Project; Papua New Guinea, Smallholder Agriculture Development Project; South Africa, Eskom Investment Support Project.

29 The detailed case analysis is part of a broader research project of the Ludwig Boltzmann Institute of Human Rights on extrajudicial complaint mechanisms, which will be completed in 2015. A pilot study was conducted in 2013. *See* Barbara Linder, Karin Lukas, & Astrid

Transparency of the Process and Enhanced Accountability

A major strength of the Inspection Panel procedure is its transparency. All Panel reports concerning eligibility and investigation (including recommendations) are publicly disclosed and accessible on the Panel's website. Similarly, all Bank Management's responses to the requests are publicly available. Rejected cases are also made public. This feature is indispensable in the "tracking" of requests received by the Panel, the number of cases accepted and rejected, and, to a lesser extent, the impacts made by the investigations.

The cases reviewed, particularly those regarding the concerns of indigenous groups and resettlement issues, show that the Panel process provided the opportunity to raise issues that seemed difficult to solve in the local or national (legal) context.[30] The complaint mechanism was at times used to draw attention to human rights–related issues that may have been ignored in the past by the respective authorities.

According to the Panel itself, its work indirectly triggered the establishment of the Bank's Quality Assurance Group, which led to increased accountability and improved Bank performance.[31]

However, the mechanism also faces a number of impediments. Many projects reviewed suffered from insufficient assessment of the project situation and lack of integration of sociocultural aspects prior to and during project implementation by Bank Management.[32] The difficulties in planning and implementing projects in former areas of conflict and/or developing countries require comprehensive baseline studies prior to project planning. Most negative effects linked to the Bank's projects were rooted in insufficient knowledge about indigenous cultures;[33] existing conflicts with the national authorities, especially in connection with land rights;[34] or informal structures in the borrowing country.[35]

Steinkellner, *The Right to Remedy* (Ludwig Boltzmann Inst. Hum. Rights 2013).

30 *See*, for example, the West African Gas Pipeline Project in Nigeria, the Mumbai Urban Transport Project, and the Land Administration Project in Honduras.

31 World Bank, *Accountability at the World Bank: The Inspection Panel 10 Years On* 79 (World Bank 2003).

32 *See*, for example, Inspection Panel Investigation Report (IPIR) Nepal Arun III (1995), 29; IPIR Ecuador Mining Project (2001), 13; IPIR Colombia Water Project (2005), 18; IPIR Private Power Generation (Bujagali) Project, Uganda (2001), 76; IPIR Paraguay/Argentina Yacyretá Hydroelectric Project (2004), xxv; IPIR Mumbai Urban Transport Project, India (2005), xi, xiii; Argentina Santa Fe Road Infrastructure Project (2009), xii.

33 IPIR Private Power Generation (Bujagali) Project, Uganda (2002), lii; IPIR Emergency Economic and Social Reunification Support Project & Transnational Support for Economic Recovery Grant Operation Democratic Republic of Congo [hereinafter DRC Reunification Project] (2007), iii, ix.

34 Inspection Panel Eligibility Report (IPER) Nepal Arun III (1994), 12; IPIR China Western Poverty Reduction Project (1999), xvii, para. 23; IPIR Coal Sector Environmental and Social Mitigation Project, India (2002), xii; IPIR Land Management and Administration Project, Cambodia (2010), xviii; IPIR Panama Land Administration Project (2010), xxi.

35 IPIR Integrated Coastal Zone Management and Clean-up Project, Albania (2007), xii.

Communication and access to information is another critical issue. Illiteracy as well as geographical distance to information and cultural centers are factors to be taken into account when devising information strategies. These factors were sometimes either not given due regard or neglected, which led to misunderstandings and flawed decisions.[36] The cultural aspects of communication are a critical element for successful World Bank project planning and implementation.[37]

Recurrent issues of controversy included land rights and compensation for resettlement, inadequate consultation, and indigenous rights. Land rights and resettlement were quantitatively the most contested issues.[38] Here, several factors culminate: the project logic that requires that areas be "cleared" of people to install required infrastructure, the communities' dependence on land as a critical income source, and the difficulties of resettlement as such. This problem area is further exacerbated by inadequate information and communication with project-affected persons.[39] Context-specific and culturally sensitive approaches in such complex settings are critical to comply with Bank policies and procedures on consultation with affected groups.

More attention seems to be paid to the assessment of the projects' ecological and environmental impacts than to their social impacts where more technical than contextualized approaches can be applied.[40]

The Significance of Human Rights for the Bank

Another fundamental issue influencing the Panel's mandate and activities is the Bank's position on human rights in general. According to the Bank's Articles of Agreement, "only economic considerations shall be relevant to [the Bank's] decisions."[41] Two legal opinions by the Bank's general counsel at the time explain that the prohibition of political activities of the Bank has to be interpreted as noninterference into a state's affairs regarding "political rights," as long as this has no demonstrable effect on the country's economy.[42] In recent years, however, there has been growing recognition by the Bank of the need to address human rights in a more explicit way. A legal opinion by the former Senior Vice-President and General Counsel, Roberto Dañino, indicates that human rights may constitute legitimate considerations for the Bank

36 IPER Ecuador Mining Development Project (2000), 9, 18; IPIR Colombia Cartagena Water Supply, Sewerage and Environmental Management Project (2004), 20.

37 *See*, in particular, IPIR Smallholder Agriculture Development Project, Independent State of Papua New Guinea (2011), xvi.

38 Of the 25 cases identified as relating to human rights issues, 19 dealt with land issues and/or resettlement.

39 India Coal Sector Environmental and Social Mitigation Project; Cambodia Forest Concession Management and Control Pilot Project; Chad Petroleum Development and Pipeline Project.

40 *See*, for example, the IPIR Smallholder Agriculture Development Project, Independent State of Papua New Guinea (2011), xvi.

41 IBRD, Articles of Agreement, art. IV (Operations), sec. 10; IDA, Articles of Agreement, Article V (Operations), sec. 6.

42 *See* World Bank, *supra* note 31, at 96.

where they have economic ramifications or impacts, and confirms the facilitative role the Bank may play in supporting its member-states to fulfill their human rights obligations.[43]

This legal opinion represents a considerable step farther; however, the Bank has not yet instituted a comprehensive approach to human rights at the policy and operational levels.[44] While there are a growing number of human rights–related safeguard policies, several gaps in human rights coverage remain.

The Panel dealt with human rights for the first time in the Chad Petroleum Development and Pipeline Project,[45] where a requester alleged that he had been tortured because of his opposition to the project. The Panel took the approach of finding "human rights implicitly embedded in various policies of the Bank," and thus within the "Panel's jurisdiction."[46] Bank Management "by and large" agreed with this approach.[47] In this case, the Panel concluded that the Bank should be "more forthcoming about articulating its role in promoting rights within the countries in which it operates . . . [and] perhaps this case should lead . . . to study [of] the wider ramifications of human rights violations as these relate to the overall success or failure of policy compliance in future Bank-financed projects."[48] Since then, steps in this direction have been made, and it remains to be seen whether the Bank safeguard policies review will further develop the current position.

The Bank's Policies and Procedures

Another decisive issue is the application of Bank policies and procedures by Bank Management and whether there is a certain margin of appreciation in their application. In some cases—such as the India Coal Sector Environmental and Social Mitigation Project, the Cambodia Forest Concession Management and Control Pilot Project, and the Chad Petroleum Development Project—Bank Management applied policies inaccurately or gave no information or misinformation. According to Elvira Nurmukhametova, one reason could lie in the Bank's view that the policies and procedures are more or less flexible rules that allow for a certain margin of appreciation.[49] The Panel, in contrast, is of the opinion that these norms, particularly environmental standards, require

---

43 Roberto Dañino, *Legal Opinion on Human Rights and the Work of the World Bank*, Jan. 27, 2006. This document is not publicly available but is referred to in several documents; *see*, for example, World Bank, *FAQ Human Rights*, http://web.worldbank.org/WBSITE/EXTERNAL/EXTSITE TOOLS/0,,contentMDK:20749693~pagePK:98400~piPK:98424~theSitePK:95474,00.html.

44 Adam McBeth, *A Right by Any Other Name: The Evasive Engagement of International Financial Institutions with Human Rights* 40 (5) Geo. Wash. Intl. L. Rev. 1101, 1103 (2009).

45 Inspection Panel, Chad: Petroleum Development and Pipeline Project (2001), Mar. 22, 2001.

46 Edward Ayensu, *Remarks of the Chairman of the Inspection Panel to the Board of Executive Directors on the Chad-Cameroon Pipeline Projects* (World Bank website, *The Inspection Panel*, Sept. 2002); World Bank, *supra* note 31, at 97.

47 World Bank, *supra* note 31, at 97.

48 *Id.*, at 98.

49 Nurmukhametova, *supra* note 19, at 419.

uniform application and are not subject to discretion. They are binding documents and should be treated as such.[50] According to Benedict Kingsbury, the operational directives have been understood to be obligatory to Bank staff within the Management structure but have been applied and enforced "flexibly" with the objective of "ameliorating project failures and learning for the future."[51] To get a more precise view of binding Bank norms and mere guidelines, the Bank has engaged in the process of developing operating policies and bank procedures (both mandatory) and good practices. The Panel has taken the approach that Bank policies are mandatory for Bank staff and hence give the margin of appreciation only when explicitly indicated.[52] Still, the exact nature and application of Bank policies are ambiguous and cause tension between the Panel and Bank Management. A former chairman of the Inspection Panel has also pointed out that the nonbinding guidelines are not subject to review by the Panel, a situation that has been seen as problematic when Bank Management and Panel interpretations of the guidelines differ in substance.[53]

The analysis of the cases reviewed shows some antagonism between the Panel's findings and Bank Management's position on whether a violation of Bank policies has occurred, particularly in the earlier years of cooperation.[54] The author observes that these conflicting views sometimes continued to exist even after the investigation had ended. An example of this can be found in the Yacyretá Hydroelectric Project case, when the Bank apparently misinterpreted the Panel's findings.[55] In a letter to a Paraguayan newspaper, the Bank's Vice President for Latin America and the Caribbean stated: "The Bank is satisfied with the conclusions of the [Inspection Panel's] report which confirm[s] that the Bank policies on resettlement, the environment, community participation and all other areas were fully met and implemented in the Yacyretá case."[56] This consequently led to an NGO campaign with the involvement of several interna-

---

50 A. G. Gualtieri, *The Environmental Accountability of the World Bank to Non-state Actors* 72 (1) British Y.B. Intl. L. 213, 245 (2001).

51 Benedict Kingsbury, *Operational Policies of International Institutions as Part of the Law-Making Process: The World Bank and Indigenous Peoples*, ch. 14 in *The Reality of International Law* (Guy S. Goodwin-Gill & Stefan Talmon eds., Clarendon 2001), cited in Stefanie Ricarda Roos, *The World Bank Inspection Panel in Its Seventh Year: An Analysis of Its Process, Mandate, and Desirability, with Special Reference to the China (Tibet) Case* vol. 5, 503 (Max Planck Y.B. U.N. L. 2001).

52 For details on the Panel's approach, *see* Roos, *supra* note 51, at 506.

53 Interview with Werner Kiene, former chair of the Inspection Panel (Apr. 25, 2012).

54 The tendency was for Management to deny that there had been a violation of policies. Sometimes Management would even challenge the eligibility of a case to prevent the Panel from examining it. For example, in Argentina's Garden Program, Management doubted the eligibility of the case, maintaining that no supervisory errors had been made and that the participants lacked standing to make a complaint. *See* Victor Abramovich, *Social Protection Conditionality in World Bank Structural Adjustment Loans: The Case of Argentina's Garden Program (Pro-Huerta)*, in *Demanding Accountability: Civil-Society Claims and the World Bank Inspection Panel* 204 (Dana Clark, Jonathan Fox, & Kay Treakle eds., Rowman & Littlefield 2003).

55 *Id.*

56 World Bank, *supra* note 31, at 67.

tional newspapers. Finally, the Bank's president, James Wolfensohn, formally apologized and made press statements expressing the "erroneous description of the findings" released.[57]

Procedural Issues

By the establishment of a two-step procedure in response to requests regarding eligibility criteria, Panel intervention is delayed in cases where serious social and environmental harm takes place. Consequently, there is no possibility for taking procedural measures in cases of imminent danger, a possibility that courts and some human rights mechanisms provide for.[58] The requirement to request the opinion of the responsible Management office can be seen as a barrier for requesters seeking a prompt solution or a timely action from the Panel. This limitation was addressed in the review of the resolution in 1996, after the creation of the Panel. In that review, the Panel clearly stated that the resolution limited the first phase of the inspection process, which ascertains the eligibility of the request, and proposed instead a "preliminary assessment" that could lead to a quick resolution without the need to ask for approval of a full investigation. This would have narrowed the time frame for the acceptance of a request for inspection by the Panel, and it would have reduced the number of days needed for approval or rejection of an investigation process based on the Board's decision. The Board, however, rejected this proposal in its clarification of 1999.

As mentioned earlier, the Panel process foresees that the Panel can formulate two reports, one on eligibility and the other on the investigation. The eligibility report is by its nature less substantial than the investigation report; it contains the reasons why the case was filed, why it was accepted, and the recommendations of the Panel on how to proceed. The investigation report analyzes the compliance or noncompliance of the Bank and the linkages to the borrowers involved. Consequently, it portrays the violations and the lack of success of the policies and performances of both branches (IBDR and IDA) and, to a limited extent, of the borrower in a specific project.

The Board is the only body that can authorize a Panel investigation. In circumstances where the Board has not approved an investigation phase, only an eligibility or final eligibility report is issued. Thus, the strongest and most substantial tool of the Panel can be used only if authorized by the Board. This rule can be seen as a considerable weakness of the procedure.[59] However, in the author's view, it is unlikely that this situation is going to change in the near

---

57 *Id.*, at 68.

58 *See*, for example, Rule 39 of the Rules of the European Court of Human Rights, which provides for interim measures "where there is an imminent risk of irreparable harm."

59 For example, in the Singrauli, Itaparica, and Yacyretá cases, the Board rejected the Panel's recommendation for a full investigation. This led to a high degree of tension. *See* Dana Clark, *Singrauli: An Unfulfilled Struggle for Justice*, in *Demanding Accountability: Civil-Society Claims and the World Bank Inspection Panel* 179 (Dana Clark, Jonathan Fox, & Kay Treakle eds., Rowman & Littlefield 2003).

future due to political reasons. Moreover, the creation of these two reports leaves a certain time gap between the Panel's recommendations and their implementation by Bank Management. As mentioned above, an action plan, or a more elaborate action program, of Bank Management can be implemented before the Panel has formulated its recommendations. In the author's view, the fact that Management can implement action plans without full recognition of the Panel's recommendations in the eligibility phase considerably weakens the mechanism at the moment that it could have the most effective impact.

Some cases reviewed show that the Panel could not propose a final investigation because Bank Management had in the meantime decided to implement an action plan (or sometimes even an action program) in response to the request. Assuming that an action plan is being implemented to settle the differences between parties, it may be considered a foreclosure on the Panel's decision on whether to conduct an investigation. In the case of NTCP India in 1997, the Panel did not fully agree with Management's action plan proposals because they ignored Panel recommendations and the potential efforts of compliance by the IBRD and IDA and the borrowers. This problem is also highlighted by the NGO network International Accountability Project:

> Bank Management will propose an "action plan" in response to the Panel claim or the Panel's report, and the Board will then authorise the Management to implement the plan, with very little oversight or independent on-site verification of the outcomes of the action plans. These plans have been problematic in the past, as they have generally not been developed in consultation with the claimants or the Panel, nor are the claimants or the Panel consulted during its implementation, nor is there sufficient oversight by the Board.[60]

The approach of Bank Management in the earlier periods of cooperation with the Panel to provide remedial action plans prior to or even at the meeting where the Board dealt with the Panel's recommendations for investigation prevented the Panel and the Board from assessing whether these plans fully addressed the requesters' concerns and the Panel's analysis.

This problem is evident in the case of the Argentina/Paraguay Yacyretá Hydroelectric Project (1996),[61] where the Executive Directors decided not to authorize an investigation that the Panel had recommended. Right before the Board's meeting to discuss the Panel's recommendation, Management presented two action plans. Hence, the Executive Directors based their decision on the argument that a number of elements had to be further defined. Serious doubts remained as to whether such speedily developed plans allowed for effective consultation as required by the Bank's policies.[62]

---

60 Friends of the Earth Intl. & Intl. Acctg. Project, *Strategic Guide for Filing Complaints with International Financial Institutions* 17 (Apr. 2004).

61 Argentina/Paraguay: Yacyretá Hydroelectric Project (1996), IBRD Loan 2854-AR/IBRD Loan 3520-AR, P006036.

62 Nurmukhametova, *supra* note 19, at 420. See also World Bank, *supra* note 31, at 63.

Such an approach affects the successful conclusion of complaints; one consequence of this has been the resubmission of complaints.[63] Bank Management should include Panel recommendations when drafting and implementing an action plan, to increase the coherence and effectiveness of both the Panel and Management, and to avoid receiving repeated requests for the same problems. In recent years, the resubmission of cases has somewhat subsided. Similarly, in recent cases, Panel investigation reports have usually been followed up in subsequent remedial action plans of Bank Management.[64]

An additional issue arises in the rare cases where the Bank withdraws from a project because the problems analyzed by the Panel could not be resolved satisfactorily. In these cases of noncompliance with Bank policies and procedures, the loan was canceled, sometimes paralleled by the granting of compensation or the creation of protected areas.[65] This situation mirrors a dilemma confronted by companies aware of human rights: Would it have been better to have stayed? The "exit solution" may leave "burnt earth" behind. As has been shown in a number of cases, the companies that took over the activities from those leaving usually were less or not at all interested in improving the human rights situation.[66]

One case illustrating this dilemma is the China Western Poverty Reduction Project. The objective of this project was to reduce absolute poverty in three provinces of China, particularly through the resettlement of over 50,000 poor farmers to an irrigation project area.[67] A complaint was brought by the International Campaign of Tibet, alleging that Tibetan and Mongolian ethnic peoples would be harmed by the project.[68] The Panel found, among other things, breaches of Bank policies on resettlement and indigenous peoples. Eventually, China withdrew its request for financing from the Bank and decided to implement the project on its own.[69]

In case an exit of the Bank is unavoidable, a constructive outcome could be reached if the cancellation of the loan were linked with remedial measures

---

63 Clark, Fox, & Treakle speak about "one of the most significant weaknesses of the Inspection Panel Process." See Clark, Fox, & Treakle, *supra* note 17, at 266.

64 Linder, Lukas, & Steinkellner, *supra* note 29, at 122–25.

65 *See,* for example, the result of the panel process in the Arun III Hydroelectric Project in Nepal, October 1994. An analysis of the case is provided by Richard Bissell, *The Arun III Hydroelectric Project, Nepal,* in *Demanding Accountability: Civil-Society Claims and the World Bank Inspection Panel* 25–44 (Dana Clark, Jonathan Fox, & Kay Treakle eds., Rowman & Littlefield 2003). A survey of possible impacts of the panel process can be found in *Demanding Accountability,* 259.

66 *See,* for example, the operations of the Canadian oil company Talisman in Sudan, whose assets were taken over by ONGC Videsh Ltd., an Indian company. See Human Rights Watch, *Sudan, Oil, and Human Rights* 16, 49 (2003), http://www.hrw.org/reports/2003/sudan1103/sudanprint.pdf.

67 IPIR China Western Poverty Reduction Project (2000), xii, para. 2.

68 *Id.,* at xiii, para. 5.

69 *See* Bank Info. Ctr., *Summary of Events Leading to the Cancellation of the China Western Poverty Reduction Project,* July 20, 2000, http://www.tew.org/development/sum.china.pov.html.

such as compensation or the creation of protected areas, depending on the situation at hand.

As already mentioned, one final, considerable shortcoming is the lack of a follow-up procedure. The Board has explicitly prohibited the Panel from overseeing Management-generated action plans.[70] Therefore, it is difficult to assess the impact of the Panel's work on the actual cases as such. It would be useful and contribute immensely to the impact of the Panel mechanism if such follow-up procedures were introduced. However, the complaint mechanism itself seems to have adequate means of communication, in that requesters appear to feel confident in using the provided channels. This implies a certain degree of trust in the complaint mechanism by the target group.

Conclusions

Overall, the Inspection Panel complaint mechanism appears to work well; the reports are impartial assessments of the Bank's work; most are followed by on-site missions, and some by follow-up reports on the progress made on the respective action plans. Despite the shortcomings analyzed in the previous sections, the Panel process is an important extrajudicial complaint mechanism.

The Inspection Panel does not have the power to take measures other than publishing a report; it is up to the Board to announce remedial measures. Nevertheless, a number of claims have had positive impacts for the requesters, such as the projects Arun, Planafloro, Jamuna, Yacyretá, Itapraica, Singrauli 1, Poverty Reduction China, and Structural Adjustment Argentina.[71] Requesters claimed compensation for being forcibly displaced; demanded the implementation of environmental protection and mitigation measures and the restoration of their livelihoods; and sought to receive support for social programs.[72] In these cases, the project was stopped, the claimants were provided with compensation, and protected areas or new project-level policies were created.

It remains to be seen how the Bank reform on safeguard policies will impact the Panel's work. Nevertheless, this reform and the work of the Panel itself are two signs of a growing human rights awareness on the part of the World Bank that may lead to a more systematic approach to addressing human rights issues in the future.

70 Clark, Fox, & Treakle, *supra* note 17, at 266.

71 *Id.*, at 257. *See* also Roos, *supra* note 51, at 514.

72 Clark, Fox, & Treakle, *supra* note 17, at 258.

Concluding Remarks

ALBERTO NINIO

Our foremost priority is the removal of poverty, hunger and malnutrition, disease and illiteracy. All social welfare programmes must be implemented efficiently. Agencies involved in the delivery of services should have a strong sense of duty and work in a transparent, corruption-free, time-bound and accountable manner.

– Pratibha Patil, former president of India
November 15, 2014

The 20th century witnessed remarkable scientific progress in almost every aspect of human life. As more nations became democratic, and as low-cost access to telecommunications dramatically expanded, more people in developing countries started to press for enhanced access to the results of this scientific and technological progress. Achieving full-fledged development, however, requires overcoming great challenges.

Over the years, development organizations have moved from a parceled approach to development to a more integrated one. More emphasis is placed on looking at the whole forest rather than at just a single tree. Decades of focusing on well-delineated and specific issues, such as agriculture, health, education, and infrastructure, have given way to a more cross-cutting, or transversal, approach to development that generates results that in one way or another impact every development issue or area. A more cross-cutting approach, for example, would involve an emphasis on broad-based themes, such as governance, the environment, human rights, and corruption, that span several discrete development areas.

This volume examines the key development concepts of voice, social contract, and accountability, all of which must be understood and incorporated into development efforts if a transversal approach to development is to work in practice. The need to integrate these three elements into the design and implementation of social and economic development was often unacknowledged or ignored in the past, and is sometimes forgotten even in current development projects. This volume strives to correct this neglect. It is the collective effort of many seasoned development practitioners and scholars, who together bring to the table both the latest legal, social, and economic theories and a wealth of practical experience in order to address the perennial conundrum of how to make development work for all and in a sustainable manner.

This succinct concluding chapter cannot hope to spotlight every chapter in this substantial, wide-ranging, and analytically rich volume. Instead, this chapter illuminates briefly some of the key issues that have a special or unique resonance in the book.

"Human Rights and Service Delivery: A Review of Current Policies, Practices, and Challenges," by Axel Marx, Siobhán McInerney-Lankford, Jan Wouters, and David D'Hollander, seems to reflect the authors' awareness, based on extensive research, that the appropriate application and effective implementation of human rights principles in development are highly dependent on *specific country contexts.* The chapter also indirectly brings to the reader's mind the reality that it is the *particular team or persons tasked with implementing human rights principles in development,* and their *knowledge and experience,* that fundamentally shape the effectiveness of development outcomes. A country or a region's political, social, and economic context affects success, but a *suitable team* must be in place to interact with such contexts and solve real-world development problems.

Rajeev Malhotra offers a unique perspective in "Delivering Development and Good Governance: Making Human Rights Count." He presents a powerful case that human rights do indeed matter for good governance, and then offers the reader a pragmatic framework for enabling human rights to feature in development efforts, and for those efforts to be measured effectively. Malhotra's approach to development is fairly new in the field of development, and although it holds much promise, its continuing evolution must be observed and, where possible, its results measured in order to form a clearer idea of the approach's effectiveness. Creating and employing methods to measure and evaluate such an approach's effectiveness will require expertise from many disciplines that intersect with development efforts.

The importance of voice is perhaps the most powerful message delivered by Emilio Viano in "The Curse of Riches: Sharing Nature's Wealth Equitably?" Viano provides a straightforward account of how indigenous peoples are often "left behind" in large infrastructure projects when their needs and voice are not taken into account. By focusing on the accountability of states, multinationals, and international financial institutions, the author makes a convincing case for "rebalancing the scale." Progress, Viano acknowledges, means bringing the voices of the dispossessed to the negotiating table of development initiatives, efforts, and discourse, such as those emanating from the Inter-American Human Rights System, the Organisation for Economic Co-operation and Development, the United Nations, and the World Bank. But, crucially, Viano also calls for greater change on the part of multilateral institutions, the private sector, and state policy makers in recognizing indigenous peoples' voice and rights in development.

This volume comes out at a time when the world is anticipating the Paris climate conference, scheduled for December 2015, at which representatives will try to reach an essential compromise on climate change and replace the Kyoto Protocol. In "Fostering Accountability in Large-Scale Environmental Projects: Lessons from CDM and REDD+ Projects," Damilola Olawuyi examines a number of critical questions regarding some of the more challenging aspects of projects designed to combat climate change. His comments make an interesting and valuable contribution to explaining how legal frameworks for large-scale projects can assist in increasing accountability and transparency.

Two chapters, "Conceptualizing Regulatory Frameworks to Forge Citizen Roles to Deliver Sustainable Natural Resource Management in Kenya," by Robert Kibugi, and "The Impact of the Legal Framework of Community Forestry on the Development of Rural Areas in Cameroon," by Emmanuel D. Kam Yogo, examine governance in a fragile area of the world, Africa. Both chapters provide practical evidence that without some sort of agreement involving the local community, the private sector, and the government, no permanent development initiative can be successfully sustained over the long term. Kenya's water resource management laws, designed to incorporate the people's voice in decision making, and Kenya's and Cameroon's forest management agreements, initiated and managed by village communities or citizens themselves, give the reader some insight into how beneficiaries' voices can be practically incorporated into legal structures that support long-term development efforts. Although many problems remain unresolved, real progress can be seen in the practical development efforts described by these two authors—efforts that work because they recognize the voice of beneficiaries in decision-making processes and are contextually sensitive.

Urban issues are well represented in this volume. Three chapters examine voice, social contract, and accountability in relation to urban issues and contexts: "Urban Law: A Key to Accountable Urban Government and Effective Urban Service Delivery," by Matt Glasser and Stephen Berrisford; "Confronting Complexity: Using Action-Research to Build Voice, Accountability, and Justice in Nairobi's Muruku Informal Settlements," by Jane Weru, Waikwa Wanyoike, and Adrian Di Giovanni; and "'Good' Legislation as a Means of Ensuring Voice, Accountability, and the Delivery of Results in Urban Development," by Maria Mousmouti and Gianluca Crispi. While each of these chapters focuses on a different topic, they share several common themes, namely, the importance of community engagement, the necessity of incorporating local voices in decision-making processes, the need for early planning, the value of collecting useful and reliable data, and the importance of workable dispute-resolution strategies and measures. With the proportion of urban dwellers predicted to soar from one-half to two-thirds of the world's population by 2050, not least because of rapid migration from rural areas to densely populated cities, these chapters spotlight critical current challenges and solutions as well as likely future needs.

The challenging issue of sexual and gender based-violence is masterfully dealt with in "Justice Sector Delivery of Services in the Context of Fragility and Conflict: What Is Being Done to Address Sexual and Gender-Based Violence?" by Waafas Ofosu-Amaah, Rea Abada Chiongson, and Camilla Gandini, and "Sexual Violence in Conflict: Can There Be Justice?" by Justice Teresa Doherty. These chapters demonstrate that long-standing historical and cultural challenges, as well as deep-seated institutional obstacles, must be tackled to change mind-sets that tolerate violence against women and to counter gender inequality and patriarchal structures that entrench such inequalities. This situation is especially prevalent in contexts where traditional mind-sets that endorse or support gender inequality have not evolved sufficiently to recognize women's rights. Ofosu-Amaah, Chiongson, and Gandini trace the international legal framework that protects women against sexual and gender-based violence, discussing measures that can be used in an integrated fashion to combat such violence. Doherty offers a superb "boots on the ground" account that focuses on her observations and experiences with the international tribunals established in the Former Yugoslavia and Sierra Leone.

Latin America receives special attention in this volume. Two chapters focus on ways to deliver justice more efficiently. "The Ministério Público of the State of Minas Gerais and the ADR Experience," by Danielle de Guimarães Germano Arlé and Luciano Luz Badini Martins, and "Courts and Regulatory Governance in Latin America: Improving Delivery in Development by Managing Institutional Interplay," by Rene Urueña, present informative accounts of two contemporary issues very much at the forefront of developments in this part of the world. Arlé and Badini identify limitations in court resources, which fuel the pressing need to engage more deeply and professionally in alternative dispute resolution systems. Urueña's chapter touches on the more visible emergence of regulatory agencies in Latin America, made possible by special support from courts, judges, judicial proceedings, and information offered by expert witnesses in such proceedings. The potential options and solutions discussed in these chapters offer an excellent starting point from which to develop further useful ideas and methods for addressing future challenges along the long developmental road that lies ahead for Latin American countries.

Several chapters deal with an ongoing and long-standing problem that impedes development efforts throughout the world: corruption. No country is completely free from corruption. "Voice and Accountability: Improving the Delivery of Anticorruption and Anti–Money Laundering Strategies in Brazil," by Fausto Martin De Sanctis, a federal Appellate Court judge, provides a critique of recent developments in anticorruption law and policy in Brazil, the most recent reforms of which are modeled on the U.S. Foreign Corrupt Practices Act of 1977. Two additional chapters, "Development-Oriented Alternatives to Debarment as an Anticorruption Accountability Tool," by Frank A. Fariello, Jr., and Giovanni Bo, and "Making Delivery a Priority: A Philosophical Perspective on Corruption and a Strategy for Remedy," by Morigiwa Yasutomo, both provide refreshingly unique approaches to addressing anticorruption issues. Fariello and Bo examine useful (but underused or unused) alternatives through which multilateral organizations can address corruption; Morigiwa offers a philosophical framework within which the problem of anticorruption can be considered and addressed.

To sum up, this volume is not simply about development. It is about how to have a better life through development efforts. As Oscar Wilde put it, "To live is the rarest thing in the world. Most people exist, that is all." Those committed to development cannot be satisfied merely because children are surviving and people are living longer. The commitment must be to improving people's quality of life—the quality of services, justice, economic goods, and other benefits that ultimately enhance that quality of life.

When considering the key development themes of voice, social contract, and accountability in development, it is impossible not to reflect on the practical mechanisms by which these elements are incorporated into development efforts to generate effective, long-term outcomes. There is also the challenge to examine essential aspects of institutional development, shaped by cultural, legal, and historical factors that need to be harnessed or, in some cases, reshaped to cultivate an appropriate context in which these three themes can be smoothly integrated into development efforts, enhancing the delivery of positive outcomes.

By intertwining the themes of voice, social contract, and accountability across several development areas, this volume provides a powerful analysis of issues critical to the developing world. The integrated approach to development challenges, it is hoped, may serve as a valuable blueprint, outlining complex development issues and practical methods to deal with them.

The words of the former president of India, Pratibha Patil, with which this chapter began, reinforce the abiding sense that in order to fully realize our goals in delivering development—in other words, to make a real, tangible, and sustainable impact on poverty—commitment to the core values discussed in this volume should be approached as a nonnegotiable requirement by development practitioners and states. Such commitment will certainly enhance the quality of the development intended to be delivered.

Index

ECO-AUDIT

Environmental Benefits Statement

The World Bank is committed to preserving endangered forests and natural resources. *The World Bank Legal Review* was printed on recycled paper with 100 percent post-consumer fiber in accordance with the recommended standards for paper usage set by the Green Press Initiative, a nonprofit program supporting publishers in using fiber that is not sourced from endangered forests. For more information, visit www.greenpressinitiative.org.

Saved:

- 17 trees
- 7 million British thermal units of total energy
- 1,424 pounds of net greenhouse gases (CO_2 equivalent)
- 7,724 gallons of waste water
- 517 pounds of solid waste

green press INITIATIVE